June 13-15, 2018
Indianapolis, IN, USA

Association for Computing Machinery

Advancing Computing as a Science & Profession

SACMAT'18

Proceedings of the 23rd ACM

Symposium on Access Control Models & Technologies

Sponsored by:

ACM SIGSAC

Supported by:

Cyber2Slab

Association for Computing Machinery

The Association for Computing Machinery
2 Penn Plaza, Suite 701
New York, New York 10121-0701

Advancing Computing as a Science & Profession

ISBN: 978-1-4503-5666-4 (Digital)

ISBN: 978-1-4503-6157-6 (Print)

Additional copies may be ordered prepaid from:

ACM Order Department
PO Box 30777
New York, NY 10087-0777, USA

Phone: 1-800-342-6626 (USA and Canada)
+1-212-626-0500 (Global)
Fax: +1-212-944-1318
E-mail: acmhelp@acm.org
Hours of Operation: 8:30 am – 4:30 pm ET

General Chair and PC Chairs' Welcome

It is our great pleasure to welcome you to the 23rd ACM Symposium on Access Control Models and Technologies (SACMAT 2018) taking place in Indianapolis, IN, USA on June 13 - 15, 2018. The SACMAT symposium series is the premier forum for presentation of research results and experience reports on leading edge issues of access control in terms of models, systems, applications, and theory. The symposium aims to share novel access control solutions that fulfill the needs of heterogeneous applications and environments, and to identify new directions for future research and development.

The call for papers attracted about 30 submissions from a variety of countries around the world. Submissions were anonymous, and each paper has been reviewed by at least three reviewers who are experts in the field. Extensive online discussions took place to make the selections for the symposium. The program committee finally accepted 12 papers as full papers and 4 papers as short ones for presentation at the symposium. The topics covered include access control in IoT, access control policy analysis and enforcement, and privacy issues in social networks.

Besides the regular research track, this year SACMAT introduced a special track, named "Blue Sky Vision", led by Elena Ferrari (University of Insubria). This track invited researchers to share promising new ideas and challenges of interest to the community which can shape the research agenda for the next 10 years. We will be hosting two Blue Sky sessions where 6 groups of researchers will present their visions. We hope to expand this track in the next editions of SACMAT.

The program is complemented by poster and demonstrations sessions, and by a panel discussion. We are also very proud to present as part of the program three exciting keynote talks by Daphne Yao (Virginia Tech), Dan Thomsen (Smart Information Flow Technologies), Omar Haider Chowdhury (the University of Iowa). We have started this year the test-of-time award for the paper published in SACMAT 10 years ago that has had the most impact. The paper selected this year was "ROWLBAC: representing role based access control in OWL" co-authored by T. Finin, A. Joshi, L. Kagal, J. Niu, R. Sandhu, W. Winsborough, and B. Thuraisingham.

Putting together SACMAT 2018 program was a team effort. We first thank the authors for preparing the papers. We are grateful to the program committee members who worked very hard in reviewing papers and providing feedback for authors. We also acknowledge the poster chair-- Jianwei, the demonstrations chair-- Axel Kern, and the panel chair -- Murat Kantarcioglu, for their contributions to SACMAT 2018 program. Finally, we thank all the conference officers involved in the different organizational aspects of SACMAT 2018: Hongxin Hu – proceedings chair; Mauro Conti – publicity chair; Barbara Carminati -- 10-Year Best Paper Award Committee Chair; Basit Shafiq – treasures; Dongwan Shin – webmaster. Last but not least we would like to thank the SACMAT steering committee, chaired by Elena Ferrari, for the constant guidance throughout the process of organizing SACMAT 2018.

We hope that you will find this program interesting and thought-provoking and that the symposium will provide you with a valuable opportunity to share ideas with other researchers and practitioners from institutions and organization around the world.

Elisa Bertino
SACMAT 2018
General Chair
Purdue University, USA

Dan Lin
SACMAT 2018
Program Co- Chair
Missouri University of Science and Technology, USA

Jorge Lobo
SACMAT 2018
Program Co- Chair
ICREA & Universitat Pompeu Fabra, Spain

Table of Contents

Session: Research Track- IoT

SACMAT 2018 Symposium Organization

General Chair:	Elisa Bertino (Purdue University, USA)
Program Chairs:	Dan Lin (Missouri University of Science and Technology, USA)
	Jorge Lobo (Universitat Pompeu Fabra, Spain)
Panels Chair:	Murat Kantarcioglu (University of Texas at Dallas, USA)
Special Track Vision/Blue Sky Thinking Chair:	Elena Ferrari (University of Insubria, Italy)
Demonstrations Chair:	Axel Kern (Beta Systems, Germany)
Poster Chair:	Jianwei Niu (University of Texas at San Antonio, USA)
Proceedings Chair:	Hongxin Hu (Clemson University, USA)
10-Year Best Paper Award Committee Chair:	Barbara Carminati (University of Insubria, Italy)
Publicity Chair:	Mauro Conti (university of Padova, Italy)
Treasurer:	Basit Shafiq (Lahore University of Management Sciences, Pakistan)
Webmaster:	Dongwan Shin (New Mexico Tech, USA)
Steering Committee Chair:	Elena Ferrari (University of Insubria, Italy)
Steering Committee:	Gail-Joon Ahn (Arizona State University, USA)
	Elisa Bertino (Purdue University, USA)
	Barbara Carminati (University of Insubria, Italy)
	Robert Deng (Singapore Management University, Singapore)
	Jorge Lobo (Universitat Pompeu Fabra, Spain)
	Ravi Sandhu (University of Texas at Sant Antonio, USA)

Data Breach and Multiple Points to Stop It

Danfeng (Daphne) Yao
Department of Computer Science
Virginia Tech
danfeng@vt.edu

ABSTRACT

Preventing unauthorized access to sensitive data is an exceedingly complex access control problem. In this keynote, I will break down the data breach problem and give insights into how organizations could and should do to reduce their risks. The talk will start with discussing the technical reasons behind some of the recent high-profile data breach incidents (e.g., in Equifax, Target), as well as pointing out the threats of inadvertent or accidental data leaks. Then, I will show that there are usually multiple points to stop data breach and give an overview of the relevant state-of-the-art solutions.

I will focus on some of the recent algorithmic advances in preventing inadvertent data loss, including set-based and alignment-based screening techniques, outsourced screening, and GPU-based performance acceleration. I will also briefly discuss the role of non-technical factors (e.g., organizational culture on security) in data protection.

Because of the cat-and-mouse-game nature of cybersecurity, achieving absolute data security is impossible. However, proactively securing critical data paths through strategic planning and placement of security tools will help reduce the risks. I will also point out a few exciting future research directions, e.g., on data leak detection as a cloud security service and deep learning for reducing false alarms in continuous authentication and the prickly insider-threat detection.

KEYWORDS[1]

Data breach; data loss prevention; access control; multiple point of prevention; inadvertent data leak; software security; system security; anomaly detection; ransomware; security practices

SACMAT '18, June 13–15, 2018, Indianapolis, IN, USA
© 2018 Copyright is held by the owner/author(s).
ACM ISBN 978-1-4503-5666-4/18/06.
https://doi.org/10.1145/3205977.3206001

BIOGRAPHY

In the past decade, Daphne Yao has been working on designing and developing data-driven anomaly detection techniques for securing networked systems against stealthy exploits and attacks. Her expertise also includes data loss prevention, program analysis for security. Dr. Yao received her Ph.D. in Computer Science from Brown University.

Dr. Yao is an Elizabeth and James E. Turner Jr. '56 Faculty Fellow and L-3 Faculty Fellow. She received the NSF CAREER Award for her work on human-behavior driven malware detection, and the ARO Young Investigator Award for her semantic reasoning for mission-oriented security work. She has several Best Paper Awards and holds multiple U.S. patents for her anomaly detection technologies.

Dr. Yao is the lead program chair of 2018 *IEEE Security Development Conference (SecDev)*. She is an associate editor of *IEEE Transactions on Dependable and Secure Computing (TDSC)*. She serves as PC members in numerous computer security conferences, including *ACM CCS* and *IEEE S&P*. She has over 85 peer-reviewed publications in major security and privacy conferences, journals, and workshops. Daphne is an active member of the security research community. She serves as the Secretary/Treasurer at ACM Special Interest Group on Security, Audit and Control (SIGSAC).

REFERENCES

[1] L. Cheng, F. Liu, and D. Yao. Enterprise Data Breach: Causes, Challenges, Prevention, and Future Directions. *WIREs Data Mining and Knowledge Discovery*. Wiley. 2017.

[2] F. Liu, X. Shu, D. Yao, and A. Butt. Privacy-Preserving Scanning of Big Content for Sensitive Data Exposure with MapReduce. In *Proceedings of the ACM Conference on Data and Application Security and Privacy (CODASPY)*. 2015.

[3] N. Meng, S. Nagy, D. Yao, W. Zhuang, and G. Argoty. Secure Coding Practices in Java: Challenges and Vulnerabilities. *International Conference on Software Engineering (ICSE)*. Gothenburg, Sweden. May, 2018.

[4] X. Shu, D. Yao, and E. Bertino. Privacy-Preserving Detection of Sensitive Data Exposure with Applications to Data-Leak Detection as a Service. *IEEE Transactions on Information Forensics & Security (TIFS)*. 10(5). 1092-1103. May 2015.

[5] X. Shu, J. Zhang, D. Yao, and W.-C. Feng. Fast Detection of Transformed Data Leaks. *IEEE Transactions on Information Forensics & Security (TIFS)*. 11(3): 528-542. 2016.

[6] X. Shu, D. Yao, and N. Ramakrishnan. Unearthing Stealthy Program Attacks Buried in Extremely Long Execution Paths. *ACM SIGSAC Conference on Computer and Communications Security (CCS)*. Denver, Colorado. Oct. 2015.

Automated Coverage-Based Testing of XACML Policies

Dianxiang Xu
Department of Computer Science
Boise State University
Boise, ID 83725, USA
dianxiangxu@boisestate.edu

Roshan Shrestha
Department of Computer Science
Boise State University
Boise, ID 83725, USA
roshanshrestha@boisestate.edu

Ning Shen
Department of Computer Science
Boise State University
Boise, ID 83725, USA
ningshen@boisestate.edu

ABSTRACT

While[1] the standard language XACML is very expressive for specifying fine-grained access control policies, defects can get into XACML policies for various reasons, such as misunderstanding of access control requirements, omissions, and coding errors. These defects may result in unauthorized accesses, escalation of privileges, and denial of service. Therefore, quality assurance of XACML policies for real-world information systems has become an important issue. To address this issue, this paper presents a family of coverage criteria for XACML policies, such as rule coverage, rule pair coverage, decision coverage, and Modified Condition/Decision Coverage (MC/DC). To demonstrate the assurance levels of these coverage criteria, we have developed methods for automatically generating tests, i.e., access requests, to satisfy the coverage criteria using a constraint solver. We have evaluated these methods through mutation analysis of various policies with different levels of complexity. The experiment results have shown that the rule coverage is far from adequate for revealing the majority of defects in XACML policies, and that both MC/DC and decision coverage tests have outperformed the existing methods for testing XACML policies. In particular, MC/DC tests achieve a very high level of quality assurance of XACML policies.

KEYWORDS

XACML, access control, coverage criteria, test generation, mutation testing

ACM Reference Format:

Dianxiang Xu, Roshan Shrestha, and Ning Shen. 2018. Automated Coverage-Based Testing of XACML Policies. In *SACMAT'18*: 23rd ACM Symposium on Access Control Models & Technologies, June 13–15, 2018, Indianapolis, IN, USA. ACM, New York, NY, USA, 12 pages. https://doi.org/10.1145/3205977.3205979

1 INTRODUCTION

XACML (eXtensible Access Control Markup Language) [1] is an OASIS standard for specifying attribute-based access control (ABAC) policies in the XML format. ABAC [2] is a new access control method where authorization elements are defined in terms of attributes, rather than identities, of subjects, actions, resources, and environments. These attributes are characteristics of subjects (e.g., job title and age), actions, resources (e.g., data, programs, and networks), and environments (e.g., current time and IP address) that are predefined and pre-assigned by an authority [3]. By combining various attributes into access control decisions, ABAC enables fine-grained access control of resources. ABAC also facilitates collaborative policy administration within a large enterprise or across multiple organizations [1]. The Federal Identity, Credential, and Access Management (FICAM) Roadmap and Implementation Plan v2.0 [4] has called out ABAC as a recommended access control model for promoting information sharing between diverse and disparate organizations. The National Strategy for Information Sharing and Safeguarding included a Priority Objective that the federal government should extend and implement the FICAM Roadmap across federal networks in all security domains [3]. Currently XACML3.0 has been used in the mainstream identity management products, such as Oracle's Identity Manager and WSO2's Identity Server.

XACML supports a variety of data types, functions, and combining algorithms for policy composition. While such expressiveness is highly desirable for representing real-world ABAC policies, it raises challenges for validating whether XACML policies indeed meet the access control requirements. When an ABAC policy is coded in XACML, defects can be introduced for various reasons, such as misunderstanding of the access control requirements, omissions, and coding errors [5]. These defects may result in unauthorized accesses, escalation of privileges, and denial of service. To reveal these defects, a major practice is to test the policy by feeding the policy together with test inputs to an XACML engine (or policy decision point) and check if the policy interpreted by the XACML engine produces correct responses. A test input is an access request that consists of attribute names, types, and values. In this paper, we assume that the implementation of the XACML engine conforms to the XACML3.0 standard. The response to an access request by a given policy is consistent with the standard.

Several methods have been proposed to generate test inputs for XACML 1.0 or 2.0 policies [6]-[14]. These methods, however, have two problems. First, their experimental results have shown that they are incapable of detecting the majority of defects and produce a large number of tests. Second, the tests generated by these methods do not achieve adequate coverage of the XACML policy under test. For example, some of them [9] [10] do not

SACMAT'18, June 13-15, 2018, Indianapolis, IN, USA
© 2018 Association for Computing Machinery.
ACM ISBN 978-1-4503-5666-4/18/06...$15.00
https://doi.org/10.1145/3205977.3205979

necessarily cover all reachable rules in the policy under test, while others [8][11] aim at selecting or generating test inputs to cover all rules. This paper will show that a test suite for rule coverage is far from adequate for quality assurance. Adequate test coverage is important because a defect in a policy element will not be revealed unless the policy element is exercised by some test. This paper demonstrates that coverage-based testing is very useful for quality assurance of XACML policies.

The contributions of this paper are as follows:

- We define a family of coverage criteria for XACML 3.0 policies, including rule coverage, decision coverage, Modified Condition/Decision Coverage (MC/DC), rule pair coverage, and permit/deny rule pair coverage. These coverage criteria are defined over the essential access control constraints in XACML 3.0 policies, including policy set target, policy target, rule target, and rule condition. They can be used to measure the adequacy of tests for an XACML policy under development and determine whether or not more tests need to be created and performed in order to achieve an expected level of quality assurance. Even for a policy in operational use (i.e., its tests are actual access requests in an operational environment), the coverage criteria can indicate the confidence levels of policy quality. For example, when the actual accesses are already MC/DC-adequate and none of them have led to security violation, we are confident that the policy is highly assured, even though it has not been tested adequately before the deployment.

- We have developed efficient methods for automatically generating tests to meet each of these coverage criteria using a constraint solver. They have been applied to a number of policies with different levels of complexity and demonstrated satisfactory time performance.

- We have conducted empirical studies to evaluate the cost-effectiveness of the coverage-based tests through comprehensive mutation analysis of XACML policies. The defect detection capability is measured by mutation score, i.e., mutant-killing ratio between the total number of policy mutants killed by a test suite and the total number of non-equivalent policy mutants. A policy mutant is a variant of the original policy with an injected fault. The injected faults represent the typical defects that may occur in XACML policies. A mutant is said to be killed if there is at least one test that reports a failure. Our experiment results have shown that both the MC/DC tests and the decision coverage tests are much more effective than the existing testing methods for XACML policies. In particular, MC/DC-adequate tests can provide high assurance of XACML policies.

The remainder of this paper is organized as follows. To make the paper self-contained, Section 2 briefly introduces XACML 3.0 policies. Section 3 defines the test coverage criteria. Section 4 describes the coverage-based test generation methods. Section 5 presents the empirical studies. Section 6 reviews related work. Section 7 concludes this paper.

2 ACCESS CONTROL POLICIES IN XACML3.0

The main components of the XACML3.0 model are rule, policy, and policy set. As the most elementary unit of policy, a rule consists of a target, a condition, and an effect. The target is a logical expression that specifies the set of requests to which the rule is intended to apply. The condition is a Boolean expression that refine the applicability of the rule established by the target. A policy comprises a policy target, a rule-combining algorithm identifier, and a list of rules. A policy set consists of a policy set target, a policy-combining algorithm identifier, and a list of policies or policy sets. The target of a rule, policy, or policy set is a conjunctive sequence of AnyOf clauses. Each AnyOf clause is a disjunctive sequence of AllOf clauses, and each AllOf clause is a conjunctive sequence of match predicates. A match predicate compares attribute values in a request with the embedded attributes. Logical expressions for match predicates and rule conditions are usually defined on four categories of attributes: subject, resource, action, and environment. They can use a great variety of predefined functions and data types.

We use the policy in Figure 1 as a running example. It is one of the sample policies in Balana, an open source implementation of XACML 3.0 [15]. For simplicity, some text is not omitted. The policy is named "KmarketBluePolicy" and the rule combining algorithm is *deny-overrides* (line 2). The policy's target (lines 3-14) means *role=blue*, where *role* is an attribute in the subject category and both *role* and *blue* are strings. There are three rules: *deny-liquor-medicine* (line 16-37), *max-drink-amount* (lines 38-61), and *permit-rule* (line 62).

The target of rule *deny-liquor-medicine* (lines 18-35) means *resource-id=Liquor* (line 19-26) $\lor$ *resource-id=Medicine* (lines 27-34), where *resource-id* is an attribute in the resource category. Because the rule's condition is omitted, the rule will result in a "deny" decision if *resource-id=Liquor* $\lor$ *resource-id=Medicine*. The target of rule *max-drink-amount* means *resource-id=Drink*, and the condition means *amount$\geq$10*. Thus the rule results in a deny decision if *resource-id=Drink* $\land$ *amount$\geq$10*. Rule *permit-rule* has neither target nor condition. It results in a permit decision whenever it is applied.

To facilitate our discussion, we use policy set as a general structure of XACML specification. Formally, a policy set *PS* is a triple < *pst, pca, [P₁, P₂,..., Pₘ]*>, where *pst* is the policy set target, *pca* is the policy combining algorithm, and *[P₁, P₂,..., Pₘ]* is the list of policies in the policy set. <*pst, pca, [P₁, P₂,..., Pₘ]*> reduces to a policy when *pst* and *pca* are omitted and *m=1*. Thus, the discussions in the subsequent sections apply to individual policies. Each policy *Pᵢ* is a triple <*ptᵢ, rcaᵢ, [R₁, R₂,..., Rₙ]*> , where *ptᵢ* is the policy target, *rcaᵢ* is the rule combining algorithm, and *[R₁, ..., Rₙ]* is the list of rules in the policy. Each rule *Rⱼ* is a triple < *rtⱼ, rcⱼ, reⱼ* >, where *rtⱼ* is the rule target, *rcⱼ* is the rule condition, and *reⱼ* ∈*{Permit, Deny}* is the rule effect. < *rtⱼ, rcⱼ, Permit*> is called a permit rule, whereas < *rtⱼ, rcⱼ, Deny*> is a deny rule. If both *rtⱼ* and *rc* are omitted (always true), then the rule < _, _, *reⱼ* > is a default rule. More specifically, < _, _, *Deny*> is a default deny rule, whereas < _, _, *Permit*> is a default permit rule.

4

```
1    <Policy xmlns="urn:oasis:names:tc:xacml:3.0:core:schema:wd-17"
2    PolicyId="KmarketBluePolicy" RuleCombiningAlgId= "...deny-
     overrides" Version="1.0">
3    <Target>
4      <AnyOf>
5        <AllOf>
6          <Match MatchId="...function:string-equal">
7            <AttributeValue
     DataType="...#string">blue</AttributeValue>
8            <AttributeDesignator AttributeId="...role"
9            Category="...subject-category:access-subject"
10           DataType="...string" MustBePresent="true"/>
11         </Match>
12       </AllOf>
13     </AnyOf>
14   </Target>
15   ...
16   <Rule Effect="Deny" RuleId="deny-liquor-medicine">
17   <Target>
18     <AnyOf>
19       <AllOf>
20         <Match MatchId="...function:string-equal">
21           <AttributeValue
     DataType="...string">Liquor</AttributeValue>
22           <AttributeDesignator AttributeId="...:resource-id"
23           Category="...attribute-category:resource"
24           DataType="...string" MustBePresent="true"/>
25         </Match>
26       </AllOf>
27       <AllOf>
28         <Match MatchId="...function:string-equal">
29           <AttributeValue
     DataType="...string">Medicine</AttributeValue>
30           <AttributeDesignator AttributeId="...resource-id"
31           Category="...attribute-category:resource"
32           DataType="...string" MustBePresent="true"/>
33         </Match>
34       </AllOf>
35     </AnyOf>
36   </Target>
37   </Rule>
38   <Rule Effect="Deny" RuleId="max-drink-amount">
39     <Target>
40       <AnyOf>
41         <AllOf>
42           <Match MatchId="...function:string-equal">
43           <AttributeValue
     DataType="...string">Drink</AttributeValue>
44             <AttributeDesignator AttributeId="...resource-id"
45             Category="...attribute-category:resource"
46             DataType="...string" MustBePresent="true"/>
47           </Match>
48         </AllOf>
49       </AnyOf>
50     </Target>
51     <Condition>
52       <Apply FunctionId="...function:integer-greater-than">
53         <Apply FunctionId="...function:integer-one-and-only">
54           <AttributeDesignator AttributeId="...amount"
55           Category="...category"
56           DataType="...#integer" MustBePresent="true"/>
57         </Apply>
58         <AttributeValue
     DataType="...integer">10</AttributeValue>
59       </Apply>
60     </Condition>
61   </Rule>
62   <Rule RuleId="permit-rule" Effect="Permit"/>
63   </Policy>
```

Figure 1: A sample XACML policy.

An access request consists of attribute names, types, and values. For an access request, a policy or policy set responds with an access decision, such as permit or deny. The semantics of a policy set $PS= < pst, pca, [P_1, P_2,..., P_m]>$ can be informally described as follows: given an access request q, PS is evaluated to produce a response (i.e., access decision) to q, denoted as $d(PS, q)$. Policy set target pst is first evaluated according to the attribute values in q. If the result of evaluation is false (or an error occurs during the evaluation), then $d(PS, q)=$ *Not-Applicable* (or *Indeterminate*), otherwise policies P_1, P_2,..., and P_m will be evaluated. $d(PS, q)$ depends on policy combining algorithm pca and the decisions of individual policies with respect to q (denoted as $d(P_i, q)$). Similarly, for an individual policy $P_i = <pt_i, rca_i, [R_1, R_2,..., R_n] >$, policy target pt_i is evaluated according to the attribute values in q. If the evaluation result is false (or an error occurs during the evaluation), then $d(P_i, q)=$ *Not-Applicable* (or *Indeterminate*), otherwise rules R_1, R_2,..., and R_n will be evaluated. $d(P_i, q)$ depends on rule combining algorithm rca and the decisions of individual rules. Decision of rule $R_j = < rt_j, rc_j, re_j >$ with respect to q, denoted as $d(R_j, q)$, is defined as follows:

- *Permit*: access is granted when $re_j = Permit$ and $rt_j \wedge rc_j$ is true with respect to q.
- *Deny*: access is denied when $re_j = Deny$, and $rt_j \wedge rc_j$ is true with respect to q.
- *NotApplicable*, or simply *N/A*: q is not applicable, i.e., $rt_j \wedge rc_j$ is false with respect to q.
- *IndeterminateD* or simply *I(D)*: An error occurred when rt_j or rc_j was evaluated and $re_j=Deny$. The decision could have evaluated to *Deny* if no error had occurred.
- *IndeterminateP*, or simply *I(P)*: An error occurred when rt_j or rc_j was evaluated and $re_j=Permit$. The decision could have evaluated to *Permit* if no error had occurred.

For a default rule $r_j= < \_, \_, re_j >$ and any access request q, $d(r_j, q) = re_j$. A syntactically valid access request may cause the occurrence of a runtime error for different reasons, such as missing an attribute value, mismatch of an attribute type, and an exception of expression and function evaluation.

In XACML 3.0, there are 11 rule combining algorithms and 12 policy combining algorithms (11 of them use the same names as respective rule combining algorithms). Four of them are for compatibility support of old versions - *Legacy Ordered-deny-overrides*, *Legacy Permit-overrides*, *Legacy Ordered-permit-overrides*, and *Legacy Ordered-permit-overrides*. In Balana [15], the implementations of *Ordered-deny-overrides* and *Ordered-permit-overrides* are the same as *Deny-overrides* and *Permit-overrides*. As such, our work focuses on five rule combining algorithms and six policy combining algorithms: *Deny-overrides*, *Permit-overrides*, *Deny-unless-permit*, *Permit-unless-deny*, *First-applicable*, and *Only-one-applicable*.

3 TEST COVERAGE CRITERIA FOR XACML

A test case for a policy set or policy is an access request (i.e., test input) together with the correct response to the request by the policy set or policy under test (i.e., oracle value). Generally oracle values for given test inputs are determined by the access control requirements. In an evolving policy development process, the actual responses of test inputs from earlier policy versions can be recorded and then used as the oracle values for testing the current or future versions if their correctness is confirmed. A test passes (or fails) if the actual response is the same as (or different from) the oracle value. Sometimes we simply refer to a test as an access request (i.e., the input part of the test). A test suite is a set of tests. In the following, we define a family of test coverage criteria for XACML policies.

3.1 Rule Coverage (RC)

Definition 1. A test suite TS for a policy set PS is said to satisfy *Rule Coverage (RC)* of PS if, for each rule R_j in each policy P_i of PS, there is as least one test q in TS that evaluates rule R_j to its specified effect re_j i.e., $d(R_j, q) = re_j$.

A test q making R_j evaluate to its specified effect re_j must satisfy the following three conditions:

(1)   Reachability of policy P_i: the test must reach policy P_i, otherwise no rule in P_i will be evaluated. This means that PS's target evaluates to true and no policy before P_i terminates the evaluation of PS. For any policy P_k $(0<k<i)$ before P_i, its evaluation will make P_i unreachable if:
- $d(P_k, q) = Deny$ when $pca = Deny\text{-}overrides$ / *Permit-unless-deny*,
- $d(P_k, q) = Permit$ when $pca = Permit\text{-}overrides$ / *Deny-unless-permit*, or
- $d(P_k, q) \neq N/A$ when $pca = First\text{-}applicable$.

(2)   Reachability of rule R_i: After P_i is reached, the test triggers the evaluation of rule R_i only if the policy target of P_i evaluates to true and no rule before R_i in P_i terminates the evaluation of P_i. For any rule R_s $(0<s<j)$ before R_j, its evaluation will make R_s unreachable if:
- $d(R_s, q) = Deny$ when $rca_j = Deny\text{-}overrides$ / *Permit-unless-deny*,
- $d(R_s, q) = Permit$ when $rca_j = Permit\text{-}overrides$ / *Deny-unless-permit*, or
- $d(R_s, q) \neq N/A$ when $rca_j = First\text{-}applicable$.

(3)   Reachability of rule effect re_j: the test makes evaluate to its specified effect only if $rt_i \land rc_i$ evaluates to true.

For instance, a test that covers rule *max-drink-amount* in the running policy example must satisfy the following conditions:
- Rule reachability: *role=blue* $\land \neg$ *(resource-id=Liquor $\lor$ resource-id=Medicine)*
- Effect reachability: *resource-id=Drink $\land$ amount≥10*

3.2 Decision Coverage (DC)

A policy set PS has different points of decision-making, such as policy set target, policy target, rule target, and rule condition. Each of these decision points can evaluate to true, false, or error. These different evaluation results lead to different access control decisions. It is desirable to test whether these decision points work correctly. In the following, we refer to policy set target, policy target, rule target, and rule condition collectively as **decision expressions**.

Definition 2. A test suite TS for a policy set PS is said to satisfy *Decision Coverage (DC)* of PS if TS covers all three decisions of each decision expression, i.e.,

(1) TS has three tests to make policy set target pst evaluate to true, false, and error, respectively,

(2)   For each policy P_i in policy set PS, TS has three tests to make policy P_i's target pt_i evaluate to true, false, and error, respectively, and

(3)   For each rule R_j in each policy P_i of PS, TS has three tests to make rule target evaluate to true, false, and error, respectively.

(4)   For each rule R_j in each policy P_i of PS, TS has three tests to make rule condition evaluate to true, false, and error, respectively.

In (1), if a test makes policy set target pst evaluate to true, then individual policies in PS will continue to be evaluated. If a test makes pst evaluate to false or error, then the evaluation of PS result in a decision of N/A or *Indeterminate*. A test that makes pst evaluate to error (called error test) refers to a valid access request that leads to the *Indeterminate* decision due to such semantic issues as missing attribute value and mismatch of attribute type. This is similar for policy targets, rule targets, and rule conditions. Section 3.5 will discuss why error tests are useful for detecting defects in XACML policies. As described before, the reachability condition of P_i is assumed in (2). The reachability condition of R_j is assumed in (3) and (4). (4) also implies that R_j's target evaluates to true. "false" and "error" do not apply to omitted rule target in (3) or omitted rule condition in (4). Consider the running example, the full decision coverage of the policy target requires a test to cover the following situations:
- *role=blue*
- $\neg$ *(role=blue)*, i.e., *role≠blue*
- an error occurs when the match predicate for *role=blue* (lines 6-11) is evaluated (e.g., if the access request contains no value for attribute *role*)

The full decision coverage of the rule target of *max-drink-amount* requires one test to cover the following constraints:
- *role=blue* $\land \neg$ *(resource-id=Liquor $\lor$ resource-id= Medicine) $\land$ resource-id=Drink*
- *role=blue* $\land \neg$ *(resource-id=Liquor $\lor$ resource-id= Medicine) $\land \neg$ (resource-id=Drink)*
- *role=blue* $\land \neg$ *(resource-id=Liquor $\lor$ resource-id= Medicine) $\land$ an error occurs when resource-id=Drink is evaluated*

The full decision coverage of the rule condition of *max-drink-amount* requires one test to cover the following constraints:
- *role=blue* $\land \neg$ *(resource-id=Liquor $\lor$ resource-id= Medicine) $\land$ resource-id=Drink $\land$ amount≥10*
- *role=blue* $\land \neg$ *(resource-id=Liquor $\lor$ resource-id= Medicine) $\land$ resource-id=Drink $\land \neg$ (amount≥10)*
- *role=blue* $\land \neg$ *(resource-id=Liquor $\lor$ resource-id= Medicine) $\land$ resource-id=Drink $\land$ an error occurs when amount≥10 is evaluated (e.g., if the access request contains no value for attribute amount)*

The full decision coverage of rule *deny-liquor-medicine'* target, *resource-id=Liquor ∨ resource-id=Medicine,* requires one test to meet each of the following constraints in addition to the rule's reachability condition *role=blue*:

- *resource-id=Liquor ∨ resource-id= Medicine*
- *¬(resource-id=Liquor ∨ resource-id= Medicine)*
- an error occurs when rule *max-drink-amount* is evaluated (e.g., if the access request contains no value for attribute *resource-id*).

Definition 2 has considered the occurrence of errors when a policy (set) target, a rule target, or a rule condition is evaluated. A variation of decision coverage is **non-error decision coverage (NE-DC)**, where error tests are not considered.

3.3 Modified-Condition/Decision Coverage

MC/DC originated from NASA's RTCA/DO-178B document [16], which is "the primary means used by aviation software developers to obtain Federal Aviation Administration (FAA) approval of airborne computer software" [17]. DO-178B requires level-A software to achieve MC/DC of the software structure. Here a condition is a primitive Boolean valued expression that cannot be broken down into simpler Boolean expressions, whereas a decision is a Boolean-valued expression made up of conditions and logic operators (e.g., ∧, ∨, and ¬). Consider rule *deny-liquor-medicine*'s target as an example: *resource-id=Liquor ∨ resource-id= Medicine* is a decision. It is composed of two conditions *resource-id=Liquor* and *resource-id= Medicine*, and the logic operator ∨. Note that, here the term "condition" is different from "condition" in XACML rules. In addition to condition coverage (i.e., make a decision true and false at least once), MC/DC requires that: (1) every condition in a decision has taken on all possible outcomes at least once, and (2) each condition has been shown to independently affect the decision's outcome. For example, MC/DC of a conjunctive decision with n conditions (e.g., $c_1 ∧...∧ c_n$) requires $n+1$ tests: one test that evaluates all conditions to true and n tests that evaluate one condition to false and other conditions evaluate to true. MC/DC of a disjunctive decision with n conditions (e.g., $c_1∨...∨c_n$) requires $n+1$ tests: one test that evaluates all conditions to false and n tests that evaluate one condition to true and other conditions evaluate to false.

In this paper, we apply MC/DC to each decision expression (i.e., policy set target, policy target, rule target, and rule condition) in XACML policies. We not only consider two truth values (i.e., true and false), but also error conditions.

Definition 3. A test suite *TS* for a policy set *PS* is said to satisfy *MC/DC* of *PS* if *TS* satisfies MC/DC of each decision expression:
(1)   *TS* satisfies MC/DC of policy set target *pst*, and has a test to make *pst* evaluate to error,
(2)   For each policy P_i in *PS*, *TS* achieves MC/DC of policy P_i's target pt_i, and has a test to make pt_i evaluate to error,
(3)   For each rule R_j in each policy P_i of *PS*, *TS* achieves MC/DC of R_j's target and has a test to make R_j's target evaluate to error.

(4)   For each rule R_j in each P_i of *PS*, *TS* achieves MC/DC of R_j's condition and has a test to make R_j's condition evaluate to error.

The reachability condition of P_i is assumed in (2), and the reachability condition of R_j is assumed in (3) and (4). (4) also implies that rule R_j's target evaluates to true. A variation of the above MC/DC is *non-error MC/DC (NE-MC/DC)*, where error tests are not considered.

Consider rule *deny-liquor-medicine*'s target: *resource-id=Liquor ∨ resource-id= Medicine*. Its MC/DC requires one test to meet each of the following constraints in addition to the rule's reachability condition *role=blue*:

- *resource-id=Liquor ∧ ¬(resource-id= Medicine)*, i.e., *resource-id=Liquor*
- *¬(resource-id=Liquor) ∧ resource-id= Medicine*, i.e., *resource-id= Medicine*
- *¬(resource-id=Liquor) ∧ ¬(resource-id= Medicine)*, i.e., *resource-id≠Liquor ∧ resource-id≠ Medicine*
- an error occurs when *resource-id=Liquor ∨ resource-id= Medicine* is evaluated, e.g., if the access request contains no value for attribute *resource-id*.

In this example, MC/DC requires one more test than decision coverage. Both of the first two tests make the expression true. Only one is needed to achieve the decision coverage.

3.4 Rule Pair Coverage (PC)

Policy combining algorithms and rule combining algorithms are meant to combining multiple conflicting decisions into a single access decision. Such conflicting decisions typically arise from different rules. Thus, testing may target the circumstances under which multiple rules evaluate to their specified effects.

Definition 4. A test suite *TS* for a policy set *PS* is said to achieve rule *Pair Coverage (PC)* of *PS* if, for each pair of rules within each policy P_i (excluding default rules), *TS* has a test to make both rules evaluate to their specified effects if feasible.

Because covering a pair of default rule and non-default rule would be the same as covering the non-default rule, Definition 4 excludes pairing of default rules. When there are default rules, rule pair coverage focuses on pairs of non-default rules. Note that, it is not always feasible to make two rules evaluate to their specified effects. In fact, different rules may deal with mutually exclusive circumstances. Consider rules *deny-liquor-medicine* and *max-drink-amount* in the running example. No test can satisfy the targets of both rules: *resource-id=Liquor ∨ resource-id=Medicine* and *resource-id=Drink*.

A variation of rule pair coverage is *Permit/Deny Rule Pair Coverage (PD-PC)*, where each rule pair consists of a permit rule and a deny rule. Testing may target such heterogeneous rule pairs in that homogeneous rule pairs do not necessarily yield conflicting decisions.

Definition 5. A test suite *TS* for a policy set *PS* is said to achieve *Permit/Deny rule Pair Coverage (PD-PC)* of *PS* if, for each pair of permit and deny rules within each policy P_i (excluding default rules), *TS* has a test to make both rules evaluate to their specified rule effects if feasible.

3.5 Relationships among Coverage Criteria

The aforementioned test coverage criteria are closely related to each other. Figure 2 shows the "subsumes" relationships between the coverage criteria. MC/DC subsumes decision coverage (DC) in that a test suite that achieves MC/DC always achieves the decision coverage. Similarly, decision coverage (DC) subsumes rule coverage, and rule pair coverage (PC) subsumes permit/deny rule pair coverage (PD-PC). In addition, MC/DC subsumes non-error (NE-) MC/DC, whereas decision coverage (DC) subsumes non-error decision coverage (NE-DC) because of the error tests. Error tests are syntactically valid access requests that make decision expressions (policy set target, policy target, and rule target/condition) evaluate to an *Indeterminate* decision. Since such an intermediate decision affects the next level decision of the containing policy element (policy set, policy, and rule), error tests are useful for detecting defects in XACML policies. Consider the following faulty policy with two deny rules (*Rule1* and *Rule2*) and a default permit rule (*Rule3*).

> <RuleCombiningAlgId = Deny-overrides >
> Rule 1: < name = "Tom", gender = "Male", deny>
> Rule 2: < name = "Lee", class = "CS221", deny>
> Rule 3: < , , deny>

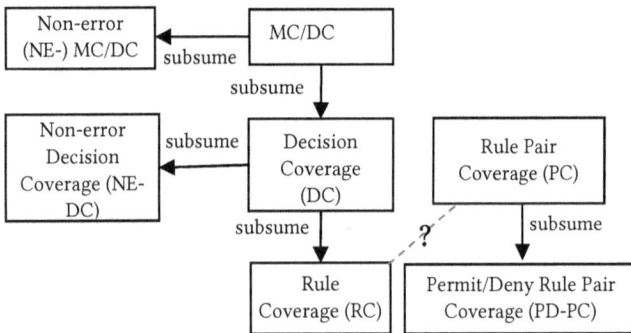

Figure 2: Relationships among test coverage criteria.

Suppose the given rule combing algorithm *Deny-overrides* is incorrect and the correct one is *Permit-unless-deny*. A non-error test that makes the two deny rules evaluate to either *NotApplicable* or *deny* requires that the access request contain a valid value for each of the three attributes: *name*, *gender*, and *class*. A request that contains no valid value for one of the attributes is an error test that would lead to an error occurrence. For example *{name = "Lee", gender="Male"}* is an error test because it contains no value for attribute *class*. *Rule 1* evaluates to *NotApplicable*, whereas *Rule 2* evaluates to *IndeterminateD*. The decision of the faulty policy is *IndeterminateD*. As the correct combining algorithm is *Permit-unless-deny*, however, the correct decision is permit. Thus, the above error test can reveal the fault. A non-error test makes *Rule 1* and *Rule 2* evaluate to either *NotApplicable* or deny. If either *Rule 1* or *Rule 2* evaluate to deny, the faulty and correct policies result in the same decision of deny. If both *Rule 1* and *Rule 2* evaluate to *NotApplicable*, the faulty and correct policies also yield the same decision of permit. Thus, non-error tests cannot reveal the fault. It is worth pointing

out that the tests in this paper (including the error tests) target faults in the policy under test, rather than error in the XACML implementations as studied by [18]. They can be useful for testing XACML implementations, though. None of the existing research on testing XACML policies has discussed the concept of error tests. Note that rule pair coverage (PC) does not necessarily subsume rule coverage (RC) although each test that covers a pair of rules also covers the individual rules in the pair. As discussed before, tests for a specific rule pair may not exist.

3.6 Application of Coverage Criteria

The test coverage criteria can be applied as follows:

- Measuring test coverage adequacy of given tests. These tests may be produced by other testing methods when a policy is developed or represent actual access requests in a running system. As will be shown in Section 5, test suites of different coverage criteria have different levels of fault detection capabilities. Measurement of coverage adequacy of tests provides important guidelines for the development of access control tests. For instance, if MC/DC is required of a policy but the current tests are not yet adequate for MC/DC, then more tests need to be developed and executed. As test suites for rule coverage have a poor record in finding defects (refer to Section 5), a test suite that does not even achieve the rule coverage cannot assure the policy quality.

- Generating access requests automatically to meet a certain coverage criterion. The proposed coverage criteria provide guidelines for automated test generation when validating XACML policies under development. As described in Section 4, we have developed methods for generating tests to satisfy the coverage criteria. They make it possible to empirically evaluate the levels of quality assurance implies by the coverage criteria. In practice, when the proposed test generation methods are applied to an XACML policy, the tester needs to define the oracle value (i.e., expected response) of each test input in order to determine if the test passes or fails.

Because it is easy to implement the measurement of coverage criteria, this paper focuses on automated test generation for the coverage criteria and empirical evaluation of their effectiveness.

4 COVERAGE-BASED TEST GENERATION

The coverage-based test generators produce access requests from a given policy set or policy to satisfy a coverage criterion. They first collect the constraints on attributes according to the criterion as described in Section 3. Then they feed each constraint to the Z3-str constraint solver, and convert the result into an access request if the constraint is solved. Z3-str [19] is an extension to Z3 [20], an efficient SMT (Satisfiability Modulo Theories) Solver freely available from Microsoft Research. SMT generalizes boolean satisfiability (SAT) by adding equality reasoning, arithmetic, fixed-size bit-vectors, arrays, quantifiers, and other useful first-order theories. Z3-str treats strings as a primitive type with common string operations.

The test generator for rule coverage aims to generate a test to cover each rule. It first composes the constraint for each rule in each policy of the given policy set and then uses Z3-str to generate an access request for the constraint. The algorithms are given below. The constraint for covering a rule includes policy set target, policy reachability condition, policy target, rule reachability condition, rule target and rule condition. Obtaining the reachability condition of each policy within the policy set and obtaining the reachability condition of each rule within a policy are described separately in Algorithms 2 and 3. Policy reachability depends on the policy combining algorithm in the policy set and rule reachability depends on the rule combining algorithm in each policy. They are reflected by the conditional statements in Algorithms 2 and 3, respectively.

Algorithm 1. *generateTestsForRuleCoverage(PS)*

Function: Generate tests for rule coverage
Input: Policy set PS= < pst, pca, $[P_1, P_2,..., P_m]$>
Output: A set of access requests Q

1    $Q \leftarrow \varnothing$
2   for each policy P_i = <pt_i, rca_i, $[R_1, R_2,..., R_n]$> in PS, do
3        $constraint \leftarrow pst$
4        $constraint \leftarrow constraint \wedge policyReachability(PS, P_i)$
5        $constraint \leftarrow constraint \wedge pt_i$
6   for each rule R_j =<rt_j, rc_j, re_j> in P_i, do
7            $ruleConstraint \leftarrow constraint \wedge ruleReachability(P_i,R_j)$
8            $ruleConstraint \leftarrow ruleConstraint \wedge (rt_j \wedge rc_j)$
9            $Q \leftarrow Q \cup \{Z3\text{-}request(ruleConstraint)\}$

Algorithm 2. *policyReachability(PS, P_i)*

Function: Generate policy reachability constraint
Input: Policy set PS= < pst, pca, $[P_1, P_2,..., P_m]$>
          Policy P_i = <pt_i, rca_i, $[R_1, R_2,..., R_n]$>
Output: *constraint*

1    $constraint \leftarrow$ ""
2   for k=1 to i-1, do
3   if P_k's target pt_k is not empty
4            $constraint \leftarrow constraint \wedge \neg (pt_k)$
5   else
6   if pca = *Deny-overrides* or *Permit-unless-deny*
7                $rules \leftarrow$ all deny rules in P_k
8   else if pca = *Permit-overrides* or *Deny-unless-permit*
9                $rules \leftarrow$ all permit rules in P_k
10   else if pca = *First-applicable*
11               $rules \leftarrow$ all rules in P_k
12   for each rule R_s =<rt_s, rc_s, re_s> in $rules$, do
13               $constraint \leftarrow constraint \wedge \neg (rt_s \wedge rc_s)$

Algorithm 3. *ruleReachability(P_i, R_j)*

Function: Generate rule reachability constraint
Input: Policy P_i = <pt_i, rca_i, $[R_1, R_2,..., R_n]$>
          Rule R_j =<rt_j, rc_j, re_j> in P_i
Output: *constraint*

1    $constraint \leftarrow$ ""
2   if rca_i = *Deny-overrides* or *Permit-unless-deny*
3        $rules \leftarrow$ all deny rules before R_j in P_i ($s<j$)
4   else if rca_i=*Permit-overrides* or *Deny-unless-permit*
5        $rules \leftarrow$ all permit rules before R_j in P_i ($s<j$)
6   else if rca_i = *First-applicable*

7    $rules \leftarrow$ all rules before R_j in P_i ($s<j$)
8   for each rule R_s =<rt_s, rc_s, re_s> in $rules$
9        $constraint \leftarrow constraint \wedge \neg (rt_s \wedge rc_s)$

To deal with MC/DC and decision coverage, we use a truth table to manage its coverage status for each decision expression (e.g., policy set target, policy target, rule target, and rule condition). Each entry consists of three parts: a truth value for each of the basic conditions that comprise the decision expression, truth value of the decision expression (TRUE, FALSE, or ERROR), and whether the entry is covered by some existing test (TRUE or FALSE). Table 1 shows a sample MC/DC truth table for decision expression *resource-id=Liquor* ∨ *resource-id= Medicine*. The four entries are corresponding the four expected MC/DC tests discussed in Section 3.3. Entry 0 represents that *resource-id=Liquor* is True and *resource-id= Medicine* is False. In this case, the decision expression *resource-id=Liquor* ∨ *resource-id= Medicine* evaluates to True. "Covered" is False because no existing test has covered this entry. Entries 1-3 can represent tests for decision coverage. Let *conditions (constraint, i)* represent the conjunction of the basic conditions in the *i*-th entry. Consider entry 0 of Table 1. *conditions (resource-id=Liquor* ∨ *resource-id= Medicine, 0)* means *(resource-id=Liquor)* ∧ ¬*(resource-id=Medicine)*. Let *decision(constraint, i)* represent the decision in the *i*-th entry and *covered(constraint, i)* represent whether or not the *i*-th entry is covered by existing tests. For convenience, the truth table of an empty decision expression (e.g., policy set target, policy target, rule target, rule condition) has one entry, where *conditions(constraint, 0)* and *decision(constraint, 0)* are both *True*.

Table 1: MC/DC Truth Table for resource-id=Liquor ∨ resource-id= Medicine

Basic Conditions		Decision	Covered
resource-id =Liquor	resource-id = Medicine	resource-id=Liquor ∨ resource-id= Medicine	
TRUE	FALSE	TRUE	FALSE
FALSE	TRUE	TRUE	FALSE
FALSE	FALSE	FALSE	FALSE
		ERROR	FALSE

When dealing with a decision expression for test generation purposes, we check each entry of its MC/DC truth table. If an entry is already covered by the existing tests, no new test is needed for the entry. If it is not covered by any existing test and the truth value of the decision expression is TRUE, the conditions in this entry will be carried to the next decision expression (e.g., if the current expression is rule target, the next is rule condition). If it is not covered by any existing test and the truth value of the decision expression is FALSE or ERROR, a new test will be generated according to the entry's conditions together with all the constraints for reaching this decision expression.

Algorithm 4 below describes how to generate MC/DC tests for a policy set. Lines 2-7 initialize MC/DC truth tables. Then we deal with four levels of MC/DC truth tables for *pst* (policy set target), pt_i (policy target of each policy), rt_j (rule target of each rule), and rc_j (for rule condition of each rule). pt_i is reachable only when pst is true (line 13). rt_j is reachable only when pst and pt_i are true (line 23). rc_j is reachable when if pst, pt_i, and rt_j are true (line 32). Therefore, at each level, we explore the next level only when the decision of the current entry is true. If the decision of current entry is false and it is not yet covered, we use Z3-str to generate a request: lines 9-10 for pst, lines 16-18 for pt_i,

lines 26-28 for rt_j, line 35 for rc_j. If the decision of the current entry is error and is not yet covered, we generate an error request (lines 11-12 for pst, lines 19-21 for pt_i, lines 29-21 for rt_j, line 37 for rc_j). After a request is generated, we update the coverage information in all MC/DC truth tables. Note that generation of a normal or error request also involves policy reachability constraint (Algorithm 2) and/or rule reachability constraint (Algorithm 3).

Algorithm 4. *generateTestsForMC/DC(PS)*
Function: Generate tests for MC/DC
Input: Policy set $PS = <\ pst, pca, [P_1, P_2,..., P_m]>$
Output: A set of access requests Q
Steps:

1     $Q \leftarrow \varnothing$
2   create MC/DC truth table for pst
3   for each policy $P_i = <pt_i, rca_i, [R_1, R_2,..., R_n]>$ in PS, do
4   create MC/DC truth table for pt_i
5   for each rule $R_j = (\ rt_j, rc_j, re_j)$ in P_i do
6   create MC/DC truth table for rt_j
7   create MC/DC truth table for rc_j
8   for each entry u of pst's truth table
9   if $decision(pst, u)$ = FALSE
10       $Q \leftarrow Q \cup \{$Z3-request$(conditions(pst, u))\}$
11   else if $decision(pst, u)$ = ERROR
2       $Q \leftarrow Q \cup \{$error-request$(\_, pst)\}$
13   else if $decision(pst, u)$ = TRUE
14   for each $P_i = <pt_i, rca_i, [R_1, R_2,..., R_n]>$, do
15   for each entry v of pt_i's truth table
16   if $decision(pt_i, v)$=FALSE & $covered(pt_i, v)$=FALSE
17         $q \leftarrow$ Z3-request$(conditions(pst, u) \wedge\ policyReachability(PS,P_i) \wedge conditions(pt_i, v))$
18   add q to Q and update truth tables
19   else if $decision(pt_i, v)$=ERROR & $covered(pt_i, v)$=FALSE
20         $q \leftarrow$ error-request$(conditions(pst, u) \wedge policyReachability(PS,P_i), pt_i)$
21   add q to Q and update truth tables
23   else if $decision(pt_i, v)$ = TRUE
24   for each rule $R_j = <rt_j, rc_j, re_j>$, do
25   for each entry w of rt_j's truth table, do
26   if $decision(rt_j,w)$=FALSE & $covered(rt_j,w)$=FALSE
27           $q \leftarrow$ Z3-request$(conditions(pst, u) \wedge policyReachability(PS,P_i) \wedge$
                $ruleReachability(P_i, R_j) \wedge conditions(pt_i, v) \wedge conditions(rt_j, w))$
28   add q to Q and update truth tables
29   if $decision(rt_j,w)$=ERROR & $covered(rt_j,w)$=FALSE
30           $q \leftarrow$ error-request$(conditions(pst, u) \wedge\ policyReachability(PS,P_i) \wedge$
                $ruleReachability(P_i, R_j) \wedge conditions(pt_i, v), pt_i)$
31   add q to Q and update truth tables
32   else if $decision(rt_j,w)$=TRUE
33   for each entry z of rc_j's truth table such that $covered(rc_j, z)$=FALSE, do
34   if $decision(rc_j,z)$!=ERROR
35             $q \leftarrow$ Z3-request$(conditions(pst,u) \wedge\ policyReachability(PS,P_i) \wedge$
                $ruleReachability(P_i, R_j) \wedge conditions(pt_i, v) \wedge conditions(rt_j, w) \wedge conditions(rc_j, z))$
36   else // $decision(rc_j, z)$ = ERROR
37             $q \leftarrow$ error-request$(conditions(pst,u) \wedge policyReachability(PS_i,P) \wedge$
                $ruleReachability(P_i, R_j) \wedge conditions(pt_i,v) \wedge conditions(rt_j,w), rc_j)$
38   add q to Q and update tables

The test generation algorithm for decision coverage is a special case of Algorithm 4. Specifically, the MC/DC truth table in Algorithm 4 is replaced with the decision table. Consider *resource-id=Liquor $\vee$ resource-id= Medicine* whose MC/DC table is shown in Table 1. Its decision table has two columns as in Table 1: Decision and Covered. It has only one decision entry for TRUE, FALSE, and ERROR.

5 EMPIRICAL STUDIES

We have implemented our approach in a Balana-based tool. It has facilitated conducting empirical studies for evaluating scalability and cost-effectiveness of the coverage-based test generation methods. This section presents experiment setup and results and discusses threats to validity.

5.1 Experiment Setup

Our experiments use a total of seven cases studies (nine XACML3.0 policies) with different levels of complexity. As shown in Table 2, the number of rules ranges from a dozen to 1,280. Kmarket is the demonstration application of Balana with three individual policies and a total of 12 rules. All other policies are from the literature.

Table 2: Subject Policies

#	Policy	#Rules	#Mutants (M14)	# Mutants (M8)
1	Kmarket [15]	12	88	67
2	fedora[2]	12	94	58
3	conf [21]	15	107	64
4	itrust[3]	64	515	259
5	itrust5 [5]	320	2,563	1,283
6	itrust10 [5]	640	5,123	2,563
7	itrust20 [5]	1,280	10,243	5,123

Our approach to the evaluation of testing effectiveness is mutation analysis of subject policies. Mutation analysis is a widely applied technique for evaluating testing methods. The main hypotheses underlying mutation analysis [22] are: (a) the mutants are based on actual fault models and are representative of real faults, (b) developers produce programs (policies) that are close to being correct, (c) tests sufficient to detect simple faults (i.e., in mutants) are also capable of detecting complex faults. Recent experiments have confirmed that mutants are indeed similar to real faults for the purpose of evaluating testing techniques [23]. As discussed below, these hypothesis are valid for mutation analysis of XACML policies in this paper.

We generated mutants of each policy by using all the mutation operators in Table 3. Each mutant is a variant of the given policy with one fault injected by a mutation operator. The mutants generated by the mutation operators in Table 3 represent a great variety of faults in XACML policies. Each mutation operator may generate a number of mutants for a given policy. For example, given a policy with n rules, CRE (Change Rule Effect) creates n mutants because it creates a mutant by changing the effect of each rule. We use M14 and M8 to denote the set of all 14 mutation operators and the set of the first 8 mutation operators, respectively. M8 represents the set of mutation operators commonly used by the majority of the existing work on XACML policy testing. It is equivalent to the 11 mutation operators in [14] because the mutation operators in

Table 3 are more coarse-grained. For instance, CRC (Change Rule/Policy Combining Algorithm. applies to both rule combining algorithm and policy combining algorithm. It represents two traditional mutation operators in [14]. M14 is based on the mutation operators in the XACML 2.0 mutant generator, XACMUT [24]. It does not include ANR (Add New Rule), RUF (RemoveUnique-nessFunction), AUF (AddUniqueness Function), CNOF (Change-N-OF-Function), and CLF (Change LogicalFunction). This paper evaluates the fault detection capabilities of the coverage-based test generation methods with both M14 and M8. Table 3 includes the numbers of non-equivalent mutants of each policy created by M14 and M8, respectively. It excludes those mutants that are equivalent to their original policy. As proven in [25], for example, the rule combining algorithms Permit-overrides and Deny-overrides make no difference with respect to a policy with permit-only (or deny-only) rules.

Table 3: Mutation Operators of XACML Policies

#	Fault Type	Mutation Operator Name	Mutation
1	Incorrect policy	PTT*	set Policy/set Target True
2	/policy set target	PTF	set Policy/set Target False
3	Incorrect rule/ policy combining algorithm	CRC	Change Rule/Policy Combining algorithm
4	Incorrect rule effect	CRE	Change Rule Effect
5	Incorrect rule	RTT	set Rule Target True
6	target	RTF	set Rule Target False
7	Incorrect rule	RCT	set Rule Condition True
8	condition	RCF	set Rule Condition False
9		ANF	Add Not Function in condition
10		RNF	Remove Not Function in condition
11	Incorrect rule	FPR	First Permit Rules
12	ordering	FDR	First Deny Rules
13	Missing rule	RER	REmove a Rule
14	Missing target element	RPTE	Remove Parallel Target Element

Our experiments use the same protocol for each subject policy. First, we generate a test suite by each of the coverage-based test generation method. Second, we run each test suite against the given policy and record the actual response of each test. It will be used as the oracle value of this test when the policy mutants are tested. Third, we generate mutants of the policy using all the mutation operators in Table 3. Fourth, we run the test suite of each test generation method against each mutant. Since mutants represent the faults that likely occur in XACML policies, mutation score is considered the main indicator of the fault-detection capability.

5.2 Results

We present the experiment results from three perspectives: time performance of test generation, fault detection capability (i.e., effectiveness), and cost-effectiveness.

---

[2] http://www.fedora.info
[3] http://agile.csc.ncsu.edu/iTrust/wiki/doku.php?id=start

5.2.1 Time performance of test generation. Table 4 shows the number of tests generated by each test generation method for each subject policy. Typically, the test suite for decision coverage has more tests than that for rule coverage, whereas the MC/DC test suite may have many more tests than those of rule coverage and decision coverage. It depends on the complexity of policy/rule targets and rule conditions. For itrustX, pair coverage and permit/deny pair coverage are not applicable because the rules are all mutually exclusive.

Table 4: Number of Generated Tests

Subject	RC	DC	NE-DC	MC/DC	NE-MC/DC	PC	PD-PC
Kmarket	12	32	19	33	20	15	9
fedora	12	27	18	33	24	25	13
Conf	15	18	16	27	25	14	14
itrust	64	66	65	197	196	N/A	N/A
itrust5	320	322	321	983	982	N/A	N/A
itrust10	640	642	641	1,965	1,964	N/A	N/A
itrust20	1,280	1,282	1,281	3,929	3,928	N/A	N/A

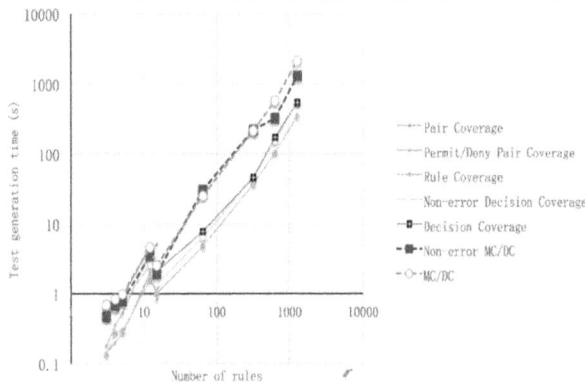

Figure 3: Test generation time.

Given a policy, the test generation time of a testing method is related to the total number of tests generated, which depends on the number and complexity of rules in the policy. Figure 3 shows the test generation time of each testing method with respect to the number of rules in all subject policies. The test generation was performed on a 64bit Ubuntu laptop (Inter Core i5-2410 @2.3 GHz, 3.8GB memory). Using a series of policies with similar rule structures (i.e., itrust, itrust5, itrust10, and itrust20) provides a good measurement of the scalability of test generation. Because MC/DC entails a much larger test suite than decision coverage and rule coverage, it also consumes more time for test generation. Nevertheless, the test generation time of each method is approximately linear to the number of rules. It is satisfactory even for the largest policy (i.e., itust20 with 1,280 rules). From the time performance perspective, all the test generation methods are applicable to large policies.

5.2.2 Fault detection capabilities. Table 5 shows the mutation scores of the coverage-based testing methods with respect to all subject policies. The mutation scores range from 50% to 63.6% for

the rule coverage tests, from 62.5% to 96.6% for the decision coverage tests, and from 97.01% to 100% for the MC/DC tests, 58.2% to 70.3% for all rule pairs tests, and 43.1% to 70.3% for all PD-pairs tests. The results demonstrate that the rule coverage tests are far from adequate for high assurance of XACML policies because they cannot reveal many faults, and that the MC/DC tests are the most capable and provide high assurance of XACML policies. Further analysis of the mutant-killing results indicates that the rule coverage tests did not kill any of the mutants created by PTT, RTT, RCT or RPTE, and some of the mutants created CRC, FPR, and FDR. The decision coverage tests did not kill all of the mutants created by RTT, FPR, FDR, and RPTE. The MC/DC tests did not kill all of the mutants created RTT, FPR and FDR. Different from the rule coverage and decision coverage tests, they killed all RPTE mutants. The error tests for MC/DC and decision coverage killed some CRC and RPTE mutants.

Table 5: Mutation Scores (%) with M14

Subject	RC	DC	NE-DC	MC/DC	NE-MC/DC	PC	PD-PC
Kmarket	63.6	96.6	89.8	97.7	90.9	63.6	63.6
fedora	56.4	94.7	90.4	97.9	97.9	56.4	47.9
conf	55.1	86.9	72	100	98.1	55.1	55.1
itrust	49.9	62.9	62.7	100	100	N/A	N/A
itrust5	50	62.6	62.5	100	100	N/A	N/A
itrust10	50	62.5	62.5	100	100	N/A	N/A
itrust20	50	62.5	62.5	100	100	N/A	N/A
Average	50.1	63.0	62.9	99.98	99.94	57.9	54.9

Table 6: Mutation Scores (%) with M8

Subject	RC	DC	NE-DC	MC/DC	NE-MC/DC	PC	PD-PC
Kmarket	58.2	97.01	88.1	97.01	88.1	58.2	58.2
fedora	56.9	100	100	100	100	56.9	43.1
conf	70.3	100	96.9	100	96.9	70.3	70.3
itrust	74.5	100	100	100	100	N/A	N/A
itrust5	74.9	100	100	100	100	N/A	N/A
itrust10	75	100	100	100	100	N/A	N/A
itrust20	75	100	100	100	100	N/A	N/A
Average	**74.68**	**99.98**	**99.89**	**99.98**	**99.89**	**61.9**	**57.7**

Table 6 shows the mutation scores using M8. The mutation scores of the rule coverage tests are similar to those in Table 5. However, the decision coverage tests and the MC/DC tests have the same high mutation scores. The decision coverage tests are highly capable of killing M8 mutants, i.e., detecting the types of faults represented by all mutation operators in M8. Both the decision coverage tests and the MC/DC tests have higher mutation scores. For the three policies (i.e., fedora, conference, itrust) that are commonly used by the related work and this paper, the decision coverage tests and the MC/DC tests have killed all the mutants. They have outperformed the existing testing methods as described in the related work section.

Table 7: **MKPT scores**

Subject	RC	DC	NE-DC	MC/DC	NE-MC/DC	PC	PD-PC
Kmarket	4.67	2.66	4.16	2.61	4.00	3.73	6.22
Fedora	4.42	3.30	4.72	2.79	3.83	2.12	3.46
Conf	3.93	5.17	4.81	3.96	4.20	4.21	4.21
itrust	4.02	4.91	4.97	2.61	2.63	N/A	N/A
itrust5	4.00	4.98	4.99	2.61	2.61	N/A	N/A
itrust10	4.00	4.99	5.00	2.61	2.61	N/A	N/A
itrust20	4.00	5.00	5.00	2.61	2.61	N/A	N/A
Average	**4.01**	**4.94**	**4.99**	**2.61**	**2.62**	**3.11**	**4.44**

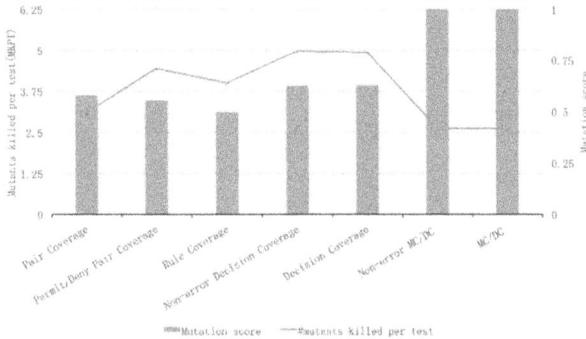

Figure 4: **Cost-effectiveness of testing methods.**

5.2.3 Cost-effectiveness. While mutation score is a good indicator of the fault detection capability of a testing method, it does not account for the testing cost. Ideally, we expect to find all potential faults in a given policy so as to achieve high assurance. In practice, this may be infeasible due to limited resources available (e.g., time and budget). Thus we need to take testing cost into consideration. Here we use the total number of tests created by a testing method as the main cost factor of testing because it often reflects the total test generation time and test execution time. We consider the average number of Mutants Killed Per Test (MKPT) as the indicator of cost-effectiveness. Table 7 shows MKPT scores for all coverage-based test generation methods. Figure 4 compares MKPT scores with mutation scores. While MC/DC is the most capable testing method in terms of mutation scores, it is not the most cost-effective. Although rule coverage is the least capable, it is more cost-effective than MC/DC. Among all the testing methods, decision coverage is the most cost-effective. The analysis of cost-effectiveness leads to the following observations: (1) when testing resources (e.g., time and budget) are very limited in the evolving process of policy development and validation, decision coverage (or even rule coverage) is a better choice than MC/DC. The tests for decision coverage (or rule coverage) should be performed first. (2) As the testing process progresses, it gets more and more expensive to find additional faults because more and more tests need to be created and executed. Nevertheless, before an XACML policy is deployed, a MC/DC-like test suite is high desirable to ensure correct enforcement of access control.

6 RELATED WORK

Martin et al. [13] defined several coverage measurements for XACML1.0/2.0 policies, such as policy hit percentage, rule hit percentage, and condition hit percentage. They used coverage information to reduce test suites produced by existing test generation methods. In comparison, this paper presents test criteria and methods for generating tests to satisfy the criteria. Decision coverage and MC/DC consider error tests for targets and conditions.

Cirg [11] generates access requests from counterexamples produced by Margrave [21] through the change-impact analysis of two synthesized versions. The difference of the two versions of a policy targets a test coverage goal, such as rule coverage or condition coverage. Because request generation from change-impact analysis may result in a large number of requests, Cirg reduces the number of tests by selecting tests based on policy structural coverage. The mutation scores of the testing methods in Cirg ranged from 30% to 60% in the case studies (except 100% for a trivial policy). Targen [12] derives access requests to satisfy all the possible combinations of truth values of the attribute id-value pairs found in a given policy. The mutation scores of Targen ranged from 75% to 79% for different case studies [7].

Access requests generated by Cirg and Targen typically use a limited number of subject, resource, action, and environment attributes. Generally, a request could use any combination of attributes. Because XACML requests are encoded in XML, they must be conforming to a specific XML Schema called the Context Schema. Bertolino et al., have developed the X-CREATE framework with multiple test generation algorithms by considering the structures of the Context Schema [9]. These algorithms can generate requests that use more than one subject, resource, action, or environment attribute. The mutation scores of the testing methods in X-CREATE ranged from 75% to 96% for several small policies. Bertolino et al., have also developed other test selection strategies, such as Simple Combinatorial and Incremental XPT [7]. The mutation scores ranged from 3% to 100%, whereas the mutation scores of the Incremental XPT strategy ranged from 55% to 100%. Bertolino et al., [8] proposed an approach to select tests from a given large test suite based on the rule coverage criterion. It selects tests to match each rule target set, which is the union of the target of the rule and all enclosing policy and policy sets targets. The mutation scores of this approach ranged from 62% to 98%. Our paper proposes several additional criteria. Our empirical studies show that decision coverage and MC/DC are more capable. Li et al., [10] have developed XPTester, which used a symbolic execution technique to generate requests from XACML policies. They convert the policy under test into semantically equivalent C Code Representation (CCR) and symbolically execute CCR to create test inputs and translate the test inputs to access requests. This approach has the same fault detection capability as the Preliminary XPT algorithm in the X-CREATE framework, but it produces smaller test suites. The mutation scores of XPTester ranged from 37% to 93% in the case studies.

This paper is different from the above work on test generation from XACML policies [6]-[14]. First, this paper targets XACML 3.0, whereas the above work all deals with earlier versions of XACML (i.e., 2.0 or 1.0). Second, this paper aims at stronger coverage criteria, i.e., decision coverage and MC/DC, whereas the existing work is only concerned with rule coverage. As discussed before, a test suite for rule coverage can be very weak at fault detection. In addition to mutation scores, this paper also provides an analysis of cost-effectiveness using average number of mutants killed per test.

Safarzadeh et al. have proposed a model-based approach for testing the implementation of access control in a system, where system functional model and access control policy are specified by extended finite state machines and XACML, respectively. This approach derives conditions from rules in the policy and the functionality and applies MC/DC to the conditions for test generation. Our approach does not rely on functional models.

7 CONCLUSIONS

We have described the test coverage criteria for XACML3.0 policies and efficient methods for generating tests to satisfy each of the coverage criteria. We have also presented the empirical studies for evaluating the scalability, fault detection capabilities, and cost-effectiveness of the coverage-based test generation methods. The results show that the coverage-based tests, especially MC/DC tests, can achieve high assurance of access control enforcement.

The empirical studies also indicate that some mutants may not be killed by a given coverage-based test suite. It is highly desirable to conduct a theoretical analysis on why they are not killed. One approach is to formalize the fault detection conditions of these mutants which must be satisfied by the tests in order to kill them. It is also interesting to investigate whether the coverage-based test suites can be reduced while maintaining the same level of fault detection capability. Our future work will also exploit the proposed coverage criteria to select tests from large test suites generated by other testing methods. For example, combinational test generation for XACML policies may produce a large number of tests. Not all of them make contributions to the fault detection. The coverage criteria can be used to select tests in order to improve cost-effectiveness.

ACKNOWLEDGMENTS

This work was partially supported by the US National Science Foundation under grants 1359590 and 1618229. The mutation tool was implemented by Mr. Jimmy Wang and Mr. Shuai Peng.

REFERENCES

[1]   OASIS. 2013. *eXtensible Access Control Markup Language (XACML)* Version 3.0, (Jan. 2013), http://www.oasisopen.org/committees/xacml/

[2]   N. Li, J.C. Mitchell, W.H. Winsborough. 2002. Design of a Role-Based Trust Management Framework. In *Proc. IEEE Symposium on Security and Privacy* (S&P 2002). 114–130.

[3]   V. Hu, D. Ferraiolo, R. Kuhn, A. Schnitzer, K. Sandlin, R. Miller, K. Scarfone. 2013. *Design of a Role-Based Trust Management Framework*. NIST Special Publication 800-162. (October 2013).

[4]   FEDCIO2: *Federal Identity, Credential, and Access Management (FICAM) Roadmap and Implementation Guidance Version 2.0.* (December 2011).

[5]   D. Xu, N. Shen, and Y. Zhang. 2015. Fault-Based Testing of Combining Algorithms in XACML3.0 Policies. In *Proc. of the 27th International Conf. on Software Engineering and Knowledge Engineering* (SEKE'15), Pittsburg, (July 2015).

[6]   A. Bertolino, F. Lonetti, and E. Marchetti. 2010. Systematic XACML Request Generation for Testing Purposes. In *EUROMICRO Conference on Software Engineering and Advanced Applications* (SEAA), Lille, (September 2010).

[7]   A. Bertolino, S. Daoudagh, F. Lonetti, and E. Marchetti. 2012. Automatic XACML Requests Generation for Policy Testing. In *The Third International Workshop on Security Testing* (SecTest 2012), Montreal, (April 2012).

[8]   A. Bertolino, Y. Le Traon, F. Lonetti, E. Marchetti, and T. Mouelhi. 2014. Automatic XACML Requests Generation for Policy Testing. In *IEEE Seventh International Conference on Software Testing, Verification and Validation Workshops (ICSTW)*. 12-21. (2014),

[9]   A. Bertolino, S. Daoudagh, F. Lonetti, and E. Marchetti. 2012. The X-CREATE Framework-A Comparison of XACML Policy Testing Strategies. In *Proc. of the 8th International Conference on Web Information Systems and Technologies* (WEBIST). 155–160.

[10] Y. Li, Y. Li, L. Wang, G. Chen. 2014. Automatic XACML Requests Generation for Testing Access Control Policies. In *Proc. of the 26th International Conf. on Software Engineering and Knowledge Engineering* (SEKE'14). Vancouver. (July 2014).

[11] E. Martin, and T. Xie. 2007. Automated Test Generation for Access Control Policies via Change-Impact Analysis. In *Proc. 3rd International Workshop on Software Engineering for Secure Systems* (SESS). 5-11.

[12] E. Martin, and T. Xie. 2006. Automated Test Generation for Access Control Policies. In *Supplemental Proc. of ISSRE*. (Nov. 2006).

[13] E. Martin, and T. Xie. 2006. Defining and Measuring Policy Coverage in Testing Access Control Policies. In *Proc. of the 8th International Conf. on Information and Communications Security*. 139-158, (December 2006).

[14] E. Martin, and T. Xie. 2007. A Fault Model and Mutation Testing of Access Control Policies. In *Proc. of the 16th International Conf. on World Wide Web* (WWW'07). 667-676, (May 2007).

[15] WSO2. 2012. *Balana: An Open Source XACML 3.0 Implementation*. http://xacmlinfo.org/2012/08/16/balana-the-open-source-xacml-3-0-implementation/

[16] RTCA/DO-178B. 1992. *Software Considerations in Airborne Systems and Equipment Certification*. RTCA, Inc., Washington, D. C., (December 1992).

[17] K. Hayhurst, D. Veerhusen, J. Chilenski, L. Rierson, 1992. *A Practical Tutorial on Modified Condition/Decision Coverage*. NASA. (May 2001).

[18] N. Li, J.H. Hwang, T. Xie. 2008. Multiple-Implementation Testing for XACML Implementations. In *Proc. of the Workshop on Testing, Analysis, and Verification of Web Services and Applications* (TAV-WEB'08), 27-33.

[19] Y. Zheng, X. Zhang, V. Ganesh. Z3-str: A Z3-based String Solver for Web Application Analysis. In *Proc. of the 9th Joint Meeting on Foundations of Software Engineering* (ESEC/FSE'13). 114-124.

[20] L. de Moura and N. Bjørner. 2008. Z3: An Efficient SMT Solver. In *Proc. of the 14th International Conference Tools and Algorithms for the Construction and Analysis of Systems* (TACAS'08), LNCS volume 4963. Springer (2008).

[21] K. Fisler, S. Krishnamurthi, L.A. Meyerovich, and M.C. Tschantz. 2005. Verification and Change-Impact Analysis of Access-Control Policies. In *Proc. of the 27th International Conference on Software Engineering* (ICSE'05). 196-205.

[22] Y. Jia, and M. Harman. 2010. An Analysis and Survey of the Development of Mutation Testing. *IEEE Trans. on Software Engineering*, Vol. 37, No. 5, 649-678.

[23] R. Just, D. Jalali, L. Inozemtseva, M.D. Ernst, R. Holmes, and G. Fraser. 2014. Are Mutants a Valid Substitute for Real Faults in Software Testing? In *Proc. of the Symposium on the Foundations of Software Engineering* (FSE'14), 654-665, Hong Kong, (November 2014).

[24] A. Bertolino, S. Daoudagh, F. Lonetti, E. Marchetti, 2013. XACMUT: XACML 2.0 Mutants Generator. In *Proc. of 2013 IEEE Sixth International Conf. on Software Testing, Verification and Validation Workshops*. 28-33.

[25] D. Xu, Y. Zhang, N. Shen, 2015. Formalizing Semantic Differences between Combining Algorithms in XACML 3.0 Policies. In *Proc. of the 2015 International Conference on Software Quality, Reliability and Security* (QRS'15), Vancouver, Canada (August 2015).

[26] M. Safarzadeh, M. Taghizadeh, B. Zamani, and B. T. Ladani. 2017. An Automatic Test Case Generator for Evaluating Implementation of Access Control Policies. *The ISC International Journal of Information Security*.

Parametric RBAC Maintenance via Max-SAT

Marco Benedetti
Bank of Italy, ICT Department
Centro Donato Menichella, Roma
marco.benedetti@bancaditalia.it

Marco Mori
Bank of Italy, ICT Department
Centro Donato Menichella, Roma
marco.mori@bancaditalia.it

ABSTRACT

In the past decade, many organizations have adopted a Role-Based Access Control model (RBAC) to reduce their administration costs and increase security. The migration to RBAC requires a role engineering phase aimed at generating "good" initial roles starting from direct assignments of permissions to users. For an RBAC approach to be effective, however, it is also necessary to update roles and keep them compliant with the dynamic nature of the business processes; not only this, but errors and misalignments between the current RBAC state and reality need to be promptly detected and fixed.

In this paper, we propose a new maintenance process to fix and refine an RBAC state when "exceptions" are detected. Exceptions are permissions some users realize they miss that are instrumental to their job and should be granted as soon as possible. They are caught by a monitoring system as unexpected "access denied" conditions and then validated by the RBAC administrator. The fix we produce aims at balancing two conflicting objectives, i.e., (i) simplifying the current RBAC state, and (ii) reducing the transition cost. Our approach is based on a Max-SAT formalization of this trade-off and it exploits *incomplete* solvers that quickly provide approximations of optimal solutions.

Experiments show good performance on real-world benchmarks.

Disclaimer: The opinions expressed and conclusions drawn are those of the authors and do not necessarily reflect the views of the authors' company.

CCS CONCEPTS

• **Security and privacy** → *Logic and verification*; *Access control*; *Authorization*;

KEYWORDS

Role Maintenance; Role Based Access Control (RBAC); Max-SAT

ACM Reference Format:
Marco Benedetti and Marco Mori. 2018. Parametric RBAC Maintenance via Max-SAT. In *SACMAT '18: The 23rd ACM Symposium on Access Control Models & Technologies (SACMAT), June 13–15, 2018, Indianapolis, IN, USA*. ACM, New York, NY, USA, 11 pages. https://doi.org/10.1145/3205977.3205987

1 INTRODUCTION

Complex organizations have to guarantee the correct access to software, systems, and data to a large number of employees involved in heterogeneous and evolving tasks. Classical access control policies based on a direct assignment of permissions to users have shown their limits: Granting and revoking individual permissions as tasks evolve and employees move is inefficient and error-prone.

Role Based Access Control - RBAC [3] has emerged as a solution to this issue and is currently widely adopted; it simplifies the management of permissions by defining *roles*, which include the permissions required to execute certain tasks. Users gain the permissions which are included in at least one of the roles assigned to them. In case users are moved to different tasks or if tasks change, it is sufficient to operate at the role level without modifying several Permission-to-User assignments. In addition, basic security principles such as *Least Privilege* and *Separation of Duties* may be easily enforced by posing conditions on roles and their assignments.

In order for an organization to adopt the RBAC model, it has to implement a *role management lifecycle* [14, 15] process, aimed at designing, implementing, and maintaining roles. To design (initial) roles, it is necessary to analyze Permission-to-User assignments and group together permissions into functional roles compactly representing the current access control policy. This is typically done via an automatic heuristic process called *role mining* [8]. While role mining supports the discovery of roles from scratch, in many cases organizations need to just *tune* or *maintain* the current set of roles: Roles may have to be revised to support new User-to-Permission assignments; or, a (possibly hand-made) RBAC state may contain errors, which need to be first discovered and then incorporated into the current state (after validation by a security administrator).

While tuning an RBAC model, the company has to consider conflicting objectives. It certainly benefits from a *simplification* of the current Permission-to-Role and Role-to-User assignments, i.e., of the so called *RBAC state*. Different metrics have been proposed in the literature to characterize the complexity of an RBAC state; they are often based on a combination of the number of roles and the number of assignments in it [1, 9]. Nevertheless, any *uninformed* simplification of a given RBAC state may heavily modify the current assignments, thus disrupting organizational processes and/or separation of duty constraints [13], not to mention the muscle memory of any human actor involved in managing and assigning roles. This may be acceptable if the organization is very small or at a preliminary stage of RBAC adoption; not so much in case of a large company with its own well-defined, perhaps "cherished" working set of roles, which have been costly defined and negotiated.

In this paper we define a new *parametric RBAC maintenance process* that supports both from-scratch design and maintenance of an existing role model. When performing maintenance, the in-place RBAC state is provided as input to the algorithm (together with new requirements to satisfy) and an adjusted model is produced as output, which accommodates the new requirements by "patching" the original state. When starting with a clean slate, a fully compliant RBAC state is grown out of the empty state by a sequence of patches.

As a key feature, the new algorithm aims at balancing two possibly conflicting metrics: *similarity* and *simplicity*. Similarity is a measure of how different the patched state is from the pre-patch state: the closer the two states the less disrupting the update. Simplicity is a measure of how close the patched state is to the unconstrained, *optimal* RBAC state: the more a patch strives for optimality, the larger the potential impact on the organization. As we will see, in our approach the RBAC administrator is provided with means to strike the best balance between these two objectives.

The algorithm generates Max-SAT [6] instances and solves them via publicly-available, state-of-the-art solvers. Several well known datasets are adapted to this new incremental setting and are used to establish the practicality of our solution in real-world cases.

The rest of this paper is organized as follows. Section 2 frames the problem and presents a working example. Section 3 defines the Max-SAT formalization and introduces two metrics we use to evaluate the quality of an RBAC state. Section 4 describes the datasets we use in the experiments and presents the results of our experimental evaluation. Section 5 discusses related works. Section 6 concludes the paper and proposes directions for future work.

2 PARAMETRIC RBAC MAINTENANCE

2.1 Preliminaries

Role mining is a preliminary step to enable the adoption of an RBAC model. It can be executed bottom-up or top-down.

The bottom-up approach takes as input an existing set of direct Permission-to-User assignments. Then, mining roles consists in defining a collection of roles (sets of permissions) and then assigning one or more roles to each user. The permissions each user is granted by any of his role(s) have to be exactly the same Permissions-to-User assignments he had before roles were introduced.

Formally, starting from a binary matrix $UPA \in \{0, 1\}^{m,n}$ representing the assignments of n permissions to m users, role mining factorizes it into a Role-to-User matrix $UA \in \{0, 1\}^{m,k}$ and a Permission-to-User matrix $PA \in \{0, 1\}^{k,n}$, for some positive integer k (number of roles), such that $UA \otimes PA = UPA$, where the boolean matrix multiplication operator $\otimes$ is defined as $UPA_{ij} = \bigvee_{l=1}^{k} (UA_{il} \wedge PA_{lj})$.

Top-down approaches—employed as an alternative or in combination with bottom-up mining—define roles starting from an analysis of the business processes to support. Top-down roles are typically hand-crafted by business stakeholders after an analysis of the organization processes and of the permissions users require to execute them. Hand-made roles, though validated and closely inspected, may of course contain (several) errors.

Whether the synthesis is top-down or bottom-up, once an *RBAC state* is in place, a *role maintenance* process is required to adapt the state to intervening organizational changes (employees move, new systems are deployed, etc.) or to fix errors that become apparent during actual usage.

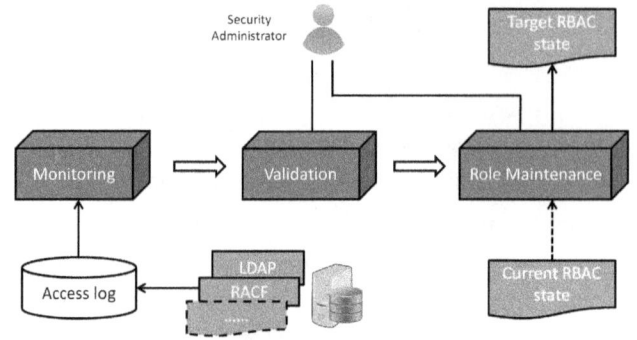

Figure 1: The Parametric Role Maintenance process.

2.2 Maintenance of an RBAC state

Errors show up as either Permission-to-User assignments that are not implied by the current state but should be, or as unnecessary permissions granted to users. In this paper, we address missing permissions only, though the formalization in Section 3 is capable of dealing with extra permissions (the issue with extra permissions is how to discover them in the first place, a subject out of scope here). Figure 1 describes the process of discovering missing permissions. The logs captured by the monitoring systems record (among the other things) events corresponding to missing permissions. The security administrator comes into play at this stage by *validating* prohibited accesses; of particular interest are false positives, i.e., permissions a user misses but should be allowed to have, which we call *exceptions*. The administrator may also directly specify further exceptions by generalizing the issue at hand.

Starting from a (validated) exception $e : p \rightarrow u$ to be incorporated into an existing RBAC state S_0, the *maintenance* phase generates a target RBAC state with the following properties:

(a) it is semantically equivalent to S_0, aside from accommodating exception e, i.e., u now has permission p;

(b) among all states that satisfy (a), it is either (i) the *most similar* to S_0, or (ii) the *simplest possible* state, or (iii) any state *in between* these two extremes.

Section 3 formalizes the meaning of "most similar", "simplest possible", and "in between". Maintenance is applied as new exceptions arrive. If necessary, several exceptions may be dealt with at once, in a single step (however, we only show the exception-by-exception workflow in the following sections). The degree of freedom at (b) is exploited by the security administrator to strike the best balance between evolving the state towards simplicity and preserving the status quo, according to criteria external to the algorithm.

2.3 Scope of application

Role maintenance may also act as a *fixing* or *mining* tool, depending on how it is applied; indeed, the state fed into it can be:

Fix A hand-made, top-down RBAC state, which despite possibly containing (several) errors cannot be radically overhauled because it has been agreed on by several stakeholders; here, role maintenance is basically used to gradually shepherd the hand-made model to the reality of business processes;

Tune An in-place, fully satisfactory RBAC state which needs to undergo maintenance to accommodate exogenous events, such as updates in business processes, deployment/replacement of information systems, relocation of employees, etc.;

Mine An empty state granting no permission to anyone; in this case, role maintenance is used as an incremental role mining procedure whereby the administrator generates a well-behaved and well-structured RBAC state by monitoring missing permissions on-line and judiciously granting them.

We focus on the "tune" use case in the rest of the paper.

2.4 A working example

Let us consider a consulting firm with dozens of employees. They use two applications that store data into a company database. The first application supports the *publishing* activity of the company. The second application is used for *marketing* purposes, specifically in the definition of campaigns for mainstream media. An independent in-house *quality assurance* process ensures the compliance of the actions taken through the publishing and the marketing platform with all relevant guidelines and regulations. Employees also use a *general*-purpose Internet service and an in-house e-mail server, through which they *communicate* with institutional stakeholders. An Intranet is available for internal communication and to access *business* applications. The *HR* department manages a database with employees' data. A *web site* describes the services offered by the company on the web. The application server and the *databases* are managed by different administrators.

An RBAC solution is in place at this company: Roles have been crafted so that each employee is enabled to perform only the task(s) he is involved in. The set of (business and technical) roles are: *publishing, marketing, quality assurance, general communication, business communication, HR management, server administration* and *database administration*. As usual, each role is associated with the set of permissions required to carry out the corresponding task(s). For example, the marketing (publishing) role entails the permission to access the marketing (publishing) application, in addition to the permission to access the shared business database. The business communication role grants the permission to use the mail server and the Intranet, while the general communication role gives access to the Internet. Finally, the database administration role is required to operate on the business and the HR databases.

Let us suppose the RBAC manager at this company is now faced with these urgent requests: An employee is about to join the marketing division and needs the corresponding permissions; at the same time, another employee who is already in that division just realized he lacks some much needed permissions to operate; another employee from the marketing division is required to (also) work in the publishing process for a while. Finally, yet another employee is to be temporarily granted permissions to help the database administrator, but only on a non-critical dataset.

The RBAC administrator would like to be supported in the process of re-configuring the RBAC state. In particular, he would like to automatically obtain good answers to questions such as:

- *"How to modify the current RBAC state to implement the necessary variations and nothing more?"*

- *"Is it possible to operate on the Permission-to-Role and/or Role-to-User assignments without adding new roles?"*
- *"Would it be better to just create new custom roles?"*
- *"Is this an occasion to merge some existing roles into less and more clear-cut business figures?"*
- *"Once I'm at it, can I simplify the current role set while keeping the solution stable w.r.t. to the desired RBAC state?"*

3 FORMALIZATION

We use the language of propositional logic to represent RBAC maintenance instances. The question we ask is not simply about the satisfiability of a logic statement by some propositional model (SAT), because we need to also express preferences between conflicting objectives (similarity and simplicity of the output RBAC state). It turns out a slightly different, "optimizing" framework perfectly suited to our needs is Max-SAT, which considers all possible truth assignments to the input formula and picks the best one according to a fitness metric defined in the Max-SAT language itself.

3.1 SAT and Max-SAT

A SAT problem [2] is solved by assigning a truth value in {*True, False*} to each Boolean variable that appears in the input propositional formula in such a way that the formula as a whole evaluates to *True*. If at least one such assignment exists, the formula is *satisfiable* and the satisfying assignment is called a *model*; otherwise, the formula is *unsatisfiable* (inconsistent) and it has no model. This problem is intractable (NP-complete) in general, yet several highly efficient solvers exist that in practice solve real-world problems with millions of variables in reasonable time.

Given any UPA matrix, its factorization into $UA \otimes PA = UPA$ for some number of roles k can be directly expressed in SAT as:

$$\bigwedge_{ij} \left[UPA_{ij} \leftrightarrow \vee_{l=1}^{k} (UA_{il} \wedge PA_{lj}) \right] \quad (1)$$

(1) is a SAT instance with $k(m + n)$ variables. Without loss of generality, most SAT solvers require input formulas in Conjunctive Normal Form (CNF), i.e., a conjunction of clauses, each clause being a disjunction of literals. By either reworking the formula (possibly enlarging its size) or adding auxiliary variables, it is possible to rewrite any non-CNF problem like (1) in CNF.

In SAT, all clauses have to be satisfied for the formula to be declared satisfiable. The *Maximum Satisfiability problem* (Max-SAT) is a variant of SAT that relaxes this premise. The goal of Max-SAT is to find an assignment that makes true the *largest possible subset* of clauses: some may remain unsatisfied. *Partial* Max-SAT is another variant in which some clauses are declared *hard* and must be satisfied no matter what, as in SAT, while others are declared *soft*: As many of them as possible must be satisfied, à la Max-SAT. Yet another variant is *Weighted* Max-SAT, that generalizes Max-SAT by associating a positive real or integer weight to each input clause: An assignment that *maximizes the sum of the weights* of satisfied clauses, rather than just their number, is sought (clauses left unsatisfied contribute nothing to the sum).

Finally, the *Weighted Partial* Max-SAT (WPMS) language combines both features: It finds an assignment that satisfies all hard clauses while maximizing the cumulated weight of satisfied soft clauses. We employ WPMS here (and call it simply Max-SAT).

3.2 Hard constraints

Hard clauses are well suited to represent invariants that must hold on any RBAC state we may possibly output, and in particular to capture condition (a) from Section 2.2.

The input RBAC state is represented by two boolean matrices UA^0 and PA^0 such that $UA^0 \otimes PA^0 = UPA^0$. UA^0 and PA^0 are respectively a $m \times k^0$ and a $k^0 \times n$ boolean matrices having non-empty roles, i.e., $\forall_{t=1,..,k^0}(\bigvee_{i=1,..,m} UA_{i,t} = True) \wedge (\bigvee_{j=1,..,n} PA_{t,j} = True)$. Given an exception $e : p_i \rightarrow u_j$ meant to grant a new permission p_i to user u_j (it was $UPA^0_{i,j} = False$), we define EXC(e) as the $m \times n$ boolean matrix that is $True$ at (i,j) and $False$ everywhere else. We then need $k(m + n)$ variables to represent the unknown elements of the updated Role-to-User (UA) and of the Permissions-to-Role (PA) matrices, where m, k, and n are the number of users, roles, and permissions.

We have to find two boolean matrices UA and PA such that:

$$UA \otimes PA = UPA^0 \oplus EXC(e) = UPA \qquad (2)$$

where $\oplus$ is the boolean matrix sum operator. In terms of the variables defining UA and PA, this can be written:

$$\bigwedge_{i,j} F_{i,j}, \text{ where } F_{i,j} := \left(\bigvee_{t \in [1,k]} UA_{i,t} \wedge PA_{t,j}\right) = UPA^0_{i,j} \vee EXC_{i,j}(e)$$

Formulas $F_{i,j}$ are not in CNF. To turn them into CNF we observe that only two cases have to be considered:

$$\begin{pmatrix} \cdots & \cdots & \cdots \\ UA_{i_0,1} & \cdots & UA_{i_0,k} \\ \vdots & \vdots & \vdots \\ UA_{i_1,1} & \cdots & UA_{i_1,k} \\ \cdots & \cdots & \cdots \end{pmatrix} \begin{pmatrix} \cdots & PA_{1,j_0} & \cdots & PA_{1,j_1} & \cdots \\ \vdots & \vdots & \vdots & \vdots & \vdots \\ \cdots & PA_{k,j_0} & \cdots & PA_{k,j_1} & \cdots \end{pmatrix} =$$

$$\begin{matrix} & j_0 & & j_1 & \\ & \begin{pmatrix} \cdots & \cdots & \cdots & \cdots & \cdots \\ i_0 \quad \cdots & False & \cdots & \cdots & \cdots \\ \vdots & \vdots & \vdots & \vdots & \vdots \\ i_1 \quad \cdots & \cdots & \cdots & True & \cdots \\ \cdots & \cdots & \cdots & \cdots & \cdots \end{pmatrix} \end{matrix}$$

If $UPA^0_{i,j} \vee EXC_{i,j}$ is $False$, such as at index (i_0,j_0) above, we have:

$$\left[\bigvee_{t \in [1,k]} (UA_{i,t} \wedge PA_{t,j}) \right] = False$$

which can be rewritten as a set of clauses by negating both sides:

$$has_{i,j}(UA, PA) := \bigwedge_{t \in [1,k]} (\neg UA_{i,t} \vee \neg PA_{t,j}) \qquad (3)$$

If $UPA^0_{i,j} \vee EXC_{i,j}$ is $True$, such as at index (i_1,j_1), we have:

$$\left[\bigvee_{t \in [1,k]} (UA_{i,t} \wedge PA_{t,j}) \right] = True$$

Here we apply the Tseytin transformation [12] by inserting k auxiliary variables $\{aux_1, \ldots, aux_k\}$, one for each disjunct:

$$\begin{cases} \bigvee_{t \in [1,k]} aux_t \\ \bigwedge_{t \in [1,k]} aux_t \leftrightarrow (UA_{i,t} \wedge PA_{t,j}) \end{cases}$$

which is equivalent to the CNF form:

$$hasnt_{i,j}(UA, PA) := \begin{cases} \bigvee_{t \in [1,k]} aux_t \\ \bigwedge_{t \in [1,k]} (\neg aux_t \vee UA_{i,t}) \wedge (\neg aux_t \vee PA_{t,j}) \\ \bigwedge_{t \in [1,k]} (aux_t \vee \neg UA_{i,t} \vee \neg PA_{t,j}) \end{cases}$$

$$(4)$$

Overall, the hard clauses that guarantee we are incorporating the exception(s) in EXC are:

$$exc(UA, PA) := \bigwedge_{i,j | UPA_{i,j}} has_{i,j}(UA, PA) \quad \wedge \bigwedge_{i,j | \neg UPA_{i,j}} hasnt_{i,j}(UA, PA)$$

$$(5)$$

3.3 Soft constraints

We use soft clauses to express contraints that we know are in trade-off and cannot always be satisfied simultaneously. In particular, we want to capture the conditions (i) and (ii) at point (b) in Section 2.2.

Identity. To express the condition that the output RBAC state (UA, PA) must be identical to the input state (UA^0, PA^0) we write:

$$\begin{cases} \bigwedge_{i \in [1,m], j \in [1,k]} UA_{i,j} \leftrightarrow UA^0_{i,j} \\ \bigwedge_{i \in [1,k], j \in [1,n]} PA_{i,j} \leftrightarrow PA^0_{i,j} \end{cases}$$

which in CNF is:

$$eq(UA, PA) := \begin{cases} \bigwedge_{i,j}(UA_{i,j} \vee \neg UA^0_{i,j}) \wedge (\neg UA_{i,j} \vee UA^0_{i,j}) \\ \bigwedge_{i,j}(PA_{i,j} \vee \neg PA^0_{i,j}) \wedge (\neg PA_{i,j} \vee PA^0_{i,j}) \end{cases}$$

$$(6)$$

Note that $exc(UA, PA) \wedge eq(UA, PA)$ is unsatisfiable by construction in the traditional SAT sense.

Sparsification. To express the condition that the output RBAC state (UA, PA) must be as "simple" as possible we need to adopt some notion of simplicity. The two simplifying conditions we consider are: *(i)* a reduction in the number of Roles-to-User and/or Permission-to-Role assignments ("sparsification"), and *(ii)* a reduction in the number of roles (see next section, "Contraction").

According to (i), the sparsest possible RBAC state would be:

$$sparse(UA, PA) := \begin{cases} \bigwedge_{i \in [1,m], j \in [1,k], UA^0_{i,j}=1} \neg UA_{i,j} \\ \bigwedge_{i \in [1,k], j \in [1,n], PA^0_{i,j}=1} \neg PA_{i,j} \end{cases} \qquad (7)$$

Contraction. Sometimes, incorporating an exception makes it possible to satisfy equation (2) with one less role than those present in (UA^0, PA^0). The soft constraint $sparse(UA, PA)$ is not sufficient to prefer a reduction in the number of roles over similarly-sized but sparse unassignments from UA. The fact that role j is no longer in use in the target RBAC state is represented by a column of 0's in the Role-to-User assignment matrix (UA); so the condition is:

$$contr(UA) := \bigwedge_{j \in [1,k]} unused_j(UA) \qquad (8)$$

where $\{unused_j\}$ are auxiliary variables telling whether role j is assigned to someone ($unused_j = False$) or not ($unused_j = True$):

$$unused_{contr}(UA) := \bigwedge_{j \in [1,k]} \left[unused_j(UA) \leftrightarrow \wedge_{t \in [1,m]} \neg UA_{t,j} \right]$$

$$(9)$$

Expansion. Dually, it is possible that the only way to incorporate an exception is by adding one role to the state, i.e., one column to UA and one row to PA. In a propositional encoding, the only way to accommodate for a possible expansion of the matrices we handle is to "reserve space" in advance for the additional row and column. This means we actually work with an RBAC state made by a matrix UA^+ with $k + 1$ columns and a matrix PA^+ with $k + 1$ rows. The condition that this additional role stays unused is:

$$noexp(UA) := unused_{k+1} \tag{10}$$

where $unused_{k+1}$ is an auxiliary variable telling whether the additional role remains unused:

$$unused_{exp}(UA) := unused_{k+1} \leftrightarrow \wedge_{i \in [1,m]} \neg UA^+_{i,k+1} \tag{11}$$

$$unused(UA) := unused_{contr}(UA) \wedge unused_{exp} \tag{12}$$

In an encoding where both contraction and expansion constraints are added, we enforce a coherent interplay between the two opposite effects by saying they must not happen simultaneously:

$$mutex(UA) := noexp(UA) \vee \neg leastcontr(UA) \tag{13}$$

where $leastcontr$ tells weather at least a role is no longer in use:

$$leastcontr(UA) := \bigvee_{j \in [1,k]} unused_j(UA)$$

3.4 The complete encoding

We have all the pieces to present the complete encoding of the RBAC maintenance problem as a Weighted Partial Max-SAT instance. First, let us list the hard constraints (HC) that any feasible solution must comply with. In addition to those from Section 3.2, all the auxiliary contraints from Section 3.3 are hard, because auxiliary propositional variables cannot cause inconsistencies on their own, yet they must always be assigned a consistent value:

$$HC(UA, PA) := exc(UA^+, PA^+) \wedge unused(UA) \wedge mutex(UA) \tag{14}$$

Soft constraints (SC) are used to express and balance two potentially conflicting objectives of the RBAC maintenance procedure:

(1) maximizing the *similarity* between the target and the origin RBAC state; in this sense, the higher the weight we assign to clauses in (6), the better;
(2) maximizing the *simplicity* of the target RBAC state (independently of the origin RBAC state); in this sense, the higher the weight we assign to clauses in (7), (8), and (10), the better.

Let us assume the weight of a given clause C is a real value[1] $w \in [0, 1]$, noted $w : C$. The notation $w : (C_1 \wedge \ldots \wedge C_n)$ is a shorthand for $w/n : C_1 \wedge \ldots \wedge w/n : C_n$, while $w_1 : (w2 : C)$ is interpreted as $(w_1 \cdot w_2) : C$. The three components (7), (8), and (10) of the "simplicity" objective are merged into one weighted set of clauses, noted $SIMP_{k^+, k^-}(UP, PA)$ and defined as:

$$v : \left[k^- : contr(UA, PA) \wedge sparse(UA, PA) \wedge k^+ : noexp(UA, PA) \right] \tag{15}$$

Here, $k^- \geq 0$ is a parameter meant to quantify how much we reward the elimination of a role versus to the sparsification of the matrix; $k^+ \geq 0$ measures our adversion to introduce a new role

if not strictly necessary. $v := (1 + k^- + k^+)^{-1}$ is a normalization factor meant to ensure the weights of the three components sum up to 1. We assume $k^- > k^+ > 1$, i.e., we value the possibility to expunge a role more than the removal of an equivalent number of assignments; adding a role is a last resort.

Finally, let $\beta \in [0, 1]$ be a balancing parameter that measures the extent to which the RBAC administrator is interested in a simplified (β closer to 1) VS a stable (β closer to 0) RBAC state; we pose:

$$SC_{\beta, k^-, k^+}(UA, PA) := (1-\beta) : eq(UA, PA) \wedge \beta : SIMP_{k^+, k^-}(UA, PA) \tag{16}$$

3.5 Solutions and their quality

Given (i) the input RBAC state (UA^0, PA^0), (ii) the exception matrix EXC to incorporate, and (iii) some specific values for the parameters β, k^+, and k^-, we submit to a Max-SAT solver the hard clauses (14) plus the soft clauses (16). The Max-SAT solver returns a *fixed* RBAC state (UA, PA), i.e., a truth assignment to all the $k(m + n)$ variables that define UA and PA. Note that the encoding is satisfiable by construction, so we always obtain a fixed state.

To assess the quality of UA, PA (both per se and w.r.t. UA^0, PA^0) we need some synthetic indicators for the two dimensions we are after: simplicity and similarity.

Similarity is computed according to the metric defined in [13], which is based on the Jaccard coefficient.

Role-to-Role similarity. The similarity between two roles r_1 and r_2 granting permissions P_1 and P_2 respectively is defined as:

$$sim_{1-1}(r_1, r_2) := \frac{|P_1 \cap P_2|}{|P_1 \cup P_2|}$$

Role-to-RoleSet similarity. The similarity between a role r and a set of roles R is defined as:

$$sim_{1-N}(r, R) := max_{r_x \in R} sim_{1-1}(r, r_x)$$

RoleSet-to-RoleSet similarity. The similarity between a set of roles R_1 and a set of roles R_2 is defined as:

$$sim_{N-N}(R_1, R_2) := avg_{r \in R_1} sim_{1-N}(r, R_2)$$

Building on these definitions, we pose:
Similarity. The similarity of the target RBAC state (with roles R) to the source RBAC state (with roles R_0) as:

$$sim(R_0, R) := \frac{sim_{N-N}(R_0, R) + sim_{N-N}(R, R_0)}{2} \tag{17}$$

This similarity function is always between 0 and 1; in particular, the value 1 is obtained iff $R \equiv R_0$.

Simplicity is defined in different ways in the relevant literature; metrics taken into account to define it include, but are not limited to, the number of roles, assignments, erroneous permission granted, relations among roles, permission assigned directly, and any combination of these metrics. We start from a definition of "absolute complexity" that grows with the number of roles and the number of assignments in UA and PA:

$$comp(UA, PA) := (|UA| + |PA|) + |R|^2 \tag{18}$$

---

[1] Some Max-SAT solvers only accept positive integer values as weights; we can map real values onto integers that are equivalent to the effect of the optimization we perform as $weight_{int} = \lceil \delta * weight_{real} \rceil$ where δ is the minimum absolute difference between the sum of the weights of any two disjoint subsets of the real weights mentioned in the formula.

where R is the set of roles, and UA and PA are the assignments of permissions and roles[2]. A *relative* complexity is then computed as the ratio between the complexity of the target state and the complexity of the "trivial" admissible state; in such state, each user is assigned one and only one custom role which entails exactly the set of permissions that user has in UPA. In this configuration, the UA matrix becomes the identity matrix, there are as many roles as users, and all the knowledge about permissions is in PA. The absolute complexity of such trivial state is thus $(|UPA| + |U|) + |U|^2$.

The (relative) simplicity[3] of a state is then:

$$opt = 1 - \frac{|UA| + |PA| + |R|^2}{|UPA| + |U| + |U|^2} \tag{19}$$

4 VALIDATION

In this section we validate our maintenance algorithm *(i)* at a *small-scale* in Section 4.1, where we apply it to our motivating example from Section 2.4; *(ii)* at a *larger scale* in Section 4.2, where we present experimental results showing its viability in real-word cases.

4.1 Maintenance of our working example

Table 1 and Table 2 formalize (a small version of) the example from Section 2.4. Table 3 represents the corresponding RBAC state as Permission-to-Role and Role-to-User assignments.

We now imagine that four exceptions to such initial RBAC state—listed in Table 4—are captured by the monitoring system or directly specified by the RBAC administrator. We have to incorporate them.

e_1: According to the first exception, it is necessary to augment the permissions of user $u4$ by granting him access to the marketing application (permission $p7$). The user already has access to the publishing application and to the business database. Different RBAC states result from different values of the balance parameter β. For example, if (i) the administrator prefers not to alter the current state too much and he submits the value $\beta = 0.1$ to the algorithm, the exception is incorporated by simply assigning role *marketing-Funct* to $u4$. The variation over the current RBAC state is minimal ($sim = 1$) and the complexity of the state is almost unchanged at $opt = 0.388$ (same number of roles and the addition of a single assignment); in case (ii) the administrator values simplicity more and sets the value $\beta = 0.5$, the algorithm again answers by assigning role *marketingFunct* to $u4$, but then carries out further simplifying and adjustments to the input state. Namely, the *busComm* role is augmented with the Internet access permission thus making it possible to reduce the assignments of role *genComm* to just $u6$ and $u7$. Simplicity raises to $opt = 0.432$ at the price of lowering the similarity to $sim = 0.958$. Let us suppose in what follows that the RBAC administrator picks option (ii).

e_2: It is now required that the marketing application ($p7$) is made accessible to user $u5$ too. Assuming (i) a high interest in similarity

($\beta = 0.1$), the algorithm assigns role *marketingFunct* to $u5$, thus maintaining a stable state ($sim = 1$) and essentially the same simplicity ($opt = 0.429$). Alternatively, (ii) the assignment $\beta = 0.5$ causes the algorithm to extend the role *publishingFunct*—which is already assigned to $u5$—with the missing permission $p7$. This is possible since no user is granted $p8$ but not $p7$ anymore. Thus, the new *publishingFunct* role enables both business applications, while *marketingFunct* gives access to the marketing application only, and is assigned to $u3$. This new RBAC state has a lower similarity at $sim = 0.958$, but only a slightly improved simplicity at 0.446. Since the optimization is marginal and it comes with a damage to similarity, the administrator picks option (i) over option (ii).

e_3: User $u3$ needs to access the publishing application (permission $p7$). It turns out that in the current state all users granted $p8$ should also have $p7$. It follows that the distinction between *marketingFunct* and *publishingFunct* makes no longer sense. It is thus not surprising that with even moderate importance assigned to simplicity ($\beta = 0.3$), the algorithm answers by joining such two roles and reducing the state complexity to $opt = 0.541$, at the price of some state variation ($sim = 0.935$). In particular, role *publishingFunct* is erased and role *marketingFunct*, already assigned to $u3$, is augmented with $p8$, thus enabling the access to both business applications.

e_4: User $u6$ is assigned the responsibility of managing the business DB (permission $p10$). A role enabling the management of all the databases (business and HR, $p10$ and $p9$) already exists: *DBAdmin*. However, $u6$ is to be granted access to the business database only; it may be necessary to augment the role set. By applying the role-maintenance algorithm with $\beta = 0.1$, we are indeed returned a target RBAC state with a new role (we call it *BussDBAdmin*) assigned to $u6$ and including permission $p10$ only. The complexity of the RBAC state is augmented since a new role is introduced ($opt = 0.452$); there is a minimal variation from the initial state ($sim = 0.958$).

4.2 Experimental Evaluation

To experiment at a larger scale we exercise our algorithm on the semi-synthetic datasets described in Section 4.2.1. Different Max-SAT solvers are compared in Section 4.2.2 to select the one that best suits our needs. Experimental results, performed on a 20-core Intel CPU with 138GB of memory, are presented in Section 4.2.3. Unless noted otherwise, we set $k^+ = k^- = 1$. All the results and datasets can be downloaded from the web site [10].

4.2.1 Synthetic datasets. In order to experiment with our maintenance procedure, we require datasets that include: *(i)* some initial RBAC state defined in terms of a set of roles and their assignment to users, and *(ii)* a list of exceptions: couples of Permission-to-User assignments that are either missing or in excess in such RBAC state. To the best of our knowledge, no public dataset provides such information. Most datasets only consist of a binary matrix of Permission-to-User assignments, with no associated RBAC state. Moreover, exception histories are never included.

In order to synthesize a benchmark for the maintenance problem, we start with four existing datasets: our example from Section 4.1, named *SmallComp* here, plus three classical problems of increasing

---

[2] By squaring the role number, we penalize the growth of roles more than linearly compared to the role and permission assignments, without introducing arbitrary weighting factors. Alternative definitions from the literature have been tested, with minimal impact on the results from Section 4.

[3] Another possibility here would be to measure the absolute complexity via (18) as a percentage of the complexity of the initial state. We prefer measure (19) because it is independent of the unknown quality of the initial state (which we'll synthesize via an approximate miner) and stays in the range [0, 1) with a clear meaning at the extremes.

U\P	p1	p2	p3	p4	p5	p6	p7	p8	p9	p10	p11
u1	1	1	0	1	0	1	1	1	0	0	0
u2	1	1	0	1	0	1	1	1	0	0	0
u3	1	1	0	1	0	1	1	$0[1]^3$	0	0	0
u4	1	1	0	1	0	1	$0[1]^1$	1	0	0	0
u5	1	1	0	1	0	1	$0[1]^2$	1	0	0	0
u6	1	0	0	0	0	0	0	0	0	$0[1]^4$	0
u7	1	0	0	0	0	0	0	0	0	0	0
u8	1	1	0	1	0	1	0	0	1	1	0
u9	1	1	0	0	0	1	1	1	0	0	1
u10	1	1	0	1	1	1	0	0	0	0	0
u11	1	1	1	0	0	1	0	0	0	0	0

Table 1: Permission-to-User assignment matrix (UPA).

Permission	Meaning
p1	Internet Access
p2	Mail Access
p3	HR DB Access
p4	Business DB Access
p5	High Perf. Comp. Resource Access
p6	Intranet Access
p7	Marketing Application Access
p8	Publishing Application Access
p9	HR DB Admin
p10	Business DB Admin
p11	Application Server Admin

Table 2: Permissions and their meaning.

R\P	p1	p2	p3	p4	p5	p6	p7	p8	p9	p10	p11	u1	u2	u3	u4	u5	u6	u7	u8	u9	u10	u11
bussComm	$0[1]^1$	1	0	0	0	1	0	0	0	0	0	1	1	1	1	1	0	0	1	1	1	1
genComm	1	0	0	0	0	0	0	0	0	0	0	$1[0]^1$	$1[0]^1$	$1[0]^1$	$1[0]^1$	$1[0]^1$	1	1	$1[0]^1$	$1[0]^1$	$1[0]^1$	$1[0]^1$
marketingFunct	0	0	0	1	0	0	1	$0[1]^3$	0	0	0	1	1	1	$0[1]^1$	$0[1]^2$	0	0	0	0	0	0
publishingFunct	0	0	0	1	0	0	0	1	0	0	0	$1[0]^3$	$1[0]^3$	$0[0]^3$	$1[0]^3$	$1[0]^3$	$0[0]^3$	$0[0]^3$	$0[0]^3$	$0[0]^3$	$0[0]^3$	$0[0]^3$
HRManagement	0	0	1	0	0	0	0	0	0	0	0	0	0	0	0	0	0	0	0	0	0	1
QualityAssurance	0	0	0	1	1	0	0	0	0	0	0	0	0	0	0	0	0	0	0	0	1	0
DBAdmin	0	0	0	1	0	0	0	0	1	1	0	0	0	0	0	0	0	0	1	0	0	0
ServerAdmin	0	0	0	0	0	0	1	1	0	0	1	0	0	0	0	0	0	0	0	1	0	0
BussDBAdmin	$[0]^4$	$[0]^4$	$[0]^4$	$[0]^4$	$[0]^4$	$[0]^4$	$[0]^4$	$[0]^4$	$[0]^4$	$[1]^4$	$[0]^4$	$[0]^4$	$[0]^4$	$[0]^4$	$[0]^4$	$[0]^4$	$[1]^4$	$[0]^4$	$[0]^4$	$[0]^3$	$[0]^4$	$[0]^4$

Table 3: Permission-to-Role matrix PA (left) and User-to-Role matrix UA^T (right).

dimension used in the role-mining literature, called *Domino*, *University*, and *Firewall1*. All these instances are defined in terms of their User-to-Permission matrix. Starting from one of these UPA matrices, we generate (purely additive) maintenance instances as follows:

(1) Given a positive integer k, we randomly select k user permissions in UPA and remove them, thus obtaining UPA^0. A random order is assigned to such permissions to obtain the list of exceptions which we ask our algorithm to incorporate;

(2) We synthesize a complete RBAC state out of UPA^0 via one of the role mining algorithms available in the literature. Given that we aim at an arbitrary (not necessarily optimal) initial state, we adopt *Fast Miner*, a heuristic procedure which returns a sub-optimal set of roles[4]. The corresponding UA^0 matrix is then iteratively generated, and the resulting RBAC state is used as initial state for the maintenance algorithm.

The resulting benchmark is described in Table 5.

---

[4] We choose Fast Miner over the alternatives–which we tried–because it quickly returns solutions of good quality to medium and large problems. In preliminary experiments done with other miners, we observed different initial absolute values but quite similar trends (as a function of beta and of the timeout) in all the experiments.

			RBAC state			
Exception	β	|UPA|	|R|	|UA| + |PA|	opt	sim
-	-	50	8	47	0.390	-
$e_1 : p7 \rightarrow u4$	0.5	51	8	40	0.432	0.958
$e_2 : p7 \rightarrow u5$	0.1	52	8	41	0.429	1
$e_3 : p8 \rightarrow u3$	0.3	53	7	36	0.541	0.935
$e_4 : p10 \rightarrow u6$	0.1	54	8	38	0.452	0.958

Table 4: List of exceptions to incorporate in the working example. In Table 1 and Table 3, we note $old[new]^i$ an assignment that is changed from value *old* to value *new* by applying exception e^i.

4.2.2 Choosing a Max-SAT solver. Max-SAT solvers are either complete or incomplete. Complete solvers always identify the optimal solution (if one exists), given enough time. Incomplete solvers determine an approximate solution, with no guarantee on how distant it is from the optimum. In practice, on satisfiable non-random instances, they often produce good approximations, and quickly. Furthermore, some solvers work as anytime algorithms, i.e., given any timeout as input, they return the best solution they could possibly find (if any) within the assigned timeout.

Complete solvers. Solving large instances of the role-maintenance problem may be unfeasible in practice for complete solvers. To check if this is the case, we chose a few of the best performers at the Max-SAT 2016 international competition[5]. Then, we exercise these promising solvers on the datasets from Section 4.2.1, imposing a time limit of 1 hour. Results are in the following table.

Solver	SmallComp	Domino	University	Firewall1
Maximo	$\beta \leq 0.5$	$\beta = 0$	$\beta = 0$	$\beta = 0$
MaxHS	$\beta \leq 0.4$	$\beta = 0$	$\beta = 0$	-
LMHS	$\beta \leq 0.3$	$\beta = 0$	$\beta = 0$	-
Ahmaxsat	$\beta \leq 0.25$	-	-	-

The table shows the maximum value of β for which solvers are able to incorporate all the exceptions. The symbol "−" means the solver failed (timeout or memout) on one or more instances.

The *SmallComp* dataset is the only one for which we obtain some results across the entire panel of solvers. Even with such dataset of small instances, as β grows most solvers quickly stop responding within the alloted timeout. For example, even the best solver of *SmallComp* (i.e., Maximo) fails instances as $\beta > 0.5$.

As expected, the larger the instances in the benchmark, the sooner complete solvers stop responding. More surprising is how

---

[5] Max-Sat competition web-site - http://maxsat.ia.udl.cat/introduction/

Dataset	#U	#P	Density	RBAC state			Max-SAT encoding			
				$\|R^0\|$	$\|UA^0\| + \|PA^0\|$	#Excs	#V	#C	$\#C_h$	$\#C_s$
SmallComp	11	11	0.207	13	65	12	$6.9 \cdot 10^2$	$3 \cdot 10^3$	$2.6 \cdot 10^3$	$3.7 \cdot 10^2$
Domino	79	231	0.039	71	1803	19	$7.4 \cdot 10^4$	$1.4 \cdot 10^6$	$1.4 \cdot 10^6$	$2.4 \cdot 10^4$
University	493	56	0.143	71	8769	10	$3.2 \cdot 10^5$	$2.6 \cdot 10^6$	$2.6 \cdot 10^6$	$4.8 \cdot 10^4$
Firewall1	365	709	0.123	580	99713	32	$1.9 \cdot 10^7$	$1.9 \cdot 10^8$	$1.9 \cdot 10^8$	$7.2 \cdot 10^5$

Table 5: Datasets in our benchmark. #U, #P, and *Density* are the number of users, permissions, and the percentage of assignments in the UPA^0 matrix, respectively, after the removal of #Excs exceptions. $|R^0|$ and $|UA^0| + |PA^0|$ are the number of roles and assignments in the initial RBAC state. #V, #C, $\#C_h$, and $\#C_s$ are the number of variables, clauses, hard clauses, and soft clauses in the Max-SAT encoding, respectively.

quickly performance deteriorates: By the time we try to solve *Firewall1*, even the best solver doesn't return solutions unless $\beta = 0$.

We conclude that it is not feasible to employ complete solvers to tackle real-world instances of our RBAC maintenance encoding, except perhaps for very small values of β.

Incomplete solvers. Let us shift our attention to state-of-the-art incomplete solvers, as represented by the best performers at Max-SAT 2016. We tested: *Dsat, CCLS2015, CCEHC, OptiRiss, Dist, WPM3*.

CCEHC [7] stands out here, because it is the only solver that: (1) showed a strong performance at Max-SAT 2016, (2) accepts command-line options to tune its solving behavior for industrial benchmarks, and (3) works as an anytime algorithm.

Let us first measure how CCEHC behaves in a case clearly beyond reach for complete solvers. We generate 90 maintenance instances of increasing size from *Firewall1* by selecting more and more of its users (i.e., rows); each instance is associated with a single exception to incorporate and generates a Max-SAT encoding of growing size. We ask CCEHC to incorporate the exception leaning strongly towards on optimized, simpler RBAC state ($\beta = 0.8$). Figure 2 shows the minimum timeout needed to obtain a feasible solution for these inputs as a function of their size.

While the minimum timeout grows exponentially, performances over instances in a real-world size range are acceptable; for example, it is possible to obtain a solution in less than one hour for a 337.2MB

formula that encodes the problem of incorporating one exception into an RBAC state with 165 users and 709 permissions.

But how good are these solutions? To provide an estimate we compare them to optimal solutions returned by complete solvers. As we have shown, *Firewall1* is completely out of reach, so we resort to *SmallComp*. Given that hard constraints are always satisfied by feasible solutions from both complete and incomplete solvers, we focus on the ability of the incomplete solver to satisfy soft constraints. In particular, we compute the average weight of satisfied soft constraints over the total sum of input weights for the 12 different exceptions in the dataset. In Figure 3 we report this metric measured after CCEHC has worked for $t = 2sec$ and then for $t = 180sec$. We include the same metric computed on optimal solutions by complete solvers, which we could obtain for $\beta \leq 0.5$ (1 hour timeout). As expected, the complete solver outputs (slightly) better answers across the line, independently of β, but CCEHC is not far. These results, though quite comforting, have to be taken with a grain of salt because the small instances in *SmallComp* may not be representative of the general behavior of CCEHC.

4.2.3 Experimental Results. Incremental Max-SAT solvers seem capable of providing good approximate solutions within reasonable time on real-world instances. In the rest of this section we use them (namely, CCEHC) to explore the behavior of our encoding. We set $k^- = 7$ and $k^+ = 2$ to prefer role reduction to matrix simplification.

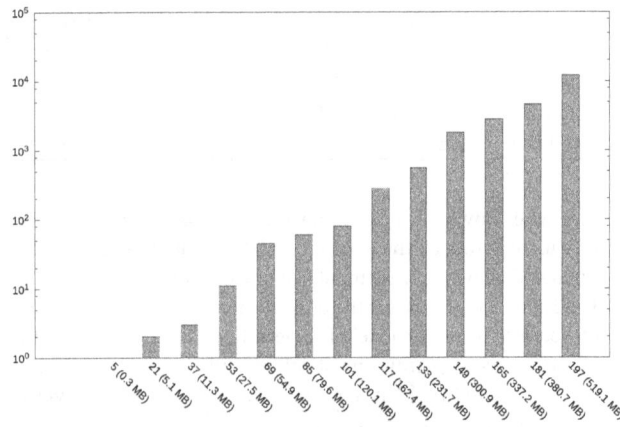

Figure 2: Minimum time to compute feasible solutions to Firewall1 (y axis, secs) as a function of the number of users (x axis). Along the x axis we also note the size of the corresponding CNF encoding in Megabytes.

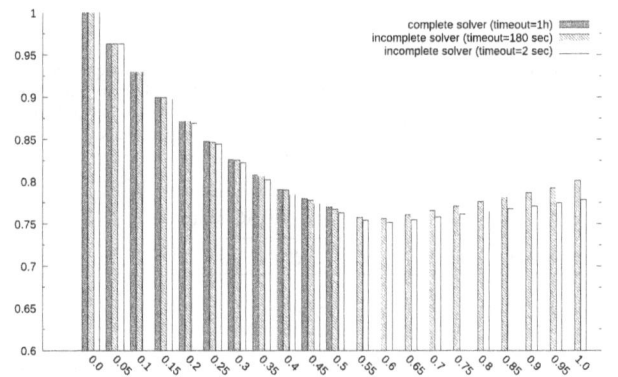

Figure 3: Average percentage of satisfied soft clauses (y axis) as a function of the balance β (x axis) in the *SmallComp* dataset.

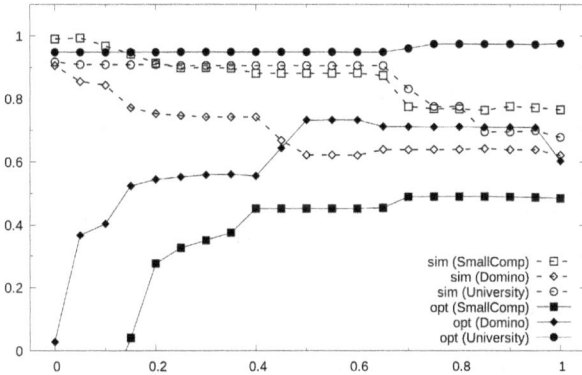

Figure 4: Average similarity and simplicity (y axis) as a function of the balance β (x axis) for different datasets. Twenty-one values of $\beta \in [0, 1]$ are sampled, at regular intervals (step 0.05).

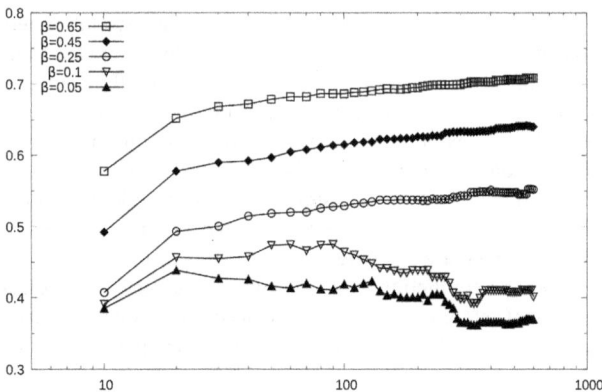

Figure 6: Average number of roles after incorporating exceptions (y axis) as a function of the balance β (x axis) for different datasets.

Impact of β. The first thing we assess experimentally is the impact the value of β has on the structure of the fixed RBAC state. Figure 4 shows that–for all datasets–similarity decreases (and simplicity increases) almost monotonically as β grows. Figure 6 shows how the corresponding number of roles decreases on average by increasing the preference towards optimized solutions (β close to 1). Conversely, if the encoding leans towards preserving the original RBAC state (β close to 0) these numbers stay close to the input values. None of the instances in the largest of the four datasets could be solved within 1 hour: Firewall1 thus constitute a *hard* problem at present (see Conclusions). Overall, by tuning β, it seems actually possible to steer the quality of the solution towards similarity or simplicity during maintenance.

Impact of timeout. We show how the output RBAC state (simplicity, similarity) changes by granting more time to the solver, at different balance points. Figure 5 and 7 show the results for timeouts in 10s–600s on the dataset *Domino* (representative of the entire benchmark). Simplicity increases for $\beta \geq 0.25$ (we are optimizing the state as a side effect of the maintenance) while it drifts towards lower values when $\beta < 0.25$ (the price we pay to avoid reworking the RBAC state too much as exceptions arrive). Conversely, similarity improves for low values of β while it remains almost stable

for $\beta \geq 0.25$. It follows that if the interest towards simplification is high, it always pays to allot more reasoning time to the solver. Conversely, if the interest is in preserving the input state, increasing the reasoning time pays for $\beta < 0.25$, where similarity increases at the expense of simplicity.

The order of exceptions. In these experiments, exceptions are incorporated sequentially, one-by-one, as they show up (though bulk incorporation is also possible, as already noted). We are interested in understanding how much the order in which they manifest affects the quality of the eventual state. In principle, the number of roles can either increase (small values of β) or decrease (large β). To confirm this, we select the *Domino* dataset and pick a string of 6 exceptions to be incorporated. We generate all their permutations (720) as incorporation sequences. For each sequence, we record the final number of roles, assignments, simplicity and similarity to the initial state (that has 73 roles). Figure 8 shows the distribution generated by 715 paths (each solvable in 60 seconds) with four different β configurations. While by construction the final states are equivalent in terms of Permission-to-User assignments, the average value and the variance of the distributions are profoundly impacted by β; the variance in particular widens as β goes close to 0; for example, with $\beta = 0.1$ the number of roles ranges from 28 to

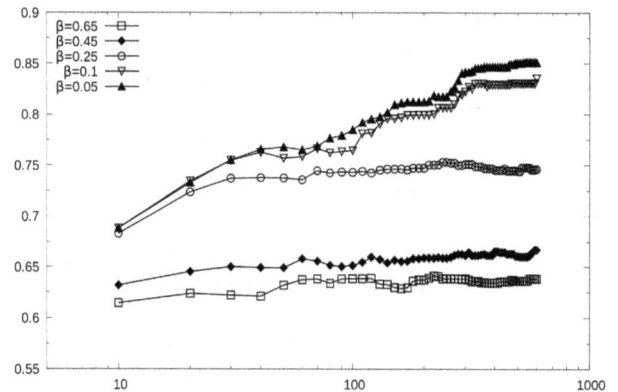

Figure 5: Average simplicity in *Domino* (y axis) as a function of the timeout (x axis, secs) at difference balance points (β).

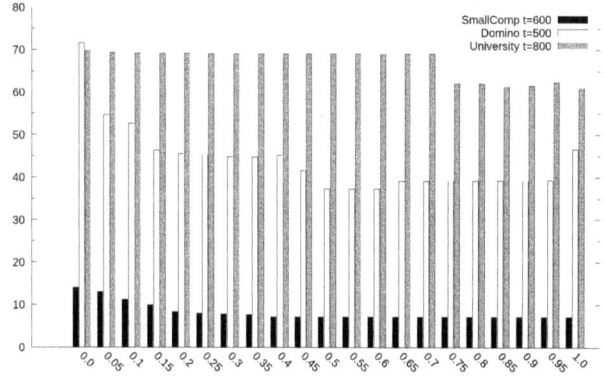

Figure 7: Average similarity in *Domino* (y axis) as a function of the timeout (x axis, secs) at difference balance points (β).

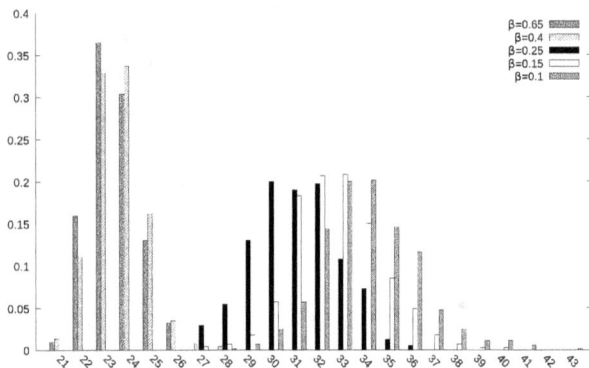

Figure 8: Distribution of the number of roles in *Domino* (x axis) after incorporating 6 exceptions in all possible orderings.

43, corresponding respectively to a 61.6% to 41.1% reduction with respect to initial RBAC state.

This behavior suggests that—independently of the order in which exceptions arrive—by leveraging β the RBAC administrator can direct the state over time to become simpler, to accumulate "clutter," or to remain stable in terms of number of roles.

5 RELATED WORK

The literature on Role Mining and RBAC state tuning is quite extensive. The works most closely related to this paper are [5, 13, 16, 17]. These approaches are similar to ours in that they aim at reconfiguring an existing set of roles with the goal of simplifying them.

In [16] the simplification procedure works as follows: A candidate set of new roles are iteratively generated starting from the trivial role set (one role per permission) and combining them in several ways (pairwise, etc.). The candidate set is kept consistent with the input RBAC state, i.e., each old role must be representable as the union of some new roles. Individual candidates with the lowest "management cost" are preferred, where the management cost is the sum of a fixed component (the same for all roles) plus a variable component which depends on the role cardinality and granularity. A parameter is introduced to balance their relative importance.

The approach presented in [13] more directly balances the quality of the new RBAC state against its similarity to the current one. It first applies a canonical role mining algorithm (Fast Miner) to generate a starting set of candidates. Then it iteratively evaluates roles according to a fitness function and selects the best ones until a solution is obtained that covers all the Permission-to-User assignments of the input RBAC state. The fitness function is a weighted sum of a measure of similarity to the original roles and a measure of coverage of the input Permission-to-User matrix. This algorithm has been extended to work with role hierarchies [4, 11].

A different perspective is adopted in [17]. This procedure analyzes logs of actual permission utilizations over time and exploits this data to inform the next RBAC state. There are two phases: The first phase applies a variant of the subset enumeration technique of Fast Miner to iteratively generate a set of roles, which are then sorted according to a fitness function. The fitness function is

where the traces of real permission usage come into play: It aims at balancing similarity to the original roles with "homogeneity" to actual permission utilization. At each iteration, top ranked roles which cover the input Permission-to-User matrix are selected; this is repeated until fixpoint (two subsequent steps result in the same set of roles) or until a maximum number of iterations is reached. The second phase then assigns roles to users based on a heuristic process which aims to contain redundancy.

A first difference between our approach and [13, 16] is that those procedures ignore how the simplified Permission-to-Role matrix they output will impact (in terms of administration costs) the correspondingly adjusted Permission-to-User assignments. This is evident because at no point those procedures take into account the UA matrix or how complex it would be for the administrator to edit it. Furthermore, in [16] the management cost of a set of roles is defined by only looking at roles per se, and not at the distance from the original. Overall, the link between the input matrices and the output matrices is very indirect: Both couples represent the same Permission-to-User relations, but the difficulty for an administrator to transform UA^0 into UA and PA^0 into PA is not modeled. Conversely, our encoding explicitly captures the difference of UA from UA^0 and PA from PA^0, so it relates more directly to the amount of work an administrator will have to do.

Another major difference from [13, 16, 17] is that our approach captures the RBAC optimization problem declaratively within a logic formalism, and neatly separates the declaration of the constraints and objective function from the search for an optimal solution. This provides several benefits and additional guarantees versus employing custom multi-phase heuristics. One advantage is that future breakthroughs from the community developing complete (and incomplete) Max-SAT solvers will result in an improved RBAC maintenance process without any change to our encoding. Another advantage is that the mechanism controlling the trade-off between quality and similarity provides strong guarantees about the output RBAC state; for example, for $\beta = 0$ we are sure that the output RBAC state is the least variation to the input that is capable of accommodating the intervening exception, whereas for $\beta = 1$ we have the guarantee that the output state is optimal w.r.t. a certain metric and that the input state has been completely ignored[6].

A logic-based formalization of the RBAC state similar to ours is presented in [5]. In that case, the Satisfiability Modulo Theory (SMT) framework is adopted; the theory used to expand the expressive power of SAT is Integer Linear Programming (ILP), employed to capture certain boolean-unfriendly quality metrics. The paper shows how to exploit SMT to solve several role mining variants, including one that generates an RBAC state optimal in terms of a combination of WSC [9] and similarity to an input RBAC state. To this end, a heuristic technique is presented to iteratively generate role sets, which are evaluated according to a fitness function that balances the conflicting WSC-vs-similarity objectives. The complete RBAC state is thus taken into account, and configurations that disrupt the Role-to-User assignments are penalized. Other

---

[6]It is worth noticing that while the *encoding* we propose offers these guarantees, we may lose them by solving the resulting problems with *incomplete* solvers.

variants consider the permission usage or the RBAC hierarchy as optimization metrics, resulting in a hybrid role mining approach.

The major difference between this approach and ours (beyond the definitions of certain quality metrics) is that we embrace the inherent nature of the role maintenance process as an *optimization procedure* by using a logic framework (Max-SAT) meant to optimize an objective function, whereas Satisfiability Modulo Theory (SMT) is a decision procedure meant to prove the consistency of statements. As a result, while the entire problem is captured by a single Max-SAT instance and the reasoning/searching/optimization stage is decoupled and offloaded to an external solver, [5] generates a long sequence of SMT problems in the context of a complex, custom algorithm to achieve the trade-off between quality and similarity. Another difference is that instead of generating candidate role sets and testing them against the original RBAC state to assess their similarity, we directly embed the original RBAC state as-is in the encoding together with penalties for diverging from it.

Another key difference from previous approaches is in when and how the RBAC reconfiguration is supposed to happen. Previous algorithms are presented as off-line procedures; administrators are supposed to first let the complexity of the RBAC state increase, perhaps by creating several ad-hoc new roles to quickly fix exceptions. Then, from time to time, a procedure is applied to simplify everything. Large discontinuities are acceptable at these "reconfiguration points". Conversely, the approach presented here can be leveraged to continuously introduce small optimizing changes: Applied on-line, in an exception-driven way, it steers the trajectory of the RBAC state towards simplicity without any costly or stakeholder-adverse update.

6 CONCLUSION AND FUTURE WORK

We presented a novel approach to perform maintenance of RBAC states, that is, to incorporate exceptions as they show up and improve the quality of the role model along the way. Based upon generating Max-SAT instances and solving them via state-of-the-art solvers, this method seems capable of dealing with real-life instances.

We are motivated to pursue optimized RBAC maintenance by actual issues at our company. Seldom there is the time and opportunity to perform large, impactful RBAC updates; conversely, errors show up on a daily basis, and if any push towards optimization can be exerted during maintenance, the RBAC state may actually start to converge to an (almost) optimal version of itself.

Directions for future work are as follows. Large datasets (e.g., *Firewall1*) still require too much time to solve; improvements to the encodings and/or the solving stage are of the essence here[7]. We haven't fully investigated yet how our technique behaves in the case of permissions in excess, to be withdrawn; these cases are indeed more difficult to capture automatically and we have less examples at our disposal. An optimal, fully-specified (and automatically synthesized) course of action for the RBAC administrator to implement a fix into an RBAC management system in use is another objective of interest, which seems within reach.

---

[7]We submitted our datasets to the organizers of the Max-SAT competition to provide them with challenging real-world instances on which to compare solvers.

ACKNOWLEDGMENTS

The authors thank Dr. Chuan Luo for supplying us with an improved and configurable version of the solver *CCEHC*; Dr. Carlos Ansótegui for the solvers *Dsat* and *WPM3*; Dr. Shaowei Cai for *Dist*.

Several colleagues from the Bank of Italy offered help: A special thanks goes to Domenico Pansini (security administrator) for providing us with examples and insights on role maintenance in a real-world setting; Oliver Giudice, Giuseppe Galano, and Roberto Favaroni (ART team) offered a great deal of support in setting up and configuring the computational infrastructure we used for our experiments; Arturo Baldo was the first to suggest the opportunity to investigate formal approaches to role maintenance. Finally, the anonymous referees helped us to produce a better and more readable contribution.

REFERENCES

[1] Alessandro Colantonio, Roberto Di Pietro, and Alberto Ocello. 2008. A Cost-Driven Approach to Role Engineering. In *Proceedings of the 2008 ACM symposium on Applied computing*. ACM, 2129–2136.
[2] Stephen A. Cook. 1971. The Complexity of Theorem-Proving Procedures. In *Proceedings of the third annual ACM symposium on Theory of computing*. ACM, 151–158.
[3] David F. Ferraiolo, Ravi Sandhu, Serban Gavrila, D. Richard Kuhn, and Ramaswamy Chandramouli. 2001. Proposed NIST Standard for Role-Based Access Control. *ACM Transactions on Information and System Security (TISSEC)* 4, 3 (2001), 224–274.
[4] Qi Guo, Jaideep Vaidya, and Vijayalakshmi Atluri. 2008. The Role Hierarchy Mining Problem: Discovery of Optimal Role Hierarchies. In *Computer Security Applications Conference, 2008. ACSAC 2008. Annual*. IEEE, 237–246.
[5] Jafar Haadi Jafarian, Hassan Takabi, Hakim Touati, Ehsan Hesamifard, and Mohamed Shehab. 2015. Towards a General Framework for Optimal Role Mining: A Constraint Satisfaction Approach. In *Proceedings of the 20th ACM Symposium on Access Control Models and Technologies*. ACM, 211–220.
[6] David S. Johnson. 1973. Approximation Algorithms for Combinatorial Problems. In *Proceedings of the fifth annual ACM symposium on Theory of computing*. ACM, 38–49.
[7] Chuan Luo, Shaowei Cai, Kaile Su, and Wenxuan Huang. 2017. CCEHC: An Efficient Local Search Algorithm for Weighted Partial Maximum Satisfiability. *Artificial Intelligence* 243 (2017), 26–44.
[8] Barsha Mitra, Shamik Sural, Jaideep Vaidya, and Vijayalakshmi Atluri. 2016. A Survey of Role Mining. *ACM Computing Surveys (CSUR)* 48, 4 (2016), 50.
[9] Ian Molloy, Hong Chen, Tiancheng Li, Qihua Wang, Ninghui Li, Elisa Bertino, Seraphin Calo, and Jorge Lobo. 2008. Mining Roles with Semantic Meanings. In *Proceedings of the 13th ACM symposium on Access control models and technologies*. ACM, 21–30.
[10] Marco Mori and Marco Benedetti. 2018. Web page with downloadable experiments and datasets. (2018). Retrieved April 19, 2018 from https://bancaditalia.github.io/sacmat2018/
[11] Hassan Takabi and James B.D. Joshi. 2010. StateMiner: An Efficient Similarity-Based Approach for Optimal Mining of Role Hierarchy. In *Proceedings of the 15th ACM symposium on Access control models and technologies*. ACM, 55–64.
[12] Grigori S. Tseitin. 1983. On the complexity of derivation in propositional calculus. In *Automation of reasoning*. Springer, 466–483.
[13] Jaideep Vaidya, Vijayalakshmi Atluri, Qi Guo, and Nabil Adam. 2008. Migrating to Optimal RBAC with Minimal Perturbation. In *Proceedings of the 13th ACM symposium on Access control models and technologies*. ACM, 11–20.
[14] Heidi L. Wachs. 2014. *How to Succeed With Role Management and Avoid Common Pitfalls*. Technical Report ID: G00262708. Gartner Technical Professional Advice.
[15] Heidi L. Wachs. 2015. *Take Control of Enterprise Role Management*. Technical Report ID: G00262285. Gartner Article.
[16] Hao Xia, Milind Dawande, and Vijay Mookerjee. 2014. Role Refinement in Access Control: Model and Analysis. *INFORMS Journal on Computing* 26, 4 (2014), 866–884.
[17] Wen Zhang, You Chen, Carl Gunter, David Liebovitz, and Bradley Malin. 2013. Evolving Role Definitions Through Permission Invocation Patterns. In *Proceedings of the 18th ACM symposium on Access control models and technologies*. ACM, 37–48.

Independent Key Distribution Protocols for Broadcast Authentication

Bruhadeshwar Bezawada
Computer Science Department
Colorado State University
Fort Collins, Colorado, USA
bru.bezawada@colostate.edu

Sandeep Kulkarni
Computer Science Department
Michigan State University
East Lansing, Michigan, USA
sandeep@cse.msu.edu

Indrajit Ray
Computer Science Department
Colorado State University
Fort Collins, Colorado, USA
indrajit.ray@colostate.edu

Indrakshi Ray
Computer Science Department
Colorado State University
Fort Collins, Colorado, USA
indrakshi.ray@colostate.edu

Rui Li
Dongguan University of Technology
Songshan Lake, Dongguan
Guangdong, P.R.China
ruili@dgut.edu.cn

ABSTRACT

Broadcast authentication is an important problem in several network settings such as wireless sensor networks and ad-hoc networks. We focus on the problem of *independent* key distribution protocols, which use efficient symmetric key signatures in distributed systems to permit (local) broadcast authentication. We focus on five types of communication graphs: (1) star, (2) acyclic, (3) planar, (4) complete bipartite, and (5) fully connected graphs. A star graph is the simplest network topology where a *central* node is transmitting authenticated broadcast messages to several *satellite* nodes. For star graphs, we show that as n, the number of satellite nodes in the star network, tends to ∞, it suffices to maintain $\log n + \frac{1}{2} \log \log n + 1$ keys at the center node, but $\log n + \frac{1}{2} \log \log n$ keys do not suffice. We establish that this is the optimal lower bound on the number of keys for a star graph. Building on this result, we describe storage efficient key distribution for acyclic, planar, and complete bipartite graphs, when compared to existing key distribution schemes. We extend our scheme for fully connected graphs and show that it is sufficient to store $O(c \log^2 N)$ keys per node where $c < 1$. We perform a detailed analysis of collusion resistance of our protocols and show the trade-offs against *internal* and *external* attacks depending on the size of storage. Finally, we demonstrate the practical applicability of our protocols for wireless sensor networks.

KEYWORDS

Key distribution, Broadcast authentication, Multiple Message Authentication Codes, Sensor Networks, Internet-of-Things

ACM Reference Format:
Bruhadeshwar Bezawada, Sandeep Kulkarni, Indrajit Ray, Indrakshi Ray, and Rui Li. 2018. Independent Key Distribution Protocols for Broadcast Authentication. In *SACMAT '18: The 23rd ACM Symposium on Access Control Models & Technologies (SACMAT), June 13–15, 2018, Indianapolis, IN, USA.* ACM, New York, NY, USA, 12 pages. https://doi.org/10.1145/3205977.3205985

1 INTRODUCTION

1.1 Background and Motivation

Consider a communication network represented by a graph $G = (V, E)$, where V is the set of nodes and $E \subseteq V \times V$ is a symmetric relation. We use the set of edges to denote the need for authenticity in the communication between the nodes connected by the edge. In other words, $(v_i, v_j) \in E$ implies that v_i needs to verify authenticity of messages received from v_j and vice versa. As an illustration, consider a sensor network consisting of a base station and a set of sensors. A sensor may *need* to communicate securely with a base station, where the communication may itself be assisted by other sensors in terms of routing. However, the intermediate sensors can neither learn the contents of the message nor can generate messages on behalf of the sender.

A similar scenario is a set of clients and servers, where each client needs to talk to (a subset of) the servers, but the clients (respectively, servers) do not need authentic communication among themselves. This is common in protocols defined for peer connections, such as the Border Gateway Protocol (BGP). Note that the set of edges in this graph are possibly application dependent, and may not be the same as those corresponding to physical communication links between nodes. Hence, other nodes in the network may be required for *routing*, although the intermediate nodes would not be able to tamper/decrypt any communication they forward.

1.2 Problem Overview

Now, consider the set $NBR = \{v_j | (v_i, v_j) \in E\}$. This is the set of nodes that v_i communicates with. We consider two types of communication: unicast, where v_i communicates with one of its neighbors and the neighbor wants to verify that the message is indeed from v_i, and (local) broadcast, where v_i sends a message to all nodes in NBR and each node wants to verify that the message is indeed from v_i. We denote this problem as local broadcast authentication.

1.3 Limitations of Prior Research

Studies [39] have shown that adopting computationally intensive public-key based authentication solutions like [2, 13, 42], can significantly impact the network lifetime of networks such as sensor networks, which consist of severely resource constrained sensor nodes. Single sender broadcast authentication solutions, such as [24, 31, 32, 49], impose additional constraints like sender-receiver synchronization and packet buffering, which are not feasible in large distributed networks. Furthermore, these solutions do not consider different types of network topologies like complete graphs where any node can be a sender as well as a receiver.

Symmetric key based solutions [5, 11, 43], also known as *Multiple Message Authentication Code* (MMAC) signature schemes, have been preferred over such solutions. In these solutions, the sender maintains a pool of secret keys and each node receives a unique subset of these keys. The sender signs a broadcast message using all the pool keys and broadcasts the resulting message with the signatures to the receivers. Each receiver can independently verify only the signatures corresponding to the sub-set of keys obtained from the sender at initialization. Relatively, these solutions are more efficient than the previous solutions, but they suffer from high sender storage and broadcast communication complexity. While there have been attempts [3] to identify the lower bounds of broadcast authentication *communication complexity* there have been no studies on identifying the lower bounds of broadcast authentication *storage complexity* in MMAC schemes. Thus far, there has been no attempt to reduce the storage complexity associated with these protocols especially when dealing with large networks with different topologies like acyclic, bipartite and complete graphs.

In this work, for the first time, we address the problem of identifying lower bounds in storage complexity in symmetric key based (MMAC) broadcast authentication protocols. Our solutions achieve optimal lower bounds for star network topology and improved storage complexities for other network topologies.

1.4 Proposed Approach

We consider the MMAC scheme paradigm of [5, 11, 43] and design key distribution protocols for broadcast authentication that are storage efficient. We consider five types of communication graphs: star, acyclic, planar, complete bipartite, and fully connected graphs. Of these, the star graph is motivated by examples such as the sensor networks scenario discussed. A planar graph is motivated by the case where nodes are distributed in a plane and a planar communication network is established for connectivity. Acyclic and complete bipartite graphs are useful in cases of client-server applications. Finally, fully connected graphs capture the case where each node may be interested in authentic communication from all other nodes in the network.

Based on these network models our approach is as follows. First, we focus on designing key distribution protocols for the star graph: a *center* node acting as a sender connected to several *satellite* nodes, which are the receivers. Our key distribution protocol ensures that the sender has the smallest possible pool of keys, and that the sender can distribute a unique subset of keys, chosen from this pool, to each receiver. Next, we use the low storage achieved in the star graph to design key distribution protocols for planar, acyclic, complete bipartite, and fully connected graphs. By leveraging the topology features of these varied graphs, we reduce the storage cost, as well as, the signature generation and verification costs for the nodes in these graphs.

1.5 Technical Challenges and Solutions

The first challenge is that, the keys assigned to nodes need to be independent, *i.e.*, one node cannot derive a key stored by another node. Independent keys permit asynchronous and periodic update where only one key is changed as needed. For example, a simple approach for such asynchronous update is to encrypt the new key with the corresponding old key and transmit it. But if some other node had to maintain a key that is dependent on k, say a hashed version of k, then the new key needs to be changed any time k is changed. In our solution, we ensure that the keys are independent by choosing the sender pool of keys uniformly at random and not imposing any relationship between any pair of keys. Each receiver gets a unique subset from this pool of keys, and therefore, the node keys are independent as well.

The second challenge is that, the *cost* of the broadcast communication should be proportional to the keys stored by the sender and the receivers in the communication graph. For example, in complete graphs, where every node is a sender as well as a receiver, it is quite essential to ensure that each receiver maintains only a small number of verification keys from other senders besides the keys it has to maintain as a sender. To address this, we focus on the star communication graphs and identify an optimal lower bound for the storage required at the sender and the receivers. We show that as n, the number of satellite nodes in the star network, tends to ∞, it suffices to maintain $\log n + \frac{1}{2} \log \log n + 1$ keys at the center node, which is a tight bound. Furthermore, as the keys are independent, our result significantly reduces the signature generation cost for the sender and the verification cost for the receivers.

The third challenge is that the network may be organized in different topologies such as acyclic, planar, complete bipartite and fully connected graphs. The key distribution protocol should ensure that the node storage depends asymptotically on the size of the network for every kind of topology. To solve this, we compose the complex network topologies as instances of star graphs and achieve the desired key distribution suitable for broadcast authentication.

Finally, since the key distribution protocols in the MMAC paradigm require that the keys are shared across multiple receivers, it is essential to address the issue of collusion among receivers. We address this by varying the different parameters of our key distribution protocol and demonstrate the collusion resistance achieved by each instance of the protocol.

1.6 Key Contributions

Our key contributions are: (1) We show that for a star graph with n satellite nodes, there exists a protocol that maintains $\log n + \frac{1}{2} \log \log n + 1$ keys at the center node, which is the optimal storage. This condition holds in virtually all network sizes of practical interest. Also, under the assumption that the number of keys maintained by the satellite nodes is identical, we show that there does not exist a protocol that maintains $\log n + \frac{1}{2} \log \log n$ keys at the center node. (2) We show that our protocols can also be extended to acyclic, planar, complete bipartite, and fully connected graphs. (3) We show that the protocol can provide higher collusion resistance than the existing protocols under different attack scenarios. (4) We show that our protocols provide tradeoff between internal and external attackers. (5) We demonstrate the applicability of our protocols in wireless sensor networks with promise for Internet-of-Things.

2 PROBLEM STATEMENT

First, we state the problem of authentication under any communication model, and then, state the problem of authentication[1] with broadcast capability and without broadcast capability.

---

[1]Unless explicitly stated, we use the terms "authentication", "authenticity" and "source authentication" interchangeably.

The Authentication Problem. For a message m transmitted from a source A to a destination B;

Message Authenticity : B should be able to verify that the source of the message is indeed A and,

Message Integrity : B should be able to verify that the message integrity has not been compromised in transit.

Threat Model. We consider impersonation as the main threat, *i.e.*, one node being able to authenticate as another node. We focus on key distribution in which a single node, using the set of stored keys, cannot impersonate another node in the network.

Problem Statement Motivation. To motivate the problem, we begin with star networks where there is one center node and other satellite nodes that only communicate with the center node. Our problem statement first focuses on defining the *number of stored keys* and then relates it to the cost of broadcast authentication. To motivate the need for such a definition, consider the following solution for key distribution in a star network.

The center node maintains a key x. and each satellite node has an ID ranging from $1, \cdots, n$. The key associated with satellite node with ID j is $f(x, j)$ where f is a one-way function. Clearly, $f(x, j)$ could be used for unicast communication to/from j and the center node. For example, $f(x, j)$ could be used to generate a message digest that the receiver can verify. Since $f(x, j)$ is known only to the center node and satellite node j, only they can generate the corresponding message digests. In this solution, the number of keys that each node *stores* is 1. While the center node has access to many keys that it can generate at run-time, they need not be stored. Thus, we need to distinguish between the number of *stored* keys and the number of *generated* keys.

A node can store two sets of keys: those that it distributes to other nodes and those that it receives from other nodes. We denote the keys stored by node v_i as $stored(v_i)$. A node can generate keys from the $stored(v_i)$ using any operation like, *XOR*, one-way hashing and so on, which can result in a potentially unbounded set of keys. We denote the set of all such operations by, *gen* and the set of all such keys that can be generated as, $generated(v_i)$. Observe that $stored(v_i) \subseteq generated(v_i)$. Based on this, we make a standard assumption about the adversary capability, *i.e.*, the adversary can combine the keys it has, *e.g.*, by XORing them/adding them, one-way hashing and so on, to generate newer keys. However, such combination does not allow the adversary to *guess* the keys that other nodes have.

While the above solution works for unicast, it is very inefficient for broadcast. For broadcast, the center node must provide a separate message authentication code using $f(x, j) \, \forall j$ where $1 \le j \le n$. Each satellite node can verify the authentication code by generating the code locally, using its key $f(x, j)$, and comparing the generated code with the code sent by the center node. Clearly, in this solution, the cost of generating authentication codes, which is $O(n)$, for broadcast is very high.

Now, consider the following scenario. Given two nodes, j and k where j has key s and k has key $f(s)$ where f is some function, a message encrypted with s cannot be decrypted by k (unless strong requirements are added for function f and the algorithm for encryption). Since we would like to allow the use of any symmetric key based encryption approaches, for j and k to communicate securely, they must share common key(s). As a result, for broadcast communication, where the sender signs the message separately with multiple keys, the receiver must have one or more of the keys

that are actually used for generating the signature. Therefore, to provide broadcast authentication capability, we impose the following constraint on the problem of key distribution in star network: We require that a sender maintain a set of keys. Whenever the sender sends a (local) broadcast message to its neighbors, it provides authentication codes using (a subset of) of the keys it has. Upon receiving the message, the receiver will verify the signatures it can verify. Note that the receiver cannot verify all signatures since it does not have all the keys used by the sender. It is required that when the receiver verifies the signatures it can, it must be the case that the message is indeed authentic.

Based on this discussion, we now clearly define the problem statements for message authentication that distinguish between unicast and broadcast capability with differing key storage scenarios. These statements allow us to describe the primary problem statement of this work, *i.e.*, independent key distribution for broadcast authentication.

Problem Statement 2.1 (Key Distribution With Broadcast Capability). Given an undirected graph $G(V, E)$ where V is the set of nodes and E is the set of edges such that given two nodes v_i and v_j in V, $(v_i, v_j) \in E$ iff v_i needs the communication with v_j to be authentic. Then, assign to each node v_i a set of keys, $stored(v_i)$, such that for any $(v_i, v_j) \in E$:

1) (Existence of Common Keys usable for broadcast): $stored(v_i) \cap generated(v_j) \ne \phi$. where $generated(v_j)$ is the set of keys that can be generated from $stored(v_j)$ (subject to constraints specified later).

2) (Authenticity): For any $v_k \in V : v_k \ne v_i \wedge v_k \ne v_j$: $(stored(v_i) \cap generated(v_j)) \not\subseteq generated(v_k)$.

Note that this problem statement requires broadcast capability, *i.e.*, if a node, say v_i, sends a message and includes a signature block that contains a signature from each of the key it stores then any node that receives this message can verify the signatures by using the keys in $stored(v_i) \cap generated(v_j)$. If all signature verifications succeed then the message is indeed from v_i. Thus, the cost of broadcast authentication is proportional to $stored(v_i)$. This implies that reducing the cost of broadcast authentication is equivalent to reducing the size of $stored(v_i)$.

Problem Statement 2.2: (Key Distribution Without Broadcast Capability.) Given an undirected graph $G(V, E)$ where V is the set of nodes and E is the set of edges such that given two nodes v_i and v_j in V, $(v_i, v_j) \in E$ iff v_i needs the communication with v_j to be authentic. Then, assign to each node v_i a set of keys, $stored(v_i)$, such that for any $(v_i, v_j) \in E$:

1) (Existence of Common Keys): $generated(v_i) \cap generated(v_j) \ne \phi$.

2) (Authenticity): For any $v_k \in V : v_k \ne v_i \wedge v_k \ne v_j$: $(generated(v_i) \cap generated(v_j)) \not\subseteq generated(v_k)$.

Lemma 2.2.1. Given any protocol that satisfies Problem Statement 2.1, there is an equivalent protocol that satisfies Problem Statement 2.2.

Proof. Let p be the protocol that satisfies 2.1. Let $stored_p(v)$ denote the secrets stored at v in protocol p. Let $generated_p(v)$ denote the secrets that can be generated at node v by using the secrets $stored_p(v)$. Let p' be a protocol such that $stored_{p'}(v) = generated_p(v)$, where $stored_{p'}(v)$ denotes the secrets stored at v in protocol p'. It is straightforward to observe that p' satisfies the constraints of Problem 2.2 □

Any shared key protocol that provides authentication meets the constraints of Problem Statement 2.2. Protocols that do not satisfy it include those that use asymmetric keys [2, 13, 42], physical security [36] and delayed authentication approaches [24, 31, 32, 49]. From Lemma 2.2.1, it follows that for any protocol that satisfies key distribution without broadcast capability, there is a corresponding protocol that provides broadcast capability. However, the protocol generated by application of this Lemma is likely to maintain a substantially larger number of keys than the original protocol. Since our goal is to reduce the keys stored at a given node, it follows that it is desirable to develop a protocol that satisfies Problem Statement 2.1. Next, we state the problem of independent key distribution for unicast.

Problem Statement 2.3: (Independent Key Distribution for Unicast)   Given an undirected graph $G(V, E)$ where V is the set of nodes and E is the set of edges such that given two nodes v_i and v_j in V, $(v_i, v_j) \in E$ iff v_i needs the communication with v_j to be authentic. Then, assign to each node v_i a set of keys, $stored(v_i)$, such that for any $(v_i, v_j) \in E$ where $v_i \neq v_j$:

Independent Common Keys: $stored(v_i) \cap generated(stored(v_j) - stored(v_i)) = \phi$.

Authenticity: For any $v_k \in V : v_k \neq v_i \wedge v_k \neq v_j : (generated(v_i) \cap generated(v_j)) \nsubseteq generated(v_k)$.

The notion of *independent common keys* captures the intuition that the keys stored or generated at v_i and v_j are truly independent of each other. The above problem statement allows us to explore solutions where refreshing or updating the keys is possible. For example, we can update a particular key in the key distribution and send it to those nodes who need that key. Removing an independent key will not affect the key sharing patterns among the nodes and therefore, we can be assured of retaining the authentication properties of the key distribution protocol that contains only independent keys. This is not possible in key distribution protocols such as [31] that rely on generated keys to achieve authentication.

Theorem 2.3.1 Let p be a key distribution that satisfies problem statement 2.1 (respectively, 2.2) and 2.3. Let k be one of the keys used in the distribution. Let k' be a new key which is not currently used in p. Now, if we replace all instances of k with k', then the corresponding key distribution also satisfies problem statement 2.1 (respectively, 2.2) and 2.3.

Proof.   Note that the common keys in p are independent of each other. This implies that changing these keys will not affect the common keys among any other nodes in the system. Hence, replacing a key in p will result in a key distribution where the corresponding nodes share a new common key and no other keys among the other nodes are affected by this change. This proves that the changed key distribution satisfies the problem statement 2.3. □

Theorem 2.3.1 shows that if the keys are independent then it is possible to change one key without affecting other keys. If the keys are not independent then this is not guaranteed. For example, if node v_i maintains a key k and node v_j maintains $f(k, ID_{v_j})$ where f is a one-way hash function then just changing k to k' is not possible as it requires the key maintained at v_j to be updated simultaneously. This problem becomes even more challenging if such hashed keys are maintained at several nodes. The independence feature is especially valuable if the key distribution utilizes a large number of keys and changing several keys in a coordinated fashion is difficult. Thus, independence allows keys to be effectively refreshed. For example, to refresh key k with k', one can just send k' by encrypting it with k. Finally, we state the problem of independent key distribution with broadcast capability, which is the focus of our work.

Problem Statement 2.4: Independent Key distribution with broadcast capability   Given an undirected graph $G(V, E)$ where V is the set of nodes and E is the set of edges such that given two nodes v_i and v_j in V, $(v_i, v_j) \in E$ iff v_i needs the communication with v_j to be authentic. Then, assign to each node v_i a set of keys, denoted by $stored(v_i)$, such that for any $(v_i, v_j) \in E$ where $v_i \neq v_j$, all the constraints of Problem Statements 2.1 and 2.3 are satisfied. We focus on this problem in our work and describe our solutions.

One of the main reasons for describing these problems is to clearly distinguish among the storage costs required for solving the authenticity problem across different communication capabilities and to establish the notion of optimal storage for key distribution. For instance, a shared key distribution protocol that solves the authenticity problem in 2.1 can solve Problem Statement 2.2, but might require a higher number of keys, because additional keys need to be generated. For instance, $stored(v_i) \cap generated(v_j) \neq \emptyset$ implies that $generated(v_i) \cap generated(v_j) \neq \emptyset$. But as shown in proof of Lemma 2.2.1, the storage required by the latter expression is higher. One other reason for these definitions is to clearly demarcate the storage capabilities of solutions proposed in literature so far.

3   RELATED WORK

Secure communication using symmetric key mechanisms has been widely studied. For fully connected network topologies, it has been shown by [1, 4, 6, 7, 12, 14, 16, 21, 23, 28, 29, 44, 45, 47], that the number of keys stored by each node can be less than $O(n)$ for a system of n nodes. In [14, 21], the authors describe a key distribution protocol which allow any two nodes to communicate securely while storing only $O(\sqrt{n})$ keys. These protocols are designed for the case where the communication graph is fully connected. Further, in [1], the authors describe a key distribution protocol that requires each node to store only $O(\log^2 n)$ keys. They show the existence of $O(\log n)$ key distribution protocol for star network like scenario without actually constructing the protocol.

Reducing the storage to logarithmic bounds has benefits in resource constrained networks such as sensor networks, ad-hoc networks and IoT networks. Examples of such resource constrained networks include sensor networks [12, 31], ad-hoc networks [18, 25] and IoT [17, 20, 35, 38, 51]. In [17], the authors discuss about the need for application data authenticity and confidentiality in IoT networks. However, in these works [1, 4, 6, 14, 21, 23, 27, 28, 34, 45, 46, 48], pair-wise confidentiality, not broadcast authentication, was the main focus. Nevertheless, these protocols can be extended for authentication by, possibly, using additional storage so that they satisfy the constraints of the authentication problem. For comparison with our approach, we have considered such extensions for the low storage schemes in [1, 11, 28] and demonstrate that our approach achieves the lowest possible storage compared to these schemes (cf. Section 5.1). Also, we have not considered the problem of confidentiality in broadcast communication [41] as it is orthogonal to the problem in this paper. While the focus of our work is on deterministic key distribution schemes, such as those mentioned above, there is significant work in probabilistic random key distribution schemes such as [7, 12, 47].

Solutions like [10] are not suited to solve Problem statement 2.1 as they do not have broadcast capability. In [5], the authors describe a probabilistic symmetric key distribution protocol, based on the results from [10], that satisfies the Problem statement 2.1.

For fully connected networks, the solution in [5] proposes a key distribution which separates senders and receivers. However, this solution does not satisfy the constraints of Problem statement 2.4. The keys distributed to the receivers are a function of the keys given to the senders to enable appropriate sender authentication. Alternatively, they describe an approach where the number of keys held by each node depends on the desired collusion resistance (w) and the acceptable probability of forging the signatures (q) and is quantified by: $O(e(w+1)ln(1/q)$. However, to achieve a low value of q, the number of sender signatures and consequently, the number of sender keys needs to be increased considerably. Another drawback in [5] is that the time taken to verify whether the key distribution has the desired property is $O(n^3)$ for a group of n nodes, which is computationally intensive for large groups, say, $n > 20000$ and if the keys need to refreshed periodically. In contrast, our protocols are deterministic and the key distributions can be generated using standard combinatorial enumeration techniques [9].

In [11], for authentication with broadcast capability, the authors describe a logarithmic key distribution protocol for a star network where the storage is logarithmic for both the center, which stores $2 \log n$ keys and the satellite nodes, which store $\log n$ keys. They extend their results to achieve logarithmic key distribution for several classes of communication networks including, star networks, acyclic networks, cycle-limited networks, planar networks and dense bipartite networks. We show that the storage used in their approach is higher than what is required in our approach and our scheme supports a larger receiver base for the same sender storage while achieving higher collusion resistance for similar storage. A major difference between [11] and our work is that, we have considered fully connected networks and describe efficient key distribution protocols, which require each node to store a small number of keys, i.e., poly-logarithmic in the size of the group.

In [31], and later in extended works like [24, 49], the authors describe broadcast authentication schemes based on one-way hash chains. The sender reveals values from a one-way hash chain at appropriate time intervals periodically. Each node verifies the authenticity of these values using a master hash value which serves as a public-key. Their scheme works essentially for star networks and requires an initialization step for every new session, i.e., setting up of a new master hash value. Such protocols, using generated keys, might appear to have the best storage solution, i.e., requiring only one (generated) key per receiver, but updating this key across sessions takes considerable effort for the sender and requires additional effort in synchronizing sender and receiver. Our solutions apply for the paradigm of Multiple Message Authentication Codes (MMAC) based solutions using independent shared keys and we focus on the optimal solution in this approach. We emphasize the notion of independent keys due to the additional security properties they provide such as updating the keys efficiently.

In [3], Boneh et al., discuss in depth regarding the lower bounds of broadcast authentication communication complexity. However, this work did not explore the storage complexity and the correlation between these two complexities. In [15], the authors explore the constructions of [5] to authenticate messages in the controller area network (CAN) broadcast serial bus for in-network communication in modern day vehicles. In such scenarios, our protocols will provide considerable storage savings and communication efficiency due to the real-time constraints in these networks. Recent efforts in diverse networks like vehicular ad-hoc networks (VANETS), e.g., in [8] have explored this problem with the help of an online centralized key distribution center, which is may not always be possible.

Several solutions [2, 19, 22, 26, 33, 40, 41, 50] exist for achieving broadcast confidentiality, i.e., these protocols concern with the establishment of a single group wide secret to secure all communications in the group. These protocols can handle dynamic group membership wherein nodes can join and leave the group, i.e., these protocols establish a new group secret in an efficient manner. There are two important differences between the solutions we describe and these solutions. First, in these solutions, confidentiality of communication is the main concern and the group wide secret is available with any group member, which makes it difficult to authenticate the sender of a particular message and might need public-key mechanisms like RSA signatures or [31, 42] to achieve source authentication. In our work, we focus on the ability of receiver to authenticate the sender of any message without ambiguity. Second, there is usually the presence of single group wide controller who handles the dynamic membership changes and re-establishes new secrets among the group members. In our work, the group controller is not assumed to be available at all times. Node additions and revocations are done by the controller in an off-line manner. More importantly, the design of our protocols ensures that nodes can be added to the group without having to change the keys across the entire group.

4 OPTIMAL SOLUTION FOR STAR NETWORK

In this section, we focus on key distribution for a star network, i.e., a center node and a set of satellite nodes that communicate with it. Let the set of keys at the center node be K and $|K| = k$. Each satellite node receives a unique subset of size l, $l > 0$, from this set. Note that, by construction, given any two distinct satellite nodes v_i, v_j, we have $K \cap generated(v_i) \nsubseteq generated(v_j)$. Thus, the constraints of Problem 2.1 are satisfied. We term this protocol instance as $p(k, l)$. Technically, $p(k, l)$ is a family of protocols. However, for brevity of presentation, we denote $p(k, l)$ as a protocol. We note that all the results in this paper attributed to protocol $p(k, l)$ are valid for any member of the $p(k, l)$ protocol family. Using $p(k, l)$, authentication can be achieved in the communication as follows.

(1) To authenticate a message m broadcast by the center node to the satellite node, the center node generates authentication codes with each of the k keys. Each authentication code consists of the message digest md of the message computed using a key held by the center. The center appends the k authentication codes thus generated to the message and broadcasts the resulting message. Now, when a satellite node receives this message, it uses its subset of l keys to compute l authentication codes. The satellite node then verifies these authentication codes with the corresponding authentication codes sent by the center node. Note that, each satellite node can verify only those authentication codes for which it has the corresponding generating key.

(2) To authenticate a unicast message m from the center to a particular satellite node, the center node first computes an XOR of the subset of the keys that this satellite node knows. Now, the center node uses the combined key to compute the message authentication code for this message. The center node appends this authentication code to the message and unicasts the message to the satellite node. The satellite node XORs its subset of keys and uses the generated key to verify the authentication code sent by the center node. Due to the

independence of keys, using XOR to combine the secrets to the secret to authenticate a message provides information-theoretic security under assumption of no collusion.

(3) To authenticate a unicast message m from a satellite node to the center, the satellite node uses the same approach used by the center node for authenticating unicast messages.

An example distribution is shown in Figure 1, where a center A distributes keys to the satellite nodes $A_1, A_2, \ldots, A_6$. By design, the set of keys given to each node is unique and hence, can be used to authenticate messages sent to that node.

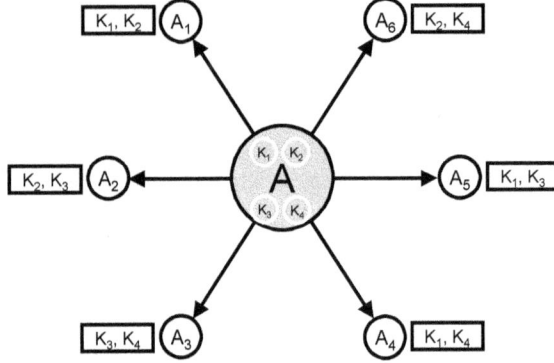

Figure 1: Example key distribution for star network

In the remaining section, we consider the case where the number of satellite nodes, n, tends to ∞: First, we show (cf. Theorem 4) that $\log n + c \log \log n$ keys do not suffice if $c < 1/2$. Using the proof of this result, we show (cf. Theorem 5) that $\log n + \frac{1}{2} \log \log n + 1$ keys suffice to handle n nodes whereas $\log n + \frac{1}{2} \log \log n$ do not.

Theorem 1. $p(k, l)$ solves Problem 2.4 in the star network.

Proof. The proof follows from the construction of $p(k, l)$. □

Theorem 2. Protocol $p(k, l)$ can accommodate up to $C(k, l)$ satellite nodes where $C(k, l)$ is the number of unique subsets of size l chosen from the pool of k keys.

Proof. This follows directly, as this $C(k, l)$ is the number of unique subsets of keys that can be generated. □

Corollary 3. For a given value of k, choosing $l = k/2$ maximizes the number of satellite nodes that can be accommodated. □

Lemma 4. As $n \to \infty$, protocol $p(k, l)$, where $k = \log n + \log \log n$ and $l = k/2$, provides authentication for the star network with n nodes.

Proof. To prove this, we show that, when $k = \log n + \log \log n$ and $l = k/2$,[2] the number of unique subsets of keys that are possible, i.e., $C(k, l) \geq n$. This implies that each satellite node receives a different subset of keys and hence, based on Theorems 1 and 2, $p(k, l)$ can be used for authentication in star network.

We use Stirling's approximation (originally attributed to Abraham de Moivre)[30, 37] for factorials which states that, for large values of n, $n! \approx (n/e)^n \cdot \sqrt{2\pi n}$. Now, $C(k, l) = \frac{k!}{(l)!(k-l)!}$. Since $l = k/2$, this values simplifies to: $\frac{k!}{(k/2)!(k/2)!}$. Now, using Stirling's approximation, we have

$$C(k, k/2) = \frac{k!}{(k/2)!(k/2)!}$$

[2]Since we are dealing with large values of n, for simplicity of presentation, we omit the floor/ceiling operations required in computing $\log n$, l, etc.

$$\approx \frac{(k/e)^k * \sqrt{2\pi k}}{((k/2e)^{k/2}\sqrt{2\pi(k/2)})^2}$$
$$= \frac{2^k . 2}{\sqrt{2\pi k}}$$

{Now, letting $k = (\log n + \log \log n)$ }

$$= \frac{2^{(\log n + \log \log n)}2}{\sqrt{2\pi(\log n + \log \log n)}}$$
$$= n \frac{2 \log n}{\sqrt{2\pi(\log n + \log \log n)}}$$

and after canceling out common terms we obtain the following term:

$$\frac{2.2^{(\log n + \log \log n)}}{\sqrt{(2\pi \log n + \log \log n)}} \geq \frac{2n \log n}{\sqrt{(2\pi 2 \log n)}} = n.\sqrt{\log n}/\sqrt{4\pi}$$

Now, as $n \to \infty$, the multiple of n tends to ∞. Hence, as $n \to \infty$, $C(k, k/2) > n$, where $k = \log n + \log \log n$. In other words, the number of subsets generated by choosing $k = \log n + \log \log n$ and $l = k/2$ is greater than or equal to n. Thus, this key distribution ensures authentication in the star network. □

Theorem 4. As $n \to \infty$, protocol $p(k, l)$ where $k = (\log n + c \log \log n)$, where $c < 1/2$ and $l = k/2$ cannot provide authentication for the star network with n nodes.

Proof. We evaluate $C(k, l)$ using Stirling's approximation and show that this value is less than n. This implies that there will at least two nodes who might receive the same subset of keys. Based on Theorems 1 and 2, this result proves this theorem. From the above proof,

$$C(k, k/2) = \frac{k!}{(k/2)!(k/2)!}$$
$$\approx \frac{(k/e)^k * \sqrt{2\pi k}}{((k/2e)^{k/2}\sqrt{2\pi(k/2)})^2}$$
$$= \frac{2^k * 2}{\sqrt{2\pi k}}$$

{Using this approximation}

$$C(k, k/2) \approx \frac{2^k * 2}{\sqrt{2\pi k}}$$

{Now, letting $k = \log n + c \log \log n$}

$$= \frac{2^{(\log n + c \log \log n)} * 2}{\sqrt{2\pi(\log n + c \log \log n)}}$$
$$= n \frac{2.2^{c \log \log n}}{\sqrt{2\pi(\log n + c \log \log n)}}$$
$$= n \frac{2.(2^{\log \log n})^c}{\sqrt{2\pi(\log n + c \log \log n)}}$$
$$= n \frac{2.(\log n)^c}{\sqrt{2\pi(\log n + c \log \log n)}}$$

This implies that there will be at least two nodes who might receive the same subset of keys. Substituting for the values of k, l in $C(k, l)$, where $k = (\log n + c \log \log n)$, $c < 1/2$ and $l = k/2$, and using Stirling's approximation, we obtain:

$$\frac{2.2^{(\log n + c \log \log n)}}{\sqrt{(2\pi \log n + c \log \log n)}}$$

This term simplifies to:

$$\frac{2n.\log n^c}{\sqrt{(2(\pi \log n + c \log \log n))}} \leq \frac{2n(\log n)^c}{\sqrt{(4\pi \log n)}} = \frac{n}{(\pi \log n)^{1/2-c}}$$

Note that, as $n \to \infty$, the multiple of n in the above formula tends to 0, where $c < 1/2$, this value is always smaller than n

due to the presence of a non-negligible denominator. Thus, for $k = (\log n + c \log \log n)$, $c < 1/2$ and $l = k/2$, the value $C(k, l)$ generates less than n unique subsets of keys. Hence, this $p(k, l)$ does not ensure authentication in star network. Therefore, as $n \to \infty$, $C(k, k/2) < n$.   □

Based on the above theorem, if $c = 1/2$ then the multiple of n is $\frac{2}{\sqrt{2\pi}}$. Since this number is less than 1, $\log n + c \log \log n$ keys do not suffice when $c = 1/2$. However, if the number of keys is $(\log n + \frac{1}{2} \log \log n + 1)$, then in the above formula, the multiple of n is $\frac{4}{\sqrt{2\pi}}$. Since this number is greater than 1, $(\log n + \frac{1}{2} \log \log n + 1)$ keys suffice for key distribution in a star network as $n \to \infty$. Thus, we have:

Theorem 5. As $n \to \infty$, protocol $p(k, l)$ where $k = (\log n + \frac{1}{2} \log \log n)$, and $l = k/2$ cannot provide authentication for the star network with n nodes. And, as $n \to \infty$, protocol $p(k, l)$ where $k = (\log n + \frac{1}{2} \log \log n + 1)$, and $l = k/2$ can provide authentication for the star network with n nodes.   □

The above results highlight an important aspect of the $p(k, l)$ protocols, *i.e.*, it takes constant time, $O(k)$, for the center node to select the subset of keys, that are given to the satellite node, from the initial pool keys. In other words, the time taken to compute the subset of keys does not depend on the number of nodes in the system but only on the size k of the initial pool of keys stored by the center node.

Theorem 6. The $p(k, l)$ distribution satisfies the constraints of Problem statement 2.1 and 2.3 and hence, solves problem 2.4.

Proof. First, the keys given to the nodes are independent of each other by design. Second, the authentication codes are generated by the center node by directly using the keys and not on a derivative of the keys. From these two points, it is straightforward to note that $p(k, l)$ satisfies the constraints of Problem statement 2.4.   □

When compared to the key distribution for star network in [11] our key distribution requires lesser number of keys. In [11], the center maintains $2 \log n$ keys and in our key distribution protocol the center only needs to maintain $\log n + O(\log \log n)$ keys. The number of keys stored by the satellite nodes is reduced as well. In [11], each satellite node maintain $\log n$ keys and in our key distribution protocol, each satellite node maintains at most $(\log n)/2 + O(\log \log n)$ keys. This value represents the upper bound for the number of keys maintained by the satellite node. Moreover, the result from the above theorem can be verified for most small values of n. In particular, we have verified that $\lceil \log n + \log \log n \rceil$ keys suffice for $5 < n < 1000$ nodes.

Also, since the above theorem applies for the case where $n \to \infty$, the natural question is about what happens for small values of n. Here, we note that we checked whether $\lceil \log n + \frac{1}{2} \log \log n \rceil$ keys suffice for $n < 50000$. For $2 \le n \le 1000$, we found this number to be insufficient for 510 values and for $1000 \le n \le 50000$, we found that this number to be insufficient for 20313 values. By contrast, if we consider $\lceil \log n + \frac{1}{2} \log \log n + 1 \rceil$ keys then this number suffices for the case where the number of nodes is less than 50000. For illustration, we refer the reader to Figure 2(a).

We would like to note that while the reduction in the number of keys is from $2 \log n$ to $\log n + O(\log \log n)$, this reduction is especially valuable when we consider the number of nodes that can be supported with a given set of keys at the center. For example, Figure 2(b) compares the number of nodes that can be supported with our scheme with that in [11]. If 10 keys are available at the center then the scheme in [11] can support up to 32 satellite nodes

whereas our protocol can tolerate upto 252 satellite nodes. Or, if 20 keys are available at the center then the scheme in [11] can support up to 1024 satellite nodes whereas our protocol can tolerate upto 184756 satellite nodes.

4.1 Optimality of Key Distribution

Consider the problem of independent key distribution in star network where the number of keys stored by the satellite nodes is equal. Thus, based on the constraints in Section 2, a solution is of the form where, for some values of k and l, the center node maintains k keys and each satellite node maintains a subset of size l from that set. In other words, a solution is of the form $p(k, l)$. Therefore, based on Theorem 5, as $n \to \infty$, $\log n + \frac{1}{2} \log \log n + 1$ is the optimal number of keys that need to be maintained by the center node.

5 KEY DISTRIBUTION FOR FULLY CONNECTED COMMUNICATION NETWORK

We describe how the protocol $p(k, l)$ can be extended to solve Problem 2.4 in all-to-all communication, *i.e.*, where communication graph is fully connected. Thus, this approach would allow any two nodes to communicate securely with each other and any node can broadcast an authenticated message using the keys it has. Our key distribution protocol is designed in stages; the first stage, Stage 1, extends the protocol $p(k, l)$ by considering a fully connected graph as a set of star graphs (or planar graphs). This stage is intended for the case where the number of nodes in the graph is small. Then, Stage 2 uses the scheme in Stage 1 in an hierarchical manner.

Stage 1. In this stage, first, we design a protocol that establishes keys for a group of d nodes. We first select a unique node, say X, and consider the star graph where X is the center node and the remaining $d-1$ nodes are satellite nodes. The center node maintains a set of $k = f(d)$ keys, where $f(d) = \lceil \log d + \frac{1}{2} \log \log d + 1 \rceil$. Each satellite node receives a unique subset of size $l = f(d)/2$ from this set. Note that this is an instance of $p(k, l)$ where $k = f(d)$ and $l = f(d)/2$.

Now, we repeat the above protocol by considering each node as a center node. Thus, for a fully connected network of d nodes, each node is a center node in one star graph and a satellite node in the $d-1$ star graphs. As a center node, each node stores $f(d)$ keys and as a satellite node it stores $(d-1).f(d)/2$ keys, one for each of the $d-1$ center nodes. Thus, we have:

Theorem 7. The number of keys stored by each node in Stage 1 is: $f(d) + \frac{d-1}{2} f(d) = \frac{d+1}{2} f(d)$.   □

Theorem 8. The key distribution in the above solution solves Problem 2.4.   □

Stage 2. Now, we consider d communication networks from Stage 1, which gives us a network of d^2 nodes, and denote this grouping by G_p. We treat each basic structure of d nodes as a single (virtual) node U_i where $1 \le i \le d$, *i.e.*, in any key distribution scheme, any key that is given to the virtual node U_i is actually given to all the nodes that are part of U_i.

With this setting, we consider the star graph where U_i is the center node for some $1 \le i \le d$ and all nodes in $G_p - U_i$ are satellite nodes. Thus, there are $d(d-1)(\approx d^2)$ satellite nodes. We instantiate $p(k, l)$ for such a network. Thus, with this approach, each node in U_i will get $f(d^2)$ keys whereas each node in $G_p - U_i$ will get $f(d^2)/2$ keys. Now, we repeat this process by considering the star

(a) Optimality of Star Network

(b) Storage Comparison With [11]

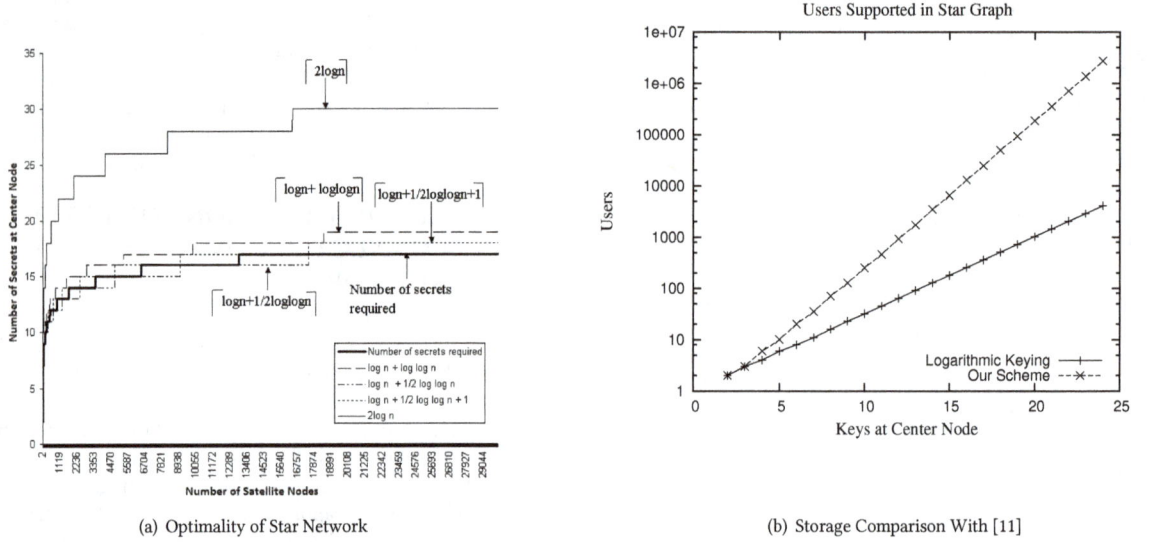

Figure 2: Independent Key Distribution in Star Network

graphs where for each i, U_i is the center node. As in Stage 1, each node is a satellite node in $d-1$ star graphs and the virtual node it is in is the center node in one star graph. Thus, each node maintains $\frac{d+1}{2}f(d^2)$ keys in Stage 2.

For an arbitrary number of nodes N, we repeat the protocol of Stage 2. Thus, at stage k we group d (virtual) nodes considered in stage $k-1$. For N nodes, the number of such stages required will be $\lceil \log_d N \rceil$ to secure communication between all the nodes. The number of keys stored by each node is: $\frac{d+1}{2}.y$ where, the term y is as shown:

$$y = f(d) + f(d^2) + \ldots + f(d^{\lceil \log_d N \rceil}) \qquad (1)$$

Theorem 9. The key distribution in the above solution solves Problem 2.4.   □

5.1 Storage Analysis

Now, we evaluate the storage at each node by evaluating formula (1), where $f(d) = \log d + \frac{1}{2}\log\log d + 1$.

$y = \log d + \log d^2 + \ldots + \log d^{\lceil \log_d N \rceil} +$

$\quad O(\log\log d + \log\log d^2 + \ldots + \log\log d^{\lceil \log_d N \rceil})$

$= \log d + 2\log d + \ldots + (\lceil \log_d N \rceil).\log d$

$\quad + O(\log_d N.\log\log_d N)$

$= \frac{(\lceil \log_d N \rceil)(\lceil \log_d N \rceil+1)}{2}(\log d) + O(\log_d N.\log\log_d N)$

$= \frac{(\lceil \log_2 N \rceil)(\lceil \log_2 N \rceil+1)}{2\log d} + O(\log_d N.\log\log_d N) \quad (2)$

Note that, when evaluating the term $O(\log_d N.\log\log_d N)$, we have used some upper bound approximations, such as $O(n!) = O(n^n)$, in the above formula and therefore, the final computed value is higher than the actual value. The storage at each node is given by: $\frac{(d+1)}{2}.y$ where the value of y is substituted from (2). By letting $d = 2$, the number of keys per node is: $\frac{3\log N(\log N+1)}{4}$.

In Figure 3, we compare the per node storage required in our approach with the best case storage cost required in the existing approaches [1, 11, 28]. The approach of Aiyer *et al.* [1] is denoted *Key Grids* and has a storage of $4\log^2 n$ keys per node. The approach by Ehab *et al.* [11] is denoted by *Logarithmic Keying* and has a storage of $\log^2 n$ keys per node. The approach by Novales *et al.* [28], which is an improvement over [11], is denoted by *Parameterized Keying* and has a storage of $\frac{3}{2}.(\log^2 n - \log n) + \log n - 3$ keys per node. The approach in [28] has higher collusion resistance than the approaches in [1, 11]. Whereas the approach from [28] uses the approach by Ehab *et al.* [11] as the base scheme for the star graph and hence, has a higher storage cost than our approach. We note that, by adjusting the parameter d in our approach it is possible to achieve similar bounds on the collusion resistance compared to the approach from [28] while keeping the storage lower than this approach. This is possible due to the optimal storage cost of the star graph as shown in Section 4. From this figure we can see that the storage required using our stage-wise approach is lower than that of previous approaches.

Signature and Verification Costs. Since our protocols use symmetric keys for generating signatures, we have not explicitly

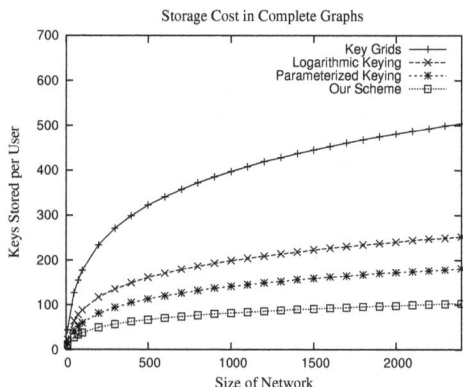

Figure 3: Storage for Fully Connected Networks

shown these costs in this paper as these costs are directly proportional to the storage cost. For the same reason we have not compared these costs against the existing approaches [1, 11, 28].

5.2 Note on Optimality of Storage

We note that, the key distribution for star networks, in Section 4, is optimal in terms of storage required. However, it is not known whether the key distribution for fully connected networks, and other networks (described next section) is optimal.

6 KEY DISTRIBUTION IN ACYCLIC, PLANAR AND COMPLETE BIPARTITE NETWORKS

In this section, we extend $p(k, l)$ for the cases where the communication graph is acyclic, planar, or complete bipartite. An acyclic network is a network whose topology is an acyclic graph. Similar definitions apply for planar and complete bipartite networks.

6.1 Acyclic Networks

In an acyclic network, a node can communicate with only those nodes that have an incident edge to this node. Two nodes not connected by an edge need not communicate with each other. Since an acyclic undirected graph consists of a set of trees, we describe the key distribution for a tree. The same algorithm can be applied for each tree separately to obtain the key distribution for acyclic graphs. Given a tree, we choose one of the nodes in it as a root and consider the corresponding rooted version. In particular, this allows us to define a parent of node in the tree and to define whether a node is a leaf. Now, consider a non-leaf node and its children in this network. This sub-network is a star graph where the non-leaf node is the center node and the children are satellite nodes. Now, we apply the $p(k, l)$ key distribution with appropriate values of k and l for this star graph. We repeat this process for each star graph obtained by considering a non-leaf node and its children in this fashion. The keys assigned to a node in the tree are the same as the union of the keys assigned to it in any star graph considered in this fashion.

In the star graph, the non-leaf node which is the center node gets $\log d + O(\log \log d)$ keys and each satellite node gets $\frac{1}{2} \log d + O(\log \log d)$ keys, where d is the degree of the center node. Furthermore, for any given non-leaf node, it is a center node in at most one star graph considered above. Likewise, it is a satellite

node in at most one star graph (where its parent is the center node) considered above. Thus, the number of keys at any node is at most $\frac{3}{2} \log d + O(\log \log d)$, which is less than that in [11] where $2 \log d$ keys are maintained.

6.2 Planar Networks

The extension to planar network is similar to that in [11]. In particular, in [11], a well-known result from graph theory [9], which states that any planar graph G can be decomposed into at most three acyclic graphs, is used. These acyclic graphs are also called *factors* where each factor has the same nodes as the original graph G and the degree of each factor is at most the degree of the original graph. We use the decomposition technique to distribute keys to the nodes. First, we decompose the graph into t factors, where $1 \le t \le 3$. Next, since each factor is an acyclic graph, we instantiate the key distribution for acyclic networks described earlier. One requirement of the key distribution is that, we need to secure each communication channel, *i.e.*, every edge that exists in the original graph. From the properties of factors, we observe that each edge occurs in at most one factor. Thus, each node in the graph receives t times the keys required in a $p(k, l)$ distribution. Note that, the number of keys held by each node can be reduced by reusing them in the different factors. Hence, for key distribution in planar networks, each node stores at most $O(t(\log d + \log \log d))$ keys where d is the maximum degree of the graph G.

6.3 Complete Bipartite Graphs

A complete bipartite graph is a graph $G(V, E)$ such that its vertex set can be partitioned into two disjoint sets, V_1 and V_2, the edge set, E is induced by these two vertex sets such that every vertex in V_1 is connected to every other vertex in V_2. No edge exists between any of the vertexes in V_1 (respectively, V_2). Example of such communication graph is one where the vertex set V_1 contains servers and the vertex set V_2 contains clients. The communication is from servers to clients and vice-versa. No server (respectively, client) needs to communicate with each other.

For this network, we employ the following key distribution technique. We treat the vertex set V_1 as a single center node, say C, and the vertex set V_2 as satellite nodes. As this represents a star network with C as star node, we instantiate a $p(k, l)$ key distribution for this network. Thus, in this distribution, the node C needs to store $\log |V_2| + O(\log \log |V_2|)$ keys. Since C represents the vertex set V_1, each of the nodes in V_1 is given all these keys. We repeat this procedure by treating the vertex set V_2 as the center node and the vertex set V_1 as the satellite nodes. This key distribution would provide an additional $\frac{1}{2} \log |V_1| + O(\log \log |V_1|)$ keys to each node in V_1. Thus, the number of keys given to nodes in V_1 is $\frac{3}{2} \log d + O(\log \log d)$, where $d = max(|V_1|, |V_2|)$ is the maximum degree of any node in the communication graph.

7 EVALUATION OF COLLUSION RESISTANCE

In this section, we evaluate the collusion resistance of our protocols. First, for star networks, we evaluate the collusion resistance gained by choosing a higher number of keys by the center node. Second, for fully connected networks, we show that the overall storage per node increases marginally as the desired level of collusion resistance increases. We considered these two topologies as they represented the two ends of the spectrum of the communication topologies. The results for other topologies are similar and we omitted due to space constraints.

We begin with a brief formal analysis for collusion resistance in star network by computing the probability of successful collusion of two nodes in $p(k, l)$ where $l = \frac{k}{2}$ and $k = \log n + \frac{1}{2} \log \log n + 1$. Let U_t be a target node and U_i, U_j be the colluding nodes that are attempting to send forged messages to U_t, posing as the center node. Let X_{sr} denote the random variable for the probability that a key $K_s \in K(U_r)$. The collusion is successful if: $K(U_i) \cup K(U_j) \supseteq K(U_t)$. From the results in [10], the expected value of this event is given by:

$$E[\Pi_{s=1}^{s=l}(1 - (1 - X_{si})(1 - X_{sj})X_{st})]$$

For $p(k, l)$, with $l = \frac{k}{2}$, we compute the probability $f = P(X_{sr} = 1)$, which is the probability of a key being part of any subset l of k. Note that the number of subsets of size l from k is given by $\binom{k}{l}$, which can be written as: $\binom{k-1}{l} + \binom{k-1}{l-1}$ where the first term is all possible l-sized sub-sets that do not include a given key and the second term is all sub-sets that include the key. When $l = \frac{k}{2}$ these two terms can be shown to be equal and hence, $P(X_{sr} = 1) = f = \frac{1}{2}$. Therefore, the probability of successful collusion is given by: $P(collusion) \leq (1 - (1 - f)(1 - f)f)^l$. Substituting for f, we get $P(collusion) \leq (7/8)^l$. Since l depends on k, which in turn depends on n, a larger value of k will achieve a higher collusion resistance for the case where $l = \frac{k}{2}$. However, if $l < \frac{k}{2}$, the collusion resistance is higher and we demonstrate this through an informal analysis in the following due to space constraints.

In Figure 4(a), for a star network, we illustrate the increase in storage at the center node for the set of protocols $p(k, k/x)$ where $x = 2, 3, \ldots, 10$. In this figure, the x-axis shows the minimum number of satellite nodes required to compromise the center node keys and the y axis show the corresponding number of center keys required for this level of collusion resistance. In Figure 4(b), we show the effect of collusion resistance on the storage for fully connected networks. Note that the increase in the number of keys for providing increased collusion resistance is small. For example, similar to the approach in [5], which has a collusion resistance of $w + 1$ nodes, it is possible to increase the collusion resistance in our scheme without increasing the storage at the nodes. The approach is as follows: the group controller chooses a large degree d for the hierarchy at the lowest level and instantiates $p(k, k/w + 1)$. Hence, at the lowest level the collusion resistance is $w + 1$ for any given sender. For higher levels of the hierarchy, the group controller chooses $d = 2$ and obtains the storage benefits. This construction shows that higher collusion resistance is possible in our approach without increasing the storage considerably.

Comparative Analysis of Collusion Resistance. Consider the scenario where in the number of keys maintained in $p(k, l)$ is equal to those maintained in the approach from [11] (respectively, approaches from [27, 28, 45]). By maintaining a larger set of keys at the center node, it is possible to maintain a smaller set of keys at the satellite nodes while still ensuring that each satellite node receives a unique set. Furthermore, the approach in [11] uses an identifier (ID) based key assignment wherein two nodes with specific IDs can break the scheme. Our approach does not have any structure and thereby, the colluding nodes need to search for suitable nodes to compromise by comparing the key sets they possess. This increases the difficulty of collusion in our scheme when compared to the scheme in [11]. Further, the schemes in [27, 28] are built by using

the scheme in [11] as the basis. Hence, the collusion resistance of the schemes in [27, 28] is proportional to the collusion resistance of the scheme in [11]. Finally, the scheme in Section 4 has, asymptotically, the same collusion resistance as the scheme in [11] (also, [27, 28], which are based on [11]). However, the scheme in Section 4 has better collusion resistance (see Figure 4(a)) when only numbers are used to measure the collusion resistance.

8 INTERNAL AND EXTERNAL ATTACKS

In this section, we show that our key distribution protocols can provide a tradeoff between handling *internal* vs *external* attacks. The storage at the node can be increased or reduced depending on the likelihood of the possible attacks. An *internal* attack is launched by two or more colluding satellite nodes that are currently part of the network. These satellite nodes combine their keys and try to compromise all the keys of the center node. The goal of an internal attack is to impersonate the center node and inject false information into the network or tamper the messages sent by the center node. Recall that, in the protocol in [11], two specifically chosen nodes are sufficient to compromise all the center node keys. An external attack is launched by an intruder who is not part of the network but is able to listen on to the communication in the network. The goal of the external attacker is to impersonate one of the nodes in the network, *i.e.*, it wants to send a message and the corresponding authentication codes, to the center node and have it accepted as a genuine message. Also, we are not concerned with replay of genuine packets, as it can be handled using standard techniques.

To illustrate the tradeoff between internal and external attacks, consider two protocols $p(k, l)$, where $l = k/3$ or $l = 2k/3$. Since $C(k, k/3) = C(k, 2k/3)$, the number of nodes that can be handled in either protocols is same. Now, consider the effect of these protocol instances on the two types of attacks.

(a) **Internal Attacks** For $p(k, k/3)$, the number of keys held by a satellite node is small. In this case, at least three internal attackers must collude to collect all the center keys. By contrast, for $p(k, 2k/3)$, the number of keys held by a satellite node is large. And, only two internal attackers can collude to collect all the center keys. Hence, for $p(k, k/3)$, an internal attacker has to perform more work to complete the attack successfully. This implies that reducing the satellite node storage provides better collusion resistance against internal attacks.

(b) **External Attacks** For $p(k, k/3)$, an external attacker only needs to generate $k/3$ valid authentication codes, but for $p(k, 2k/3)$, an external attacker needs to generate $2k/3$ valid authentication codes. This issue needs to be considered especially if weak authentication codes are used due to resource constraints, *e.g.*, when only a small number of bytes generated by a hash function are included. For $p(k, 2k/3)$, the number of keys held by a satellite node is large. For an external attacker, this key distribution increases the difficulty in compromising all the keys of a particular satellite node. Hence, when $p(k, 2k/3)$ is deployed, the external attacker has to perform more work to compromise the satellite node. Thus, increasing the storage at the satellite node provides better resistance against external attacks.

The above discussion shows that our key distribution protocol provides tradeoffs for handling internal and external attacks. These tradeoffs can be generalized as $p(k, k/c)$ and $p(k, k(1 - 1/c))$ where $c > 1$ where the value of c can be appropriately chosen to achieve the desired attack resilience.

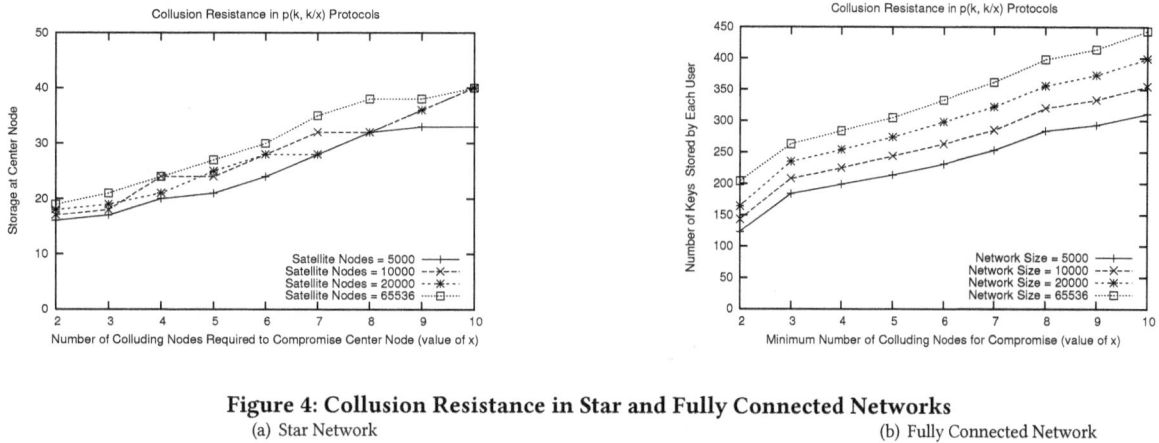

Figure 4: Collusion Resistance in Star and Fully Connected Networks
(a) Star Network   (b) Fully Connected Network

9 APPLICATION IN SENSOR NETWORKS

One scenario in sensor networks that requires authentication is reprogramming of sensor nodes. In reprogramming, the base station transmits a new program that needs to be executed in place of the currently running program. Since the base station may not be able to reach all the sensor nodes, the sensors that receive the program instructions propagate them further up in the network. The intermediate sensors are only required to propagate the received instructions without adding or removing any information. Hence, in this scenario, the network is a star network where there is a single sender, the base station, and several satellite nodes in the form of sensors. If the sensor network has multiple base stations then the resulting graph would be bipartite then, each base station communicates with a different part of the network and transmits the program. In this scenario, the network resembles a bi-partite graph where the base stations are in one partition and the sensors are there in the other partition. Therefore, it is important for the sensor nodes to be able to verify that the instructions they receive are indeed sent by (some) base station and that the integrity of the instructions is intact. Hence, protocol such as $p(k, l)$ (or its extension to bipartite graphs) can be used to provide authentication in such sensor networks.

Sensor nodes have limited battery resources and need to reduce the number of transmissions as message transmission is a battery intensive operation. It has been observed that cost of transmitting a single packet using public keys pair is more expensive than transmitting 3-4 KB of data [39]. The additional cost comes from the various public-key operations involved in preparing the data. Using $p(k, l)$, for a group of 1024 sensors, it requires transmission of approximately 5KB of data with a 512-bit secure hash function being used for signature generation. The size of the signatures can be further reduced if only a few bits from each signature are included. For instance, if only 384-bits of each signature are included then size of the data reduces by 25% to 3.75KB, where the number of bits to include depends on the desired level of security. Since the success of an adversary depends on forging *all* the sender signatures, the forgery resistance of this curtailed signature scheme can be verified to be secure in most practical situations. A hash functions like SHA-256, which yields 256-bit output, is very secure in most scenarios

and hence, can further reduce the signature size in $p(k, l)$. Even if the sensor network utilizes IEEE 802.15.4 for communication, which has an MTU of 127 bytes and payload of 104 bytes, our solutions still provide the smallest possible signature and verification cost when compared with other existing solutions.

10 CONCLUSION

In this paper, we considered the problem of independent key distribution for broadcast authentication. Our key distribution is such that it allows each node to provide authentication for unicast communication as well as broadcast communication where it sends a message to all nodes it intends to communicate with. We presented solutions for the cases where the communication graph is a: (1) star graph, (2) acyclic graph, (3) complete bipartite graph and (4) fully connected graph. For the star graph, we presented an optimal lower bound on key distribution with broadcast capability. We showed that this lower bound is indeed achievable and tight. In particular, we showed that as $n \to \infty$, $\log n + \frac{1}{2} \log \log n + 1$ keys at the center node suffice for virtually all cases of practical interest. Using $p(k, l)$, we showed that it is possible to reduce the keys maintained in an acyclic, planar, complete bipartite and fully connected communication graphs. However, the optimality of the number of keys for these graphs is still an open question. We demonstrated the security of our protocols by analyzing their collusion resistance and considering different attack scenarios. We demonstrated the applicability of our protocols in wireless sensor networks.

One of the future work in this area is to identify lower bounds for keys in different network topologies, which form the core of various communication networks. Another future direction is to explore possibility of applications in Internet-of-Things networks. Such an analysis has been done by Zhao *et al.* in [48] for the random key distribution protocols [12], but is an open problem for deterministic key pre-distribution protocols.

ACKNOWLEDGEMENT

The work of Bezawada was supported in part by funds from NSF under Award No. CNS 1650573, CableLabs, AFRL, Furuno Electric Company, SecureNok and National Natural Science Foundation of China Grant 61672156. The work of Indrajit Ray and Indrakshi

Ray was supported in part by funds from NSF under Award No. CNS 1650573, CableLabs, AFRL, Furuno Electric Company, and SecureNok. The work of Rui Li was supported in part by grant from National Natural Science Foundation of China Grant 61672156.

REFERENCES

[1] Amitanand Aiyer, Lorenzo Alvisi, and Mohamed Gouda. 2006. Key grids: A Protocol Family for Assigning Symmetric Keys. In *Proc. IEEE Int. Conf. on Network Protocols (ICNP)*. 178–186.
[2] E. Ayday and F. Fekri. 2012. A Secure Broadcasting Scheme to Provide Availability, Reliability and Authentication for Wireless Sensor Networks. *Ad Hoc Networks* 10, 7 (2012), 1278–1290.
[3] Dan Boneh, Glenn Durfee, and Matt Franklin. 2001. Lower Bounds for Multicast Message Authentication. In *Advances in Cryptology (EUROCRYPT)*. Vol. 2045. 437–452.
[4] Seyit A. Camtepe and Bülent Yener. 2007. Combinatorial Design of Key Distribution Mechanisms for Wireless Sensor Networks. *IEEE/ACM Trans. on Networking* 15, 2 (2007), 346–358.
[5] Ran Canetti, Juan Garay, Gene Itkis, Daniele Micciancio, Moni Naor, and Benny Pinkas. 1999. Multicast security: a taxonomy and some efficient constructions. In *Proc. of the IEEE Joint Conf. on Computer Communications (INFOCOM)*. 708–716.
[6] Taehwan Choi, Hrishikesh B. Acharya, and Mohamed G. Gouda. 2013. The Best Keying Protocol for Sensor Networks. *Pervasive and Mobile Computing* 9, 4 (2013), 564–571.
[7] Jacek Cichon, Zbigniew Golebiewski, and Miroslaw Kutylowski. 2012. From Key Predistribution to Key Redistribution. *Theoretical Computer Science* 453 (2012), 75–87.
[8] Pedro Cirne, André Zúquete, and Susana Sargento. 2018. TROPHY: Trustworthy VANET routing with group authentication keys. *Ad Hoc Networks* 71 (2018), 45–67.
[9] C. J Colbourn. 1987. *The Combinatorics of Network Reliability*. Oxford University Press.
[10] Martin E. Dyer, Trevor I. Fenner, Alan M. Frieze, and Andrew Thomason. 1995. On Key Storage in Secure Networks. *Journal of Cryptology* 8, 4 (1995), 189–200.
[11] Ehab S. Elmallah, Mohamed G. Gouda, and Sandeep S. Kulkarni. 2008. Logarithmic Keying. *ACM Trans. on Autonomous Adaptive Sys.* 3, 4 (2008), 1–18.
[12] Laurent Eschenauer and Virgil D. Gligor. 2002. A Key-management Scheme for Distributed Sensor Networks.. In *Proc. of the ACM Conf. on Computer and Communications Security (CCS)*. 41–47.
[13] G. Gaubatz, J.-P. Kaps, E. Ozturk, and B. Sunar. 2005. State of the Art in Ultra-low Power Public Key Cryptography for Wireless Sensor Networks. In *Proc. of the IEEE Conf. on Pervasive Computing and Communications (PerCom) Workshops*. 146–150.
[14] Li Gong and David J. Wheeler. 1990. A Matrix Key-Distribution Scheme. *Journal of Cryptology* 2, 1 (1990), 51–59.
[15] Bogdan Groza, Stefan Murvay, Anthony Van Herrewege, and Ingrid Verbauwhede. 2017. Libra-can: Lightweight broadcast authentication for controller area networks. *ACM Trans. on Embedded Computing Sys. (TECS)* 16, 3 (2017), 90.
[16] Kevin J. Henry, Maura B. Paterson, and Douglas R. Stinson. 2013. Practical Approaches to Varying Network Size in Combinatorial Key Predistribution Schemes. In *Selected Areas in Cryptography (Lecture Notes in Computer Science)*, Vol. 8282. 89–117.
[17] Mahmud Hossain, Ragib Hasan, and Anthony Skjellum. 2017. Securing the Internet of Things: A Meta-Study of Challenges, Approaches, and Open Problems. In *Proc. of IEEE Int. Conf. on Distrib. Computing Sys. Workshops (ICDCSW)*. IEEE, 220–225.
[18] Jean-Pierre Hubaux, Levente Buttyán, and Srdan Capkun. 2001. The Quest for Security in Mobile Ad Hoc Networks. In *Proc. of the ACM Int. Symp. on Mobile Ad Hoc Networking and Computing (MobiHoc)*. 146–155.
[19] Michelle Kendall, Keith M. Martin, Siaw-Lynn Ng, Maura B. Paterson, and Douglas R. Stinson. 2012. Broadcast-enhanced Key Predistribution Schemes. *IACR Cryptology ePrint Archive* 2012 (2012), 295.
[20] Jun Young Kim, Wen Hu, Dilip Sarkar, and Sanjay Jha. 2017. ESIoT: Enabling Secure Management of the Internet of Things. In *Proc. of the ACM Conf. on Security and Privacy in Wireless and Mobile Networks (WiSec)*. 219–229.
[21] Sandeep S. Kulkarni, Mohamed G. Gouda, and Anish Arora. 2006. Secret instantiation in Ad-Hoc Networks. *Computer Communications* 29 (2006), 200–215.
[22] Hartono Kurnio, Safavi-Naini Rei, and Huaxiong Wang. 2002. Efficient Revocation Schemes for Secure Multicast. In *Proc. of the Int. Conf. on Information Security and Cryptology (ICISC)*, Vol. 2288. Springer, 160–177.
[23] Jooyoung Lee and Douglas R. Stinson. 2005. Deterministic Key Predistribution Schemes for Distributed Sensor Networks. In *Selected Areas in Cryptography*. 294–307.
[24] Dongang Liu and Peng Ning. 2003. Efficient Distribution of Key Chain Commitments for Broadcast Authentication in Distributed Sensor Networks. In *Proc. of the Network and Distributed System Security Symposium (NDSS)*.
[25] Yi Mu and Vijay Varadharajan. 1996. On the Design of Security Protocols for Mobile Communications. In *Information Security and Privacy*. Lecture Notes in Computer Science, Vol. 1172. 134–145.
[26] Dalit Naor, Moni Naor, and Jeffery Lotspiech. 2002. Revocation and Tracing Schemes for Stateless Receivers. *Electronic Colloquium on Computational Complexity (ECCC)* (2002).
[27] Ramon Novales and Neeraj Mittal. 2009. TASK: Template-Based Key Assignment for Confidential Communication in Wireless Networks. In *Proc. of the IEEE Symp. on Reliable Distrib. Sys. (SRDS)*. 209–216.
[28] Ramon Novales and Neeraj Mittal. 2011. Parameterized Key Assignment for Confidential Communication in Wireless Networks. *Ad Hoc Networks* 9, 7 (2011), 1186–1201.
[29] Maura B. Paterson and Douglas R. Stinson. 2014. A Unified Approach to Combinatorial Key Predistribution Schemes for Sensor Networks. *Designs, Codes and Cryptography* 71, 3 (2014), 433–457.
[30] Karl Pearson. 1924. Historical Note on the Origin of the Normal Curve of Errors. *Biometrika* 16 (1924), 402–404.
[31] Adrian Perrig, Ran Canetti, J.D. Tygar, and Dawn Song. 2002. The TESLA Broadcast Authentication Protocol. *RSA CryptoBytes* 5 (2002).
[32] Adrian Perrig, Robert Szewczyk, J. D. Tygar, Victor Wen, and David E. Culler. 2002. SPINS: Security Protocols for Sensor Networks. *Wireless Networks* 8, 5 (2002), 521–534.
[33] Di Pietro, L. V. Mancini, Y. W. Law, S. Etalle, and P. J. M. Havinga. 2003. LKHW: A Directed Diffusion-Based Secure Multicast Scheme for Wireless Sensor Networks. In *Proc. of the Int. Conf. on Parallel Processing Workshops (ICPP)*. 397–406.
[34] Rodrigo Roman, Cristina Alcaraz, Javier Lopez, and Nicolas Sklavos. 2011. Key Management Systems for Sensor Networks in the Context of the Internet of Things. *Computers & Electrical Engineering* 37, 2 (2011), 147–159.
[35] Rodrigo Roman, Jianying Zhou, and Javier Lopez. 2013. On the Features and Challenges of Security and Privacy in Distributed Internet of Things. *Computer Networks* 57, 10 (2013), 2266–2279.
[36] Lifeng Sang and Anish Arora. 2008. Spatial Signatures for Lightweight Security in Wireless Sensor Networks. In *Proc. of the IEEE Joint Conference on Computer Communications (INFOCOM)*. 2137–2145.
[37] Ivor Schneider. 2005. Abraham De Moivre, The Doctrine of Chances (1718, 1738, 1756). *Grattan-Guinness, I., Landmark Writings in Western Mathematics 1640–1940* (2005).
[38] Sabrina Sicari, Alessandra Rizzardi, Luigi Alfredo Grieco, and Alberto Coen-Porisini. 2015. Security, Privacy and Trust in Internet of Things: The Road Ahead. *Computer networks* 76 (2015), 146–164.
[39] Arvinderpal S. Wander, Nils Gura, Hans Eberle, Vipul Gupta, and Sheueling Chang Shantz. 2006. Energy Analysis of Public-Key Cryptography for Wireless Sensor Networks. In *Proc. of Int. Conf. on Pervasive Computing and Communications (PerCOM)*. 324–328.
[40] Pan Wang, Peng Ning, and Douglas S. Reeves. 2004. Storage-Efficient Stateless Group Key Revocation. In *Proc. of Int. Conf. on Information Security (ISC) (Lecture Notes in Computer Science)*, Vol. 3225. Springer.
[41] Chung Kei Wong, Mohamed Gouda, and Simon S. Lam. 2000. Secure Group Communications Using Key Graphs. *IEEE/ACM Trans. on Networking* 8, 1 (February 2000), 16–30.
[42] Chung Kei Wong and Simon S. Lam. 1999. Digital Signatures for Flows and Multicasts. *IEEE/ACM Trans. on Networking* 7, 4 (1999), 502–513.
[43] Taojun Wu, Yi Cui, Brano Kusy, Akos Ledeczi, Janos Sallai, Nathan Skirvin, Jan Werner, and Yuan Xue. 2007. A Fast and Efficient Source Authentication Solution for Broadcasting in Wireless Sensor Networks. In *New Technologies, Mobility and Security*. Springer, Dordrecht, 53–63.
[44] Yang Xiao, Venkata Krishna Rayi, Bo Sun, Xiaojiang Du, Fei Hu, and Michael Galloway. 2007. A Survey of Key Management Schemes in Wireless Sensor Networks. *Computer Communications* 30, 11-12 (2007), 2314–2341.
[45] Y.E. Yang and J.D. Touch. 2008. Protocol Family for Optimal and Deterministic Symmetric Key Assignment. In *Proc. of the Int. Conf. on Networking (ICN)*. 207–212.
[46] Xuan Zha, Wei Ni, Kangfeng Zheng, Ren Ping Liu, and Xinxin Niu. 2017. Collaborative Authentication in Decentralized Dense Mobile Networks with Key Predistribution. *IEEE Trans. on Information Forensics and Security* 12, 10 (2017), 2261–2275.
[47] Junqi Zhang and Vijay Varadharajan. 2010. Wireless sensor network keymanagement survey and taxonomy. *Journal of Network and Computer Applications* 33 (2010), 63–75.
[48] Jun Zhao. 2017. Probabilistic key predistribution in mobile networks resilient to node-capture attacks. *IEEE Trans. on Information Theory* 63, 10 (2017), 6714–6734.
[49] Yun Zhou and Yuguang Fang. 2006. BABRA: Batch-based Broadcast Authentication in Wireless Sensor Networks. In *Proc. of the IEEE Global Telecommunications Conf. (GLOBECOM)*.
[50] Sencun Zhu, Sanjeev Setia, Shouhuai Xu, and Sushil Jajodia. 2006. GKMPAN: An Efficient Group Rekeying Scheme for Secure Multicast in Ad-Hoc Networks. *Journal of Computer Security* 14, 4 (2006), 301–325.
[51] Jan Henrik Ziegeldorf, Oscar Garcia Morchon, and Klaus Wehrle. 2014. Privacy in the Internet of Things: Threats and Challenges. *Security and Communication Networks* 7, 12 (2014), 2728–2742.

Self-Generation of Access Control Policies

Seraphin Calo
IBM Research
Yorktown Heights, New York, USA

Dinesh Verma
IBM Research
Yorktown Heights, New York, USA

Supriyo Chakraborty
IBM Research
Yorktown Heights, New York, USA

Elisa Bertino
Purdue University
West Lafayette, Indiana, USA

Emil Lupu
Imperial College
London, UK

Gregory Cirincione
Army Research Labs
Adelphi, Maryland, USA

ABSTRACT

Access control for information has primarily focused on access statically granted to subjects by administrators usually in the context of a specific system. Even if mechanisms are available for access revocation, revocations must still be executed manually by an administrator. However, as physical devices become increasingly embedded and interconnected, access control needs to become an integral part of the resources being protected and be generated dynamically by the resources depending on the context in which they are being used. In this paper, we discuss a set of scenarios for access control needed in current and future systems and use that to argue that an approach for resources to generate and manage their access control policies dynamically on their own is needed. We discuss some approaches for generating such access control policies that may address the requirements of the scenarios.

KEYWORDS

Dynamic Security, IoT, Machine Learning, AI, Autonomic Access Control

ACM Reference Format:
Seraphin Calo, Dinesh Verma, Supriyo Chakraborty, Elisa Bertino, Emil Lupu, and Gregory Cirincione. 2018. Self-Generation of Access Control Policies. In *SACMAT '18: The 23rd ACM Symposium on Access Control Models & Technologies (SACMAT), June 13–15, 2018, Indianapolis, IN, USA*. ACM, New York, NY, USA, 9 pages. https://doi.org/10.1145/3205977.3205995

1 INTRODUCTION

Access control is a fundamental part of security in IT systems, and various approaches to properly authenticate and control access to sensitive resources have been developed [9], including role based [7] and attribute based [13] access control schemes, and their numerous variants [2, 8, 14]. While the need for dynamic access control is recognized, the solutions proposed for dynamicity have been grafted over a static access control paradigm [6, 11, 12]. Nevertheless, current approaches for access control tend to be relatively static, have to be managed by human administrators, and in many cases imposed as an external security mechanism to wrap around the operation of a resource.

ACM acknowledges that this contribution was authored or co-authored by an employee, contractor, or affiliate of the United States government. As such, the United States government retains a nonexclusive, royalty-free right to publish or reproduce this article, or to allow others to do so, for government purposes only.
SACMAT '18, June 13–15, 2018, Indianapolis, IN, USA
© 2018 Association for Computing Machinery.
ACM ISBN 978-1-4503-5666-4/18/06...$15.00
https://doi.org/10.1145/3205977.3205995

As information systems become more dynamic, virtualized, grow in size and scale, and are increasingly used to interconnect physical systems, existing access control mechanisms may turn out to be inadequate to deal with the resulting complexities. In this paper, we argue that we need to envision a new type of access control paradigm, one in which resources determine their own access control policies from a dynamic assessment of their context of operations, the risks versus utility trade-off imposed in a specific situation and learn how to adapt their behavior. Static access control paradigms and supporting dynamicity by grafting dynamic access control post-facto, e.g., using a management system for dynamic access control, is no longer going to be sufficient. The intelligence to provide access control in a dynamic manner needs to be embedded within the resources themselves.

We begin this paper with a discussion of several scenarios in which existing access control paradigms may prove to be inadequate. These scenarios motivate the need for resources to create their own access control policies in a dynamic manner. Finally, we discuss some approaches by which the vision of resources that generate their own policies can be attained and conclude with a discussion about when each approach may be applicable.

2 SCENARIOS

The scenarios that we discuss below are ones that are going to be real in the imminent future. In some cases, one can even assert that the situation described is already present in many environments. In all the scenarios, we argue that the current access control mechanisms will be inadequate to address the security needs of the scenario.

Current access control mechanisms are derived primarily from a model in which "subjects"[1] try to access resources and a complete set of subjects and resources can be specified in advance in an access control matrix [19]. Access control is enforced by either considering the set of subjects that are allowed access to a resource (by maintaining an access control list) or by considering the set of resources a subject is allowed to access (capabilities). On this basic mechanism, one can add definitions of "roles" to group subjects and/or resources; or arrange these subjects and resources in different hierarchies to simplify the task of representing the access control matrix. However, the matrix remains relatively static, and rarely considers the fact that resources interact with each other and may require a continuously changing access control matrix. More recent attribute-based access control models [13], of which XACML[2] is a well-known example, try to provide richer access

---

[1] A subject can be a human user, a process, an application, a device and so forth.
[2] http://docs.oasis-open.org/xacml/3.0/xacml-3.0-core-spec-os-en.html

based on values of properties (e.g. attributes) characterizing subjects and resources and are also able to take context into account. However, permissions in such models are usually static and need to be issued by an administrator. Furthermore, these models require the acquisition of trusted attribute information. The static nature of access control may be inadequate in many situations. There are models which take into account context information. Some attention has been given to add dynamicity as an after-thought through management systems or as part of a federation architecture. For example, roles are delegated in a dynamic manner to deal with dynamic coalitions [11], an intelligent network management system reacts to current threat to adjust network security policies [6], higher level workflows are used to determine access control [12], or dynamic attributes like location are used to determine roles [3]. However, the context information is usually limited to location and time and even for this limited context there are no effective approaches for dealing with rapidly changing contexts (which is relevant especially for mobile systems). In order to cope up with the rapid dynamicity in the system, the use-cases below require resources to be able to determine their own access control policies.

2.1 Car Navigation Systems

A car navigation system has several types of information available to the driver, and information such as the home location and previous destinations is available to any person who is able to access the car. However, open access to this information creates known security exposures, e.g., a thief may break into a car parked at a movie theater, drive the car to the home location, open the garage door using the remote control in the car, and rob the house under the likely scenario that the home is unoccupied.

Adding a static access control paradigm to the information, e.g., defining the role of a driver and/or passenger, and assigning role or attribute-based access control permissions does not solve this problem. Similarly, identifying the driver using visual recognition with a camera and only allowing access to home location and/or recent destinations to the authorized driver is not a viable solution. The car may be driven on occasions by the spouse, children or neighbor of the most frequent driver, and authorizing each one to the car systems would be tedious. If a policeman or paramedic needs to take the driver, who may be sick, back to his or her home, they should be authorized to get the home information. If the driver is in the passenger seat of the car, the access should probably be authorized. On the other hand, if a previously unseen person has broken the window of the car to enter, that is likely to be a burglar, access should be denied. The starting location of the car, the presence/absence of the most frequent driver (see [3] for a preliminary notion of proximity-based access control), and the status of the car, all contribute to the decision as to whether the access to information in a navigation system (or other systems in the car) should be allowed. If we add the other issues which arise when a car is used by rental companies, where there is no normal driver, but an authorized driver or a set of authorized drivers has temporary authorization to drive the car, thus requiring configuration of the car access control systems on each rental, and revocation of the authorization when the car is returned, the situation becomes even more complex.

Dealing with all the dynamic contexts which could arise in the automobile and combinations of drivers cannot be achieved by means of current access control mechanisms. A dynamic access control scheme, where the navigation system, the car remote, and the car ignition system, make their own access control rules based on the current context is needed. The intelligence cannot be put into a management system since the connectivity of the car to the management system would frequently be interrupted depending on the usage pattern of the car.

2.2 Partner Information Access

Modern enterprise and university research has become more and more collaborative. Whether it is research, product development, or operational service creation, it is very common for several organizations to collaborate together to engage in a joint task. Each such cooperation requires access to resources and services that only the members of the alliance are allowed to access.

Most enterprise and government systems, however, remain bound to the concept of a static access control, where users outside the enterprise are considered potential threats and restricted in which services they can use. Although the use of client-side scripts and programs (e.g., Java or JavaScript code for video meetings) is prevalent, static protection systems would prevent such code from entering the enterprise network, and access to many useful services would thus be eliminated. The situation is made worse since many users frequently work remotely, so access control based on source and destination network addresses of users proves woefully inadequate.

Without denying the need for security for the enterprises, the identity, business arrangements and trust relationships must be considered to determine the dynamic context of a network access request, and enhanced access to services provided to trusted partners. Given the myriad of partnerships, alliances and collaborations any large organization engages in, the access granted needs to depend on the context and sensitivity of the information, and may need to consider history of previously granted accesses or previously accessed information.

The situation is shown in Figure 1. Organizations A and B have an existing agreement which allows them to share a set of common services. When employee X from Organization A tries to access a web conferencing service which is operated in an authorized manner by organization D under authorization by organization B, organization A's firewall access control policies should be smart enough to allow access to the client-side code that is needed for service participation on X's machine, as long as the web conferencing session includes an employee Y from the partner organization. However, if the same web conferencing service is being used by Organization C, which does not have an existing agreement with Organization A, any session which is an attempt by employee X to access the service with an employee of organization C should be denied. So even though the end-points of the communication for the two requests are the same, the context of operation, and the identities and affiliations of who else is in the conference as well as the relationships between organizations, need to be taken into account to determine whether access is to be allowed or not, and whether the code being sent by organization D is a threat to organization A.

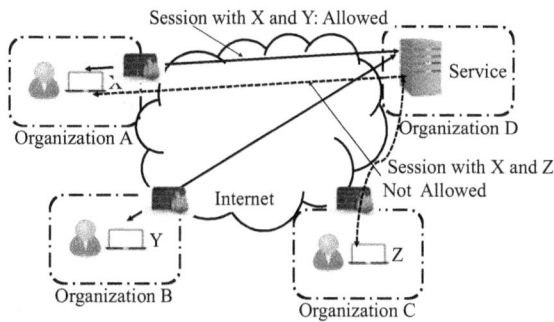

Figure 1: Partner Information Access Scenario

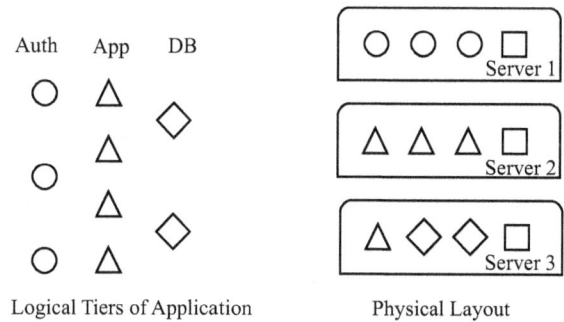

Figure 2: Elastic Data Center

While the software in an enterprise would typically be able to contact a management server and get the required dynamic access control policy, there are several organizations where partners cannot assume constant connectivity to a management service. Some examples include coalitions operating in a remote region, companies exploring for oil or minerals jointly in a remote area, or ships from different navies conducting a joint exercise.

2.3 Elastic Data Centers

Technologies such as virtual machines, Docker containers, Kubernetes and microservices-based architectures enable the concept of elastic services. In elastic services, a service may be running as multiple parallel tasks (a task being either a virtual machine, a container or a parallel service or micro-service instance).

Static access control mechanisms require setting up access control rules in different components of the system. With the high degree of dynamicity in the environment, manual configuration of such access control policies is challenging. An alternative would be to have a centralized system which generates access controls for the configuration as it changes. The master control would then be responsible for keeping track of the current configuration of a dynamic system and ensuring that the right access controls are in place.

However, centralizing the access control, while simple in concept, can be fraught with challenges when the set of virtual components are changing rapidly, and each change requires accessing a central location. There will be race conditions where the master configuration is out of sync with the actual configuration of the dynamic system, especially if every configuration change requires accessing the master server. It would be highly desirable that such central access be made for less dynamic aspects of the environment, while more dynamic issues such as access control for each device be able to be determined automatically by each element in the system.

An illustrative example is shown in Figure 2, in which an application running at the data center consists of three tiers of applications, let us say a tier of authentication services (circle shape), a tier of web application services (triangle shape), and a tier of database services (rhombus shape). The square shapes are for services that

may belong to some other applications. Each tier consists of one or more services performing the task required of it. The authentication services, the application services and the database services are all virtual machines (or other virtual entities) which need to be configured physically so they allow access only to the other virtual machines belonging to the same application. The triangles permit access to the circles, and the rhombuses permit access to the triangles. The circles, triangles and the rhombuses should not permit access to the squares. The number of circles, triangles, rhombuses and even the squares in the system can vary over time.

Physically, the services can be running on physical servers in any configuration and share the physical capacity of the system. A possible configuration is shown to the right of Figure 2. This gives the ability of squares to send requests to the triangles, circles and rhombuses on the same or other machines. However, each virtual machine needs to protect itself to only allow requests from the tier ahead of it. This protection needs to be updated as new instances are added in each tier.

While the data centers do have a good connectivity to a local server that can provide them with dynamic access control guidelines, the rapid rate of changes in the system may make it more efficient if the virtual machines/containers could generate their own access control policies under a slower-rate supervision of the management server.

2.4 Coalition Resource Sharing

Military coalitions are becoming common with different countries joining forces in order to deal with the challenges of an increasingly complex world. When such military coalitions are formed, they often need to form dynamic communities of interest (CoI). A CoI consists of people, resources and infrastructure established for a relatively short period of time, e.g., a CoI may consist of a group of U.S. and UK soldiers that will be distributing food packets to a remote village which has been impacted by floods, and the operation will last for a couple of days. When a CoI contains local civilian organizations or NGOs, the degree of trust among organizations can vary widely.

An example of a CoI is provided in Figure 3, in which partner *A* provides people, drones and a mule, partner *B* provides people,

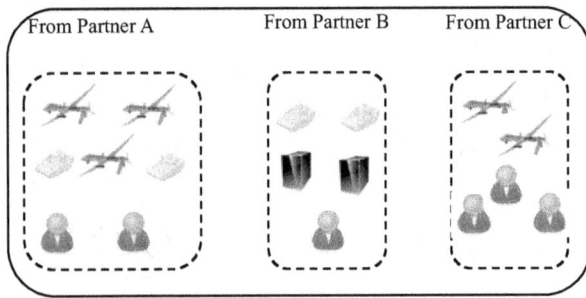

Figure 3: A Community of Interest

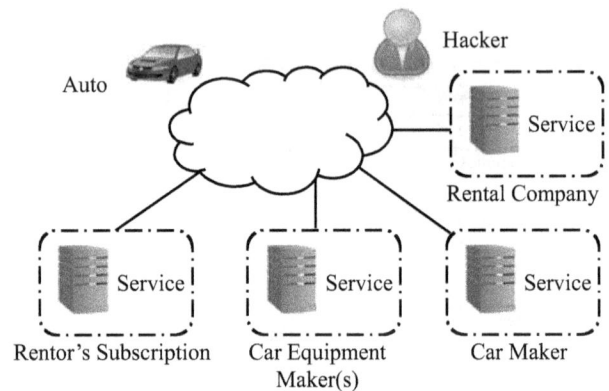

Figure 4: Client Side IoT Security Scenario

computing infrastructure and automated mules, and partner *C* provides drones and people. When dynamic CoIs are formed, resources among different coalition partners need to be shared and pooled together for the common task. The access control and authorizations for access to the shared resources need to be granted dynamically as these CoIs are formed and removed as the CoIs disband. Since the resources that are used for the CoI may also be used for other operations that a country may not want to share with other coalition partners, access to resources needs to be granted based on the situation. If the humanitarian mission mentioned above comes under an attack, and an attack drone with U.S. controls needs to expand its access control to its UK colleagues, then that access control ought to be provided based on the context. Given the range of dynamic situations that can arise in the context of a military operation, access control must be determined by resources themselves on a dynamic basis depending on the context, and re-evaluated as the context changes.

2.5 Client Side IoT Security

Devices that used to deal with physical processes, e.g. heaters, coolers, elevators, automobiles, centrifuges etc., are getting connected to Internet based services at an exponentially growing pace. This is happening in several domains, ranging from industrial manufacturing, automobiles, and semiconductor foundries to banking and homes. The benefits of connecting the devices to Internet based services is immense, allowing for dynamic updates to software and firmware, sharing of insights gained from different devices, the ability to mine the data for insights into operational efficiency, quick trouble-shooting and improved productivity. However, as more and more of these devices are getting connected, the risks associated with Internet based black hat attackers gaining access to these devices, and causing irreparable damage is also increasing.

As these devices are being accessed from the Internet, they need to be safeguarded. The accesses being provided to them must not cause a security risk, for example, being compromised and used in botnets [1], or even worse a safety risk. When safety is at risk, e.g. in an emergency situation, security norms may need to be violated. Static access control, which allows for restricted access to services from users on the Internet is inadequate for the task at hand. The person accessing the service from the Internet can steal credentials and masquerade as an authorized user. The IoT system

which is being accessed must be able to protect itself when given dangerous commands over the Internet. This determination needs to be dynamic and based on the current context in which the device is being used. A simple and innocuous command, e.g., asking an automobile to accelerate from a service that appears to be from the manufacturer of the automobile, may be perfectly fine if the car is parked imperfectly in a parking lot, but would be dangerous if that causes the car to hit something in front of it, and is being sent by a hacker.

An illustrative example of the access control that an IoT device needs to enforce is shown in Figure 4. An automobile is being operated by a rental car company and is currently rented out to a driver. The automobile is connected via a cellular network to the Internet, and interacts with: (a) a tracking service run by rental company; (b) a maintenance and diagnostic service run by the maker of the car; (c) a maintenance and diagnostic service run by the supplier of the car; and, (d) an independent service that provides emergency assistance for which the renter has a subscription. Since the cellular network provider can change across different regions within which the car is driven, the car needs its own protection service.

Each of the services is allowed its own set of data restrictions which can change over time. The tracking service may be allowed access to the location of the car when the car is not rented out, but the tracking of an individual renter location when the car is rented out is prohibited. Each of the subcontractors who provided material to the car may be running a service, but they are only allowed access to some of the services within the car. Furthermore, the diagnostics that are permitted on the car have to be performed when the car is not being driven. Access control to car functions for services that need subscription from the renter needs to be added dynamically.

Furthermore, any requests to control the car from any of the service providers over the Internet needs to be validated to see that: (a) they are indeed from a valid service and not a hacker on the Internet; and, (b) they are permissible under the current context that the car is operating in. Similarly, any request going out from the car needs to be checked to ensure that: (a) it is going to one of the authorized services relevant to the car; (b) it is not leaking sensitive information about the current user of the car; and, (c) is not due to the car being used for malicious purposes such as becoming part of a botnet. All these decisions vary over time depending on the rental status, the car location, and the condition of the automobile and its components.

Because of the dynamic nature of the access required, the car needs to be able to decide for itself which accesses are allowed, and which ones are not. The car is in the best position to assess its state, decide whether the requests coming from the Internet are worth addressing, and thus protect itself. Interactions with other cars in the neighborhood may also play a role in the decisions made by a single car.

In addition to the car, similar dynamic access control concerns may arise in many other IoT environments. Wearable health-care systems worn by a patient and the health-care providers may need to interact together, and each interaction may require adjustment in access control rules. In [5], a system which generates new access control rules when new devices are encountered is described. While they do not change access control rules, an environment in which people leave hospital premises would also require modification and changes in the access control rules.

The key requirement for access control as shown by these scenarios is that the right access control is very dependent on the context in which a request is being made. The same access request (i.e., from the same subject to the same resource) may be safe (or desirable) to grant in some conditions, while it may be undesirable to grant in other conditions. The resource being accessed is usually in the best position to determine whether the request should be allowed, and we need to develop access control mechanisms by which the resources themselves are able to decide whether a subject access request should be granted. We refer to these types of access control requests as dynamic access control approaches.

3 DYNAMIC ACCESS CONTROL APPROACHES

The previous section argued that we need to enhance static access control models, including role-based access control and more recent attribute-based access control, to deal with more dynamic scenarios. In this section, we present some potential approaches for a dynamic access control which depends on the local context. In order to do so, we introduce the abstraction of a device, which is a collection of resources and subjects. The devices can host subjects that can access resources on the same or on other devices. One way to understand the concept of the device is to consider each device as a collection of long running services. Each service can invoke other services, acting both as subjects as well as resources. Our end goal is to have each device be capable of determining the access control policies for its resources depending on the context in which the device finds itself.

3.1 Dynamic Refinement from Environment Specification

One approach to allow devices to generate their own access control policies is to provide them with a description of the environment in which they are operating, giving them a high-level guidance on

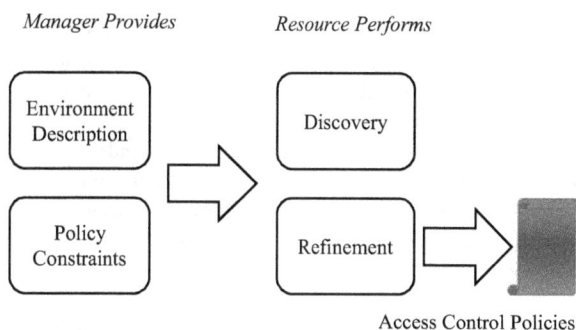

Figure 5: Dynamic Policy Refinement

how they ought to operate as regards to providing access control to other entities in the system. As an example, a manager can provide devices with information about other types of devices that are found in the system, and mechanisms to validate the new devices entering the system. The devices could then discover other devices in the system, and then decide to give them access on the basis of the restrictions provided by the manager, and also based on information about the devices (such as type of device [18], and organization or user owning the device).

The concept of dynamic refinement is schematically described in Figure 5. A set of guidelines from a management system provides each resource with a description of the environment in which it could expect to operate. This description would include the other types of subjects and resources it should expect to encounter during operation, and the properties expected of those other types of subjects/resources. Each device would also have a discovery process which would allow it to discover other entities in the system, both the other types of subjects, and other resources that are present in the environment. During the discovery process, resources may share accesses made by different subjects and thus maintain a distributed log of accesses that are made.

Each resource would also be provided with a set of constraints on the type of access control policies that they should explore. These constraints could be used to check the validity of the policies that the resource uses for its operation, some examples being a policy generation grammar, or a template for policies. The resource uses a refinement process to translate the constraints into a set of access control policies, which can then be used on a per request basis to determine access. The policies could be regenerated either periodically, or when a specific event happens, e.g., new subjects or resources are discovered in the environment. As the policies are regenerated, the high-level constraints are mapped (refined) into a part of the access control matrix with the currently discovered set of subjects, resources, their attributes and/or roles, and the history of the previous requests. The high level constraints may be defined in a teleo-reactive manner [5].

Such a system is described in [21], in which the manager defines the roles that devices may play within a large group, and provides each device with an interaction graph with the different roles in the system. The devices act as subjects for accessing services present on other devices, with the services playing the role of resources. Each device is also provided with a template that allows it to generate access control policies based on the roles assigned to a new system. The combination of the three techniques, namely: (a) defining an interaction graph among different roles; (b) providing a way for devices to discover other devices in the environment and validate their roles; and, (c) providing each device with a mechanism to generate policies, e.g., a policy template or a policy generation grammar, allows devices the ability to generate access control policies in a dynamic manner.

Such dynamic refinement allows devices to generate their own policies in scenarios where the set of other subjects/resources in the environment fall into a few broad classes with known relationships among them, and the set of specific subjects/resources can be easily discovered. Examining the various scenarios presented in Section 2, the scenarios for dynamic data centers and coalition resource sharing can be supported well by dynamic refinement approaches.

3.2 Device Model based Access Control

Another approach for devices to determine their own access control is to provide them with a model of how their safety would be impacted if they were to allow any operation to be executed on them. For example, use of computation intensive services may deplete the energy resources of a device making it unable to answer some critical requests. The devices can use such a model to determine whether or not they should allow access to any resource or service that is being requested of them.

If we consider each resource as a collection of services, to which requests are being made by an external entity, the access control problem can be seen as a go/no-go decision on every attempt by the external entity to access a specific service. If the device has a model that determines whether the result of that particular service invocation would be safe or unsafe for that device, it can use that model to determine whether or not that access ought to be allowed.

The approach is described in Figure 6, where the device model is used to assess the validity of each request. On each request, the model of the device is used to understand the impact of approving for the requesting subject to access the requested resource. The device determines its state by reading its own sensors (including the status of the resources present on the device, and any prior history of requests from other subjects) and executes the model to assess the impact of the request. The assessment can be done by means of the digital twin paradigm [10], in which the device performs a simulation to understand the impact of the request.

As an example, if we consider that physical devices have a specific model that can map any state they have into a safe/unsafe classification, then every request can be run through a simulation of the model to determine whether the result of that service invocation is safe or not. Some of the simulations may be run when a device is put into operation, resulting in a static set of access control policies. Other types of requests would be done in a dynamic manner when a new request is received, and the resulting new state computed for the device as a function of the current state and the new request. This allows for a dynamic generation of the access control rules on a per-request basis.

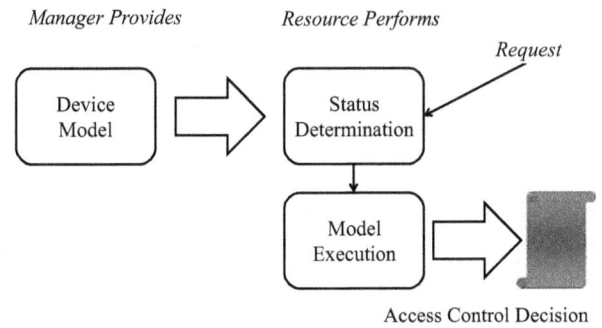

Figure 6: Model based Access Control

It is important to notice that such an approach is also critical for devices that are actuators and thus can execute actions that may impact the physical environment and thus undermine safety. Furthermore, since simulations of the systems can be time-consuming, the devices may choose to run simulations periodically to generate a set of access control policies which can be used as a faster way to do the determination of access on a per request basis. For access control decisions which can be modeled well, and the focus of securing access is on a specific device, model based access control can be very useful. It can be used effectively for physical safety of client-side IoT devices and be a building block for assuring safety, partner information access, and coalition resource sharing.

3.3 Networked Environment Model driven Access Control

While the previous subsection has discussed the model of individual devices, many security scenarios may involve considering the state of the other devices that are in the environment as well. The safety of a device may depend not just on its own state, but on the state of other devices in the environment. In addition, when dealing with a networked system of devices, many of which have actuation capabilities, assuring safety becomes even more challenging as the safety analysis becomes more complex as one must collectively consider the combined effects of several actions, each of which when executed alone is safe but when combined may introduce safety risks.

At a high level this system would work as shown in Figure 7. The manager provides an environment description to the device, and also provides models for understanding the behavior of each device. The device runs a discovery process which allows it to determine the set of other devices that are present in the system. The model execution phase performs the simulation after reading the status of all the devices in the system, and the simulation would consider the impact of all the devices in order to determine its final go/no-go decision.

As an example, if a building cooling system and a building heating system are controlled by independent controls, it is possible to launch an attack on the system by setting them both to run continuously, asking the cooling system to maintain a temperature below a threshold and asking the heating system to maintain a temperature

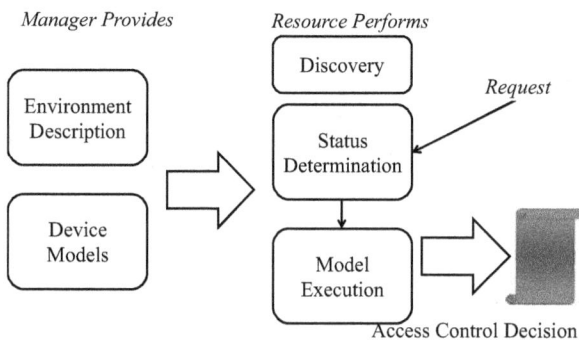

Figure 7: Networked Environment Model

above that threshold. On the other hand, if the devices have a way to discover other systems in the environment and their state, they could determine that a request made in this manner could lead to an unsafe situation and one or the other could adjust their settings to avoid running continuously. Therefore, in such context the devices must coordinate their access control decisions, rather than taking these decisions independently. Thus, some form of coordinated access control is required [20], combined with models of the devices and their deployment environments.

Networked environment models can be used to secure scenarios like car navigation systems and client side IoT security. They can also be used to provide dynamic access control for scenarios that use dynamic refinement such as elastic data centers and coalition resource sharing.

3.4 Machine Learning based Access Control

Whenever a model needs to be deployed, its specification and construction can be a difficult and tedious task. In some environments, models can be automatically built for the devices using machine learning techniques. In these cases, an initial specification could define the safe and unsafe state of devices to the best possible ability of a human. As the system operates in live environments, its state variables are recorded and the impact of any service request on the state variables also recorded. The system could then build the model for the device based on its actual operation.

Machine learning can also be used to characterize the behavior of external entities who are using the system. External entities which are using the system frequently with benign impact can be allowed access to the system. Such access has to be balanced against the threat of someone launching a reputation-based attack on the system. Similarly, entities which are present/endorsed by such an entity can be provided access. However, an unknown entity would be denied access to the system, unless it is in the presence of a known entity.

The machine learning aspect can be added to all three of the previous approaches described in this section. The machine learning algorithms can be used as the mechanism to refine the policy constraints into a set of access control policies or be used to make the determination on a request by request basis [17]. In the specific scenario of the car navigation system, a machine learning based system can recognize the faces of people who are present frequently with the driver in the car and provide them access to all required information. An unknown entity that tries to operate the car with the company of a known entity is also provided access. However, a completely unknown entity can be refused access to car navigation systems. Dynamic learning of entities using machine learning can provide a much better approach to handle access control policy generation than the other approaches discussed above.

3.5 Sharing of Models

While machine learning allows the ability for devices to determine their own models, it would provide a greater flexibility if devices could share the models that they have learnt with each other. This sharing of knowledge on how to determine policies in general has been introduced in [4] and can be used to further improve dynamic access control policy determination.

Devices in this model act like a community of managers of other devices. By contrast, in all previous approaches a (human) manager is typically responsible for providing some information to the devices. The devices can use that information to dynamically update any models that they have received. In a model sharing approach, instead, each device gets models from its peers and can update them locally – so the peer group is acting like several managers feeding models to each other.

One a device has updated its model, it can share the updated model and the conditions under which the updated model is best suited. Each device can use the set of models shared with it to determine if it should use the new model, the original model provided to it, or the model it has learned, the choice dependent on the conditions that accompany each model.

While the manager-provided original model would be the default mode of operation, such sharing of conditions and models would allow the devices to quicken the pace at which new models are created in the system. Models built on machine learning approaches could take a significant amount of time to be created – until sufficient data has been observed. The sharing of models allows the learning process to become much faster and efficient.

As with the machine learning approach, the model sharing approach can be used in conjunction with any of the three earlier approaches that were described.

4 RESEARCH CHALLENGES

We can generalize the various approaches for resources to generate their own access control policies described in Section 3 into an abstract one. In this abstract approach, each of the resources is provided some "high-level guidance" from a system manager; the resources then conduct a "discovery process" to determine their "situational context" of operation and generate their access control policies using some type of "learning" approach.

In order to enable the resources to learn their own access policies, several research challenges need to be addressed. Some of these challenges include:

(1) Defining the right "high-level guidance": Access control policies were introduced as the general approach for simplifying the application of access control mechanisms to a divergent

set of use-cases. We need to define a similar concept for "high level guidance" which will be applicable to various scenarios and contexts in a general way. The semantics to be used for high-level guidance needs to be defined. While that semantics can be defined for each of the different generation approaches discussed in Section 3, an open challenge remains that of identifying the abstraction that will create the concept of the "high level guidance" that will be applicable to a broad set of use-case scenarios regardless of the approach used to generate policies.

(2) Defining the right discovery process: Generating the right access control policy requires each of the resources in the environment to be aware of the other devices in the environment. Given the lack of widely adopted standards for discovery of resources, and the many security exposures that may result from a flawed discovery process, new discovery techniques that can provide sufficient security in many dynamic contexts are needed.

(3) Determining the situational context: The definition of the situational context, as well as its determination, remains a hard and open research challenge. Access control needs to account for not only the other resources that any given resource interacts with, but also for the resources that may indirectly use the information provided by that resource. Understanding the situation on the ground in sufficient detail to provide workable security is a challenge that can be solved on a case-by-case basis, but a general formulation remains an open challenge.

(4) Policy deconfliction without human guidance: When access control policies are generated by the resources, they may conflict among themselves, or with other policies that are imposed on the system to meet other requirements, such as performance, reliability or availability requirements. In the presence of a human, such conflicts can be resolved and deconflicted using the human provided input. Similar algorithms, which can operate without a human in the loop, need to be developed.

(5) Controlling emergent behavior: When resources create their own policies, there is a danger of uncontrolled emergent behavior [15]. Emergent behavior is behavior shown by a collection of systems which was not originally designed but happens due to the dynamic interactions among different intelligent systems. Such emergent behavior can be controlled, but the design needs to account for that. The control of emergent behavior in complete generality remains an open challenge, but there may be solutions that can be developed for specific domain of access control.

(6) Learning-related challenges: The approach used by resources to learn their access control policy has to use some type of learning approach, which creates a generalization based on its past experiences, but such learning mechanism has its challenges. The set of experiences for access control in each use-case has only a few small data points to draw from, which means that either existing learning techniques that use only a few data points need to be used, or new learning techniques requiring small data for training needs to be created. Learning also exposes new threats, e.g., a malicious actor may manipulate the data so as to force the device to learn an invalid model which could lead to generation of insecure access control policies. Solutions to such adversarial learning in uncontrolled environments need to be developed.

(7) Increase in attack surface. The increase in complexity due to autonomous generation of policies by devices can lead to new types of security vulnerabilities and threats, e.g. the adversarial learning example given above. This could lead to challenges with established assurance processes in enterprise and government networks, and the right way to provide assurance for systems using dynamically generated access control policies need to be developed.

(8) Power, computation and communication efficiency. While in the past several years there have been tremendous advantages in the computational capacity of small devices, devices that need to learn and manage their own policies may find themselves unable to use approaches that require specialized hardware, or significant computational power, e.g. learning mechanisms based on deep neural networks. For any solution developed with dynamic access control policies, system design should incorporate mechanisms that take into account the limitations on a resource, which usually manifests itself as limited amount of battery power, computational capacity or the ability to communicate at high bandwidth rates.

A more general discussion on research challenges associated with devices that try to generate their security policies in a broader context can be found in [16].

5 DISCUSSION

In this paper, we have looked at different scenarios that require a dynamic approach for access control, and require devices to generate their own policies, usually based on the context in which they are operating. The devices may operate under the constraints provided by a management system, or they may use models provided by a management system to determine their own access control policies. They can also use machine learning to learn their own models or improve upon the model that is provided to them by a machine learning system. Also access control mechanisms need to be tightly coupled with authentication systems so that access control can also be based on trusted information about the identity and the properties of the entities requiring access to devices.

Of the approaches discussed in this paper, the approach for dynamic refinement is closest to the current approaches for access control management. It can be viewed as an adaptation of role-based access control for dynamically formed groups that have a well-defined discovery process. Model based approaches provide more flexibility in the access control generation but face the challenge that a good model should accompany each device. The approach to use machine learning to learn the models for devices, and have the system determine its model and context is the most flexible option among all of them. Sharing the learned models among different devices can further improve the ability of devices to dynamically determine their context.

We believe that each of these approaches holds immense promise for improving access control for future systems and can be built upon to show their effectiveness in more details in several scenarios.

ACKNOWLEDGEMENTS

This research was sponsored by the U.S. Army Research Laboratory and the U.K. Ministry of Defence under Agreement Number W911NF-16-3-0001. The views and conclusions contained in this document are those of the authors and should not be interpreted as representing the official policies, either expressed or implied, of the U.S. Army Research Laboratory, the U.S. Government, the U.K. Ministry of Defence or the U.K. Government. The U.S. and U.K. Governments are authorized to reproduce and distribute reprints for Government purposes notwithstanding any copyright notation hereon.

REFERENCES

[1] E. Bertino and N. Islam. 2017. Botnets and Internet of Things Security. *IEEE Computer* 50, 2 (2017), 76–79.

[2] E. Bertino, P. Bonatti and E. Ferrari. 2001. TRBAC: A Temporal Role-based Access Control Model. *ACM Transactions on Information and System Security (TISSEC)* 4, 3 (2001), 191–233.

[3] M. S. Kirkpatrick, M. L. Damiani and E. Bertino. 2011. Prox-RBAC: a Proximity-Based Spatially Aware RBAC. In *Proceedings of the 19th ACM SIGSPATIAL International Symposium on Advances in Geographic Information Systems (ACM GIS)*. ACM, 339–348.

[4] E. Bertino, G. de Mel, A. Russo, S. Calo and D. Verma. 2017. Community-based Self Generation of Policies and Processes for Assets: Concepts and Research Directions. In *Proceedings of the 2017 IEEE International Conference on Big Data (BigData)*. IEEE Computer Society, 2961–2969.

[5] S. Marinovic, K. Tiwdle, N. Dulay and M. Sloman. 2010. Teleo-Reactive Policies for Managing Human-centric Pervasive Services. In *Proc. International Conference on Network and Service Management*. 80–87.

[6] A. K. Nayak, A.Reimers, N. Feamster and R. Clark. 2009. Resonance: Dynamic Access Control for Enterprise Networks. In *Proceedings of the 1st ACM Workshop on Research on Enterprise Networking*. ACM, 11–18.

[7] R. Sandhu , E. Coyne, H. Feinstein and C. Youman. 1995. Role-based Access Control Models. *Computer* 29, 2 (1995), 38–47.

[8] M. Bartoletti, P. Degano, G. L. Ferrari, and R. Zunino. 2015. Model Checking Usage Policies. *Mathematical Structures in Computer Science* 25, 3 (2015), 710–763.

[9] M. Gilbert. 1993. An Examination of Federal and Commercial Access Control Policy Needs. In *Proceedings of National Computer Security Conference on Information Systems Security*.

[10] M. Grieves and J. Vickersg. 2017. Digital Twin: Mitigating Unpredictable, Undesirable Emergent Behavior in Complex Systems. *Transdisciplinary Perspectives on Complex Systems* (2017), 85–113.

[11] E. Freudenthal, T. Pesin, L. Port, E. Keenan and V. Karamcheti. 2002. dRBAC: Distributed Role-based Access Control for Dynamic Coalition Environments. In *Proceedings 22nd International Conference on Distributed Computing Systems (ICDCS)*. IEEE Computer Society, 411–420.

[12] K. Knorr. 2000. Dynamic Access Control through Petri Net workflows. In *Proceedings of the Annual Computer Security Applications (ACSAC)*. ACM, 159–167.

[13] V. Hu, R. Kuhn, and D. Ferraiolo. 2015. Attribute-based Access Control. *Computer* 48, 2 (2015), 85–88.

[14] G. Wang, Q. Liu, and J. Wu. 2010. Hierarchical Attribute-based Encryption for Fine-Grained Access Control in Cloud Storage Services. In *Proceedings of the 17th ACM conference on Computer and Communications Security (CCS)*. 735–737.

[15] M. Mataric. 1993. Designing Emergent Behaviors: from Local Interactions to Collective Intelligence. In *Proceedings of the Second International Conference on Simulation of Adaptive Behavior*. 432–441.

[16] S. Calo, E. Lupu, E. Bertino, S. Arunkumar, G. Cirincione, B. Rivera and A. Cullen. 2017. Research Challenges in Dynamic Policy-based Autonomous Security. In *Proceedings of the 2017 IEEE International Conference on Big Data (BigData)*. IEEE Computer Society, 2970–2973.

[17] Q. Ni, J. Lobo, S. Calo, P. Rohatgi and E. Bertino. 2009. Automating Role-based Provisioning by Learning from Examples. In *Proceedings of the 14th ACM Symposium on Access Control Models and Technologies (SACMAT)*. 75–84.

[18] M. Miettinen, S. Marchal, I. Hafeez, N. Asokan, A.-R. Sadeghi and S. Tarkoma. 2017. IoT SENTINEL: Automated Device-Type Identification for Security Enforcement in IoT. In *Proceedings of the 37th IEEE International Conference on Distributed Computing Systems (ICDCS)*. IEEE Computer Society, 2177–2184.

[19] R. Sandhu and P. Samarati. 1994. Access Control: Principle and Practice. *IEEE Communications Magazine* 32, 09 (1994), 40–40.

[20] A. C. Squicciarini, M. Shehab and F. Paci. 2009. Collective Privacy Management in Social Networks. In *Proceedings of the 18th International Conference on World Wide Web, WWW*. ACM, 521–530.

[21] D. Verma, S. Calo, S. Chakraborty, E.Bertino, C. Williams, J. Tucker and B. Rivera. 2017. Generative Policies for Autonomic Management. In *Proceedings of 1st IEEE International Workshop on Distributed Analytics InfraStructure and Algorithms for Multi-Organization Federations (DAIS)*.

Multi-Party Access Control: Requirements, State of the Art and Open Challenges

Anna Cinzia Squicciarini
Pennsylvania State University
asquicciarini@ist.psu.edu

Sarah Michele Rajtmajer
Quantitative Scientific Solutions
sarah.rajtmajer@qs-2.com

Nicola Zannone
Eindhoven University of Technology
n.zannone@tue.nl

ABSTRACT

Multi-party access control is gaining attention and prominence within the community, as access control models and systems are faced with complex, jointly-owned and jointly-managed content. Traditional single-user approaches lack the richness and flexibility to accommodate these scenarios, resulting in undesired disclosure of sensitive data and resources. Moving forward fundamental work in this area is critical. In particular, as personal data amasses and algorithms for data mining improve, personally identifiable information is more readily inferred and the practical implications of privacy decisions are relatively opaque. This is true even at the individual level, but the parallel problem for jointly managed content involves the cross product of these complex outcomes. In this presentation, we discuss fundamental requirements of successful multi-party access control mechanisms and contextualize these concepts with respect to the state of the art. Based on this analysis, we identify open challenges and draw a roadmap for future work.

CCS CONCEPTS

• **Security and privacy** → **Access control**; • **Human-centered computing** → **Collaborative and social computing systems and tools**;

KEYWORDS

Collaborative access control; data governance; literature study.

ACM Reference Format:
Anna Cinzia Squicciarini, Sarah Michele Rajtmajer, and Nicola Zannone. 2018. Multi-Party Access Control: Requirements, State of the Art and Open Challenges. In *SACMAT '18: The 23rd ACM Symposium on Access Control Models & Technologies (SACMAT), June 13–15, 2018, Indianapolis, IN, USA.* ACM, New York, NY, USA, 1 page. https://doi.org/10.1145/3205977.3205999

1 SUMMARY

In the highly connected networks typifying today's online communities, the sharing of content attributable to multiple owners or stakeholders is increasingly frequent. Users need to make collaborative decisions about content-sharing, while adequate multi-party decision mechanisms are not yet in place.

Traditional, single-user access control policies currently supported by main-stream services and collaborative environments are insufficient for jointly-managed content in important ways. They focus on confidentiality rather than facilitating controlled sharing. Access decisions are often binary, or based on inflexible policies. This inflexibility can inhibit mission-critical information sharing, e.g., in hospitals, intelligence departments, fire departments, and the military – organizations that commonly handle and protect sensitive, private data, but also rely on sharing that data appropriately.

Furthermore, single-user driven policies make it difficult, if not impossible, to determine whether a given disclosure meets the privacy expectations of all involved parties, and as such threaten to violate the expectations of both content owners and stakeholders. Along these lines, the impacts of collaborative decision making on users' behaviors and dynamic user interactions are largely unexplored. In particular, we have yet to understand how individuals' sharing decisions change over time, who are the most influential users, how they benefit from it, and the privacy gains and losses from a collective perspective.

This current gap in research may be the result of several (related) causes. To our knowledge, proposed content sharing models to date have not been translated into practical features or applications, as social networks provide minimal support for joint decision-making scenarios. Hence, an exploration in the wild of the effects of multi-party sharing is fundamentally hard. In addition, work to date on multi-party sharing has adopted a micro-scale view of the interactions among users (i.e., one-on-one and one-shot interactions), in an attempt to minimize discomfort and other security properties one interaction at a time. However, it is possible that group dynamics at the collective scale are distinct from the aggregation of one-on-one interactions between members within the group. While literature on collective behavior abounds, these considerations have yet to find their place within the discourse of multi-party access control.

In this presentation, we outline what we believe to be plausible steps forward for the research community to address community-centric access control. We discuss fundamental requirements of developed solutions with respect to policy specification, governance, usability and transparency, and we contextualize these requirements within the state of the art. We discuss both state of the science as well as the state of practice, with direct comparison of existing methods, their capabilities and limitations. We identify open challenges, and in doing so, aim to provide a roadmap of key points for future work in the community. This presentation is based on [1].

Acknowledgement Work from Dr. Squicciarini is partly funded by NSF Grant 1453080. Work from Dr. Zannone is partially funded by the ITEA projects M2MGrids (13011) and APPSTACLE (15017).

REFERENCES

[1] Federica Paci, Anna Squicciarini, and Nicola Zannone. 2018. Survey on Access Control for Community-Centered Collaborative Systems. *ACM Comput. Surv.* 51, 1, Article 6 (2018), 38 pages. https://doi.org/10.1145/3146025

Securing Named Data Networks:
Challenges and the Way Forward

Elisa Bertino
Purdue University
West Lafayette, Indiana
bertino@cs.purdue.edu

Mohamed Nabeel
Qatar Computing Research Institute
Doha, Qatar
mnabeel@qf.org.qa

ABSTRACT

Despite decades of research on the Internet security, we constantly hear about mega data breaches and malware infections affecting hundreds of millions of hosts. The key reason is that the current threat model of the Internet relies on two assumptions that no longer hold true: (1) Web servers, hosting the content, are secure, (2) each Internet connection starts from the original content provider and terminates at the content consumer. Internet security is today merely patched on top of the TCP/IP protocol stack. In order to achieve comprehensive security for the Internet, we believe that a clean-slate approach must be adopted where a content based security model is employed. Named Data Networking (NDN) is a step in this direction which is envisioned to be the next generation Internet architecture based on a content centric communication model. NDN is currently being designed with security as a key requirement, and thus to support content integrity, authenticity, confidentiality and privacy. However, in order to meet such a requirement, one needs to overcome several challenges, especially in either large operational environments or resource constrained networks. In this paper, we explore the security challenges in achieving comprehensive content security in NDN and propose a research agenda to address some of the challenges.

KEYWORDS

Named Data Networks, Edge Computing, Access Control, Security, Confidentiality, Integrity, Privacy

ACM Reference Format:
Elisa Bertino and Mohamed Nabeel. 2018. Securing Named Data Networks: Challenges and the Way Forward. In *SACMAT '18: The 23rd ACM Symposium on Access Control Models & Technologies (SACMAT), June 13–15, 2018, Indianapolis, IN, USA.* ACM, New York, NY, USA, 9 pages. https://doi.org/10.1145/3205977.3205996

1 INTRODUCTION

The current IP based end-to-end Internet architecture [20] designed in 1970's is fundamentally broken as the way we use the Internet has changed drastically over the last four decades. Nowadays, the Internet usage is dominated by content distribution mainly due to video streaming and billions of things connected to the Internet. As a solution, the notion of Named Data Networking (NDN) [61] has been proposed. NDN is a general-purpose, information-centric network architecture [55], that uses names to identify resources in the Internet, similar to the REST architecture [29], and provides native support for content caching at edge nodes. While NDN provides many benefits compared to the traditional network architectures, in order to gain its full potential and make it practical, one needs to address security, efficiency and scalability.

Key requirements for NDN security is to assure that data managed by the system is not tampered with and also that data is kept confidential and only accessed by authorized parties. In addition, privacy is critical.

NDN defines two types of network packets, possessing highly asymmetric properties. Clients send *interest packets*, which contain only a name and a minimal set of additional control fields. Servers respond with *data packets*, which contain the data associated with the name in the corresponding interest. By looking at interest packets of an individual, a malicious party can infer privacy-sensitive information about the individual. Even though today we have a huge body of security and privacy techniques, applying these techniques to NDN, especially when deployed on 5G networks, is challenging due to stringent real time requirements and the scale, and highly dynamic nature of the systems.

In order to provide a comprehensive framework for data security and privacy in NDN, it is critical to address three main requirements. The first requirement focuses on designing efficient digital signature techniques; this is a critical security building block for NDN in order to ensure authenticity and integrity of data packets. The second requirement focuses on access control techniques to allow selective sharing of the data packets with end-to-end encryption enforced. Finally, the third requirement focuses on privacy which is perhaps the most challenging issue.

NDN requires data producers to digitally sign every data packet so that data consumers can verify the data without caring about the locations from which the data packets are delivered. Specifically, a valid digital signature gives data consumers reason to believe that the data was created by a known data producer (authentication), that the data producer cannot deny having transmitted the data (non-repudiation), and that the data was not altered in transit (integrity). However, considering that the data consumers can be mobile devices or small Internet of Things (IoT) devices with limited resources, it is critical to minimize the signature generation/verification latency and the signature size and enhance the efficiency of all operations related with the management of data signature processes.

Access control is critical in NDN systems in order to selectively share data among users. Access control has been widely investigated (we refer to [15] for a survey of access control for database systems). At a higher level, an access control system is based on an access control model (such as the discretionary model and the mandatory model [15]). When a discretionary model is adopted, the system uses a set of permissions to decide whether access to a protected resource can be granted. In this paper, we argue that the most suitable model is what we refer to as "name-based access control" model. In addition to differing with respect to access control model, access control systems differ with respect to the enforcement approaches used (e.g.: access control lists, and encryption). The actual enforcement mechanism to be adopted depends in turn from the system architecture and the types of actions to be controlled. A critical issue in designing an access control system for NDN is to select a proper enforcement mechanism. Such a mechanism has to be decentralized, as having to contact some centralized server for access control enforcement is not suitable when there are real-time constraints and does not follow the decentralized distributed architecture of NDN. Further, the mechanism must exploit caching mechanisms to support caching of information needed for access control.

Ensuring privacy for both content producers and content users is a very important as well as a challenging step towards building practical NDN. We identify three key requirements to ensure privacy: (1) communication annonymity, that is, making it difficult for an attacker to trace back to a sender of a message received by a destination; (2) search privacy, that is, hiding the content of the interest packets sent by content users from intermediaries in the NDN infrastructure and attackers; (3) cache privacy, that is, making it difficult for a data consumer to infer information about the content consumption patterns of other consumers in the physical proximity based on cached contents. It should be noted that even if data packets are end-to-end encrypted, the privacy of data packets is ensured only if the privacy of the interest packets is also preserved. The reason is that the content of the interest packet, which includes the name of the content users want to consume, may reveal information about the encrypted data packets even though intermediaries cannot decrypt such packets.

In what follows based on the characteristics of NDN systems, we propose possible approaches to meet the content security and privacy requirements that we have outlined. Further, we critically evaluate the existing solutions proposed for some of the security challenges. We also identify and discuss open research challenges that have to be addressed in order to build practical and secure NDN systems.

The rest of the paper is organized as follows. Section 2 presents an overview of NDN with an emphasis on security. In Section 3, we critically evaluate the existing solutions to address some of the security problems discussed in this paper. We identify challenges in supporting scalable and efficient digital signatures on data packets and discuss possible directions to solve such challenges in Section 4. Section 5 identifies challenges in decentralized access control in NDN and possible solutions to address such challenges. Finally, in Section 6, we discuss privacy requirements in details and challenges in addressing such requirements.

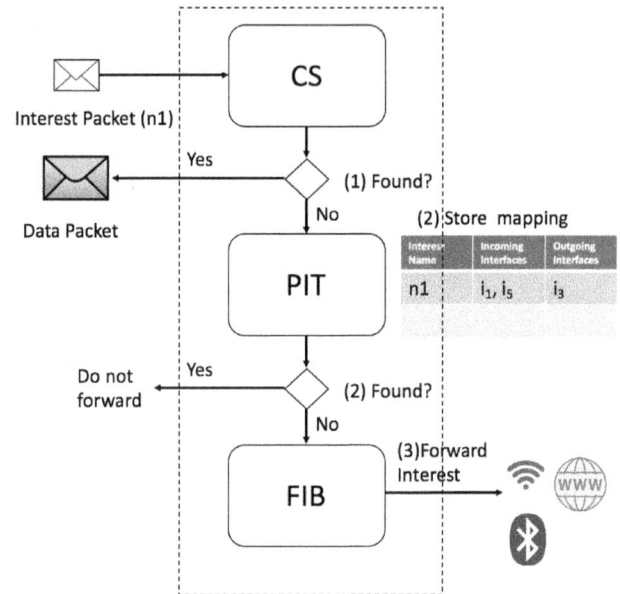

Figure 1: An NDN Node

2 NAMED DATA NETWORKING

NDN [34, 61] is one instance of a more general next generation network architectures called Information Centric Networking [55]. The Internet Research Task Force (IRTF) established an ICN research working group [4] in 2012 in order to further advance the research and standardization of ICN. NDN has its roots in an earlier projected called Content-Centric Networking (CCN) proposed by Van Jacobson. He publicly presented his work at Google Tech talk in 2006 [33].

NDN changes the Internet's communication model from delivering packets to an end host to retrieving content for a given name. The communication in NDN is driven by receivers, i.e. data consumers, based on a pull model. They exchange two types of packets: Interest and Data. Both types of packets carry a name that uniquely identifies a piece of data.

In order to fetch data, a data consumer creates an interest packet adding the name of the data packet it needs and sends it to the network. The routers in NDN use the name in the data packet to push the interest packet towards data producer(s). Once the interest packet reaches a network node that has the requested data packet, signed by the producer's private key, the node pushes the data packet to the consumer following the reverse path that the interest packet took.

Both types of packets carry a name that uniquely identifies an information item in NDN within the given scope and context. NDN names are opaque to the network meaning that NDN does not attribute any meanings to the names. Thus, it allows applications to choose their own naming conventions and evolve independently of the network. However, NDN does assume that names are hierarchically structured. For example, a whitepaper produced by QCRI may have the name /qa/org/qcri/papers/whitepaper.pdf, where '/' separates the name components in text representations similar to

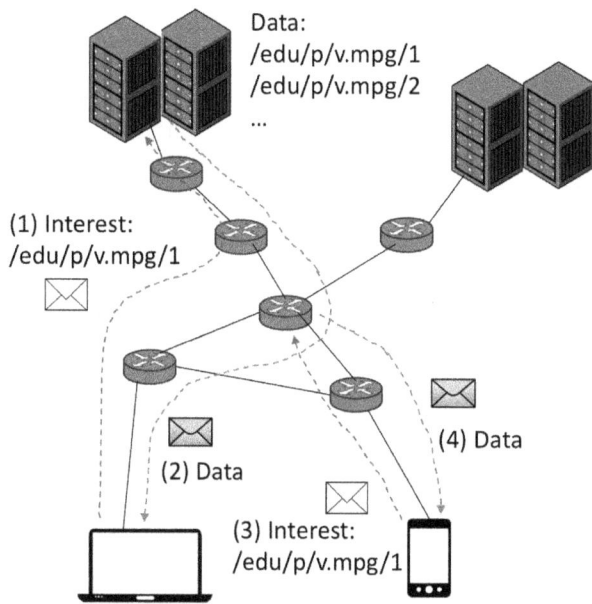

Figure 2: Routing and Caching in NDN

RESTful resources. Large objects, e.g., a video, that cannot be carried as a single component, are segmented into multiple packets. For example, /edu/purdue/cs/keynote.mpg/2 may represent the second segment of a particular keynote video from Purdue University.

As mentioned earlier, names in NDN need to be unique within the scope and context only, very much like the concept of public and private IPs. For example, two organizations may use the same name /iotdevices/smartlights/room1 in their own private context, but if the name is used in the global context, it should be unique universally.

As NDN routes packets based on names, it eliminates two issues in current IP based routing architecture: address space exhaustion, and address management. Unbounded namespace eliminates the address space exhaustion problem. Local address assignment and management are no longer required as NDN does away with IP addresses.

As shown in Figure 1, an NDN node maintains three data structure to move packets around the network: a Forwarding Information Base (FIB), a Pending Interest Table (PIT), and a Content Store (CS). As mentioned earlier, in order to request some data, a consumer sends an interest packet containing the name of the data. These interest packets are forwarded along routes by the FIB in each node. When an interest packet arrives at a node, the node first checks its CS to see if the data is cached; if this is the case, the node returns the data packet to the interface from which the interest packet had been received. Otherwise, the node checks if the data is available in the PIT; if a matching entry is available, the node simply appends the interface of this request to the existing entry and waits for the reply from upstream nodes. If an entry does not exist, the node creates an entry in PIT, and consults the FIB to find the nodes towards data producer(s) in order to forward the request. When a data packet

arrives at the node, it follows the reverse path. In order to mitigate Distributed Denial of Service (DDoS) attacks, the node accepts only those data packets which it anticipates to receive as recorded in the PIT. Based on the caching policy, the node may or may not cache the data packet after forwarding it to the corresponding interfaces. Figure 2 shows the typical caching based routing in NDN.

The current connection-based approach to security (Transport Layer Security (TLS)) inexplicably ties the security of the content to trust in the server that stores the content. This approach is widely recognized as a significant problem as the trust that the consumer gets is essentially transient leaving no reliable traces on the content after the connection is over. For example, in order to have some confidence over the data, one always needs to retrieve the data from the original server, not from any intermediaries. NDN is designed to address this issue by moving to a content-based security model instead of a connection-based one. In fact, a central tenant of NDN is that data consumers do not care if a data packet was served from a network node caching the content or from the original producer. Similarly, data producers do not care from where and when data consumers receive the data packet. Thus, the trust in data is decoupled from the time when the data was originally obtained and from the location(s) from which the data was obtained. This content-based design demands mechanisms to validate the integrity, and authenticity of data packets by data consumers and ensure confidentiality.

3 RELATED WORK

NDN security can broadly be classified along two dimensions: infrastructure security and content security. As this paper focuses on the latter, we only provide a summary of the former as we believe that most of the infrastructure security issues can be addressed using the same techniques used to protect traditional IP network infrastructures.

Content based security is at the core of NDN design. NDN specifies that all data packets must be secured by cryptographically signing them. However, designing mechanisms that are efficient, scalable, and usable in order to meet the security requirements of integrity, authenticity, confidentiality and privacy are very much open problems that a few researchers have started to research on. [7, 52, 59]. A issue in meeting these requirements is to establish trust in the keys utilized for enforce the security mechanisms. Diana et al. [52] proposes a PKI based scheme to verify the authenticity and integrity of names associated with contents. They further elaborate on the level of trust one place on the keys used to sign data packets together with their names. Going one step further, Yu et al. [59] proposes the notion of trust schemas that can provide data consumers an automatic way to discover which keys to use for authentication and data producers to identify which keys to use for the signatures. However, it is not clear from their work how data consumers can correctly identify trust schemas or trust anchors, and bootstrap trust. A more serious issue is that there is no provision for key revocation and reflecting key revocation in trust schemas. Afanasyev et al. [7] have investigated how to utilize secure NDNs to replace the current connection based Web infrastructure. They discuss security issues in HTTPS especially with the prevalence of CDNs and HTTPS termination, and propose a research agenda to solve these issues by using content-based security over NDN. It should be noted that their focus areas are different from what we discuss in this paper. They mainly focus on supporting cryptographic protocols in browsers, key management for data producers and consumers, and establishing trust in keys.

Akin to the routing and lookup infrastructures in TCP/IP based architecture, NDN does require a set of always available services in order to operate across multiple networks. Recently, Afanayev et al. [8] proposed a DNS like name service for NDN to identify the need to look up names. While the proposed system has features similar to DNSSEC [9] and to security extensions of DNS, they show that their design differs from the DNS design mainly due to how NDN operates and NDN caching mechanisms. DNS operates at the application layer, whereas NDN works on names at the network layer itself. Gasti et al. [30] analyze the resilience of NDN to DDoS attacks and identify some new types of attacks specific to NDN, such as interest flooding. Due to the design of NDN, they show that current DDoS attacks such as bandwidth depletion, reflection attacks [46], and black-holing by prefix hijacking [12], are ineffective in NDN systems. As you may recall, NDN supports built-in caching to accelerate content delivery and these caching nodes are an attractive target for attackers. Securing these NDN caching nodes is also an active research area [23, 37].

Privacy protection in NDN [21] is a seldom explored topic. While some features of NDN, such as the lack of source/ destination addresses and cached content retrieval, improve privacy, a closer look at the design choices of NDN reveals a number of open privacy issues: name privacy, cache privacy [5, 6], and certificate privacy are some of the issues that need further attention from the privacy research community.

Content security is not a new topic. In the last couple of decades, numerous research efforts concerning systems and models have focused on content based security, mainly confidentiality. Such efforts include end-to-end encrypted messaging systems [27], encrypted content dissemination [50], encrypted cloud storages [44], encrypted query processing systems (e.g.: CryptDB, DBMask, Monomi, TrustedDB, and Cipherbase), encrypted publish-subscribe systems [24, 40], encrypted web application platforms (e.g.: Mylar, and ShadowCrypt), encrypted email systems [47], computation over encrypted data, and end-to-end integrity over web [36]. While some of the building blocks developed as part of the above systems (e.g. attribute based group key management [41]) can be applied to secure NDN systems, most of the cryptographic techniques utilized in these systems are either known be broken under practical threat models or too inefficient to meet performance and response time requirements. While content based security, especially encryption, satisfies the necessary security requirements, encryption comes with a cost, namely broken functionality. The above systems utilize a new class of algorithms that try to strike a balance between these two conflicting goals of security and functionality. They are collectively called property preserving encryption schemes: searchable encryption schemes [17, 53], order preserving encryption schemes [38], and format preserving encryption schemes [13]. Most of the above property preserving schemes are known to leak information to various degrees based on auxiliary information available and broken under honest-but-curious threat model [19, 45].

4 DIGITAL SIGNATURES

A valid digital signature gives data consumers reason to believe that the data was created by a known data producer (authentication), that the data producer cannot deny having transmitted the data (non-repudiation), and that the data was not altered in transit (integrity). However, considering that the data consumers can be mobile devices or small IoT devices with limited resources, it is critical to minimize the signature generation/verification latency and the signature size and enhance the efficiency of all operations related with management of data signature processes. In particular the design of a suitable digital signature for NDN should follow three different orthogonal strategies: (1) adopt the most efficient signature scheme(s); (2) devise scalable and efficient strategies for the management of information required by the adopted scheme(s) (such as public encryption keys); (3) support the concurrent execution of multiple authentication operations. Adoption of these strategies is particularly critical for NDN deployed over 5G networks in that in these networks connection times are extremely short. In what follows, we discuss approaches that can be adopted and extensions to these approaches to meet scalability and stringent time requirements.

Signature Schemes: Over the past decades, various digital signature schemes have been devised. NIST recommends the RSA signature algorithm, the Digital Signature Algorithm (DSA), and its elliptic curve variant ECDSA as the digital signature standards and specifies their parameters for various security levels [2]. Each such algorithm has its unique properties. The RSA signature algorithm has the fastest signature verification time, but the slowest signature generation time. DSA is slower in verifying, but faster in signing than the RSA signature algorithm. A DSA key of the same strength as the RSA signature algorithm generates a smaller signature. The elliptic curve-based algorithms have moderate signature generation/verification time (see the details in [3]). However, compared with the RSA algorithm, the size of ECDSA signatures/keys is much smaller than the size of the RSA signatures/keys. Recently, Bernstein et al. [14] developed the Edwards-curve Digital Signature Algorithm (EdDSA) using a variant of Schnorr signature based on Twisted Edwards curves. It is designed to be faster than existing digital signature schemes without sacrificing security. EdDSA is included in OpenSSH and GnuPG. Therefore, when designing the security framework of NDN, it is crucial to adopt the best digital signature scheme according to the specific NDN application scenario. For efficiency, we should also consider signature aggregation. Given n signatures on n distinct messages, by different n users, it is possible to aggregate all these signatures into a single signature [18]. Aggregate signatures may be useful for reducing the size of data signatures in NDN. To minimize signing cost, Merkle Hash Trees [39] can be used to aggregate many data contents and sign them all together.

In order to develop digital signature schemes that are very efficient in terms of response time, one possible approach is to select the most efficient representative digital signature techniques and combine them with pre-computation techniques. Such strategy is based on the observation that the signature aggregation operation for some signature schemes is several magnitudes of times faster than that of their signature generation. One can leverage this observation to shift off-line expensive operations of the signature generation phase. That is, we off-line compute a set of signatures on the bit-structures of the hash output domain. Later, these pre-computed signatures very efficiently. An approach based on the combination of pre-computation techniques and signature aggregation protocols has been recently proposed [57].

However, as the most efficient scheme depends on the specific scenario, it is important to develop scenarios for different applications, such as augmented reality, and IoT systems, and identify the most effective scheme(s) for each scenario. Based on these scenarios, one can design and implement a multi-schema digital signature service that can support different signature schemes for different applications.

Scalable Infrastructure for Signature Management: In 5G NDN networks, even small devices (such as IoT devices) can be data producers and, thus, must have their own private/public keys (as most common schemes are based on public-key cryptography). Considering the large number of such devices, a scalable key management scheme is thus required. The traditional Certificate-Authority-based Public Key Infrastructure (CA-PKI) is not well-suited for NDN since it can be a single-point-of-failure problem due to its centralized nature. Therefore, it is important to design a distributed/scalable PKI with an appropriate key management scheme. In order to address such an issue, one possible approach is to utilize the blockchain technology so that the role of the traditional CAs (i.e., binding an ID with a public key by signing them) is replaced with the proof-of-work of the blockchain networks. One can also consider a hybrid approach combining CA-PKI with the blockchain-based PKI or PGP Web-of-Trust [1] in order to support various NGN applications. However in order to achieve very small response times for retrieving information authentication information from blockchain, it is critical not only to adopt the most efficient blockchain technologies, but also to investigate caching strategies that can further improve such approaches and conduct experimental assessment of the various approaches.

Concurrent Execution of Signature Operations:
Many NDN applications, especially in the context of 5G networks, may require the same device to transmit/receive data from many different devices within a very short time. It is thus critical that the device be able to simultaneously execute many different signature operations (e.g. verifying a digital signature, or generating a digital signature). To address this issue, a possible approach is to use hardware-based acceleration techniques, such as techniques based on the use of GPU [56] available for example on systems-on-chip of vehicles.

5 ACCESS CONTROL

At a higher level, an access control system is based on an access control model (such as the discretionary model and the mandatory model [15]). When a discretionary model is adopted, the system uses a set of permissions to decide whether access to a protected resource can be granted.

Permission Specification: A permission typically consists of three components: (subject-specification,
object-specification, action-specification). For example, the permission (Bob, ND, Read) states that user Bob can read the data packet

with name ND. Many variations exist with respect to such specifications. We now explore each of the items in this specification below.

Object Specification: It specifies the object(s) to which a subject is granted a given action. There are many variations for specifying objects. For example, the object can be specified by name (name-based access control) or by content (content-based access control). We argue that name-based access control combining the name of the packet and its namespace is the most suitable for NDN as every object has a unique name within a given namespace. Further, it is consistent with the name based matching of interest packets to data packets in NDN.

Subject Specification: Even more options are possible for subject specification; the most notable being: user-ids, roles (as in the popular RBAC model [48] which has been standardized by NIST [28]), and attribute-based denotations (as in the ABAC [60] model adopted by the XACML standard [15]). Out of all the above subject specification options, ABAC is the most expressive and flexible specification which can support fine-grained access control in NDN.

Action Specification: It indicates which actions a subject can perform on a given object. Depending on the application, context, and/or the system, various action specification schemes are utilized. For example, create, read, update and delete (CRUD) operations are commonly supported by persistent storage systems and PUT, GET and UPDATE operations are frequently supported by RESTful web APIs. The most important operation in NDN is the "read" action by which data consumers can read the protected data according to the permissions in the system. Thus access control should be optimized for "read" action by data consumers and "write" action by data producers. One may extend the system to support other actions such as "update" and "delete" at the expense of additional mechanisms in place.

Enforcement Mechanism: In addition to differences with respect to the access control model, access control systems differ with respect to the enforcement approaches. Well known approaches include access control lists, and encryption. The actual enforcement mechanism to be adopted depends however from the system architecture and the types of actions to be controlled. Since NDN follows a decentralized link-to-link communication model compared to a connection based one, it is important to choose an enforcement mechanism whose reference monitor is not centralized. Especially in the context of NDN over 5G networks, having to contact some centralized server for access control enforcement is not suitable when there are real-time constraints. Further, the enforcement mechanism must be able to exploit caching mechanisms in NDN to support caching of information needed for access control. Thus, we argue that an encryption based enforcement mechanism can satisfy these enforcement requirements that the NDN specification demands. In addition to controlling access to data packets, encryption enforces confidentiality of data packets at content level which current transport level security protocols such as HTTPS fail to support due to inherent limitations of the current Internet architecture. For example, today, many CDNs and middleboxes intercept HTTPS traffic in order to make routing and content optimization decisions violating HTTPS's model of an end-to-end encrypted connection. With encryption at content level, confidentiality of data packets is guaranteed irrespective of how those packets arrived at data consumers.

Designing and developing an efficient and flexible access control system for NDN that meets the above mentioned access control requirements with strict performance guarantees and scalability is challenging. In what follows we discuss a possible approach to address the access control challenge.

Encryption based Access Control System for NDN: As mentioned earlier, one suitable enforcement strategy is based on encryption. An important design decision one needs to make is which cryptosystem to utilize to encrypt data packets. There are two main choices: public key cryptosystems (PKC) and symmetric key cryptosystems (SKC).

PKC based approaches can be mainly classified into three groups: (1) traditional PKI based schemes such as RSA, (2) Proxy Re-Encryption (PRE) [11] schemes, and (3) Attribute Based Encryption (ABE) [16, 31] schemes. However, such schemes have several weaknesses: they cannot efficiently handle the addition and/or the revocation of subjects, and policy changes; they require to keep multiple encrypted copies of the same key; they incur high computational cost. On the other hand, SKC based schemes, such as AES and Blowfish, are orders of magnitude faster than PKC based schemes and thus are the preferred to cryptosystem for NDN. However, SKC schemes have their own limitations. One needs to consider the challenge of how to generate a minimal number of keys to enforce the access control policies, how to enforce the access control policies over encrypted data, how to efficiently manage keys especially in a dynamic environment where new users join and existing users leave frequently, how to scale the key management scheme to a large number of names, data producers and data consumers, and how to efficiently deliver the keys to data consumers.

In a SKC based system, each data packet D is encrypted with a symmetric key K. Subjects authorized to read D receive the symmetric key for decrypting D, whereas the non-authorized subjects do not receive such key. Therefore, even if a non-authorized subject gets a copy of D (for example by intercepting messages transmitting D), it would not be able to decrypt D. Note that different data packets may be encrypted with different symmetric keys, depending on the authorizations associated with each data. The adoption of such a strategy however requires a mechanism to distribute the symmetric keys to the authorized users. An out-of-band communication channel is required to do so. One research challenge is thus to devise possible options to efficiently deliver the keys to data consumers. One approach is to utilize a PKC scheme, such as a traditional PKI scheme or an attribute-based encryption (ABE) scheme, to encrypt the symmetric keys using the public keys of data consumers. Another approach is to utilize a hybrid approach where a minimal number symmetric keys are delivered to data consumers utilizing a PKC scheme and then utilize the same underlying SKC scheme to deliver the remaining keys. As discussed in Section 4, a scalable and distributed PKI infrastructure is thus critical and is an open research challenge.

While the above scheme works well in a static environment where users and authorization policies are predefined and do not change over time, it is unable to efficiently handle user and authorization policy dynamics. A possible solution is to adopt and extend

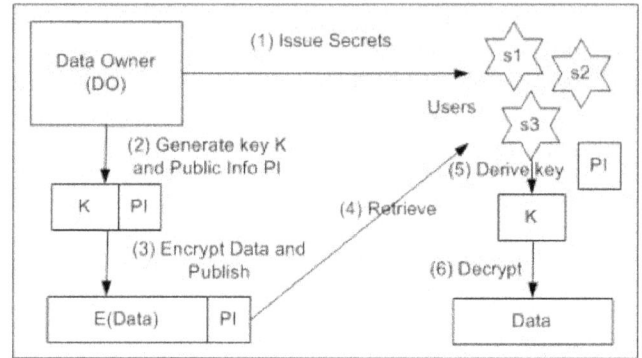

Figure 3: Broadcast Group Key Management Scheme

an approach based on our earlier work [41, 44]. Our previous approach is based on the idea that instead of directly distributing to the authorized subjects the symmetric keys for decrypting the data packets, one can allow the subjects to dynamically derive the keys at the time of decryption.

As shown in Figure 3, the basic idea of such an approach, referred to as *Broadcast Group Key Management* (BGKM), is to generate and distribute secrets to users based on their identity attributes (such as user-id, role, etc.) and later allow them to derive actual symmetric keys based on their secrets and some public information. Having only the public information in data packets does not allow data consumers to derive the underlying key used to encrypt the data packet. The ability to derive the key depends on whether a given data consumer satisfies the authorization policy encoded in the public information. A key advantage of the BGKM scheme is that adding users/revoking users or updating the permission can be performed efficiently and only requires updating the public information attached to subsequent data packets.

The BGKM scheme satisfies several requirements: minimal trust, key indistinguishability, key independence, forward secrecy, backward secrecy, and collusion resistance with minimal computational, space, and communication cost. We now provide a brief technical description of this primitive. The key idea of BGKM is to hide the symmetric data encryption key into a public data structure that is generated as a function of the secrets of the authorized users. These secrets map one on one to the attributes that data consumers possess (e.g. driver license, age, and the role played at work). Therefore, only users that have those secrets can extract the key. The two basic operations of BGKM are: generation of the public information hiding the key; and key derivation to get at the data decryption key. Below, we provide a high-level technical presentation of the adapted BGKM solution for NDN. We refer the reader to [44, 51] for additional technical details and proofs.

Let the data producer be DP [1] and a set of data consumers $DC_i, i = 1, 2, \ldots, n$.

paramgen It generates the parameters required to initialize. DP takes a security parameter ℓ. DP chooses an ℓ-bit prime number q, a positive integer $N \geq n$ which represents the maximum allowed

---

[1]There can be many data producers, but for simplicity of presentation only one is considered.

number of group members, and a cryptographic hash function

$$H(\cdot) : \{0, 1\}^* \to \mathbb{F}_q,$$

where $\mathbb{F}_q$ is a finite field with q elements, which can be represented by $\{0, 1, \ldots, q - 1\}$ with modular arithmetic. DP sets the keyspace $\mathcal{KS} = \mathbb{F}_q$. $param = \langle \mathcal{KS}, N, H(\cdot), \rangle$. where $param$ consists of all public parameters.

secgen It generates secrets for each DC. For each $1 \le i \le n$, DP chooses a random bit string $s_i \in \{0, 1\}^*$ as a secret for each DC_i, and sends s_i to DC_i. DP saves these s_i together with the group's membership information locally. Without loss of generality, we also assume that $s_i \ne s_j$ for $i \ne j$. In practice, an s_i is chosen long enough (e.g., ≥ 80 bits) so that guessing becomes infeasible.

keygen It generates public information (PI) embedding data decryption key. DP picks a random $K \in \mathcal{KS}$ as the shared group key. DP chooses N random bit strings $z_1, z_2, \ldots, z_N \in \{0, 1\}^*$. DP creates an $n \times (N + 1)$ $\mathbb{F}_q$-matrix

$$A = \begin{pmatrix} 1 & a_{1,1} & a_{1,2} & \ldots & a_{1,N} \\ 1 & a_{2,1} & a_{2,2} & \ldots & a_{2,N} \\ 1 & a_{3,1} & a_{3,2} & \ldots & a_{3,N} \\ \vdots & \vdots & \vdots & \vdots & \vdots \\ 1 & a_{n,1} & a_{n,2} & \ldots & a_{n,N} \end{pmatrix},$$

where

$$a_{i,j} = H(s_i || z_j), 1 \le i \le n, 1 \le j \le N. \tag{1}$$

DP then solves for a nonzero $(N+1)$-dimensional column $\mathbb{F}_q$-vector Y such that $AY = 0$. Note that such a nonzero Y always exists as the nullspace of matrix A is nontrivial by construction. Here we require that DP chooses Y from the nullspace of A uniformly randomly. DP constructs an $(N + 1)$-dimensional $\mathbb{F}_q$-vector which we call an *access control vector*

$$ACV = K \cdot e_1^T + Y,$$

where $e_1 = (1, 0, \ldots, 0)$ is a standard basis vector of $\mathbb{F}_q^{N+1}$, v^T denotes the transpose of vector v, and K is the pre-chosen shared group key. DP lets $PI = \langle ACV, (z_1, z_2, \ldots, z_N) \rangle$, and broadcasts PI via the broadcast channel.

keyder This method derives the data decryption key based on a set of secret a user possesses. Having s_i and PI, DC_i computes $a_{i,j}, 1 \le j \le N$, as in formula (1) and sets an $(N + 1)$-dimensional row $\mathbb{F}_q$-vector

$$v_i = (1, a_{i,1}, a_{i,2}, \ldots, a_{i,N}).$$

DC_i derives the group key as $K' = v_i \cdot ACV$.

update It updates PI to reflect the user dynamics of leaving and joining. DP runs the *keygen* phase again with respect to the current group users, creates a new group key $\hat{K}$ and random $\hat{z}_i, 1 \le i \le N$, and broadcasts $\widehat{PI} = \langle \hat{X}, (\hat{z}_1, \hat{z}_2, \ldots, \hat{z}_N) \rangle$ via the broadcast channel. A current DC derives the shared group key by following the same procedure specified in the *keyder* phase.

An important practical issue is how to support expressive access control policies over encrypted data. This requires encoding an access control policy into the above PI data structure. One possible approach is that that an access control policy is represented as an access tree, where each node in the tree can be represented using an instance of BGKM. Data consumers who have secrets

to climb up the tree from leaf nodes all the way up to the root node are able to get the key to decrypt the associated data packets. Therefore, an interesting direction is to adapt and extend such an approach supporting expressive access control policies over encrypted data [41] in order to provide expressive policies over NDN.

Another interesting extension is based on the fact that names in NDN follow a hierarchical structure. An important consideration is whether we can leverage this fact to enhance the BGKM based access control mechanism with respect to the number of secrets that need to be shared. A key challenge is to design meaningful and efficient schema mappings similar to the concept of trust schemas [59] in order to identify hierarchically ordered data packets and the corresponding keys.

With the scale of operations, data producers may find it challenging to keep up with the access control requirements. Another important practical consideration is that how to efficiently delegate some of the access control enforcement functionality to intermediaries without compromising confidentiality. One possible approach is to utilize a two layer encryption approach where data producers enforce a coarse grained access control over data and intermediaries enforce fine grained access control over data. One research direction is thus to extend our previous approach on delegated encryption based access control on cloud based systems [42] and adapt a similar approach in NDN in order to reduce the load on data producers.

In order to make the scheme practical, one must overcome usability challenges involved in using encryption based access control mechanisms. The mechanism should be as transparent as possible to users of the system. One possible direction in this regard is to utilize browser based proxies, similar to current password managers, to hide the complexity of key management, encryption and decryption operations from users.

6 PRIVACY

As we mentioned in the introduction, comprehensive privacy in NDN requires combining different techniques that we discuss in what follows.

Anonymous Communication: Lack of such a mechanism makes it easy for an attacker to trace back to a sender of a message received by a destination, and vice versa. One possible approach is to utilize a network anonymizer that supports anonymous communications; a very well known example of such an anonymizer is represented by Tor [25]. An anonymizer makes it much more difficult for an attacker to trace back to the sender of a message received by the destination.

Starting from the notion of Onion routing, on which Tor was implemented, several other network anonymizers have been proposed. However, most existing anonymizers have scalability and performance issues. Recent approaches, like LAP [32] and [49] have addressed performance issue, but at the expense of reduced security. A recent scheme, HORNET, by Chen et al. [22] has addressed the problem of high performance and stronger security. In particular, HORNET uses only symmetric key encryption, which enhances efficiency. Scalability in HORNET is ensured by the fact that HORNET routers do not keep per-flow state or perform computationally expensive operations. A major issue in applying HORNET to NDN is that it requires the client to know in advance the IP address of the destination, whereas in a NDN the client only needs to know the searched data name. One research direction is to investigate the use of HORNET in the context of NDN to identify additional issues, and design caching approaches that can allow the client to determine the possible paths leading to a given data.

Private Searches: Anonymous communication is not sufficient to ensure privacy because by looking at the interest packets and/or data packets of the requested data, an attacker may combine this information with other available information and link back the request to a specific subject. In other words, a network anonymizer only prevents an attacker from knowing from which IP address a given data was requested, not which data was requested. Further, setting up a communication anonymizer requires setting up a set of anonymizing routers from the client which must choose the path to follow and setting up such a network anonymizer may not be always possible. Therefore, a complementary mechanism to actually hide the actual data, in both interest packets and data packets, is required.

Efficient and effective countermeasures must be taken to prevent the data consumer's interests from being inferred according to the submitted interest packets. Several approaches could be adopted, including techniques for private-retrieval [58], but such techniques are not scalable and efficient for use in NDN systems, especially over 5G networks. One alternative approach is the use of the cover file notion proposed by Arianfar et al. [10]. Under such an approach a file F of interest is split into different chunks and the content of each chunk is randomized by combining it, through an exclusive OR operation, with another chunk. The latter can be a chunk from the same file F or from another file, referred to as cover file. This approach also includes a strategy for generating secure names for the various transformed chunks. A major issue in the use of this approach is that data users need to know the cover blocks used for generating the blocks of the file to be retrieved. The approach by Arianfar et al. does not indicate how such information is transmitted to the data users. To address this issue one possible approach is the use of encryption-based access control mechanisms, such as the one, described in the previous section. Information about the cover blocks for a given file would be encrypted and the encryption key made available only to authorized users. An additional research direction is the design of techniques by which one can select more than one blocks of actual interest by retrieving more chunks than needed in order to support a level of plausible deniability. We note however that the solution of Arianfar et al. does not work when one of the authorized users is a malicious party trying to infer privacy sensitive information about other authorized users. To address such scenario, one can explore privacy-preserving publishing techniques [40, 43].

In all the privacy approaches that we outlined, search patterns are revealed to intermediate NDN routing nodes, especially if network anonymization is not utilized. Oblivious RAM (ORAM) [54] is one of the best tools we have today for hiding such access patterns. Although ORAM is currently slow, an open challenge is how to build faster schemes specifically for NDN routing. If developed, such a technique can be added on top of existing privacy and security techniques proposed for NDN to hide the access patterns in NDN routing.

Cache Privacy: One important NDN feature is router-side content caching. While it helps to reduce congestion and improve throughput/latency, it can leak the interests of data consumers to nearby curious or malicious users. The most effective counter measure against cache sniffing attacks has been to randomize the caching strategy [5, 35]. Such approaches delay response time and increase congestion. Further, the privacy they provide is not well defined. It is thus an open challenge to support caching privacy with concrete privacy guarantees, such as the one defined by the differential privacy model [26] without degrading the response and the throughput.

7 CONCLUSIONS

NDN is a promising next-generation content-centric network architecture proposed for content distribution. Unlike current connection based security which is patched on top of the TCP/IP protocol stack, NDN takes a clean-slate approach to incorporate security from the beginning. However, achieving the security goals of NDN networks is challenging due to performance requirements, the scale and the highly dynamic behavior of users and content. In this paper, based on the characteristics and design goals of NDN, we identify security and privacy requirements, and propose possible directions towards meeting those requirements. There may well be other practical issues related to content security that we may have overlooked. We believe this research agenda will serve as a basis to identify other practical requirements as well as help make secure NDN a reality by addressing the challenges discussed in this paper.

ACKNOWLEDGEMENTS

This work was supported by the NSF grant CNS-1719369, and Intel as part of the NSF/Intel ICNWEN program.

REFERENCES

[1] https://www.gnupg.org/gph/en/manual/book1.html. (????).
[2] Digital Signature Standard (DSS). http://csrc.nist.gov/publications/fips/archive/fips186-2/fips186-2.pdf. (????).
[3] eBACS: ECRYPT Benchmarking of Cryptographic Systems. http://bench.cr.yp.to/results-sign.html. (????).
[4] 2006. IETF ICN Working Group. https://goo.gl/wVHPWg. (2006).
[5] N. Abani and M. Gerla. 2016. Centrality-based caching for privacy in Information-Centric Networks. In *MILCOM 2016 - 2016 IEEE Military Communications Conference*. 1249–1254.
[6] G. Acs, M. Conti, P. Gasti, C. Ghali, and G. Tsudik. 2013. Cache Privacy in Named-Data Networking. In *2013 IEEE 33rd International Conference on Distributed Computing Systems*.
[7] Alexander Afanasyev, J. Alex Halderman, Scott Ruoti, Kent Seamons, Yingdi Yu, Daniel Zappala, and Lixia Zhang. 2016. Content-based Security for the Web. In *Proceedings of the 2016 New Security Paradigms Workshop (NSPW '16)*. ACM, 49–60.
[8] A. Afanasyev, X. Jiang, Y. Yu, J. Tan, Y. Xia, A. Mankin, and L. Zhang. 2017. NDNS: A DNS-Like Name Service for NDN. In *2017 26th International Conference on Computer Communication and Networks (ICCCN)*. 1–9.
[9] R. Arends, R. Austein, M. Larson, D. Massey, and S. Rose. 2005. Resource Records for the DNS Security Extensions. https://tools.ietf.org/html/rfc4034. (2005).
[10] Somaya Arianfar, Teemu Koponen, Barath Raghavan, and Scott Shenker. 2011. On preserving privacy in content-oriented networks. In *2011 ACM SIGCOMM Workshop on Information-Centri Networking, ICN 2011, Toronto, Canada, August 19, 2011. Proceedings*. 19–24.
[11] Giuseppe Ateniese, Kevin Fu, Matthew Green, and Susan Hohenberger. 2006. Improved Proxy Re-encryption Schemes with Applications to Secure Distributed Storage. *ACM Transactions on Information System Security* (2006), 1–30.
[12] Hitesh Ballani, Paul Francis, and Xinyang Zhang. 2007. A Study of Prefix Hijacking and Interception in the Internet. In *Proceedings of the 2007 Conference on Applications, Technologies, Architectures, and Protocols for Computer Communications (SIGCOMM '07)*. ACM, 265–276.

[13] Mihir Bellare, Thomas Ristenpart, Phillip Rogaway, and Till Stegers. 2009. Format-Preserving Encryption. In *Selected Areas in Cryptography*. Springer Berlin Heidelberg, 295–312.

[14] Daniel J. Bernstein, Niels Duif, Tanja Lange, Peter Schwabe, and Bo-Yin Yang. 2012. High-speed high-security signatures. *J. Cryptographic Engineering* 2, 2 (2012), 77–89.

[15] Elisa Bertino, Gabriel Ghinita, and Ashish Kamra. 2011. Access Control for Databases: Concepts and Systems. *Foundations and Trends in Databases* 3, 1-2 (2011), 1–148.

[16] J. Bethencourt, A. Sahai, and B. Waters. 2007. Ciphertext-Policy Attribute-Based Encryption. In *2007 IEEE Symposium on Security and Privacy (SP '07)*. 321–334.

[17] Dan Boneh, Giovanni Di Crescenzo, Rafail Ostrovsky, and Giuseppe Persiano. 2004. Public Key Encryption with Keyword Search. In *Proceedings of the International Conference on the Theory and Applications of Cryptographic Techniques*, Christian Cachin and Jan L. Camenisch (Eds.). Springer Berlin Heidelberg, 506–522.

[18] Dan Boneh, Craig Gentry, Ben Lynn, and Hovav Shacham. 2003. Aggregate and Verifiably Encrypted Signatures from Bilinear Maps. In *Advances in Cryptology - EUROCRYPT 2003, International Conference on the Theory and Applications of Cryptographic Techniques, Warsaw, Poland, May 4-8, 2003, Proceedings*. 416–432.

[19] David Cash, Paul Grubbs, Jason Perry, and Thomas Ristenpart. 2015. Leakage-Abuse Attacks Against Searchable Encryption. In *Proceedings of the 22Nd ACM SIGSAC Conference on Computer and Communications Security*. ACM, 668–679.

[20] V. Cerf and R. Kahn. 1974. A Protocol for Packet Network Intercommunication. *IEEE Transactions on Communications* 22, 5 (1974), 637–648.

[21] Abdelberi Chaabane, Emiliano De Cristofaro, Mohamed Ali Kaafar, and Ersin Uzun. 2013. Privacy in Content-oriented Networking: Threats and Countermeasures. *SIGCOMM Computer Communication Review* 43, 3 (2013), 25–33.

[22] Chen Chen, Daniele Enrico Asoni, David Barrera, George Danezis, and Adrian Perrig. 2015. HORNET: High-speed Onion Routing at the Network Layer. In *Proceedings of the 22nd ACM SIGSAC Conference on Computer and Communications Security, Denver, CO, USA, October 12-6, 2015*. 1441–1454.

[23] Mauro Conti, Paolo Gasti, and Marco Teoli. 2013. A Lightweight Mechanism for Detection of Cache Pollution Attacks in Named Data Networking. *Computer Networking* 57, 16 (2013), 3178–3191.

[24] Giovanni Di Crescenzo, Brian Coan, John Schultz, Simon Tsang, and Rebecca N. Wright. 2014. Privacy-Preserving Publish/Subscribe: Efficient Protocols in a Distributed Model. In *Proceedings of the 8th International Workshop on Data Privacy Management and Autonomous Spontaneous Security*, Joaquin Garcia-Alfaro, Georgios Lioudakis, Nora Cuppens-Boulahia, Simon Foley, and William M. Fitzgerald (Eds.). Springer Berlin Heidelberg, Berlin, Heidelberg, 114–132. DOI: http://dx.doi.org/10.1007/978-3-642-54568-9_8

[25] Roger Dingledine, Nick Mathewson, and Paul F. Syverson. 2004. Tor: The Second-Generation Onion Router. In *Proceedings of the 13th USENIX Security Symposium, August 9-13, 2004, San Diego, CA, USA*. 303–320.

[26] C. Dwork, F. McSherry, K. Nissim, and A. Smith. 2006. Calibrating Noise to Sensitivity in Private Data Analysis. In *Proceedings of the Third Conference on Theory of Cryptography*. Springer-Verlag, 265–284.

[27] Ksenia Ermoshina, Francesca Musiani, and Harry Halpin. 2016. End-to-End Encrypted Messaging Protocols: An Overview. In *Internet Science*. Springer International Publishing, 244–254.

[28] David F. Ferraiolo, Ravi Sandhu, Serban Gavrila, D. Richard Kuhn, and Ramaswamy Chandramouli. 2001. Proposed NIST Standard for Role-based Access Control. *ACM Transactions on Information Systems Security* 4, 3 (2001), 51.

[29] Roy Fielding. Architectural styles and the design of network-based software architectures. https://goo.gl/tDx9JZ. (????).

[30] P. Gasti, G. Tsudik, E. Uzun, and L. Zhang. 2013. DoS and DDoS in Named Data Networking. In *2013 22nd International Conference on Computer Communication and Networks (ICCCN)*. 1–7.

[31] Vipul Goyal, Omkant Pandey, Amit Sahai, and Brent Waters. 2006. Attribute-based Encryption for Fine-grained Access Control of Encrypted Data. In *Proceedings of the 13th ACM Conference on Computer and Communications Security (CCS '06)*. ACM, 89–98.

[32] Hsu-Chun Hsiao, Tiffany Hyun-Jin Kim, Adrian Perrig, Akira Yamada, Samuel C. Nelson, Marco Gruteser, and Wei Meng. 2012. LAP: Lightweight Anonymity and Privacy. In *IEEE Symposium on Security and Privacy, SP 2012, 21-23 May 2012, San Francisco, California, USA*. 506–520.

[33] Van Jacobson. 2006. A new way to look at networking. https://goo.gl/VGwkUu. (2006).

[34] Van Jacobson, Diana K. Smetters, James D. Thornton, Michael F. Plass, Nicholas H. Briggs, and Rebecca L. Braynard. 2009. Networking Named Content. In *Proceedings of the 5th International Conference on Emerging Networking Experiments and Technologies (CoNEXT '09)*. ACM, 1–12.

[35] M. Jakobsson and S. Stamm. 2007. Web Camouflage: Protecting Your Clients from Browser-Sniffing Attacks. *IEEE Security Privacy* 5, 6 (2007), 16–24.

[36] N. Karapanos, A. Filios, R. A. Popa, and S. Capkun. 2016. Verena: End-to-End Integrity Protection for Web Applications. In *2016 IEEE Symposium on Security and Privacy (SP)*. 895–913.

[37] D. Kim, J. Bi, A. V. Vasilakos, and I. Yeom. 2017. Security of Cached Content in NDN. *IEEE Transactions on Information Forensics and Security* 12, 12 (2017), 2933–2944.

[38] Kevin Lewi and David J. Wu. 2016. Order-Revealing Encryption: New Constructions, Applications, and Lower Bounds. In *Proceedings of the 2016 ACM SIGSAC Conference on Computer and Communications Security*. ACM, 1167–1178.

[39] Ralph C. Merkle. 1987. A Digital Signature Based on a Conventional Encryption Function. In *Advances in Cryptology - CRYPTO '87, A Conference on the Theory and Applications of Cryptographic Techniques, Santa Barbara, California, USA, August 16-20, 1987, Proceedings*. 369–378.

[40] Mohamed Nabeel, Stefan Appel, Elisa Bertino, and Alejandro Buchmann. 2013. Privacy preserving Context Aware Publish Subscribe Systems. In *Network and System Security - 7th International Conference, NSS 2013, Madrid, Apain, June 3-4, 2013. Proceedings*. 465–478.

[41] Mohamed Nabeel and Elisa Bertino. 2014. Attribute Based Group Key Management. *Trans. Data Privacy* 7, 3 (2014), 309–336.

[42] M. Nabeel and E. Bertino. 2014. Privacy Preserving Delegated Access Control in Public Clouds. *IEEE Transactions on Knowledge and Data Engineering* 26, 9 (2014), 2268–2280.

[43] Mohamed Nabeel, Ning Shang, and Elisa Bertino. 2012. Efficient Privacy Preserving Content Based Publish Subscribe Systems. In *Proceedings of the 17th ACM Symposium on Access Control Models and Technologies (SACMAT '12)*. ACM, New York, NY, USA, 133–144. DOI: http://dx.doi.org/10.1145/2295136.2295164

[44] Mohamed Nabeel, Ning Shang, and Elisa Bertino. 2013. Privacy Preserving Policy-Based Content Sharing in Public Clouds. *IEEE Trans. Knowl. Data Eng.* 25, 11 (2013), 2602–2614.

[45] Muhammad Naveed, Seny Kamara, and Charles V. Wright. 2015. Inference Attacks on Property-Preserving Encrypted Databases. In *Proceedings of the 22Nd ACM SIGSAC Conference on Computer and Communications Security*. ACM, 644–655.

[46] Christian Rossow. 2014. Amplification Hell: Revisiting Network Protocols for DDoS Abuse. In *In Proceedings of the 2014 Network and Distributed System Security Symposium, NDSS*.

[47] Mark D. Ryan. 2014. Enhanced certificate transparency and end-to-end encrypted mail. In *In Network and Distributed System Security Symposium (NDSS). Internet Society*.

[48] R. S. Sandhu, E. J. Coyne, H. L. Feinstein, and C. E. Youman. 1996. Role-based access control models. *Computer* 29, 2 (1996), 38–47.

[49] Jody Sankey and Matthew K. Wright. 2014. Dovetail: Stronger Anonymity in Next-Generation Internet Routing. In *Privacy Enhancing Technologies - 14th International Symposium, PETS 2014, Amsterdam, The Netherlands, July 16-18, 2014. Proceedings*. 283–303.

[50] N. Shang, M. Nabeel, F. Paci, and E. Bertino. 2010. A privacy-preserving approach to policy-based content dissemination. In *Proceedings of the IEEE 26th International Conference on Data Engineering*. 944–955.

[51] N. Shang, M. Nabeel, F. Paci, and E. Bertino. 2010. A Privacy-Preserving Approach to Policy-Based Content Dissemination. In *ICDE '10: Proceedings of the 2010 IEEE 26th International Conference on Data Engineering*.

[52] Diana Smetters and Van Jacobson. 2009. Securing network content. (2009).

[53] Dawn Xiaodong Song, David Wagner, and Adrian Perrig. 2000. Practical Techniques for Searches on Encrypted Data. In *Proceedings of the IEEE Symposium on Security and Privacy*. IEEE Computer Society.

[54] Emil Stefanov and Elaine Shi. 2013. ObliviStore: High Performance Oblivious Cloud Storage. In *Proceedings of the 2013 IEEE Symposium on Security and Privacy*. IEEE Computer Society, 253–267.

[55] G. Xylomenos, C. N. Ververidis, V. A. Siris, N. Fotiou, C. Tsilopoulos, X. Vasilakos, K. V. Katsaros, and G. C. Polyzos. 2014. A Survey of Information-Centric Networking Research. *IEEE Communications Surveys Tutorials* 16, 2 (2014), 1024–1049.

[56] Attila Altay Yavuz. 2014. An Efficient Real-Time Broadcast Authentication Scheme for Command and Control Messages. *IEEE Transactions on Information Forensics and Security* 9, 10 (2014), 1733–1742.

[57] Attila Altay Yavuz, Anand Mudgerikar, Ankush Singla, Ioannis Papapanagiotou, and Elisa Bertino. 2017. Real-time digital signatures for time-critical networks. *IEEE Transactions on Information Forensics and Security* 12, 11 (2017), 2627–2639.

[58] Sergey Yekhanin. 2010. Private Information Retrieval. *Communication of ACM* 53, 4 (2010), 68–73.

[59] Yingdi Yu, Alexander Afanasyev, David Clark, kc claffy, Van Jacobson, and Lixia Zhang. 2015. Schematizing Trust in Named Data Networking. In *Proceedings of the 2Nd ACM Conference on Information-Centric Networking (ACM-ICN '15)*. ACM, 177–186.

[60] E. Yuan and J. Tong. 2005. Attributed based access control (ABAC) for Web services. In *IEEE International Conference on Web Services (ICWS'05)*. 569.

[61] Lixia Zhang, Alexander Afanasyev, Jeffrey Burke, Van Jacobson, kc claffy, Patrick Crowley, Christos Papadopoulos, Lan Wang, and Beichuan Zhang. 2014. Named Data Networking. *SIGCOMM Computer Communication Review* 44, 3 (2014), 66–73.

Privacy-Aware Risk-Adaptive Access Control in Health Information Systems using Topic Models

Wenxi Zhang
Institute of Software Chinese Academy of Science
University of Chinese Academy of Sciences
Beijing, China
zhangwenxi@is.iscas.ac.cn

Hao Li*
Institute of Software Chinese Academy of Science
Beijing, China
lihao@tca.iscas.ac.cn

Min Zhang
Institute of Software Chinese Academy of Science
Beijing, China
mzhang@tca.iscas.ac.cn

Zhiquan Lv
National Computer Network Emergency Response
Technical Team/Coordination Center of China
Beijing, China
lvzhiquan@cert.org.cn

ABSTRACT

Traditional role-based access control fails to meet the privacy requirements for patient data in medical systems, as it is infeasible for policy makers to foresee what information doctors may need for diagnosis and treatment in various situations. The universal practice in hospitals is to grant doctors unlimited access, which in turn increases the risk of breaching patient privacy. In this paper, we propose a dynamic risk-adaptive access control model for health IT systems by taking into consideration the relationships between data and access behaviors. By training topic models to portray individual and group-level access behaviors, we quantify the risk for each user over a certain period of time. Malicious users are supposed to get higher risk scores than honest users due to improper requests. Thus their further access would be denied under our access control scheme. The topic model and risk scores are periodically updated to advance the self-adaptability of the system. Experimental results have shown that our solution could effectively distinguish malicious doctors even if they deliberately conceal the misconducts.

CCS CONCEPTS

• **Security and privacy** → **Access control**; **Privacy-preserving protocols**; **Privacy protections**; • **Computing methodologies** → *Topic modeling*; *Latent Dirichlet allocation*; • **Applied computing** → Health care information systems; Health informatics;

KEYWORDS

Access Control, Privacy, Risk Quantification, Topic Model, Healthcare

*Hao Li is the corresponding author.

ACM Reference Format:
Wenxi Zhang, Hao Li, Min Zhang, and Zhiquan Lv. 2018. Privacy-Aware Risk-Adaptive Access Control in Health Information Systems using Topic Models. In *SACMAT'18: 23rd ACM Symposium on Access Control Models & Technologies, June 13–15, 2018, Indianapolis, IN, USA*. ACM, New York, NY, USA, 7 pages. https://doi.org/10.1145/3205977.3205991

1 INTRODUCTION

Healthcare is one of the most important social and economic issues worldwide. With the widely application of electronic healthcare systems, a major problem has aroused that medical records typically include detailed patient information with high risks of privacy disclosure. Privacy threats, unlike in many other situations, mainly come from authorized users within health IT systems[4, 14]. Physicians, doctors or nurses might use legitimate access to release sensitive information to untrustworthy environments or third parties. Europe is at the forefront for personal privacy protection. The new EU regulation GDPR has been designed to enforce privacy requirements in the processing of data. It is imperative to implement effective and practical access control models in clinical systems to meet the actual needs.

Obviously, hospitals should not assign doctors full permission of access to virtually everything about patients. It seems possible to limit access scope based on identities or roles. Ophthalmologists, for instance, may only have access to eye-correlated data according to the theory of role-based access control. Or access to a patient's medical records may be restricted to his physician-in-charge. However, it is impractical and infeasible for hospitals to do so. Medical diagnosis and treatment require multiple kinds of data, and rely heavily on knowledges of concrete fields. General policy makers could hardly determine what information is needed for a specific domain. However, from a data perspective, this task is achievable by considering the relationships between data and access behaviors to quantify the risk of data access. Intuitively, doctors in the same medical department tend to follow similar medical treatment principles even though they may apply personal research experience. In the long term, the data they process follow a relatively stable pattern, with reasonable fluctuations allowed for individual differences.

Thus a risk assessment process that uses the group-level pattern of access as a benchmark would fit the realistic demands in healthcare systems. As machine learning methods have played an important role in recognition of the intrinsic relationship between data objects and behaviors, it is possible to settle privacy issues in the health system through these approaches. When dealing with a medical case, doctors make a prejudge and choose medical data subconsciously from experience. This process is like writing an article, when we need to describe things or state views. The writer then seek sufficient evidences and form the language to support the contention. Topic model is a type of statistical model for discovering the abstract topics that occur in a collection of documents. Each doctor is like writing an article. With the help of topic models, we might discover the subconscious patterns under which doctors selecting materials for a certain disease or prejudgement. And doctors following bizarre patterns from the general level might be further exposed on suspension of privacy invasion.

Static risk-aware access control frameworks could hardly meet the changing requirements. Healthcare data are piling up at a staggering rate. Medical treatment principles keep transforming owing to scientific innovations, healthcare policies, or even season alternating. In this paper, we propose a dynamic risk-adaptive access control model. Data-accessing activities are associated with quantified risk scores computed from a topic model, which is updated over a certain period of time. Request to accessing a resource is granted if doing so will not make the user's aggregated risk exceed tolerance threshold set by the system; otherwise, the request is denied. We use time-adjusted risk quotas to set the tolerance threshold. Our model allows users to access data on condition that their temporal aggregated risk is at an acceptable level. For simplicity, we use the word doctors to refer to healthcare practitioners in various roles.

The contributions of this paper are summarized as follows:

- We define a comprehensive adversary model for health IT systems. In this model, we describe in detail the exceeding access behaviors of malicious doctors and how they may take advantage of system vulnerabilities to conceal misconducts. The behaviors are depicted through statistical approaches.
- We design a novel risk-quantification approach by adopting the method of topic models. By drawing an analogy between medical diagnosis and writing, our approach discovers relationships between medical records and therapeutic goals. Risk scores are calculated based on group-level and individual patterns.
- We propose a dynamic risk-adaptive access control model by updating the topic model and the baseline tolerance periodically. We also provide a novel way to adjust risk quotas to enhance the timeliness of the system.
- We have implemented our approach on health care data according with real-world medical records provided by hospitals. Our method has achieved excellent performance comparing to the existing approach, and has shown effectiveness and superiority in protection of patient privacy.

The rest of this paper is organized as follows. Section 2 gives an overview of related work. In Section 3, we define a comprehensive adversary model. An advanced risk-quantification method is provided in Section 4. Section 5 presents a dynamic access control scheme. In Section 6, we describe the experimental procedure in detail and analyse experiment results. We draw conclusions and outline opportunities for future work in the last section.

2 RELATED WORK

Risk access control is one of the most representative technologies in adaptive access control. By evaluating the risk of access behaviors, risk access control makes a trade-off between risk and profit. In this way, implementing access control policy based on risk quantification guarantees strong self-adaptability.

Primary work from MCJP Office introduces risk quantification into access control[17]. Researchers have defined the concepts of computing risks and access quotas as well as given some guiding principles and requirements that risk-based information systems should meet. In terms of risk measurement, Ni and Cheng et al. have proposed a method of measuring static risk based on the sensitivity of the target object, the number of objects, the mutually exclusive relationship between the objects, the security level of the access subjects and so on[5, 19]. Han et al. evaluate risk by measuring rank differences between roles and users, which has extended the traditional framework of role-based access control[9].

Other work include the mechanism design and improvements of the risk threshold and the risk quota. Cheng et al. propose the concept of risk band by defining partial permission between full permission and rejection[5]. These work extend and enhance the applicability of access control in various situations.

In further work, the risk value is calculated through collaborative filtering, that is, by quantifying the difference between the access of a subject and that of other subjects. Wang et al.[21] exploit the concept of Shannon entropy from information theory to compute risk scores of access requests. As malicious users access all kinds of data while honest users only access necessary data, the larger diversity of access of the former leads to a larger entropy. Their work greatly improves the flexibility of access control and provides possibility for further research on the implementation of access control in big data scenarios. However, this method could hardly adapt to comprehensive adversary models and fulfill the changing demands from medical environment.

3 ADVERSARY MODEL

In this section, we first introduce a plain adversary model as is defined by Wang et al.[21], and then enrich the model by defining more realistic and comprehensive attacks in detail. Users in the models are doctors or physicians who have access to patients' medical information.

3.1 A plain model

While a patient's medical information of all kinds may be available, it is desirable for honest doctors to access only information that is relevant to the current task so as to comply with the requirements of need-to-know, whereas malicious doctors sometimes additionally access irrelevant information.

The relationship between a healthcare task t and a medical record m is described as a hypothetical function $\theta(t, m)$, called the relevance-relation function. The higher $\theta(t, m)$ is, the more useful m is in diagnosis with respect to t. Doctors' overall decisions on information needs in various conditions should approximately reach the group-level θ.

Let D_θ be the distribution of $\theta(t, m)$. An honest doctor's choice of records would follow distribution D_θ, as those records match his current treatment purpose well; Let ϵ_1 be the probability of exceptions including wrong clicks or when doctors may need information to handle special conditions. In contrast, with probability $(1 - \epsilon_2)$ a malicious doctor behaves identically as an honest doctor, as they perform their job duty; with probability ϵ_2, he accesses irrelevant medical data. Both ϵ_1 and ϵ_2 are expected to be small in practice. In particular, the information access behaviors of the two groups of doctors are defined as follows:

Honest doctors: Given a patient p_i and a treatment purpose t_j, let $M_{i,j}$ be the set of medical records chosen by an honest doctor. For each record entry $m_k \in M_{i,j}$, with probability $(1 - \epsilon_1)$, the selection of m_k follows the distribution D_θ; with probability ϵ_1, m_k is chosen uniformly random among all the available records of patient p_i, where $\epsilon_1 \in [0, 1]$.

Malicious doctors: Given a patient p_i and a treatment purpose t_j, let $M_{i,j}$ be the set of medical records chosen by a malicious doctor. For each record entry $m1_k \in M_{i,j}$, with probability $(1 - \epsilon_1)(1 - \epsilon_2)$, the selection of $m1_k$ follows the distribution D_θ; with probability $\epsilon_1(1 - \epsilon_2) + \epsilon_2$, $m1_k$ is chosen uniformly random among all the available records of patient pi, where $\epsilon_1, \epsilon_2 \in [0, 1]$.

3.2 A more comprehensive model

Unlike most adversary models where attackers focus on cracking the system, malicious doctors could only implement infringement acts with reliance on the integrity of the system. Yet still they would try to figure out ways to cover the track of improper behaviors once they understand the system mechanisms.

Some different entries in medical record materials provide the same or similar information albeit in altered forms. Generally, an initial electronic medical record is made up of[1]:

- A set of personal information(name, age, occupation, etc.)
- A list of problems with dates of diagnosis and current activity
- A list of treatments with start and end dates and dosages
- A list of tests and measurements with dates and results

Although medical records usually contain much more information than listed above, this is a reasonable minimum amount of information to expect from an electronic summary.

However, these record entries are not unique and irreplaceable for the information behind them. Personal information is interrelated due to social attributes. Finances, social backgrounds and even daily routines could be inferred from one's address or occupation. Some record entries directly reveal multiple information at the same time, such as ID numbers revealing age and location. Medical examinations designed to reveal different aspects of one disease might be conducted several times for observation and certainty. Symptoms of several similar diseases are also highly relevant and exhaustively depicted. Thus from a smaller part of the medical records, experienced readers could somehow infer many hidden messages behind those unread. Complete and detailed clinical records could actually provide alternative information.

As described in Section 2, the more one conducts exceeding access activities, the higher his entropy of activities become, which

leads to an increment of his risk score. Given the knowledge of such a mechanism, some malicious doctors would accordingly modulate improper behaviors. If record entry 1 to 10 provide alternative information, they may intentionally always visit entry 1 to 6 and never read entry 7 to 10. Malicious doctors decrease the overall entropy by applying this rule to all record entries, while honest doctors would not narrow the range deliberately. Thereby they sustain the acts of prying into patients' privacy.

This type of dishonest doctors are defined as concealed doctors. In particular, the behaviors of concealed doctors are defined as:

Concealed doctors: Given a patient p_i and a treatment purpose t_j, let $M1_{i,j}$ be the set of medical records chosen by a malicious doctor. For each record entry $m_{1k} \in M1_{i,j}$ let h be a range parameter and LG be the set of record entries with the same label m_{1k}, concealed doctors would randomly pick a record entry m_{2k} in set $smallLG$, which contains the forward section of LG and satisfies:

$$\frac{|smallLG|}{|LG|} = h \qquad (1)$$

Thus the m_{2k} corresponding to $m_{1k} \in M1_{i,j}$ constitute $M2_{i,j}$, set of medical records chosen by a concealed doctor, where $h \in (0, 1]$.

4 RISK QUANTIFICATION

Our approach to computing risk is based on probabilistic topic models. The steps are summarized in the following:

(1) In a preliminary step, each piece of record entry has a label indicating its category. An access log is generated for each doctor of his activities in the same department. During each activity, a doctor accesses one labelled record entry.

(2) A topic model is trained based on access logs over a relatively long period. Topics related to a treatment process are extracted. The behavior pattern of a doctor is characterized by the distribution of his access log on those topics.

(3) The risk score is computed from the distance between the distribution vector of a doctor's log and training data.

4.1 Labeling of the medical records

The International Classification of Diseases (ICD) is designed as a classification system, providing diagnostic codes for classifying diseases. Major categories are designed to include a set of similar diseases[18]. The ICD is revised periodically and ICD-10 is currently in use by the WHO and most countries. ICD-10 covers more than 15,5000 different codes including new diagnoses[12, 20]. Usually, medical records are automatically labeled in electronic systems.

4.2 Topic modeling of access logs

4.2.1 Topic Model. Topic models are powerful tools initially developed to characterize text documents, but can be extended to other collections of discrete data[2]. The intuition behind topic models is that documents are represented as random mixtures over latent topics and each topic is characterized by a distribution over words.

In this paper we adopt the Latent Dirichlet Allocation(LDA) model[3]. In the LDA model, each document in a corpus exhibits multiple topics, and each word in a document supports certain

Table 1: A Summary for Mapping from Access Logs to Documents

Document $\mathbf{w}$	Access log of a doctor
Word w	Labelled medical record entries
Topic z	A subconscious access pattern
$p(\mathbf{z}\|\mathbf{w})$	Distribution on topics of an access log
$p(w\|z)$	Probability of a record entry belonging to a topic

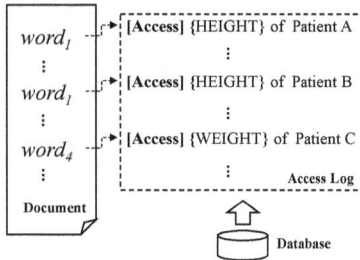

Figure 1: An Analogy between A Document and An Access Log for A Doctor in A Certain Period

topics. Given all the words of each document in a corpus as observations, we can train a topic model to infer the hidden thematic structure behind the observations[11].

4.2.2 Intuition of Using Topic Model. We highlight the intuition in Table 1. An access log could reveal multiple subconscious access patterns. We map the pattern in our problem to the concept of topic. A record entry provides information appears in different subconscious access patterns. This is equivalent to the polysemy phenomenon in topic model: a word serves diverse topics.

In Figure 1, we draw a analogy between a document and an access log for a doctor in a certain period. When a document contains multiple words and an access log includes multiple medical record entries, we equivalently map the concepts of document and word in the topic model to access log and labelled medical records respectively.

We train a topic model to express the group-level and individual access behavior patterns in a mathematical way. The distribution vector of an access log on the topics shows how a doctor follows the universal principles of choosing medical records, and would effectively expose the abnormal behaviors of malicious even if they conceal the acts painstakingly.

4.3 Risk quantification based on the topic model

4.3.1 The Methodology for Calculating Risk Scores. Once the topic model has been trained based on previous data, we analyse a new document using its distribution vector on the topics. Figure 2 shows the process. We compute the distance between the distribution vector of this document and previous documents as the risk value.

Let $p(\mathbf{z}|\mathbf{w})$ be the distribution of a document $\mathbf{w}$ on the topics $\mathbf{z}$. The distribution vector of training document $\mathbf{w_i}$ is $p(\mathbf{z}|\mathbf{w_i})$, and for the test document $\mathbf{w_{test-k}}$ the distribution vector is $p(\mathbf{z}|\mathbf{w_{test-k}})$.

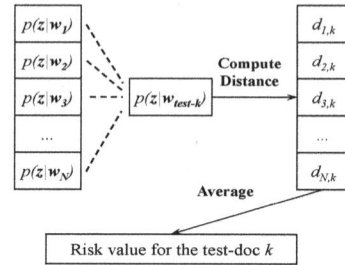

Figure 2: The Methodology for Calculating Risk Scores

To measure the risk level of a new access log, we compute the distance $d_{i,k}$ between each pair of vector $p(\mathbf{z}|\mathbf{w_{test-k}})$ and vector $p(\mathbf{z}|\mathbf{w})$, $i = 1, 2, ..., N$. The risk score for the access log is defined as the average of $d_{i,k}$

$$Risk\_Score(\mathbf{w_{test-k}}) = \sum_{i=1}^{N} d_{i,k}/N \qquad (2)$$

We use the distance instead of similarity between two vectors. The more differently a doctor acts from his colleagues, the less similar his distribution vector would be to those of others, which naturally leads to a larger distance value and a higher risk score.

4.3.2 Distance Measure. We adopt the Jensen-Shannon(JS) divergence, which has ever been used as a distance measure for documents, to compute the distance between two vectors. If the feature vector of a document is considered as probability distribution over features, JS divergence measures the similarity between the two probability distributions[8]. It outperforms common measures including cosine similarity based on document clustering[7]. JS divergence is based on Kullback-Leibler(KL) divergence. For discrete probability distributions P and Q, the KL divergence from Q to P is defined to be[10, 15, 16]:

$$D_{KL}(P||Q) = \sum_{i} P(i) log \frac{P(i)}{Q(i)} \qquad (3)$$

In the simplest case, a KL divergence of 0 indicates that we can expect similar, if not the same, patterns of two different distributions, while a KL divergence of 1 indicates that the two distributions behave in a different manner. The JS divergence from discrete probability distributions Q to P is defined to be:

$$D_{JS}(P||Q) = \frac{1}{2}D_{KL}(P||\frac{P+Q}{2}) + \frac{1}{2}D_{KL}(Q||\frac{P+Q}{2}) \qquad (4)$$

Similarly, the less similar two distributions are, the larger the JS divergence would become.

5 DYNAMIC ACCESS CONTROL

In this section, we propose a dynamic access control model incorporating the concept of timeboxing and iteration. The timeboxing technique allocates a fixed time period to each planned iteration activity[13, 22]. Here the access control schedule is divided into a series of separate long time periods (long timeboxes). As is shown in Figure 3, a long timebox L_i is divided into k fixed short timeboxes. At the beginning of L_i, a new topic model is trained with accumulated feedback from the previous period L_{i-1}. The matrix

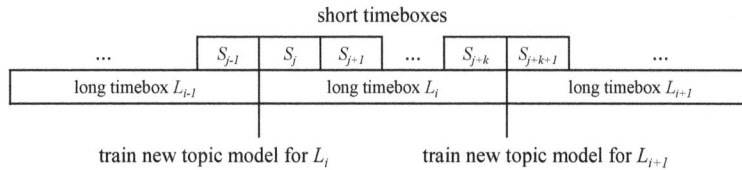

Figure 3: Update of Topic Models Periodicly

of document-topic for training data, which serves as a benchmark in the risk quantification process, is synchronously updated along with the new topic model.

At the beginning of a period, doctors are granted a certain quantity of access quotas. The system shall have detailed logs showing the labels of all accesses that doctors conduct. After every short timebox, the risk score for each doctor is computed and deducted from his quota account. Further access requests are allowed if the doctor still has remaining quotas; otherwise he has to either apply for more quotas or just wait till the next long timebox, which is certainly not feasible in reality.

The number of quotas granted to a doctor essentially specifies a threshold the system can tolerate for him over k short timeboxes. Suppose the number of quotas $Quota(L_i)$ for L_i is fixed as the average amount of quotas for a doctor in L_{i-1}. If the general level of risk is decreasing during L_i, $Quota(L_i)$ would be excessive for almost all doctors. In that case, malicious doctors could continue misconducts without being discovered. Conversely, if the general level of risk is increasing during L_i, $Quota(L_i)$ would be insufficient even for honest doctors, thus the normal treatment process would be interrupted. Since conditions vary from place to place, the length of timeboxes shall be set against reality.

To guarantee the timeliness of the system, we design an automatic mechanism to adjust the number of quotas after each short timebox using a sliding window scheme[6]. Let S_j be the jth short timebox. $Mdoctor(S_j)$ is the number of doctors submitting information requests during S_j, and $Mquota(S_j)$ is the total amount of quotas consumed by these doctors in S_j. Suppose the current short timebox is S_t, we compute $Quota(S_t)$ as.

$$Quota(S_t) = \frac{\sum_{j=t-k}^{j=t-1} Mquota(S_j)}{\sum_{j=t-k}^{j=t-1} Mdoctor(S_j)} \quad (5)$$

Thus $Quota(S_t)$ of quotas would be assigned to every current doctor in the system. After each short timebox, the number of quotas also changes according to the overall risk level. At the beginning of the next short timebox S_{t+1}, $Quotas(S_{t+1})$ is updated to be:

$$Quota(S_{t+1}) = \frac{\sum_{j=t-k+1}^{j=t} Mquota(S_j)}{\sum_{j=t-k+1}^{j=t} Mdoctor(S_j)} \quad (6)$$

In reality, the number quotas is adjusted before S_{t+1} by:

$$\Delta Quota(S_{t+1}) = Quota(S_{t+1}) - Quota(S_t) \quad (7)$$

If the overall risk scores increase, $\Delta Quota(S_{t+1})$ would be positive and doctors would achieve extra quotas automatically. Otherwise, certain amount of quotas would be deducted from everyone's account. By adjusting the number of quotas assigned to each doctor,

our method manages to improve timeliness and accuracy to meet the changing requirements in the medical environment.

Once a doctor consumes all the quotas before the next offering, he may ask for more. If a doctor rarely asks for more quotas in the past, we may consider he runs out of quotas due to exceptional conditions. The system may automatically grant the doctor more quotas so that he can continue with his job. However, if a doctor runs out of quotas frequently, his risk scores must be higher than group-level, which provides strong evidence for improper acts.

6 EXPERIMENT

6.1 Experiment settings

Our experimental dataset is generated on the real-world medical history records dataset containing 2.9 million access activities. Let b_i be the label of the current medical record entry. Let $B1_i$ and $B2_i$ be the main category and the sub-category of b_i, and B be the set of all main categories in ICD-10, respectively. Thus we have $b_i \in B2_i$, $B2_i \subseteq B1_i$, and $B1_i \subset B$. Naturally, the labels in the set $B2_i$ are more likely to be relevant to l_i than those in $B1_i - B2_i$. Labels in $B1_i - B2_i$, however, are more likely to be related to b_i than those in $B - B1_i$. With probability 68%(i.e. the probability of falling in one standard deviation from the mean of a normal distribution), the target label of the medical record entry is in $B2_i$. With probability $(1 - \epsilon 1)$, the target label of the access request is in $B1_i$. With probability $\epsilon 1$, the target label is randomly selected among all the labels we have seen for the current patient's records. The value of $\epsilon 1$ is set to be 5%, as the probability $(1 - \epsilon 1)$ captures how a value falls in two standard deviations from the mean of a normal distribution. This simulates access activities made by mistake or due to exception. As to a malicious doctor, there is a probability $\epsilon 2$ that the target label is randomly selected, and there is a probability $(1 - \epsilon 2)$ that the selection of the target label follows the above process for honest doctors. Finally, a concealed doctor's selection process is the same as a malicious doctor, besides he transforms each selection following the concealment method as described in Section 3.2.

The access logs are divided into training cases and test cases. The LDA topic model is trained on the dataset of 5400 doctors, 10% (i.e. 540) of whom are malicious doctors while the others are honest doctors. The test dataset contains 542 doctors, 10% (i.e. 54) of whom are malicious doctors while the others are honest. The probability factor $\epsilon 2$ is set to be 5% to reflect the real level of exceeding access percentages. We implement Wang et al.'s method on the same dataset.

Finally, we define the criteria used for evaluation. The precision@k of a result is the percentage of certain group of doctors among the top k users; the recall@k is the percentage of certain

Table 2: Measure Values of Top X Results for Malicious Doctors and Concealed doctors

(a) Our Method

Measure	Doctor Group	Top 10	Top 20	Top 30	Top 40	Top 50
P	Both groups	1.00	1.00	1.00	0.90	0.74
	Malicious	0.70	0.65	0.73	0.65	0.54
	Concealed	0.30	0.30	0.23	0.25	0.20
R	Both groups	0.19	0.37	0.56	0.67	0.70
	Malicious	0.16	0.30	0.50	0.59	0.61
	Concealed	0.30	0.60	0.70	1.00	1.00
F1	Both groups	0.31	0.54	0.71	0.77	0.73
	Malicious	0.26	0.41	0.59	0.62	0.57
	Concealed	0.30	0.40	0.35	0.40	0.33

(b) Wang et al.'s Method

Measure	Doctor Group	Top 10	Top 20	Top 30	Top 40	Top 50
P	Both groups	1.00	0.95	0.90	0.825	0.72
	Malicious	1.00	0.95	0.87	0.80	0.70
	Concealed	0	0	0.033	0.025	0.02
R	Both groups	0.19	0.35	0.50	0.61	0.67
	Malicious	0.23	0.43	0.59	0.73	0.80
	Concealed	0	0	0.10	0.10	0.10
F1	Both groups	0.32	0.51	0.64	0.70	0.69
	Malicious	0.37	0.59	0.70	0.76	0.75
	Concealed	0	0	0.05	0.04	0.033

(c) After Adjustments

Measure	Doctor Group	Top 10	Top 20	Top 30	Top 40	Top 50
P	Both groups	1.00	1.00	1.00	0.90	0.76
	Malicious	0.80	0.70	0.77	0.65	0.56
	Concealed	0.20	0.30	0.23	0.25	0.20
R	Both groups	0.23	0.45	0.68	0.82	0.84
	Malicious	0.18	0.32	0.52	0.59	0.64
	Concealed	0.30	0.70	0.80	1.00	1.00
F1	Both groups	0.37	0.62	0.81	0.86	0.79
	Malicious	0.30	0.44	0.62	0.62	0.60
	Concealed	0.30	0.47	0.40	0.40	0.33

group of doctors that are among the top k users. We use F1 score, which is the harmonic mean of precision and recall, to measure the overall performance among different values of k.

6.2 Experimental Results

6.2.1 Malicious Doctors. The experimental results are given as doctor group *Malicious* in Table 2(a)(b). Our result for top 20 doctors is slightly lower in precision than Wang et al.'s but still approaches 70%. As for top 30, top 40 and top 50 doctors, our method has obtained the results which are very close to theirs in F1 score. As the single indicator of entropy is sensitive to malicious behaviors, Wang et al.'s method shows effectiveness in Top 20 malicious(not concealed) detection. But it is defeated by our method in general performance, since LDA could distinguish both types.

6.2.2 Concealed Doctors. The second experiment is designed to test the effectiveness of our solution over concealed doctors. Among the malicious doctors, 20% are concealed doctors who are adept at hiding the improper behaviors. The range parameter h for concealment behaviors is 0.6. The experimental results are given as doctor group *Concealed* in Table 2(a)(b). The results show that our risk-quantification method is a completely valid way of detecting

concealed doctors. As is disclosed in recall values, we successfully recognize all the concealed doctors in top 40 results. Meanwhile, Wang et al.'s method fails to recognize any of the concealment behaviors in top 20 and finds only 10% of concealed doctors in top 50 results.

6.2.3 Both Groups. In this experiment we test the effectiveness of our solution over two groups of doctors. We use the same database as described in the second experiment, which contains both malicious doctors(about 8%) and concealed doctors(about 2%). The experimental results are given as doctor group *Bothgroups* in Table 2(a)(b). As is revealed in precision, all top 30 and about 90% of top 40 are either malicious doctors or concealed doctors. The recall value shows about 70% of both groups of doctors have been distinguished from the dataset in the top 50 results. The results demonstrate that our method is effective for detection of malicious doctors and concealed doctors.

6.2.4 Improving Search Effectiveness. We analyse the influences of diverse topics on distinguishing different groups of doctors. A vector with equal weights on each document is defined as a useless weight vector. For example, $[0.1, 0.1, ..., 0.1]$ is a useless weight vector for 10 documents. That means, if all documents relate to topic i to an equal extent, then the topic-document vector for i is the useless weight vector.

We quantify a topic's importance as the non-similarity between its topic-document vector and the useless weight vector. In particular, we define the weight of a topic i as

$$Weight_i = D_{JS}(v_i||V) \qquad (8)$$

Where V is the useless weight vector and v_i is the topic-document vector respectively. $D_{JS}(v_i||V)$ refers to the value of JS divergence between the two vectors.

Table 2(c) shows the improvement on detection of malicious doctors. Only precision@10 slightly decrease, the general performance has improved as recall values and F1 scores have increased.

7 CONCLUSION

We propose a dynamic risk-adaptive access control scheme for health IT systems. By updating the risk scores and tolerance threshold periodically, this method provides a continuously available solution for the ever-changing medical environment. We adopt topic models to grasp the relationships between medical records and treatment tasks and achieve good performance in traditional scenes comparing to the existing work.

Our work have obtained an early application of topic models in access control. As data volume increases, we believe that further research on applying machine learning methods would help solve privacy issues and improve effectiveness of access control.

ACKNOWLEDGMENTS

The authors would like to thank Yaojie Lu for giving guidance on the formatting of this paper and the refinement of the pictures.

The authors would also like to thank the anonymous referees for their valuable comments and helpful suggestions. The work is supported by the National Natural Science Foundation of China under Grant No. 61402456 and No. U1636216, and the Science and Technology Projects of State Grid Corporation of China.

REFERENCES

[1] Kim Binsted, Alison Cawsey, and Ray B. Jones. 1995. Generating Personalised Patient Information Using the Medical Record. In *AIME '95 Proceedings of the 5th Conference on Artificial Intelligence in Medicine in Europe: Artificial Intelligence Medicine*. 29–41.

[2] David M. Blei. 2012. Probabilistic topic models. *Communications of The ACM* 55, 4 (2012), 77–84.

[3] David M. Blei, Andrew Y. Ng, and Michael I. Jordan. 2003. Latent dirichlet allocation. *Journal of Machine Learning Research* 3 (2003), 993–1022.

[4] Sofiene Boulares, Kamel Adi, and Luigi Logrippo. 2016. Insider Threat Likelihood Assessment for Access Control Systems: Quantitative Approach. In *International Symposium on Foundations and Practice of Security*. 135–142.

[5] Pau-Chen Cheng, Pankaj Rohatgi, Claudia Keser, Paul A. Karger, Grant M. Wagner, and Angela Schuett Reninger. 2007. Fuzzy Multi-Level Security: An Experiment on Quantified Risk-Adaptive Access Control. In *2007 IEEE Symposium on Security and Privacy (SP '07)*. 222–230.

[6] Mayur Datar, Aristides Gionis, Piotr Indyk, and Rajeev Motwani. 2002. Maintaining Stream Statistics over Sliding Windows. *SIAM J. Comput.* 31, 6 (2002), 1794–1813.

[7] Bent Fuglede and Flemming TopsÃÿe. 2004. Jensen-Shannon divergence and Hilbert space embedding. In *International Symposium onInformation Theory, 2004. ISIT 2004. Proceedings*. 31.

[8] I. Grosse, P. Bernaola-Galvan, P. Carpena, R. Roman-Roldan, J. Oliver, and H. E. Stanley. 2002. Analysis of symbolic sequences using the Jensen-Shannon divergence. *Physical Review E* 65, 4 (2002), 41905.

[9] Weili Han, Qun Ni, and Hong Chen. 2009. Apply Measurable Risk to Strengthen Security of a Role-Based Delegation Supporting Workflow System. In *2009 IEEE International Symposium on Policies for Distributed Systems and Networks*. 45–52.

[10] John R. Hershey and Peder A. Olsen. 2007. Approximating the Kullback Leibler Divergence Between Gaussian Mixture Models. In *2007 IEEE International Conference on Acoustics, Speech and Signal Processing - ICASSP '07*, Vol. 4. 317–320.

[11] Thomas Hofmann. 1999. Probabilistic latent semantic indexing. In *Proceedings of the 22nd annual international ACM SIGIR conference on Research and development in information retrieval*, Vol. 51. 50–57.

[12] Robert A. Israel. 2005. International Classification of Diseases (ICD). *Encyclopedia of Biostatistics* (2005).

[13] Pankaj Jalote, Aveejeet Palit, Priya Kurien, and V. T. Peethamber. 2004. Timeboxing: a process model for iterative software development. *Journal of Systems and Software* 70 (2004), 117–127.

[14] Kyoungyoung Jee and Gang Hoon Kim. 2013. Potentiality of big data in the medical sector: focus on how to reshape the healthcare system. *Healthcare Informatics Research* 19, 2 (2013), 79–85.

[15] Solomon Kullback. 1962. Information theory and statistics. *Population* 17, 2 (1962), 377.

[16] S Kullback and R A Leibler. 1951. ON INFORMATION AND SUFFICIENCY. *Annals of Mathematical Statistics* 22, 1 (1951), 0–0.

[17] Office Program M.C.Jason. [n. d.]. HORIZONTAL INTEGRATION: Broader Access Models for Realizing Information Dominance. ([n. d.]).

[18] Sartorius N, UstÃijn Tb, Korten A, Cooper Je, and van Drimmelen J. 1995. Progress toward achieving a common language in psychiatry. II: Results from the international field trials of the ICD-10 Diagnostic Criteria for Research for mental and behavioral disorders. *American Journal of Psychiatry* 152, 10 (1995), 1427–1437.

[19] Qun Ni, Elisa Bertino, and Jorge Lobo. 2010. Risk-based access control systems built on fuzzy inferences. In *Proceedings of the 5th ACM Symposium on Information, Computer and Communications Security*. 250–260.

[20] Geoffrey M. Reed. 2010. Toward ICD-11: Improving the Clinical Utility of WHO's International Classification of Mental Disorders. *Professional Psychology: Research and Practice* 41, 6 (2010), 457–464.

[21] Qihua Wang and Hongxia Jin. 2011. Quantified risk-adaptive access control for patient privacy protection in health information systems. In *Proceedings of the 6th ACM Symposium on Information, Computer and Communications Security*. 406–410.

[22] Liu Zhi-yong. 2007. Research and application of TimeBox development. *Technological Development of Enterprise* (2007).

"Kn0w Thy Doma1n Name": Unbiased Phishing Detection Using Domain Name Based Features

Hossein Shirazi
Computer Science Department
Colorado State University
Fort Collins, Colorado, USA
shirazi@colostate.edu

Bruhadeshwar Bezawada
Computer Science Department
Colorado State University
Fort Collins, Colorado, USA
bru.bezawada@colostate.edu

Indrakshi Ray
Computer Science Department
Colorado State University
Fort Collins, Colorado, USA
indrakshi.ray@colostate.edu

ABSTRACT

Phishing websites remain a persistent security threat. Thus far, machine learning approaches appear to have the best potential as defenses. But, there are two main concerns with existing machine learning approaches for phishing detection. The first is the large number of training features used and the lack of validating arguments for these feature choices. The second concern is the type of datasets used in the literature that are inadvertently biased with respect to the features based on the website URL or content. To address these concerns, we put forward the intuition that the *domain name* of phishing websites is *the tell-tale* sign of phishing and holds the key to successful phishing detection. Accordingly, we design features that model the relationships, visual as well as statistical, of the domain name to the key elements of a phishing website, which are used to snare the end-users. The main value of our feature design is that, to bypass detection, an attacker will find it very difficult to tamper with the visual content of the phishing website without arousing the suspicion of the end user. Our feature set ensures that there is minimal or no bias with respect to a dataset. Our learning model trains with only seven features and achieves a true positive rate of 98% and a classification accuracy of 97%, on sample dataset. Compared to the state-of-the-art work, our per data instance classification is 4 times faster for legitimate websites and 10 times faster for phishing websites. Importantly, we demonstrate the shortcomings of using features based on URLs as they are likely to be biased towards specific datasets. We show the robustness of our learning algorithm by testing on unknown live phishing URLs and achieve a high detection accuracy of 99.7%.

KEYWORDS

Phishing, Phishing detection, Domain name, Machine Learning, Biased datasets

ACM Reference Format:
Hossein Shirazi, Bruhadeshwar Bezawada, and Indrakshi Ray. 2018. "Kn0w Thy Doma1n Name": Unbiased Phishing Detection Using Domain Name Based Features. In *SACMAT '18: The 23rd ACM Symposium on Access Control Models & Technologies (SACMAT), June 13–15, 2018, Indianapolis, IN, USA.* ACM, New York, NY, USA, 7 pages. https://doi.org/10.1145/3205977.3205992

1 INTRODUCTION

1.1 Motivation

Phishing attacks continue to be of persistent and critical concern to users, online businesses and financial institutions. A phishing website lures users into divulging their sensitive information such as passwords, pin numbers, personal information, and credit card numbers, and uses such information for financial gains. According to current estimates, the annual financial losses due to phishing attacks surpasses $3 billion. Especially, for users, a phishing attack can mean a lot more than just financial losses as the loss of sensitive personal information has long term future ramifications as well.

The major problem in detecting phishing attacks is the adaptive nature of strategies used by the phishers. Generating a phishing website has not only become trivial, but also the attackers are able to bypass most defense strategies with relative ease. For instance, the evolution of *extreme phishing* [21], a complex form of phishing that targets the identity of users shows the severity and intensity of phishing attacks. Therefore, there is a need for developing phishing detection approaches that demonstrate robustness and resiliency against the adaptive strategies being used by the phishers.

1.2 Problem Statement

We focus on the general problem of determining if a target website is a phishing website or not, based on the standard definitions of a phishing website from literature [1, 5]. Typically, the content of a phishing website is textually and visually similar to some legitimate website. Based on this, the problem statement we examine is, to determine the features that quantify the attacker strategies in terms of the content found in the phishing website. Such features will be used to train a machine learning model to classify between phishing and legitimate websites.

1.3 Limitations of Past Work

Content-based approaches [3, 4, 7, 8, 10, 11, 14, 17, 18, 20] perform in-depth analysis of content and build classifiers to detect phishing websites. These works use features extracted from the page content as well as from third-party servers, search engines and DNS servers. However, these approaches are not efficient due to the large number of training features and the dependence on third-party servers. Using third-party servers violates user privacy. Furthermore, in most these approaches, except [10], there is a critical issue of using biased datasets (see Section 1.4 for detailed discussion) and the design of features that seem to work well for such datasets.

The URL-based approaches [2, 6, 9, 16] analyze various features based on the target URL such as length of the URL, page rank of the URL, presence of special characters in the URL, host name features like IP address, DNS properties, and geographic properties. While the intuition in these approaches is sound, *i.e.*, the URL is a good indicator of phishing attacks, the structural changes of modern day

URLs negates several lexical features identified by these approaches. For instance, these days, the URLs generated by websites like Google and Amazon, are long and contain many non-alphabetic characters, which dilute the lexical similarity of legitimate URLs. For this reason, the URL based approaches inadvertently tend to be biased towards the datasets being used and are likely to be ineffective in the future. A few hybrid detection mechanisms [15, 19] combine content and URL features, but suffer from the same problems.

1.4 Bias in Datasets

There are two reasons for bias in datasets: *dataset usage* and *URL based features*. First, to create a labeled dataset, many researchers [8, 14, 16–18, 20] used Alexa.com website to create the list of legitimate websites. Alexa.com publishes the list of highly ranked *domain names* and a researcher generates the dataset based *only* on the index pages of these ranked websites. But, for the phishing dataset, they used anti-phishing sites like PhishTank.com or Openphish.com, which list the entire URLs of the phishing web pages. For instance, many phishers use 000webhost.com, a free hosting service to host their phishing sites whereas this domain name itself is ranked highly in Alexa.com. For instance, for a feature defined as *number of sub-domains* in the URL, the legitimate URL instances obtained from Alexa.com will not have any sub-domains while many of phishing URL have sub-domains.

The second reason is that URL based detection [2, 6, 9, 16] does not guarantee good distinguishers between legitimate and phishing URLs. This is because adversaries have complete control over URL composition, excepting domain name, and can obfuscate against any number of measures. For instance, features like URL length, number of dots (".") in URL, presence of special characters *etc.* can easily be manipulated by phishers. In fact, this the reason for the high true negative rate (TNR) in existing works.

Except the work by Marchal *et al.* [10] where they used unbiased datasets made available by Intel security, no other work in literature has specifically addressed this concern. Furthermore, our work achieves similar classification accuracy with only seven features compared to the 200+ features used in [10].

1.5 Proposed Approach

Our work is the first solution to be entirely focused on the domain name of the phishing website. In our work, the domain name is the string before the top-level domain identifier, *e.g.*, for the URL google.co.uk, the domain name is google. We only concern ourselves with examining the landing page of this website, and with the information that can be extracted from this page without the help of third-party servers, search engines or DNS servers.

Our approach is based on the intuition that the domain name of the phishing websites is a key indicator of a phishing attack. We design several features that are based on the domain name and train a machine learning classifier based on sample data. The trained classifier is used to test a suspicious website against these features. Next, we describe the key challenges in our proposed approach and our solutions.

The primary challenge is to justify the design of domain name based features. Towards this end, first, we highlight the subtle distinctions between impact of the domain name and the URL of a phishing website. A phisher has much control over the formation and structure of the URL and therefore, can generate noisy URLs that can bypass most machine learning approaches. On the other hand, the phisher has limited control over the domain name, *i.e.*, the adversary can generate several types of URLs with the same domain, but the domain name remains fixed throughout. Second, domain name based features are likely to be more independent of the content in the phishing pages. The structure of the page layout, the HTML tags and the dynamic content will no longer be a major part of the detection algorithm. Third, a phishing domain name typically can contain additional characters or numbers to give the illusion of a legitimate website, *e.g.*, gooogle.com. These variations are subtle and are likely to provide sufficient statistical distinctions between legitimate and phishing websites. Hence, based on these arguments, we claim that the domain name based features are likely to exhibit more regularity than URL based features.

The next challenge is that the detection features could be data driven, that is, they can be biased with respect to the training data. To address this, our features mainly model the relationship between the domain name and the *visible content* of the web page. For instance, one feature calculates the rank of the domain name against all visible words on the web page, which is low for almost all phishing websites, as the attacker doesn't wish to reveal the suspicious domain name to the user. Importantly, such feature design ensures that an attacker finds it difficult to tamper with these features without arousing the suspicion of the user. But, designing such features is non-trivial and requires deep analysis of the phishing websites over a period of time. Therefore, for higher detection accuracy, we combine them with other statistical features based on observations of phishing domain names reported on PhishTank.com and from observations in existing research. Also, since our features are based on the domain names, we redesign the existing features to derive new features that correlate with the domain name of the website.

The penultimate challenge concerns the validity of the features. We performed a statistical validation against a small sample of the data to verify the utility of the features across the phishing and legitimate websites. We were able to eliminate several features and our final classifier consists of only seven features.

The final challenge is testing the resiliency of the domain based features to detect unknown or zero-day phishing attacks. To address this, we tested the classifier against a blacklist of URLs taken from the latest updates on OpenPhish.com. Our approach showed excellent resiliency and was able to detect up to 99.7% of the URLs.

1.6 Key Contributions

Our key contributions are: (a) We describe a machine learning (ML) based approach for phishing detection that relies entirely on domain name based features. Our approach is the first approach that has the combination of several benefits such as not using third party servers, search engines, suspicious words and URL specific features. (b) Our approach achieves 97% accuracy on a set of 2000 URLs with a five-fold cross-validation. (c) Our approach achieves 97-99.7% detection rate on live blacklist data from OpenPhish.com, validating our base hypothesis of bias in datasets and at the same time, demonstrating the remarkable robustness of our learning model against phisher induced noise. (d) The run-time detection speed of our approach is 4 times faster for legitimate websites and 10 times faster than the state-of-the-art work [10] in this domain. (e) We demonstrate the bias induced in the learning model by certain features, such as URL length, which raises the need for revisiting many of the existing works in literature.

2 RELATED WORK

Cui *et al.* [4] tried to find similarities between different attacks during a 10 month study by monitoring around 19000 websites. The study showed that 90% of phishing websites have similar HTML Document Object Model (DOM) structure and over 90% of these attacks were actually replicas or variations of other attacks in the database. Hong *et al.* [20] created a dataset to make use of the well-known term frequency inverse document frequency (TF-IDF) algorithm to find the top-5 important words in a web page and cross-checked using the Google® search engine. If the website appears in the very first list of results, then it is considered genuine.

Zhang *et al.* [18] created a framework using a Bayesian approach for content-based phishing web page detection. The model takes into account textual and visual contents to measure the similarity between the protected web page and suspicious web pages. But, this process is expensive and often results in false positives.

Ma *et al.* [9] described an approach on URL classification using statistical methods to discover the lexical and host-based properties of malicious web site URLs. They use lexical properties of URLs and registration, hosting, and geographical information of the corresponding hosts to classify malicious web pages at a larger scale. However, this approach requires a large feature set and extracts host information with the help of third-party servers.

Miyamoto *et al.* [12] provide an overview of nine different machine learning techniques and analyzed the accuracy of each classifier on the CANTINA dataset [20], reporting a maximum accuracy of 91.34% using AdaBoost. Abdelhamid *et al.* [1] experimentally compare large number of ML techniques on real phishing datasets with respect to different metrics.

Xiang *et al.* [17] proposed a layered anti-phishing solution with a rich set of features. They used machine learning techniques with 15 features, based on the HTML DOM structure, search engine capabilities, and third-party services, to detect phishing attacks. The key shortcoming of this approach is that the experiments were conducted with biased datasets as discussed in Section 1.4.

In 2015, Verma *et al.* [16] described an approach based on textual similarity and frequency distribution of text characters in URLs. For instance, they examined the character frequencies in phishing URLs and the presence of suspicious words as features. However, this approach is entirely based on URLs and is likely to be biased in the modern day context.

Jain *et al.* [8] described a machine learning based approach that extracts the features from client side only. However, their method of dataset creation is biased as discussed in Section 1.4.

Al-Janabi *et al.* [2] described a supervised machine learning classification model to detect the distribution of malicious content in online social networks (OSNs). These URLs direct users to websites that contain malicious content, phishing, and scams. Their features cannot be extracted locally and cannot guarantee the security of users outside of that network during regular browsing.

Recently, Marchal *et al.* [10, 11] propose a client-side detection approach using custom datasets from Intel security and tried to eliminate bias in datasets. However, their approach uses over 200+ features for classification, which indicates a significant time for feature extraction and classification.

There has been a rise in *extreme* phishing attacks [21] on financial institutions where the phishing website mimics the legitimate website to an alarming degree. The high level of noise in such websites is likely to defeat most content-based machine learning

approaches in the past. Compared to past work, our approach relies on a nominal set of features for classification and does not examine the content of the websites in depth.

3 DOMAIN NAME BASED FEATURES

In Figure 1, we demonstrate some of the distinguishing domain name based features of legitimate and phishing websites.

3.1 Feature Engineering and Validation

As far as possible, our feature design attempts to be content-agnostic, *i.e.*, the feature design attempts to model the principles of phishing attacks and reduce the dependence of the features on specific data values. Our feature set consists of two types of features: binary, *i.e.*, the feature value is 0 or 1, and non-binary, *i.e.*, the feature is real-valued. In summary, the key principle of our feature engineering is that, all features depend on the domain name of the website and the relationships, visual and statistical, of the domain name with the content of the website. These aspects ensure that our features are not affected by biased datasets and are robust to noise.

To validate the intuition behind each feature, we tested the empirical cumulative distribution function (ECDF) of the feature for 1000 phishing websites against 1000 legitimate websites. We show sample ECDF plots for a few features. We also indicate if the features are "New", meaning designed by us, or "Existing", meaning that other researchers have designed it.

3.2 Non-binary Features

3.2.1 Feature 1 (New) : Domain Length. The attackers who want to register domain for phishing have to choose longer domain name in comparison with the legitimate website. The length of domain name is the number of characters in the domain name string. As shown in Figure 2(a), the ECDF of this feature shows sufficient distinction between the legitimate websites and the phishing websites.

3.2.2 Feature 2 (Existing) : URL Length. The URL length is a popular feature among all known phishing detection approaches and is based on the intuition that phishing URLs are longer than legitimate URLs. We describe this feature here primarily to highlight the issue of dataset bias discussed in Section 1.4. In Figure 2(b), we show the ECDF of this feature. On the surface, it seems an excellent feature, however, it is completely data dependent and most existing works have generated results that are likely to be heavily influenced by the distribution of this feature in the phishing and legitimate datasets. We generated two sets of classification results: with and without the URL length, to demonstrate the impact of classification due to this feature. The average accuracy of classification increases by 2% because of this feature and reaches 99%, which matches the state-of-the-art result when only accuracy is considered. Furthermore, if the feature extraction time is also considered, we show that our results are better than the state-of-the-art.

3.2.3 Feature 3 (Existing) : Link Ratio in BODY. This feature is defined as the ratio of the number of hyper-links pointing to the same domain to the total number of hyper-links on the web page. The intuition is that, in the process of making a phishing website similar to the legitimate website, the attackers refer the hyper-links on the landing page to a legitimate domain name, which is different from the domain name displayed in the address bar of the browser. This feature is content-agnostic as the ratio can computed for any phishing website that exhibits this behavior. For example,

(a) Legitimate site

(b) Phishing site

Figure 1: Domain name features for legitimate and phishing websites

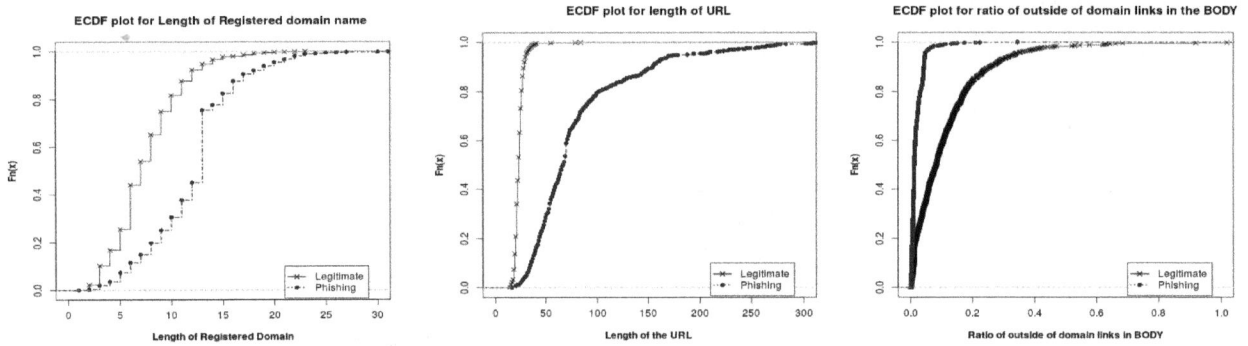

(a) Domain Name Length

(b) URL Length

(c) Link Ratio in BODY

Figure 2: Domain Name Length, URL Length, and Link Ratio in BODY

the phishers create a phishing page to mimic a well-known payment service where all links on the page are to a legitimate website except the login-form in which the users need to enter their information. Accordingly, the ratio of the links referring to current domain compared to all links found in the website will be different when compared between a phishing website and a legitimate website. To evaluate this feature, we find all of links in the page and the ratio of links referring to the current page over the number of all links found on the page. However, some legitimate websites also exhibited this behavior and therefore, we used a scaling process to derive the final value of the feature. For instance, if for a given website the ratio was in the range $[0.1, 0.2]$, we assigned the value 20 to this feature. Figure 2(c), shows the ECDF of this feature, of the raw ratios, with sufficient separation between the two distributions.

3.2.4 Feature 4 (New) : Frequency of Domain Name. This feature counts the number of times the domain name appears as a word in the visible text of the web page. The intuition is that many web pages repeat the domain name several times in their web page, as part of disclaimers, privacy terms and so on. Therefore, if the domain name does not appear at all in the web page, then there is something suspicious about such a web page. This is a key feature that captures the visual relationship of the domain name to the web page. In practice, we find this feature to be very indicative and useful in detecting phishing websites. Note that, for classification purpose, we converted this feature into a binary feature, *i.e.*, if the domain name does not appear in the web page, we set it to 0 and if it appears more than once, we set it to 1.

Table 1: Binary Feature Distribution

Feature	Legitimate	Phishing
HTTPS Present	0.92	0.23
Non-alphabetical Characters	0.05	0.36
Copyright Logo Match	0.26	0.0
Page Title Match	0.87	0.03

3.3 Binary Valued Features

Table 1 summarizes the percentage distribution of the binary features in the sample dataset.

3.3.1 Feature 5 (Existing) : HTTPS Present. An SSL certificate is issued for a particular domain name. Most legitimate websites used SSL certificates and operated over HTTPS protocol. Therefore, if a website uses HTTPS, the feature value is 1 and if not, it is 0. Recently, phishing websites are using HTTPS as well and this explains the relative high distribution.

3.3.2 Feature 6 (New) : Non-alphabetical Characters in Domain Name. Attackers use non-alphabetical characters, like numbers or hyphen, to generate newer phishing domain names, which are very similar to legitimate domain names. If the domain name has any non-alphabetic character, this feature is set to 1 and 0, otherwise. Past works [8, 16] have considered a variant of this feature, *i.e.*, they examined the number of special characters in the entire URL. However, as discussed earlier, generating customized noisy URLs is a relatively easy task for the attackers.

3.3.3 Feature 7 (New) : Domain Name with Copyright Logo. Many legitimate websites use the copyright logo to indicate the trademark ownership on their organization name. Usually, the domain name is placed before or after the copy right logo for such websites. To generate this feature, we considered up to 50 characters before and after the copyright logo, removed the white spaces, and checked for the presence of the domain name in the resulting string. Surprisingly, we found that none of the phishing websites placed their actual domain names along with the copyright logo. To do so, would have aroused the suspicion of any web user and therefore, we found this feature to be an excellent distinguisher.

3.3.4 Feature 8 (New) : Page Title and Domain Name Match. Many legitimate websites repeat the domain name in the title of web page. We found that many phishing websites used this feature to deceive users into believing that they were visiting legitimate websites. But, clearly, a phishing website would not use the phishing domain name in the title page as it would be clearly visible to the user. As shown in Table 1, our intuition proved right and we found that less than 3% of the phishing websites were using this feature, but over 87% of legitimate websites had this feature.

A Comparison with [10]. In [10], although the authors have alluded to the use of the domain name as *one* of the factors and described several features, they did not base their approach entirely on this aspect as we have done in our work. Some of the features common with our work are Feature 4, the frequency of occurrence of domain name, and Feature 8, the match of domain name with title along with some more domain name based features. Furthermore, the approach in [10] uses many other features, over 200, to perform the final classification and even ignored some domain name based features. For instance, they ignored Feature 7, domain name match with copyright logo, which we found very useful in detecting phishing websites.

4 EXPERIMENTAL EVALUATION

4.1 Experimental Methodology

We conducted two sets of experiments to assess the performance of our model trained with various machine learning classifiers. The first set of experiments were conducted on a prepared dataset and the second set of experiments were conducted on live unknown phishing dataset from OpenPhish.com. Only one past work [16] demonstrated a similar result on unknown datasets with a detection rate of 95%. In contrast, our approach achieves much higher detection accuracy, close to 99.7%.

During classification, total phishing websites correctly classified are denoted by, true positive (TP) and incorrectly classified as legitimate sites are denoted by, false negatives (FN), and total legitimate sites correctly classified are denoted by, true negatives (TN) and incorrectly classified as phishing websites are denoted by, false positive (FP). We report the standard classification metrics such as, positive predictive value, $PPV = \frac{TP}{TP+FP}$; true positive rate, $TPR = \frac{TP}{TP+FN}$; and accuracy, $ACC = \frac{TP+FN}{TP+FP+FN+TN}$. We show the time taken to extract the feature values for each website, the training time for each classifier, and the time taken by the classifier to predict whether a website is phishing or not.

We implemented our approach using the Sci-kit [13] library in Python 2.7 on a desktop running Fedora 24 OS with Intel Core® 2 Duo CPU E8300© 2.4 GHz processor with 6 GB RAM.

4.2 Datasets

For the list of legitimate websites, we obtained the 1000 top ranked websites from the Alexa.com and assumed them as legitimate. For the phishing websites, we got 1000 phishing websites from PhishTank.com and 2013 phishing websites from OpenPhish.com. Data was collected during the first week of January 2018.

Dataset 1: DS-1 This set includes 1000 legitimate websites from Alexa.com and 1000 phishing websites from PhishTank.com. In the experiments, we trained and tested on this dataset with 80% data for training and 20% data for testing using five-fold cross validation.

Dataset 2: DS-2 This dataset includes 1000 legitimate websites from Alexa.com and 3013 phishing websites from PhishTank.com and OpenPhish.com. For this dataset, we considered 1000 legitimate and 1000 phishing websites for training without cross-validation. The remaining 2013 websites were used for testing.

4.3 Experiment 1: Performance on DS-1

We designed two different experiments to evaluate the accuracy of classifiers on DS-1. In the first experiment, we used all the features described in Section 3 except URL length. In the second experiment, to show bias of URL based features, we included URL length and demonstrated the increase in classification accuracy. The URL length feature is one such biased feature that exhibits significantly different distribution for phishing and legitimate URLs, as phishing URLs are typically longer in publicly available datasets.

Results without URL Length Feature. *Our domain name based approach achieves 97% accuracy and validates our basic hypothesis.* We show the results in Figure 3. For each of the parameters, we show the maximum value achieved and the average value across all the validations. Gradient Boosting performed the best with a maximum accuracy of 99.55% percentage and an average accuracy of 97.74%. For Gradient Boosting and Majority Voting, the TPR is very high, 98.12% and 97.46%, respectively, and so is the PPV, 97.8% and 97.55%, respectively, showing the high phishing detection capability of the classifiers. We note that, our average accuracy of 97.74% is very high when compared several existing works that used a rather large and diverse set of features.

Results with URL Length Feature. *This feature results in higher accuracy and clearly demonstrates the bias due to the dataset.* We show the results of these experiments in Figure 4. There is an increasing trend across all the classifiers for all the parameters considered. There is clear increase in PPV where four classifiers reported an average of 98% and above with Majority Voting reporting 99%. Excepting Gaussian Naive Bayes, all other classifiers recorded an average TPR of 98% and above, with the maximum of 100% for three classifiers. The accuracy also showed an increasing trend with the average accuracy increasing to 98.8% for Gradient Boosting, and the maximum accuracy of 99.55% for several other classifiers. This experiment clearly shows that features like URL length tend to impact classification accuracy depending on the dataset.

4.4 Timing Analysis for DS-1

Feature Extraction Timings. *Our feature extraction time is very low, of the order of few milli-seconds, and demonstrates the efficiency of our feature set.*

Table 2 shows the results of our feature extraction. The total time for extracting features of a legitimate website is about 0.117 seconds and for a phishing website is 0.02 seconds, which indicates the real-time nature of our approach. This is extremely low compared to the

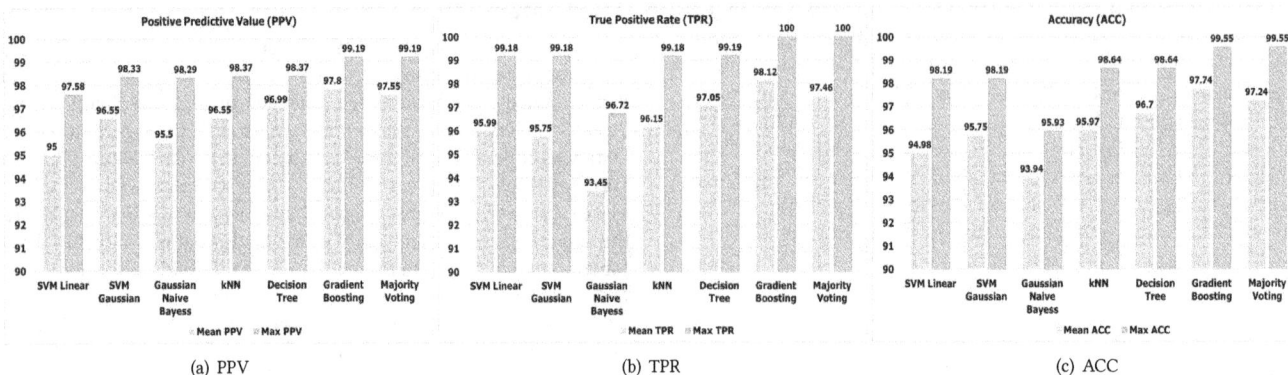

Figure 3: PPV, TPR and ACC on DS-1 without URL Length Feature

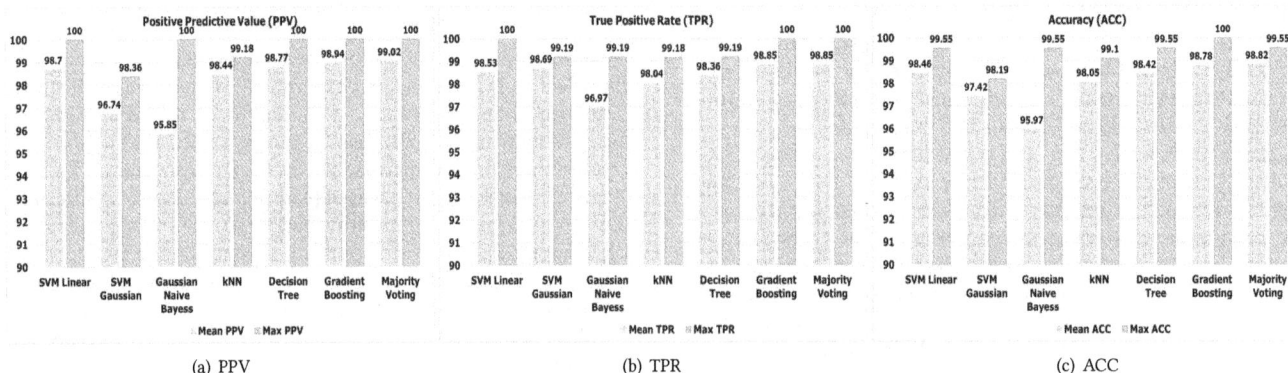

Figure 4: PPV, TPR and ACC on DS-1 with URL Length Feature

state-of-the-art approach in [10] where the extraction time was in the order of a few seconds. We emphasize that the average loading time of a web page like msn.com, is around 1 second and our feature extraction adds only a few milliseconds overhead to this process.

Training and Classification Timings. *Our classifier training and classification times are very low, of the order of few micro-seconds, and again demonstrates the efficiency of our approach.*

The testing times reported are the average across the five-fold cross validation and do not include the feature extraction time. The training can be done off-line and the testing takes a few microseconds to perform, after the feature extraction. Given that cumulative time for feature extraction and testing is less than 2 milliseconds, we claim that our approach can be deployed in practice as a client-side browser plug-in.

4.5 Experiment 2: Performance on DS-2

In this experiment, we examine robustness of our learning approach on unknown and unseen data. We obtained a list of 2013 live phishing websites from OpenPhish.com. Although, a higher number of sites were listed, many sites were unavailable and few were blocked by the corresponding ISPs. We trained the classifier in two modes: without including the URL length feature and with the URL length feature included. Finally, we tested the resulting classifier on the 2013 data instances and show the results in Table 4. These results show the remarkable performance of our approach. Unlike the previous approach [16], which attempted a similar experiment, for many of our classifiers, the TPR largely remains *unchanged* across

both the experiments and even shows a slight increase for Decision tree and Gradient Boosting classifiers. Furthermore, when including URL length, the TPR even reaches 99.7%(!) for kNN and Gradient Boosting. This result also confirms our hypothesis that domain name based features can accurately capture the nature of a phishing website.

4.6 Comparison with Previous Work

We compare our results empirically with existing state-of-the-art solutions in Table 5. Our basis for comparison is the number of features, the accuracy, whether client-side features only are used or third-party features are included and average accuracy. We did not include the run-times of the approaches as that is a system specific metric. However, we note that our scheme reports micro-second level feature extraction and classification time, even when run on a relatively low performance laptop with Core 2 Duo processor.

5 CONCLUSION

In this work, we described the first approach towards the design of *only* domain name based features for detection of phishing websites using machine learning. Our feature design emphasized on the elimination of the possible bias in classification due to differently chosen datasets of phishing and legitimate pages. Our approach differs from all previous works in this space as it models the relationship of the domain name to the intent of phishing. With only seven features we are able to achieve a classification rate of 97% with cross-validated data. Furthermore, we were able to show a detection rate of 97-99.7% for live black-listed URLs from OpenPhish.com.

Table 2: Feature Extraction Timings

Feature	Legitimate (μs)	Phishing (μs)
HTTPS Present	4.12	3.87
Domain Length	63.45	66.45
Page Title Match	26.9	32.3
Frequency Domain Name	333.8	33.09
Non-alphabetic Characters	32.64	13.68
Copyright Logo Match	2737.56	450.48
Link Ratio in Body	114482.87	19445.67
URL Length	0.3576	0.5066
Total Time (in seconds)	0.117	0.02

Table 3: Training/Testing Timings

Classifier	Train (in ms)	Test (in μs)
SVM Linear	1339.85	6.74
SVM Gaussian	703.62	38.32
Gaussian Naive Bayes	2.28	1.47
kNN	7.36	14.85
Decision tree	2.49	0.80
Gradient Boosting	2737.56	450.48
Majority Voting	177.73	3.25

Table 4: True Positive Rate for DS-2

Classifier	Without URL Length	With URL Length
SVM Linear	94.09	94.24
SVM Gaussian	92.75	90.81
Gaussian Naive Bayes	91.06	92.75
kNN	93.74	**99.7**
Decision tree	97.91	97.27
Gradient Boosting	**98.21**	**99.75**
Majority Voting	95.33	97.67

Table 5: Comparison with State-of-the-art Approaches

Approach	♯ of Legitimate sites	♯ of Phishing Sites	♯ of features	Accuracy	Client Side
Cantina [20]	2100	19	7	96.97	No
Cantina+ [17]	1868	940	15	97	No
Verma *et al.* [16]	13274	11271	35	99.3	Partial
Off-the-Hook [10]	20000	2000	210	99.9	Yes
Our approach without URL Length	1000	3013	7	97.7	Yes
Our approach with URL Length	1000	3013	8	98.8	Yes

This shows that our approach is able to adapt to the complex strategies used by phishers to evade such detection mechanisms. As our features explore the content found in the visible space of the web page, an attacker will need to put a huge effort to bypass our classification. In trying to bypass our approach, an adversary may end up designing a page that will make any user suspicious. Furthermore, we demonstrated the shortcoming of using URL features such as URL lengths, that seem to give higher accuracy but may not do so in the near future. Our feature extraction and classification times are very low and show that our approach is suitable for real-time deployment. In future, we wish to explore the robustness of machine learning algorithms for phishing detection in the presence of newer phishing attacks. We are also developing a real-time browser add-on that will provide warnings when visiting suspicious sites.

ACKNOWLEDGEMENT

This work was supported in part by funds from NSF under Award No. CNS 1650573, CableLabs, AFRL, Furuno Electric Company, and SecureNok.

REFERENCES

[1] Neda Abdelhamid, Fadi A. Thabtah, and Hussein Abdel-jaber. 2017. Phishing Detection: A Recent Intelligent Machine Learning Comparison Based on Models Content and Features. In *Proc. of the IEEE Int. Conf. on Intelligence and Security Informatics (ISI).* 72–77.

[2] Mohammed Al-Janabi, Ed de Quincey, and Peter Andras. 2017. Using Supervised Machine Learning Algorithms to Detect Suspicious URLs in Online Social Networks. In *Proc. of the IEEE/ACM Int. Conf. on Advances in Social Network Analysis and Mining (ASONAM).* 1104–1111.

[3] Ram B. Basnet, Srinivas Mukkamala, and Andrew H. Sung. 2008. Detection of Phishing Attacks: A Machine Learning Approach. In *Soft Computing Applications in Industry. Studies in Fuzziness and Soft Computing.* Vol. 226. Springer, 373–383.

[4] Qian Cui, Guy-Vincent Jourdan, Gregor V Bochmann, Russell Couturier, and Iosif-Viorel Onut. 2017. Tracking Phishing Attacks over Time. In *Proc. of the Int. World Wide Web (WWW) Conf.* 667–676.

[5] Z. Dou, I. Khalil, A. Khreishah, A. Al-Fuqaha, and M. Guizani. 2017. Systematization of Knowledge (SoK): A Systematic Review of Software-Based Web Phishing Detection. *IEEE Communications Surveys Tutorials* 19, 4 (2017), 2797–2819.

[6] Sujata Garera, Niels Provos, Monica Chew, and Aviel D Rubin. 2007. A Framework for Detection and Measurement of Phishing Attacks. In *Proc. of the ACM Workshop on Recurring Malcode (WORM).* ACM, 1–8.

[7] R. Gowtham and Ilango Krishnamurthi. 2014. A Comprehensive and Efficacious Architecture for Detecting Phishing Webpages. *Computers and Security* 40 (2014), 23–37.

[8] Ankit Kumar Jain and B. B. Gupta. 2017. Towards Detection of Phishing Websites on Client-side Using Machine Learning Based Approach. *Telecommunication Systems* (December 2017), 1–14.

[9] Justin Ma, Lawrence K. Saul, Stefan Savage, and Geoffrey M. Voelker. 2009. Beyond Blacklists: Learning to Detect Malicious Web Sites from Suspicious URLs. In *Proc. of the ACM Int. Conf. on Knowledge Discovery and Data Mining (KDD).* ACM, 1245–1254.

[10] Samuel Marchal, Giovanni Armano, Tommi Grondahl, Kalle Saari, Nidhi Singh, and N. Asokan. 2017. Off-the-Hook: An Efficient and Usable Client-Side Phishing Prevention Application. *IEEE Trans. on Computers* 66, 10 (2017), 1717–1733.

[11] Samuel Marchal, Kalle Saari, Nidhi Singh, and N Asokan. 2016. Know Your Phish: Novel Techniques for Detecting Phishing Sites and Their Targets. In *Proc. of IEEE Int. Conf. Distributed Computing Systems (ICDCS).* IEEE, 323–333.

[12] Daisuke Miyamoto, Hiroaki Hazeyama, and Youki Kadobayashi. 2008. An Evaluation of Machine Learning-based Methods for Detection of Phishing Sites. In *Proc. of the Int. Conf. on Neural Information Processing (ICONIP).* Springer, 539–546.

[13] Fabian Pedregosa, Gaël Varoquaux, Alexandre Gramfort, Vincent Michel, Bertrand Thirion, Olivier Grisel, Mathieu Blondel, Peter Prettenhofer, Ron Weiss, Vincent Dubourg, and others. 2011. Scikit-learn: Machine Learning in Python. *Journal of Machine Learning Research* 12, Oct (2011), 2825–2830.

[14] Routhu Srinivasa Rao and Alwyn Roshan Pais. 2018. Detection of Phishing Websites using an Efficient Feature-based Machine Learning Framework. *Neural Computing and Applications* (January 2018).

[15] Choon Lin Tan, Kang Leng Chiew, KokSheik Wong, and San Nah Sze. 2016. PhishWHO: Phishing webpage detection via identity keywords extraction and target domain name finder. *Decision Support Systems* 88, C (2016), 18–27.

[16] Rakesh Verma and Keith Dyer. 2015. On the Character of Phishing URLs: Accurate and Robust Statistical Learning Classifiers. In *Proc. of ACM Conf. on Data and Applications Security and Privacy (CODASPY).* 111–122.

[17] Guang Xiang, Jason Hong, Carolyn P. Rose, and Lorrie Cranor. 2011. CANTINA+: A Feature-Rich Machine Learning Framework for Detecting Phishing Web Sites. *ACM Trans. Information and Systems Security (TISSEC)* 14, 2 (September 2011), 1–28.

[18] Haijun Zhang, Gang Liu, Tommy W. S. Chow, and Wenyin Liu. 2011. Textual and Visual Content-Based Anti-Phishing: A Bayesian Approach. *IEEE Trans. on Neural Networks* 22, 10 (2011), 1532–1546.

[19] Wei Zhang, Qingshan Jiang, Lifei Chen, and Chengming Li. 2017. Two-stage ELM for Phishing Web Pages Detection Using Hybrid Features. *World Wide Web* 20, 4 (2017), 797–813.

[20] Yue Zhang, Jason I Hong, and Lorrie F Cranor. 2007. Cantina: A Content-based Approach to Detecting Phishing Web Sites. In *Proc. of the World Wide Web (WWW) Conf.* ACM, 639–648.

[21] Rui Zhao, Samantha John, Stacy Karas, Cara Bussell, Jennifer Roberts, Daniel Six, Brandon Gavett, and Chuan Yue. 2017. Design and Evaluation of the Highly Insidious Extreme Phishing Attacks. *Computers & Security* 70 (2017), 634 – 647.

A blockchain-based Trust System for the Internet of Things

Roberto Di Pietro
HBKU-CSE
rdipietro@hbku.edu.qa

Xavier Salleras
UPF
xavier.salleras@upf.edu

Matteo Signorini
Nokia Bell Labs
matteo.signorini@nokia.com

Erez Waisbard
Nokia Bell Labs
erez.waisbard@nokia.com

ABSTRACT

One of the biggest challenges for the Internet of Things (IoT) is to bridge the currently fragmented trust domains. The traditional PKI model relies on a common root of trust and does not fit well with the heterogeneous IoT ecosystem where constrained devices belong to independent administrative domains.

In this work we describe a distributed trust model for the IoT that leverages the existing trust domains and bridges them to create end-to-end trust between IoT devices without relying on any common root of trust. Furthermore we define a new cryptographic primitive, denoted as *obligation chain* designed as a credit-based Blockchain with a built-in reputation mechanism. Its innovative design enables a wide range of use cases and business models that are simply not possible with current Blockchain-based solutions while not experiencing traditional blockchain delays. We provide a security analysis for both the obligation chain and the overall architecture and provide experimental tests that show its viability and quality.

CCS CONCEPTS

• **Security and privacy → Access control**; **Distributed systems security**;

KEYWORDS

IoT, Blockchain, Distributed Ledger, Access Control, Security

ACM Reference Format:
Roberto Di Pietro, Xavier Salleras, Matteo Signorini, and Erez Waisbard. 2018. A blockchain-based Trust System for the Internet of Things. In *SACMAT '18: The 23rd ACM Symposium on Access Control Models & Technologies (SACMAT), June 13–15, 2018, Indianapolis, IN, USA.* ACM, New York, NY, USA, 7 pages. https://doi.org/10.1145/3205977.3205993

1 INTRODUCTION

The true potential of the Internet of Things (IoT) will be unleashed when billions of devices are be connected to the Internet, and able to interact with each other. However, while it is true that more and more devices are becoming connected [4], the grand vision

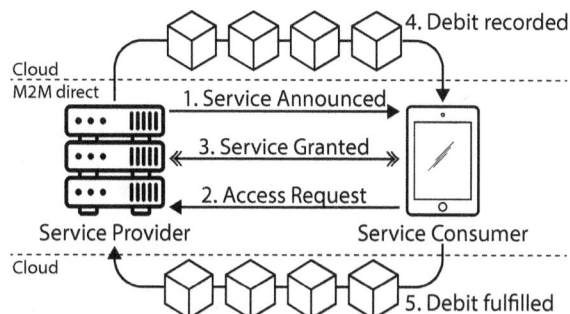

Figure 1: Our solution in brief.

of IoT is still far from being achieved since these devices do not communicate with each other mainly due to a lack of trust between devices, which is essential for establishing secure communication. Indeed, the trust model that works well for the Internet does not fit the scale and diversity of the IoT, where there is no common root of trust. Instead, we see different domains in which manufacturers create a root of trust that allows devices within each single domain to communicate securely. We refer to these domains as *Islands of Trust*, where the trust is provided and regulated by an entity independent from those administering other domains.

Industry consortia such as the Open Connectivity Foundation (OCF) [8] attempt to solve this problem by agreeing on a common root of trust but do not cover the entire IoT landscape. As a result, the current IoT consists individual manufacturers and platforms that can communicate securely only if they agree on a common root of trust (e.g. through a consortium) or if they establish direct mutual trust through bilateral agreements.

In this work we take a new approach for bridging trust between the above domains (i.e. the islands) by leveraging blockchain technologies [5] to create a distributed trust mechanism. We start by introducing a new tool, named *Obligation Chain*, which is a new platform for a distributed credit-like system (in contrast to the cash-like Bitcoin [11]). Furthermore, our credit system has a built-in reputation mechanism [13] that allows peers to decide whether or not to accept obligations based on the credit history of a consumer. Figure 1 shows an overview of our main scheme in which a service provider interacts with a service consumer providing real time services while postponing the obligation fulfillment.

The benefits of our construction can best be seen through the following use case: a service provider offers a service, together with its terms of use. For example, let us consider a small coffee-shop that wishes to offer WiFi services for customers (for an additional fee). Currently, major operators and major coffee chains have bilateral agreements that allow this, but there is no solution that fits any small/family run coffee-shops. We would like to have a solution that allows anyone to consume these services simply by providing a public obligation for fulfilling the terms of use as specified by the service provider. Following good practices, the service provider is not expected to automatically accept an obligation from anyone, but it is expected to first assess the risk of accepting that obligation. Naturally, a large part of potential consumers might not have enough reputation to access the service. This is indeed where many reputation systems fail in practice [9] and this is why our system goes a step further to leverage existing trust. In the above example, we have leveraged the trust these users already have with their mobile operator and the fact that the mobile operator already has a well established reputation. Furthermore there is already a full fledged public key infrastructures (PKIs) in place mediating between the mobile operator and its customers. By bridging trust between the coffee shop and the mobile operator, we are able to provide a complete path of trust between any customer of the mobile operator and the service provider.

The coffee shop simply needs to publish the terms of use for accessing the WiFi service. Any large mobile operator that wishes to grant free access of the WiFi services to its customers can sign an obligation to fulfill the terms of use. The users would get the signed obligation based on their existing trust relationship with their operators. The users would then present the signed obligations to the coffee shop that would need to decide whether or not to grant access based on the public credibility of the signing operator. As the entire history of obligation fulfillment is available on the immutable blockchain, the service provider can make its decision of whether or not to accept the obligation. If the obligation is accepted and later fulfilled then the service provider would report it on the blockchain. By doing so, it would increase the operators' credibility.

The solution described in this paper allows every service provider to conduct its own assessment based on the credit history of the obligation's signer, the service value and any other element it could deem relevant. Thus, one service provider may decide to accept an obligation from a certain consumer, while another one may not. Furthermore it has the flexibility to offer complex business models that may depend on the actual consumption of the service while requiring minimal capabilities from the end devices.

The rest of this paper is organized as follows. In Section 2 we summarize the building blocks leveraged in this paper. In Section 3 we introduce the core elements and main concepts defined in this solution, paving the way to Section 4, where we describe our solution. In Section 5 we provide a security analysis of our solution and compare its performances against the well-known Bitcoin system (the measurements are done over our reference implementation[1] that was developed in the context of the production of the paper[6] and is available on GitHub). Section 7 concludes the paper.

2 BACKGROUND

Trust is generally perceived as a belief that an entity is honest and will not harm other entities. This belief is subjective and based on

[1] https://github.com/xevisalle/IslandsOfTrust

past experiences. On the other hand, reputation is a global perception of an entity's behavior based on the trust that other entities have established [13]. The goal of a Trust and Reputation System (TRS) is then to guarantee that actions taken by entities in a system reflect their reputation values and cannot be manipulated by unauthorized entities [2, 3, 12]. TRSs can be generalized as composed by entities, observers, disseminators and reputation servers [9] and have been shown to be threatened by different attacks [9]. In this paper, we focus on how to design a blockchain based TRS which allows for bridging of trust between secure domains.

2.1 Blockchain Technology

In the last few years, a new technology named *Blockchain* [5, 18] which first emerged with Bitcoin [11], has had great success in many areas. This technology can be roughly described as a digital ledger that sits at the core of decentralized ecosystems and keeps track of any changes by holding a new record for each transaction. In a more abstract way, the blockchain can be seen as an ordered and back-linked list of blocks carrying transactions which encode exchanged information between two or more participants. Each block consists of a collection of transactions and is linked to the previous block in the blockchain, thus creating a chronological order of blocks that all together build a chronological order of transactions.

3 SETTINGS AND DEFINITIONS

The main goal of our solution is to build an access control system that leverages consumers' reputation and that is used by service providers. To this end, our basic setup is made by a *service provider* (SP) and a *service consumer* (SC). Given a SCD seeking to access some service from a SPD we seek to establish trust between the SCB and SPB and then pass that trust down to the devices. The scenario can be enriched in complexity, but for the sake of exposition we will stick to the simple model just introduced. Each of the two entities has access to powerful *back-ends* and more constrained *end-devices* (respectively SPB/D and SCB/D). All internal communications inside the SP and the SC are secured leveraging the existing trust within the same Island of Trust (i.e. same domain) while external communications between SP and SC are secured using our solution.

Symbol	Description
SP	service provider
SPD	service provider end-device
SPB	service provider back-end server
SC	service consumer
SCD	service consumer end-device
SCB	service consumer back-end server

Table 1: Table of symbols

SC and SP has a self-generated public key, used to sign messages and as an ID, recognized by others. The reputation is associated with this ID. We stress that in our solution there is no certification authority (CA) that manages these IDs. Instead, they are self-generated within each Island of Trust and may be replaced at any time. However, as explained in the rest of this paper, both SCs and SPs are usually keen to keep the same IDs as needed to claim their reputation. SPs and SCs mainly cooperate by exchanging *terms of use* (TERMS) and *obligations*. The former are created by service providers and signed by both service providers and consumers. They are here intended as rules that SCs must agree to abide to in order to access services provided by SPs. The latter are tokens leveraged by SCs to publicly state that all the conditions listed within TERMS will be fulfilled as *per* what has been specified by SPs.

As usual in life, building a good reputation is much harder than ruining it, which mitigates the attack where an SC builds a good reputation over a long time only later sign an obligations it does not intend to fulfill. We note that reputation is built on honored obligation thus wandering on the security of the bootstrap phase. Luckily, bootstrapping in trust and reputation management systems has been extensively treated in the literature in the past (for instance, in the context of P2P systems). And the topic is also being addressed by leveraging blockchain technologies [1].

4   OUR SOLUTION

We now show how TERMS and obligations can be used by SPs and SCs to set up trusted interactions between untrusted devices. To this end, we have designed a new blockchain named *obligation chain* that is linked to to another blockchain and used to build a tamper-proof reputation system. In this section we first introduce this new chain and then describe how we have leveraged it to bridge the different islands of trust (i.e. different domains).

4.1   Obligation Chains

Being based on the blockchain technology, our obligation chain is eventually agreed upon by the whole network. It can be seen as a distributed ledger storing obligations of commitments signed by SCs to access SPs' services without immediately paying for them. For the sake of simplicity, we can imagine our obligation chain as an append only log database where obligations and TERMS are kept. However, unlike other solutions, our chain does not contain digital assets which have to be recognized and verified by other peers at run-time (as for bitcoins in the Bitcoin blockchain). Indeed, our obligation chain contains obligations that are *locally* accepted by SPs and then shared to the rest of the network via the same SP.

Obligations are generated by SCBs and initially contain only the TERMS and their signature. They are then downloaded to SCDs which will later exchange them, in the form of an obligation transaction, to get access to services provided by SPs. Obligation transactions contain, among others: the TERMS which have been previously published by SPBs and agreed to by SCBs, a unique ID of the obligation and all the signatures provided by SP/SC entities.

Obligation transactions are leveraged to keep track (on the chain) of the agreements that are established (off the chain) between SCs and SPs. As such, as both SCs and SPs built their reputation on the chain, they both need tools to prevent fraudulent interactions. On the one hand, the proof of commitment described above is the tool used by SPs against malicious SCs. On the other hand, the *proof of*

fulfillment is the tool we have designed for honest SCs which have to protect themselves against malicious SPs.

The proof of fulfillment has been realized by linking our obligation chains with standard blockchains. Obligations' fulfillment is not public since obligations are accepted locally by SPs. As such, a TERM signed by SP_i and SC_j serves as a proof that SC_j owes some money to SP_i. Nothing else is needed by others SPs to decide on SC_j reputation. It would have been also possible to use smart contracts within a single blockchain. However, although using smart contract is indeed a possibility that does not change the framework set by the proposed solutions, our solution does not require smart contracts which are more costly and limited to certain platforms.

For the sake of simplicity, we will consider a toy example in which services provided by SPs need some kind of payment in order to be accessed. To this end, throughout the rest of the paper, we have put forward the Bitcoin solution as a concrete example to cite. However, as we describe in the remaining of this section, our solution is agnostic with respect to the payment solution and the adopted technology and it can be applied to any other blockchain. Furthermore, it is also important to highlight that the validity of an obligation and the acceptance of the transaction containing that obligation are different concepts. Obligations are accepted if signed appropriately by the participating parties. Namely, by the SCB, SCD and SPD. If the transactions is created and signed by SP_i, since the obligation validity is locally taken, then the transaction per-se is considered valid.

As detailed in Section 4.2, the update of SCs' reputations might be synchronous and/or asynchronous. On the one hand, in the asynchronous approach, SPs cannot always remain updated on both the obligation and the Bitcoin blockchains. As such, they connect to them and download new blocks only when they need to update service consumers' reputation scores. As an example, the first time that a given service consumer C approaches a service provider requires the latter to read the obligation and bitcoin chains from their origin in order to bootstrap C's reputation. Contrariwise, for all those service consumers for which a service provider does not have updated info on their reputations, only the new blocks need to be accessed. On the other hand, in the synchronous (or Cached) approach, SPs always receive the latest obligation and Bitcoin blocks in the chains. As such, there is no need to build the local reputation scores for their service consumers from scratch. Hence, given a service consumer C only new blocks in which C's obligations and payments are stored will need to be downloaded.

4.2   Islands of Trust

Now that we have described the obligation chain and how it is leveraged to store SCs' obligations, we can introduce the concept of *bridging the trust* between different islands of trust, i.e. different secure domains. In our solution, we assume that each island of trust has a full local PKI and CA. Such a PKI is not recognized or trusted by other islands and it is only used for the internal device management. However, PKI information (such as the public keys) are used as publicly available IDs. Reputations are built on top of such IDs. Furthermore, we assume that each device has a certificate that was issued by its local CA and that is used to secure the communications between end-devices and back-ends within the same island. Each device belonging to either the SPB or the SCB can be uniquely identified by them thanks to unique IDs.

The protocol that we have designed for the trust bridging is a three-way handshaking protocol composed by *setup*, *spend*, and *fulfilling* phase. During the *setup*, SCBs generate (and sign) obligations based on the TERMS published by SPBs. These obligations are passed to SCDs to be used when interacting with SPDs. In the *spend* phase, end-devices coming from both SPs and SCs interact with each other and exchange their own version of TERMS. If they match, the obligations created in the *setup* phase are passed to the SPB. If the SPB decides to accept the obligations based on the local SC's reputation score, the SCD receives access to the service from SPD and its obligations are broadcast to the rest of the network to be included in the obligation blockchain. In the final step, SCs make a connection between the Bitcoin and the obligation chain by paying for them. This final step causes all the local reputation scores within all the SPs to be updated which also increases the likelihood of SC's new obligations to be accepted in the future. It has to be noted that even though a PKI and CA is used to access the blockchain, such access can be multi-tenant (as provided by IBM Hyperledger). As such, no root of trust is needed to provide SPs with a tool to compute local SC reputation scores.

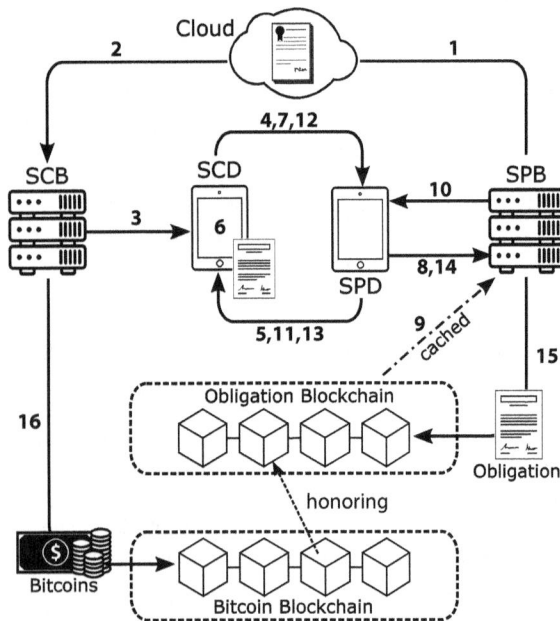

Figure 2: Protocol Overview.

Figure 2 depicts our three-way handshaking protocol and highlights each individual operation executed by both SC and SP entities (both end-devices and back-ends). In our proof of concept we implemented SPB and SCB to be miners, both for Multichain and Bitcoin. However, as for all the current blockchain-based systems, this is a matter of choice. SPB and SCB might be either miners or clients. The latter assumes other peers are maintaining the chain. The complete flow is as follows (see also Figure 3):

(1) The SPB publishes the TERMS[2] with all the required details (e.g. the price);

(2) The SCB downloads SP TERMS and creates obligations. The obligations contain all the details written within the TERMS and are signed by the SCB;

(3) The above obligations are downloaded within the SCDs that intend to use them;

(4) The SCD sends a service request to the SPD ;

(5) The SPD sends the TERMS to the SCD;

(6) The SCD compares the TERMS to the ones in its obligation to ensure they match;

(7) If the TERMS match the SCD passes the obligation to the SPD, otherwise it ABORT;

(8) The SPD sends the obligation to its SPB;

(9) The SPB looks at the obligation chain and payment chain to assess the credibility of the obligation issuer. Depending on the approach being used (which can be either *synchronous* or *asynchronous* as described above) a complete bootstrap or an update of the consumer's reputation are executed accordingly. The result is an updated knowledge of SC's trustworthiness. This result is local to the SP that is computing it and is based on an arbitrary trust score evaluation which is beyond the scope of this work. The SPB also verifies the signature w.r.t. the public key of the issuer;

(10) If the signature is valid, the TERMS match, and the SPB decides to trust the SC based on his obligations history and thus his reputation, then the SPB sends an OK to the SPD. Otherwise, it sends ABORT. SPB also generates and sends back to the SPD a new payment address. As we are considering the toy example of a service provisioning that requires Bitcoin payments, this new address will be a new Bitcoin address. This address needs to be sent back to the SCD and SCB as it will be later used to fulfill the obligation;

(11) The SPD either conveys the reply to the SCD, if it has received an OK from its SPB, or it ABORT the protocol;

(12) The SCD signs the obligation;

(13) The SCD passes the signed obligation to the SPD (this is to allow the SCB to keep track of used obligations);

(14) The SPD verifies the SCD signature. If the signature is valid, then it gives access to the service otherwise ABORT;

(15) The SPD signs the obligation just received from the SCD;

(16) The SPD sends its signature back to the SCD (to serve as a receipt of the transaction);

(17) The SPD conveys the signed obligation to the SPB;

(18) The SPB broadcasts the obligation to the other peers in the obligation chain network in order for the obligation to be added in the obligation chain;

(19) The SCB periodically monitors the obligation chain looking for its obligations which are then fulfilled by issuing payment transactions to the exact Bitcoin addresses that have been created by the SPB at step 9. This allows the SP to monitor those addresses and to detect new bitcoin incomes. The result

---

[2]We do not specify exactly how these TERMS are published. We envision them to be posted on the service provider's web site, but any other solution would do. We also note that the TERM may change over time and that the SCB is the solely responsible for keeping track of changes.

is for the SP to remove the pending obligation from its internal database, thus also updating the SC's reputation.

It is again important to highlight that, whilst all the aforementioned steps are executed at run-time, the step number 8 can also be executed off-line in the *asynchronous* mode (see Section 4.1 for more details). In this mode, SPs can update SCs' reputations each time they receive a new block head for the obligation chain. This makes the whole process faster as SPs are already aware of SCs' reputations even before they receive new SCs' requests. During our experimental tests we have used the asynchronous mode as it represents the worst case scenario—the SP has to rebuild the consumer's reputation every time. However, even in the worst case scenario our solutions proved to be faster than standard blockchain based payment systems such as Bitcoin.

One of the main advantages of this solution is that service providers and consumers do not have to explicitly establish a contractual agreement. SPs publish the possible business models as part of their TERMS while SCs pick the ones that best suit their needs. Then the decision on whether or not to accept the obligations is left to the SPs. Another key advantage of the proposed solution is the establishment of self-enforced and tamper-resistant reputations. Indeed, as we are assuming that SCs and SPs do not know each other in advance, they can judge each other's trustworthiness only based on the reputations stored within our obligation chain. In this work the reputation is meant as the average of obligations fulfilled on time. This information is accessible to anyone having access to both the obligation blockchain and the Bitcoin blockchain as it is only required to check how many obligations have been fulfilled by using the new Bitcoin addresses created in step 9 of our protocol. Hence, peers with a high frequency of interactions with others will create many obligations and will need to fulfill them as established with the SP. If they do so, they will have a good reputation, otherwise they will not. Furthermore, TERMS also contain the time by which the payment needs to be completed. A consumer that does not pay or that delays the payment will lose credibility and will be rejected by others in the future.

4.3 Privacy

So far we argued about the benefits of having all transactions publicly recorded as part of a distributed reputation platform. However, this also raises some privacy concerns. As such, we have used encryption to provide confidentiality of the obligations between the parties by encrypting TERMS. Naturally SPs and SCs would both have the keys to decrypt TERMS and their signatures. However, keeping the keys solely between a SP and a SC would not enable others to assess the reputation of the latter. Thus, when a SC approaches a new SP, he would need to disclose the decryption keys (which is also used nowadays when users need to present their bank records and credit history when asking for a loan).

This enables the new SP to see SC's good credit history while also allowing the latter to hide bad credit history. We solved such a problem by publishing the obligations that were not fulfilled in an unencrypted form (i.e. along with their keys) and linking them to the previous encrypted ones. The result is that some obligations are encrypted (i.e. revealed by SCs only to the right SPs) while all the non-fulfilled obligations are public.

5 ANALYSIS

5.1 Security

Trust and reputation systems (TRS) have been suggested as an effective security mechanism for open and distributed environments. However, it has also been shown that such mechanisms can be threatened by different attacks as described by Fraga et al. [9] who identified information gathering, calculation and dissemination attacks. Based on such classification, we have analyzed attacks in our solution that might threaten i) how SPs gather information on SCs, ii) how SPs access the obligation blockchain and make decisions on SCs' reputations as well as iii) how it is possible to thwart the process in which SCs' information is shared among SPs.

As a first result it has to be noted that, all the attacks targeting observers, reputation servers, or entities in classical TRSs, do not apply here as they are part of the islands. Hence, as defined in Section 3, those elements belong to a single domain and thus assumed secure. Furthermore, even attacks based on data manipulation do not apply due to the blockchain technology. However, other classical (i.e. non TRS specific) attacks might still occur. *Privilege escalation* might be one of those in which a malicious SC creates and uses a big set of obligations to build a temporary good reputation for malicious purposes. Our solution mitigates this attack as new obligations do not affect SC's reputation until a payment is validated within the Bitcoin chain that links to it.

A complementary attack might also be unleashed in the presence of operators that refuse to endorse their clients thus producing a denial of service (DoS) attack. Although this theoretically is a possibility, it already exists in current systems (e.g. Gmail denying access to the inbox of some clients). However, in this setting it is unlikely that rational service providers will be keen on compromising their reputation by playing a DoS on their users or cheating them since their own (social) reputations could be jeopardized. Still this is an interesting point to address in future works. Ballot stuffing attacks can be easily mitigated as well via obligations' fees or watch-dog systems. This will reduce the incentive for the attacker to generate fake transactions and detect them within the chain.

A full and detailed comparison against the state of the art in TRS attacks will be given in the extended version of our paper.

5.2 Performance

In this section we present a performance analysis of our solution on the time required for SPs to compute SCs' reputations where the creation and validation of obligations have been accomplished by using the *SigningKey*, *SECP256k1* and *VerifyingKey* python functions from the *ecdsa* library. This analysis is indeed required to show if, as expected, the proposed solution provides a virtual zero-latency user experience. The above test has been conducted in the worst case scenario (the one in which SPs have to always rebuild SCs' reputation from scratch) and compared it to the Bitcoin best case scenario (i.e. the smallest block acceptance delay witnessed in the last year). To implement such a worst case scenario, we have automated 1460 handshake protocols between a SC and a SP (i.e. the Bitcoin blocks created between Oct. 2016 and Sept. 2017).

The results clearly showed that our acceptance delay is always shorter than Bitcoin even in the case in which all the 1460 new

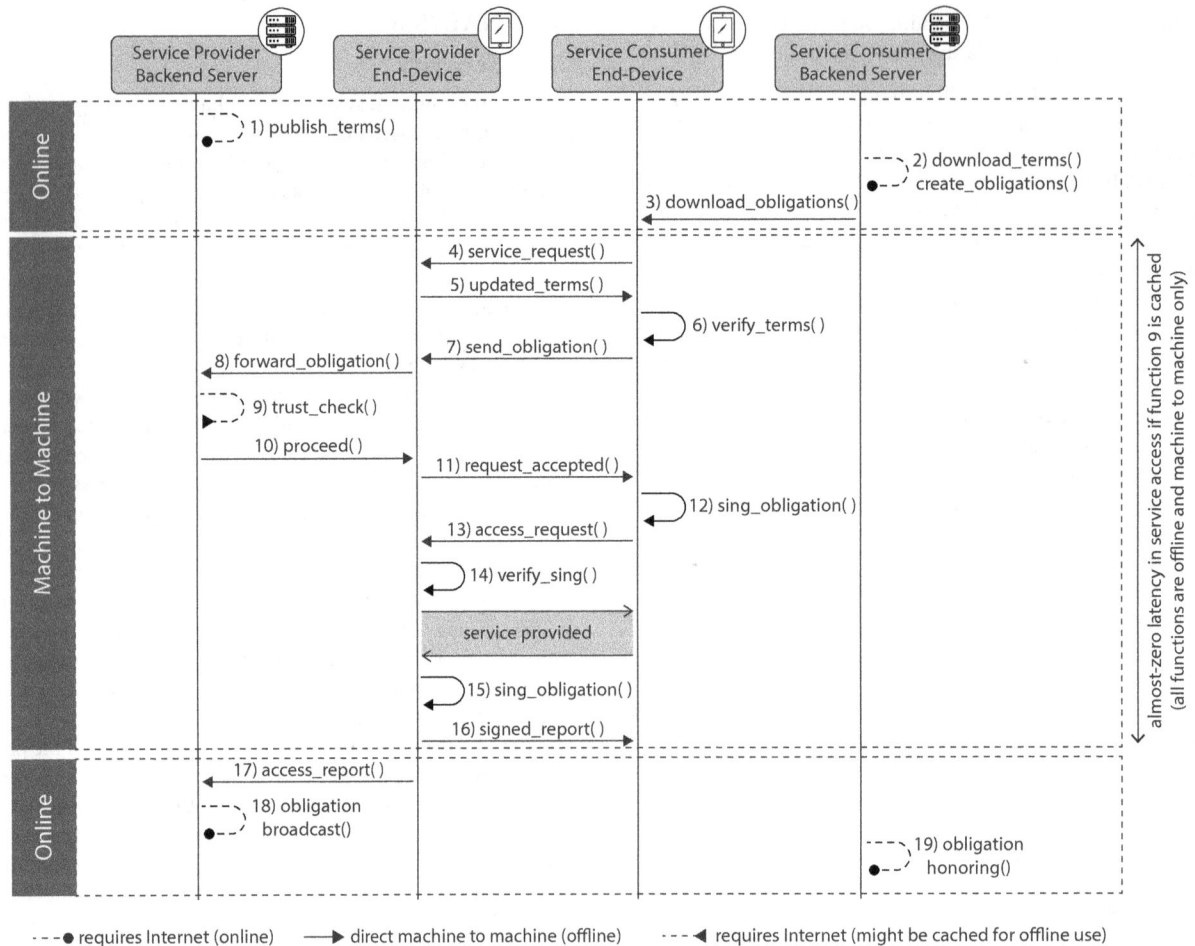

Figure 3: Protocol sequence diagram.

obligations are verified at the same time (we refer to the asynchronous approach described in Section 3). Indeed, checking the reputations of 1460 service consumers took as much time (6.9 minutes) as needed by Bitcoin to add a single block to the chain. Taking also into account that a new Bitcoin block usually requires one hour to be considered valid and that updating SCs' reputations in a synchronous environment (see Section 3) only required less than a second, finally shows that we have achieved a zero latency user experience.

6 RELATED WORK

Recently, in the academic world, there is a trend towards redesigning rating systems (i.e. TRSs) given the rise of the new blockchain era. As examples, Schaub et al. [15] and Soska-Christin [16] have both designed users' privacy-aware solutions based on the blockchain technology. However, the aforementioned approaches were not focused on TRS specific attacks but rather on general blockchain vulnerabilities. In this paper we are more focused on reputation attacks such as *rating frauds* in which a malicious user tries to seek inappropriate profits from the system. Such attacks occur both in

content-driven and non-computational TRS systems but can be mitigated by using the blockchain technology as a source of immutable and non-repudiable rating information.

In the last few years, different proposals have been published to that end. Dennis et al. [14] proposed a solution in which the human rating factor (usually associated to *feedback*) has been removed. The result is a binary rating system in which either the service has been provided or not. Such an approach, however, weakens the rating system as it removes the *service quality* aspect. Indeed, the final goal of TRSs is to help SCs in understanding sellers. As such, if we only keep track of whether the product/service has been delivered, we will lose other factors and information which are as important as the delivery. In our solution we create commitments on the service quality which are signed by both SPs and SCs. As such, although we use a binary feedback (an obligation can be either fulfilled or not fulfilled) we maintain services' quality information within the obligation.

Other works tried to mitigate rating fraud by raising rate costs. This approach has been largely used in the past for standard TRSs. As examples, Douceur et al. prevented sybil attacks by binding accounts to unique IPs [7] while Yu et al. [17] increased the difficulty in controlling multiple accounts. Another example of raising costs or complexity has been designed by Yosang and Ismail [10]. In this solution, raters are encouraged to provide honest rates by sharing incomes with them. However, such kind of solutions are not effective if the perceived benefit from the attacks is greater than its cost. In traditional Cloud services (such as *Amazon.com* or *Expedia.com*), this problem is solved by using *verified transaction* labels but requires trust to be centralized.

The immutable and eventually agreed database held by the blockchain technology can be used to mitigate the aforementioned rating attacks. As an example, Schaub et al. [15] proposed an interesting approach against bad mouthing attacks. In their solution, they kept the user feedback while allowing only peers who actually received tokens from seller to rate them. Compared to this approach, our solution solves the same problem but with a different perspective. Indeed, whilst Schaub et al. try to protect SCs from malicious SPs, we defend the latter from frauds. The main reason why we focus on this open challenge is that our solution is based on credits. As such, SPs accept *payment obligations* and make a decision on whether to trust the SC. Unlike what has been proposed by Schaub et al. in which SCs can take their time before making transactions with SPs, we need to take immediate (i.e. zero latency) decisions. In our scenario, SPs do not know at what time SCs will contact them and do not even know their identities. Still, they want to accept obligations while being sure to not be cozen.

TRSs can also be threatened by *ballot stuffing* sybil attacks in which the service provider colludes with SCs to gain reputations. Usually, these attacks leverage small fraudulent purchases. As such, a traditional way to mitigate them is to remove the *verified purchase* label on top of discounted transactions. As shown by Schaub et al., the blockchain technology can be used against ballot stuffing attacks as well. However, in their solution, SPs are limited in the number of tokens (feedback) that can be used. Although this approach was proved to be effective (as it creates a trade-off between ratings and profit), it limits the overall business model. In our solution we do not assume any limitation on the number of obligations that can be created by SCs and accepted by SPs.

7 CONCLUSION

In this paper we have shown a solution that enables trust establishment among devices belonging to different domains. In particular, our solution is suited for the IoT context, given its unique features of being fully decentralized, and requiring both security and negligible overhead on end devices. These features are achieved in our proposal by leveraging the idiosyncratic properties of blockchain technologies, combined with a new architecture design that avoids the pitfalls inherited by this technology, while unleashing its advantages. In particular, as the performance of our implementation shows, all the above features are achieved in a very efficient way, and significantly faster when compared to the standard Bitcoin based solution —hence enabling those use cases that otherwise could not work when facing long delays.

It is worth noting that our solution supports rich and flexible business models and use cases. Indeed, by allowing a seamless level of trust and cooperation among actors belonging to different domains, it removes entry-barriers to service providers thus introducing a disruptive degree of innovation. Finally, the obligation chain enables a wide range of credit based use cases.

We believe that the flexibility of our solution in supporting different business models, its degree of innovation, combined with its efficiency and overall deployability has a clear potential for opening further research threads in the highlighted directions.

ACKNOWLEDGMENT

We like to thank Louis Shekhtman for his help in improving the editorial quality of this paper.

REFERENCES

[1] Muneeb Ali, Jude Nelson, Ryan Shea, and Michael J. Freedman. 2016. *Bootstrapping Trust in Distributed Systems with Blockchains*. Technical Report. Blockstack.
[2] Sulin Ba and Paul A. Pavlou. 2002. Evidence of the Effect of Trust Building Technology in Electronic Markets: Price Premiums and Buyer Behavior. *MIS Quarterly* 26, 3 (sep 2002), 243.
[3] Gary E. Bolton, Elena Katok, and Axel Ockenfels. 2004. How Effective Are Electronic Reputation Mechanisms? An Experimental Investigation. *Management Science* 50, 11 (nov 2004), 1587–1602.
[4] V. Daza, R. Di Pietro, I. Klimek, and M. Signorini. 2017. CONNECT: CONtextual NamE disCovery for blockchain-based services in the IoT. In *2017 IEEE International Conference on Communications (ICC)*. IEEE, Paris, France, 1–6.
[5] Christian Decker and Roger Wattenhofer. 2013. Information propagation in the Bitcoin network. In *IEEE P2P 2013 Proceedings*. Institute of Electrical and Electronics Engineers (IEEE), Trento, Italy, 1–10.
[6] Roberto di Pietro, Xavier Salleras, Matteo Signorini, and Erez Waisbard. 2018. A blockchain-based Trust System for the Internet of Things - Extended. https://cri-lab.net/wp-content/uploads/2018/04/IslandsOfTrust-Clean.pdf
[7] John R. Douceur. 2002. The Sybil Attack. In *Revised Papers from the First International Workshop on Peer-to-Peer Systems (IPTPS '01)*. Springer-Verlag, London, UK, UK, 251–260.
[8] Open Connectivity Foundation. 2017. Online: https://openconnectivity.org/.
[9] D. Fraga, Z. Bankovic, and J.M. Moya. 2012. A Taxonomy of Trust and Reputation System Attacks. In *2012 IEEE 11th International Conference on Trust, Security and Privacy in Computing and Communications*. Institute of Electrical and Electronics Engineers (IEEE), Liverpool, UK, 41–50.
[10] Audun Josang and Roslan Ismail. 2002. The beta reputation system. In *In Proceedings of the 15th Bled Conference on Electronic Commerce*. Electronic Commerce Center, Bled, Slovenia.
[11] Sergio Martins and Yang Yang. 2011. Introduction to Bitcoins: A Pseudo-anonymous Electronic Currency System. In *Proceedings of the 2011 Conference of the Center for Advanced Studies on Collaborative Research (CASCON '11)*. IBM Corp., Riverton, NJ, USA, 349–350.
[12] Do-Hyung Park, Jumin Lee, and Ingoo Han. 2007. The Effect of On-Line Consumer Reviews on Consumer Purchasing Intention: The Moderating Role of Involvement. *International Journal of Electronic Commerce* 11, 4 (jul 2007), 125–148.
[13] Paul Resnick, Ko Kuwabara, Richard Zeckhauser, and Eric Friedman. 2000. Reputation systems. *Commun. ACM* 43, 12 (dec 2000), 45–48.
[14] Dennis Richard and Owenson Gareth. 2016. Rep on the Roll: A Peer to Peer Reputation System Based on a Rolling Blockchain. *International Journal of Digital Society (IJDS)* 7 (3 2016), 1123–1134.
[15] Alexander Schaub, Rémi Bazin, Omar Hasan, and Lionel Brunie. 2016. A Trustless Privacy-Preserving Reputation System. In *ICT Systems Security and Privacy Protection*. Springer Nature, Cham, 398–411.
[16] Kyle Soska and Nicolas Christin. 2015. Measuring the Longitudinal Evolution of the Online Anonymous Marketplace Ecosystem. In *Proceedings of the 24th USENIX Conference on Security Symposium (SEC'15)*. USENIX Association, Berkeley, CA, USA, 33–48.
[17] Haifeng Yu, Michael Kaminsky, Phillip B. Gibbons, and Abraham Flaxman. 2006. SybilGuard: Defending Against Sybil Attacks via Social Networks. In *Proceedings of the 2006 Conference on Applications, Technologies, Architectures, and Protocols for Computer Communications (SIGCOMM '06)*. ACM, New York, NY, USA, 267–278.
[18] Guy Zyskind, Oz Nathan, and Alex' Sandy' Pentland. 2015. Decentralizing Privacy: Using Blockchain to Protect Personal Data. In *2015 IEEE Security and Privacy Workshops*. Institute of Electrical and Electronics Engineers (IEEE), San Jose, CA, USA, 180–184.

Distributed Usage Control Enforcement through Trusted Platform Modules and SGX Enclaves

Paul Georg Wagner
Karlsruhe Institute for Technology,
Karlsruhe, Germany
paul.wagner@student.kit.edu

Pascal Birnstill
Fraunhofer IOSB, Karlsruhe, Germany
pascal.birnstill@iosb.fraunhofer.de

Jürgen Beyerer
Fraunhofer IOSB, Karlsruhe, Germany
juergen.beyerer@iosb.fraunhofer.de

ABSTRACT

In the light of mobile and ubiquitous computing, sharing sensitive information across different computer systems has become an increasingly prominent practice. This development entails a demand of access control measures that can protect data even after it has been transferred to a remote computer system. In order to address this problem, sophisticated usage control models have been developed. These models include a client side reference monitor (CRM) that continuously enforces protection policies on foreign data. However, it is still unclear how such a CRM can be properly protected in a hostile environment. The user of the data on the client system can influence the client's state and has physical access to the system. Hence technical measures are required to protect the CRM on a system, which is legitimately used by potential attackers. Existing solutions utilize Trusted Platform Modules (TPMs) to solve this problem by establishing an attestable trust anchor on the client. However, the resulting protocols have several drawbacks that make them infeasible for practical use. This work proposes a reference monitor implementation that establishes trust by using TPMs along with Intel SGX enclaves. First we show how SGX enclaves can realize a subset of the existing usage control requirements. Then we add a TPM to establish and protect a powerful enforcement component on the client. Ultimately this allows us to technically enforce usage control policies on an untrusted remote system.

CCS CONCEPTS

• **Security and privacy** → **Access control**; *Privacy-preserving protocols*; *Digital rights management*; *Information flow control*;

KEYWORDS

Usage Control, Access Control, Trusted Reference Monitor, Trusted Platform Module, SGX, Secure Remote Computation

ACM Reference Format:
Paul Georg Wagner, Pascal Birnstill, and Jürgen Beyerer. 2018. Distributed Usage Control Enforcement through Trusted Platform Modules and SGX Enclaves. In *SACMAT '18: The 23rd ACM Symposium on Access Control Models & Technologies (SACMAT), June 13–15, 2018, Indianapolis, IN, USA.* ACM, New York, NY, USA, 7 pages. https://doi.org/10.1145/3205977.3205990

1 INTRODUCTION

Most modern computer systems rely on mechanisms that can restrict the access to certain system resources like files and services. Especially in the context of mobile and ubiquitous computing, digitally managing the access to sensitive information clearly plays an essential role in designing data processing systems that are both secure and privacy friendly. Traditional access control models are generally implemented through a reference monitor that is invoked whenever a subject requests access to a particular object. The reference monitor then evaluates available access control policies and enforces the resulting access control decision on the subject. However, for some use cases it is not sufficient to merely control the access to information once at the time of data request. Sometimes a generalized model is necessary that can continuously monitor and control the actual *usage* of information over an extended period of time. Such a model includes solutions to many questions of digital rights management (DRM) and it may also allow for the implementation of privacy enhancement technologies that monitor and control the usage of personal data after it has been released. To adequately reflect these important requirements, Park and Sandhu [8] developed the notion of usage control (UC). Furthermore, distributed usage control models have been proposed [9] that tackle the problem of transferring information across different usage control domains. In these scenarios, the data access should be continuously controlled on a remote computer system even after the data has left the domain of the data provider. In order to achieve this, the data provider deploys usage control policies to a client-side reference monitor (CRM) before the data access is granted on the server. Afterwards the CRM is responsible for enforcing the deployed policies on the data. The policies that should be enforced on the client side can be of different nature.

- Restricting access: The user of the client system should only be allowed to access the files in certain situations or at certain times.
- Usage control: The user of the client system may be allowed to access the data, but their use is restricted. For example, the user should not be able to disseminate the data further.
- Secure computation: The user must never access the transmitted data directly. Instead, a trusted module on the client side performs a computation on the data, after which the user can get access.

While most usage control models focus on policies that mainly reflect the former two cases, the latter is of great use when implementing privacy protecting mechanisms. For example, a provider of personally identifiable information could issue usage control policies that enforce data anonymization on the client before the critical information is used otherwise. With powerful usage control models already established, it is still an open question how to implement and protect a client-side reference monitor in a possibly hostile environment. Previous suggestions utilize Trusted Platform Modules (TPMs) to establish a trusted computing base, but this solution has drawbacks and is not sufficient to appropriately protect the transmitted data. This work proposes a CRM implementation that establishes trust by using TPMs along with Intel SGX enclaves running on an untrusted system. Ultimately this allows us to technically enforce usage control policies on a remote system, whose user we do not trust. In section 2 we will present existing propositions of a CRM design, which are based on TPMs, and discuss their drawbacks. In section 3 we present a simple CRM design that uses the well researched secure remote computation features of Intel SGX. However, this design cannot enforce arbitrary usage control policies. Afterwards in section 4 we generalize the design by adding another TPM, which yields a solution that can enforce all mentioned usage control policies. We finally conclude in section 5.

2 RELATED WORK

Implementing a reference monitor in a possibly hostile environment requires a Trusted Computing Base on the target system. This can be achieved by a Trusted Platform Module (TPM). A TPM is a dedicated hardware chip that extends a computer with basic security related features [6]. It uses volatile platform configuration registers (PCRs) to *measure* the current hardware and software configuration as an unforgeable hash. This allows the system to *seal* confidential data to a certain TPM state. Furthermore, remote parties can verify that the target system is in a certain state by *attesting* to certain PCR values. Hence a TPM can be used to protect system components in an untrusted environment.

Sandhu and Zhang [11] introduced the notion of a trusted reference monitor (TRM) inside the client-side operating system. The TRM is a reference monitor that operates in an untrusted environment, but is protected from external modification by a TPM. Implemented as a kernel module, the TRM is part of the measurement chain during the boot process. Before transmitting any data or policies, the data provider remotely attests to the PCR values of the client system. Only if the remote system is in a trustworthy state (i.e. the TRM is unmodified and running), information is transmitted. Since we focus on implementing a trusted reference monitor on client systems, in the following sections we will use TRM and CRM synonymously. Based on the work of Sandhu and Zhang, Sevinç et al. [12] developed a protocol that relies on a TPM to remotely verify the integrity of the client software stack. In this protocol, secrets are only transmitted to the client if the attestation is successful and the remote system can show the correct PCR values. Furthermore, the server binds the secret data to a key that is sealed to the required PCRs. That way the transmitted data can only be unsealed and used as long as the client system is in a trustworthy state. However, by relying only on TPMs, Sevinç's protocol has several drawbacks that have not yet been addressed. For example, the TPM cannot distinguish between trusted and untrusted processes. Even in trusted system states (i.e. the TRM is running and has not been tampered with) there will be untrusted user processes active in the system. In that case only trusted processes, such as the TRM itself, should be able to unseal the data. If the sealed data is intercepted during transmission, or is in any way available later on, any user process can request the TPM to unseal the data if only

the PCRs still have the correct values. This bypasses TRM control on a software level. In order to distinguish trusted from untrusted processes, the TRM design may include operating system based protection mechanisms, such as access rights on files and directories. There are techniques available to include executable content and security extended file attributes into the TPM measurement chain, such as the integrity measurement system and the extended verification module for Linux [10]. However, since in this case the user of the client system is an attacker, TPM based mechanisms are not sufficient to protect the sealed data that way. The user can mount the hard drive and access the sealed data in a secondary operating system. Even though the sealed data cannot be unsealed in this untrusted system state, the user can still make a copy of the encrypted data without changing the original file meta data. When booting the unmodified operating system, the PCRs are filled with the correct values and the user can unseal the copied data.

To conclude, the proposed solutions for a secure TRM implementation rely on establishing trust using a TPM, but are not sufficient to properly protect the transmitted data. This is mainly a result of the attacker model, which includes valid users of the client system itself, who can use the TPM, launch untrusted system processes and have physical access to the hardware.

3 IMPLEMENTATION WITH INTEL SGX

Intel's Software Guard Extensions (SGX) consist of a set of processor instructions extending the x86 architecture, along with special hardware that is included in newer Intel CPUs. SGX can provide integrity and confidentiality, even if privileged software such as the operating system is malicious. This is achieved by executing user code in a protected container called *enclave*, which cannot be accessed by other user processes or even by the operating system itself. The enclave is executed by trusted hardware and is isolated from the rest of the system (reverse sandboxing). It uses encrypted memory to protect the confidentiality of data and can verify the integrity of the code by communicating with the Intel Attestation Service (IAS). Because the runtime state of the enclave cannot be influenced from the outside, SGX represents a trusted computing design. SGX allows to encapsulate critical software, for example cryptographic libraries or key management services, in protected shells that will behave in expected ways. Architectural details of SGX and a comprehensive analysis of its security is provided in [5].

3.1 Secure Remote Computation

SGX has been designed to ease the implementation of secure remote computation. Secure remote computation is the problem of using a remote computer, owned by an untrusted party, to perform some computation on certain confidential data. In our case a remote service provider needs to provision secrets to untrusted clients, who run trusted code inside an enclave. Before transmitting the data, the service provider has to convince himself that he is communicating with a certain enclave, which is running in a secure environment. With SGX-enabled processors, this can be achieved by initiating a remote attestation process. This process consists of four phases [1].

(1) *Enclave Launch*: The untrusted system launches code inside an enclave. During the launch, code and data are cryptographically hashed. This hash is called the enclave's *measurement*.

(2) *Attestation*: The enclave contacts the remote service provider and signals that it is ready for provisioning. The enclave produces a signed quote that includes the enclave measurement. This quote is sent to the service provider.

(3) *Provisioning*: The service provider verifies the quote by contacting the IAS. This ensures that the service provider is indeed communicating with the correct enclave. The service provider uses the attestation protocol to establish a secure channel to the enclave and transmits the sensitive data.

(4) *Sealing/Unsealing*: The enclave receives the sensitive data and seals it to its current state. Sealed data is encrypted and can be securely stored outside the enclave (e.g. in files). It can only be decrypted by the same enclave in the same state.

After the attestation process, the enclave received all necessary data and performs the desired computations while protecting both confidentiality and integrity. The necessary secure channel is established by a modified Sigma protocol that facilitates a Diffie-Hellman Key Exchange (DHKE) between the enclave and the service provider. During the remote attestation process the enclave sends a quote containing its enclave measurement to the service provider. The service provider forwards the quote to the IAS, where it can be verified. If the quote verifies correctly, the service provider is confident that he communicates with the right enclave (measurement is correct) and that only the enclave knows the established Diffie-Hellman key. Both parties can then derive a symmetric secret from the Diffie-Hellman key and use it to encrypt their communication for the provisioning phase. In [7] the remote attestation protocol is explained in greater detail. A similar protocol is also possible between two enclaves that reside on one SGX platform. This is called *local attestation*. It can be used to locally verify the integrity of another enclave and establish a secure channel between them.

3.2 TRM Design

Trusted Reference Monitors can be implemented on SGX-enabled processors by using the remote attestation functionality. The TRM is realized as a trusted enclave that is running on the client. A data provider (DP) can remotely attest to the identity and integrity of the enclave (via the IAS), and hence establish trust in the remote reference monitor. The sigma protocol instance authenticates the channel and gives both sides a shared secret, which the data provider uses to encrypt the data. The untrusted software on the client acts as a man in the middle, but can neither decrypt nor modify any messages between enclave and data provider. Once the secure channel has been established, the data provider deploys the signed access control policies at the remote TRM and transmits the encrypted data. On the client side, the enclave verifies the signature of the policies and seals the received data. Untrusted processes can request data access at the enclave, which evaluates the policies and enforces the resulting access control decisions. Figure 1 shows the resulting sequence of data request, transmission and access control enforcement at the client. Of course, the TRM can also enforce complex access control policies that require computation on the data before access can be granted. For example, a provider of personally identifiable information can instruct the TRM to remove personal information from the data for certain requests.

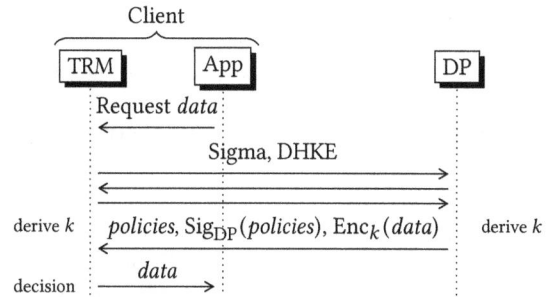

Figure 1: TRM implementation with SGX.

3.3 Security Analysis

In terms of the attacker model we have to distinguish between *internal* and *external* attackers. Internal attackers are the untrusted parts of the client system, outside the trusted enclave. This includes any untrusted user process running on the client, as well as privileged software like the operating system. The goal of internal attackers is to bypass the policy enforcement and directly access the protected data without access control restrictions. External attackers reside outside the client system and can intercept and modify messages between the data provider and the client. Their goal is to extract information about the protected data from the exchanged messages.

Based on this attacker model, the security of the TRM design immediately reduces to the design of the SGX remote attestation procedure as well as the security of the used cryptographic schemes. The integrity of the enclave code is ensured because the data provider verifies the quote containing the enclave measurement with the IAS. Only the TRM enclave is able to generate a quote that is correctly signed. An internal attacker, who tampers with the TRM code before launching the enclave, changes the enclave measurement in the process, which will fail the quote verification step on the data provider. The communication channel between the data provider and the trusted enclave is established by the sigma protocol. The resulting channel is authenticated by digital signatures provided by the enclave and the data provider. The data provider signs his messages with his private key. The enclave can verify the signatures by using the data provider's public key that is usually hard coded into the enclave software. Since the public key is part of the enclave code, its integrity is protected by the enclave measurement. The enclave is authenticated by the correct quote signature. The quote contains the public part of an asymmetric key pair that the enclave generated for communicating with the data provider. This key is used for authenticating further messages to the data provider. Furthermore, a shared Diffie-Hellman key is established between the enclave and the data provider. Since the channel is authenticated, no external or internal attacker is able to intercept the Diffie-Hellman key exchange and hence does not know the shared secret after the sigma protocol finishes. Under the assumption that the key derivation function and the used encryption scheme are secure, the protected data cannot be decrypted on the way to the enclave. On the client system, the SGX-enabled hardware ensures that no internal attacker can access any data residing in an enclave. The integrity of the included access control policies is assured by the digital signature of the data provider. Since the SGX specification includes hardware protection mechanisms, such as reserved memory areas for enclaves, physical attacks become less feasible for internal attackers. The security of the remote attestation and the underlying SGX design are analyzed in greater detail in [1, 5].

3.4 Problems

Since the security of the proposed design is based on the security of the SGX architecture, attacks against SGX hardware or protocols immediately impact the TRM implementation. As shown in [3, 14], SGX has certain weaknesses against side channel information leakage attacks. This could allow internal attackers to extract knowledge about enclave data. However, recent research has attempted to prevent such information leakage by detecting external intervening in enclave execution [4, 13]. Another problem is the remote policy deployment mechanism of the access control system. In order to remotely deploy new policies at the TRM, the data provider needs to connect to the client system and transmit the encrypted policies. An internal or external attacker could block respective messages from the data provider to the TRM, and thereby prevent policy updates. In that case the TRM does not know about the new policies and will continue to evaluate old ones for access control decisions. The data provider will notice the failed policy deployment, but has no way of notifying the enclave if the attacker severs all communication. This is a general problem of distributed access control systems and it also affects access right revocation. A possible solution is for the TRM to regularly query policy updates at the data provider and deny accesses if the data provider is not reachable. The downside of this solution is the increased communication overhead. It also requires a suitable challenge-response protocol in order to prevent replay attacks. Finally, implementing a TRM inside an enclave leaves only limited options with regard to policy enforcement. Most importantly, the TRM cannot enforce policies on data that has been released outside the enclave. Once an access is granted and data leaves the enclave into untrusted space, no further control on the copied data is possible. Therefore this TRM design is sufficient for remote access control, but not for cross-domain usage control. Of course, the TRM can also enforce computations on the protected data (e.g. remove sensitive personal information) before they are released without further restrictions. However, due to the isolation of the enclave against the rest of the untrusted system, the TRM implementation has only limited resources available. Enclaves can only use a modified version of the standard C library, along with a limited amount of protected memory. Hence it is unfeasible to perform complex calculations (e.g. anonymize privacy impacting images) inside an enclave. All in all, using SGX to protect a TRM results in a design that can remotely enforce access control policies and provide secure computation. However, this solution is not sufficient for enforcing distributed usage control in general.

4 IMPLEMENTATION WITH SGX AND TPM

As shown in the previous sections, neither TPMs nor SGX enclaves alone are sufficient to securely implement a powerful TRM on a remote client system. TPMs offer a single isolation container that covers all the software running on the computer, including the operating system. This makes it possible to protect the integrity of kernel modules that can enforce complex policies on a low system level. Such a powerful kernel level component is necessary to implement distributed usage control systems. However, TPMs cannot sufficiently protect the integrity of policies and the confidentiality of data in this use case (see section 2). SGX-enabled processors can be used to implement a TRM design based on enclaves. A TRM enclave can use the SGX remote attestation protocol to perform remote policy deployment and secure remote computation. On the other hand, the SGX enclave is technically isolated from the rest of the system, which makes it impossible to enforce usage control policies on data outside the enclave. Therefore SGX enclaves cannot implement a TRM for general usage control purposes. A possible solution is to combine SGX enclaves with a separate TPM that is protecting the rest of the system. An external enforcement component is realized as a standard kernel module and gets measured by a separate TPM. The TRM itself consists of SGX enclaves that communicate with the data provider and evaluate the deployed policies. The enclaves verify the integrity of the external enforcement component using the local attestation mechanism of the TPM.

4.1 TRM Design

We base our TRM design on the well researched XACML architecture [2]. The TRM components are shown in figure 2.

Policy Enforcement Point. The PEP is the enforcement component of the TRM. It intercepts data accesses in the system and enforces usage control decisions on it. The PEP cannot be isolated in a SGX enclave, because it needs to track data flows and enforce policies throughout the system. Hence the PEP is implemented as a dedicated kernel module. Its integrity is protected by a TPM measurement during the boot sequence.

Policy Decision Point. The PDP evaluates a set of deployed policies for each requested data access in order to reach an access decision for the request. It is implemented as a trusted SGX enclave. It communicates with the external PEP to announce access control decisions. The PEP notifies the PDP about an intercepted event, the PDP evaluates the respective policies and returns the resulting decision, which the PEP enforces on the requester.

Policy Retrieval Point. The PRP is the part of the TRM that securely receives policies and data from remote data providers. It is also the main component that establishes trust with the remote data provider. This includes verifying the integrity of the other parts of the TRM, especially the PEP and the PDP. The PRP is implemented as an enclave on the client system and can use the SGX remote attestation protocol to prove its integrity to the data provider.

Policy Information Point. The PIP is a user space application that provides information about the current system state for the policy evaluation. It encapsulates the PDP and PRP enclaves and acts as an interface between PEP and PDP. The PIP holds a data flow model, which maps a representation of the protected data existing on the computer to a set of containers, e.g. files or user processes that contain this information. The data flow model gives a comprehensive overview of the current system state with regard to the distribution of protected data. The PIP is notified by the

PEP about system events that can initiate a data flow, for example certain system calls, and updates the data flow model accordingly. The PDP can use this information in order to come to an access control decision for a particular access request.

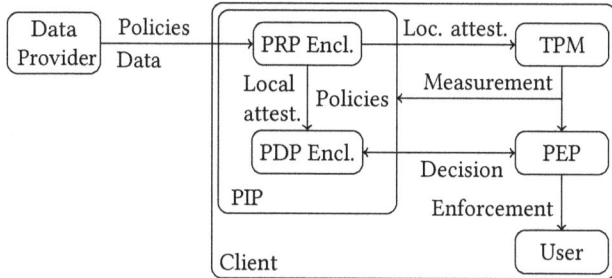

Figure 2: TRM design with TPM and SGX.

The TRM protocol consists of four phases (see figure 3).

(1) *Initialization:* During the boot sequence of the client system, the TPM measures the PEP kernel module as well as the PIP application in oder to detect tampering. The PIP application launches the PRP and the PDP enclaves.

(2) *Establishing trust:* In order to verify the integrity of the client system, a remote data provider initiates the remote attestation protocol with the PRP enclave. Three sigma messages S1-S3 are exchanged between the data provider and the PRP enclave (see section 3.1). If the sigma protocol is successful, the data provider trusts the remote PRP implementation and a shared symmetric key sk is established. The PRP enclave is responsible for verifying the integrity of the other trusted components of the TRM. First, the PRP checks the PCR values of the external TPM in order to establish trust in the PEP and the PIP implementations. If the PCR values match a known value, the components are unmodified and can be trusted. Then, the PRP uses the SGX local attestation protocol to verify the state of the PDP enclave. If this attestation is successful, the PDP enclave has been launched unmodified. In that case a transitive trust relationship is established, since the data provider trusts the PRP, and the PRP trusts the PDP and PEP. Finally, the trusted PRP notifies the data provider that the remote platform is trustworthy.

(3) *Policy deployment:* The data provider uses the established secure channel to transmit the protection policies to the PRP enclave. The policies are signed by the data provider and the PRP verifies the signature. Then the PRP deploys the policies to the PDP, using the locally established secure channel between the two enclaves. After the protection policies have been successfully deployed on the remote system, the data provider transmits the sensitive data to the PRP enclave. In order to prevent information leakage, the protected data is encrypted with the shared symmetric key. Finally, the PIP is notified about the existence of new data and updates its data flow model accordingly.

(4) *Policy enforcement:* The active PEP kernel module intercepts data requests of users in the system and notifies the PIP about respective events. The PIP can update the mappings of its data flow model according to the triggered event (e.g. a read() system call), and then forwards the event to the PDP enclave for

decision. The PDP evaluates the deployed policies for the intercepted event and may query the data flow model in the process. The resulting access control decision is returned via the PIP to the PEP, which finally enforces it on the requester. Unlike in the XACML architecture, the PIP is also responsible for initially forwarding the protected data to the requester. A user process can request access to the data that the remote data provider has transmitted to the client system. If the PDP access control decision is positive, the PIP releases the protected data. Afterwards, the usage of the released data in the memory of untrusted user processes is supervised by the PEP. The PIP then merely updates the data flow model by changing the mapping of the data to containers based on the intercepted PEP events.

4.2 Security Analysis

The attacker model for this TRM design is the same as for the previous, SGX-based solution. We distinguish between internal attackers, most importantly the user of the client system, and external attackers that eavesdrop on the communication between data provider and client. However, unlike in the previous section, we now assume that an internal attacker does not have root access to the client system. The most important issue with this TRM design is how the trust relationship between the remote data provider and the TRM on the client system is established. This is achieved in a transitive fashion. The first trust relationship to consider is between the remote data provider and the PRP enclave. This relationship is established using the SGX remote attestation protocol. The sigma protocol identifies the PRP enclave and ensures that it has not been altered. It has already been analyzed in the previous chapter. After the sigma protocol finishes, the server trusts the PRP implementation, as well as the established key. Furthermore, the SGX hardware prevents modifications and information leaks while the enclave is running. As presented in the previous section, SGX-enabled processors provide some security guarantees against both internal and external attackers. The other trust relationships are established between the PRP enclave and the other parts of the TRM design. The PRP enclave has the responsibility to issue the policy deployment and to only release the data outside the protected enclave if it is protected by the usage control system. For this, the enclave verifies the integrity of the PIP and PEP external modules by comparing the PCRs of the external TPM to known "good" values. During the boot sequence, the TPM measures both the PEP and the PIP components. If an internal attacker modifies the PEP or PIP module in order to influence the TRM implementation, the measurements will change and the PCR verification fails. In that case, the PRP will not release any sensitive data outside the enclave. An internal attacker could try to launch the PRP enclave inside an untrusted system process instead of the PIP and retrieve the protected data after the policy deployment step. This is prevented by measuring each start of an enclave individually. The PIP launches each TRM enclave exactly once during startup, and launching any more instances will result in changed PCR values. Furthermore, the reference monitor of the operating system ensures that any non-root system user (i.e an internal attacker) cannot tamper with the modules after the system is booted and the measurement is performed. This presupposes that the operating system is properly configured and the client user

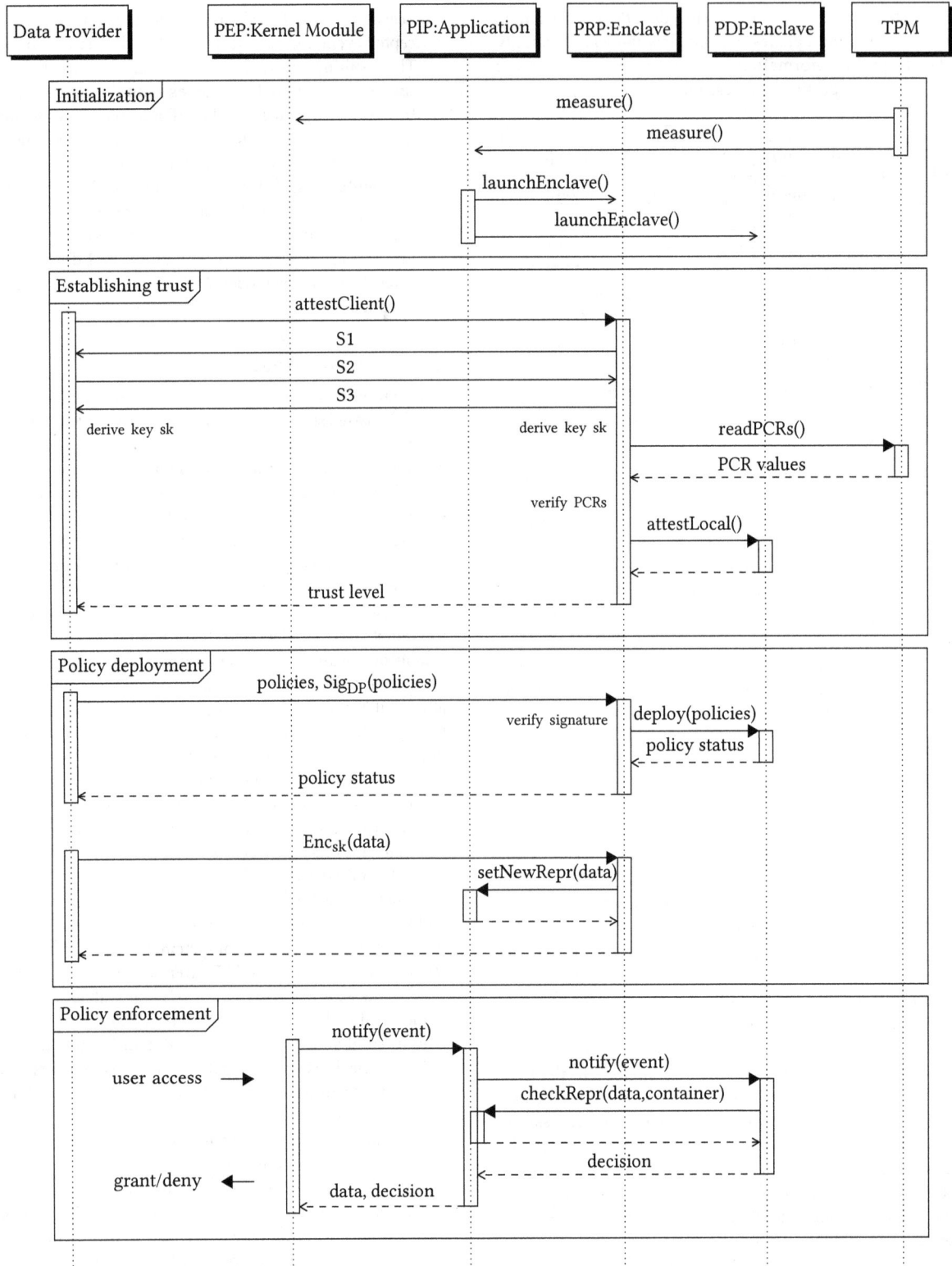

Figure 3: Sequence diagram of TRM protocol interaction.

does not have root rights at the system, which is a common demand for TPM protected systems (c.f. section 2). External attackers are not relevant for this trust relationship, since no messages between the TRM modules ever leave the client system. Finally, the trust relationship between the PRP and the PDP has to be established. Since the PDP is also an enclave, this is achieved by a SGX local attestation. The local attestation protocol verifies the integrity of the enclave code, which prevents internal attackers from tampering with the PDP implementation. After the enclave is launched, the SGX hardware isolates it from the rest of the system. Hence internal attackers cannot influence the PDP component during runtime. Again, external attackers are not relevant for this trust relationship, because no messages leave the client system.

4.3 Open Issues

The main problems of the proposed general TRM design arise from the fact that it includes a TPM, as opposed to the purely SGX-based solution. However, including a TPM is necessary in order to implement general distributed usage control. A powerful PEP, which can enforce usage control policies throughout the whole system, can only be implemented outside a SGX enclave. Hence the trust anchor of this design, unlike with many SGX-enabled applications, is not just the set of SGX enclaves alone, but also includes the TPM and the operating system. This ultimately leads to weaker security guarantees. Depending on the policies and the way of the data usage, hardware attacks may become a problem again. Only the SGX enclaves are protected against information leakage by hardware mechanisms, so data that exited the enclaves can be intercepted at the hardware bus. Furthermore, the TRM design requires additional assumptions that SGX-based designs do not necessarily demand. Unlike before, the operating system's reference monitor has to be trusted. If the operating system is vulnerable, an untrusted user could influence the user space TRM modules, for example the PEP or the PIP, during runtime. For the same reason, the client system user must not be root. Even though a root user cannot forge TPM measurements, he still can influence the non-enclave TRM modules after the measurement has been done. Those TPM-related assumptions are much stronger than those required with purely SGX-based designs, but they are common for usage control systems. Other unsolved questions concern the actual implementation of the proposed TRM design. It is not yet clear how the PCR values of an external TPM can be checked from inside an enclave. Intel does not provide an interface to access external TPMs from inside an enclave, because in the standard use cases, the SGX hardware replaces traditional TPMs. In our use case however, SGX cannot replace the external TPM, since we require to take measurements during the boot sequence. Of course it is possible to use an OCALL invocation in order to query the external PCR values from outside the enclave, but in that case the returned PCR values might be vulnerable to modification by an untrusted system process. Moreover, the TPM needs to be able to measure every SGX enclave launch separately, in such a way that each enclave launch changes the PCR values. Otherwise the user can easily impersonate a PIP, launch a second PRP enclave instance and retrieve the data himself. It is not yet clear how this mechanism can be realized in a SGX-enabled system that also features a TPM.

5 CONCLUSION

In this work we showed that it is possible to achieve secure computation as well as remote access control with SGX-enabled processors. However, enforcing distributed usage control on remote client systems requires a Policy Enforcement Point that can intercept events on an operating system level. This component cannot be implemented as an isolated SGX enclave. Therefore we proposed a TRM design with separate, but interdependent components that reside inside as well as outside of isolated enclaves. An additional TPM establishes the required trust outside of SGX enclaves. Before transmitting sensitive data to a client, the data provider uses the SGX remote attestation protocol to verify the integrity of the enclave software that is running on the client. The enclave then evaluates the measurements of the external TPM, thereby ensuring the integrity of the TRM parts that reside inside the operating system kernel. Ultimately, a transitive trust relationship is established that enforces deployed usage control policies on remote systems.

Necessary future work towards a full working implementation includes analyzing the size of various PRP and PDP code bases. Currently SGX enclaves are still quite limited in size, which could make an SGX implementation of advanced applications unfeasible. Furthermore, the ways of communication between the TPM and the SGX enclaves have to be researched further.

REFERENCES
[1] Ittai Anati, Shay Gueron, Simon Johnson, and Vincent Scarlata. 2013. Innovative technology for CPU based attestation and sealing. In *Proceedings of the 2nd international workshop on hardware and architectural support for security and privacy*, Vol. 13.
[2] Anne Anderson, Anthony Nadalin, B Parducci, D Engovatov, H Lockhart, M Kudo, P Humenn, S Godik, S Anderson, S Crocker, et al. 2003. extensible access control markup language (xacml) version 1.0. *OASIS* (2003).
[3] Ferdinand Brasser, Urs Müller, Alexandra Dmitrienko, Kari Kostiainen, Srdjan Capkun, and Ahmad-Reza Sadeghi. 2017. Software Grand Exposure: SGX Cache Attacks Are Practical. *arXiv preprint arXiv:1702.07521* (2017).
[4] Sanchuan Chen, Xiaokuan Zhang, Michael K Reiter, and Yinqian Zhang. 2017. Detecting privileged side-channel attacks in shielded execution with Déjà Vu. In *Proceedings of the 2017 ACM on Asia Conference on Computer and Communications Security*. ACM, 7–18.
[5] Victor Costan and Srinivas Devadas. 2016. Intel SGX Explained. *IACR Cryptology ePrint Archive* 2016 (2016), 86.
[6] Trusted Computing Group. [n. d.]. TCG architecture overview. (TCG Specification). ([n. d.]).
[7] Intel. 2016. Intel®Software Guard Extensions Remote Attestation End-to-End Example. (2016). https://software.intel.com/en-us/articles/intel-software-guard-extensions-remote-attestation-end-to-end-example
[8] Jaehong Park and Ravi Sandhu. 2004. The UCON ABC usage control model. *ACM Transactions on Information and System Security (TISSEC)* 7, 1 (2004), 128–174.
[9] Alexander Pretschner, Manuel Hilty, and David Basin. 2006. Distributed usage control. *Commun. ACM* 49, 9 (2006), 39–44.
[10] Reiner Sailer, Xiaolan Zhang, Trent Jaeger, and Leendert Van Doorn. 2004. Design and Implementation of a TCG-based Integrity Measurement Architecture.. In *USENIX Security Symposium*, Vol. 13. 223–238.
[11] Ravi Sandhu and Xinwen Zhang. 2005. Peer-to-peer access control architecture using trusted computing technology. In *Proceedings of the tenth ACM symposium on Access control models and technologies*. ACM, 147–158.
[12] Paul Sevinç, Mario Strasser, and David Basin. 2007. Securing the distribution and storage of secrets with trusted platform modules. *Information Security Theory and Practices. Smart Cards, Mobile and Ubiquitous Computing Systems* (2007), 53–66.
[13] Ming-Wei Shih, Sangho Lee, Taesoo Kim, and Marcus Peinado. 2017. T-SGX: Eradicating controlled-channel attacks against enclave programs. In *Proceedings of the 2017 Annual Network and Distributed System Security Symposium (NDSS), San Diego, CA*.
[14] Yuanzhong Xu, Weidong Cui, and Marcus Peinado. 2015. Controlled-channel attacks: Deterministic side channels for untrusted operating systems. In *Security and Privacy (SP), 2015 IEEE Symposium on*. IEEE, 640–656.

My Friend Leaks My Privacy: Modeling and Analyzing Privacy in Social Networks

Lingjing Yu[1,2], Sri Mounica Motipalli[3], Dongwon Lee[4], Peng Liu[4],
Heng Xu[4], Qingyun Liu[1,2], Jianlong Tan[1,2], and Bo Luo[3]

[1] Institute of Information Engineering, Chinese Academy of Sciences, Beijing, China
[2] University of Chinese Academy of Sciences, Beijing, China
[3] Department of Electrical Engineering and Computer Science, The University of Kansas, USA
[4] School of Information Science and Technology, The Pennsylvania State University, USA
yulingjing@iie.ac.cn, srimounica.motipalli@ku.edu, dlee@ist.psu.edu, pliu@ist.psu.edu,
hxu@ist.psu.edu, liuqingyun@iie.ac.cn, tanjianlong@iie.ac.cn, bluo@ku.edu

ABSTRACT

With the dramatically increasing participation in online social networks (OSNs), huge amount of private information becomes available on such sites. It is critical to preserve users' privacy without preventing them from socialization and sharing. Unfortunately, existing solutions fall short meeting such requirements. We argue that the key component of OSN privacy protection is protecting (sensitive) content – privacy as having the ability to control information dissemination. We follow the concepts of *private information boundaries* and *restricted access and limited control* to introduce a *social circle* model. We articulate the formal constructs of this model and the desired properties for privacy protection in the model. We show that the social circle model is efficient yet practical, which provides certain level of privacy protection capabilities to users, while still facilitates socialization. We then utilize this model to analyze the most popular social network platforms on the Internet (Facebook, Google+, WeChat, etc), and demonstrate the potential privacy vulnerabilities in some social networks. Finally, we discuss the implications of the analysis, and possible future directions.

CCS CONCEPTS

• Security and privacy → Social network security and privacy; Privacy protections; Usability in security and privacy;

KEYWORDS

Privacy; Social Networks; Social Circles

ACM Reference Format:
Lingjing Yu[1,2], Sri Mounica Motipalli[3], Dongwon Lee[4], Peng Liu[4], Heng Xu[4], Qingyun Liu[1,2], Jianlong Tan[1,2], and Bo Luo[3]. 2018. My Friend Leaks My Privacy: Modeling and Analyzing Privacy in Social Networks. In *Proceedings of The 23rd ACM Symposium on Access Control Models & Technologies (SACMAT) (SACMAT '18)*. ACM, New York, NY, USA, 12 pages. https://doi.org/10.1145/3205977.3205981

1 INTRODUCTION

In recent years, many online social network services (SNSs) such as Facebook have become extremely popular, attracting a large number of users to generate and share diverse (personal) contents. With the advancement of information retrieval and search techniques, on the other hand, it has become easier to do web-scale identification and extraction of users' personal information from SNSs. Therefore, malicious or curious users could take an advantage of these techniques to collect others' private and sensitive information. In fact, we have been overwhelmed by news reports on the problems caused by the lack of social network privacy. Let us illustrate a real-world case where one's private information is being leaked.

Example 1.1. **(Private Information Disclosure)** As shown in Fig. 1 (a), the owner of information, say Alice, shares two photos on Google+. She is cautious about her privacy so that she configures the album to be available only to a limited audience (i.e., small circle of friends), which includes Mallory. However, in Google+ and other SNSs, friends are often allowed to re-share their friends' photos, which potentially redefines the privacy setting set by the original content owner. In this example, although Mallory receives a warning when she attempts to re-share Alice's photo (Fig. 1 (b)), she can simply ignore the warning and re-share the photo with a different circle (Fig. 1 (c)). Now, Chuck, who is not a member of Alice's circle (so that he could not see Alice's original post), is able to see the photos from Mallory's wall (Fig. 1 (d)). Worst of all, if Alice is not a member of Mallory's circle, she does not get notified of the re-share (Fig. 1 (e)). Although, it is possible for Alice to disable re-share, that function is not obvious to regular users and it needs to be explicitly invoked for each post, which significantly degrades the level of usability.

As we have demonstrated, for various design rationales and business decisions, some SNSs promote information sharing aggressively, to the extend that introduces privacy vulnerabilities. Similar privacy breach has existed in Facebook until 2014, without the warning message or the function to disable forwarding, ever since such functions were introduced [29, 66]. However, as we will demonstrate later, private information leakage is common in many SNSs including Google+ and Sina Weibo.

In the literature, other privacy protection models and mechanisms, such as k-anonymity [61] and differential privacy [16], have been developed for privacy-preserving data analysis. Such solutions protect individual user's identity information in statistical

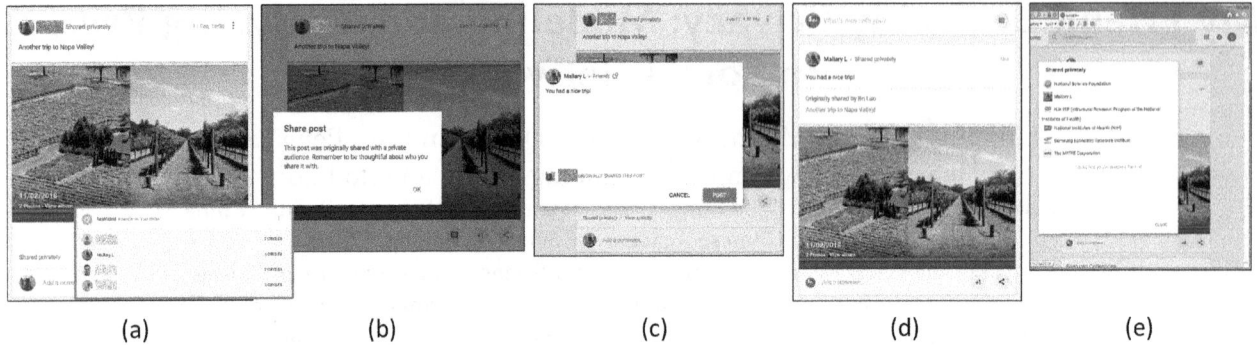

Figure 1: The demonstration of privacy breach on Google+ (Example was captured on 02/01/2018): (a) information owner (Alice) posts photos to a circle of 4 users, including Mallory; (b) Mallory attempts to re-share and sees a warning; (c) Mallory ignores the warning and re-shares the photos; (d) Chuck, who cannot see Alice's post, now sees the photos from Mallory; (e) The photos are re-shared to a completely different circle, which *excludes* Alice.

databases, so that adversaries cannot easily re-identify a user from sanitized datasets. However, they are not suitable to protect (sensitive) user contents in the settings of online social networks, where user IDs (or screen names) are revealed. Moreover, an ideal privacy protection solution for SNSs is *not* to discourage the socialization such as sharing photos with friends. In this context, behavioral researchers and practitioners argue that privacy could be defined as *having the ability to control the dissemination of (personal) information*. Recently, the concept of social circles have been adopted in the research community [44, 54, 55] and in commercial products [30, 64]. The key idea is that new messages are posted to designated audience (i.e., social circles) and the message owners have a full control of the information boundary, where information is conceptually bounded by the social circle. Meanwhile, social circles are also expected to promote information sharing, since they give users the perception of security and privacy. However, social circles are neither clearly defined nor strictly enforced (e.g., circle leakage in Example 1.1). [64] also indicates that use of social circles is limited due to lack of users, and users are unaware of how information could spread beyond circles in Google+. We argue that current adoptions of social circles have significant drawbacks: (1) the social circle model was loosely defined and there was no formal underpinning to support the model; (2) There was no systematic analysis of the requirements, properties, and issues associated with the model; (3) There is a major usability issue that prevents users from adopting social circles: it is labor-intensive and tedious to manually arrange existing users into circles, and to identify the appropriate circle for every new message; and (4) There is no available solution to detect leaky circles (as in Example 1.1) – users are more vulnerable since their perceived protection boundaries are often quietly violated.

The contributions of this paper are three-fold: (1) we have formalized a *social circle* model for social network privacy protection, which is based on the notions of *private information boundaries* and *restricted access and limited control*. The social circle model facilitates socialization while allows users to control the dissemination of their information belongings; (2) Using the social circle model as the basis of analysis, we have carefully examined the privacy enforcement mechanisms of six leading social networking platforms; and (3) We further discuss the implications of our findings. The proposed model and analysis is expected to serve as a blueprint

of technological approaches to improve the validity, usability and efficiency of social network privacy protection solutions.

2 THE SOCIAL CIRCLE MODEL

2.1 Preliminaries

Adoption of user privacy control presents not only a *technical* challenge, but also a *social* one. Studies have shown that even users with high concern about privacy do not always take appropriate actions even when those measures are fairly easy to perform. This phenomenon is known as the **Privacy Paradox**–i.e., users state high levels of privacy concerns but behave in ways that seemingly contradict their privacy attitudes [1, 2, 46]. Two complementary theoretical explanations have been proposed. First, Acquisti *et al.* argued that the dichotomy between privacy attitude and behavior is due to *bounded rationality*–i.e., human agents are unable to have absolute rationality because they either do not have the proper knowledge to process the risks, or they underestimate the risks by discounting the possibility of future negative events [1, 2]. Second, privacy control features make users' online profiles less visible, and thus can work against developing social relationships. This causes privacy control to be viewed as an additional cost in terms of social-relational concerns [17]. In either theoretical explanation, privacy control features will not be utilized if the costs are perceived to be greater than the benefits, despite users' privacy concerns. Therefore, an ideal privacy protection model that addresses the privacy paradox is expected to have sufficient rigor and expressiveness to satisfy the privacy expectations of the users, while it should also be easily understandable and highly usable.

There has been a movement toward the conceptualization of privacy as "the ability of individuals to control the terms under which their personal information is acquired and used" [13] (p.326). This concept of privacy-as-control originated in Westin's [65] and Altman's [3] theories of privacy, which have since entered the mainstream of privacy research in information systems, HCI, marketing, and sociology. The notion of privacy as control has, however, been criticized for its vagueness with regard to (1) the types of personal information over which people can expect to have control; and (2) the amount of control they can expect to have over their personal information [62]. These problems in defining privacy as control spurred the formulation of a modified notion of privacy as control and restricted access, which advocates for the provision of different levels of restricted access to different people for different types of information in different situations [62]. From this perspective, a privacy model known as *restricted access and limited control (RALC)* [62] has emerged. This new model highlights the need for the creation of a privacy protection boundary to enable people to restrict others from accessing their personal information [62].

2.2 The Social Circle Model

Drawing on the privacy theory of RALC, we argue that privacy is a multifaceted concept that should be analyzed with the considerations of: (1) degree of control over information dissemination; and (2) the extent to which their privacy (protection) expectations are met (perceived protection "boundaries"). The theoretical distinction between control and information boundary seems readily understood. However, most users in practice may conflate these two dimensions by having an "illusion" of control on the information they reveal: Because they have control over the information publication, they believe they also have control over the accessibility and use of that information by others. Such "illusion" could be explained by the optimistic bias where users overestimate their control over information dissemination, and meanwhile underestimate the future to their shared information by others. In addition, the optimistic bias may also be caused by the gap between users' perceived information boundary and the actual boundary enforced by their privacy settings. The gap might be caused by: (1) the social network sites often adopt over-simplified privacy models, which fail to accurately capture users' perceptions; or (2) when more powerful privacy models are adopted, the actual implementations fail to correctly enforce the models.

The above social science theoretical perspectives reveal different but interrelated approaches to conceptualize a privacy model. When looking across these different aspects, we find that individual privacy is better viewed as a multifaceted concept with the considerations of: **(1)** the extent to which users can control over the disclosure, dissemination, and transitive propagation of their personal information (the strength of deployed privacy control mechanisms); **(2)** the extent to which their privacy (protection) expectations are met (perceived protection "boundaries"); and **(3)** the subjective estimation of the gap between users' perceptions of protection boundary and the actual boundary enforced by their privacy settings (optimistic bias).

Based on these findings, now, we formalize the model termed as **Social Circles** to integrate the *control perspective* and the *restricted access to information boundary perspective* as follows:

Definition 2.1 (Social Network Identity (SNID)). A social network identity (SNID) is defined as the identity a specific end user adopts for a given SNS (or social application). It consists of two attributes, the name of the SNS and the name the user has adopted for that site–e.g., $SNID_1$=(facebook, dul13);

In practice, automatically linking SNIDs from different social networks to the same real-world identity is a difficult problem, unless such a link is explicitly available in social network profiles. Note that SNID owners may explicitly reveal their offline identity to the public or to their friends, especially in closed social networks

such as Facebook or WeChat, where friends are often connected offline as well. This fact also supports our original claim that the primary goal should be protecting sensitive content instead of protecting identity. In this paper, we consider SNIDs from different social networks as independent – Alice from Twitter and Alice from Facebook are considered unrelated. The rationale is that the privacy protection mechanism from each OSN platform only handles SNIDs, posts, and information flow within its platform. That is, a cross-platform privacy protection mechanism does not exist yet.

Definition 2.2 (Social Circle). A **social circle (SC)** is simply a set of SNIDs that is conceptually grouped together by a user and used for some purpose–i.e., SC = $\{SNID_1, SNID_2, ..., SNID_n\}$.

The owner of the circle does not own the SNIDs in the circle–rather, she groups her contacts/friends in circles. A social circle represents the fact that every social network post is intended for a targeted group, where users in the group has inherent social ties or similarities. Posts on similar topics are often intended for the same group. For example, Professor Alice may share research news with *colleagues* ($SC_{Alice,C}$) and *students* ($SC_{Alice,S}$), but only shares her baby's photos with *personal friends*. Three different (potentially overlapping) circles are implied here. In the rest of the paper, we use *Alice* to denote the owner of multiple circles. We also assume that SNIDs in the same circle all belong to the same OSN. The implication is that we do not concern partially overlapping social circles from different platforms. For example Alice may use her Google+ SNID to interact with dancing buddies and a LinkedIn SNID to interact with professional colleagues. In this scenario, they are considered two unrelated SNIDs with two unrelated social circles, although a member in the Google+ circle and a member in the LinkedIn circle may be owned by the same offline friend.

Definition 2.3 (Information Belongings). A user's **information belongings** (I), defined as his or her personal attributes (e.g., birth-date, SSN), content created (e.g., writings, photos), or traces of online social activity (e.g., joining a club, adding a friend).

In our model, information belongings are categorized as: (a) attributes, which often contain sensitive information (e.g., date of birth, SSN); (b) user-generated information (e.g., writings, photos, videos); (c) public content forwarded or re-posted by the SNID (i.e. Alice posts a news article to her wall); (d) social activities (e.g. Alice joins a club); and (e) information generated in response to another information belonging (e.g., Bob replies to Alice's post).

All original attributes and messages (type-a and b) from Alice are considered her privacy. Different content may pose different levels of privacy concern (e.g., a blog post about a park vs. a blog post about family members). However, as none of the existing social networks provides the capability of autonomous content analysis and content-based protection, all information belongings in each category are subject to the same privacy protection mechanism.

Meanwhile, a type-c information belonging (third-party message) is usually considered as *not* private, however, any comment from the user is private. Moreover, the fact that the user forwarded the message is a type-d information belonging (social activity), which is also private. For example, forwarding and commenting on a news report about the presidential election may reveal Alice's political opinions, even though the news itself is non-private.

Last, the type-e information belongings – small pieces of information attached to another (seed) information belonging – are the trickiest. When Bob "likes" or replies to Alice's post, it is both conceptually and practically unclear about the controller of the type-e information belonging. Although the content is generated by Bob (i.e. Bob is the owner), it is impractical for Bob to explicitly specify a social circle for each reply. In practice, different social networks handle them differently, while some implementations introduce potential privacy issues (to be elaborated in Section 3).

Definition 2.4 (Protection Boundary). The protection boundary of an element within a user's information belongings is defined as the union of the social circles within which the element is shared.

The core component of the social circle model is the protection boundary. We assume that when a user posts one or more belongings to a social circle, the individual who owns the social circle and the belongings are one and the same. That says, only Alice could post an information belonging to her own social circle. Another SNID in Alice's circle, Bob, could "reply to" (or "like") this information belonging, however, when Bob attempts to "forward" the information belonging to his own circle (i.e., outside of Alice's original circle), there may be a potential privacy leakage.

When Alice distributes an information belonging to one of her social circles, she essentially creates a mapping between the information belonging I_i and all the SNIDs in the circle. This is a many-to-many mapping, which should only be determined by Alice. In practice, the SNIDs who see the information belongings should exactly match Alice's sharing intention. That is, the *perceived* protection boundary (SC_p), the *specified* protection boundary (SC_s), and the *enforced* protection boundary (SC_e) should all be identical.

2.3 Properties of the Social Circle Model

With the definition of the key concepts of the social circle model, now we elaborate the desired properties for a social network privacy protection mechanism. In particular, the protection boundaries that determine who can access the information belongings should be controlled by the user and enforced in a non-leaky manner. What the user perceives as her protection boundaries should be consistent with what she specifies to the social network provider.

Property 1 (Control). The protection boundary of an information belonging should be fully controllable by its owner.

This property states that the social circle owner controls the enforced circle (SC_e). This is the most fundamental property of the social circle model. It implies that nobody, including the social network platform, should violate the information sharing intentions of the owner of the information belonging. Example 1.1 in Section 1 presents a typical violation of this property, in which the user lost control of her protection boundary. When a member in any social circle attempts to move information from its origin to his/her own circles, it is the online version of "social gossips", which results a violation of *Property Control*.

The *Control* property provides a theoretical guidance on how *forward* functions should be implemented in social networks. When Alice posts a message to her designated social circle (SC_A), which includes Bob, Bob should: (1) be disallowed to forward the message; (2) be allowed to forward the message to its original (Alice's) circle SC_A; or (3) be allowed to forward the message to a smaller circle, i.e. a subset of SC_A defined by Bob. Option (2) is the design choice of some social network platforms. Although it does not violate Alice's protection boundary, it discloses the fact that "Bob is Alice's friend and he forwarded the message" to people who are not Bob's friends (i.e., SC_A SC_B). If Bob is unaware of this fact and makes a different assumption (that the message is only visible to his friends), it may violate Bob's sharing intention. Option (3) is usually implemented in this way: Bob selects a protection boundary (SC_B) for the forwarded message, and the new *enforced boundary* would be the intersection of two circles $SC_A \cap SC_B$. This appears to be the best option, which ensures that Alice's information belonging does not escape from its original circle, and also gives Bob enough control to his type-d information belonging.

Meanwhile, as we have discussed, type-c information belongings (third party messages such as news articles) are generally not considered to be private. But the corresponding type-d information belongings are private. That says, when Alice forwards a news article to a designated circle (SC_{Ai}), Bob should: (1) be able to forward the original article itself to his designated circle, which is unrelated to Alice or SC_{Ai}; (2) be able to forward the article, with Alice tagged to it, in the same way as Alice's other private information belongings, i.e., same as options (2) and (3) as described above.

Last, for simplicity and usability concerns, there is no explicit control of type-e information belongings, i.e., when Bob replies to Alice's post, he cannot control who sees the reply. One option is to apply the same protection boundary as the seed – whoever sees the seed message sees all the replies. This may violate Bob's information sharing intention, when he does not want non-friends to see his reply. Another model is to implement a *default circle* for every user, so that the reply is visible to the intersection of original circle for this message and Bob's default circle: $SC_{Ai} \cap SC_{B,F}$

Property 2 (Consistency). The user-perceived protection boundary should be consistent with the protection boundary enforced by a social network site: $SC_p = SC_s = SC_e$.

This property reiterates the concepts of the *perceived boundary*, the *specified boundary*, and the *enforced boundary*. To correctly enforce Alice's information sharing intention, we expect $SC_p = SC_s = SC_e$. In particular, when there is inconsistency between perceived and specified boundaries ($SC_p \neq SC_s$), it implies a potential usability issue with the privacy modeling of the social network platform. When there is inconsistency between specified and enforced boundaries ($SC_s \neq SC_e$), it indicates an implementation error, which often causes leaky boundaries.

Property 3 (Usability). The designs of the system should facilitate relatively easy specification and utilization of social circles that are consistent with users' perceptions. The designs of the system should not obscure the scope and extent of socialization and sharing.

The usability issues occur throughout the design and implementation of social network privacy protection mechanisms. In the social circle model, the usability concerns are: (1) it should be easy to define social circles; (2) the defined social circles should be consistent with user perceptions; (3) it should be easy to select a circle in posting messages. The core of the proposed *Usability* property is to ensure $SC_p = SC_s$ through a user-friendly mechanism.

A major drawback in the adoption of the social circle model is the usability problem–it is tedious and labor-intensive to assign hundreds of existing friends into circles or lists. To tackle this problem, it was proposed that the owner may specify attribute values or credentials so that qualified SNIDs are automatically admitted to the circle. However, such delegation may suffer from discrepancies between user perceptions and specifications. Therefore, undesired SNIDs may be introduced to a circle due to faultily or incompletely specified credentials. There are also proposals to automatically identify social circles based on friendship connections, content and socialization activities (e.g., [32, 69]). Such proposals are not yet adopted in commercial OSN products. Meanwhile, they do not guarantee 100% accuracy – human adjustments are still needed.

Property 4 (Clean Deletion). Assume that an information belonging I is posted at time t_1 and deleted at time t_2, a user views the owners' space at $T > t_2$ and sees V, the deletion is clean iff $P(I = i) = P(I = i|V), \forall U$.

Information belongings posted to social circles may need to be deleted/recalled, such as the "regretted messages" [63]. The *Clean Deletion* property says that when the owner of an information belonging (I) deletes it, users should not learn any information about I when they look at the owner's space after the deletion. This property implies the full control of the social circle owner over the deletion of information. The deletion should be clean that no SNIDs in the circle should see any "phantom post", and no SNIDs in the circle could be able to infer anything about the deleted post.

Different types of information belongings may be deleted differently. In particular, when a type-b information belonging is deleted, all of its instances (e.g. forwarded or re-posted instances) should be completely erased. Its related replies, "likes", and "notifications" (e.g., Bob receives a notice when Alice posts a new message) should be erased too. Meanwhile, there is the concept of *forward privacy* in messages deletions: when Alice posts a message and deletes it before Bob logs in, Bob should be completely unaware of the existence of the deleted message. On the other hand, deleting a type-c information belonging only removes the copy of the message, but should not affect the original message. Last, if an SNID is closed, all of its information belongings should become invisible.

Property 5 (Non-leaky). A user's information dissemination activity D is defined as a 3-tuple: $D = \{U_A, I, SC_s\}$: user U_A disseminates information belonging I to social circle SC_s. The protection boundary for I is non-leaky iff $P(I = i) = P(I = i|D), \forall U_o \notin SC_s$.

The property says that, for any SNID U_o that is outside the specified protection boundary SC_s, his probability of guessing the information belongings before I and after I is posted should stay unchanged. As a complement to the *Usability* property, the Non-leaky property is to ensure that the enforced boundary equals the specified boundary $SC_s = SC_e$ – users outside the specified boundary cannot access the information. Many social network sites enforce privacy protection as "messages are only accessible within the owner's circle." However, violations of properties 1–4 all result in leaky boundaries. Examples include mal-functioning applications (e.g., Example 1.1 1 in Section 1). In fact, non-leaky models and the non-leaky enforcement are two very different concepts. When pragmatic tradeoffs between usability and privacy have to be done,

online social networks may often enforce a non-leaky model in a leaky way. In general, most of the leaky-boundary issues are caused by message forwarding and non-clean deletion. In the next section, we will examine the most popular social network platforms on the Internet, and discuss the privacy leakages we discovered.

3 ANALYSIS OF SOCIAL NETWORK PRIVACY MECHANISMS

In this section, we use the social circle model to examine the privacy protection functions for information dissemination in six popular social networks. We do not include public social networks, such as Twitter, that do not provide mechanisms to restrict access to user-generated content. We focus on the following: (1) The definition (configuration) of social circles, especially the usability issues when adding users into circles; (2) The control of information dissemination, and the consistency between specified and enforced circles; (3) The security of the protection boundaries, especially, whether the boundaries are leaky when the information belongings are being forwarded; (4) The handling of Type-e information belongings (e.g., likes and replies); and (5) The clean deletion of information belongings. Unless specified otherwise, all the experiments discussed in this section were conducted in December 2017 and January 2018.

3.1 Facebook

Facebook is reported to be the largest online social network platform, with 2 billion monthly active users. Facebook started as an internal social networks for Harvard College students, and later expanded to more universities and eventually to the public. As the business interest of Facebook is to facilitate socialization and sharing, their privacy policy used to be quite loose, such as: "*The default privacy setting for certain types of information you post on Facebook is set to 'everyone.'*" With years of development, the privacy protection mechanisms in Facebook have evolved significantly.

Defining Social Circles: Initially, Facebook's privacy settings were based on the concept of "networks", which include schools, geography, etc. For example, when a user registered with an @cmu.edu email, she became part of the "CMU network". Although many users perceived their protection boundary to be "friends", however, by default, profiles and activities were open to their networks (e.g., entire University network) [23]. In this case, everyone has several default circles, but she has no control over the membership of such circles (violation of Property 1. Control).

The current privacy protection mechanism of Facebook allows users to organize friends into *custom lists*, which are equivalent to social circles. Lists could be created by adding users one-by-one. Meanwhile, since Facebook explicitly collects user attributes such as location, education, work, etc, it also creates *smart lists* for users (e.g., all friends from CMU are placed into one list). Other than the smart lists, users cannot add friends in batch operations.

Control: When a user posts a message, she could choose a protection boundary, including public, friends, friends of friends, or a custom list. This allows a user to define any arbitrary protection boundary for each message. When a friend is explicitly *tagged* in a message, he/she is automatically added to the enforced circle and cannot be removed. However, this function could be confusing that: (1) when a custom list (SC_c) is selected and a friend (f_i) is tagged, the actual protection boundary is the *custom list + anyone tagged*, i.e., $SC_c \cup \{f_i\}$; however, (2) when the default list of *friends* (SC_F) is selected and a friend (f_i) is tagged, the new protection boundary is *friends + anyone tagged + friends of anyone tagged*, i.e. $SC_F \cup f_i \cup SC_{f_i, F}$, unless the user explicitly un-checks "friends of anyone tagged" in custom settings. Note that f_i owns circle $SC_{f_i, F}$. Therefore, the user is posting information to someone else's circle, which is out of her control (violation of Property Control). This practice may not seem intuitive/appropriate to all users.

Forwarding: In the current version of Facebook, an information belonging that has restricted access (non-public) cannot be re-shared/forwarded, except for type-c information belongings. Type-c information belongings could always be re-shared, but the previous sharer's information is excluded in re-sharing. That is, when Alice shares an ESPN news article to SC_A, Bob could re-share it, but he is actually re-sharing from ESPN, without any indication that Alice also shared it. Meanwhile, when Alice posts a Type-b information belonging to *public* and Bob re-shares it, Bob could specify the protection boundary of his re-share. Bob's friend Cathy could re-share from Bob's wall, but she is actually re-sharing Alice's seed information belonging. The fact that Bob re-shared the message is not further re-shared.

Replies: In Facebook, all *replies* and *likes* (Type-e information belongings) inherent the protection boundary of the seed content. Therefore, the actual owner of the type-e information belongings has no control over the enforced protection boundary. For example, when Bob replies to Alice's message, the enforced boundary of the reply ($SC_{e, Bob}(R)$) is the same as the protection boundary of the original message ($SC_{e, Alice}(M)$), which is defined by Alice. It would be interesting to examine if/how Bob's perceived boundary ($SC_{p, Bob}(R)$) would be different from the enforced boundary $SC_{e, Bob}(R)$. In practice, Bob's reply could be viewed by total strangers of Bob, which could be considered a potential privacy leakage. In the literature, [42] also mentioned that users might be unaware of the possibility of privacy leakage in replies in Twitter.

Clean deletion: Facebook supports clean deletion. In particular, when Alice posts a message that tags Bob, and deletes the message before Bob logs in. Bob will not receive any notification about the message or the tagging. Meanwhile, when a seed information belonging is deleted, all re-shares are also erased.

The Main Takeaway: Facebook, as one of the largest online social networks, has implemented a privacy model that supports social circles. It provides rich functions in defining circles and control protection boundaries. Sometimes there could be inconsistency between perceived and enforced protection boundaries, mainly due to the complications with tagging and the default circle of Friends. The enforced boundaries are non-leaky. In summary, we feel that Facebook's implementation of the social circle model is mostly correct, as long as the users use it correctly.

3.2 Google Plus (Google+)

Google plus, launched in 2011, is an Internet based social network that is operated by Google with 375 million active users as of August 2017. Circles is one of the core functions in Google+.

Define Circles: The default circles in Google+ are friends, family, acquaintances, and following. Users could create new circles and add any arbitrary set of users to any circle. Note that adding a user into a circle, even into the Friends circle, does not require mutual following relationship. Each user needs to be added manually, while there is no mechanism to add a bulk of followers into one circle.

On the other hand, Google+ also has the concept of "Communities" and "Collections". Each community is like a discussion room for people with similar interests. The owner of the community has full control of the membership of the community. Collections are used as a container for posts, where all the posts in the collection inherit the same protection boundary as the collection.

Control: When a user posts a message, she could choose one of the following as the destination: (1) a community, (2) a collection, or (3) a set of circles and users (followings and followers). In option (3), the enforced protection boundary is the union of all selected circles and users: $SC_e = SC_s = (\bigcup_i SC_i) \cup (\bigcup_j U_j)$. It is not possible to specify other operations such as $(SC_i \cap SC_j)$ or $(SC_F \setminus \{Alice\})$. In options (2) and (3), the user has full control of the protection boundaries. On the other hand, all Type-e information belongings inherit the protection boundary from the seed.

Although communities are not intended for access control, a user could choose a community as the destination when she posts a message (in the same way she chooses circles as destinations). However, for communities not owned by her, she has no control over who sees the post now and in the future. The fact that communities and circles could be selected in the same way as the destination of a post could be confusing to the users, and may cause potential privacy issues (Potential violation of Property 2. Consistency).

Forwarding: Unless the owner explicitly disables re-sharing, any user is allowed to forward Type-b and Type-c information belongings that she has access to. For an information belonging that is not posted to public ($SC_e(M) \neq U$), a warning will be displayed at the re-share attempt, but it could be ignored. Meanwhile, when $SC_e(M) \neq U$, it cannot be forwarded to the public. However, the protection boundary for M' could be any arbitrary set of circles or users defined by the re-sharer, and it could even exclude the original owner. As a result, the original users' information is easily leaked beyond the originally specified protection boundary.

Google+ does not distinguish Type-b and Type-c information belongings in re-sharing. That is, when Alice shares a public news article to a non-public circle, people in the circle will have two options in re-sharing this article: (1) Directly re-share from Alice: this is the same as re-sharing any Type-b information from Alice: the warning will be displayed, and the article can only be re-shared to non-public circles. (2) Click on the original article and re-share from there, so that it could be re-shared to public. For both options, the article displayed on the re-sharer's wall will be the same – although he re-shared from Alice in Option (1), there would be no indication of Alice in the re-shared post.

Clean Deletion: Google plus doesn't support Clean deletion. When the seed information is deleted, the re-shares are not deleted. For instance, when Bob re-shares a post from Alice and later Alice deletes the post, Bob's re-share will still exist, showing that it was from Alice. Interestingly, Bob's re-share is not allowed to be further re-shared if the seed information is deleted. Last, if Bob deletes a comment and undo the '+1' action (similar to 'like' in Facebook) made to Alice's post, the notification of the comment will disappear, but the notification of the '+1' will be kept.

The Main Takeaway: Google+ implements a social circle model, in which users have full control in defining circles and posting to circles. The protection boundary gets leaky when posts are forwarded by followers. Although the leakage could be prevented by disabling forwarding, usability appears to be an issue. The community mechanism is not intended for access control. However, it gives users a feeling that it could be used to control information dissemination, but the boundary is out-of-control and leaky.

3.3 VKontakte

VKontakte (VK) is an online social networking service that is very popular in Russian. As of January 2018, VK ranked 17th in Alexa-aâĂŹs global top 500 sites, and is 5th among social networking sites. VKontakte is more akin to Facebook.

Defining Social Circles: VKontakte allows users to organize friends into default lists (Best Friends, Co-Workers, Family, University Friends and School Friends) or custom lists. VK also has another function similar to social circles named groups, which can be open (anyone can join), closed (can request to join or by invitation) or private (can join on invitation). However, similar to Google+'s communities, this function is not designed for privacy protection.

Control: In VKontakte, the social circles could be used in general privacy settings to define an information boundary for each category of information, such as: "Who can view photos of me", "Who can view the Saved photos album". However, the general privacy settings does not include Type-b information belongings, whose protection boundary needs to be configured for each information belonging. When a user attempts to post a status update, she can only choose between Public ($SC = U$) or Friends (SC_F). When she creates an album as a container for photos, she can select fine-grained protection boundaries such as one or more social circles ($SC = \bigcup SC_i$). In VK, privacy settings are very complicate, for instance, hiding your profile does not hide your birthday – you can only configure your birthday to be shown to public or completely hidden in profile editing. Last, all Type-e information belongings inherit the protection boundary of seed message.

Forwarding: In VK, a user can re-share a public Type-b or Type-c information belonging to: her wall, a community she is in, or via a private message to any friend. For a private wall post that is accessible to her (i.e., she is within the protection boundary), she can share it as a private message to any friend, even the ones who are outside of the protection boundary of the post. Meanwhile, for a private photo, she can share it as a private message or directly on her wall. In the latter case, the photo becomes accessible to anyone who sees her wall, which could be public. In either case, there is no warning regarding the privacy of the original owner of the photo. This shows that the enforced protection boundaries could be easily broken, and the social circle is leaky.

Clean Deletion: In VK, when a wall post is re-shared and then deleted, all the re-shared copies will continue to exist, and they can be further re-shared. That says, when an information belonging is re-shared, a copy is made and its control belongs to the re-sharer.

The Main Takeaway: VK does not do a good job in protecting user privacy, especially in message forwarding. VK used similar designs with Facebook. The privacy vulnerability during forwarding existed on Facebook in 2014 and earlier. Facebook fixed this vulnerability

and enforced tighter privacy restrictions, unfortunately, VK did not follow. Meanwhile, clean deletion is not supported in VK, which means once a post/photo has been forwarded, the original owner completely loses control to the information belonging.

3.4 Sina Weibo

Sina Weibo is a social media platform with over 361 million active users in the second quarter of 2017. It is considered as a micro-blogging service similar to Twitter. The design is intended to be open to encourage sharing and socialization. For instance, all followings and followers are open to public. However, it added limited privacy protection functions for microblogs.

Defining Social Circles: Sina Weibo has three mechanisms to manage followers or followings in groups. Not all of them are designed for privacy protection, or can be used to control information dissemination. (1) Friend circle: "Friends" are defined as followers who are also followed by the owner (i.e. mutual followers). All friends are automatically added into this circle, while the owner could remove friends from this circle. She cannot add non-friends into this circle. Each user has only one *friend circle*, and she has full control over the membership. This circle could be used for control the boundary of information dissemination. (2) Weibo Groups: They are designed as chat groups, but it is possible to post microblogs to groups. A user could create chat groups by adding followers into the chat. Owners have full control over group membership. She can configure the group to be open or allow members to invite others. Members could leave the group at any time, but they do not have control over the membership of others. (3) Groups of followings: user can group the accounts that she is following into groups, so that she could view mricroblogs from a specified group. This function is designed for managing information consumption, not for information dissemination – users cannot post to such groups.

Control: When a user posts a microblog message, she could choose a protection boundary as: public, friend circle (SC_F), or a chat group. The friend circle is a true social circle that (1) the owner has full control over the membership, and (2) the enforced protection boundary is exactly the members in this circle $SC_s = SC_e = SC_F$.

Meanwhile, a message could be posted to any Weibo (chat) group that the user participates. Although this provides a means of information boundary, the mechanism is inconsistent with the social circle model or any other privacy model for social network information dissemination. In particular, a user may post to a group that is not owned by her, and she has no control over the membership of the group. Moreover, since the groups are dynamic and the user does not have full control over group membership, the perceived boundary SC_p could be dramatically different from the actually enforced boundary SC_e. This is a violation of Property Control.

Forwarding: In Weibo, messages maybe forwarded by others, while the forwarding history is maintained. That is, when Bob forwards a message from Alice, his friend Charlie will have two options: (1) forwarding from Bob's wall, so that the forwarded message shows a *forward chain* like "forwarded from Bob who forwarded from Alice". This chain could be very long in practice; (2) directly forwarding from Alice, so that the chain shows "forwarded from Alice". A Type-b or Type-C information belonging that is *not* available to public (e.g. a message to SC_F) cannot be forwarded.

Meanwhile, when an original information belonging is public, but forwarded by someone to her SC_F, this forwarded message cannot be re-forwarded. However, anyone who has access to ancestor nodes in the forwarding chain could still forward from there.

Replies: In Sina Weibo, there are two different notions of (1) who can reply and (2) who can see the replies. The SNID could configure who can reply to a post, such as everyone, followers, etc. Meanwhile, the protection boundary of Type-e information belongings is the intersection of the protection boundary of the seed message and the circle which is chosen by users to determine who could reply.

Clean Deletion: In Sina Weibo, when a type-b information belonging is deleted, all its replies and notifications of replies are erased. However, if the message has been forwarded, then the forwarder's wall will show a message like "this post has been deleted by the original user", but it does not reveal the SNID of the user. However, when Alice forwards a post, Bob re-forwards it, and Alice later deletes her forwarded post, Bob's message will remain on his wall with the complete forwarding chain which shows that it is re-forwarded from Alice. That is, a user can (almost) cleanly delete an original post, but cannot cleanly delete a forwarded post.

The Main Takeaway: Sina Weibo provides one mechanism that implements a limited social circle model. It supports only one circle for each user, who has full control over this circle. The circle is non-leaky, except potential issues with the inherited protection boundaries of the type-e information belongings. On the other hand, although the Chat Group mechanism could be utilized for access control of microblog posts, it was not intended for this function, and it creates issues with Consistency, Usability, and Control.

3.5 QZone

Tencent Qzone is a public social network platform for Tencent's instant messaging software named QQ. It allows QQ users to publish diverse types of content, such as blogs (journals), microblogs ("Shuoshuo"), photo, music, etc. It had over 606 million monthly active users in the second quarter of 2017.

Defining Social Circles: Users could define custom lists in QZone, which are expected to work as social circles. Users could extract any subset of friends from QQ into custom lists.

Control: A user could define a protection boundary for the entire QZone $SC(Z)$ as public (to all QQ users), friends, or a subset of friends. Only users in this boundary could access the QZone. In the QZone, different privacy protection mechanisms are developed for different media type: (1) The default specified protection boundary for blogs and microblogs is public. The owner could specify a new boundary $SC_s(M)$ by including or excluding a subset of friends. The actually enforced protection boundary will be $SC_e(M) = SC(Z) \cap SC_s(M)$. (2) Users could set protection boundaries for albums, so that all photos in the album will inherit the same protection boundary $SC_e(Albumn) = SC(Z) \cap SC_s(Album)$. Last, just like Facebook, all Type-e information belongings such as replies inherit the protection boundary from the seed content.

Forwarding: There are two types of forwarding activities in QZone: "Re-share" and "Reprint". Re-sharing is like creating a link to the original information belonging (except that microblogs are copied). The protection boundary of re-shared information belongings inherits the protection boundary of the re-sharer's QZone, which

cannot be re-configured. Meanwhile, reprinting is making a copy of the original message (for blogs and photos), where a new protection boundary could be set by the reprinter.

When a non-public protection boundary is specified for a microblog, it cannot be re-shared. However, in the case that the specified protection boundary is public ($SC_s(M) = U$) but the QZone is not open to public (i.e. $SC_e(M) = SC(Z) \neq U$), the message could be re-shared. The re-shared microblog breaks the originally enforced protection boundary – whoever could view the re-sharer's QZone sees the re-shared message: $SC_e(M') = SC_{Bob}(Z) \neq SC_e(M)$.

A blog message could always be re-shared regardless of the originally specified protection boundary. The new boundary will inherit the boundary of the re-sharer's QZone ($SC_e(M') = SC_{Bob}(Z)$). The title and the first few lines of the blog (and thumbnails of images) are shown in the re-sharer's QZone, with a link to the original blog – a user in $SC_e(M') \setminus SC_e(M)$ could see all these information, but will get an error clicking on the link. A blog could also be reprinted, so that a new copy of the blog is created on the reprinter's wall with a new protection boundary specified during reprint. The reprinted blog becomes completely out of the control of its original owner.

Clean Deletion: In Qzone, deleting a blog will not erase its re-shares – the title, abstract and thumbnail will stay in the re-sharer's space, but the link will point to an error message. Reprints are not affected when the original blog is deleted – they are not controlled by the original creator. On the other hand, deleting a microblog will erase all its re-shares. However, when a photo without text description is attached to a microblog, the text content of the microblog will be copied to the description. Deleting the microblog (not deleting the photo from the album) will not affect the description of the photo, and it will continue to be visible with the photo.

The Main Takeaway: QZone implements the social circle model, where any arbitrary circle could be specified when the user posts an information belonging. However, the circles become leaky when information belongings are re-shared or reprinted. Meanwhile, when an information belonging is deleted, not all its occurrences are erased. These vulnerabilities could post serious privacy threats to the owners of the information belongings.

3.6 WeChat

WeChat is an instant messenger and social networking software developed by Tencent. Its monthly active users reached 963 million in the second quarter of 2017. In this paper, we focus on the social networking component embedded in WeChat: the *Moments*, in which users may share: (1) a text message with 0 to 9 photos; or (2) a third party resource (link) such as a news article.

Defining Social Circles: Social networks are defined using tags – SNIDs (friends) carrying the same tag are considered in the same circle. Circles may have overlapping SNIDs. Since WeChat integrates instant messenger with social networking, users could add all the friends from group chats to the same circle.

Control: When a Type-b or c information belonging is posted, the default boundary is *all friends*. The user could set a customized protection boundary by *including* or *excluding* a subset of circles. That is, the specified boundary could be: (1) $SC_s = SC_{Alice,F}$; (2) $SC_s = \bigcup_i SC_{Alice,i}$; or (3) $SC_s = SC_{Alice,F} \setminus (\bigcup_i SC_{Alice,i})$, where $\bigcup_i$ denotes the union of the circles SC_i. No other set operations are supported. In particular, users cannot specify $SC_s = SC_i \cap SC_j$ or $SC_s = SC_i \setminus SC_j$, unless they explicitly define a circle as $SC_i \cap SC_j$.

Forwarding: Users cannot forward others' type-b information belongings, i.e., original messages and pictures. Users could forward Type-c information belongings regardless of the original access control settings. However, when Bob forwards a Type-c information belonging from Alice's moments to his own moments, he is actually forwarding from the original source – Alice is never associated with the re-post, so that her privacy is not violated.

Replies and Likes (type-e information belongings): In WeChat moments, protection boundary of type-e information belongings cannot be explicitly specified. The enforced circle is the intersection of the specified circle of the seed message and the replier's default circle. For example, Alice posts a photo to the colleagues circle: $SC_s(M) = SC_{Alice,C}$. Bob, who is a member of $SC_{Alice,C}$, comments on the photo. Bob's comment is only visible to Alice's colleagues who are also friends of Bob. That is, the enforced protection boundary of Bob's reply is $SC_e(R) = SC_s(M) \cap SC_{Bob} = SC_{Alice,C} \cap SC_{Bob,F}$. This model is more restricted than Facebook's model for Type-e information belongings, where $SC_e(R) = SC_s(M)$.

Clean Deletion: In WeChat, deleting an information belonging from the moment may not erase all its traces. In particular, we found that notifications are not cleanly erased when the seed information belongings are deleted. This vulnerability may result undesired recovery of deleted posts on some versions of WeChat.

(1) Deletion of Type-e information belongings. When Bob likes or comments on Alice's message (i.e., Bob posts a Type-e information belonging), Alice receives a notification of the activity. When Bob unlikes or deletes the comment (i.e. deletes the Type-e information belonging), Alice still sees a notification saying that "the comment has been deleted" – the notification is updated upon the deletion of the Type-e information belonging, but not deleted correspondingly.

(2) Deletion of Type-b information belonging. Deleting the original message will result the deletion of all attached Type-e information belongings, but not the deletion of corresponding notifications. The notifications become dangling that the seed messages no longer exist. Meanwhile, users may be able to access the deleted message (phantom message) through the dangling notifications. In our experiment, a WeChat user posted a picture to his moment (WeChat V6.5.18 on iOS), as shown in Fig. 2 (a). His friends liked the picture, hence, he received notifications about the event. Later, he decided to delete the picture (Fig. 2 (b)). The picture and the likes disappeared, however, the notifications of the likes, including a thumbnail of the first picture, still existed, (Fig. 2 (c)). To make things worse, clicking on dangling notification would lead to a phantom copy of the original message (Fig. 2 (d)) – the likes were gone, but the text message and the picture(s) were all shown. We name this the *Dangling notifications and Phantom posts* vulnerability of WeChat moments. This bug does not appear on all versions of WeChat. In our experiments, clicking on the dangling notifications in the Android version of WeChat (V6.5.14) will not load the phantom post. However, clicking on the thumbnail of the dangling notification will always load a phantom picture (original size).

The Main Takeaway: WeChat Moments implement a social circle model, in which each user has a default circle consists all her friends. Circles could be extracted from group chats, which is a plus from the usability perspective. Users have full control over their circles and circles are implemented non-leaky. Type-b information belongings cannot be forwarded, which is somewhat restrictive from usability perspective, but it improves privacy. For Type-e information belongings, unlike other social networks that inherits the protection boundary from their seed posts, WeChat utilizes the repliers' default circles to further tighten the boundary for each reply/like. This is more desirable compared with all other social networks we examined. Last, we found a vulnerability in clean deletion, which may be caused by caching.

4 IMPLICATIONS AND DISCUSSIONS

4.1 Implications

Privacy Model. In this paper, we have articulated the social circle model. We show that this model has sufficient rigor and expressiveness to satisfy the needs for controlling the boundary of information dissemination in social networks. It is also easily understandable and highly usable for non-expert users. Several popular OSNs have adopted privacy models that resemble the social circle model. Although the concept of social circles appears to be straight forward, the three-way interactions between *social circles*, *different types of information belongings*, and *operations on the information belongings* may be confusing to both developers and users. In practice, the implementation/enforcement of the social circle model could be problematic, as we have demonstrated in Section 3.

Enforcement. From our investigation on six popular social networking sites, we can see that none of them developed a perfectly non-leaky privacy protection mechanism. Some platforms implemented more things right, while some made serious mistakes. In particular, *forwarding* has been a big challenge – some sites set relaxed restrictions on forwarding to encourage socialization, which resulted in leaky boundaries when a post is forwarded outside its original circle ($SC(M') \setminus SC(M) \neq \Phi$); while some sites enforce more restrictions on forwarding, so that privacy leaks are less likely. *Clean deletion* has been another issue, where we have identified leakages in the models and inconsistencies in the implementations.

Usability. A privacy protection mechanism needs to be used and used properly in order to be effective. In our investigation, we found that not all privacy mechanisms are easily understandable and convenient to use. For example, in several social networks, the forwarding function needs to be explicitly disabled using a "hidden" checkbox for each post, even for posts to private circles. Otherwise the post may be forwarded out of its original circle without the consent of the owner of the information belonging. The lack of usability directly leads to privacy threats. Meanwhile, some mechanisms that are not intended for privacy protection (e.g., Google+'s Community and QZone's Chat Group functions) also have features similar to social circles that could confuse the users.

4.2 Discussions

Overlapping vs. Non-overlapping Circles. Overlapping circles means two social circles have members in common: $SC_i \cap SC_j \neq \Phi$. Most of the social networks allow overlapping circles since such overlapping exists in real-world relationships, e.g., Bob could be your classmate as well as colleague. However, SNIDs in the intersection of two circles have the privilege to access information disseminated to both circles, which may have the potential to cause

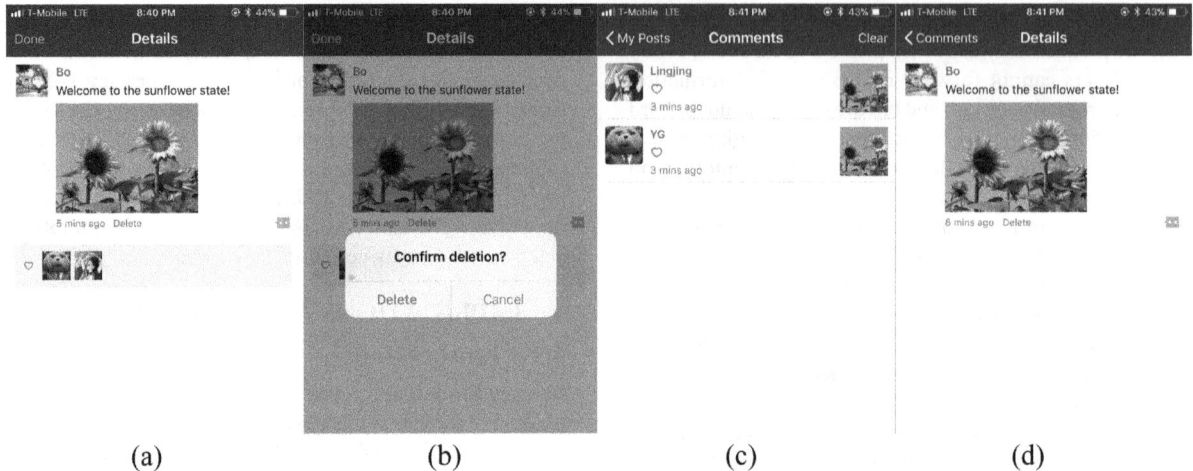

Figure 2: Non-clean deletion in WeChat: (a) User posts a picture, which was liked by two friends; (b) user deletes the message; (c) user could still see notifications that his friends "liked" the picture; (d) user could further click on the notifications to retrieve a phantom copy of the deleted message, but the "likes" were gone.

privacy threats. However, the models for overlapping circles and non-overlapping circles are convertible: two overlapping circles SC_1 and SC_2 could be translated into three non-overlapping circles: $SC_1 \cap SC_2$, $SC_1 \setminus SC2$, and $SC_2 \setminus SC_1$.

Co-ownership and Multi-party Sharing. Information belongings may be co-owned by multiple users, such as a photo with several people in it. We consider explicit and implicit co-ownerships: (1) When Alice tags Bob on a photo, Bob becomes the explicit co-owner. In this case, the desired protection boundary should be the intersection of two specified boundaries: $SC_{Alice,s} \cap SC_{Bob,s}$. However, this is impractical in real world social networking platforms. For instance, Facebook allows users (Alice) to tag friends (Bob) on a photo, however, the tagged friends: (i) do not have any control over the original photo – Alice still retain full ownership of I; (ii) can configure if photos with himself in them are automatically displayed on his own timeline; and (iii) can forward the photo even if the photo is non-public. (2) When Alice shares a photo with Bob in it, or Alice and Bob shares the same photo, the implicit co-ownership needs to be identified before enforcing multi-party access control. To our best knowledge, identification of implicit co-ownership is not supported in existing OSNs. To learn more about co-owned content and multi-party sharing, please refer to the literature, e.g., [48, 56, 58, 59] .

Leaky boundary monitoring. Besides the leaky enforcement of protection boundaries, an active attacker within one social circle could always copy-paste or even make a screen capture of a post, and repost as a new message to a new circle of his/her own. Defending against this attack will require prediction of user behaviors, active monitoring of high-risk nodes (friends who are "gossipy") and content-based detection of similar messages. Such attacks bypass all the privacy protection mechanisms from the SN platform, hence, they are outside the scope of this paper.

Circle Updates. Although social circles are relatively stable – similar to roles in RBAC, they still get updated, especially with newly introduced friends or changes in social status/relationships. When a social circle is reconfigured (by adding/removing members), different social networks take different approaches in managing the protection boundary of existing messages in this circle. For example, Google+ will update the protection boundary to the new circle, while WeChat choose to keep the original protection boundary. That is, when Alice posts a message to a circle and later adds Bob into the circle, Bob sees the message if they were using Google+, but he does not see the message if they were using WeChat. Each of these two design options has its pros and cons, which we cannot provide in-depth discussions here due to space constraints.

Other Perspectives of Social Network Privacy. In the literature, researchers study OSN privacy protection from different angles: (1) protecting user identity in data collection and data publishing (e.g., k-anonymity, differential privacy); (2) access control models and enforcement mechanisms for sharing private information; and (3) preventing users from posting extremely sensitive or regrettable content. In this paper, we follow the second thrust, in which we attempt to identify and evaluate a model that both facilitates information sharing and prevents undesired privacy leakage. We examine the dissemination of potentially private information, and find models and enforcement mechanisms that are able to contain information dissemination as specified by the user.

5 RELATED WORKS

1. Privacy Threats with SN Platforms and Communication. [8] and [73] build social networks from multiple resources while ensuring the privacy of participants. [5] introduces a privacy-preserving social network platform that stores and exchanges encrypted content, and access is enforced through key management. [51] builds a platform that enforces privacy control on third party applications. Meanwhile, users implicitly reveal their identity (e.g., IP address) through network communications. Anonymous communications are proposed to hide user identities [14, 20, 49].

2. Privacy Threats within Social Network Sites. *(1) Private information disclosure.* Personal information may be mistakenly disclosed from trusted social networks: publicly-available archives of closed social networks [18], social network stalkers [15], code errors, add-ons and apps [11, 28, 31]. Meanwhile, people publicize private information if they feel "somewhat typical or positively atypical compared to the target group" [27]; 80% of the Facebook users adopt identifiable or semi-identifiable profile photos, and less than 2% made use of the privacy settings [23]. Users' privacy settings violate their sharing intentions [38, 41], and they are unable or unwilling to fix the errors [41]. [33, 50] studies the discrepancies between users' perceived privacy disclosure and the actual exposure allowed by privacy policies. [42] explores three types of private information (e.g., medical conditions) shared in the textual content of tweet messages. Users may also post messages and later regret doing so for various reasons [47, 53, 63]. Impersonation attacks have been proposed [7] to steal private (friends-only) attributes by faking user identities. *(2) Information aggregation attacks.* We introduced information aggregation attacks in [34, 39, 70]: significant amount of privacy is recovered when small pieces of information submitted by users are associated. In particular, people are highly identifiable with very little information [21, 60], which make cross-network aggregations quite feasible. [6] confirms that a significant amount of user profiles from multiple SNSs could be linked by email addresses. *(3) Inference attacks.* Hidden attributes are inferred from friends' attributes with a Bayesian network [25, 26]. Unknown user attributes could be accurately inferred when as few as 20% of the users are known [45]. Friendship links and group membership information can be used to (uniquely) identify users [67] or infer sensitive hidden attributes [74], e.g., membership of a local engineer society discloses user's location and profession [74].

3. Privacy Threats in Published Social Network Data. *(1) Attribute re-identification attacks.* When social network data sets are published for legitimate reasons, user identities are removed. Some well-known techniques include *k-anonymity* [61], *l-diversity* [40] and *t-closeness* [35]. *(2) Structural re-identification attacks.* Graph structure from anonymized social network data could be utilized for re-identification (survey: [76]). Notably, [4] identifies the problem that node identities could be inferred through passive and active attacks. *Topological anonymity* quantifies the level of anonymity using the topology properties [52]. Adversaries with knowledge of user's neighbors could re-identify the user from network graph [75]. *k-degree anonymity* requires each node to have the same degree with at least $k-1$ other nodes [36]. [24] models three types of adversary knowledge that could be used to re-identify vertexes from an anonymized graph. [37] handles social network as a weighted graph, in which edge labels are also considered sensitive.

4. Social Network Privacy Models. Access control protocols and models have been proposed for social networks, such as [9, 10, 12, 22]. With the observation that it is difficult to explicitly define access control for large number of friends, tools have been built to manage privacy settings: *Privacy Wizards* [19] builds a machine learning model to predict and configure privacy rules, and *PViz* [43] is proposed to help users comprehend their privacy configurations based on the automatically labeled groups. [57] predicts privacy policies for newly uploaded images based on their content

similarities with existing images with known policies. Other approaches [68, 71, 72] help users group their contacts by exploiting the topology relationships among friends. However, none of the above mentioned approaches prevents privacy leakage during normal socialization, and some of them lack theoretical foundations from sociological perspectives and/or formal constructs.

6 CONCLUSION

With the extreme popularity of online social networks, it is crucial to protect private content without preventing users from normal socialization. In this paper, we articulate the social circle model, which aims to protect the boundary of information dissemination in social networks. We then use this model to examine six popular social networks: Facebook, Google+, VK, Tencent QZone, Weibo, and WeChat. We show that all social network platforms have issues in their implementations of the social circles that may put users' privacy at risk. Some of them pose severe vulnerabilities as their protection boundaries are leaky and sensitive information could flow out of the circle to a significantly larger audience. We also briefly discuss the implications of our findings, and other important issues that are relevant to the social circle model.

ACKNOWLEDGMENTS

The authors would also like to thank the anonymous referees for their valuable comments and helpful suggestions. This work was supported in part by: National Key R&D Program of China under 2016YFB0801300, International Collaboration Project of Institute of Information Engineering, Chinese Academy of Sciences under Grant Y7Z0511101, US National Science Foundation under NSF CNS-1422215, CNS-1422206 and DGE-1565570.

REFERENCES

[1] A. Acquisti. 2004. Privacy in Electronic Commerce and the Economics of Immediate Gratification. In *Proceedings of the 5th ACM Electronic Commerce Conference*.
[2] A. Acquisti and J. Grossklags. 2005. Privacy and Rationality in Decision Making. *IEEE Security and Privacy* (2005).
[3] I. Altman. 1975. *The Environment and Social Behavior: Privacy, Personal Space, Territory, and Crowding*. Brooks/Cole Publishing, Monterey, CA.
[4] Lars Backstrom, Cynthia Dwork, and Jon Kleinberg. 2007. Wherefore art thou r3579x?: anonymized social networks, hidden patterns, and structural steganography. In *WWW*.
[5] Randy Baden, Adam Bender, Neil Spring, Bobby Bhattacharjee, and Daniel Starin. 2009. Persona: an online social network with user-defined privacy. *SIGCOMM Comput. Commun. Rev.* 39, 4 (2009), 135–146.
[6] Marco Balduzzi, Christian Platzer, Thorsten Holz, Engin Kirda, Davide Balzarotti, and Christopher Kruegel. 2010. Abusing Social Networks for Automated User Profiling. In *Recent Advances in Intrusion Detection*. Vol. 6307. 422–441.
[7] L. Bilge, T. Strufe, D. Balzarotti, and E. Kirda. 2009. All your contacts are belong to us: automated identity theft attacks on social networks. In *WWW*.
[8] Gary Blosser and Justin Zhan. 2008. Privacy Preserving Collaborative Social Network. In *International Conference on Information Security and Assurance*.
[9] B. Carminati, E. Ferrari, R. Heatherly, M. Kantarcioglu, and B. Thuraisingham. 2009. A semantic web based framework for social network access control. In *ACM SACMAT*.
[10] B. Carminati, E. Ferrari, and A. Perego. 2009. Enforcing access control in web-based social networks. *ACM TISSEC* 13, 1 (2009).
[11] Pete Cashmore. 2009. Privacy is dead, and social media hold smoking gun. CNN. (October 2009).
[12] Y. Cheng, J. Park, and R. Sandhu. 2012. A user-to-user relationship-based access control model for online social networks. In *DBSec*.
[13] M.J. Culnan and J.R. Bies. 2003. Consumer Privacy: Balancing Economic and Justice Considerations. *Journal of Social Issues* 59, 2 (2003).
[14] Roger Dingledine, Nick Mathewson, and Paul Syverson. 2004. Tor: the second-generation onion router. In *USENIX Security Symposium*.
[15] Byron Dubow. 2007. Confessions of 'Facebook stalkers'. USA Today. (2007).

[16] Cynthia Dwork. 2008. Differential privacy: A survey of results. In *International Conference on Theory and Applications of Models of Computation*. Springer, 1–19.

[17] N.B. Ellison, C. Steinfield, and C. Lampe. 2007. The Benefits of Facebook "Friends:"Âś Social Capital and College Students' Use of Online Social Network Sites. *Journal of Computer-Mediated Communication* 12, 4 (2007), 1143–1168.

[18] Gunther Eysenbach and James E Till. 2001. Ethical issues in qualitative research on internet communities. *BMJ* 323 (2001), 1103–1105.

[19] Lujun Fang and Kristen LeFevre. 2010. Privacy Wizards for Social Networking Sites. In *International World Wide Web conference(WWW)*.

[20] David Goldschlag, Michael Reed, and Paul Syverson. 1999. Onion Routing for Anonymous and Private Internet Connections. *Commun. ACM* 42, 2 (1999).

[21] Philippe Golle. 2006. Revisiting the uniqueness of simple demographics in the US population. In *ACM WPES*. 77–80.

[22] L. González-Manzano, A. González-Tablas, J. de Fuentes, and A. Ribagorda. 2014. Extended U+ F social network protocol: Interoperability, reusability, data protection and indirect relationships in web based social networks. *Journal of Systems and Software* 94 (2014).

[23] Ralph Gross and Alessandro Acquisti. 2005. Information revelation and privacy in online social networks (The Facebook case). In *ACM WPES*. 71–80.

[24] Michael Hay, Gerome Miklau, David Jensen, Don Towsley, and Philipp Weis. 2008. Resisting structural re-identification in anonymized social networks. *Proc. VLDB Endow.* 1, 1 (2008), 102–114. https://doi.org/10.1145/1453856.1453873

[25] Jianming He and Wesley W. Chu. 2008. Protecting Private Information in Online Social Networks. In *Intelligence and Security Informatics*. 249–273.

[26] Jianming He, Wesley W. Chu, and Zhenyu Liu. 2006. Inferring Privacy Information from Social Networks. In *IEEE International Conference on Intelligence and Security Informatics*. 154–165.

[27] Bernardo A. Huberman, Eytan Adar, and Leslie R. Fine. 2005. Valuating Privacy. *IEEE Security and Privacy* 3, 5 (2005), 22–25.

[28] M Irvine. 2008. Social network users overlook privacy pitfalls. USA Today. (April 2008).

[29] Haiyan Jia and Heng Xu. 2016. Autonomous and interdependent: Collaborative privacy management on social networking sites. In *ACM CHI*.

[30] Sanjay Kairam, Mike Brzozowski, David Huffaker, and Ed Chi. 2012. Talking in circles: selective sharing in Google+. In *ACM CHI*.

[31] Balachander Krishnamurthy and Craig E. Wills. 2009. On the leakage of personally identifiable information via online social networks. In *ACM WOSN*.

[32] C. Lan, Y. Yang, X. Li, B. Luo, and J. Huan. 2017. Learning Social Circles in Ego-Networks based on Multi-View Network Structure. *IEEE TKDE* 29, 8 (2017).

[33] Yann Le Gall, Adam J. Lee, and Apu Kapadia. 2012. PlexC: a policy language for exposure control. In *ACM SACMAT*.

[34] Fengjun Li, Jake Y. Chen, Xukai Zou, and Peng Liu. 2010. New Privacy Threats in Healthcare Informatics: When Medical Records Join the Web. In *Proceedings of the 9th International Workshop on Data Mining in Bioinformatics (BIOKDD)*.

[35] Ninghui Li, Tiancheng Li, and Suresh Venkatasubramanian. 2007. t-Closeness: Privacy Beyond k-Anonymity and l-Diversity. In *Proceedings of the 23rd International Conference on Data Engineering*. 106–115.

[36] Kun Liu and Evimaria Terzi. 2008. Towards identity anonymization on graphs. In *Proceedings of the 2008 ACM SIGMOD international conference on Management of data*.

[37] Lian Liu, Jie Wang, Jinze Liu, and Jun Zhang. 2008. *Privacy Preserving in Social Networks Against Sensitive Edge Disclosure*. Technical Report CMIDA-HiPSCCS 006-08. University of Kentucky.

[38] Yabing Liu, Krishna P. Gummadi, Balachander Krishnamurthy, and Alan Mislove. 2011. Analyzing facebook privacy settings: user expectations vs. reality. In *Proceedings of the 2011 ACM SIGCOMM conference on Internet measurement conference (IMC '11)*. ACM, New York, NY, USA, 61–70.

[39] Bo Luo and Dongwon Lee. 2009. On Protecting Private Information in Social Networks: A Proposal. In *IEEE ICDE Workshop on Modeling, Managing, and Mining of Evolving Social Networks (MMSN)*.

[40] Ashwin Machanavajjhala, Daniel Kifer, Johannes Gehrke, and Muthuramakrishnan Venkitasubramaniam. 2007. L-diversity: Privacy beyond k-anonymity. *ACM Trans. Knowl. Discov. Data* 1, 1 (2007), 3. https://doi.org/10.1145/1217299.1217302

[41] M. Madejski, M. Johnson, and S. M. Bellovin. 2011. *The failure of online social network privacy settings*. Technical Report CUCS-010-11. Columbia University.

[42] Huina Mao, Xin Shuai, and Apu Kapadia. 2011. Loose tweets: an analysis of privacy leaks on twitter. In *Proceedings of the 10th annual ACM workshop on Privacy in the electronic society (WPES '11)*. ACM, New York, NY, USA, 1–12.

[43] Alessandra Mazzia, Kristen LeFevre, and Eytan Adar. 2012. The PViz comprehension tool for social network privacy settings. In *Proceedings of the Eighth Symposium on Usable Privacy and Security*. Article 13, 12 pages.

[44] Julian McAuley and Jure Leskovec. 2012. Discovering social circles in ego networks. *TKDD'13* (2012).

[45] Alan Mislove, Bimal Viswanath, Krishna P. Gummadi, and Peter Druschel. 2010. You are who you know: inferring user profiles in online social networks. In *Proceedings of the third ACM international conference on Web search and data mining (WSDM '10)*. ACM, 251–260. https://doi.org/10.1145/1718487.1718519

[46] P.A. Norberg, D.R. Horne, and D.A. Horne. 2007. The privacy paradox: Personal information disclosure intentions versus behaviors. *Journal of Consumer Affairs* 41, 1 (2007).

[47] Sameer Patil, Greg Norcie, Apu Kapadia, and Adam J Lee. 2012. Reasons, rewards, regrets: Privacy considerations in location sharing as an interactive practice. In *Proceedings of the Eighth Symposium on Usable Privacy and Security*. ACM, 5.

[48] S. Rajtmajer, A. Squicciarini, C. Griffin, S. Karumanchi, and A. Tyagi. 2016. Constrained social-energy minimization for multi-party sharing in online social networks. In *AAMAS*.

[49] Michael K. Reiter and Aviel D. Rubin. 1998. Crowds: anonymity for Web transactions. *ACM Trans. Inf. Syst. Secur.* 1, 1 (1998), 66–92. https://doi.org/10.1145/290163.290168

[50] Roman Schlegel, Apu Kapadia, and Adam J. Lee. 2011. Eyeing your exposure: quantifying and controlling information sharing for improved privacy. In *SOUPS*.

[51] Kapil Singh, Sumeer Bhola, and Wenke Lee. 2009. xBook: Redesigning Privacy Control in Social Networking Platforms. In *USENIX Security Symposium*.

[52] Lisa Singh and Justin Zhan. 2007. Measuring Topological Anonymity in Social Networks. In *GRC '07: Proceedings of the 2007 IEEE International Conference on Granular Computing*.

[53] M. Sleeper, J. Cranshaw, P. Kelley, B. Ur, A. Acquisti, L. Cranor, and N. Sadeh. 2013. I read my Twitter the next morning and was astonished: a conversational perspective on Twitter regrets. In *ACM CHI*.

[54] Anna Squicciarini, Sushama Karumanchi, Dan Lin, and Nicole DeSisto. 2013. Identifying hidden social circles for advanced privacy configuration. *Computers & Security* (2013).

[55] Anna Squicciarini, Dan Lin, Sushama Karumanchi, and Nicole DeSisto. 2012. Automatic social group organization and privacy management. In *CollaborateCom*.

[56] A. Squicciarini, M. Shehab, and J. Wede. 2010. Privacy policies for shared content in social network sites. *VLDBJ* 19, 6 (2010).

[57] Anna Cinzia Squicciarini, Smitha Sundareswaran, Dan Lin, and Josh Wede. 2011. A3P: adaptive policy prediction for shared images over popular content sharing sites. In *Proceedings of the 22nd ACM conference on Hypertext and hypermedia*.

[58] J. Such and N. Criado. 2016. Resolving multi-party privacy conflicts in social media. *IEEE TKDE* 28, 7 (2016).

[59] J. Such and M. Rovatsos. 2016. Privacy policy negotiation in social media. *ACM TAAS* 11, 1 (2016).

[60] Latanya Sweeney. 2000. Uniqueness of Simple Demographics in the U.S. Population. (2000).

[61] Latanya Sweeney. 2002. k-anonymity: a model for protecting privacy. *Int. J. Uncertain. Fuzziness Knowl.-Based Syst.* 10, 5 (2002), 557–570. https://doi.org/10.1142/S0218488502001648

[62] H.T. Tavani. 2007. Philosophical Theories of Privacy: Implications for an Adequate Online Privacy Policy. *Metaphilosophy* 38, 1 (2007).

[63] Y. Wang, G. Norcie, S. Komanduri, A. Acquisti, P. Leon, and L. Cranor. 2011. I regretted the minute I pressed share: A qualitative study of regrets on Facebook. In *SOUPS*. ACM, 10.

[64] Jason Watson, Andrew Besmer, and Heather Richter Lipford. 2012. + Your circles: sharing behavior on Google+. In *ACM SOUPS*.

[65] A.F. Westin. 1967. *Privacy and Freedom*. Atheneum, New York.

[66] Pamela Wisniewski, Heng Xu, and Yunan Chen. 2014. Understanding user adaptation strategies for the launching of facebook timeline. In *ACM CHI*.

[67] Gilbert Wondracek, Thorsten Holz, Engin Kirda, and Christopher Kruegel. 2010. A Practical Attack to De-anonymize Social Network Users. In *IEEE Symposium on Security and Privacy*.

[68] Qian Xiao, Htoo Htet Aung, and Kian-Lee Tan. 2012. Towards ad-hoc circles in social networking sites. In *Proceedings of the 2nd ACM SIGMOD Workshop on Databases and Social Networks (DBSocial '12)*. 19–24.

[69] Yuhao Yang, Chao Lan, Xiaoli Li, Bo Luo, and Jun Huan. 2014. Automatic social circle detection using multi-view clustering. In *ACM CIKM*.

[70] Yuhao Yang, Jonathan Lutes, Fengjun Li, Bo Luo, and Peng Liu. 2012. Stalking Online: on User Privacy in Social Networks. In *ACM Conference on Data and Application Security and Privacy (CODASPY)*.

[71] H. Yildiz and C. Kruegel. 2012. Detecting social cliques for automated privacy control in online social networks. In *IEEE PERCOM Workshops*.

[72] A.S. Yuksel, M.E. Yuksel, and A.H. Zaim. 2010. An Approach for Protecting Privacy on Social Networks. In *Systems and Networks Communications (ICSNC), 2010 Fifth International Conference on*. 154 –159.

[73] Justin Zhan, Gary Blosser, Chris Yang, and Lisa Singh. 2008. Privacy-Preserving Collaborative Social Networks. In *Pacific Asia Workshop on Intelligence and Security Informatics (PAISI)*.

[74] Elena Zheleva and Lise Getoor. 2009. To Join or not to Join: The Illusion of Privacy in Social Networks with Mixed Public and Private User Profiles. In *WWW*.

[75] Bin Zhou and Jian Pei. 2008. Preserving privacy in social networks against neighborhood attacks. In *Proceedings of the 24th International Conference on Data Engineering (ICDE)*.

[76] Bin Zhou, Jian Pei, and WoShun Luk. 2008. A brief survey on anonymization techniques for privacy preserving publishing of social network data. *SIGKDD Explor. Newsl.* 10, 2 (2008), 12–22.

Sensing or Watching? Balancing Utility and Privacy in Sensing Systems via Collection and Enforcement Mechanisms

Adam J. Lee
University of Pittsburgh
Pittsburgh, PA, USA
adamlee@cs.pitt.edu

Jacob T. Biehl
FXPAL
Palo Alto, CA, USA
biehl@fxpal.com

Conor Curry
University of Pittsburgh
Pittsburgh, PA, USA
clc231@pitt.edu

ABSTRACT

Devices with embedded sensors are permeating the computing landscape, allowing the collection and analysis of rich data about individuals, smart spaces, and their interactions. This class of devices enables a useful array of home automation and connected workplace functionality to individuals within instrumented spaces. Unfortunately, the increasing pervasiveness of sensors can lead to perceptions of privacy loss by their occupants. Given that many instrumented spaces exist as platforms outside of a user's control—e.g., IoT sensors in the home that rely on cloud infrastructure or connected workplaces managed by one's employer—enforcing access controls via a trusted reference monitor may do little to assuage individuals' privacy concerns. This calls for novel enforcement mechanisms for controlling access to sensed data.

In this paper, we investigate the interplay between sensor fidelity and individual comfort, with the goal of understanding the design space for effective, yet palatable, sensors for the workplace. In the context of a common space contextualization task, we survey and interview individuals about their comfort with three common sensing modalities: video, audio, and passive infrared. This allows us to explore the extent to which discomfort with sensor platforms is a function of *detected states* or *sensed data*. Our findings uncover interesting interplays between content, context, fidelity, history, and privacy. This, in turn, leads to design recommendations regarding how to increase comfort with sensing technologies by revisiting the mechanisms by which user preferences and policies are enforced in situations where the infrastructure itself is not trusted.

CCS CONCEPTS

• **Security and privacy** → **Access control**; **Privacy protections**;

ACM Reference Format:
Adam J. Lee, Jacob T. Biehl, and Conor Curry. 2018. Sensing or Watching? Balancing Utility and Privacy in Sensing Systems via Collection and Enforcement Mechanisms. In *SACMAT '18: The 23rd ACM Symposium on Access Control Models & Technologies (SACMAT), June 13–15, 2018, Indianapolis, IN, USA.* ACM, New York, NY, USA, 12 pages. https://doi.org/10.1145/3205977.3205983

1 INTRODUCTION

The world is becoming an very connected place. Advancements in the Internet of Things (IoT) and wearable technologies are extending the reach of technology into daily life. This is resulting in the collection of huge amounts of data about people, instrumented spaces, and the interactions between people and spaces. One promising class of technologies within this space is workplace awareness tools. The development, deployment, and study of these types of systems is a rich space within the intersection of the IoT and sensing research communities. By leveraging instrumented spaces, these types of systems are able to provide details and assistance about co-workers' location and availability, as well as contextualize how shared spaces are being used. Deployments of these technologies have shown their value in increasing timely communication among peers and promoting a greater sense of community in the work environment (e.g., [7, 11, 21, 23, 34]).

However, these systems also expose workers to a variety of potential security and privacy risks, especially when users are suspicious of the operators of the system. For instance, a vengeful manager could use data that was collected to help foster collaboration in ways that were not envisioned and are potentially detrimental to the employee. These concerns are legitimate, and are often reported as a major barriers to adoption or widespread use in the studies of these systems. As Patil et al. [31] noted, *"user opposition due to privacy concerns can translate into minimal use or even the abandonment of the system."* Similarly, Biehl et al. [6] found that *"Violations of their model [of data use], or even uncertainty as to how the data are being used, negatively impacts use"* of these types of systems. Interestingly, standard approaches to access control are unlikely to increase user comfort if the system enforcing these controls is not trusted by the user specifying preferences or policies regarding the collection and use of their information.

This presents an interesting tension: namely, balancing appropriate uses of these technologies while protecting individuals' privacy. There are many approaches that have been proposed for mitigating this tension, ranging from the use of formal policies, to controls for reciprocity and awareness. An alternate take on this issue appeals to Saltzer and Schroeder's oft-cited principle of least privilege: *Every [component] of the system should operate using the least set of privileges necessary to complete the job* [36]. Viewed through this lens, it is unsurprising that privacy and sensing are intrinsically linked: systems that have an imbalance in the amount, fidelity, or type of data that is collected to support a given sensing task can lead to actual (i.e., realized) or perceived (i.e., potential) privacy violations. For instance, a system that counts people in a space using video will always have the potential to collect and, in the worst case, share the broader—and perhaps sensitive—contexts of and goings-on within that space. These violations can be malicious or, more likely, accidental.

This exposes an important technical challenge: preserving some notion of least privilege by mitigating privacy concerns at the sensing level, while supporting functionality and usability at the application level. We explore three modalities of presence sensors typically found in the workplace: those built using video, audio, or motion monitors. Given minimal performance differences between sensors built using each of these modalities in common workplace scenarios, we carry out a broad and representative evaluation exploring user-level discomfort arising from privacy concerns with these technologies across a variety of contexts of use.

In this work, we show that the privacy and utility gap can be narrowed such that there is better alignment between the technologies deployed and individuals' concerns over privacy. We conclude that complex policy controls may not be the best solution to the challenge of balancing privacy and utility in these workplace awareness scenarios, and perhaps broader IoT contexts. We further posit that these controls should be supplemented by the careful selection of sensing technologies used, in accordance with the principle of least privilege. We support this conclusion through a series of lessons for the design of future systems for enabling workplace awareness that balance accuracy with the privacy needs of individuals within an instrumented space.

2 RELATED WORK

We now highlight key areas of related work that provide context for the class of sensing problems that we study, raise privacy issues associated with ubiquitous and social systems, or propose solutions to the privacy problems emergent in these types of environments.

2.1 Awareness Technologies

Sensor driven awareness systems have a rich history in this research community. Early work on Portholes [11], a tool for sharing video feeds of colleagues' offices, pioneered the concept of workplace awareness tools. This work has inspired researchers to better understand the importance and conveyance of rhythms and activities in the workplace. For instance, Begole et al. [2] and Reddy and Dourish [33] both observed that workers exhibit periodic, predictable behaviors, or rhythms, and these signals become well understood in long term co-working environments and are often used in deciding how or when to establish contact.

Many systems have been developed to transition these findings into technological solutions. These include BlueSpace [28], ConNexus [40], MyVine [16], SideShow [7], InteruptMe [21], MyUnity [46], and many more. Many of these systems have been studied through broad deployment. Throughout the findings, there is consensus from this body of work that awareness systems are perceived by workers as useful tools in workplace. Further, their use has also been shown to effect many positive workplace communication behavior changes such as decreased time spent on email and an increase in more productive face-to-face meetings [7, 21, 46].

2.2 Privacy Issues in Ubiquitous and Social Systems

Ubiquitous and social computing systems are home to unique privacy problems [24]. These systems differ from traditional computing systems in that information is gathered continuously, rather than being created by individuals in distinct editing sessions. Further, individual users must behave as policy administrators and govern their own data sharing, rather than relying on trained security administrators to set policy for them. This pervasive collection of information and near seamless sharing make it easy to accidentally post information to unintended audiences [12], which can lead individuals to harbor feelings of regret [32, 44], cause feelings of embarrassment or humiliation [39], or even loss of employment [38].

Much research has been conducted into the factors leading to discomfort with the sharing of contextual information. Many studies have shown that a user's relationship with the data consumer to impact their comfort in sharing information (e.g., [9, 29]). The granularity at which information is accessed (e.g., city- vs. GPS-level access to location) has been found to be an important factor governing comfort (e.g., [6, 9, 30]), as has the frequency with which data is accessed by others (e.g., [6, 37]). Whether or not data is stored historically or simply shared ephemerally has also been shown to contribute to individuals' comfort with these systems [6]. Similarly, the purpose with which information is accessed has a major impact on individuals' comfort with sharing (e.g., [6, 9, 41]). These and other factors lead to a myriad of potential privacy issues in context sharing systems.

Of particular note are studies of sensing within the context of smart homes. The literature contains general discussions of privacy as being an important factor to consider in the design of smart homes (e.g., [27]), survey studies of behaviors in the home (e.g., [8]), and the development of purpose-built sensors for detecting home activities (e.g., [15]). Like our work, the above highlight the important role that context and fidelity play in perception of privacy. However, this body of work tends to focus either on privacy in a general sense, or the perceived implications of a particular sensing technology. Our work assesses the privacy implications of a variety of sensing technologies for a single type of sensing task across multiple contexts: to our knowledge, this is a unique contribution.

2.3 Privacy Controls for Ubiquitous and Social Systems

Given the complexity of issues surrounding privacy in these types of systems, a diversity of work has been done on developing solutions to provide users with some measure of control over their data sharing. Much work has gone into designing access controls and policy languages that can be used to govern data and context sharing in these types of systems, many of which provide controls for the above types of factors influencing individual comfort (e.g., [10, 17, 19, 22]). Others, however, recognize that individuals are often not trained as policy administrators, and instead seek to use machine learning to automate the process of setting privacy policies for location or social networking systems (e.g., [14, 35]).

Systems that make use of reciprocity in sharing are becoming more prevalent in this space. For instance, the privacy settings on

LinkedIn[1] allow users to see who has viewed their profile only if they are willing to share their identity with individuals whose profiles they visit. Similar efforts have been explored in the context of location sharing [3]. Other systems like Facebook Messenger[2], WhatsApp[3], and Google Hangouts[4] provide notifications to senders when messages are read by their recipients, making for reciprocal data sharing between the sender and receiver.

In addition to controls for who can access information, others have looked at building awareness regarding *when* information is accessed. This has a long history in the ubiquitous computing space [4], and has recently been explored in the context of social [43] and location sharing [37, 42] systems. These systems may make use of explicit, log-like records of accesses to an individual's data [42], or make use of summary techniques in an effort to preserve the privacy of individuals requesting information [37].

Finally, we note that the types of privacy controls explored our work occur at the sensor level, before the data to be shared with a system is even computed. As such, the resulting awareness information is amenable to any of the above-described approaches to further protect individual privacy.

3 WORKPLACE ACTIVITY SENSORS

In this paper, we seek to study the utility and privacy attitudes that people harbor towards sensing technologies that have application in the workplace. To this end, we describe a particular sensing task that enables a variety of smart-space functionality, identify three sensor modalities that are typical in today's workplaces, and explore the relative trade-offs between these types of sensors. These sensing modalities will form the basis of a survey and interview study aimed at understanding the design space for sensing systems that people trust to balance these types of trade-offs.

3.1 Scenario and Technologies

A key functionality of awareness platforms, and smart offices in general, is the ability to automatically assess the occupancy or utilization of a space. This functionality can help individuals locate colleagues for the purposes of interaction or collaboration (e.g., *Is Chris in his office?*), as well as contextualize spaces (e.g., *Is Chris alone in his office, or holding a meeting? Is anyone using the 4th floor conference room?*). For the purposes of our investigation, we focus on the following sensing problem:

PROBLEM (SPACE CONTEXTUALIZATION). *Given a space S, determine whether S is unoccupied, in use by a single individual, or being used by multiple individuals.*

In the event that (some) spaces are controlled by individual users, the above problem can help with certain classes of localization: e.g., if Chris' office is occupied, Chris is probably in it. Furthermore, presence sensors are used in a variety of tasks including security monitoring, building automation, energy conservation, space-based analytics, etc. A principle aspect of building smart workspaces is understanding whether and to what degree spaces are occupied. As

[1]http://www.linkedin.com/
[2]https://www.messenger.com/
[3]https://www.whatsapp.com/
[4]https://hangouts.google.com/

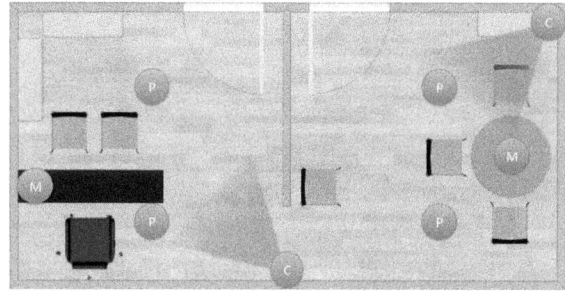

Figure 1: Office floor plan with sensor placements (C = Camera, M = Microphone, P = PIR housing)

such, the space contextualization problem is a foundational enabler for a variety of applications.

We note that locating a single user is easily accomplished via the use of indoor localization techniques (e.g., based upon ultrasonic sound [18], infrared [45], RFID [20], WiFi/Bluetooth [5], or coded light [13] transmissions). However, leveraging indoor localization techniques to address the space contextualization problem is tricky. First, this requires buy-in from *all* individuals that may potentially use a space; this is likely unreasonable in situations with individuals not deriving value from this tracking (e.g., customers at a bank, or undergraduate students attending office hours). Second, these systems can enable persistent employee tracking in ways that other sensing platforms may not.

3.2 Prototypical Sensor Platforms

Rather than surveying user perceptions of purely hypothetical sensors, we sought to ground our study in reality. We began by carrying out an informal assessment of the types of sensors commonly deployed in office environments. In the end, three sensing modalities emerged as pervasive in these environments: video, audio, and passive infrared (PIR). The use of both video and audio processing date back to early work in presence literature (e.g., the Portholes system [11]), and readily support object and conversation detection. Further, these three sensing technologies are widely deployed in existing workplaces: cameras are deployed in many workplace security systems; microphones are increasingly deployed as part of networked meeting spaces and voice assistants (e.g., Apple's Siri, Google Home, or Amazon Echo); and most office spaces use PIR sensors to automatically control lighting and other environmental systems. Although individuals may not have each of these technologies in their personal workspace, it is likely that their pervasiveness means that individuals have a general sense of familiarity with these technologies.

One thing that was unclear from our assessment was the degree to which these sensing modalities might differ in terms of accuracy for the sensing task at hand. If this were the case, accuracy differences between technologies would likely dictate deployment decisions, thereby overriding ancillary benefits of one technology over another (e.g., user privacy considerations). To explore this, we ran a small experiment in which we instrumented an office (Figure 1) with three prototype sensors (one per sensing modality). These prototypes were informed by the presence literature, and

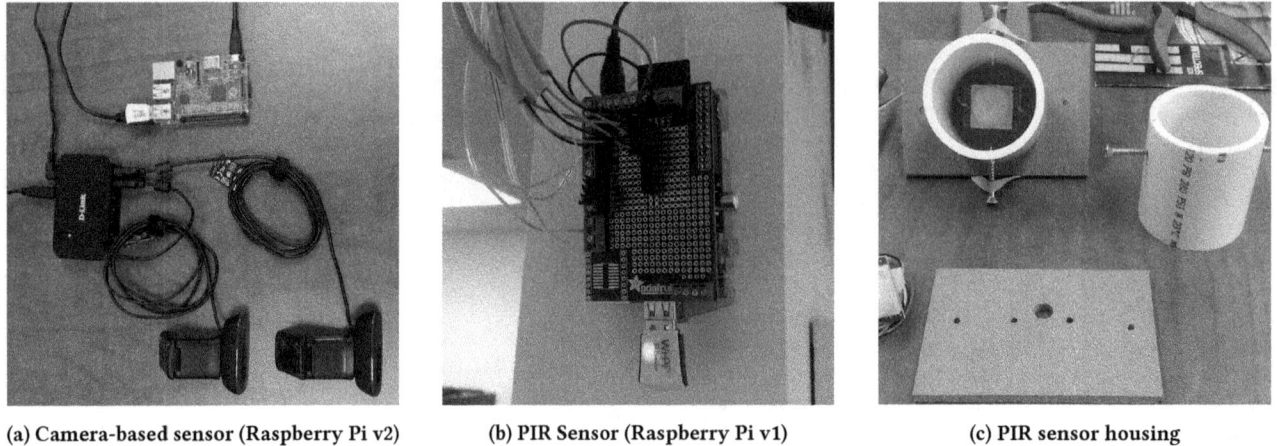

(a) Camera-based sensor (Raspberry Pi v2)   (b) PIR Sensor (Raspberry Pi v1)   (c) PIR sensor housing

Figure 2: Prototype sensor hardware. The camera- and PIR-based sensors were developed using the Raspberry Pi platform to allow for easy incorporation into the physical environment. The housings used in the PIR sensor package allow for the monitoring of smaller office sub-regions, rather than the office as a whole. The audio sensor (not pictured) was a software-only implementation installed on computers already existing in the space.

are shown in Figure 2. We evaluated sensor accuracy in this context over the course of a typical work week, and found only minor variations in accuracy across a variety of workplace activities. This indicates that, even at the prototype level, accuracy alone should not, solely, dictate sensor selection.

3.3 Trade-offs

These types of sensors represent a range of utility and privacy affordances. The camera-based sensor package provides easy deployability in spaces already outfitted with cameras. However, processing high resolution images of a space to detect a three-value state carries a high potential for privacy "collateral damage" if the camera feed is compromised or stored. Audio sensor packages would likely require slight modifications to room-based microphone systems, as the microphones must sample continuously, rather than only when activated by the user. The audio sensor that we deployed was designed to prevent the capture of entire conversations via sampling, although we have not formally studied whether it is possible to reconstruct words (or even emotional states) from the snippets that are captured and processed. Finally, the PIR sensor package has the lowest potential for privacy violation, although this comes with the most overhead in terms of deployment. Typical PIR sensor configurations in office spaces are designed to scan the entirety of the space, not the targeted areas used by our application.

The literature (e.g., [4, 6]) highlights the need for tunable participation in awareness systems to help balance privacy and utility. This is in terms of enabling opt-in or opt-out of various sensors, as well as balancing the frequency, fidelity, and archival of information captured. Clearly, providing more information leads to higher quality presence states. However, privacy must be considered, otherwise invasive sensors will simply be turned off, reducing the quality of data brokered by the system. Despite this observation, the research community has largely been focused on understanding and improving the performance of individual technologies. Our hope is that reducing the privacy collateral damage associated with

sensing by appealing to the principle of least privilege will lead to greater sensor opt-in, which increases the quality of information provided by the system. *That is, we believe that sensors designed for privacy can actually beget utility.* In support of this sentiment, we now turn our research towards understanding how the selection of these potential technologies could impact workplace privacy expectations and sentiments.

4 SURVEY OF CONTEXT SENTIMENT

In the previous section, we examined various technologies for workplace presence detection tasks. While this effort provides a good grounding for gaging trade-offs of one technology over another for a given context of use, it also raises many meta-level questions about how sensing technologies are *chosen* for deployment. Specifically, the varying tension between ease of deployment and accuracy vs. perceived invasiveness could help guide the deployment of awareness systems that balance the need for high quality information with the privacy of the individuals using monitored spaces. Towards building a broader understanding of this tension, we conducted a large-scale survey that examines user sentiment and concerns across a variety of contexts of use.

4.1 Contexts of Use

With breadth as the goal, we designed our survey to gage user sentiment regarding presence sensing technologies across four broad contexts of use. Three contexts were situated within a workplace setting. In each context, the workplace was introduced in the following way: *"Consider that you work in a workspace where each worker has his/her own office, and a presence system is in use to help facilitate person-to-person communication within the workplace."* We further specified the context of use into three categories, described to users as follows:

- **Personal office (PO):** *Consider the use of [presence] technologies within your own office.*

- **Colleague's office, work (CW):** *Consider the use of [presence] technologies while you are visiting a colleague's office to attend a work related meeting.*
- **Colleague's office, social (CS):** *Consider the use of [presence] technologies while you are visiting a colleague's office for the purpose of a brief social interaction.*

A fourth context of use focused on use in workplaces a person may visit as a **Customer to a Business (B)**. It was defined to users as follows: *"Consider you are visiting a place that you do business with (e.g., a bank or insurance office), and a presence system is in use to manage the distribution of incoming clients to representatives of the business. Consider the use of these technologies while you meet with a representative in his/her personal office."*

4.2 Presence Technologies

In the survey, we asked about the same technologies explored in the previous section: video camera (C), audio microphone (A), and motion sensor (M). As noted before, our motivation for selecting these technologies is that they are already in pervasive use in workplaces today and, perhaps as a result, are technologies that everyday users are likely to understand.

We prepared a series of short video explanations to (i) explain the purpose of data collection, (ii) situate how the technologies are used, and (iii) provide details about what information each technology collected, and the events that it could detect. These videos showed a typical office workplace (see Figure 1) and illustrated how each specific technology would be deployed in that environment. A short explanation was then given to demonstrate how each sensor collected and processed information. We note that the order in which technologies were presented in these videos was dictated by a 3x3 Latin Square (see "Participants, Calibration, and Counterbalance," below). We believe that these videos were important to ensure that our survey respondents all had the same understanding of not only the technologies' capabilities, but also the context in which they were deployed and used. The video for the C-A-M ordering condition can be found online[5]; the other videos are identical, modulo technology ordering.

4.3 Survey Questions

Our survey contained a mix of free-form and Likert rating questions. Questions were organized so that participants were asked to give their opinion and sentiment for each of the technologies (C, A, and M) across the various contexts of use (PO, CW, CS, and B). This provided an in-depth understanding across various dimensions, which included:

- Comfort with each technology and specific context of use
- Differences in comfort with the technology across contexts of use
- Differences in comfort with the technology when sensed data may be stored for historical or archival purposes
- Differences in comfort with the technology as a factor of respondents' overall privacy concerns
- Expectation of notification and/or awareness that technologies are deployed and in use

- Differences in notification and/or awareness preferences across contexts of use

A copy of our survey instrument (ordered for the C-A-M condition) is available in the Appendix.

4.4 Interviews

For a subset of survey participants, we conducted follow up in-person interviews. To ensure that responses were still fresh in the minds of participants, these interviews were conducted within 24 hours of the survey being completed. The format of the interview generally followed a process of reviewing responses with participants, and then asking them to verbally provide a rationale or explanation for their rating. Through these interviews, we were able to a gain an even deeper, more contextual explanation for what motivated users concerns and preferences.

4.5 Participants, Calibration, and Counterbalance

Participants who only participated in the survey were recruited using the internal Amazon Mechanical Turk worker solicitation tools. Workers were restricted to being from the United States and over the age of 18. A total of 240 participants participated in the survey, which was conducted over a two day period in the spring of 2015. 50% were female. We did not collect absolute age of participants, but had them respond based on range: 15.4% 18-24, 32.9% 25-34, 26.3% 35-44, 15.4% 45-54, 8.8% 55-64, 1.3% 65+. Education level was also diverse; 11.3% high school or less, 10.0% attended college but no degree, 6.6% attended trade schools or programs, 10.4% earned associate degree, 35.8% bachelors, 7.1% masters, 2.0% professional degree, and 0.4% doctorate. Upon competition of the survey, participants received $1.

Nine of these participants were recruited using convenience sampling using organizational-level email solicitations in two organizations: a computer science department and a corporate research laboratory, both of which have sensor deployments to support the use of awareness systems by employees. These participants participated in the survey and follow-up interviews. The average interview time was 15:06 (SD=3:04). The age distribution for this group was comparable to the broader group, 22.2% 18-24, 55.5% 25-34, 11.1% 35-44, 11.1% 55-64. Given the additional time commitment of participating in the follow-up interview, these participants received $5 compensation.

All participants also completed a qualitative rating survey [25], categorizing them on Westin's three-level privacy sensitivity scale [1]. Across all participants, 29.6% categorized as Privacy Fundamentalists, 67.9% Privacy Pragmatists, and 2.5% Privacy Unconcerned. Compared to prior large population privacy studies (e.g., [25]), this distribution is similar except for a slightly lower than normal proportion of Privacy Unconcerned individuals. This difference is likely attributed to two factors. First, past research has shown that Mechanical Turk workers trend more privacy conscious than the broader population [26]. Second, during the time that the survey was administered, the United States NSA phone tapping and tracking activities were popular national news. We, however, believe this population to still be valid and representative, given the nature

---

[5]http://bit.ly/1R36Ldu

of our investigation. Higher attention and interest to privacy concerns will likely lead to more articulate and detailed explanations in survey responses.

To prevent ordering bias, the presentation of the technologies and the ordering of the scenarios of use considered were counterbalanced. At the beginning of the survey, the ordering of technologies described in the short introductory video was counterbalanced using a 3x3 Latin Square. For each participant, the ordering of technologies in their video was preserved through all of the context of use scenario questions. The ordering of the four context of use scenarios was randomized using mechanisms in the Qualtrics survey software[6]. In our analysis, we checked for ordering effect on all responses. No significant differences were found, and we do not report on this further.

5　RESULTS

From our broad survey, we found several consistencies in the responses across the variety of technologies and scenarios of use that were investigated. An unsurprising, but important, high-level result showed that comfort ratings were neutral to slightly negative as a whole. Specifically, collapsing across use and scenario conditions, the mean comfort score was 2.87 (SD=1.43, n=2880) on a 5-point scale ranging from very uncomfortable (1) to very comfortable (5), with a neutral condition (3).

Demographics, specifically the respondents' gender, age, and education level did not have a significant effect on comfort rating. While not significant (p=0.060), the data showed a small, negative trend between level of education and comfort rating. That is, respondents with higher levels of education trended lower in their ratings.

Also, perhaps as expected, we found that the Westin Privacy response had significant impact on comfort ratings ($F_{(2,237)}=10.999$, $p<0.0001$, participant as random effect). A post hoc Tukey HSD test ($\alpha=0.050$, Q=2.359) revealed significance between each Westin category. Privacy fundamentalists were most concerned (M=2.56, SD=0.11), followed by pragmatists (M=2.95, SD=0.07) and unconcerned (M=4.13, SD=0.36).

A two-way ANOVA was performed with scenario and technology as independent variables and participant as a random effect. Technology ($F_{(2,2629)}=489.312$, $p<0.001$) and scenario ($F_{(3,2629)}=48.677$, $p<0.001$) both had main effects. Interaction was just short of significance ($F_{(6,2629)}=2.061$, $p=0.0546$). In short, technology and scenario both showed significant differences, when accounting for participant variance. That is, it is not the case that one explains the outcome of the other, it is likely these two factors contribute uniquely to a person's privacy concerns. Thus, in this investigation, we look at both factors in detail.

To better situate the results, we organize further analysis of the main effects within broader categorizations of our findings, including context provided by the qualitative measures.

5.1　Sensor Fidelity Matters

As the above main effect indicates, technology had a large and significant impact on participants' ratings of comfort. A post hoc Tukey HSD test ($\alpha=0.050$, Q=2.345) revealed significance across

---

[6]http://www.qualtrics.com/

all technologies. Microphone was rated lowest (M=2.42, SD=0.06). Followed closely, but significantly different from, camera (M=2.53, SD=0.06). Motion sensors, interestingly, were rated *above* neutral (M=3.64, SD=0.06).

Participants were asked in the survey to provide explanation for each of their comfort ratings. This qualitative channel provided some context for the difference in ratings. Many indicated that a large amount of discomfort with microphones and cameras stemmed from the fact that they captured data that could reveal a person's identity. As one participant stated, *"I would be uncomfortable with any technology that would collect and/or store any information that is identifiable or traceable back to any specific person."* This person further explains, *"I'm comfortable with the motion sensor because there is no identifying information tied to it other than simply motion was detected or not."*

While similar, others expressed discomfort because microphones and cameras could detect actions. For instance, one participant stated, *"I tend to talk to myself when I'm alone, I may say inappropriate things out loud that [could be captured]."* Similarly, another participant noted, *"Maybe [if] I fall asleep and snore briefly. Maybe I'm overwhelmed and sit and rest my head as I pull together from a busy task. This can be [captured] and taken out of context."*

5.2　Personal vs. Professional Personas

Scenario was also observed to have a main effect on participants' comfort ratings. A post hoc Tukey HSD test ($\alpha=0.050$, Q=2.571) revealed significance across all scenarios. Personal office (PO) was rated lowest (M=2.61, SD=0.06). Followed by colleague's office for social interactions (CS) (M=2.74, SD=0.06), colleague's office for work (CW) (M=2.95, SD=0.06), and external business as a customer (B) (M=3.17, SD=0.06).

While scenarios were significantly different from each other, the quantitative results revealed that participants were less comfortable with the presence of sensing technology when the space was being used for personal or non-professional activities. In contrast, for true work-related interactions, the concerns were more neutral.

This observation also emerged in the qualitative data. One participant articulated his comfort ratings in this way: *"It would depend on how intimate and private of a situation I would be facing. If I were talking about something personal, I would need more privacy."* Many participants were very direct about the personal interactions that concerned them the most: family. For instance, one participant stated *"Personal visits from family/friends are more private and demand greater protections, making these technologies more intrusive."* Another stated, *"If I have my friend or family visiting, presence of these technologies would be considered like personal invasion, espionage."*

5.3　Content and Context

Despite not having a true statistical interaction, there are aspects of the data that point to an interesting relationship between scenario and technology. In line with a weak interaction effect, we found that despite the overall comfort scores across scenarios being significantly different (as noted above), the variance of comfort scores within a particular scenario are quite similar (SD=1.44, 1.40, 1.42,

1.37, for PO, CW, CS, and B scenarios, respectively). Indeed the differences between the highest rated technology (motion) and lowest (audio) have similar mean distances across all scenarios (1.26, 1.24, 1.22, 1.18, for PO, CW, CS, and B, respectively). That is, the spread of comfort ratings across technologies was consistent across scenarios, but not the means (overall, or individually by technology).

It is likely that this result emerges based on the influence that a scenario has on the type of conversations and interactions that occur within it. For instance, the higher comfort with all technologies in the external business scenario is likely the result of participants believing they are less likely to have sensitive interactions within these spaces. As one participant stated, *"an office is a setting where professionalism is always the expectation."* Another participant was even more explicit, stating *"Whether I was visiting the CEO or another associate at the same level as myself I wouldn't be bothered by these technologies. When a person is at work all interactions should be professional."*

In contrast, not all participants expressed this relationship. For instance one participant stated, *"It matters not the office of the person I am visiting. What matters is the purpose of the visit."* Another expressed, *"It depends on what kind of meeting it is and what kind of conversation we're going to have."*

5.4 History Matters

When asked about their overall comfort when sensing technologies are used in situations where information would be kept for historical use, participants' overall comfort ratings (collapsed across scenarios and technologies) were lower (M=2.40, SD=1.08, n=2880) compared to the mean comfort score reported above. A paired t-test (with user as grouping) showed a significant difference (paired t(2879)=-23.9615, p<0.0001). That is, across the board, historical use of sensor data negatively impacted users' comfort.

We saw a similar pattern in the regression tests on comfort ratings for historical use as we did for the question where historical use was not identified in the question, albeit with lower means. We conducted a two-way ANOVA with scenario and technology as independent variables, and participant as a random effect. A main effect was observed for technology (F(2,2629)=247.621, p<0.0001) and scenario (F(3,2629)=30.566, p<0.0001). No interaction effect was observed.

A post hoc Tukey HSD test (α=0.050, Q=2.345) showed significant differences between motion sensor (M=2.83, SD=0.05) and the other technologies. Interestingly no difference existed between audio (M=2.18, SD=0.05) and camera (M=2.20, SD=0.05). Similarly a post hoc Tukey HSD test (α=0.050, Q=2.571) showed a significant difference between the external business (B) scenario (M=2.59, SD=0.05) and other scenarios, a difference between colleague's office for work interaction (CW) (M=2.45, SD=0.05) and other scenarios, but no difference between colleague's office for social interaction (CS) (M=2.28, SD=0.05) and personal offices (PO) (M=2.28, SD=0.05).

Over all of these statistics, the means are all below the neutral mark. Further, the post hoc comparisons show less contrast between technologies and scenarios. These result suggest that historical use of data likely eliminates any neutral to mild comfort participants could have with any workplace sensing deployment. This is overwhelming supported by the qualitative feedback as well. One user

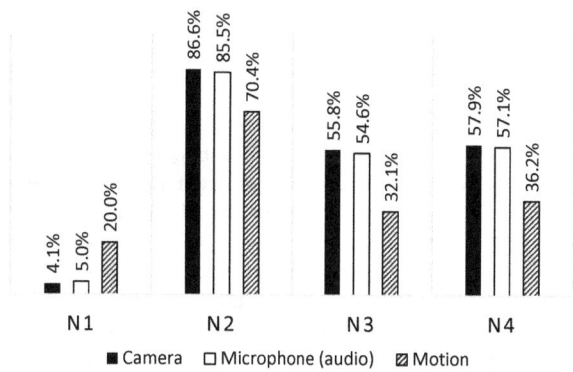

Figure 3: Agreement rates for N1–N4.

stated, that if the data *"was being collected then there is a possibility it could be used in the future, that makes me uncomfortable."* Similarly, another stated *"the amount of social interaction could be tracked [over time] and used to judge me negatively as being idle."* One participant stated *"... [historical] camera data scares me, images can be fatal to careers."*

5.5 Benevolent Sensing

Finally, we wanted to understand whether participants harbored any expectation that notifications should be provided if these types of technologies were in use in their own workplace, or in workplaces that they visited. For each of the three sensing technologies, participants were asked for binary agreement with each of the following statements:

- **N1:** No notification necessary for [cameras, microphones, motion sensors]
- **N2:** Signs in the space indicating [cameras, microphones, motion sensors] are in use
- **N3:** Signs indicating the position of [cameras, microphones, motion sensors] in the space
- **N4:** Light or other indicator that the [camera, microphone, motion sensor] was current in active use

In addition, the participants were given an "other" option in which they could fill their own statement regarding notification. A free form section was also provided to allow participants to explain or summarize their agreement ratings across all the technologies. A summary of our results is shown in Figure 3.

In relation to overall comfort scores, it was not surprising that very few participants agreed with N1 (No notifications necessary). Only 4.1% and 5.0% of respondents felt that no notification was necessary for camera and microphone sensors, respectively. 20.8% of participants indicated no notification was necessary for motion sensors, perhaps a reflection of their greater overall comfort with this sensor technology. The difference across technologies was significant (F(2,478)=36.430, p<0.0001). Post hoc Tukey HSD (α=0.050) revealed motion sensors were significantly different from camera and microphone. No other differences were observed.

Agreement with N2 (Signs) was very high for camera (86.6%) and microphone (85.8%). Motion sensors had comparatively lower agreement at (70.4%). The difference across technologies was significant ($F(2,478)=26.699$, $p<0.0001$) and post hoc Tukey HSD ($\alpha=0.050$) showed the difference between motion and the other technologies was significant.

With respect to N3 (Position indicators), 55.8%, 54.6%, and 32.1% of participants agreed for camera, microphone, and motion sensors, respectively. The result was significant across technologies ($F(2,478)=44.464$, $p<0.0001$) with post hoc Tukey HSD ($\alpha=0.050$) showing significance between motion and other sensors. N4 (Lights or other indicators) followed a similar pattern, with 57.9%, 57.1% and 36.2% agreement for camera, microphone, and motion sensors, respectively (also significant $F(2,478)=34.972$ $p<0.0001$ across technologies with post hoc significant between motion and other sensors).

Qualitative feedback from participants provided a very clear concern to inform suspecting colleagues and visiting family. Comments from participants capturing this sentiment included statements like *"I would want to make sure that the individual in the office is aware of the presence of these devices.";* *"I feel the person visiting me would feel uncomfortable, and that in turn would make me feel uncomfortable.";* and *"I would like to know it was there when visiting any office. I feel like I am ok with this but think there should be a way to make sure people know these things are there."*

6 DISCUSSION AND IMPLICATIONS

We now reflect upon and interpret our findings in the context of designing more effective workplace sensing technologies and mechanisms for enforcing user preferences in a trusted manner.

6.1 Design for Assurance

The neutral to mildly positive valence for individual comfort with the PIR sensors across contexts of use is a potential indicator that unease with sensing in the workplace is not due to the deployment of presence systems in general, but rather with the specific sensing technologies deployed to support presence detection. For instance, when discussing the audio sensor, one interviewee noted *"... when you tell me that it's only 1 or 0 that's being uploaded from the microphone [indicating conversation], I wouldn't believe you.",* indicating doubts that sensed environmental data may actually be stored or misused by the sensor.

To explore this notion further, we asked interviewees more directly about their perceived trust of a hypothetical "unhackable" sensor that carried out image or audio processing within a trusted component and emitted only a presence state. Across the board, individuals reported that such a sensor would cause them to re-think their comfort with camera- and audio-based sensors. As one individual responded when asked about the value of this potential technology in her interview, *"... it would be a nice thing to do to increase peoples' trust in the system".* This qualitative result combined with individuals' quantitative preference for PIR sensing as a technology, indicate two promising approaches toward designing sensor systems that provide individuals with high assurances regarding the privacy of their actions within a space: securing sensor components themselves, and further exploring the use of low-fidelity sensors.

While "unhackable" sensors may not be technically feasible, steps can be taken to design inexpensive sensor packages that make surreptitious access to the environmental inputs used to derive presence states markedly more difficult. For example, our camera-based sensor currently processes the video feeds from two webcams on a Raspberry Pi v2 single-board computer, transmitting the derived presence state to our awareness system via a USB WiFi adapter. An alternate—and only marginally more expensive—approach to this would be to remove the WiFi adapter, and instead leverage an output-only pin on the Raspberry Pi as a makeshift data diode that transmits computed presence states to a Bluetooth or WiFi system-on-a-chip (e.g., Electric Imp[7]). This SoC can handle relaying presence states to our awareness system, without having the ability to, itself, access raw environmental data. Such an architectural shift on the sensor side would make unauthorized access to raw environmental data much more difficult—likely requiring physical access to the sensor—and perhaps increase individuals' comfort with sensing technologies that are typically viewed as invasive.

A second approach worth studying is the design of other low-fidelity sensor packages for common presence sensing tasks. For instance, ultrasonic ingress/egress counters could be useful for spaces with clearly demarcated entrances or exits. Similarly, force sensing resistors could be used to instrument chairs in meeting spaces or common areas to register when individuals are using the space. Given the potential for privacy harm related to high-fidelity sensors that was noted by the individuals that we surveyed, the onus is on system designers to consider these less invasive—and often inexpensive—alternatives to rich sensing modalities like image processing.

6.2 Locality of Control

One possible explanation for the noted decrease in comfort with sensed data being stored for historical use, as well as the use of higher-fidelity sensing modalities (i.e., camera and audio), could be a perceived loss of control by individuals as they are monitored by these systems. This is reflected by many of the participant quotes in the "Personal vs. Professional Personas," "Content and Context," and "History Matters" subsections of the Results section.

As historical information has been shown to be a useful feature of awareness systems [2, 33], it would be worthwhile to explore the impacts that "opt in" policies for historical data collection and/or the ability for an individual to edit the historical information stored about them may have on individuals' comfort with these features. Similarly, it could be useful to provide users with the ability to temporarily shut off awareness sensors in response to their personal determination of a private context (e.g., having a sensitive discussion or a visit from a family member). Providing individuals with some (perhaps time- or task-limited) measure of control over *when* they are sensed may enable the use of higher fidelity sensing in certain situations, without impinging on individuals' comfort with their participation in an awareness system.

---

[7]https://www.electricimp.com/

6.3 Mixed Method Deployments

In the specific context of workplace sensing, our investigation of sensing modalities and survey findings indicate that a one-size-fits-all solution to the problem of deploying a highly-effective presence system that maximizes individual comfort across contexts is unlikely to exist. For instance, the PIR sensor package was shown to elicit the highest level of comfort from survey participants, as well as perform well in an office environment. This type of environment is often largely static, however, with individuals having seated discussions or working collaboratively using whiteboards within relatively small sensing zones. We expect that these types of sensors would perform poorly in environments where motion across large areas—and thus multiple sensing zones—is typical (e.g., kitchens or break rooms). By contrast, camera-based sensors handle motion well, but come at the cost of being a significantly more invasive technologies.

One potential solution to this problem that is worth investigating is the use of mixed method sensor deployments. Rather than relying on a homogeneous sensor deployment throughout an organization, the particular sensors deployed could be chosen to balance accuracy and comfort. For instance, PIR sensors would be reasonable to deploy in personal office spaces or small meeting rooms in which individual motion is typically limited and sensitive or personal topics may be discussed. Meanwhile, camera-based sensors could be used in common areas or larger meeting spaces where individuals are perhaps more mobile, but would likely have lower expectations of privacy, as supported by our findings. Such a deployment would allow system designers to balance the overall accuracy of the data used by the presence system system with the per-space privacy concerns of the individuals occupying these spaces.

6.4 Study Limitations

One limitation of our study is that we considered a single sensing problem within the broader context of workplace awareness, and a small set of sensing technologies for addressing this problem. This was an intentional choice, made to keep our survey short ($\approx$10 minutes on average) and to allow respondents to give deeper attention to a specific problem, rather than considering "monitoring" in general. However, it would be worthwhile to explore individuals' sentiments towards other sensing tasks in the workplace, as well develop a deeper understanding of how a broader class of sensing technologies (including those noted above) impact individuals' perceptions of privacy loss.

Another limitation of our study is our use of Amazon Mechanical Turk for the recruitment of survey respondents. It has been shown that Mechanical Turk workers tend to be more privacy conscious than the general public [26], a fact that is reflected in the distribution of Westin scores reported on previously. However, there are also two potential strengths to soliciting more privacy-conscious respondents for this study. First, these individuals are likely to have more well-defined mental models of privacy, which could lead to more authentic responses to our hypothetical contexts of use. Second, this allows us to effectively lower-bound the comfort with these technologies that we would expect to see in a survey of the general population. For instance, that a more privacy-conscious population expresses a positive valence for comfort with low-fidelity sensing

provides strong justification for further pursuing the use of these types of technologies in workplace awareness systems. Nonetheless, a broader survey of the general public would enhance our findings, and make for interesting future work.

7 CONCLUSIONS

Embedded sensors are here to stay: IoT devices, wearable computers, smartphones, and instrumented smart spaces have revolutionized the ways that people learn about themselves, interact with others, and manage spaces. Despite the benefits of these technologies, pervasive sensing has the potential for privacy harms if the collection, analysis, and dissemination of data is left unchecked. In the rush to maximize productivity and utility, this cannot be overlooked. To this end, we investigated the accuracy and comfort trade-offs that exist in common space contextualization tasks leveraged by workplace awareness systems in an effort to uncover design recommendations for sensing systems that provide users with a sense of agency when in instrumented spaces.

We surveyed and interviewed individuals to examine their comfort with sensors designed to use three sensing modalities often deployed in workplace environments (video, audio, and motion) across a variety of workplace contexts. Across all contexts, sensor fidelity and a sensor's ability to capture ancillary context were found to have a significant impact on user comfort with awareness technologies. In fact, the use of low-fidelity PIR sensors was associated with neutral to mildly positive comfort ratings, while higher fidelity sensors—which are more likely to capture private contexts—were associated with negative comfort ratings. This indicates that discomfort with awareness technologies may have less to do with specific sensing tasks, and more to do with the means by which these tasks are carried out.

Our findings signal an important message to researchers and developers in the access control space: the exploration of access control enforcement mechanisms that do not rely on a trusted reference monitor are of increasing importance as the amount of personal data processed by third-party and/or untrusted infrastructure increases. To this end, our qualitative findings show that individuals are significantly more comfortable with low-fidelity sensors in situations where raw sensed data could be accessible to the platform. Further, our qualitative findings indicate that users would be reasonably comfortable with high-fidelity sensors like camera-based platforms if they could be provided with strong assurances that only derived states (e.g., occupancy count) and not raw data (e.g., images) would be exposed to the broader platform, for instance via hardware isolation mechanisms. Given the increasing prevalence of instrumented spaces, incorporating these insights into the design of flexible sensor packages that isolate sensitive data from derived information will be instrumental in increasing the utility that can be derived from these spaces without overly impinging upon user privacy and agency.

Acknowledgments. This work was supported in part by the National Science Foundation under award no. CNS−1253204.

A SURVEY QUESTIONS (C-A-M ORDERING)

Introduction. Please watch the following short (2 minute) video further explaining how specific presence detection technologies may be deployed within a workspace.

[The video for the C-A-M ordering can be viewed at http://bit.ly/1R36Ldu.]

Personal Office. You work in a workspace where each worker has his/her own office, and a presence system is in use to help facilitate person-to-person communication within the workplace. Consider the use of these technologies **within your own personal office**.

- **Q1.** How comfortable are you with **camera sensors** being used for this specific context of use?
  - Very uncomfortable
  - Somewhat uncomfortable
  - Neutral
  - Somewhat comfortable
  - Very comfortable
- **Q2.** How comfortable are you with **microphone sensors** being used for this specific context of use?
  - Very uncomfortable
  - Somewhat uncomfortable
  - Neutral
  - Somewhat comfortable
  - Very comfortable
- **Q3.** How comfortable are you with **motion sensors** being used for this specific context of use?
  - Very uncomfortable
  - Somewhat uncomfortable
  - Neutral
  - Somewhat comfortable
  - Very comfortable
- **Q4.** In addition to using the sensed **camera data** (e.g., images) for determining current presence state, this data **may also be stored for historical or archival purposes**. Would this use change your comfort with a particular technology?
  - Very negatively
  - Somewhat negatively
  - Neutral
  - Somewhat positively
  - Very positively
- **Q5.** In addition to using the sensed **microphone data** (e.g., audio snippets) for determining current presence state, this data **may also be stored for historical or archival purposes**. Would this use change your comfort with a particular technology?
  - Very negatively
  - Somewhat negatively
  - Neutral
  - Somewhat positively
  - Very positively
- **Q6.** In addition to using the sensed **motion sensor data** (e.g., on/off readings for each sensor) for determining current presence state, this data **may also be stored for historical or archival purposes**. Would this use change your comfort with a particular technology?
  - Very negatively
  - Somewhat negatively
  - Neutral
  - Somewhat positively
  - Very positively
- Would your opinion about these technologies change depending on the **person visiting your office**? For instance, whether this person is a colleague, outside customer, friend or family? If so, please explain.
  - *[Free text input box]*

Colleague's Office (Work). You work in a workspace where each worker has his/her own office, and a presence system is in use to help facilitate person-to-person communication within the workplace. Consider the use of these technologies while you are **visiting a colleague's office to attend a work-related meeting**.

- *[Repeat questions Q1–Q6.]*
- Would your opinion about these technologies change depending on the **person whose office you were visiting**? If so, please explain.
  - *[Free text input box]*

Colleague's Office (Social). You work in a workspace where each worker has his/her own office, and a presence system is in use to help facilitate person-to-person communication within the workplace. Consider the use of these technologies while you are **visiting a colleagueâĂŹs office for the purpose of a brief social interaction**.

- *[Repeat questions Q1–Q6.]*
- Would your opinion about these technologies change depending on the **person whose office you were visiting**? If so, please explain.
  - *[Free text input box]*

Visiting a Business. Consider the scenario in which you are **visiting a place that you do business with (e.g., a bank or insurance office)**, and a presence system is in use to manage the distribution of incoming clients to representatives of the business. Consider the use of these technologies while you meet with a representative in his/her personal office.

- *[Repeat questions Q1–Q6.]*
- Would your opinion about these technologies change depending on the **type of business you were visiting**? If so, please explain.
  - *[Free text input box]*

Notifications.

- Do you feel that workspaces outfitted with presence sensing technologies should provide notification to individuals who may be monitored by these systems?
  - Yes
  - No
- Please select all notifications that you feel are appropriate if **camera sensors** are deployed.
  - No notification is necessary
  - Signs indicating the use of cameras
  - Clear indications of camera positions
  - Lights or other indicators of "record" status
  - Other (please specify)

- Please select all notifications that you feel are appropriate if **microphone sensors** are deployed.
  - No notification is necessary
  - Signs indicating the use of microphones
  - Clear indications of microphone positions
  - Lights or other indicators of "record" status
  - Other (please specify)
- Please select all notifications that you feel are appropriate if **motion sensors** are deployed.
  - No notification is necessary
  - Signs indicating the use of motion sensing technologies
  - Clear indications of motion sensor positions
  - Lights or other indicators of whether sensors are active
  - Other (please specify)

REFERENCES

[1] Privacy on and off the internet: What consumers want. Technical Report 15229, Harris Interactive, Feb. 2002. http://www.ijsselsteijn.nl/slides/Harris.pdf.

[2] J. Begole, J. C. Tang, R. B. Smith, and N. Yankelovich. Work rhythms: analyzing visualizations of awareness histories of distributed groups. In *Proceeding of the ACM Conference on Computer Supported Cooperative Work (CSCW)*, pages 334–343, 2002.

[3] P. Bellavista, A. Küpper, and S. Helal. Location-based services: Back to the future. *IEEE Pervasive Computing*, 7(2):85–89, 2008.

[4] V. Bellotti and A. Sellen. Design for privacy in ubiquitous computing environments. In *Proceedings of the Third Conference on European Conference on Computer-Supported Cooperative Work*, ECSCW'93, pages 77–92, 1993.

[5] J. T. Biehl, A. J. Lee, G. Filby, and M. Cooper. You're where? prove it!: towards trusted indoor location estimation of mobile devices. In *Proceedings of the 2015 ACM International Joint Conference on Pervasive and Ubiquitous Computing (Ubi-Comp)*, pages 909–919, 2015.

[6] J. T. Biehl, E. G. Rieffel, and A. J. Lee. When privacy and utility are in harmony: towards better design of presence technologies. *Personal and Ubiquitous Computing*, 17(3):503–518, 2013.

[7] J. J. Cadiz, G. Venolia, G. Jancke, and A. Gupta. Designing and deploying an information awareness interface. In *Proceedings of the 2002 ACM Conference on Computer Supported Cooperative Work*, CSCW '02, pages 314–323, 2002.

[8] E. K. Choe, S. Consolvo, J. Jung, B. L. Harrison, and J. A. Kientz. Living in a glass house: a survey of private moments in the home. In *13th International Conference on Ubiquitous Computing (UbiComp)*, pages 41–44, 2011.

[9] S. Consolvo, I. E. Smith, T. Matthews, A. LaMarca, J. Tabert, and P. Powledge. Location disclosure to social relations: why, when, & what people want to share. In *Proceedings of the 2005 Conference on Human Factors in Computing Systems (CHI)*, pages 81–90, 2005.

[10] A. K. Dey. *Providing Architectural Support for Building Context-Aware Applications*. PhD thesis, College of Computing, Georgia Institute of Technology, Dec. 2000.

[11] P. Dourish and S. A. Bly. Portholes: Supporting awareness in a distributed work group. In *Conference on Human Factors in Computing Systems (CHI)*, pages 541–547, 1992.

[12] N. B. Ellison, J. Vitak, C. Steinfield, R. Gray, and C. Lampe. Negotiating privacy concerns and social capital needs in a social media environment. In *Privacy Online - Perspectives on Privacy and Self-Disclosure in the Social Web.*, pages 19–32. 2011.

[13] M. Fan, Q. Liu, H. Tang, and P. Chiu. Hifi: Hide and find digital content associated with physical objects via coded light. In *Proceedings of the 15th Workshop on Mobile Computing Systems and Applications*, HotMobile '14, pages 6:1–6:6, 2014.

[14] L. Fang and K. LeFevre. Privacy wizards for social networking sites. In *Proceedings of the 19th International Conference on World Wide Web, WWW 2010, Raleigh, North Carolina, USA, April 26-30, 2010*, pages 351–360, 2010.

[15] J. Fogarty, C. Au, and S. E. Hudson. Sensing from the basement: a feasibility study of unobtrusive and low-cost home activity recognition. In *Proceedings of the 19th Annual ACM Symposium on User Interface Software and Technology (UIST)*, pages 91–100, 2006.

[16] J. Fogarty, J. Lai, and J. Christensen. Presence versus availability: the design and evaluation of a context-aware communication client. *International Journal of Humam-Computer Studies*, 61(3):299–317, 2004.

[17] Y. L. Gall, A. J. Lee, and A. Kapadia. Plexc: a policy language for exposure control. In *17th ACM Symposium on Access Control Models and Technologies (SACMAT)*, pages 219–228, 2012.

[18] A. Harter, A. Hopper, P. Steggles, A. Ward, and P. Webster. The anatomy of a context-aware application. *Wireless Networks*, 8(2/3):187–197, 2002.

[19] U. Hengartner and P. Steenkiste. Protecting access to people location information. In *Proceedings of the First International Conference on Security in Pervasive Computing*, pages 25–38, Boppard, Germany, Mar. 2003.

[20] J. Hightower, R. Want, and G. Borriello. Spoton: An indoor 3d location sensing technology based on rf signal strength. Technical Report UW CSE 00-02-02, University of Washington, Department of Computer Science and Engineering, 2000.

[21] J. D. Hincapié-Ramos, S. Voida, and G. Mark. A design space analysis of availability-sharing systems. In *Proceedings of the 24th Annual ACM Symposium on User Interface Software and Technology (UIST)*, pages 85–96, 2011.

[22] J. I. Hong and J. A. Landay. An architecture for privacy-sensitive ubiquitous computing. In *Proceedings of MobiSys 2004*, pages 177–189, June 2004.

[23] G. Hsieh, K. P. Tang, W. Y. Low, and J. I. Hong. Field deployment of *IMBuddy* : A study of privacy control and feedback mechanisms for contextual IM. In *9th International Conference on Ubiquitous Computing (UbiComp)*, pages 91–108, 2007.

[24] G. Iachello and J. I. Hong. End-user privacy in human-computer interaction. *Foundations and Trends in Human-Computer Interaction*, 1(1):1–137, 2007.

[25] C. Jensen, C. Potts, and C. Jensen. Privacy practices of internet users: Self-reports versus observed behavior. *International Journal of Human-Computer Studies*, 63(1–2):203 – 227, 2005.

[26] R. Kang, S. Brown, L. Dabbish, and S. Kiesler. Privacy attitudes of Mechanical Turk workers and the U.S. public. In *Symposium On Usable Privacy and Security*, pages 37–49, July 2014.

[27] C. D. Kidd, R. J. Orr, G. D. Abowd, C. G. Atkeson, I. A. Essa, B. MacIntyre, E. D. Mynatt, T. Starner, and W. Newstetter. The aware home: A living laboratory for ubiquitous computing research. In *The Second International Workshop on Cooperative Buildings, Integrating Information, Organization, and Architecture (CoBuild)*, pages 191–198, 1999.

[28] J. C. Lai, A. Levas, P. B. Chou, C. S. Pinhanez, and M. S. Viveros. Bluespace: personalizing workspace through awareness and adaptability. *International Journal of Humam-Computer Studies*, 57(5):415–428, 2002.

[29] S. Lederer, J. Mankoff, and A. K. Dey. Who wants to know what when? privacy preference determinants in ubiquitous computing. In *Extended abstracts of the 2003 Conference on Human Factors in Computing Systems (CHI)*, pages 724–725, 2003.

[30] S. Patil, Y. L. Gall, A. J. Lee, and A. Kapadia. My privacy policy: Exploring end-user specification of free-form location access rules. In *Financial Cryptography and Data Security (FC) Workshops*, pages 86–97, 2012.

[31] S. Patil and A. Kobsa. Privacy considerations in awareness systems: Designing with privacy in mind. In *Awareness Systems - Advances in Theory, Methodology and Design*, pages 187–206. 2009.

[32] S. Patil, G. Norcie, A. Kapadia, and A. J. Lee. Reasons, rewards, regrets: privacy considerations in location sharing as an interactive practice. In *Symposium On Usable Privacy and Security (SOUPS)*, page 5, 2012.

[33] M. C. Reddy and P. Dourish. A finger on the pulse: temporal rhythms and information seeking in medical work. In *Proceeding of the ACM Conference on Computer Supported Cooperative Work (CSCW)*, pages 344–353, 2002.

[34] N. Romero, G. McEwan, and S. Greenberg. A field study of community bar: (mis)-matches between theory and practice. In *Proceedings of the 2007 International ACM Conference on Supporting Group Work*, GROUP '07, pages 89–98, 2007.

[35] N. M. Sadeh, J. I. Hong, L. F. Cranor, I. Fette, P. G. Kelley, M. K. Prabaker, and J. Rao. Understanding and capturing people's privacy policies in a mobile social networking application. *Personal and Ubiquitous Computing*, 13(6):401–412, 2009.

[36] J. H. Saltzer and M. D. Schroeder. The protection of information in computer systems. *Proceedings of the IEEE*, 63(9):1278–1308, 1975.

[37] R. Schlegel, A. Kapadia, and A. J. Lee. Eyeing your exposure: Quantifying and controlling information sharing for improved privacy. In *Proceedings of the 2011 Symposium on Usable Privacy and Security (SOUPS)*, pages 14:1–14:14, July 2011.

[38] I. Simpson. Maryland prisons official fired for facebook joke about being groped, Feb. 2015. http://www.huffingtonpost.com/2015/02/20/maryland-prisons-official_n_6722366.html (Accessed 09/19/2016).

[39] B. Smallwood. Parents and oversharing on social media, May 2015. http://wivb.com/2015/05/19/parents-and-oversharing-on-social-media/ (Accessed 09/19/2016).

[40] J. C. Tang, N. Yankelovich, J. Begole, M. V. Kleek, F. C. Li, and J. R. Bhalodia. Connexus to awarenex: extending awareness to mobile users. In *Proceedings of the Conference on Human Factors in Computing Systems (CHI)*, pages 221–228, 2001.

[41] K. P. Tang, J. Lin, J. I. Hong, D. P. Siewiorek, and N. M. Sadeh. Rethinking location sharing: exploring the implications of social-driven vs. purpose-driven location sharing. In *12th International Conference on Ubiquitous Computing (UbiComp)*, pages 85–94, 2010.

[42] J. Y. Tsai, P. Kelley, P. Drielsma, L. F. Cranor, J. Hong, and N. Sadeh. Who's viewed you?: The impact of feedback in a mobile location-sharing application. In *Proceedings of the SIGCHI Conference on Human Factors in Computing Systems*, pages 2003–2012, New York, NY, USA, 2009.

[43] Y. Wang, P. G. Leon, K. Scott, X. Chen, A. Acquisti, and L. Cranor. Privacy nudges for social media: an exploratory Facebook study. In *WWW 2013 Companion*,

2013.

[44] Y. Wang, G. Norcie, S. Komanduri, A. Acquisti, P. G. Leon, and L. F. Cranor. "I regretted the minute I pressed share": a qualitative study of regrets on facebook. In *Symposium On Usable Privacy and Security (SOUPS)*, page 10, 2011.

[45] R. Want, A. Hopper, V. Falcão, and J. Gibbons. The active badge location system. *ACM Trans. Inf. Syst.*, 10(1):91–102, Jan. 1992.

[46] J. Wiese, J. T. Biehl, T. Turner, W. van Melle, and A. Girgensohn. Beyond 'yesterday's tomorrow': towards the design of awareness technologies for the contemporary worker. In *Proceedings of the 13th Conference on Human-Computer Interaction with Mobile Devices and Services (Mobile HCI)*, pages 455–464, 2011.

Solving Multi-Objective Workflow Satisfiability Problems with Optimization Modulo Theories Techniques

Clara Bertolissi
Aix Marseille Univ. & CNRS
clara.bertolissi@lis-lab.fr

Daniel R. dos Santos
Eindhoven University of Technology
d.r.dos.santos@tue.nl

Silvio Ranise
Fondazione Bruno Kessler
ranise@fbk.eu

ABSTRACT

Security-sensitive workflows impose constraints on the control-flow and authorization policies that may lead to unsatisfiable instances. In these cases, it is still possible to find "least bad" executions where costs associated to authorization violations are minimized, solving the so-called Multi-Objective Workflow Satisfiability Problem (MO-WSP). The MO-WSP is inspired by the Valued WSP and its generalization, the Bi-Objective WSP, but our work considers quantitative solutions to the WSP without abstracting control-flow constraints. In this paper, we define variations of the MO-WSP and solve them using bounded model checking and optimization modulo theories solving. We validate our solutions on real-world workflows and show their scalability on synthetic instances.

CCS CONCEPTS

• **Security and privacy** → **Software security engineering**; *Formal methods and theory of security*;

KEYWORDS

Business process, Workflow Satisfiability, Optimization Modulo Theories

ACM Reference format:
Clara Bertolissi, Daniel R. dos Santos, and Silvio Ranise. 2018. Solving Multi-Objective Workflow Satisfiability Problems with Optimization Modulo Theories Techniques. In *Proceedings of The 23rd ACM Symposium on Access Control Models & Technologies (SACMAT), Indianapolis, IN, USA, June 13–15, 2018 (SACMAT '18),* 12 pages.
https://doi.org/10.1145/3205977.3205982

1 INTRODUCTION

A workflow specifies a collection of tasks, whose execution is initiated by humans or software agents executing on their behalf, and the constraints on the order of execution of those tasks. Security-related dependencies are specified as authorization policies, stating which users can execute which tasks, and authorization constraints imposed on task execution, e.g., Separation of Duties (SoD) whereby two distinct users must execute two tasks.

Authorization policies and constraints are crucial to ensure the security of workflow systems and to avoid errors and frauds [28], but they may also lead to situations where a workflow instance cannot be completed because no task can be executed without violating either the authorization policy or the constraints. These deadlocks are conflicts between compliance and continuity which may be resolved by administrators granting additional permissions to users (thus hindering compliance) or canceling the execution (precluding continuity). Depending on the scenario, it may be preferable to guarantee either security or continuity. In all cases, it is desirable to have "minimal" (in some sense) violations. The Multi-Objective Workflow Satisfiability Problem (MO-WSP), considered in this paper, amounts to strike the best possible trade-off between security and continuity while minimizing the costs of violations to a policy or constraints.

The **main contributions** of this paper are the definition and solution of the MO-WSP using Bounded Model Checking (BMC) and Optimization Modulo Theories (OMT). The MO-WSP is inspired by the Valued WSP [12] and its generalization, the Bi-Objective Workflow Satisfiability Problem (BO-WSP) [13], but our work considers quantitative solutions to the WSP with an ordered execution of tasks, i.e., without abstracting the control-flow constraints. Our symbolic solution is also able to handle control-flow patterns [33], such as alternative execution, since we can encode these patterns directly in the transition system used by BMC (instead of splitting a workflow into multiple deterministic instances, as in [11, 14]). The use of off-the-shelf OMT solvers, instead of custom algorithms, provides a uniform toolkit to explore different optimization modes (such as Pareto and those based on linear cost functions), thereby gaining the freedom to evaluate the trade-offs offered by different optimization strategies. **Another contribution** is the implementation and evaluation of the proposed solution on real and synthetic workflows. The results show that the technique has a good performance due to an ingenious encoding of the problem that exploits the parallel executions of tasks in the workflow.

The rest of this paper is organized as follows. Sec. 2 discusses the original Workflow Satisfiability Problem and its valued versions; Sec. 3 presents our solution to the MO-WSP; in Sec. 4, we evaluate the performance of our solution; Sec. 5 discusses related work; and Sec. 6 concludes the paper.

2 WORKFLOW SATISFIABILITY

Given the control-flow (e.g., a task should be executed before all the others) and the authorization constraints (e.g., two tasks should be executed under the responsibility of two distinct users, known as Separation of Duties), a (decision) problem is to check for the existence of an assignment of the tasks to entitled users such that all the control-flow and authorization constraints are satisfied. In the literature, this is called the (ordered version of the) Workflow Satisfiability Problem (WSP) [34].

Example 2.1. The goal of the Trip Request Workflow (TRW) is to request trips for employees in an organization. TRW is composed of five tasks: Trip request ($t1$), Car rental ($t2$), Hotel booking ($t3$), Flight reservation ($t4$), and Trip validation ($t5$). The execution of the tasks is constrained as follows: $t1$ must be executed first, then $t2$, $t3$ and $t4$ can be executed in any order, with $t4$ being an optional task (only performed for long trips), and when all have been performed, $t5$ can be executed. Overall, there are six possible task execution sequences of length 5, in which the first is always task $t1$, the last is always task $t5$, and—in between—there is any one of the six permutations of $t2$, $t3$ and $t4$; there are also 2 sequences of length 4: $t1$, $t2$, $t3$, $t5$ and $t1$, $t3$, $t2$, $t5$.

The TRW can be modeled in BPMN [35] as shown in Figure 1: the circle on the left represents the start event (triggering the execution of the workflow), whereas that on the right represents the end event (terminating the execution of the workflow), tasks are depicted by labeled boxes, the constraints on the execution of tasks are shown as solid arrows for sequence flows and diamonds labeled by '+' for parallel flows or by 'X' for alternative flows.

Besides control-flow constraints, the BPMN in Figure 1 shows also authorization constraints. The man icon inside the box of a task t means that t must be executed under the responsibility of a user u according to an access control policy TA, specified by the table in Figure 1: a user u is entitled to execute t iff there is a line of the table in which u is associated with t.

A dashed line labeled by $\neq$ connecting two tasks t and t' denotes a Separation of Duties (SoD) constraint (see, e.g., [10]), i.e. there must exist two distinct users $u, u' \in U$ such that u executes t and u' executes t'. SoD constraints are typically used to prevent frauds. In Figure 1, five SoD constraints are depicted, requiring the following pairs of tasks to be executed by distinct users in any sequence of task executions of the workflow: $(t1, t2)$, $(t1, t4)$, $(t2, t3)$, $(t2, t5)$, and $(t3, t5)$. □

To formalize the WSP, we need to introduce some preliminary notions. Given a finite set T of tasks and a finite set U of users, an *execution scenario* (or, simply, a *scenario*) is a finite sequence of pairs of the form (t, u)—also written as $t(u)$—for $t \in T$ and $u \in U$. The intuitive meaning of a scenario $\eta = t_1(u_1), \ldots, t_n(u_n)$ is that task t_i is executed before task t_j for $1 \leq i < j \leq n$ and that task t_k is executed by user u_k for $k = 1, \ldots, n$. Among the scenarios in a workflow, we are interested in those that describe successfully terminating executions. Since the notion of successful termination depends on the application, from now on we consider only successfully terminating behaviors scenarios. A *workflow* $W(T, U)$ is a (finite) set of scenarios. To illustrate, consider the TRW in Example 2.1 and let $TRW(T, U)$ be its formalization. Then, among the following scenarios:

$$\eta_1 = t1(a), t2(a), t3(c), t4(a), t5(b); \quad \eta_4 = t1(c), t3(c), t2(a), t5(b)$$
$$\eta_2 = t1(c), t2(a), t3(c), t4(a), t5(b); \quad \eta_5 = t1(a), t2(b), t3(b);$$
$$\eta_3 = t1(a), t3(c), t2(a), t5(b); \quad \eta_6 = t2(b), t3(b), t4(a), t5(b);$$

only $\eta_1, \ldots, \eta_4$ are in $TRW(T, U)$ because they represent sequences of task executions that are compliant with the BPMN in Figure 1; whereas η_5 and η_6 cannot be in $TRW(T, U)$ as the execution of task

$t5$ and of task $t1$, respectively, is missing and thus the scenarios are not compliant with the BPMN specification.

Given a workflow $W(T, U)$, an *authorization relation* TA is a sub-set of $U \times T$ where $(u, t) \in TA$ means that u is entitled to execute task t. Following [15], we call *authorized* a scenario η of a workflow $W(T, U)$ according to TA iff (u, t) is in TA for each $t(u)$ in η. For instance, η_1 and η_3 are authorized, whereas η_2 and η_4 are not (since $(c, t1) \notin TA$). An *authorization constraint* over a workflow $W(T, U)$ is a tuple $(t_1, t_2, \bowtie)$ where $t_1, t_2 \in T$ and $\bowtie$ is a sub-set of $U \times U$. For instance, a SoD constraint between tasks t and t' can be formalized as $(t, t', \neq)$ with $\neq$ being the complement of the identity relation over U. A scenario η of $W(T, U)$ *satisfies* the authorization constraint $(t_1, t_2, \bowtie)$ over $W(T, U)$ iff for $t_1(u_1)$ and $t_2(u_2)$ in η we have that $(u_1, u_2) \in \bowtie$. Let K be a (finite) set of authorization constraints, a scenario η satisfies K iff η satisfies each constraint of K. Again following [15], we call *eligible (according to a set K of authorization constraints)* a scenario η of a workflow $W(T, U)$ iff η satisfies K. For instance, η_2 and η_4 are eligible, whereas η_1 and η_3 are not (since there is a SoD between $t1$ and $t2$, but they are executed by the same user, a).

Following [3], we call *security-sensitive workflow* (SSW) the triple $(W(T, U), TA, K)$ where $W(T, U)$ is a workflow, TA an authorization relation, and K a (finite) set of authorization constraints. The SSW $(W(T, U), TA, K)$ defines a sub-set of the scenarios in $W(T, U)$ that are both authorized with respect to TA and eligible with respect to K.

Given a SSW $(W(T, U), TA, K)$, the WSP consists of checking whether there exists an execution scenario in $W(T, U)$ which is both authorized and eligible. To illustrate, consider again the Example 2.1: it is easy to verify that the execution scenarios $\eta_1, \ldots, \eta_4$ presented above are not solutions to the WSP because they are either not authorized or not eligible. On the other hand, $t1(b), t3(c), t4(a), t2(a), t5(b)$ is both authorized (with respect to the TA shown in the table of Figure 1) and eligible (with respect to the five SoD constraints shown in the figure), and is thus a solution to the WSP.

2.1 Multi-objective Workflow Satisfiability

The solvability of the WSP provides some evidence about the possibility to find the best trade-off between security (by satisfying all authorization policies and constraints) and business continuity (by considering only successfully terminating executions). In some situations, this may be too restrictive. For instance, if we delete the lines containing $(a, t2)$ and $(b, t2)$ from the table in Figure 1 specifying the authorization policy (imagine that users a and b cannot access the TRW for some reason), the WSP for the TRW is no more solvable since no user is entitled to execute task $t2$. For the sake of business continuity, it would be important to understand which users can execute task $t2$ (despite none being entitled to do so) to ensure termination while minimizing security issues. This becomes possible as soon as we define the cost of violating an authorization policy and, in the general case, an authorization constraint.

Example 2.2. Recall the authorization policy TA defined in Example 2.1. Let $TA' := TA \setminus \{(a, t2), (b, t2)\}$. Following [12], we introduce a cost function w_P such that $w_P(u, t) = 1$ if $(u, t) \notin TA'$ and $w_P(u, t) = 0$ if $(u, t) \in TA'$. The idea is to associate a cost of

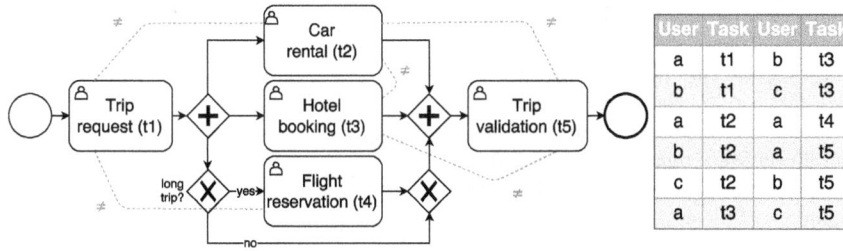

Figure 1: TRW in BPMN with an associated authorization policy

one to the situation in which a user executes tasks which they are not entitled to execute according to TA'; instead, if users are entitled to execute tasks, then the cost is zero since there is no violation of the policy TA'. To measure the cost of the violations to the policy TA' over the execution of an entire scenario, a possibility is to take the sum of the costs of each violation (if any); formally, $w_P(\eta) = \Sigma_{(u,t)\in\eta} w_P(u,t)$. We are now interested to find the scenarios in TRW (containing task $t4$) that minimize the cost function w_P. For instance, the two scenarios $\eta_1 = t1(b), t3(c), t4(a), t2(a), t5(b)$ and $\eta_2 = t1(b), t3(c), t4(b), t2(a), t5(b)$ are such that $w_P(\eta_1) = w_P(\eta_2) = 1$. Notice that one is the optimal cost as there is no scenario η' such that $w_P(\eta') < 1$.

In the same spirit, we can introduce an additional cost function w_C for the authorization constraints in K such that $w_C(\eta)$ is equal to the cardinality of the set $\{k \in K \mid \eta \text{ does not satisfy } k\}$ where K contains the SoD constraints of Figure 1. Intuitively, w_C counts how many authorization constraints are violated by the scenario under consideration; in the case of the TRW, this means to identify all pairs (u,t) and (u,t') such that $(t,t',\neq) \in K$. We are then interested to find the scenarios in TRW that minimize both cost functions w_P and w_C. There are several reasonable ways to solve this problem. For instance, one can minimize the combined cost of w_P and w_C (e.g., by taking their sum) or minimize each one of them. In the first case, the execution scenario η_2 above has a cost of 2 (1 for the violation w.r.t. TA and 1 for the violation w.r.t. K) whereas η_1 has a cost of 1 (as there is a violation w.r.t. TA and none w.r.t. K). In the second case, η_2 has a cost of $(1,1)$ whereas η_1 has a cost of $(1,0)$. Thus, η_1 is an optimal solution with respect to both criteria. □

In some situations, it may be unclear which solutions to consider as optimal. Consider, for instance, the criterion of minimizing the two cost functions at the same time and the situation in which two scenarios have costs $(1,2)$ and $(2,1)$, respectively: the former is better than the latter with respect to the first cost function, but it is worse with respect to the second cost function. An obvious question arises: which solution should be preferred? In order to address this kind of questions, we have decided to define a quantitative version of the WSP, by borrowing some notions from the framework of Multi-Objective Optimization (MOO) problems [30].

Indeed, the main goal of MOO techniques is to simultaneously optimize a collection of cost functions. In general, this is impossible since (as shown in the example above) a solution that minimizes one cost may not minimize another. In general, for any non-trivial MOO problem, there is no single solution that is simultaneously optimal for every objective. Instead, there may exist (possibly infinitely)

many solutions that can be considered equally good, called Pareto optimal (see, e.g., [30]). Formally, a scenario η^* is Pareto optimal iff there is no scenario $\eta \neq \eta^*$ such that $w_C(\eta) \leq w_C(\eta^*)$, $w_P(\eta) \leq w_P(\eta^*)$, and $w_C(\eta) < w_C(\eta^*)$ or $w_P(\eta) < w_P(\eta^*)$. I.e. a scenario is Pareto optimal if there does not exist another scenario that improves one cost function without detriment to the other.

Several methods have been devised to help the process of choosing one or more solutions among those that are Pareto optimal (see, e.g., [30, 32]); we discuss some of them and show how they relate to quantitative versions of the WSP that have been studied in the literature.

Definition 2.3. Given a SSW $(W(T,U), TA, K)$ with functions w_P and w_C associating scenarios in $W(T,U)$ with the costs of violating the authorization policy TA and the authorization constraints in K, respectively; the *Multi-Objective WSP* (MO-WSP) amounts to

$$\underset{\eta}{\text{minimize}} \quad (w_P(\eta), w_C(\eta)) \quad \text{subject to} \quad \eta \in S$$

where $S \subseteq W(T,U)$ is the set of *scenarios of interest.* □

The MO-WSP is a MOO problem that consists of optimizing—at the same time—the two functions w_P and w_C that measure the costs of violating the authorization policy and the authorization constraints, respectively, of a SSW while considering the sub-set S of scenarios in $W(T,U)$. The definition of the set S requires some care as it may be meaningless to solve the MO-WSP for all scenarios in $W(T,U)$ when some of these are executed only as alternatives. To understand why this is so, consider Example 2.1: it is not appropriate to solve the MO-WSP with S being the set of all scenarios in TRW as those containing task $t4$ are likely to have higher costs than those not containing it; in fact, $t4$ is included in a scenario only when *long trip* is true, and it is not so when *long trip* is false. It would be desirable to solve two distinct MO-WSPs: one for the set of scenarios in TRW when *long trip* is true and another when *long trip* is false. Then, one can compare the resulting solutions and, if appropriate, take their maximum. Similar observations can be found in [14]. We will elaborate on this issue further in Section 3.

Since the MO-WSP is a MOO problem, to solve it, we can reuse the cornucopia of techniques available in the literature (see, e.g., [8, 30, 32]). Many of these transform a MOO problem into one or more optimization problems whose solutions are Pareto optimal (under reasonable additional assumptions). In the rest of this section, we discuss the application of such techniques to the MO-WSP.

Weighted sum. This technique translates the MO-WSP into a standard optimization problem that amounts to minimizing a single cost function defined as the weighted sum of w_P and w_C, i.e. $a \cdot w_P(\eta) + b \cdot w_C(\eta)$, provided that $\eta \in \mathcal{S}$. The constants a and b, called *weights*, model the severity of violating the authorization policy and constraints, respectively. We assume $a > 0$ and $b > 0$ to guarantee that the solution of the transformed problem belongs to the set of Pareto optimal solutions of the original problem.

In the security literature, the use of the weighted sum of w_P and w_C to define a quantitative version of the WSP, called the Valued WSP, has been introduced in [12]. There are two main differences between the MO-WSP and the Valued WSP. First, the set $W(T, U)$ may contain scenarios of various lengths (because of the presence of conditionals) whereas the class of workflows for which the Valued WSP is defined gives rise to scenarios with the same length (as it cannot specify conditional executions). Second, the MO-WSP takes into consideration control-flow constraints whereas the Valued WSP does not. A solution to the Valued WSP is an optimal plan (a function assigning tasks to users), whereas a solution to the MO-WSP is an optimal execution scenario. In general, there are valid plans which cannot become valid execution scenarios, as observed in [11].

The main problem with using the weighted sum technique to solve the MO-WSP is the *a priori* selection of non-arbitrary values for the weights a and b. To make the technique usable in practice, it would be interesting to study the several methods available in the literature to guide the weight selection process (see again [30] for a brief introduction and pointers to the relevant literature) and adapt them to the solution of the MO-WSP.

Lexicographic. This technique is used when assigning values to the weights a and b is difficult (or even impossible) but, according to some qualitative criterion, the order of importance between the cost functions w_P and w_C is clear, reflecting the fact that it is preferable to violate either the authorization policy or the authorization constraints over the other. The first step is to find the solution η^* to the following optimization problem:

$$\underset{\eta}{\text{minimize}} \quad f_1(\eta) \quad \text{subject to} \quad \eta \in \mathcal{S}$$

where f_1 is the first according to the order of importance between the two cost functions w_P or w_C. The second step is to solve another optimization problem

$$\underset{\eta}{\text{minimize}} \quad f_2(\eta) \quad \text{subject to} \quad \eta \in \mathcal{S} \,\& \, f_2(\eta) \leq f_2(\eta^*)$$

where f_2 is the second according to the order of importance between the two cost functions w_P and w_C. The term $f_2(\eta^*)$ in the additional constraint $f_2(\eta) \leq f_2(\eta^*)$ of the second problem represents the optimal value for the first problem. The value $f_2(\eta^*)$ is not necessarily the same as the independent minimum of $f_2(\eta)$.

To the best of our knowledge, this variant of the MO-WSP has never been considered before in the literature about quantitative approaches to the WSP. Because of the difficulties in selecting weights, we believe this to be an interesting alternative to the weighted sum technique discussed above. We show our preliminary experience with solving this variant of the MO-WSP in Section 4.

Bounded cost. The first step of the technique consists of identifying f_1 and f_2 as the more and less (respectively) important function between the cost functions w_P and w_C. Then, it requires to solve the following optimization problem:

$$\underset{\eta}{\text{minimize}} \quad f_1(\eta) \quad \text{subject to} \quad \eta \in \mathcal{S} \,\& \, l \leq f_2(\eta) \leq u$$

where l and u are the lower and upper bounds on f_2. Usually, l is omitted unless the intent is to achieve a goal or fall within a range of values for f_2 rather than to determine a minimum. When omitting l, it is possible to obtain a collection of Pareto optimal solutions by a systematic variation of the upper bound u.

In the security literature, the use of the bounded cost technique to define a quantitative version of the WSP, called Bi-Objective WSP Pareto Optimal (BO-WSP-PO), has been considered in [13]. The main differences with the MO-WSP are similar to those discussed above for the Valued WSP.

Boxed. When even establishing an order of importance between the two cost functions w_P and w_C is difficult or there is no preference in violating the authorization policy or the authorization constraints, it is possible to consider the following two separate single-objective optimization problems

$$\underset{\eta}{\text{minimize}} \quad w_C(\eta) \quad \text{subject to} \quad \eta \in \mathcal{S}$$

$$\underset{\eta}{\text{minimize}} \quad w_P(\eta) \quad \text{subject to} \quad \eta \in \mathcal{S} \,.$$

Indeed, the solutions of these problems are the best possible ones for the two cost functions when considered in isolation and provide bounding box values for the set of Pareto optimal solutions of the original MOO problem (cf. Definition 2.3).

Similarly to the lexicographic method, also this variant of the MO-WSP has never been considered before in the literature about the WSP. Preliminary results about using the boxed technique are in Section 4.

Pareto front. While the boxed optimization method can provide decision-makers with a first idea of what optimal solutions for the MO-WSP look like, an approach returning a set of Pareto optimal solutions is more desirable. In this way, decision-makers can pick one of the available solutions a posteriori rather than a priori as done with the approaches above. In the context of the MO-WSP, a *Pareto front* is a maximal set of Pareto optimal scenarios that are not pairwise weight-equal. A pair of scenarios η and η' is *weight-equal* iff $w_P(\eta) = w_P(\eta')$ and $w_C(\eta) = w_C(\eta')$.

In the security literature, the use of the Pareto front technique to define a quantitative version of the WSP, called Bi-Objective WSP Pareto Front (BO-WSP-PF), has been introduced in [13]. The main differences with the MO-WSP are similar to those discussed above for the Valued WSP.

3 ENCODING THE MO-WSP AS AN OMT PROBLEM

To encode the MO-WSP as an OMT problem, we translate—by using the approach in [22]—the Petri net semantically associated to a BPMN workflow—see, e.g., [18]—to a symbolic representation in (a fragment of) first-order logic. The latter is enriched with the authorization policies and constraints, also expressed in (a fragment of) first-order logic—see, e.g., [1]—together with the cost functions, and used as input to an OMT solver. The model returned by the

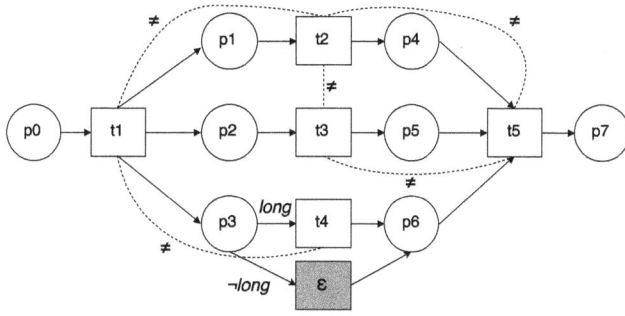

Figure 2: The Petri net for the TRW

solver represents an execution of the workflow that is optimal w.r.t. the input problem.

Background on Petri nets. A tuple (P, T, F) is a *(Place/Transition) Petri net* [16] for P a set of places, T a set of transitions disjoint from P, and $F \subseteq (P \cup T) \times (P \cup T)$ the flow relation such that $F \cap (P \times P) = F \cap (T \times T) = \emptyset$. The *pre-set* ${}^\bullet x$ and the *post-set* $x^\bullet$ of $x \in (P \cup T)$ are the sets $\{y \mid (y, x) \in F\}$ and $\{y \mid (x, y) \in F\}$, respectively. A *marking* m is a mapping from the set P of places to the natural numbers. A transition $t \in T$ is *enabled* by a marking m if $m(p) > 0$ for each $p \in {}^\bullet t$. If a transition $t \in T$ is enabled by a marking m, its occurrence transforms m into m' such that

$$m'(p) := \begin{cases} m(p) - 1 & \text{if } p \in {}^\bullet t \setminus t^\bullet \\ m(p) + 1 & \text{if } p \in t^\bullet \setminus {}^\bullet t \\ m(p) & \text{otherwise.} \end{cases}$$

We write $m \xrightarrow{t} m'$ when t is enabled by marking m with m' being the marking obtained by the occurrence of t. A *(finite) sequence* $t_1, \ldots, t_k$ of transitions in T is a *(finite) occurrence sequence enabled at marking* m if there exist markings $m_1, \ldots, m_k$ such that $m \xrightarrow{t_1} m_1 \xrightarrow{t_2} \cdots \xrightarrow{t_k} m_k$. A marking m' is *reachable* from m when there exists an occurrence sequence enabled at m whose last marking is m'; also written as $m \xrightarrow{t_1, \ldots, t_k} m'$. The Petri net (P, T, F) with the marking m is *1-bounded* when each place in P contains at most 1 token in any marking reachable from m. Here, we consider only 1-bounded Petri nets as it is known that most business processes have associated such a type of net as their semantics; see, e.g., [18]. Notice that it is possible to express iteration in 1-bounded Petri nets; see again [18].

Example 3.1. A Petri net can be graphically shown as a bipartite graph where places are drawn as circles and transitions as squares that are connected by arrows either from places to transitions or from transitions to places. Figure 2 shows a Petri net corresponding to the BPMN of the TRW at the left of Figure 1. The dashed lines labeled by $\neq$ in the Figure represent authorization constraints, whereas the arrows labeled by 'long' and '¬long' represent conditional branches. Notice that the Petri net in Figure 2 has an "extra" transition, represented by a gray box labeled by ϵ. This is an automatic transition, that is fired instead of $t4$ for short trips. □

Symbolic representation. We show how to represent a Petri net (P, T, F) and an initial marking m_i with a symbolic transition system (S, I, Tr) where S is the set of state variables, I is a symbolic description of m_i, and Tr is a symbolic description of F. We use formulae of (a fragment of) first-order logic to represent I and Tr.

Since we consider only 1-bounded nets, the set S of state variables contains a Boolean variable p for each place $p \in P$ and a Boolean variable d_{ti} for each transition $ti \in T$ for $i = 1, \ldots, K$ and $K > 0$ is the number of transitions in T. The variable p encodes the presence of a token in place p whereas d_{ti} represents the fact that transition ti has been executed. The initial state formula I is induced by the initial marking m_0 as follows:

$$I := \bigwedge_{m_0(p)=1} p \wedge \bigwedge_{m_0(p)=0} \neg p \wedge \bigwedge_{i=1}^{K} \neg d_{ti}.$$

Following [22], we derive Tr from F by taking the conjunction of the following formulae:

$$\bigvee_{i=1}^{K} d_{ti} \tag{1}$$

$$\left(\bigvee_{i=1}^{j-1} d_{ti} \right) \Rightarrow \neg d_{tj} \qquad \text{for } 2 \leq j \leq K \tag{2}$$

$$d_{ti} \Rightarrow \left(\bigwedge_{p \in {}^\bullet ti} p \right) \qquad \text{for } 1 \leq i \leq K \tag{3}$$

$$d_{ti} \Rightarrow \left(\bigwedge_{p \in {}^\bullet ti} \neg p' \wedge \bigwedge_{p \in ti^\bullet} p' \right) \qquad \text{for } 1 \leq i \leq K \tag{4}$$

$$\left(\neg \bigvee_{t \in ({}^\bullet p \cup p^\bullet)} d_t \right) \Rightarrow (p' \Leftrightarrow p) \qquad \text{for each } p \in P \tag{5}$$

where an unprimed (primed) variable in S denotes its content immediately before (after) the execution of the transition. Intuitively, (1) and (2) require that exactly one transition is executed; (3) that only enabled tasks are executed; (4) and (5) that the execution of ti transforms the symbolic representation of a marking m_1 into the symbolic representation of marking m_2 where $m_1 \xrightarrow{ti} m_2$.

It is possible to represent conditionals (as it is the case for the execution of tasks $t4$ and ϵ in Figure 1) by considering an extra (disjoint from S) set Π of Boolean variables and then appending an additional conjunct to the consequent of the implication (3) with the appropriate Boolean expression. For instance, in case of $t4$, (3) is instantiated as $d_{t4} \Rightarrow p3 \wedge long$ whereas for ϵ as $d_\epsilon \Rightarrow p3 \wedge \neg long$.

Adding authorization policies and constraints. It is easy to include an authorization policy TA and a set K of authorization constraints in the symbolic representation introduced above. It is sufficient to add to S a state variable h_{ti} such that $h_{ti}(u)$ holds whenever u has executed the transition ti and assume the availability of a predicate a_{ti} such that $a_{ti}(u)$ holds whenever $(u, ti) \in TA$ for each $ti \in T$. The intuition is that the a_{ti}'s are defined so as to represent the authorization policy TA and do not change over time (there is a rich literature about using logic to represent a variety of authorization conditions; see, e.g., [1]). The initial formula I

is extended by conjoining $\forall u.\neg h_{ti}(u)$ expressing the requirement that users have executed no tasks. The formula Tr is modified by conjoining the following two formulae to (1), (2), (3), (4), and (5):

$$d_{ti} \Rightarrow \exists u. \left(\begin{array}{c} a_{ti}(u) \wedge \bigwedge_{\{ti,tj\} \in K} \neg h_{tj}(u) \wedge \\ h'_{ti}(u) \wedge \forall w.w \neq u \Rightarrow h'_{ti}(w) \Leftrightarrow h_{ti}(w) \\ \text{for } 1 \leq i \leq K \end{array} \right) \quad (6)$$

$$\bigwedge_{i=1}^{K} \left(\neg d_{ti} \Rightarrow \forall w.h'_{ti}(w) \Leftrightarrow h_{ti}(w) \right) \quad (7)$$

where $\{ti, tj\} \in K$ abbreviates "for each $(ti, tj) \in K$ and for each $(tj, ti) \in K$." Intuitively, (6) says that task ti can be executed when there exists a user u entitled to do so (cf. $a_{ti}(u)$), no SoD constraints in which ti is involved are violated (cf. $\bigwedge_{\{ti,tj\} \in K} \neg h_{tj}(u)$), it is recorded that u has executed ti and no other user has done so (cf. $h'_{ti}(u) \wedge \forall w.w \neq u \Rightarrow h'_{ti}(w) \Leftrightarrow h_{ti}(w)$) and (7) asserts that all the history variables associated to a task that is not executed are unchanged.

An authorization constraint is called user-independent if it does not depend on identities of users. In particular, SoD constraints are user-independent. We observe that, instead of just SoD constraints, we could include arbitrary user-independent constraints (see, e.g., [27]) because of the expressiveness of (the fragment of) first-order logic that we use, as explained in [19]. Also, notice that, since the set U of users is finite, the existential and universal quantifiers in the formulae above are equivalent to disjunction and conjunction, respectively, over U. Below, we call *extended* a Petri net with authorization policies, authorization constraints, or additional Boolean variables to simplify the representation of control-flow constructs in BPMN.

Bounded Model Checking (BMC). Before explaining how to encode the MO-WSP into an OMT problem, we discuss how BMC [7] relates to the WSP. To this end, observe that the satisfiability of the formula

$$[I(S_0)]_U \wedge [Tr(S_0, S_1)]_U \wedge \cdots \wedge [Tr(S_{\tau-1}, S_\tau)]_U \wedge G(S_\tau) \quad (8)$$

amounts to establishing the reachability in $\tau \geq 1$ steps of the goal formula G from the initial formula I by means of the transition formula Tr. In (8), the expressions $I(S_0)$ and $G(S_\tau)$ denote the formulae obtained from I and G, respectively, by replacing the variables in S and G with renamed copies with subscripts 0 and τ, respectively; the expression $Tr(S_{t-1}, S_t)$ denotes the formula obtained from Tr by replacing the variables in S and their primed versions with renamed copies with subscripts $t - 1$ and t, respectively, for $t = 1, \ldots, n$; finally, $[X]_U$ denotes the formula obtained from X by expanding the universal or existential quantification over the set U of users as a (finite) conjunction or disjunction (respectively) over U for X being I or $Tr(S_{t-1}, S_t)$. The idea to construct formula (8) is to make "timed" copies of the state variables so that the variables in S_t represent the t-th state in a bounded execution of length τ.

When (S, I, Tr) encodes an (extended) 1-bounded Petri net corresponding to a security-sensitive workflow $(W(T, U), TA, K)$ and G characterizes the set of final markings, it is clear that (8) is satisfiable iff the security-sensitive workflow has an execution of $\tau \geq 1$ steps, i.e. a scenario of the form $t_1(u_1), \ldots, t_\tau(u_\tau)$ such that $m_i \xrightarrow{t_1, \ldots, t_\tau} m_f$ for m_i an initial marking and m_f a final marking. By increasing

the value τ, we can explore the whole set $W(T, U)$ of execution scenarios and check if they are both eligible and authorized. To mechanize this process, we need a Satisfiability Modulo Theories (SMT) solver, or simply a SAT solver after encoding (8) into a purely Boolean formula (which is possible because the set U of users is finite). Furthermore, it is possible to reconstruct an authorized and eligible scenario of length τ from the assignment returned (if the case) by the solver.

Symbolic representation of scenarios of interest. It is easy to symbolically represent the set S of scenarios of interest in $W(T, U)$ (recall Definition 2.3) by means of a first-order formula. To illustrate, consider the TRW in Example 2.1: by simply conjoining the formula *long* to the corresponding instance of (8), it is possible to consider only those scenarios for which the trip requires the execution of task $t4$. In general, given the set S of scenarios of interest, it is possible to build a formula $[S_t]_\Pi$ corresponding to a Boolean assignment to the variables in the set Π representing the conditionals of the 1-bounded Petri net for each time instant $t = 0, \ldots, \tau$. It is then sufficient to conjoin the formula $\bigwedge_{t=0}^{\tau} [S_t]_\Pi$ to (8).

Causal nets. We now identify a sub-class of 1-bounded Petri nets for which it is possible to solve the WSP by checking the satisfiability of (8) for finitely many values of τ.

A *causal net* [16] is a Petri net (P, T, F) satisfying the following properties: (i) F is acyclic (i.e. no path with at least two elements leads from an element to itself), (ii) for each $p \in P$, the cardinality of both ${}^\bullet p$ and $p^\bullet$ is at most one, (iii) only finitely many places $p \in P$ have an empty pre-set, (iv) for each transition $t \in T$, both ${}^\bullet t$ and $t^\bullet$ are finite and non-empty, and (v) for each element $x \in P \cup T$, only finitely many different paths lead to x. A causal net induces a partial order $\geq$ on its elements as follows: $x \geq x'$ iff there exists a path leading from x to x'. An element x is *maximal* (*minimal*) with respect to $\geq$ iff there is no element x' such that $x' \geq x$ ($x \geq x'$, respectively) and $x \neq x'$. A *canonical initial marking* m_i (*final marking* m_f) of a causal Petri net assigns to each maximal/minimal (w.r.t. $\geq$) place one token and no token to all other places. Notice that m_f enables no transition. Three important properties of a causal net are that (P1) it is 1-bounded when considered with its canonical initial marking, (P2) each transition of an occurrence sequence can eventually occur, and (P3) no transition occurs more than once in an occurrence sequence [16]. Because of (P1), we can derive a symbolic representation from a causal net as described above. (P2) can be lifted to augmented causal nets provided that any user entitled to execute a task does not delay its execution once this has become enabled. (P2) and (P3) set an upper bound on the length of the scenarios of an augmented causal net to the cardinality of the largest set of transitions that are totally ordered with respect to $\geq$. Because of (P1), (P2), and (P3), the following method is a decision procedure for the WSP. For $\tau = 0, \ldots, L$, if (8) is satisfiable, return that the WSP is solvable. If $\tau = L$ and no formula has been found satisfiable, return that the WSP is unsolvable.

In the rest of the paper, we consider only causal nets. We notice that some of the most important control flow patterns in BPMN for parallel and non-deterministic/conditional executions can be expressed in this class of nets; see, e.g., [18]. One of the most important omissions is iteration (as considered in, e.g., [14]), which we leave as future work. The advantage of considering causal nets is a simplified symbolic representation of the set $\mathcal{S}$ of the scenarios of interest. In fact, the conditionals (such as *long* in TRW) can be executed only once and we can drop the subscript t from the formula $[\mathcal{S}_t]_\Pi$ corresponding to their Boolean assignment (see paragraph 'Symbolic representation of scenarios of interest' above). It is thus sufficient to conjoin the formula $[\mathcal{S}]_\Pi$ to (8).

3.1 From the MO-WSP to the OMT Problem

Optimization Modulo Theories (OMT) is an extension of SMT which aims to solve the problem of finding a model for an input formula φ which is optimal with respect to one or more objective functions.

An important sub-case of OMT is the *(weighted partial) Min-SMT problem* that can be stated as follows. A clause is a disjunction of literals, i.e. atoms or their negations, over some theory. A soft clause is a pair consisting of a clause with a weight (a non-negative number). A hard clause is a pair consisting of a clause with an infinite weight. Given a formula of the form $\varphi_h \wedge \varphi_s^1 \wedge \cdots \wedge \varphi_s^q$, where φ_h is a conjunction of hard clauses and φ_s^k is a conjunction of soft clauses for $k = 1, \ldots, q$, the *(weighted partial) Min-SMT problem* amounts to finding a model of φ_h that minimizes the tuple $(w_s^1, \ldots, w_s^q)$ of weights obtained by taking the sum of the weights of the satisfied soft clauses in $\varphi_s^1, \ldots, \varphi_s^q$, respectively.

We now explain how to reduce the MO-WSP to a Min-SMT problem. The idea is to consider the formula (8) $\wedge [\mathcal{S}]_\Pi$, take $q = 2$ sets φ_s^1 and φ_s^2 of soft clauses representing the constraints imposed by the authorization policy and the authorization constraints, respectively, and associate to each clause in these sets a weight derived from the functions w_P and w_C. The details of the reduction can be summarized in the following six steps.

(1) From an instance of the MO-WSP (c.f. Definition 2.3), build the formula φ as the conjunction of (8) and $[\mathcal{S}]_\Pi$.

(2) Replace all the atoms of the forms $a_{ti}(u)$ and $h_{tj}(u)$, for some $u \in U$, that occur in φ as instances of the atoms in (6) with fresh Boolean variables b_a and b_h; let φ' be the resulting formula and *Abs* be the set of all pairs $(b_a, a_{ti}(u))$ and $(b_h, h_{tj}(u))$.

(3) Transform φ' into an equisatisfiable conjunction φ_h of clauses by using well-known logical transformations (see, e.g., [23]); the size of φ_h can be linear in the size of φ'.

(4) Take φ_s^1 to be a conjunction of clauses of the form $\neg b_a \vee a_{ti}(u)$ for each $(b_a, a_{ti}(u))$ in *Abs* and φ_s^2 to be a conjunction of clauses of the form $\neg b_h \vee h_{tj}(u)$ for each $(b_h, h_{tj}(u))$ in *Abs*.

(5) Assign weights w_{ai} to each b_a and w_{hj} to each b_h, such that $w_s^1 = \sum w_{ai}$ and $w_s^2 = \sum w_{hj}$ encode the cost functions $w_P(\eta)$ and $w_C(\eta)$, respectively. Notice that the cost functions are defined on execution scenarios, whereas we need "local" weights w_{ai} and w_{hj}. As a reasonable simplification, we assume that $w_P(\eta)$ and $w_C(\eta)$ are linear combinations of terms that depend only on a task t being executed, the user u executing t, and the execution history of u and another task t'[1]. Then, we can map each term in a cost function to a weight

w_{ai} or w_{hj} or ask the user directly for the weights. Recall the cost functions in Example 2.2: in this case, $w_{ai} = w_{hj} = 1$ for each b_a and b_h.

(6) Find a model of $\varphi_h \wedge \varphi_s^1 \wedge \varphi_s^2$ that minimizes the pair (w_s^1, w_s^2). The model can be used to compute one or more scenarios that are solutions to the MO-WSP (how to do this is illustrated in an example below).

Observe that formula φ' computed at step 2 is an over-approximation of (8) as it abstracts away from the constraints imposed by the authorization policies and authorization constraints (that are replaced by fresh Boolean variables), thus guaranteeing only the control-flow constraints of the SSW. Also notice that, since the fresh Boolean variables b_a's and b_h's are constrained by the soft clauses in φ_s^1 and φ_s^2, respectively, the solver is free to choose their truth value to minimize the pair of weights (w_s^1, w_s^2) according to one of the criteria discussed in Section 2.1.

3.2 Parallel encoding

The transition formula *Tr* presented above uses an interleaving semantics for the execution of tasks in a workflow, i.e. it assumes that only one task is executed at each step τ (parallel tasks can be executed in any order).

We now explore an optimized encoding of *Tr* based on a $\forall$-step semantics, as defined in [22], which exploits the parallelism in workflow specifications to model the execution of (possibly) several tasks in one step, thus compressing the number of steps in *Tr*. It also uses properties of causal nets to encode in each step only those tasks that may actually be executed. This encoding is slightly more complex to understand and requires a pre-processing phase, but it is also faster for an OMT solver (see Section 4.3).

To formalize the encoding, we need to introduce some preliminary notions. An *anti-chain* is a sub-set of the elements in a partial order $\geq$ in which no two distinct element are comparable, i.e. neither $t \geq t'$ nor $t' \geq t$ for every pair of elements in the sub-set. A *cut* of a causal net is a maximal (w.r.t. inclusion) set of elements in $P \cup T$ that are pairwise not ordered by $\geq$ (where $\geq$ is the partial order induced by the net).

PROPERTY 1. *Let N be the causal net associated to a security-sensitive workflow $(W(T, U), TA, K)$. Then, if C is a cut of N, then $C \cap T$ is a maximal anti-chain of $\geq$.*

To encode the fact that more than one task can be executed in a given step of *Tr*, we can reuse formulae (1) and (3–5). We only need to change formula (2), the one that says that only one task is executed in each step. The revised version of (2) is

$$\left(\bigvee_{i=1}^{j-1} dt_i \right) \Rightarrow \bigwedge_{p \in t_i{}^\bullet \cap\, {}^\bullet t_j} \neg dt_j \quad \text{for } 2 \leq j \leq K \qquad (9)$$

which means that possibly all tasks can be executed at each step. This formula delegates to the OMT solver the job of finding a satisfying assignment that respects the control-flow constraints of the workflow.

---

[1] Defining cost functions on scenarios is more general, as it allows us to have different costs for specific user-task pairs or costs that depend on the order of execution of the tasks. It is possible to define complex cost functions as local weights by encoding the

clauses b_a and b_h using, e.g., if-then-else conditions, but that increases the complexity both for humans to express and for solvers to find optimal models.

We obtain the sets of tasks that can be executed in parallel at each step of Tr in (8) by computing the lattice of maximal anti-chains (see, e.g., [24]) and traversing it breadth-first. We construct the BMC encoding by starting from the bottom of the lattice and, in each level (which corresponds to a step in Tr), we encode only the tasks in the anti-chain of that level in (9). If there is more than one anti-chain in a level, this is encoded as an exclusive disjunction. The number of steps in Tr becomes equal to the number of maximal anti-chains, instead of equal to the number of tasks in the workflow.

After discharging the BMC formula to an OMT solver, the resulting model is a compact representation of several possible interleaving executions, which can be linearized. We illustrate how this is done by an example.

Example 3.2. We consider TRW and assume that *long* is true, i.e. we want to execute $t4$ (for the sake of simplicity, we omit the conjunct *long* in the formulae below). In this case, we have 3 anti-chains: $\{t1\}$, $\{t2, t3, t4\}$, and $\{t5\}$, each representing a set of tasks that can be executed in parallel. Using the original interleaving encoding, we would have modeled the TRW with 5 steps, one for each task (considering that either $t4$ or ϵ can be executed). With the parallel encoding, we model it using 3 steps, one for each anti-chain. Step 0 is obtained by applying (1), (9), (3), (4), and (5) only to task $t1$:

$$d_{t1}^0 \wedge \left(\bigwedge_{j=2}^{5} d_{t1}^0 \Rightarrow \neg d_{tj}^0 \right) \wedge \left(d_{t1}^0 \Rightarrow p0^0 \right) \wedge$$

$$\left(d_{t1}^0 \Rightarrow \neg p0^1 \wedge p1^1 \wedge p2^1 \wedge p3^1 \right) \wedge \left(\neg \bigvee_{j=2}^{5} d_{tj}^0 \Rightarrow \bigwedge_{j=4}^{7} pj^1 = pj^0 \right),$$

where the first line indicates that only $t1$ can be executed and it must be enabled, whereas the second line specifies both the variables that are updated and those that remain unchanged. Step 2 is obtained by applying the same formulae only to $t5$:

$$d_{t5}^2 \wedge \left(\bigwedge_{j=1}^{4} d_{t5}^2 \Rightarrow \neg d_{tj}^2 \right) \wedge \left(d_{t5}^2 \Rightarrow p4^2 \wedge p5^2 \wedge p6^2 \right) \wedge$$

$$\left(d_{t5}^2 \Rightarrow \neg p4^3 \wedge \neg p5^3 \wedge \neg p6^3 \wedge p7^3 \right) \wedge \left(\neg \bigvee_{j=1}^{4} d_{tj}^2 \Rightarrow \bigwedge_{j=0}^{3} pj^3 = pj^2 \right)$$

and the meaning of the formula is similar to the previous one (replacing $t1$ by $t5$). Step 1 encompasses $t2$, $t3$, $t4$, and ϵ and is encoded as follows:

$$\left(\bigvee_{j=2}^{4} d_{tj}^1 \vee d_{\epsilon}^1 \right) \wedge \left(\bigvee_{j=2}^{4} d_{tj}^1 \vee d_{\epsilon}^1 \Rightarrow \neg d_{t1}^1 \wedge \neg d_{t5}^1 \right) \wedge$$

$$\left(\begin{matrix} d_{t2}^1 \Rightarrow p1^1 \wedge \\ d_{t3}^1 \Rightarrow p2^1 \wedge \\ d_{t4}^1 \Rightarrow long \wedge p3^1 \wedge \\ d_{\epsilon}^1 \Rightarrow \neg long \wedge p3^1 \end{matrix} \right) \wedge \left(\begin{matrix} d_{t2}^1 \Rightarrow \neg p1^2 \wedge p4^2 \wedge \\ d_{t3}^1 \Rightarrow \neg p2^2 \wedge p5^2 \wedge \\ d_{t4}^1 \Rightarrow \neg p3^2 \wedge p6^2 \wedge \\ d_{\epsilon}^1 \Rightarrow \neg p3^2 \wedge p6^2 \end{matrix} \right) \wedge$$

$$\left(\neg (d_{t1}^1 \vee d_{t5}^1) \Rightarrow p0^3 = p0^2 \wedge p7^3 = p7^2 \right).$$

A model for the BMC formula constructed as above assigns True to the following variables (and False to all the others):

$$d_{t1}^0, d_{t2}^1, d_{t3}^1, d_{t4}^1, d_{t5}^2, p0^0, p1^1, p2^1, p3^1, p4^2, p5^2, p6^2,$$

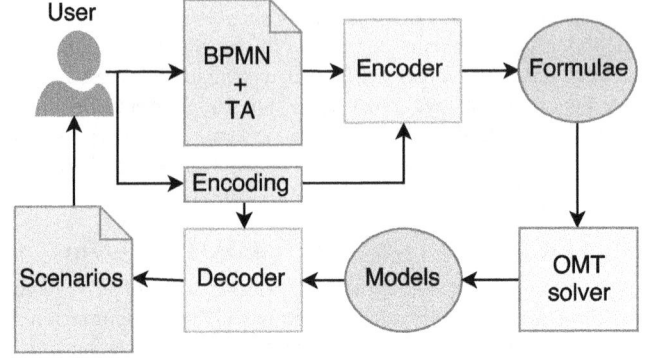

Figure 3: Architecture of the implementation

$$h_{t1}^0(b), h_{t2}^1(a), h_{t3}^1(c), h_{t4}^1(a), h_{t5}^2(b), long$$

which represents the following scenarios:

$$\eta_1 = t1(b), t2(a), t3(c), t4(a), t5(b);$$
$$\eta_2 = t1(b), t2(a), t4(a), t3(c), t5(b);$$
$$\eta_3 = t1(b), t3(c), t2(a), t4(a), t5(b);$$
$$\eta_4 = t1(b), t3(c), t4(a), t2(a), t5(b);$$
$$\eta_5 = t1(b), t4(a), t2(a), t3(c), t5(b);$$
$$\eta_6 = t1(b), t4(a), t3(c), t2(a), t5(b).$$

$\square$

4 EVALUATION

We implemented a prototype and experimented with two sets of benchmarks: real-world workflows and synthetic, randomly generated, ones. The benchmarks contain only causal nets and sets of scenarios of interest that refer to parallel executions of tasks (e.g., those either containing $t4$ or not in TRW).

4.1 Implementation

Figure 3 shows the architecture of our implementation. The user inputs a *BPMN model* of the workflow (including authorization constraints), an authorization policy, and an *Encoding*. The Encoding includes the option of semantics to use for the transition system (interleaving or parallel), the costs associated to violating the policy and constraints, and the optimization mode. These artifacts are given to an *Encoder*, which translates the model and options to a set of formulae that can be fed to an *OMT solver*. The solver outputs one or more optimal models, which are passed to a *Decoder* module to transform them into actual execution scenarios that are presented to the user.

We used Python, PySMT [25], and SageMath [17] to implement the Encoder and Decoder and interface with the OMT solvers. We support the solvers OptiMathSAT [32] and Z3 [8]. Both natively support Boxed, Lexicographic, and Pareto optimization. Weighted sum and Bounded cost optimization can be easily encoded, but we skip this in the experiments for the sake of space.

4.2 Real-world workflows

We applied our approach to two workflows inspired by real-world examples[2] (ITIL and ISO, shown in Figure 4), besides the TRW presented before. These examples include all the basic workflow control-flow patterns [33] (sequential, parallel, and exclusive executions). Each workflow has 10 users authorized for each task, except for the last task, which has no authorized users, so that the workflow becomes unsatisfiable.

Table 1 shows the results.[3] For each workflow instance, we used 12 configurations, obtained from the combinations of: 2 encodings ('Interleaving' and 'Parallel'); 2 OMT solvers ('OptiMathSat' and 'Z3'); and 3 modes of optimization ('Lexic.' for Lexicographic, 'Boxed', and 'Pareto'). Each configuration was executed 10 times and we report the median execution time (in seconds).

All solutions are found in less than 1 second (most in less than 0.5 seconds). It is easy to see that the parallel encoding has a superior performance in every case (far superior, in many cases). It is also clear that Pareto is the slowest optimization mode, while Boxed and Lexicographic have almost the same performance, and that Z3 is faster than OptiMathSAT when both are using the same optimization mode, except for two cases (ITIL and ISO with the interleaving encoding and Boxed optimization).

These results show that solving the MO-WSP with optimization modulo theories is feasible for average instances found in real-world use cases. To further test the effects of the parallel encoding and the scalability of the techniques in larger instances, we consider synthetic benchmarks.

4.3 Synthetic benchmarks

We adapted the random workflow generator used in [6] to generate workflows with TA's and SoD constraints that are not satisfiable. The tool generates workflows with a given number of tasks n, $10n$ users, TA's with up to 5 tasks with no authorized users, and at least 1 unsatisfiable SoD constraint. There are two more parameters: d is the number of user-task pairs in TA out of the possible number (e.g., with 100 users and 10 tasks, there could be 1000 user-task pairs; if $d = 10\%$, the tool generates 100 of those); e is similar and specifies the (relative) number of authorization constraints out of the number of tasks. The generated workflows have sequential and parallel tasks (for every task in a workflow, there is a 15% probability to branch).

Encodings. To confirm that the parallel encoding is superior to the interleaving encoding even as the size of the input workflow grows, we ran an experiment where we generated workflows with 10, 13, 16, 19 tasks (100, 130, 160, 190 users). We tested with the same 12 configurations as before (2 encodings, 2 solvers, 3 optimization modes) and a fixed $d, e = (10\%, 10\%)$. Again, each configuration was executed 10 times and we report the median execution time (in seconds).

Table 2 shows the results. The parallel encoding is always superior and the gains obtained with it become more substantial as the workflow size grows in most configurations. The time to compute the lattice of maximal anti-chains used for the parallel encoding is negligible and not reported separately (it is already included in the time reported for the execution with the parallel encoding).

For workflows with 20 or more tasks, we started observing timeouts in the execution of the solvers when using the interleaving encoding (we set the timeout to 1 hour). To show the scalability of the technique beyond 20 tasks, we used only the parallel encoding and expanded our tests to include different d, e configurations.

Scalability. We generated workflows with 10 to 30 tasks (100 to 300 users) and the d, e configurations $\{(10\%, 10\%), (10\%, 30\%), (20\%, 10\%), (20\%, 30\%)\}$, as done in [13]. For each configuration, we generated 10 random workflows and solved the MO-WSP using the parallel encoding, both OMT solvers and the three optimization modes (Lexicographic, Boxed, and Pareto).

Figure 5 shows the results. Each graph shows the results of one OMT solver in one optimization mode, where the x axes show the number of tasks, the y axes show the median time to solve an instance, and each line represents a (d, e) configuration. Notice that the scales are different for each graph.

There is an (expected) exponential growth in the time to solve the MO-WSP, nevertheless, even for workflows of up to 30 tasks and 300 users—large configurations for realistic use cases—the solution is found in under 30 seconds. The time to compute a lattice of maximal anti-chains and obtain the scenarios from the generated models is negligible (less than 100 ms) and thus not reported. It

---

[2]http://www.signavio.com/reference-models/

[3]All the experiments in this paper were performed on a laptop with a quad-core 2.6GHz Core i7 processor and 16GB of RAM running Ubuntu 16.04.

Table 1: Results for real-world workflows (in seconds)

Encoding	OptiMathSAT			Z3		
	Lexic.	Boxed	Pareto	Lexic.	Boxed	Pareto
TRW						
Interleaving	0.178	0.302	0.192	0.045	0.046	0.155
Parallel	0.034	0.032	0.035	0.019	0.019	0.024
ITIL						
Interleaving	0.498	0.280	0.615	0.034	0.033	0.255
Parallel	0.051	0.056	0.061	0.021	0.021	0.031
ISO						
Interleaving	0.502	0.301	0.731	0.045	0.045	0.255
Parallel	0.049	0.048	0.051	0.025	0.025	0.037

Table 2: Results for synthetic workflows (in seconds)

Encoding	OptiMathSAT			Z3		
	Lexic.	Boxed	Pareto	Lexic.	Boxed	Pareto
$n = 10$ tasks						
Interleaving	1.219	1.325	1.209	0.429	0.083	0.708
Parallel	0.117	0.125	0.123	0.030	0.024	0.061
$n = 13$ tasks						
Interleaving	5.353	6.335	5.948	3.330	32.093	3.771
Parallel	0.270	0.224	0.234	0.054	0.045	0.078
$n = 16$ tasks						
Interleaving	19.058	18.021	17.721	5.243	157.120	28.551
Parallel	1.053	0.699	0.516	0.158	0.110	0.291
$n = 19$ tasks						
Interleaving	71.607	50.214	128.333	5.496	216.106	50.075
Parallel	2.062	0.906	1.127	0.298	0.140	1.224

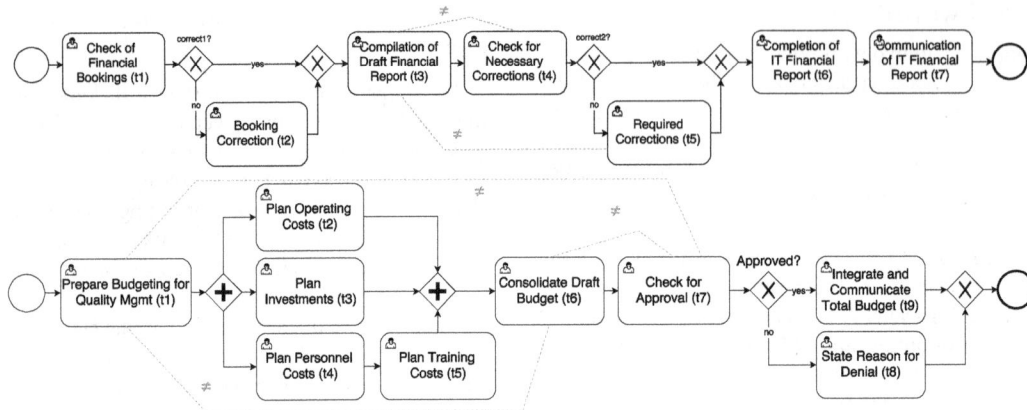

Figure 4: ITIL process (top) and ISO process (bottom) in extended BPMN.

is also clear that Z3 is faster than OptiMathSAT in almost every instance.

4.4 Discussion

In many cases, off-the-shelf solvers provide greater flexibility at the cost of decreased performance when compared to ad hoc algorithmic solutions, since the latter can be optimized for specific applications. However, in [27] it is shown that the difference in performance for moderate-size WSP instances can be practically insignificant if appropriate modelling of constraints is used. In our experiments, off-the-shelf solvers show good performance, however more experiments would be needed to confirm that our solution can outperform bespoke algorithms for the kinds of WSPs considered.

The algorithmic solution that is closest to our work is that of [13]. However, it is hard to directly compare our experiments with those reported in [13] because the settings are different. First, they consider a wide family of user-independent constraints—i.e. those constraints whose satisfaction does not depend on the identity of the users—whereas we only experiment with SoD constraints. Second, the platforms on which the experiments were run are different, e.g., they do not exploit concurrency, whereas the solvers that we use do exploit this feature. Nevertheless, to give an idea of the orders of magnitude, while our average worst case execution time for workflows of 30 tasks was under 30 seconds, they report times of 10^3 seconds in the worst case. On the other hand, their best case scenarios (for workflows of 10 tasks) run in 10^{-4} seconds, whereas our best performance for a similar configuration was 10^{-2} seconds. A systematic comparison using the available code and benchmarks of [13] is planned as future work.

5 RELATED WORK

The seminal work of Bertino et al. [5] described the specification and enforcement of authorization constraints in workflow management systems. Wang and Li [34] showed that the WSP is NP-complete even with simple constraints and reduced the problem to SAT. See [20, 26] for a survey on workflow satisfiability approaches. Bertolissi et al. [6] presented a solution to the run-time WSP that relies on pre-computing all eligible execution scenarios of a security-sensitive workflow as a symbolic reachability graph. This graph is

refined in [21] to find execution scenarios that satisfy properties defined by the user. It is not possible to reuse the solutions in [6, 21] to solve the MO-WSP because the pre-computed graphs do not consider constraint violations.

Basin et al. [4] studied how to optimally modify an authorization policy to render a workflow instance satisfiable, by associating a cost to each possible change to the policy. On the other hand, Crampton et al. [12, 13] first studied how to find minimal violating assignments of users to tasks, without changing the policy. They first defined the Valued WSP [12] and later the BO-WSP [13], then solved both using a bespoke algorithm and showed that their solution is superior to a mixed integer programming approach in terms of performance. The authors also showed how to solve two related problems by encoding them as cost functions: the quantitative resiliency problem [29], which amounts to assigning a probability to the successful termination of a workflow even in the absence of some users; and the Cardinality-constrained Minimum User Problem (CMUP) [31], which consists in finding the minimum number of users required to satisfy a workflow instance. The main difference between our work and Crampton et al. [12, 13] is that we consider an ordered execution of workflows, whereas they take as solution a valid plan, which is an unordered assignment of tasks to users. They also considered user-independent constraints in their experiments, which we did not implement, but, as already observed in Section 3, can be expressed in the fragment of first-order logic that we use.

Crampton et al. [14] extended their algorithmic solution to support conditional workflows with release points—which specify that a constraint may be active only for some scenarios—by splitting a workflow instance into many deterministic ones. We believe that release points can also be incorporated in our solution by using an approach similar to [4]; we leave this to future work. A challenge is to adapt the parallel encoding of Section 3.2 to this generalized problem so to have better scalability. For this, we believe that the techniques in [22] can be useful.

6 CONCLUSION

We have motivated, defined, and solved the MO-WSP. This work is the first to consider quantitative solutions to the WSP with an

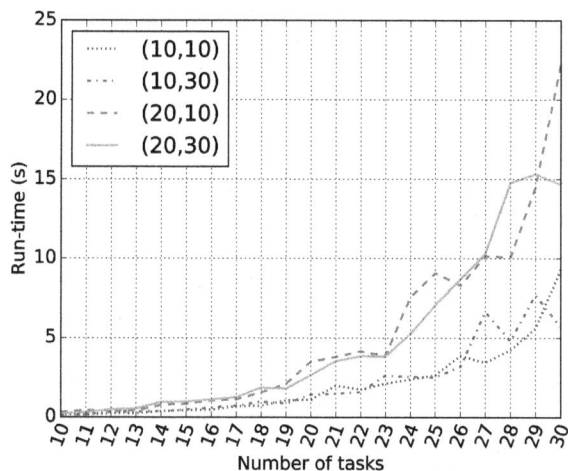

(a) OptiMathSAT/Lexicographic

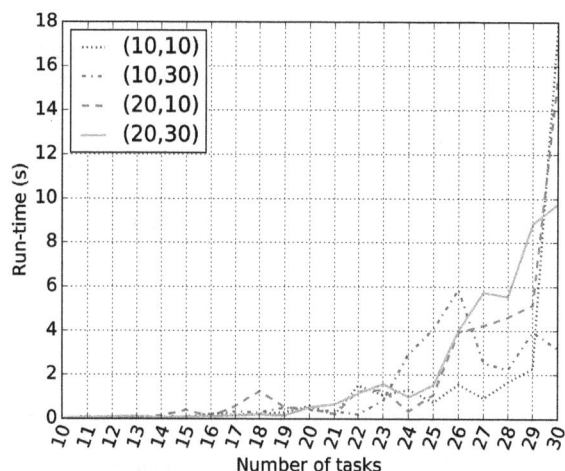

(b) Z3/Lexicographic

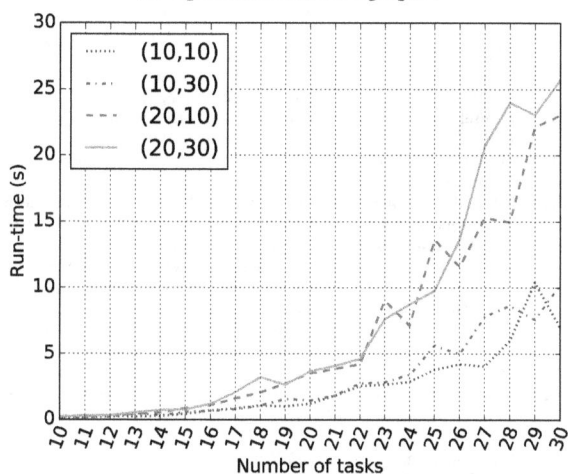

(c) OptiMathSAT/Boxed

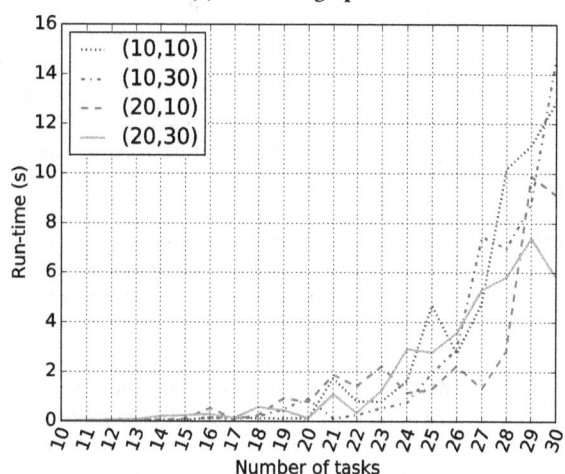

(d) Z3/Boxed

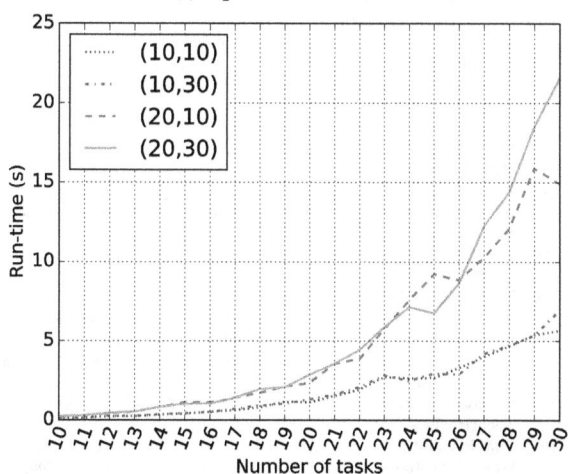

(e) OptiMathSAT/Pareto

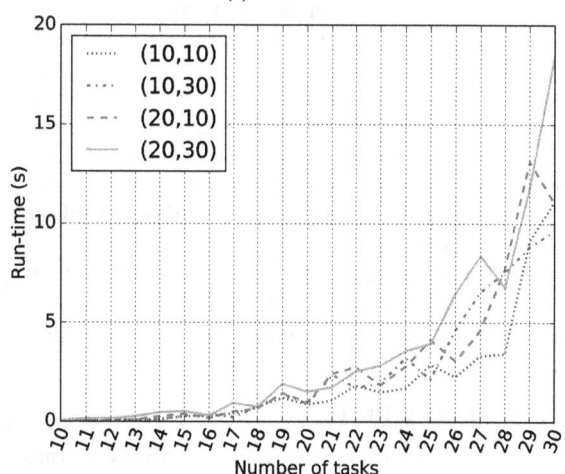

(f) Z3/Pareto

Figure 5: Scalability benchmarks

ordered execution of tasks, i.e., without abstracting the control-flow constraints, and control-flow patterns such as alternative execution. Our solution, based on the use of off-the-shelf OMT solvers is flexible enough to handle several version of the problem by simply alternating between optimization modes.

The solution was also implemented and evaluated on real and synthetic instances of the problem, showing good performance due to the use of an ingenious encoding of the problem that exploits the parallel executions of tasks in the workflow.

6.1 Future work

We plan to investigate a generalization of the MO-WSP that considers all scenarios at the same time, not restricting to the set of scenarios of interest as done in Definition 2.3. The idea is to return either all optimal solutions associated to alternatives (e.g., the set of optimal solutions for the scenarios including $t4$ and another set for those not including $t4$ in TRW) or the maximum of the optimal solutions. We intend to generalize the approach in Section 3 to solve also this problem as follows. First, use the encoding in Section 3.1 by taking (8) only as the formula φ (i.e. disregarding the formula $[S]_\Pi$ representing the set S of scenarios of interest) and solve the resulting optimization problem. Take the assignment of the Boolean variables in Π and negate them; let δ be the resulting formula. Then, take the conjunction of (8) and δ as φ and solve the new (refined) OMT problem: the solver will search for optimal solutions that refer to an assignment of the variables in Π that is different from the previous one. We repeat the process until no more assignments to the variables in Π are found. The main challenge to make the approach practical is to reduce the number of OMT problems to solve in the worst case, which is equal to the number $2^{|\Pi|}$ of alternative execution scenarios induced by the Boolean variables in Π. To this end, we plan to develop heuristics to synthesize formulae expressing the fact that sequences of tasks contained in alternative scenarios are equivalent with respect to the costs considered. Such formulae will be conjoined to (8) to hopefully avoid the complete enumeration of the exponential number of alternative scenarios.

As already mentioned throughout the paper, we intend to study how to support iterations and release points. Another line of future work is to consider a version of the MO-WSP where deviations from the modeled control-flow are allowed. In practice, control-flow deviations are common in, e.g., healthcare systems [2] and finding executions that are optimal w.r.t. control-flow, authorization policies, and authorization constraints may further expand the applicability of our technique.

Finally, we intend to integrate our work into a workflow management system, so that users can get solutions with the push of a button in an integrated environment (as done for run-time monitoring in [9]).

ACKNOWLEDGEMENTS

We thank the reviewers for their useful comments and criticisms that significantly contributed to improvement of the manuscript.

REFERENCES

[1] M. Abadi. *Logic in Access Control (Tutorial Notes)*. Springer, 2009.
[2] A. Adriansyah, B. van Dongen, and N. Zannone. Controlling break-the-glass through alignment. *ASE Science Journal*, 2(4):198–212, 2013.
[3] A. Armando and S.E. Ponta. Model checking of security-sensitive business processes. In *Proc. of FAST*, 2009.
[4] D. Basin, S.J. Burri, and G. Karjoth. Optimal workflow-aware authorizations. In *Proc. of SACMAT*, 2012.
[5] E. Bertino, E. Ferrari, and V. Atluri. The specification and enforcement of authorization constraints in workflow management systems. *TISSEC*, 2(1):65–104, 1999.
[6] C. Bertolissi, D.R. dos Santos, and S. Ranise. Automated synthesis of run-time monitors to enforce authorization policies in business processes. In *Proc. of ASIACCS*, 2015.
[7] A. Biere, A. Cimatti, E. Clarke, and Y. Zhu. Symbolic model checking without bdds. In *Proc. of TACAS*, 1999.
[8] N. Bjørner, A. Phan, and L. Fleckenstein. νz - an optimizing SMT solver. In *Proc. of TACAS*, 2015.
[9] L. Compagna, D.R. dos Santos, S.E. Ponta, and S. Ranise. Cerberus: Automated synthesis of enforcement mechanisms for security-sensitive business processes. In *Proc. of TACAS*, 2016.
[10] J. Crampton. A reference monitor for workflow systems with constrained task execution. In *Proc. of SACMAT*, 2005.
[11] J. Crampton and G. Gutin. Constraint expressions and workflow satisfiability. In *Proc. of SACMAT*, 2013.
[12] J. Crampton, G. Gutin, and D. Karapetyan. Valued workflow satisfiability problem. In *Proc. of SACMAT*, 2015.
[13] J. Crampton, G. Gutin, D. Karapetyan, and R. Watrigant. The bi-objective workflow satisfiability problem and workflow resiliency. *JCS*, 25(1):83–115, 2017.
[14] J. Crampton, G. Gutin, and R. Watrigant. On the satisfiability of workflows with release points. In *Proc. of SACMAT*, 2017.
[15] J. Crampton, G. Gutin, and A. Yeo. On the parameterized complexity of the workflow satisfiability problem. In *Proc. of CCS*, 2012.
[16] J. Desel and W. Reisig. Place or transition petri nets. In *Lectures on Petri Nets I: Basic Models, Advances in Petri Nets*. Springer, 1996.
[17] The Sage Developers. *SageMath, the Sage Mathematics Software System*, 2017. http://www.sagemath.org.
[18] R.M. Dijkman, M. Dumas, and C. Ouyang. Semantics and analysis of business process models in bpmn. *Inf. and Soft. Tech.*, 50(12):1281 – 1294, 2008.
[19] D.R. dos Santos and S. Ranise. On run-time enforcement of authorization constraints in security-sensitive business processes. In *Proc. of SEFM*, 2017.
[20] D.R. dos Santos and S. Ranise. A survey on workflow satisfiability, resiliency, and related problems. *CoRR*, abs/1706.07205, 2017.
[21] D.R. dos Santos, S. Ranise, L. Compagna, and S. E. Ponta. Assisting the Deployment of Security-Sensitive Workflows by Finding Execution Scenarios. In *Proc. of DBSec*, 2015.
[22] J. Dubrovin, T.A. Junttila, and K. Heljanko. Exploiting step semantics for efficient bounded model checking of asynchronous systems. *Sci. Comput. Program.*, 77(10-11):1095–1121, 2012.
[23] H.B. Enderton. *A Mathematical Introduction to Logic*. Academic Press, New York-London, 1972.
[24] V.K. Garg. Maximal antichain lattice algorithms for distributed computations. In *Proc. of ICDCN*, 2013.
[25] M. Gario and A. Micheli. pysmt: a solver-agnostic library for fast prototyping of smt-based algorithms. In *SMT Workshop*, 2015.
[26] J. Holderer, R. Accorsi, and G. Müller. When four-eyes become too much: a survey on the interplay of authorization constraints and workflow resilience. In *Proc. of SAC*, 2015.
[27] D. Karapetyan, A. J. Parkes, G. Gutin, and A. Gagarin. Pattern-based approach to the workflow satisfiability problem with user-independent constraints. *CoRR*, abs/1604.05636, 2016.
[28] M. Leitner and S. Rinderle-Ma. A systematic review on security in process-aware information systems–constitution, challenges, and future directions. *Inf. and Soft. Tech.*, 56(3):273–293, 2014.
[29] J.C. Mace, C. Morisset, and A. Moorsel. Quantitative workflow resiliency. In *Proc. of ESORICS*, 2014.
[30] R.T. Marler and J.S. Arora. Survey of multi-objective optimization methods for engineering. *Structural and Multidisciplinary Optimization*, 26(6):369–395, 2004.
[31] A. Roy, S. Sural, A.K. Majumdar, J. Vaidya, and V. Atluri. Minimizing organizational user requirement while meeting security constraints. *ACM Trans. Manage. Inf. Syst.*, 6(3):12:1–12:25, 2015.
[32] R. Sebastiani and P. Trentin. OptiMathSAT: A Tool for Optimization Modulo Theories. In *Proc. of CAV*, 2015.
[33] W.M.P. van der Aalst, A.H.M. ter Hofstede, B. Kiepuszewski, and A.P. Barros. Workflow patterns. *Distributed Parallel Databases*, 14(1):5–51, 2003.
[34] Q. Wang and N. Li. Satisfiability and resiliency in workflow authorization systems. *TISSEC*, 13, 2010.
[35] M. Weske. *Business Process Management: Concepts, Languages, Architectures*. Springer, Secaucus, NJ, USA, 2007.

Network Policy Enforcement Using Transactions: The NEUTRON Approach

Dan Thomsen
SIFT, LLC
Minneapolis, MN 55401, USA
dthomsen@sift.net

Elisa Bertino
Purdue University
West Lafayette, IN 47907, USA
bertino@purdue.edu

ABSTRACT

We propose a tool to capture applications requirements with respect to the enforcement of network security policies in an object-oriented design language. Once a design captures clear, concise, easily understood network requirements new technologies become possible, including *network transactions* and *user-driven policies* to remove rarely used network permissions until needed, creating a *least privilege in time* policy. Existing security enforcement policies represent a model of all allowable behavior. Only modeling allowable behavior requires that any entity that *may* need a permission, be granted it *permanently*. Refining the modeling to distinguish between common behavior and rare behavior will increase security. The increased security comes with costs, such as requiring users to strongly authenticate more often. This paper discusses those costs and the complexity of increasing security enforcement models.

KEYWORDS

security enforcement policy; network transactions; user-driven policy; network security; policy design.

ACM Reference format:
Dan Thomsen and Elisa Bertino. 2018. Network Policy Enforcement Using Transactions:
The NEUTRON Approach. In *Proceedings of The 23rd ACM Symposium on Access Control Models & Technologies (SACMAT), Indianapolis, IN, USA, June 13–15, 2018 (SACMAT '18),* 8 pages.
https://doi.org/10.1145/3205977.3206000

1 INTRODUCTION

Modern computing relies heavily on the network as a flexible utility to increase the flow of information, adapting to outages and new protocols quickly. Unfortunately, the complexity of network traffic has grown so that it is nearly impossible to map each IP packet back to the application that spawned it. Firewall policies often grow out of date when applications are retired. Administrators fear tightening network security because user applications may fail, if not immediately, possibly in the future when exercising a rarely used permission. At the other end of the spectrum, end users have no idea how network outages or firewall changes will impact their applications, and thus have difficulty adapting. These problems stem from poor understanding of an applications network requirements.

A solution requires capturing the network requirements of every application in a simple to use form that end users can understand. This paper proposes an approach to capture that knowledge in an object-oriented design approach. Policy designers can designate classes as "tasks" which represent capabilities end users can drag and drop in a straightforward interface to build capabilities they need.

Like any design process, policy design requires human effort. To minimize this effort generic patterns should be designed independent of any local network topology. Tools can then compile the enforcement pattern into the actual enforcement policy for the local topology. This will allow application network requirements to be written, shared, and refined like open source software.

When considering the enforcement permissions as a whole, they can be thought of as an approximate model of allowable behavior. Often the implementation details of the enforcement policy hide this perception of security. For example, if an organization wanted to prevent sensitive information being exfiltrated through email they could force all outgoing email to a specific server that filters the email. However, sending the email to any other properly configured server with the same filter provides the same risk mitigation. Yet the enforcement policy ties the user to a single named server. Policy designers create security enforcement policy to mitigate risks; there maybe many alternative enforcement policies that provide the same risk mitigation. Different enforcement policies can represent different models of human behavior, distinguishing between common, rare and alternative approaches to risk mitigation. Once you have a solid understanding of an applications network requirements and the risks it was designed to mitigate, you can explore new security paradigms like network transactions and user-driven policy.

Network transactions capture the permissions used only for rare network behavior. For example, if a user performs an audit one day a month, the system can remove the user's access to the audit server, and restore it only when the user performs the audit. This reduces the likelihood of a virus spreading from the user to audit server. While similar to Task based RBAC [3], this approach relies on existing enforcement mechanisms and a separate system that pushes and retracts permissions as needed. This solution requires the user to authenticate the start of the rare transaction so that the system can push out the required policy changes. Without strong authentication, a malicious process could simply request the permissions be restored, resulting in no gain of security.

User-driven policies provide a second model that allows the user to change the enforcement policy to meet the needs of a changing

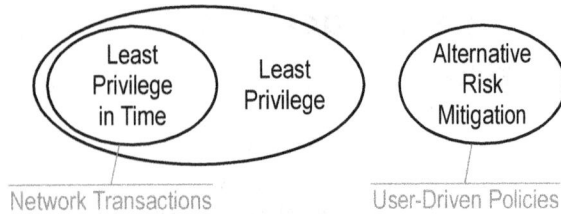

Figure 1: A Venn diagram comparing the set of permission for network transactions, user-driven policy and a least privilege policy.

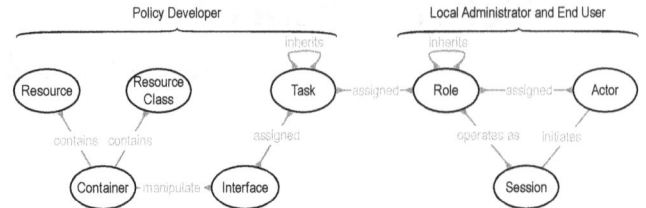

Figure 2: The NEUTRON policy design model, extended from the NIST RBAC model.

situation, by allowing alternate risk mitigation policies. User-driven policy captures the unneeded but allowed permissions inherent in the system, such as the alternate email filter discussed above. By associating a time-out with user-driven policy, the original policy can automatically be restored when the novel situation ends. User-driven policy also requires strong authentication to ensure that malicious code does not drive the policy change. A user-driven policy requires the local administrators to set up a policy boundary that limits the amount of changes the end user can make to the enforcement policy. Figure 1 provides a Venn diagram view of how the set of permissions changes with network transactions and user-driven policy.

User-driven security policy could be considered a library of contingency plans the user can implement under different circumstances. The open research question is how to define the security policy boundary, and control the flexibility of the end-user to solve novel circumstances that were not foreseen by the administrators. Administrators can define equivalent risk mitigation strategies, for example replacing one identical server with another, but there are classes of alternative enforcement policy that mitigate risk in subtly different ways. Defining security policy to mitigate risk requires many decisions with complex trade-offs. Most end users will not have the experience to make those complex trade-off decisions. Guiding user-driven security policies to mitigate the risks the administrator cares about is another open research question we hope to address in the future.

Currently security enforcement policy models all allowed behavior. This paper refines that model to include rare and commonly executed permissions, as well alternative permissions that still mitigate the intended risks.

2 POLICY DESIGN ENVIRONMENT

Capturing the network requirements of every application means capturing complex design patterns. Object-oriented programming excels at capturing complex pattern relationships, providing clarity and the ability to capture the *motivation* and the *importance* of the policy to the application, through both organizational and descriptive comments on the pattern. Figure 2, shows the core class hierarchy extending from the NIST RBAC model [5].

We have refined how the NIST model expressed permissions, to better capture observed patterns in enforcement policies. A *container* contains a set of *resources*. Resources can be files, database tables, or web pages. Interfaces determine resource access patterns. For example the interface for a file system container might have

an *owner* interface of read, write and an *auditor* interface of only read. A *resource class* is simply a set of resources that have been defined programatically, for example the user's scripts executed on login. Resources exist in only one container, and can only be accessed through the interfaces. Policy designers select the container structure that best captures design patterns of the application.

Semantically *tasks* and *roles* are similar, but separate local policy definitions from enterprise spanning generic patterns for each application. Tasks group permissions into patterns of access for an application, while roles represent patterns of access given to people. Tasks become the base library of permission patterns created by application developers that local administrators can build on.

Network permissions provide a special case of policy design because network communications involve multiple parties. Policy design must consider both the permissions the source and target applications need to successfully communicate. This communication pattern provides many challenges. For example, a network server may or may not be under the policy designer's control. Also the local network topology may vary greatly between organizations. The policy designer could easily specify the policy needed for a specific local network topology, preventing the policy from being used in by other organizations. To maximize the reuse of their effort, policy designers must specify an application's network requirements independent of the local topology. Tools similar to a compiler can take the generic specification and compile into the enforcement mechanisms present in the local topology.

In a client server example, the core requirement is the client must communicate with the server through a given port. However there are a number of supporting requirements. For example, most applications specify a host name and use DNS to turn that host name into an IP address. Thus the client application also requires access to a DNS server, which in turn needs access to the network of DNS servers.

Networks also pose a special problem because they "flatten" many communications to look the same. For example, a web server may support many different tasks, some very powerful and rarely executed. However, most network protocols will connect to the web server over port 80 providing no way to separate common and rare network traffic. However, if the two tasks were on separate servers, the policy could separate common and rare tasks based on destination. Arbitrary separation does increase security if the servers were connected on the backend by a vulnerable channel. Thus the most benefit will arise from services that are already isolated from each other on the network.

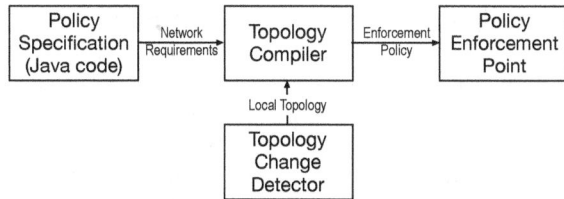

Figure 3: Application requirements can be separated from local network topology, but require translation into the local topology.

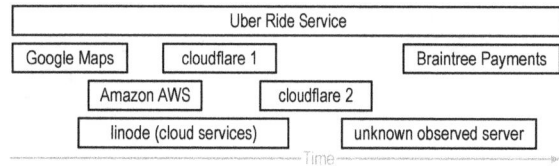

Figure 4: Booking a ride with Uber triggers a hierarchy of eight different network transactions.

The benefit of separating local topology from application requirements allows the application requirements to be specified once and shared between organizations. However, that separation requires the ability to apply the requirements to the local topology, and detect changes to the topology to update the policy.

Rather than create a new language to capture all these complex flexible network requirements, we elected to specify them in Java. The ESPANOLA program proved that capturing policy in Java added clarity and could express any enforcement mechanism policy [10, 11]. Using Java we can create methods to describe complex patterns, and that respond to changes in the network topology. These methods can translate the model into the specific enforcement mechanisms for the target system. For example, on a Unix system it will create a command script that sets the owners, groups and permissions bits correctly. For networks, the translators must create the necessary switch and firewall commands to generate the policy. Specifying policy details in Java often looks like GUI programming where the programmer users the interface to manage many implementation details, like color and border width. Pushing policy to existing enforcement mechanisms creates a low cost evolutionary path from existing systems to more secure systems.

Networks deserve special attention because reduction in the network attack surface can, if properly architected, increase security. In summary, the application policy must separate network communication requirements from permissions on the communication target. The policy must also be defined in terms of general network capabilities and then be compiled into the local network topology.

3 NETWORK TRANSACTIONS

Network transactions represent a new way of describing application dependencies on network services by relating all traffic back to the application it supports. A network transaction represents the security permissions for communications to traverse a network segment. This may include firewall and router policies, as well as filters on a host to control outbound and inbound network traffic. Complex applications spawn a number of network transactions to obtain multiple network services. For example, Figure 4 shows the network transactions spawned by a mobile device using Uber to search for a ride to a destination. The request caused the app to connect to multiple Uber servers, braintreepayments.com, Amazon AWS, Google Maps, and others.

While transactions provide a revolutionary way of looking at network security, they also introduce a number of complex issues. For example, Database Management Systems (DBMS) use transactions

to provide correctness and robustness in the face of failure. DBMS transactions ensure that a set of atomic actions either all execute, or none of them execute. This ensures that when transferring money between accounts, both the action of decrementing money from one account and the increment action in the target account occur. To improve performance, the DBMS allows transactions to occur at the same time. Certain overlaps of transactions conflict, such as writing data based on outdated data that another transaction changed after the first transaction read it. A DBMS transactions system must detect these conflicts and ensure that the transactions execute correctly.

Network transactions will face equally complex, but unique challenges. Database applications explicitly encode the start and end of transactions. If applications encoded network transaction start and end events to increase security, implementing network transactions would be straightforward. However to research the impact of controlling network transactions we must experiment on existing applications that do not define their activity in terms of transactions. In fact, often the required network activity for an application is poorly understood. We will first look at developing the necessary fine-grained dynamic security policies and models to support network transactions, and second adapting the models to work with legacy applications.

3.1 Defining Network Transactions

A network transaction represents a set of expected network traffic actions to accomplish an application task. Each network transaction has an action that starts the transaction, and one that signals the end of the transaction. In response to the transaction start event, the system pushes the network enforcement policy to support that entire transaction to the network enforcement points. When the transaction ends, the system removes the transaction policy (policy retraction), see Figure 5.

When looking at permissions as a model of behavior, a single network permission may support many different actions. So granting one network permission may enable multiple actions. Consider, a transaction with *send(data:A, server:X), send(data:B, server:X)*. Once the application has permission to *send(A)* it does not need additional permission for the *send(data:B, server:X)* action. Conversely removing the permission to *send(data:A, server:X)* would remove the permission to perform the other action as well.

As the Uber example shows, a network transaction may contain a hierarchy of supporting transactions. We plan to incorporate this structure using similar approaches to capturing a role hierarchy. The policy designer has the option of creating one transaction for all the supporting operations, or dividing the transaction into

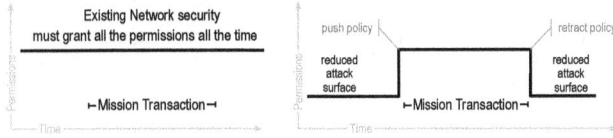

Figure 5: Retracting rarely used permissions, and resetting them just before user reduces the attack surface.

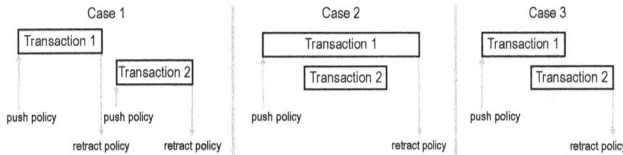

Figure 6: Concurrent transactions determine when and if the network policy needs adjustment.

smaller supporting transactions. Smaller transactions increase security, but require a deeper understanding of the network transaction hierarchy. We plan to use existing enforcement mechanisms, so the approach should have minimal impact to performance. The implementation challenge will be to ensure that the needed policy is in place before the transaction starts. Legacy applications will fail if the necessary permissions are not in place. In the future we envision network transaction aware applications that can retry an action if it failed for permission reasons.

3.2 Concurrent Transactions

Applications often execute network transactions concurrently, and a single application may execute many network transactions simultaneously. The system must understand the active policies and how to adjust the policies as new transactions start or end. For example, Figure 6 shows three simple cases where two network transactions require the same DNS permissions on the router. When the transactions start and stop determines when policy changes occur.

Network activities inherently include non-determinism as packets may take different routes and arrive at their destination out of order. Security policy updates must be active at the enforcement point before the application needs them, otherwise an application could fail. A complete system with applications that implement network transactions will support full redundancy using techniques similar to DBMS transactions to ensure the security policy updates never cause application failure. To enhance flexibility and resilience of network transactions more advanced transaction models can be adopted, such as the nested transaction model, where a transaction is organized into atomic sub-transactions. Unlike database transactions, a transaction can still decide to commit even if one of its sub-transactions aborts. This makes it possible to support alternative executions in case of failures of sub-transactions, thus enhancing resilience.

3.3 Designing Network Transaction Policy

Network transactions consist of communications actions between hosts on the network. The policy does not need to define all of these communications, but simply the permissions necessary to allow the communications to occur. The communication may transition over multiple network segments and require multiple policy updates to support bi-directional communication between the hosts. Figure 7 shows how the network transaction *start* and *end* actions trigger NEUTRON to push and retract a policy to the enforcement points shown in gray. Figure 7 shows a policy enforcement point on each host that controls the flow of information between the host and the network. If an enclave does not provide this level of control, the system must adjust its policy to push out only supported permissions, then warn the policy designers of the impact of the actual policy versus what they requested.

3.4 Network Transactions for Legacy Applications

Legacy applications do not encode the start and stop of network transactions. However, by integrating with a network sensor, we can allow legacy applications and enclaves to benefit from the enhanced security of network transactions. For example, by analyzing legacy applications and watching for specific network activity, the system could detect the start of a network transaction. Once detected, the system will then push out the network security policy to support the remaining actions in the network transaction.

Since there will be a delay detecting the start and end of transactions, supporting legacy applications cannot reduce the attack surface as much as it will for network transaction aware applications. To ensure a legacy application transaction will execute normally, the permanent policy must always allows the first several actions of transactions to execute. For example, if an application transaction starts by sending a request to a specific web server, the policy must ensure the application always has permission to send that request. Once it senses that action, it will signal the start of the transaction and push out the remaining permissions for that transaction. By trading off some reduction of attack surface, the system could improve performance by pushing the policy for *expected* transactions and all their supporting sub-transactions. Each policy push will have a built in timer that automatically retracts the policy if the transaction end action is not detected. More research needs to be done to determine the actual reduction in attack surface that can be achieved without impacting legacy applications. This approach provides an evolutionary approach that will allow applications to

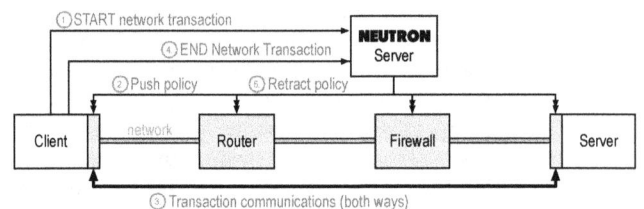

Figure 7: The steps to push and retract policy in response to start and end actions.

gain some security benefit for low cost. If it proves successful it could motivate more wide scale integration of applications into network transactions. Another key benefit is that network transactions provide a deeper understanding of application network dependencies that will enable, better administration and intrusion detection.

One secure solution requires humans to strongly authenticate any time they are going to execute a rare network transaction. For legacy applications the user will have to use a system outside the application to authenticate. For network transaction aware applications they can integrate the authentication process with the workflow. Authentication prevents malicious software from triggering the reinstating the permissions they hope to exploit. However, proper application of cryptography may allow additional security with no impact to humans, by integrating non-spoofable identifiers for applications. For example, suppose an application was assigned 1 authentication token for a task that occurs only once a month. Rather than have the user authenticate the application could use the authentication token, which would be replenished the following month. If malicious software executed the transaction and used the token, the legitimate user would not be able to complete the transaction without authenticating. This erroneous situation could be easy audited and flagged to administrators. This would limit attackers to one shot at the rare transaction as well. Many attacks succeed simply because the attacker can repeatedly attempt a privileged action.

3.5 Transaction Discovery

Most legacy applications have poorly described security designs. As a result, creating a network transaction policy for legacy applications represents a serious effort of reverse engineering the network requirements with only the running code as guidance. We postulate tools can be created to monitor network traffic and reverse engineer approximate network transactions. While not perfect they will allow an evolutionary path for incorporating legacy applications. The results can be encoded in the NEUTRON object-oriented design language for applications designed with network transactions in mind, and integrated with the human designed network requirements. This allows transaction discovery results to be integrated into human policy designs.

Simply executing an application has no guarantee that all of the network requirements will be exercised. By applying concolic testing we can increase code coverage, increasing the chance of exposing all the network requirements. Concolic testing takes applications and constructs test inputs using symbolic execution to exercise all code paths [4, 8]. Currently executing all the code paths for a large application is not feasible, however, by focusing on paths with network calls, concolic testing could provide better coverage for the code segments that impact network requirements. Such testing cannot guarantee discovery of all network requirements, but it should still provide practical results.

Ideally the application would be tested alone on a quiet network. However a realistic network simulation requires the communication targets, which may be generating their own network traffic. Thus the end results are likely to be noisy containing many communications not part of the transaction hierarchy. Multiple runs of

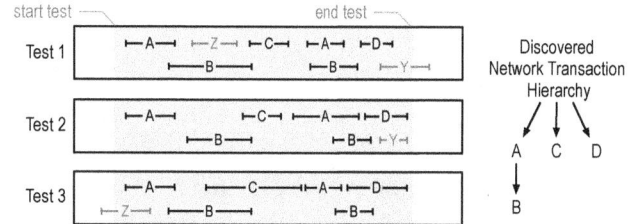

Figure 8: Running the application with the same inputs will yield different results, which must be analyzed to produce a transaction hierarchy.

the testing environment will reduce, but not eliminate the impact of noise. The power of concolic testing will greatly enhance the repeatability of the tests allowing focused tests to eliminate the noise by conducting multiple runs with the same input. Figure 8 illustrates how, after multiple runs, the spurious network traffic will be easily identified.

The concolic test cases will also provide an ability to regression test new security policies to understand the impact on the application. In the future, automated testing would include security policy changes, just as if they were critical code modules.

4 USER-DRIVEN POLICY

User-driven policy attempts to balance the security needs of the network with the flexibility to react to novel situations. Additional security measures tend to reduce the flexibility of the network to respond to novel situations. User-driven policy allows users to reinstate the retracted network transaction permissions needed to solve a problem. The model results in no more permissions than were in the original policy. In this section we will also discuss extending the capability to allow users to activate permissions not in the original policy, as long as they still implement the same mitigation strategy. Users reinstate permissions on their own authority, and with the understanding that the system will log their policy actions and they will have to answer for any abuses of the mechanism. Since the system will limit the number of user-driven policy changes, the number of cases administrators will have to review is small. As always strong authentication will be deployed to prevent abuse by malicious programs acting on the user's behalf. By definition, user-driven policy changes happen only in rare tactical situations, so the burden of doing an additional authentication will be minimal.

Network transactions are one type of user-driven policy where the user determines when to restore rarely used permissions. Consider an existing organization's legacy network enclave without a user-driven policy. This enclave will have granted all the necessary permissions for its applications, all the time. Let us assume the administrators created a least privilege policy where every permission they granted is needed. Therefore, if one permission were removed, some aspect of the application software would fail in the future. Network transactions provide a *least privilege in time* policy, removing permissions the user does not need immediately. When a network transaction requires the permission, the retracted permissions are reinstated. This approach never results in more permissions than were in the original policy, see Figure 9. At any point in time the network transaction policy represents the least privilege policy at that moment. Creating a least privilege in time

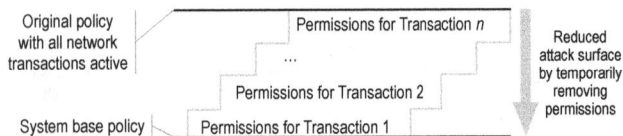

Figure 9: To provide least privilege in time, remove permissions not needed for the application's current transactions. If all transactions were active the resulting policy would be identical to that of the policy without network transactions.

policy has more impact for network permissions, because of the greater exposure network services face from attack.

The network transactions are defined as task objects in Java, meaning all the permissions necessary to complete the task are bundled in the task object. To create a user-driven policy, the user can select from any of the transaction tasks and activate them. They do not need to understand or manipulate the Java code, the task can be treated like a capability that the user simply turns on. As a result, the user cannot make a policy more permissive than the original policies, and their choices are limited to the defined transactions. Good object-oriented design and naming will allow the user to quickly find the task needed to accomplish their goal.

User-driven policy allows the user to reinstate permissions up to the level of the original enforcement policy as shown in Figure 9. Thus, the enclave faces no increased risk in security. While applications could fail if permissions are not restored in time, a robust application would notify the user and the user could push the policy and try again. Users bare the most significant cost for this increased security. User intervention in application operations is a high cost, and only becomes acceptable if user action is rare, hence limiting policy retraction to rare operations. Least privilege in time is different from dynamic policy models that allow actions when certain conditions are met, such as team formation, time of day, or other temporal constraints. The other models allow the action to take place if the condition is met, giving malicious code acting on the user's behalf a window to perform the actions unnoticed. Network transactions force the end user to restore the permissions, greatly limiting the impact of malicious code.

The approach also reduces the risk from malicious insiders. Before, if insiders exploited permissions, the exploit would go unnoticed. This design require the malicious insider to authenticate to turn on permissions, making it impossible to hide if they are repeatedly using permissions associated with a rare event. The approach makes classes of malicious insider activity obvious, and provides proof of malicious activity for prosecution.

Now consider the case outlined in Figure 1 where users can make policy changes that add permissions not present in a strict least privilege policy. The goal is to allow the user to specify a broad range of security policies to address policy situations that arise, without involving the security administrator to grant them special permission to perform the action. Network transactions are one form of user-driven policy we identified as least privilege in time. Below we discuss four different types of user-driven policy laid out

on a continuum of how much control the system maintains over the risk mitigation strategy of the policy, see Figure 10.

The first type is designed contingency plans which allow the administrator to develop alternate enforcement policy for likely scenarios. For example, suppose the policy requires users to use the printer on their floor. Often printers break down right when a critical document needs printing. The user could take it on their own authority to send the printout to another floor if the policy was designed to handle this contingency. This allows the administrator to define a library of contingency policies the user can choose from. This approach provides a clear policy boundary defined by the administrator. The administrator can think and reason about the impact of each contingency plan, and determine if the risks the policy addresses are sufficiently mitigated.

The designed contingency approach results in a clear and easy to understand set of enforcement policies for the end user to choose from. Automatic policy translation, automatic time-out of policy and strong authentication of the policy change are also required to make the approach viable, while minimizing the impact on the end user.

The building block contingency plan approach gives the end user parameterized policy components that can be combined to solve novel situations without an administrator. The administrator provides a set of policy elements that the end user can combine to accomplish some task. Automation could look at the all the possible combinations of these policy components and compare the resulting permissions sets, such as the Margrave tool [6]. This building block approach to policy building allow the end user adaptability for solving policy problems while still limiting their ability to change policy by limiting the policy building blocks. For example, such a policy could allow the end user to migrate a service to identical or more secure servers. Object-oriented encoded policies could be compared to determine if the security policies are compatible. The flexibility comes at a cost of understanding the transitive closure of all the building block and parameter combinations. This presents an open research question on understanding the kinds policies possible and understanding the impact of all the policies. We suspect the building block user-driven policy could be subdivided into further sub-classes in future work. For example, can a set of flexible building blocks be created that guarantees the same risk mitigation strategy? How about different but similar risk mitigation strategies?

Finally for completeness we consider free form policy modification. This approach allows the user to design the policy change. The problem with this approach is that end users focus on functional requirements, not security requirements. Most end users do not have the background to understand the impact of policy changes. End users will likely create overly permissive policy that increases organizational risk. We would expect such a system to be extremely

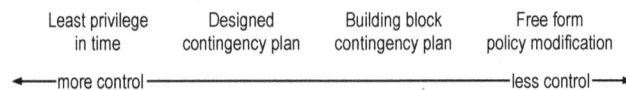

Figure 10: Four different types of user-driven policy laid out on a continuum of control.

limited. An experienced administrator balances functional and security considerations to develop an acceptable risk mitigation strategy. If the complexity of specifying the policy grows too high it will simply be best for the end users to ask the administrator to design a solution to meet their new requirements. For some organizations, ensuring this happens rarely, is always investigated, and automatically reverts to the original designed policy within a few hours may sufficiently mitigate their risks. However, not understanding and controlling the risk mitigation of the enforcement policy will be unacceptable for most organizations.

In summary, user-driven policy protects mission critical networks by:

(1) Ensuring only humans can initiate user-driven policy changes, preventing exploits from malware
(2) Limiting user-driven policy changes to ensure critical enclave policies always remain in place
(3) Ensuring that the enforcement policy never becomes a road block preventing the end users from accessing critical resources in a timely matter using acceptable risk mitigation strategies

5 RELATED WORK

Even though the framework proposed in this paper is unique, related techniques have been proposed in different areas that we discuss in what follows.

The first relevant area is the area of access control models and mechanisms. Many access control models have been proposed and even standardized - the most notable being RBAC and XACML. The latter standardizes attribute-based access control by which subjects, protected resources, and contexts are specified in terms of Boolean combinations of predicates against the properties of these subjects, resources, and contexts. Access control mechanisms are typically implemented as part of operating systems and DBMS. The XACML standard has however been proposed as a service-oriented architecture by which access control can be "externalized", thus supporting a more modular and centralized management of application-level access control enforcement.

With respect to the area of access control models, the models most relevant to NEUTRON are, in addition to RBAC, the temporal RBAC [3] (TRBAC) and the hierarchical models. TRBAC supports the association of temporal periods (both absolute and periodic) with roles; thus, roles even though present in the access control system may be used (e.g. activated) only within the periods associated with them. The second and most relevant feature of TRBAC is the notion of automatic activation and de-activation of roles based on the activation/de-activation of other roles. An interesting direction within the context of NEUTRON is to extend such automatic activation/de-activation of roles to the occurrence of other events, in particular network-related events. Temporal authorizations, by which temporal periods are associated with authorizations, have also been widely investigated by research and are today supported by commercial systems. A notable example is represented by Oracle VPD which uses a query modification approach to support temporal constraints on authorizations.

The hierarchical models have been developed with the goal of reducing the number of authorizations that administrators have to enter into the access control system. In such models, authorizations are categorized into: *explicit authorizations* that are issued by an administrator; and *implicit authorizations* that are automatically derived through some derivation rules from the explicit authorizations. Such models have been introduced to manage authorizations where the protected resources are complex and hierarchically organized. The first such model was introduced in the context of the Orion object-oriented DBMS [9] to reduce the cost of managing authorizations given the complexity of the Orion data model. A hierarchical access control model is also implemented by SQL Server. By using such a model, one can grant, for example, a user a read access to an entire database and this authorization implicitly grants this user access to all relations and other objects in the database. On the other hand, one can grant a user access to a single relation and such authorization does not imply any other authorization. In the context of NEUTRON, such hierarchical access control model would allow one to further reduce the cost of authorization administration. Supporting such a model in NEUTRON would however require the specification of an authorization propagation graph [9] indicating which authorization on which protected object automatically propagates to which other objects. In both Orion and SQL Server these propagation graphs are built-in into the authorization systems and thus cannot be modified. By contrast in NEUTRON one would need to allow security administrators and application specialists to define these graphs.

The second relevant area is represented by transaction models and systems. Transactions have been widely investigated in the area of DBMS, both centralized and distributed. Based on the pioneer notion of transactions proposed for DBMS, transactional monitors have been developed as part of middleware and used to coordinate distributed application executions. Whereas the area of transactions provides one of the basic foundations of the NEUTRON approach, NEUTRON is the first to propose the use of transactions for the management of network security based on application requirements.

The third relevant area is represented by firewall systems. These systems are characterized by the use of rules (referred to as firewall rules) filtering packets based on characteristics of the packets, such as IP source. Research has focused on analysis techniques to verify properties of sets of firewall rules, such as that rules do not conflict and are properly ordered [1]. However, firewalls do not have ability to automatically issue/remove rules nor they support any notion of transaction. NEUTRON could thus address specifically such gap by providing agents that can sit at firewalls to automatically push and retract firewall rules. It is however important to notice that firewall rules generated and managed by NEUTRON will also have to be analyzed to ensure that they verify relevant properties. In this respect, methods for the analysis of firewall rules are relevant to NEUTRON and should be integrated into it.

Finally, the last relevant area is represented by software defined networks (SDN) [2]. The main goal of SDN is to support an application-based management of packet transmissions in networks. An SDN typically consists of two components: the control plane which monitors and controls the entire network state, and the forwarding plane which defines the low-level behavior of each network element (switch, router, access point, base station). The forwarding plane receives rules, expressed in terms of a rule language such as OpenFlow [7], from the control plane and has corresponding code to enforce these rules. Actions that can be specified by these rules include drop, forward, modify, and enqueue packets. SDN are an interesting context in which NEUTRON would fit naturally. However, NEUTRON wold require extending the rule language with rules for pushing/retracting permissions and other security configurations to the various network elements. Such an extension would be an interesting and novel research direction.

6 CONCLUSION

In this paper we have proposed a novel approach for looking at network security that captures application network requirements and provides a revolutionary, dynamic, fine-grained level of network access control. Our approach is based on two novel concepts. The first is the concept of network transactions, by which all network security related enforcement actions related to the execution of a given application are grouped together. Such an approach reduces security enforcement costs and increases security and reliability. The second is the concept of user-driven policies that allows one to drive the security enforcement activities based on the application semantics. Policies in our proposed framework are automatically issued and retracted, so to minimize the policy administration costs and increase security, as policies are automatically issued only when needed and retracted when not any longer needed. The approach reduces the network attack surface, increasing the security of the entire enterprise. Our proposed framework will allow one to effectively and efficiently manage security in the face of rising complexity in network traffic. In particular, the reduced attack surface, will greatly improve the security of IoT and edge computing.

7 ACKNOWLEDGMENTS

Amazon, Braintree, Cloudflare, Google, Linode and Uber are all trademark names of their respective companies.

This research was supported by the Air Force Research Laboratory, Rome NY under contract number FA8750-18-C-0052.

REFERENCES

[1] Ehab Al-Shaer. 2014. *Automated Firewall Analytics - Design, Configuration and Optimization.* Springer, USA.
[2] Kamal Benzekki, Abdeslam El Fergougui, and Abdelbaki Elbelrhiti Elalaoui. 2016. Software-defined networking (SDN): a survey. *Security and communication networks* 9, 18 (2016), 5803–5833.
[3] Elisa Bertino, Piero Andrea Bonatti, and Elena Ferrari. 2001. TRBAC: A temporal role-based access control model. *ACM Transactions on Information and System Security (TISSEC)* 4, 3 (2001), 191–233.
[4] Lorenzo Bossi, Elisa Bertino, and Syed Rafiul Hussain. 2017. A System for Profiling and Monitoring Database Access Patterns by Application Programs for Anomaly Detection. *IEEE Transactions on Software Engineering* 43, 5 (2017), 415–431.
[5] David F Ferraiolo, Ravi Sandhu, Serban Gavrila, D Richard Kuhn, and Ramaswamy Chandramouli. 2001. Proposed NIST standard for role-based access control. *ACM Transactions on Information and System Security (TISSEC)* 4, 3 (2001), 224–274.
[6] Kathi Fisler, Shriram Krishnamurthi, Leo A Meyerovich, and Michael Carl Tschantz. 2005. Verification and change-impact analysis of access-control policies. In *Proceedings of the 27th international conference on Software engineering.* ACM, New York, NY, USA, 196–205.
[7] Nick McKeown, Tom Anderson, Hari Balakrishnan, Guru Parulkar, Larry Peterson, Jennifer Rexford, Scott Shenker, and Jonathan Turner. 2008. OpenFlow: enabling innovation in campus networks. *ACM SIGCOMM Computer Communication Review* 38, 2 (2008), 69–74.
[8] David J Musliner, Jeffrey M Rye, Dan Thomsen, David D McDonald, Mark H Burstein, and Paul Robertson. 2012. Fuzzbuster: A system for self-adaptive immunity from cyber threats. In *Eighth International Conference on Autonomic and Autonomous Systems (ICAS-12).* 118–123.
[9] Fausto Rabitti, Elisa Bertino, Won Kim, and Darrell Woelk. 1991. A model of authorization for next-generation database systems. *ACM Transactions on Database Systems (TODS)* 16, 1 (1991), 88–131.
[10] Dan Thomsen. 2007. Patterns in Security Enforcement Policy Development. In *18th International Workshop on Database and Expert Systems Applications, 2007. DEXA'07.* IEEE, 744–748.
[11] Dan Thomsen. 2011. Practical policy patterns. In *Proceedings of the first ACM conference on Data and application security and privacy.* ACM, New York, NY, USA, 225–230.

A Deep Learning Approach for Extracting Attributes of ABAC Policies

Manar Alohaly
Dept. of Computer Science and
Engineering
University of North Texas
Denton, TX, USA
Princess Nourah bint Abdulrahman
University
ManarAlohaly@my.unt.edu

Hassan Takabi
Dept. of Computer Science and
Engineering
University of North Texas
Denton, TX, USA
Takabi@unt.edu

Eduardo Blanco
Dept. of Computer Science and
Engineering
University of North Texas
Denton, TX, USA
eduardo.blanco@unt.edu

ABSTRACT

The National Institute of Standards and Technology (NIST) has identified natural language policies as the preferred expression of policy and implicitly called for an automated translation of ABAC natural language access control policy (NLACP) to a machine-readable form. An essential step towards this automation is to automate the extraction of ABAC attributes from NLACPs, which is the focus of this paper. We, therefore, raise the question of: how can we automate the task of attributes extraction from natural language documents? Our proposed solution to this question is built upon the recent advancements in natural language processing and machine learning techniques. For such a solution, the lack of appropriate data often poses a bottleneck. Therefore, we decouple the primary contributions of this work into: (1) developing a practical framework to extract ABAC attributes from natural language artifacts, and (2) generating a set of realistic synthetic natural language access control policies (NLACPs) to evaluate the proposed framework. The experimental results are promising with regard to the potential automation of the task of interest. Using a convolutional neural network (CNN), we achieved - in average - an F1-score of 0.96 when extracting the attributes of subjects, and 0.91 when extracting the objects' attributes from natural language access control policies.

CCS CONCEPTS

• Security and privacy → Access control;

KEYWORDS

access control policy, attribute based access control, policy authoring, natural language processing, relation extraction, deep learning

ACM Reference Format:
Manar Alohaly, Hassan Takabi, and Eduardo Blanco. 2018. A Deep Learning Approach for Extracting Attributes of ABAC Policies. In *SACMAT '18: The 23rd ACM Symposium on Access Control Models Technologies (SACMAT),*

June 13–15, 2018, Indianapolis, IN, USA. ACM, New York, NY, USA, 12 pages. https://doi.org/10.1145/3205977.3205984

1 INTRODUCTION

The concept of access control mechanisms has been around since Lampson's access matrix was coined in the late 1960s [31]. Thereafter, dozens of models have been proposed upon the shortage of others. Most of these models, however, have shown forms of inadequacy in withstanding the ever-increasing complexity of today's business environments or safeguard the compliance demand of dynamic organizations. From within this dilemma, attribute based access control (ABAC) has emerged as a good fit. The National Institute of Standards and Technology (NIST) Special Publication 800-162 "Guide to Attribute based Access Control (ABAC) Definition and Considerations" testifies to ABAC's potential to promote information sharing among enterprises with a heterogeneous business nature [23]. In fact, it is predicted that "by 2020, 70% of enterprises will use attribute based access control... as the dominant mechanism to protect critical assets" [17]. Despite the promising potential, the ABAC policy authoring task has stood out, among other factors, as a costly development effort. This is anything but a new challenge. In fact, the complex syntax of what has become the standard ABAC policy language, namely XACML [40], has been well understood since the earliest days of ABAC. Hence, it was presumed that "XACML is intended primarily to be generated by tools", said in 2003 [1]. This is where the policy authoring tools come into play.

XACML is a generic policy language framework ratified by OASIS to provide an abstraction layer for defining access control policies (ACPs) as machine-readable authorization rules [40]. It promotes standardization, expressiveness, granularity, interoperability, and efficiency [4]. This flexibility, on the other hand, has introduced implementation complexity. Solutions proposed to aid in the ABAC policy authoring task have ranged from GUI policy authoring tools to APIs and plug-ins [6, 46]. These tools generally provide a higher abstraction level that obscures much of XACML's syntax complexity. The former set of tools, i.e. the GUI aids, are designed as fill-in forms or spreadsheets that present policy authors with lists, or other graphical formats, populated with valid options of policy elements (i.e. subjects and objects attributes). The assumption is that a non-IT specialist would easily be able to construct a policy by selecting its constituent attributes from drop-down menus [46]. The latter set of tools is mainly designed for developers as it has borrowed

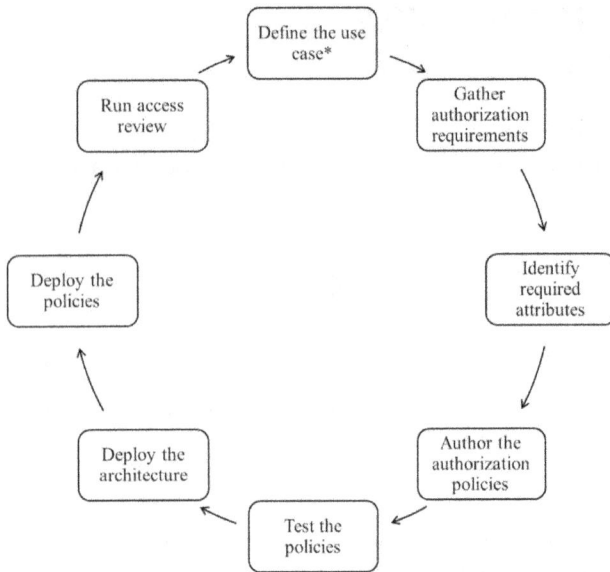

Figure 1: The authorization policy lifecycle (adopted from [10]). *Asterisk marks the beginning of the cycle

much of its structure from common programming languages [6]. Either way, the goal is to have XACML equivalent policies be automatically generated with the help of the tools. While such aids can possibly provide a better authoring experience, they heavily rely on the presence of back-end attribute exchange providers. This strong assumption sheds some light on the question of: where do the required attributes come from? Upon a closer inspection of the ABAC authorization policy lifecycle (Figure 1), policies are introduced to a system at the earliest stages of its development lifecycle as use-cases. At this point, access control policies, as well as other security and functional requirements, are components of specifications documents, which are almost always written in natural language. To identify the policy elements required to build the machine-readable authorization rules, the current practice assumes that a security architect, policy author or system analyst should manually analyze the existing documentations to extract the relevant information [10]. The fact that these requirements are often elicited from a pool of natural language statements, e.g. interview transcripts, blurs the boundaries between the policies and other requirements. Hence, manually deriving the attributes along with other policy elements needed to feed the previously mentioned policy authoring tools is rather a repetitive, time-consuming and error-prone task.

The necessity to automate this manual process has motivated several studies in developing automated tools to derive elements of access control rules directly from the natural language policies [35, 37, 43, 44, 48]. Previous research efforts have mostly been restricted to two areas: (1) automatic identification of the access control policy sentences from natural language artifacts, and (2) automatic extraction of the subject, object and action triples from these sentences. To the best of our knowledge, no detailed investigations of this automation, in the context of extracting ABAC

attributes, have been conducted. Therefore, we strive to answer the question of how the attributes extraction task can be automated.

The ABAC model groups the authorization attributes into categories which represent the grammatical function of the element being described by the underlying attributes. Going from this observation, we design our attributes identification framework as a relation extraction problem [19, 25]. The relation in this context, is what chains an element (namely, subject and object), with the attributes that modify this element. We view this work as an essential step towards the automated transformation of ABAC natural language policies to a machine-readable form. The primary contributions of this paper are as follows:

(1) We design a practical framework to automate the attributes extraction task, which is, by itself, an entire phase of the ABAC policy authoring lifecycle (Phase 3 in Figure 1). To the best of our knowledge, this is the first evaluated effort to address this problem.

(2) We construct a realistic synthetic dataset, annotated with the attributes of the subject and object elements of access control policies. We use this corpus to evaluate our proposal, and it will be made available to the research community, aiming to advance the work in this field.

The remainder of this paper is organized as follows: Section 2 provides the background information needed to establish an understanding of the problem domain. In Section 3, we present the proposed framework and discuss our methodology to automate the attributes extraction task. Section 4 describes the procedure to construct the required corpus. Our experimental results are reported in Section 5. We review the related work in Section 6. Section 7 discusses the limitations of the proposed approach. In Section 8, we conclude our study with the recommendations for future work.

2 BACKGROUND

In the following subsections, we define key terminology used in this study. Then, we provide background information regarding ABAC policy authoring process and the underlying techniques of our proposed framework.

2.1 Overview of ABAC Definition and Terminology

NIST defines ABAC as "An access control method where subject requests to perform operations on objects are granted or denied based on assigned attributes of the subject, assigned attributes of the object..." [23]. The following list provides a high-level definition of terms relevant to our study. We, also, exemplify each element using the illustrative example shown in Figure 2, whenever possible.

- Subject: an entity that initiates access requests to perform actions on objects, e.g. patient.
- Subject attribute: a characteristic of the subject, e.g. registered.
- Object: anything upon which an action might be performed by a subject, e.g. health record.
- Object attribute: a characteristic of the object, e.g. full.

Herein, we use the terms "authorization requirement", "access policy" and "access control policy" interchangeably to refer to natural

Subject Att. status   Object Att. status

A registered patient can access his/her full health record

Subject Att. subjectType   Object Att. objectType

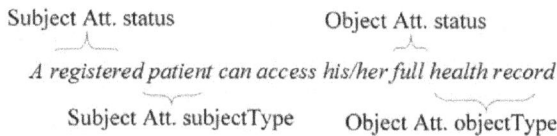

Figure 2: Attribute identification scenario

language access control policy (NLACP). We, also, use "policy elements" as well as "elements" to refer to subject and object elements of the authorization requirement, while we use "attributes" to refer to their corresponding characteristics.

2.2 ABAC Policy Authoring

Brossard et al. have designed a systematic approach for implementing ABAC [10]. The authors' proposed model is composed of an iterative sequence of phases shown in Figure 1. Several studies have researched challenges and opportunities that face the natural language processing (NLP) applications in the automation of the second phase of the cycle, named "gather authorization requirements" [35, 37, 43, 44, 48]. To complement this prior effort, our work aims to aid policy authors in the process of deriving required attributes from natural language authorization requirements, which is mainly the third phase of the lifecycle. We, therefore, zoom into the details of this phase to establish an understanding of the problem domain and to identify key activities with the potential to be automated. This, in turn, provides insights on the essential building blocks needed to design a practical ABAC attribute identification framework.

The goal of the "identify required attributes" phase (see Figure 1) is to identify attributes that jointly build up an ABAC access control rule. Each attribute is defined by the following pieces of information, as suggested by [10]:

- **Short Name**: a key a policy author would use to refer to an attribute while writing policy. From Figure 2, subjectType objectType, and status are all examples of short names.
- **Category**: the class to which an attribute belongs. The core categories are subject and object [40]. From the previously used example, the attribute subjectType, for instance, would belong to the subject category.
- **Data type**: this property tells what type of data an attribute's value would be. The most common data types are: string, boolean, numerical, and date and time. In our example, string would be a valid type of subjectType.
- **Value constraints**: this provides a range or discrete list of values that can possibly be assigned to an attribute. For instance, patient is a possible value of subjectType attribute, as well as registered is a possible value of status (of subject category).

There exist additional properties that are either optional or language dependent. Thus, deriving these properties is out of the scope of this paper. However, we refer the interested readers to [10]. In light of this description, an automated ABAC attributes identification tool is presumed to infer properties needed to define each

attribute, and make them available to the back-end attributes exchange. Hence, we design the framework, shown in Figure 3 , that leverages natural language processing (NLP), relation extraction (RE) and machine learning (ML) techniques in order to facilitate an automated analysis of authorization requirements and as well as the inference of information needed to define ABAC attributes.

2.3 Natural Language Processing Techniques

This section provides an overview of the underlying natural language processing, relation extraction and machine learning techniques used in our framework.

2.3.1 Relation Extraction (RE). Relation extraction is a central task in natural language processing. The aim of this task is to answer whether it is possible to detect and characterize a semantic relation between pairs of co-occurring entities, also known as relation mentions, mostly within a sentence. Throughout the literature, RE problem has been often addressed as a classification task where the goal is to assign a predefined relation to pair of entities [25]. This approach is mainly organized into two stages. First is the identification of candidate relation instances phase, and then the classification phase. Techniques to identify candidate instances can be feature-based or kernel-based [11, 12, 15, 19, 26, 30, 33, 49, 51]. Either way, the presence of entities alone does not guarantee that relation is validly expressed. Both strategies, therefore, require a classification phase. As a standard classification task, classifiers are built upon training corpus in which all relations and its participating entities have been manually annotated. The annotated relations are used as positive training examples, whilst the rest of

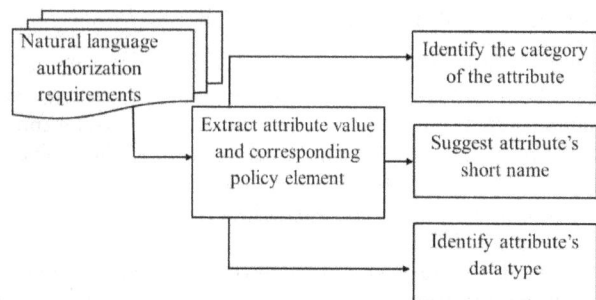

Figure 3: High level overview of the proposed attributes extraction approach

co-occurring pairs that are not labeled are deemed as negative training examples. Classical learning algorithms such as support vector machines can then be used to train relation extraction classifiers.

2.3.2 Natural Language Processing (NLP) in RE. Four key natural language techniques have influenced relation extraction studies including: tokenization, Part of Speech (POS) tagging, named entity recognition and syntactic parsing.

Tokenization is an essential starting point for almost any NLP task. It splits a text segment into tokens which are words or punctuation marks. Considering English language, rule-based text tokenization, using spaces or punctuations, is a straightforward task.

However, abbreviation-like structures introduce a level of complexity to this process.

POS taggers determine the corresponding POS tag for each word in a sentence [9]. It is a sequential labeling problem. In the context of RE, POS is used to detect relations between candidate pair of entities in a sentence by matching patterns over its POS tags. POS are also useful in providing lexical information needed to design RE model. In attribute relation extraction, for example, attributes are usually adjectives and policy elements are nouns or combination of nouns.

Named entity recognition (NER) aims to detect phrases that express some real-world entities such as people, organizations, locations, times, events, etc. [45]. in a given segment of text. Oftentimes, this task requires more than simple matching against predefined dictionaries or gazetteers. Real-world applications, thus, combine heuristics, probabilistic matching, and sequential learning techniques [32]. RE has adopted NER to identify pairs that can potentially form a candidate instance. It is also used to encode semantic knowledge of participating entities.

Syntactic parsing techniques provide a mediation between the lexical representation of a sentence and its meaning. The two dominant syntactic parsing strategies are constituency and dependency parsers. The first of these strategies constructs the explicit syntactic constituents (e.g. noun phrases and verb phrases) that formally define a sentence [52]. The latter, on the other hand, reflects the grammatical structure of a given sentence [22]. Both representations have been used in the literature of relation extraction to encode patterns that link pair of entities of a particular relation [15, 25, 49, 51]. However, relation extraction studies have empirically shown that patterns drawn from a dependency tree are more resilient to lexical inconsistency among different domains [27].

2.3.3 Convolutional Neural Network (CNN) in RE. CNN has recently been used in solving a wide range of applied machine learning problems. In RE, CNN can be used to model syntactic and semantic relations between words within a sentence while reducing the dependence on manually designed features. Generally speaking, the use of CNN-based models in various NLP tasks has achieved impressive results [14, 29, 50].

The architecture of a typical CNN consists of a stack of layers which can be (1) an input layer that encodes words in each relation instance by real-valued vectors using the lookup tables; (2) a convolutional layer to the capture the contextual features, e.g. n-grams, in the given input; (3) the pooling layer to determine the most relevant features and, (4) an output layer which is the fully connected layer that performs the classification. Subsection 3.1.3 provides a detailed discussion of each layer as well as the overall structure of our CNN.

3 THE PROPOSED METHODOLOGY

As mentioned earlier in the background section, attributes in ABAC model are defined via short name, potential value(s), the data type and category to which an attribute belongs. Out of these four dimensions, the property that is usually expressed in a natural language authorization requirement is the attribute value. Looking back to our illustrative example shown in Figure 2, *registered*, for instance, refers to the status of the authorized subjects. *Full* as well describes

the status of health record that can be accessed by the registered patient. From the natural language standpoint, clauses/phrases that express such characteristics follow certain grammatical patterns to modify particular elements of the policy sentence. Therefore, our approach leverages the grammatical relations holding between policy elements and constituents that modify these elements, to view this task as a relation extraction problem [19, 25]. Extracting the value of an attribute, say *registered*, and associating this value with the corresponding policy element, e.g. *patient*, equates finding the value and category properties of two attributes, namely status and subjectType as described later in this section. However, deriving the short name, e.g. status, as well as the data type, e.g. string, requires further analysis. Figure 3 shows an overview of our framework where rectangles depict the four main modules and arrows point in the direction of data flow. The overall approach consists of four parts. It begins with analyzing the natural language authorization requirement to locate modifiers of each policy element. Then, it proceeds towards three independent tasks of identifying attributes' category, their data type and suggesting an appropriate attribute short name.

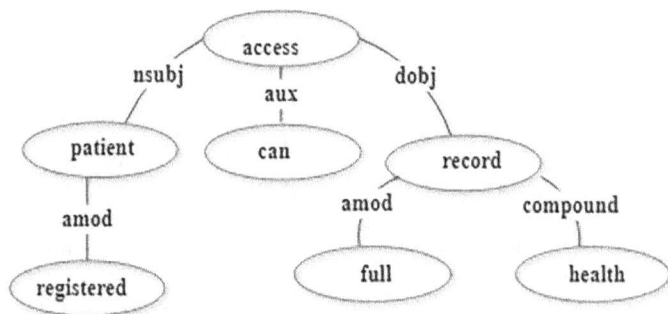

Figure 4: Dependency tree representation

3.1 Module 1: Attribute extraction

We define two element-specific relations, named subject-attribute and object-attribute. These relations exist between policy elements and a phrase or clause that expresses a characteristic of this particular element. To capture the target relations, we first identify the grammatical patterns that can possibly encode each relation. Using the most common patterns, we generate lists of candidate instances, which are then fed into a machine learning classifier to determine whether or not a candidate instance encodes the relation of interest. The following subsections provide the details of each step.

It is worth mentioning that capturing relations of interest can be addressed as a multi-class learning task. However, results obtained from this experiment design were less promising. This motivates our design decision of using two separate binary classifiers, one for each relation.

3.1.1 Identify patterns encoding the target relations. An authorization requirement is deemed to involve a subject-attribute relation if there exists at least one modifier that describes a characteristic of an authorized subject in this particular requirement.

Input sentence with marked entities of object-attribute relation

A registered patient can access his/her [full#e1OA][health record#e2OA]

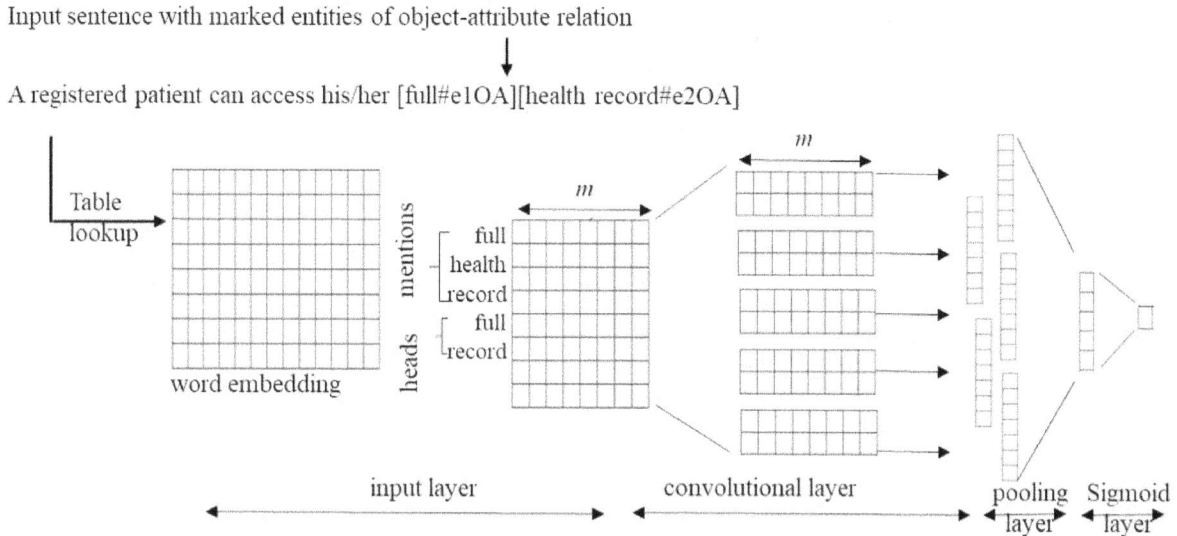

Figure 5: The architecture of the CNN model. The marked entities (or mentions) of an object-attribute instance are obtained using one of the patterns identified in 3.1.1. The mentions and the corresponding heads of the instance are concatenated and fed to the network using the word embeddings representation.

The same applies to object-attribute relation, but with respect to the object element. Knowing whether this relation holds for the subject, or object is essential to assign the appropriate category of the detected attributes, hence the use of the two element-specific relations.

Identifying patterns encoding these relations requires a structured representation of the textual authorization requirement. The constituency parse tree and the dependency tree are both valid options. However, relation extraction studies have empirically shown that patterns drawn from the dependency tree are more resilient to lexical inconsistency among different domains[27]. We, therefore, represent policy sentences with the typed dependency tree as shown in Figure 4 for the sentence "A registered patient can access his/her full health record." In this tree, each vertex represents a word from the sentence, whilst edges represent the grammatical relationship between two words. *patient*, for instance, functions as the nominal subject (nsubj) for *access* and *record* is the direct object (dobj) to be accessed. In this tree, the path that connects *registered* to *patient* is of a special interest as it encodes subject-attribute relation. Similarly, the path between *full* and *record* encodes an object-attribute relation. In other words, the shortest dependency path that links subject or object elements with their attributes is deemed as a relation pattern. To extract such patterns, we refer to our manually annotated data in which we explicitly annotate the authorization attributes of both subjects and objects as described in corpus creation, Section 4. From the entire set of resulted patterns, we follow the recommendation of Berland et al. to focus on the most frequent ones [8].

3.1.2 Generate candidate instances. After identifying the most frequent patterns for the target relations, we search through our dataset to find all matching instances. In this study, we target two

relations that are encoded with two different sets of patterns. Matching against these patterns produces two lists of candidates instances of subject-attribute and object-attribute relations. For both relations, instances are presented with the tuple R(E, AV). R defines the overall relation. Depending on the pattern used for generating the instance, E, which stands for element, could either be the subject or object. AV is the value of an attribute associated with E. The pair E and AV represent entities linked via the set of patterns that encode the relation R. Note that candidate instances do not always encode a valid relation. We, therefore, feed instances to a machine learning classifier(s) to decide whether or not a candidate instance encodes the relation of interest.

3.1.3 Classify candidate instances using CNN-based model. The extracted candidate instances are now used to build the CNN-based classifiers for both relations. Particularly, the combination of entities of each candidate instance, also known as the relation mentions, and the head of each mention is what will be fed to the model, as illustrated in Figure 5. Since CNNs can only accept fixed length inputs, we compute the maximum length of entity mentions and choose the input width to be more than twice as long as the maximum length (to account for both mentions and the heads). Inputs longer than the predefined length are trimmed, while shorter inputs are padded with special tokens. Figure 5 shows the overall architecture of our CNN. Further, in the followings, we provide the rationale for each layer of the model.

• **Input layer:** at the very first layer, the two relation mentions as well as their heads are concatenated to form the vector $x = [x_1, x_2, \ldots, x_n]$ where x_i is the i-th word in this sequence, as seen in Figure 5. Before being fed into the CNN, each word x_i in x must be encoded in a real-valued vector e of m dimensions using word embedding table $\mathbf{W}$. The embeddings table $\mathbf{W}$ can either be learned as a part of the model or loaded from a pretrained word embeddings. Following the recommendation of Chen et al. [13], which calls for the latter approach, we build our model using the GloVe pretrained word embeddings [24]. The output of this layer is a matrix $\mathbf{x} = [\,x_1, x_2, \ldots, x_n\,]$. The size of $\mathbf{x}$ is $m \times n$ where m is the dimensionality of the word embedding vectors, and n is the length of the input sequence x.

- **Convolution layer:** to learn a higher level syntactic and semantic features, the matrix $\mathbf{x}$, representing the given input, is passed through a convolution layer with filter $\mathbf{f} = [\,f_1, f_2, \ldots, f_w\,]$ of size $m \times w$ where w is the width of the filter. The filter convolves over the input sequence to learn the contextual features from the w adjacent terms in the input. The convolution of the two matrices, $\mathbf{x}$ and $\mathbf{f}$, results in a "windowed" average vector $\mathbf{h} = [\,h_1, h_2, \ldots, h_{n-w+1}\,]$ as defined in Equation 1:

$$h_i = g\left(\sum_{j=0}^{w-1} f_{j+1}^T x_{j+i}^T + b\right) \qquad (1)$$

Here g is an optional activation function and b is a bias term. The trained weights of $\mathbf{f}$ would then be used to detect the features of the relations of interest.

- **Pooling layer:** the pooling layer is mainly used for dimensionality reduction purposes. Its two basic types are the max and average pooling. Max pooling is known to be useful in the relation extraction task as it only passes the salient features of the vector $\mathbf{h}$ to the subsequent layers, and filters out the less informative ones [42]. Hence, we apply a max operation to the result of each filter in our model. The application of the max pooling over the vector $\mathbf{h}$ produces a scalar $p = max(\mathbf{h}) = max \{h_1, h_2, \ldots, h_{n-w+1}\}$

- **Fully connected layer:** in this step, the pooling scores obtained from the previous layer are concatenated into a single feature vector $\mathbf{z}$. The vector $\mathbf{z}$ is then fed into a sigmoid layer to perform the classification task.

Upon the successful completion of this module, a pair (E , AV) classified as valid member of relation R will then be used to derive values along with the category of ABAC attributes as shown in Algorithm 1 and further explained in Module 2-4. It is imperative to note that values that are explicitly expressed in the natural language sentence are the ones that are necessary to generate the executable form of the policy. Consider for instance a natural language policy sentence that begins with, "A patient of 18 years of age or older can ..." and its equivalent machine-readable form, shown in Figure 6, one can assume that the actual values of the attribute (e.g. age) that go beyond what the sentence may include are obtained from the policy information point to be used later for evaluation in the policy decision point as suggested in [23]

3.2 Module 2: Identifying the category of an attribute

A straightforward method to determine the attribute category is to refer to the type of relation by which the attribute is detected. The categories subject and object correspond the relations subject-attribute and object-attribute, respectively.

```
policies {
    attribute {
        category = subjectCat
        id = "age"
        type = numerical}
    attribute {
        category = subjectCat
        id = "subjectType"
        type = string}
    policy someAction{
        target clause subjectType == "patient"
        rule allow {
        condition on age >= 18
            permit}
        }
    }
```

Figure 6: The machine-readable form of a policy sentence that begins with "A patient of 18 years of age or older can etc."

Input : The function takes the relation R along with E and AV, e.g. (subject-attribute , patient , registered)

Output : List of attributes defined by key, value, category and data type, e.g. [(subjectType, patient, subject attribute , string) , (status, registered , subject attribute , boolean)]

Function *addNewAttributes (R,E,AV)*
    values = [E, AV];
    category = R.type();
    for *v in values* **do**
        key = getShortName(E,v);
        value = v;
        dataType = getDataType(v);
        attributes.add(key,value,category,dataType);
    end

Algorithm 1: Define the attributes out of detected relations

3.3 Module 3: Suggesting an attribute's short name

This module takes as input the pair (E, AV), produced by Module 1. E and AV are both values of ABAC attributes. Since E always expresses a value of a core policy element, its short name is defined to be either subjectType or objectType depending on the type of relation by which E is captured. However, naming the attribute valued by AV, e.g. status, requires more complex reasoning process. There are several approaches in the literature that could be used to address this task [7, 20, 21], and are beyond the scope of this paper.

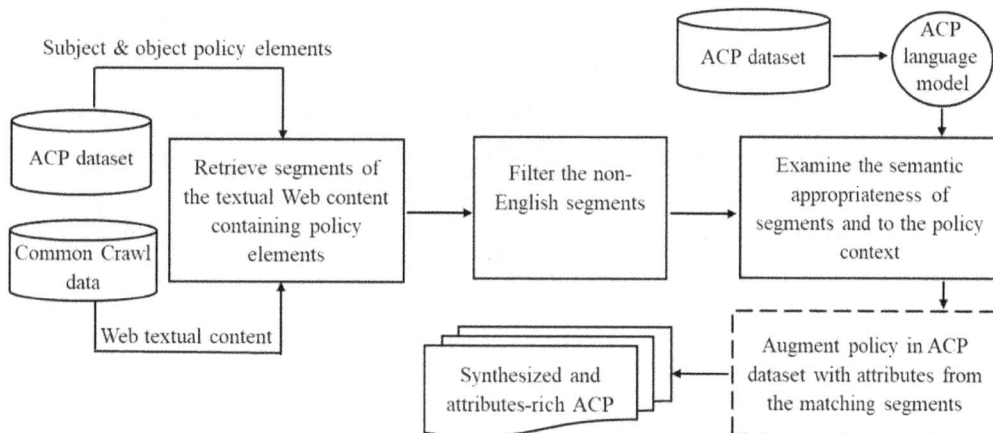

Figure 7: Synthetic data generation framework. The dashed box indicates the manual task in this process.

3.4 Module 4: Identifying an attribute's data type

We currently employ a heuristics-based approach to infer the data type of an attribute. Our heuristics are directly derived from the named entity (NE) type assigned to either E or AV. That is, a NE tagger can recognize information units such as a person, organization, location, time, date, money and many more. An example of such heuristic is "if the NE type of AV is money, then the data type is numeric". An obvious limitation of this approach is that it can infer a data type of an attribute only if NE tagger successfully captures NE type of its value, i.e. E or AV. We, therefore, plan to extend this module in order to move towards a more robust approach.

4 CORPUS CREATION

While the advancements of ML and NLP techniques can provide ABAC policy authors and security architects with powerful tools to address requirements analysis and attributes extraction tasks, the effective adoption of these techniques is restricted by the lack of appropriate datasets. One reason for this dearth of data is that the requirement specifications in general, and authorization requirements in particular are meant to be proprietary except for a few software projects for which requirements are publicly available. This results in a lack of authorization requirements that are rich with attributes. Meaning that the majority of the available natural language policy documents often express authorization rules by the means of roles, actions and resources, e.g. "a patient chooses to view his or her access log." While some of these elements could be considered as attributes, they mainly capture the core policy elements. Hence, these are not enough to train an automated attribute extraction model. To remedy the lack of appropriate data, we construct a synthetic natural language policy dataset such that the authorization rules are expressed by the means of attributes. We then use this dataset to evaluate the proposed approach.

Two information sources have been used to fuel the synthetic data generation framework. The first is the datasets obtained from the prior efforts in natural language access control policy (NLACP)

collection. These datasets were constructed to study various aspects of the automated translation of NLACPs to machine-readable code. The most representative examples of these datasets are :

(1) iTrust: is a patient-centric application for maintaining an electronic health records [5].
(2) IBM Course Management App: is a registration system for colleges [2].
(3) CyberChair: is a conference management system [47].
(4) Collected ACP: is a dataset consists of combined access control policy sentences collected by Xiao et al. [48].

Herein we refer to these documents collectively as ACP dataset[1]. The authoring style of the authorization requirements in the ACP dataset is tuned more towards the role-based access control than attribute based access control. Hence, these datasets do not have enough attributes for the purpose of our study. To address this limitation, we augment either the subjects or objects elements of the policies with additional descriptive context derived from a general purpose textual data, namely Common Crawl [3], which composes our second information source. The purpose of injecting this additional context is to change the tone of the policy so it reads as if it was written with ABAC model in mind. For example, before injecting the descriptive context, a policy sentence might be written as "faculty can access library materials", while after injection, it becomes "*retired USD* faculty can access the *unrestricted* library materials." The latter sentence ties together the core policy elements with their attributes, i.e. USD, retired and unrestricted, to mimic the type of authorization requirements ABAC model is meant to capture.

Figure 7 shows the overall synthetic data generation framework. We start the process with the subject and object elements of access control sentences in ACP dataset as they were identified by the original authors. Next, we search through the Common Crawl web content to retrieve segments of text that contain the elements of interest, i.e. the subject and the object. We limit the language of the

---

[1]These documents can be downloaded from:
https://sites.google.com/site/accesscontrolruleextraction/documents

Table 1: Examples of the synthesized natural language policies. Column A contains the original policies as obtained from ACP datasets, and B shows the policies after being augmented with attributes.

A	B
A lab technician can update the status ...	A **full-time first shift** lab technician can update the status ...
Professor must be able to access the system to ...	Professor, **of economics at University of NSW,** must be able to access the system ...
Program Committee (PC) must be selected to review the papers.	Program Committee (PC) must be selected to review the **"border line"** papers.

retrieved segments to English. Intuitively, not all of the matching segments appropriately fit with the semantic of policies in ACP dataset. To filter irrelevant matches, we first build a language model using the ACP dataset . Then, we use the conditional probability of each segment under the computed language model to determine the semantic fitness of a segment to the context of ACP dataset. Next, we manually augment policy sentence with the relevant portion of text from the matching segment and make necessary changes. The injection process ends once we collect as much of the relevant segments as needed to inject sentences of ACP dataset with the synthetic attributes.

One might argue that the data generation process can be done entirely manually, by recruiting individuals to do so. An obvious motivation for the automation is to generate the synthesized policies as natural as can be. This is to say that data generated manually by individuals in a controlled experiment settings might be biased by the individuals' writing styles, their background knowledge as well as their comprehension of the data generation instructions. However, using a content drawn from a general purpose content repository, such as Common Crawl, captures the natural context that normally contains the elements of interests. Scalability, in terms of the volume of data and the variety of domains, is another motivation. The reason is that an automated means of data generation is designed to at least partially eliminate the need of domain experts. Table 1 shows examples of the synthesized policies which if generated manually would require a certain level of domain-specific knowledge.

To this end, we introduce our synthetic natural language policy dataset of four different domains. It contains a total of 851 sentences with manual annotations of 867 subject-attribute and 912 object-attribute instances. Table 2 summarizes the number of elements along with their attributes in our dataset. To capture the subject and object elements of ABAC policy along with their attributes, we develop the following annotation scheme:

(1) e2SA: stands for element2 in Subject Attributes Relation. A segment of the sentence that is tagged with this label corresponds to a value of a core policy element named subjectType
(2) e1SA: stands for element1 in Subject Attributes Relation. This label is used to tag the part of the sentence that expresses a value of an attribute that modifies e2SA

We similarly define e2OA, e1OA to label objects and object attributes, respectively. Figure 8 presents the format for an annotated ACP sentence.

A [registered#e1SA][patient#e2SA]can access his/her [full#e1OA][health record#e2OA]

Figure 8: Annotated ACP sentence

Table 2: The corpus built for the experiment

Dataset	ACP sentences	# Subject-Attribute	# Object-Attribute
iTrust	466	511	514
Collected ACP	112	144	100
IBM App	163	140	195
CyberChair	110	72	103
Total	851	867	912

5 EXPERIMENTAL RESULTS AND PERFORMANCE EVALUATION

We next present the evaluation we conducted to assess the effectiveness of the Attribute Extraction module, i.e. Module 1. In our evaluation, we address two main research questions:

- **RQ1:** What are the possible patterns that link policy elements and their attributes?
- **RQ2:** How effectively, in terms of precision, recall and F1-score, does our approach extract attributes of subjects and objects?

To answer RQ1, we first generate the dependency tree representation of each sentence. The resulted representation is augmented with annotation information needed to explore patterns encoding either subject-attribute or object-attribute relations. Our analysis has shown that there exist 125 unique patterns to encode subject-attribute relation, while the object-attribute relation is encoded with 240. Table 3 shows the five most frequently occurring patterns for each relation as per our corpus. The remaining patterns accounts for very few valid instances. Thus, we only consider the top 5 ones. Matching against these top 5 patterns generates the two sets of candidate instances, one for each relation. Table 4 shows, for each relation, the total number of candidate instances as well as the number of valid matches in each set. It is worth mentioning that identifying these patterns can be not only valuable to the purpose of this study, but also it can be used as seeds to establish an inductive approach to semi-automate the process of learning patterns of our target relations [28].

In response to RQ2, we build our CNN model with a total of 4 layers of which two are convolution layers with dropout of 0.2 followed by one max pooling layer and the sigmoid layer. Throughout

Table 3: Five most occurring patterns in each relation (for more information regarding components of each pattern,e.g. nsubj, see [16])

Subject-Attribute		Object-Attribute	
Patterns	% of Occurrence	Patterns	% of Occurrence
nsubj,amod	32%	dobj,amod	24%
nsubj,prep	8%	pobj,amod	9%
nsubjpass,amod	7%	dobj,prep	6%
nsubj,compound	5%	dobj,compound	4%
nsubj,ROOT,amod	4%	nsubjpass,amod	3%

Table 4: Valid matches versus the total number of candidate instances using the top 5 patterns shown in Table 3.

Dataset		Subject-Attribute	Object-Attribute
iTrust	valid	265	288
	total	570	1207
Collected ACP	valid	84	70
	total	350	162
IBM App	valid	90	139
	total	299	312
CyberChair	valid	52	65
	total	148	207

Table 5: Results of the proposed models (P, R, F1 represent precision, recall and F1-score, respectively). The first four rows show the performance of the model when tested on in-domain data whilst the last row represents how the system would perform on out-of-domain data.

Dataset	Subject-Attribute			Object-Attribute		
	P	R	F1	P	R	F1
iTrust	0.97	0.99	0.98	0.91	0.90	0.90
Collected ACP	0.93	0.93	0.93	0.93	0.95	0.94
IBM App	0.95	0.96	0.96	0.92	0.92	0.92
CyberChair	0.97	0.98	0.97	0.88	0.87	0.88
Document fold	0.91	0.80	0.85	0.75	0.69	0.71

the experiment, we utilize the publicly available GloVe pretrained word embeddings of 300 dimensions. GloVe embeddings are trained on 42 billion words of Common Crawl data using the global word-word co-occurrence statistics [24, 41]. For the convolutional layer, we use Relu as an activation function and 128 filters with a window of size 2. All further parameters, e.g. batch size and kernel initializer, are left as default. The models (i.e. subject-attribute and object-attribute) are trained for 10 epochs.

To evaluate the performance of our CNN, we employ a 3-fold stratified cross-validation as well as document fold validation. In the document fold, the models are trained on three documents and tested on the forth. The rational of such evaluation setting is to evaluate how the system will perform on out-of-domain data.

A general observation with regard to the performance behavior is that the subject-attribute relation extraction model surpasses the performance of object-attribute model. A possible interpretation of the overall strength of the subject-attribute relation is rooted in the nature of the instances of this relation. More specifically, the subject-attribute relation is meant to chain system's users, which are mostly human entities, with their corresponding attributes. This introduces a level of semantic consistency between instances belonging to this particular relation. However, this is not the case in the object-attribute relation as it can possibly apply on wide variety of entity types. Hence, there will be more clusters of instances of this relation, which makes it less likely to be learned from a relatively small data size. We, therefore, expect that the accumulation of more labeled instances can substantially improve the performance.

The first four rows of Table 5 show the means of the 3-fold cross validation across 10 runs. Scores represent the performance of the model in detecting the valid instances of both relations, i.e. the performance over the positive class. The variance of these means ranges between 0.01 to 0.1. This experiment, the n-fold, represents the performance of the model on in-domain data. The high score of the precision and recall indicates model's ability to infer the semantic consistency among candidate instances. To evaluate how the model would perform when tested on out-of-domain data, we conduct a document fold experiment. Here, the model is trained on 3 documents and tested on the fourth that belongs to a different domain. The results of this experiment have shown an expected drop in the values of precision and recall. However, the loss is more significant in the case of object-attribute relation. A potential justification for this behaviour is that despite the domain differences, there are common attributes of subjects, e.g. location, age .. etc. that are shared across domains. Such similarity is less likely to occur between objects across domains. For instance, a model trained

on data from a medical domain would not be certain about the attributes of, say, courses and class as does with medical records. It is also worthy to note that we have experimented with several other classical learning algorithms, e.g. SVM and Naive Bayes, trained on manually engineered features; but, the CNN outperforms other models. The results are omitted here due to space limit.

6 RELATED WORK

Several studies have researched various aspects of the automated analysis of natural language ACPs. In order to review these prior efforts, we introduce six comparison dimensions along which each related work has been characterized: (1) the building blocks of the proposed framework; (2) the underlying techniques used for each component; (3) indicators or features used in case a learning approach is employed; (4) the dataset used for the validation; (5) size of the dataset (measured by the number of sentences), and (6) the average of available performance metrics. Table 6 presents a summary of the findings, while the rest of this section discusses each study separately.

Xiao et al. [48] have first introduced an automated approach, named Text2Policy, to construct access control policy rules out of natural language artifacts. Their approach was built upon matching against 4 predefined patterns to discern ACP sentences from other types of sentences. Heuristics were defined based on the same set of patterns to extract instances that jointly compose ACP rules. The extraction task is followed by transformation process in which a formal representation of the extracted rule is generated. The reported results achieved an average recall of 89.4% with a precision

Table 6: ACP extraction from natural language artifacts in the related work. In this table, N/A stands for not applicable while N/R means not reported.

Study	Components of Framework	Underlying Tech.	Features	Dataset	Size	Performance
[48]	ACP sentence identification	Semantic patterns matching	N/A	iTrust , IBM App	927	Prec:88.7% Rec:89.4%
	ACP elements extraction	Heuristics over the patterns	N/A	Access control sentences in: iTrust, IBM App,and collected ACP	241	Accu:86.3%
	Transformation to formal model	Heuristics	N/A	N/R	N/R	N/R
[43]	ACP sentence identification	Majority vote of K-NN, Naive Bayes and SVM classifiers	Words, synonyms, POS, named entities, and Levenshtein distance in the case of K-NN	iTrust	1159	Prec:87.3% Rec:90.8%
	ACP elements extraction	RE using bootstrapping; seeding patterns are derived from dependency tree	N/A	Access control sentences in: iTrust	409	Prec:46.3% Rec:53.6%
		Naive Bayes classifier of candidate instances	Were not clearly reported			
[44]	ACP sentence identification	K-NN	Levenshtein distance	iTrust, IBM App, Cyberchair, collected ACP	2477	Prec:81% Rec:65%
	ACP elements extraction	RE using bootstrapping; seeding patterns are derived from dependency tree	N/A	Access control sentences in: iTrust, IBM App, Cyberchair, collected ACP	1390	N/R
		Naive Bayes classifier of candidate instances	Pattern itself, relationships to resource and subject, POS of subject and resource			
[34]	ACP sentence identification	Naive Bayes and SVM classifiers	A total of 821 features categorized into: pointwise mutual information, security, syntactic complexity, and dependency features	iTrust, IBM App, Cyberchair, collected ACP	2477	Prec:90% Rec:90%
[35]	ACP sentence identification	Deep recurrent neural network	Word embedding	ACPData, iTrust ,IBM App, Cyberchair, collected ACP	5137	Prec:81.28% Rec:74.21%
[37]	ACP elements extraction	Semantic role labeler(SRL)	N/A	Access control sentences in: iTrust, IBM App, Cyberchair	726	Prec:58.3% Rec:86.3%
[36]	ACP elements extraction	Semantic role labeler(SRL)	N/A	Access control sentences in: iTrust, IBM App, Cyberchair, collected ACP	841	Prec:63.5% Rec:86.25%

of 88.7% in the identification phase and an accuracy of 86.3% on the extraction. Evaluation results of the transformation phase were not reported. However, their approach cannot capture ACP sentences that do not follow the predefined patterns; and, it has been shown that only 34.4% of ACPs can be captured with Text2Policy's patterns [44].

Slankas et al. [43] have proposed Access Control Relation Extraction (ACRE), a machine learning based approach for ACP elements extraction from natural language documents. ACRE can be broken down to ACP sentence identification phase followed by ACP elements extraction. In the identification phase, the authors have investigated whether words, words' synonyms, POS and named entities could be used as indicators to identify ACP sentences. In elements extraction phase, a bootstrapping technique built upon patterns drawn from dependency tree representation of sentence has been adopted to extract ACP instances. Slankas et al. have empirically validated the proposed approach on a version of iTrust that contains 1159 sentences. Their approach achieved a recall of 90.8% with a precision 87.3% in the identification phase, whereas in ACP rule extraction authors reported 46.3% precision with a recall of 53.6% as the best performance they can achieve.

Slankas et al. [44] have extended ACRE, which was first introduced in [43]. The main components of the framework, as well as the underlying techniques, are similar to their original proposal with only subtle modifications. What clearly distinguishes this work from its predecessor is the evaluation. In [44], Slankas et al. have validated the proposed approach against larger datasets collected from 5 sources of policy data that have been previously used in the

literature. For the identification phase, K-nearest neighbor (K-NN) learning approach was employed to discern ACP sentence from other types of sentences. Further, the authors have achieved an average classification precision and recall of 81% and 65%, respectively. For elements extraction phase, on the other hand, performance was reported per dataset, meaning the overall average scores were not reported.

Narouei et al. [34] designed a new set of features to distinguish ACP from non-ACP sentences. Using the proposed feature set and following the classical machine learning pipeline, the authors reported an average precision and recall of 90%.

Narouei et al. [35] proposed a top-down policy engineering framework to particularly aid ABAC policy authoring. They have adopted the following pipeline: ACP sentence identification followed by policy elements extraction phase. For the identification task, the authors have used a deep recurrent neural network that uses pre-trained word embedding to identify sentences that contain access control policy content; and, they achieved an average precision of 81.28% and 74.21% for recall. For policy elements extraction, the authors have suggested the use of semantic role labeler (SRL), but no evaluation results were reported [35]. Using the language of ABAC model, the authors regarded the arguments of SRL tagger as the attribute values while argument definitions were seen as the keys or what are so called short names. Consider for instance the two ACPs sentences : (1) A registered patient can access his/her full health record and (2) A registered patient can read his/her full health record. Following the approach of Narouei et al [35], attributes would be represented as follows:

- accessor = patient
- reader = patient

where *reader* and *accessor* are the arguments definition obtained from the SRL tagger. Such a direct mapping from the SRL output (i.e. arguments and argument definitions) to attribute values and short names of ABAC model is insufficient. This is mainly because of two reasons. First, SRL labels arguments only with respect to the predicate, e.g. *access* and *read*. Therefore, attributes of subjects and objects such as *registered* and *full* will not be captured using this approach. Second, from the SRL perspective, an argument definition, e.g. *accessor* and *reader*, describes the semantic relation between an argument and a predicate in a sentence. This description, however, might not be an appropriate short name of an attribute as can be seen in the above-mentioned example. That is from ABAC standpoint, *patient* is a value of one attribute called subjectType, or any semantically similar attribute name, rather than the two attribute names —*reader* and *accessor*— suggested by the SRL tagger.

Narouei et al. [36, 37] have proposed a new approach for extracting policy elements from ACP policy sentences using semantic role labeler (SRL). The performance of SRL approach was evaluated per dataset. The authors reported that they were able to achieve higher extraction recall (88%), on their test data, when compared to ACRE [44]. This boost of recall, however, comes at the cost of precision. While we are aware that the lack of benchmark dataset makes the comparison task non-trivial, the reported results suggest that a combination of policy extraction approaches by Slankas et al. [44] and Narouei et al. [37] can potentially balance both precision and recall values. Further, Narouei et al. [38] have investigated the idea of improving SRL performance using domain adaptation techniques. The authors reported that they were able to identify ACP elements with an average F1 score of 75%, which bested the previous work by 15%.

Turner designed an ABAC authoring assistance tool that allows a security architect to configure an ABAC expression as a sequence of fields, namely subject, subject attributes, object, and object attribute, etc. [46]. The natural language ABAC policy will then be provided to the tool according to the predefined fields. The aim is to create an ABAC authoring environment of business-level user experience while delegating the transformation of the provided input to machine-readable ABAC rules to the application. Unlike our proposal, following Turner's approach the task of extracting information that are relevant to the ABAC rule from the NLACP is still done manually. Although it is mentioned that this task could be automated, the presented approach is manual. Additionally, unlike our approach that works with unrestricted natural language documents, Turner's approach constrains the NLP's context-free grammar.

7 LIMITATIONS

Evaluating the proposed approach on real-world requirements would be ideal. Hence, the use of the synthetic data might impose a limitation on this work. However, acquiring the real data from real organizations might not be feasible considering the privacy-sensitive nature of the data. We, therefore, develop our synthetic data that, while not real, are intended to be realistic. Particularly, to ensure that our synthetic data preserves the key characteristics of

real data, we made the following design decisions: (1) the data was built upon real requirement documents, (2) the injected attributes were obtained from the Web content in an attempt to capture the real-world context of a particular policy element, and (3) the manual part of the injection process was conducted by Ph.D. students with expertise in access control domain. Hence, we believe that our synthetic data is representative of the real-world data and so is the performance. Generally speaking, the nature of privacy-sensitive content is a major challenge in devising data-driven security/privacy solutions, such as insider threat detection or clinically-relevant text analysis tools, to name few. In such situations the synthetic content has been considered as an alternative [18, 39]. Another limitation of this work is that our evaluation mainly focuses on attribute extraction module (see subsection 3.1) and other modules of the proposed framework are discussed briefly. Note that this module constitutes the basis for our framework and this work is the first step towards developing the proposed framework; developing and evaluating Modules 2-4 is part of our ongoing research and the results will be reported in future work.

8 CONCLUSIONS AND FUTURE WORK

A practical framework was proposed to analyze natural language ACPs, and automatically identify the core properties needed to define the attributes contained in these policies. To the best of our knowledge, this is the first evaluated effort to solve this problem. When extracting the attributes of subject and object elements of access control policy, our approach achieved an average F1-score of 0.96 and 0.91, respectively. The high values of the F1-measure indicate that our proposed method is promising. While the current results are encouraging, further data collection effort is needed to improve the performance over out-of-domain data. The future research directions are focused on devising an automated means in order to provide support to ABAC authorization policy lifecycle.

9 ACKNOWLEDGMENT

The work of the first author has been partially supported by Princess Nourah bint Abdulrahman University, Riyadh, Saudi Arabia.

REFERENCES

[1] 2003. XACML – A No-Nonsense Developer's Guide. (2003). http://www.idevnews.com/stories/57
[2] 2004. IBM 2004. Course Registration Requirements. (2004).
[3] 2017. Common Crawl. (September 2017). http://commoncrawl.org/
[4] Ryma Abassi, Michael Rusinowitch, Florent Jacquemard, and Sihem Guemara El Fatmi. 2010. XML access control: from XACML to annotated schemas. In *Communications and Networking (ComNet), 2010 Second International Conference on*. IEEE, 1–8.
[5] Laurie Williams Andrew Meneely, Ben Smith. 2011. iTrust Electronic Health Care System: A Case Study. (2011). http://bensmith.s3.amazonaws.com/website/papers/sst2011.pdf
[6] Axiomatics. 2017. Attribute Based Access Control (ABAC). (2017). https://www.axiomatics.com/attribute-based-access-control/
[7] Omid Bakhshandeh and James Allen. 2015. From Adjective Glosses to Attribute Concepts: Learning Different Aspects That an Adjective Can Describe.. In *IWCS*. 23–33.
[8] Matthew Berland and Eugene Charniak. 1999. Finding Parts in Very Large Corpora. In *Proceedings of the 37th Annual Meeting of the Association for Computational Linguistics on Computational Linguistics (ACL '99)*. Association for Computational Linguistics, Stroudsburg, PA, USA, 57–64. https://doi.org/10.3115/1034678.1034697
[9] Eric Brill. 1995. Transformation-based Error-driven Learning and Natural Language Processing: A Case Study in Part-of-speech Tagging. *Comput. Linguist.* 21, 4 (Dec. 1995), 543–565. http://dl.acm.org/citation.cfm?id=218355.218367

[10] David Brossard, Gerry Gebel, and Mark Berg. 2017. A Systematic Approach to Implementing ABAC. In *Proceedings of the 2Nd ACM Workshop on Attribute-Based Access Control (ABAC '17)*. ACM, New York, NY, USA, 53–59. https://doi.org/10.1145/3041048.3041051

[11] Yee Seng Chan and Dan Roth. 2010. Exploiting Background Knowledge for Relation Extraction. In *Proceedings of the 23rd International Conference on Computational Linguistics (COLING '10)*. Association for Computational Linguistics, Stroudsburg, PA, USA, 152–160. http://dl.acm.org/citation.cfm?id=1873781.1873799

[12] Yee Seng Chan and Dan Roth. 2011. Exploiting Syntactico-semantic Structures for Relation Extraction. In *Proceedings of the 49th Annual Meeting of the Association for Computational Linguistics: Human Language Technologies - Volume 1 (HLT '11)*. Association for Computational Linguistics, Stroudsburg, PA, USA, 551–560. http://dl.acm.org/citation.cfm?id=2002472.2002542

[13] Danqi Chen and Christopher Manning. 2014. A fast and accurate dependency parser using neural networks. In *Proceedings of the 2014 conference on empirical methods in natural language processing (EMNLP)*. 740–750.

[14] Ronan Collobert, Jason Weston, Léon Bottou, Michael Karlen, Koray Kavukcuoglu, and Pavel Kuksa. 2011. Natural language processing (almost) from scratch. *Journal of Machine Learning Research* 12, Aug (2011), 2493–2537.

[15] Aron Culotta and Jeffrey Sorensen. 2004. Dependency Tree Kernels for Relation Extraction. In *Proceedings of the 42Nd Annual Meeting on Association for Computational Linguistics (ACL '04)*. Association for Computational Linguistics, Stroudsburg, PA, USA, Article 423. https://doi.org/10.3115/1218955.1219009

[16] Marie-Catherine De Marneffe and Christopher D Manning. 2008. *Stanford typed dependencies manual*. Technical Report. Technical report, Stanford University.

[17] Gartner. 2013. Market Trends: Cloud-Based Security Services Market, Worldwide, 2014. (October 2013). https://www.gartner.com/doc/2607617

[18] J. Glasser and B. Lindauer. 2013. Bridging the Gap: A Pragmatic Approach to Generating Insider Threat Data. In *2013 IEEE Security and Privacy Workshops*. 98–104. https://doi.org/10.1109/SPW.2013.37

[19] Zhou GuoDong, Su Jian, Zhang Jie, and Zhang Min. 2005. Exploring Various Knowledge in Relation Extraction. (2005), 427–434. https://doi.org/10.3115/1219840.1219893

[20] Matthias Hartung and Anette Frank. 2010. A Structured Vector Space Model for Hidden Attribute Meaning in Adjective-noun Phrases. In *Proceedings of the 23rd International Conference on Computational Linguistics (COLING '10)*. Association for Computational Linguistics, Stroudsburg, PA, USA, 430–438. http://dl.acm.org/citation.cfm?id=1873781.1873830

[21] Matthias Hartung, Fabian Kaupmann, Soufian Jebbara, and Philipp Cimiano. 2017. Learning Compositionality Functions on Word Embeddings for Modelling Attribute Meaning in Adjective-Noun Phrases. In *Proceedings of the 15th Meeting of the European Chapter of the Association for Computational Linguistics (EACL)*, Vol. 1.

[22] Mary Hearne, Sylwia Ozdowska, and John Tinsley. 2008. Comparing constituency and dependency representations for smt phrase-extraction. (2008).

[23] Vincent C Hu, David Ferraiolo, Rick Kuhn, Arthur R Friedman, Alan J Lang, Margaret M Cogdell, Adam Schnitzer, Kenneth Sandlin, Robert Miller, Karen Scarfone, et al. 2013. Guide to attribute based access control (ABAC) definition and considerations (draft). *NIST special publication* 800, 162 (2013).

[24] Christopher D. Manning Jeffrey Pennington, Richard Socher. 2017. GloVe: Global Vectors for Word Representation. (2017). https://nlp.stanford.edu/projects/glove/

[25] Jing Jiang. 2012. Information Extraction from Text. In *Mining Text Data*, Charu C. Aggarwal and ChengXiang Zhai (Eds.). Springer US, Boston, MA, 11–41. https://doi.org/10.1007/978-1-4614-3223-4_2

[26] Jing Jiang and ChengXiang Zhai. 2007. A Systematic Exploration of the Feature Space for Relation Extraction.. In *HLT-NAACL*. 113–120.

[27] Richard Johansson and Pierre Nugues. 2008. Dependency-based Semantic Role Labeling of PropBank. In *Proceedings of the Conference on Empirical Methods in Natural Language Processing (EMNLP '08)*. Association for Computational Linguistics, Stroudsburg, PA, USA, 69–78. http://dl.acm.org/citation.cfm?id=1613715.1613726

[28] Daniel Jurafsky and James H Martin. 2009. Speech and Language Processing: An Introduction to Natural Language Processing, Computational Linguistics, and Speech Recognition. (2009).

[29] Nal Kalchbrenner and Phil Blunsom. 2013. Recurrent Convolutional Neural Networks for Discourse Compositionality. *CoRR* abs/1306.3584 (2013). arXiv:1306.3584 http://arxiv.org/abs/1306.3584

[30] Nanda Kambhatla. 2004. Combining Lexical, Syntactic, and Semantic Features with Maximum Entropy Models for Extracting Relations. In *Proceedings of the ACL 2004 on Interactive Poster and Demonstration Sessions (ACLdemo '04)*. Association for Computational Linguistics, Stroudsburg, PA, USA, Article 22. https://doi.org/10.3115/1219044.1219066

[31] Butler W. Lampson. 1974. Protection. *SIGOPS Oper. Syst. Rev.* 8, 1 (Jan. 1974), 18–24. https://doi.org/10.1145/775265.775268

[32] James H Martin and Daniel Jurafsky. 2000. Speech and language processing. *International Edition* 710 (2000).

[33] Raymond J Mooney and Razvan C Bunescu. 2006. Subsequence kernels for relation extraction. In *Advances in neural information processing systems*. 171–178.

[34] Masoud Narouei, Hamed Khanpour, and Hassan Takabi. 2017. Identification of Access Control Policy Sentences from Natural Language Policy Documents. In *Data and Applications Security and Privacy XXXI*, Giovanni Livraga and Sencun Zhu (Eds.). Springer International Publishing, Cham, 82–100.

[35] Masoud Narouei, Hamed Khanpour, Hassan Takabi, Natalie Parde, and Rodney Nielsen. 2017. Towards a Top-down Policy Engineering Framework for Attribute-based Access Control. In *Proceedings of the 22Nd ACM on Symposium on Access Control Models and Technologies (SACMAT '17 Abstracts)*. ACM, New York, NY, USA, 103–114. https://doi.org/10.1145/3078861.3078874

[36] Masoud Narouei and Hassan Takabi. 2015. Automatic Top-Down Role Engineering Framework Using Natural Language Processing Techniques. In *Information Security Theory and Practice*, Raja Naeem Akram and Sushil Jajodia (Eds.). Springer International Publishing, Cham, 137–152.

[37] Masoud Narouei and Hassan Takabi. 2015. Towards an Automatic Top-down Role Engineering Approach Using Natural Language Processing Techniques. In *Proceedings of the 20th ACM Symposium on Access Control Models and Technologies (SACMAT '15)*. ACM, New York, NY, USA, 157–160. https://doi.org/10.1145/2752952.2752958

[38] M. Narouei, H. Takabi, and R. Nielsen. 2018. Automatic Extraction of Access Control Policies from Natural Language Documents. *IEEE Transactions on Dependable and Secure Computing* (2018), 1–1. https://doi.org/10.1109/TDSC.2018.2818708

[39] Mayuresh Oak, Anil Behera, Titus Thomas, Cecilia Ovesdotter Alm, Emily Prud'hommeaux, Christopher Homan, and Raymond W Ptucha. 2016. Generating Clinically Relevant Texts: A Case Study on Life-Changing Events.. In *CLPsych@ HLT-NAACL*. 85–94.

[40] OASIS. 2013. eXtensible Access Control Markup Language (XACML) Version 3.0. (January 2013). http://docs.oasis-open.org/xacml/3.0/xacml-3.0-core-spec-os-en.html

[41] Jeffrey Pennington, Richard Socher, and Christopher Manning. 2014. Glove: Global vectors for word representation. In *Proceedings of the 2014 conference on empirical methods in natural language processing (EMNLP)*. 1532–1543.

[42] Yelong Shen, Xiaodong He, Jianfeng Gao, Li Deng, and Grégoire Mesnil. 2014. Learning Semantic Representations Using Convolutional Neural Networks for Web Search. In *Proceedings of the 23rd International Conference on World Wide Web (WWW '14 Companion)*. ACM, New York, NY, USA, 373–374. https://doi.org/10.1145/2567948.2577348

[43] John Slankas and Laurie Williams. 2013. Access Control Policy Identification and Extraction from Project Documentation. *Academy of Science and Engineering Science* 2, 3 (2013), p145–159.

[44] John Slankas, Xusheng Xiao, Laurie Williams, and Tao Xie. 2014. Relation Extraction for Inferring Access Control Rules from Natural Language Artifacts. In *Proceedings of the 30th Annual Computer Security Applications Conference (ACSAC '14)*. ACM, New York, NY, USA, 366–375. https://doi.org/10.1145/2664243.2664280

[45] Erik F. Tjong Kim Sang and Fien De Meulder. 2003. Introduction to the CoNLL-2003 Shared Task: Language-independent Named Entity Recognition. In *Proceedings of the Seventh Conference on Natural Language Learning at HLT-NAACL 2003 - Volume 4 (CONLL '03)*. Association for Computational Linguistics, Stroudsburg, PA, USA, 142–147. https://doi.org/10.3115/1119176.1119195

[46] Ronald C. Turner. 2017. Proposed Model for Natural Language ABAC Authoring. In *Proceedings of the 2nd ACM Workshop on Attribute-Based Access Control (ABAC '17)*. ACM, New York, NY, USA, 61–72. https://doi.org/10.1145/3041048.3041049

[47] Richard Van De Stadt. 2012. CyberChair: A Web-Based Groupware Application to Facilitate the Paper Reviewing Process. *CoRR* abs/1206.1833 (2012). arXiv:1206.1833 http://arxiv.org/abs/1206.1833 Withdrawn.

[48] Xusheng Xiao, Amit Paradkar, Suresh Thummalapenta, and Tao Xie. 2012. Automated Extraction of Security Policies from Natural-language Software Documents. In *Proceedings of the ACM SIGSOFT 20th International Symposium on the Foundations of Software Engineering (FSE '12)*. ACM, New York, NY, USA, Article 12, 11 pages. https://doi.org/10.1145/2393596.2393608

[49] Dmitry Zelenko, Chinatsu Aone, and Anthony Richardella. 2003. Kernel methods for relation extraction. *Journal of machine learning research* 3, Feb (2003), 1083–1106.

[50] Daojian Zeng, Kang Liu, Siwei Lai, Guangyou Zhou, Jun Zhao, et al. 2014. Relation Classification via Convolutional Deep Neural Network.. In *COLING*. 2335–2344.

[51] Min Zhang, Jie Zhang, and Jian Su. 2006. Exploring Syntactic Features for Relation Extraction Using a Convolution Tree Kernel. In *Proceedings of the Main Conference on Human Language Technology Conference of the North American Chapter of the Association of Computational Linguistics (HLT-NAACL '06)*. Association for Computational Linguistics, Stroudsburg, PA, USA, 288–295. https://doi.org/10.3115/1220835.1220872

[52] Muhua Zhu, Yue Zhang, Wenliang Chen, Min Zhang, and Jingbo Zhu. 2013. Fast and Accurate Shift-Reduce Constituent Parsing. In *Proceedings of the 51st Annual Meeting of the Association for Computational Linguistics (Volume 1: Long Papers)*. Association for Computational Linguistics, Sofia, Bulgaria, 434–443. http://www.aclweb.org/anthology/P13-1043

Efficient Extended ABAC Evaluation

Charles Morisset
Newcastle University
charles.morisset@newcastle.ac.uk

Tim A. C. Willemse
Eindhoven University of Technology
t.a.c.willemse@tue.nl

Nicola Zannone
Eindhoven University of Technology
n.zannone@tue.nl

ABSTRACT

A main challenge of attribute-based access control (ABAC) is the handling of missing information. Several studies show that the way standard ABAC mechanisms (*e.g.*, XACML) handle missing information is flawed, making ABAC policies vulnerable to attribute-hiding attacks. Recent work addressed the problem of missing information in ABAC by introducing the notion of extended evaluation, where the evaluation of a query considers all possible ways of extending that query. This method counters attribute-hiding attacks, but a naïve implementation is intractable, as it requires an evaluation of the whole query space. In this paper, we present an efficient extended ABAC evaluation method that relies on the encoding of ABAC policies as multiple Binary Decision Diagrams (BDDs), and on the specification of query constraints to avoid including the evaluation of queries that do not represent a valid state of the system. We illustrate our approach on two real-world case studies, which would be intractable with the original method and are analyzed in seconds with our method.

CCS CONCEPTS

• **Security and privacy** → **Access control**; *Formal security models*;

KEYWORDS

Policy evaluation, ABAC; missing attributes; PTaCL; BDD

ACM Reference Format:
Charles Morisset, Tim A. C. Willemse, and Nicola Zannone. 2018. Efficient Extended ABAC Evaluation. In *SACMAT '18: The 23rd ACM Symposium on Access Control Models & Technologies (SACMAT), June 13–15, 2018, Indianapolis, IN, USA*. ACM, New York, NY, USA, 12 pages. https://doi.org/10.1145/3205977.3205980

1 INTRODUCTION

Attribute-Based Access Control (ABAC) is emerging as the de facto paradigm for the specification and enforcement of access control policies. In ABAC, policies and access requests are defined in terms of attribute name-value pairs. This provides an expressive, flexible and scalable paradigm that is able to capture and manage authorizations in complex environments.

Despite providing a powerful paradigm for the specification and evaluation of access control policies, ABAC has some intrinsic

drawbacks related to the handling of missing information [3, 16]. As shown in [4], these drawbacks make ABAC policies vulnerable to attribute hiding attacks where users can obtain a more favorable decision by hiding some of their attributes. The main problem lies in the fact that all the information necessary for policy evaluation should be available to the policy decision point.

Recent years have seen the emergence of authorization mechanisms that go beyond the view of a centralized monitor with full knowledge of the system. Authorization mechanisms increasingly rely on external services to gather the information necessary for access decision making (*e.g.*, Amazon Web Services rely on third-party identity providers and federated identity systems, the OAuth 2.0 protocol enables delegation of authorization). The use of external services makes it difficult to guarantee and, in some cases, even to check that all necessary information has been provided. Moreover, in some domains like IoT, it might be difficult and costly to gather (accurate) information needed for policy evaluation. Missing information can significantly influence query evaluation and pose significant risks to a large range of modern systems.

eXtensible Access Control Markup Language (XACML) [14], the de-facto standard for attribute-based access control, provides a mechanism to deal with missing attributes, but Crampton et al. [5] showed that the evaluation of a query can yield a decision that does not necessarily provide an intuitive interpretation on whether access should be granted or not due to the fact that some information needed for the evaluation might be missing. They subsequently proposed a novel approach that allows for an extended evaluation of ABAC policies. In a nutshell, they suggest that the evaluation of a given query is calculated using the evaluation of all queries that can be constructed from that query. However, their approach requires exploring the state space for all possible queries, which is exponential in the number of attribute values, and therefore not particularly efficient.

In this paper, we present a new approach for the extended evaluation of ABAC policies that addresses this drawback. We first encode ABAC policies using binary decision diagram (BDD)-based data structures, which provide a compact encoding for storing the decisions for each query and for efficient policy evaluation [1, 8, 9]. We then propose a new method to compute the extended evaluation directly on the BDD structure, taking into account *query constraints*, which are used to exclude those queries that are not possible within the system from the query space. We demonstrate our approach on two complex case studies, where a naïve approach would deal with a query space comprising several millions of states, whereas our approach compiles in a few seconds a compact decision diagram.

The remainder of this paper is structured as follows. The next section presents preliminaries on ABAC and the notion of extended evaluation. Section 3 introduces a motivating example and provides a formulation of the problem. Section 4 presents the notion of query constraints. Section 5 presents a novel algorithm to compute the extended query evaluation. Section 6 provides a validation of our approach on two real-world case studies. Finally, Section 7 discusses related work and Section 8 concludes the paper. We provide the proofs of the theorems in appendix.

2 PRELIMINARIES

This section presents a general view of how Attribute-Based Access Control (ABAC) policies and queries are evaluated using the PTaCL language [4], which is an abstraction of the XACML standard [14]. We first present the syntax of PTaCL, which is based on two different languages: one for targets, which is used to decide the applicability of a policy to a query, and another for policies, which is used to specify how policies are combined together. We then present the different evaluation functions for PTaCL: the standard one, introduced in [4] and the extended one, introduced in [5].

2.1 ABAC Syntax

We consider here the ABAC paradigm, where queries are defined as sets of attribute values (instead of the traditional triple subject, object, access mode). More precisely, let $\mathcal{A} = \{a_1, \ldots, a_n\}$ be a finite set of attributes, and given an attribute $a \in \mathcal{A}$, let $\mathcal{V}_a$ be the domain of a. Given a set of attributes $\mathcal{A}$, we write $\mathcal{V}_{\mathcal{A}}$ for the union of all attribute domains, i.e. $\mathcal{V}_{\mathcal{A}} = \bigcup_{a \in \mathcal{A}} \mathcal{V}_a$. The set of queries $Q_{\mathcal{A}}$ is then defined as $\wp(\bigcup_{i=1}^{n} a_i \times \mathcal{V}_{a_i})$, and a *query* $q = \{(a_1, v_1), \ldots, (a_k, v_k)\}$ is a set of attribute name-value pairs (a_i, v_i) such that $a_i \in \mathcal{A}$ and $v_i \in \mathcal{V}_{a_i}$. A query encompasses both a specific request for access, and a current view of the world relative to the different entities concerned by that request.

The PTaCL language is *tree-based*, i.e. policies are either atomic or constructed by composing other policies. This vision follows the traditional "separation of concerns" principle: each policy might regulate accesses to a specific sub-domain of an organization, or regulate accesses done by a specific category of users or in specific contexts. In order to identify which policies are applicable to which targets, PTaCL introduce a target language $\mathcal{T}_{\mathcal{A}}$, such that a target $t \in \mathcal{T}_{\mathcal{A}}$ is defined as:

$$t = (a, v) \mid \text{op}(t_1, \ldots, t_n)$$

where (a, v) is an attribute name-value pair, and op is an n-ary operator, defined over the set $\mathcal{D}_3 = \{1, 0, \bot\}$, indicating that the target matches the query, that the target does not match the query, and that it is indeterminate whether the target matches the query or not (the semantical evaluation of targets is described below). Crampton and Williams showed that the set of operators $\{\neg, E_1, \tilde{\sqcup}\}$ is canonically complete [6], i.e. any 3-valued operator can be constructed using these three operators. Table 1 presents these operators, as well as operators commonly used in ABAC languages.

PTaCL also defines a policy language $\mathcal{P}_{\mathcal{A}}$, where a policy $p \in \mathcal{P}_{\mathcal{A}}$ is defined as:

$$p = 1 \mid 0 \mid (t, p) \mid \text{op}(p_1, \ldots, p_n)$$

where 1 and 0 represent the *allow* and *deny* decisions respectively, (t, p) is a target policy and op is a n-ary operator, also defined on the three-valued set $\{1, 0, \bot\}$, where $\bot$ represents the *not-applicable* decision. Although this set is syntactically equivalent to the one used for targets, the meaning of the values in the set depends on

d_1	d_2	$\neg d_1$	$\sim d_1$	$E_1(d_1)$	$d_1 \tilde{\sqcap} d_2$	$d_1 \sqcap d_2$	$d_1 \triangle d_2$	$d_1 \tilde{\sqcup} d_2$	$d_1 \sqcup d_2$	$d_1 \triangledown d_2$
1	1	0	1	$\bot$	1	1	1	1	1	1
1	0	0	1	$\bot$	0	0	0	1	1	1
1	$\bot$	0	1	$\bot$	$\bot$	$\bot$	1	1	$\bot$	1
0	1	1	0	0	0	0	0	1	1	1
0	0	1	0	0	0	0	0	0	0	0
0	$\bot$	1	0	0	0	$\bot$	0	$\bot$	$\bot$	0
$\bot$	1	$\bot$	0	1	$\bot$	$\bot$	1	1	$\bot$	1
$\bot$	0	$\bot$	0	1	0	$\bot$	0	$\bot$	$\bot$	0
$\bot$	$\bot$	$\bot$	0	1	$\bot$	$\bot$	$\bot$	$\bot$	$\bot$	$\bot$

Table 1: Operators on the set $\mathcal{D}_3 = \{1, 0, \bot\}$

whether it is used as a target or as a policy. This should always be clear from the context in the remainder of this paper.

2.2 ABAC Evaluation

Given the set of policies $\mathcal{P}_{\mathcal{A}}$, the set of queries $Q_{\mathcal{A}}$ and a set of decisions $\mathcal{D}$, an evaluation function is a function $\llbracket \cdot \rrbracket : \mathcal{P}_{\mathcal{A}} \times Q_{\mathcal{A}} \to \mathcal{D}$ such that, given a query q and a policy p, $\llbracket p \rrbracket(q)$ represents the decision of evaluating p against q. PTaCL has three main policy evaluation functions, which handle missing attributes in a different way. For the sake of uniformity, hereafter we might use different notations than those in the original publications.

2.2.1 Standard Evaluation $\llbracket \cdot \rrbracket_P$: The standard evaluation consists in evaluating a target to $\bot$ when the attribute is completely missing from the query, to 0 if the attribute is present in the query, but without the appropriate value, and to 1 otherwise. A policy then evaluates to a set of decisions within $\mathcal{D}_7 = \wp(\{1, 0, \bot\}) \setminus \emptyset$ where 1 and 0 indicate that access should be granted or denied respectively, and $\bot$ that the policy is not applicable to a given query. Non-singleton decisions are returned when the query does not provide the information necessary to evaluate a target (i.e., the target evaluates to $\bot$). Intuitively, non-singleton decisions correspond to the Indeterminate decision in XACML [12].

More formally, the semantics of a target t is given by the function:

$$\llbracket \cdot \rrbracket_T : \mathcal{T}_{\mathcal{A}} \times Q_{\mathcal{A}} \to \mathcal{D}_3$$

$$\llbracket (a, v) \rrbracket_T(q) = \begin{cases} 1 & \text{if } (a, v) \in q \\ \bot & \text{if } \forall v' \in \mathcal{V}_a : (a, v') \notin q \\ 0 & \text{otherwise} \end{cases}$$

$$\llbracket \text{op}(t_1, \ldots, t_n) \rrbracket_T(q) = \text{op}(\llbracket t_1 \rrbracket_T(q), \ldots, \llbracket t_n \rrbracket_T(q))$$

The standard semantics of a policy p is given by the function:

$$\llbracket \cdot \rrbracket_P : \mathcal{P}_{\mathcal{A}} \times Q_{\mathcal{A}} \to \mathcal{D}_7$$
$$\llbracket 1 \rrbracket_P(q) = \{1\}$$
$$\llbracket 0 \rrbracket_P(q) = \{0\}$$

$$\llbracket (t, p) \rrbracket_P(q) = \begin{cases} \llbracket p \rrbracket_P(q) & \text{if } \llbracket t \rrbracket_T(q) = 1 \\ \{\bot\} & \text{if } \llbracket t \rrbracket_T(q) = 0 \\ \{\bot\} \cup \llbracket p \rrbracket_P(q) & \text{otherwise} \end{cases}$$

$$\llbracket \text{op}(p_1, \ldots, p_n) \rrbracket_P(q) = \text{op}^{\uparrow}(\llbracket p_1 \rrbracket_P(q), \ldots, \llbracket p_n \rrbracket_P(q))$$

where, given an operator op $: \mathcal{D}_3 \times \mathcal{D}_3 \to \mathcal{D}_3$ and any non-empty sets $X, Y \subseteq \mathcal{D}_3$, $\text{op}^{\uparrow} : \mathcal{D}_7 \times \mathcal{D}_7 \to \mathcal{D}_7$ is defined as

$op^\uparrow(X, Y) = \{op(x, y) \mid x \in X \wedge y \in Y\}$. Intuitively, $op^\uparrow$ corresponds to operator op extended in a point-wise way to sets of decisions.

2.2.2 Simplified Evaluation $[\![\cdot]\!]_B$: Crampton et al. [5] have shown that the standard evaluation, which is the one used by XACML, might yield a set of decisions that does not necessarily correspond to an intuitive interpretation of what those decisions mean due to missing attributes. In other words, given a policy, it is possible for a query to evaluate to a set of decisions D such that there exists a decision $d \in D$ for which the query extended with additional attribute values would not evaluate d, while there could be some decision $d' \notin D$ for which the query extended with some additional attribute values would evaluate to d'.

The authors have addressed the problem of missing attributes by proposing a novel evaluation mechanism based on non-deterministic attribute retrieval[1]. The fundamental intuition behind non-deterministic attribute retrieval is to model the fact that a query might represent a partial view of the world, whereby some attribute values are missing. In order to define the extended evaluation function, they first introduce the simplified evaluation function:

$$[\![\cdot]\!]_B : \mathcal{P}_\mathcal{A} \times Q_\mathcal{A} \to \mathcal{D}_3$$

$$[\![1]\!]_B(q) = 1$$

$$[\![0]\!]_B(q) = 0$$

$$[\![(t, p)]\!]_B(q) = \begin{cases} [\![p]\!]_B(q) & \text{if } [\![t]\!]_T(q) = 1 \\ \bot & \text{otherwise} \end{cases}$$

$$[\![op(p_1, \ldots, p_n)]\!]_B(q) = op([\![p_1]\!]_B(q), \ldots, [\![p_n]\!]_B(q))$$

The simplified evaluation function ignores missing attributes[2], and therefore always returns a single decision.

2.2.3 Extended Evaluation $[\![\cdot]\!]_E$: The intuition behind the extended ABAC evaluation is that a query should evaluate to all possible decisions that can be obtained by adding possibly missing attributes. Hereafter, we represent a query space as a directed acyclic graph (save for self-loops) $(Q_\mathcal{A}, \to)$, where $Q_\mathcal{A}$ is a set of queries, and $\to \subseteq Q_\mathcal{A} \times Q_\mathcal{A}$ is a relation such that, given two queries $q, q' \in Q_\mathcal{A}$, $q \to q'$ if, and only if $q' = q \cup \{(a, v)\}$ for some attribute a and some value v.

However, it was identified that some extensions of q may not be possible. For instance, for a given Boolean attribute, it might not make sense to have in the same query both *true* and *false* for that attribute. Hence, Crampton et al. introduce in [5] the notion of negative attribute value to explicitly indicate that an attribute cannot have a certain value in a given context and the notion of well-formed predicate wf : $Q_\mathcal{A} \to \mathbb{B}$ over queries to ensure that a query does not contain both an attribute value and its negation. Based on these notions, they define the extended evaluation function as:

$$[\![\cdot]\!]_E : \mathcal{P}_\mathcal{A} \times Q_\mathcal{A} \to \mathcal{D}_8 = \wp(\{1, 0, \bot\})$$

$$[\![p]\!]_E(q) = \{[\![p]\!]_B(q') \mid q \to^* q' \wedge \text{wf}(q')\}$$

where $\to^*$ denotes the reflexive-transitive closure of $\to$. With the restrictions imposed on $\to$, the relation $\to^*$ reduces to the subset

relation on queries. It is worth observing that $[\![\cdot]\!]_E$ returns the empty set for any query that does not satisfy wf.

3 PROBLEM STATEMENT

As discussed before, the standard ABAC evaluation function $[\![\cdot]\!]_P$ can yield a decision that does not necessarily provide an intuitive interpretation on whether access should be granted or not due to the fact that some information needed for the evaluation might be missing. To overcome the drawbacks of function $[\![\cdot]\!]_P$, given a policy p and a query q, a policy enforcement point (*i.e.*, the point in the system in charge of enabling an access query or not) can decide to evaluate $[\![p]\!]_E(q)$ in addition to $[\![p]\!]_B(q)$, to see whether any missing attribute could change the evaluation. However, the extended evaluation $[\![\cdot]\!]_E$ can lead to a very large query space to be explored, making policy evaluation inefficient. We exemplify these issues in the following example.

Consider a system wherein access is based on the nationality of users. In particular, the system allows Belgians to access system resources, whereas the Dutch are not. This policy can be represented as follows:

$$p = ((\textbf{nat}, \textsf{BE}), 1) \vartriangle ((\textbf{nat}, \textsf{NL}), 0)$$

Consider now a user submitting the query $q = \{(\textbf{nat}, \textsf{BE})\}$: this query evaluates to $[\![p]\!]_P(\{(\textbf{nat}, \textsf{BE})\}) = \{1\}$, *i.e.* the access would be granted. However, it is possible for a user to have multiple nationalities, and in some cases, it might be possible for a user to hide some nationalities[3]. In our case, the user might be hiding that she also has a Dutch nationality, in which case the access should have been denied since $[\![p]\!]_P(\{(\textbf{nat}, \textsf{BE}), (\textbf{nat}, \textsf{NL})\}) = \{0\}$.

To address this issue, we can use the extended evaluation function $[\![\cdot]\!]_E$. In particular, we obtain $[\![p]\!]_E(\{(\textbf{nat}, \textsf{BE})\}) = \{1, 0\}$ indicating that there exists a query (*i.e.*, a view of the world) reachable from q that should be denied. Computing $[\![p]\!]_E(q)$, however, requires evaluating all the queries that can be constructed from the initial query q. There are 206 sovereign states recognized by the United Nations,[4] and users can have more than one nationality. This leads to two main problems:

- A naïve implementation of $[\![\cdot]\!]_E$ requires evaluating 2^{205} queries (*i.e.*, the queries that can be constructed from the initial query $\{(\textbf{nat}, \textsf{BE})\}$), which is clearly infeasible.
- Some combination of nationalities are not possible, due to specific country restrictions on dual nationality, which can lead to misleading decisions.

Concerning the first problem, it is worth observing that, although there is no limit on the number of nationalities individuals can hold according to international laws, this number is usually limited. For the sake of exemplification, we assume here that individuals cannot hold more than three nationalities. Accordingly, the number of queries to be constructed from the initial query $\{(\textbf{nat}, \textsf{BE})\}$ and evaluated is $21, 116$.[5] Although this is still a large number, it is

---

[1]They also consider probabilistic attribute retrieval, which is beyond the scope of this paper.

[2]In XACML, this would correspond to no attribute indicated as *must-be-present*.

[3]For instance illustrated in 2017 with the Australian parliament, where seven members of parliament were revealed to hold dual nationalities and therefore were not eligible.

[4]https://en.wikipedia.org/wiki/List_of_sovereign_states

[5]The number of queries to be evaluated is the number of combinations of at most three nationalities where one nationality is Belgian, *i.e.* $\sum_{k=0}^{2} \binom{205}{k}$.

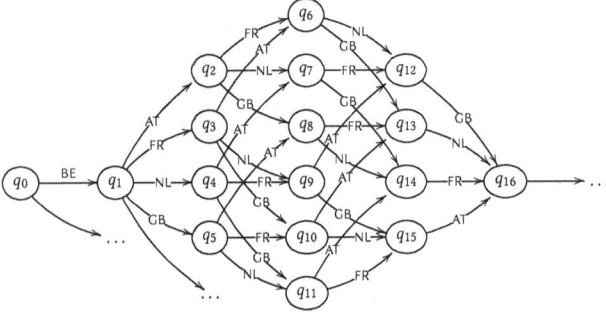

Figure 1: Portion of the query space

negligible with respect to the number of requests that have to be constructed without considering this domain constraint.

To visually represent the problem, consider (the portion of) the query space in Fig. 1, which is explored in the evaluation of p. In the figure, nodes represent queries (with q_0 the empty query) and edges are annotated with a label indicating how a query has been extended, *i.e.* $q_i \overset{\text{NL}}{\longrightarrow} q_j$ denotes $q_j = q_i \cup \{(\mathbf{nat}, \text{NL})\}$. If we consider that no user has more than three nationalities, then all queries formed by four or more attribute name-value pairs are not reachable from the initial state (*i.e.*, queries q_{12} to q_{16} in Fig. 1) as they are not plausible views of the world.

More importantly, ignoring domain constraints can result in decisions that cannot be reached in practice, thus providing misleading information for decision making. Suppose for instance that Austria does not allow dual nationality with the Netherlands[6]. In this case, we should exclude from the state space any query containing $\{(\mathbf{nat}, \text{NL}), (\mathbf{nat}, \text{AT})\}$, in which case, given the query $\{(\mathbf{nat}, \text{AT})\}$, we have $[\![p]\!]_E(\{(\mathbf{nat}, \text{AT})\}) = \{1, \bot\}$. In other words, it is impossible for this request to be denied, even if some attribute is missing. Note that, according to the standard evaluation, $[\![p]\!]_P(\{(\mathbf{nat}, \text{AT})\}) = \{\bot\}$ regardless the existence of the domain constraint.

In the remainder of the paper, we will exploit these observations to establish the foundations for the design of practical policy engines supporting the extended evaluation of attribute-based access control policies. In particular:

- We introduce the notion of *query constraints* to identify which views of the world are plausible based on domain specific requirements and assumptions, thus constructing a realistic query space (Section 4).
- We investigate practical approaches for the computation and representation of the extended evaluation $[\![\cdot]\!]_E$ of a given policy (Section 5).

4 QUERY CONSTRAINTS

As shown above, a non-deterministic evaluation of ABAC policies requires the construction of all possible views of the world from a given query, leading to a huge number of queries to be evaluated. However, many of these views may not be possible in practice. In fact, a system can be characterized by domain requirements and assumptions that determine which views of the world are plausible

---

[6]Actual rules for dual-nationality tend to be very complex, and we do not go into any detail here.

and which are not. The main problem lies in the fact that domain requirements and assumptions are typically defined outside the authorization mechanism and, thus, not available for policy evaluation.

It is worth emphasizing here that there is a fundamental distinction between queries that are not possible and queries that should be denied. In the previous section, a query including both Austrian and Dutch nationalities is neither denied or granted, but considered instead as not possible.

To address this issue, we introduce the notion of *query constraint*. Intuitively, query constraints encode domain requirements and are used to reduce the portion of the query space to be explored (*i.e.*, the number of queries that are reachable from the initial query).

Syntactically speaking, the language for constraints $C_{\mathcal{A}}$ is such that a constraint $c \in C_{\mathcal{A}}$ is defined as:

$$c = (a, v) \mid \text{op}(c_1, \ldots, c_n)$$

where a is attribute, v in an attribute value, and op is a Boolean operator. The only difference between $C_{\mathcal{A}}$ and $\mathcal{T}_{\mathcal{A}}$ (defined in Section 2.1) is that we do not consider three-valued operators for constraints. We therefore have $C_{\mathcal{A}} \subseteq \mathcal{T}_{\mathcal{A}}$, since any Boolean operator trivially corresponds to a three-valued operator. The evaluation of a constraint is given by the function:

$$[\![\cdot]\!]_C : C_{\mathcal{A}} \times Q_{\mathcal{A}} \to \mathbb{B}$$

$$[\![(a, v)]\!]_C(q) = \begin{cases} 1 & \text{if } (a, v) \in q \\ 0 & \text{otherwise} \end{cases}$$

$$[\![\text{op}(t_1, \ldots, t_n)]\!]_C(q) = \text{op}([\![t_1]\!]_C(q), \ldots, [\![t_n]\!]_C(q))$$

Example 1. Some countries such as Singapore, Austria and India, do not allow dual nationality, leading to automatic loss of citizenship upon acquiring another nationality. Other countries restrict dual nationality to certain countries. For instance, Pakistan allows double nationality only with 16 countries and Spain allows only with certain Latin American countries, Andorra, Portugal, the Philippines and Equatorial Guinea. These requirements can be modeled using query constraints. For instance, the following constraint indicates that it is not possible to have both Austrian and Dutch citizenships: $\neg((\mathbf{nat}, \text{AT}) \wedge (\mathbf{nat}, \text{NL}))$.

Some constraints might be more complex to build. For instance, we might want to have cardinality constraints specifying the maximum number of values a particular attribute can take. However, there is no Boolean operator expressing directly such constraints. Instead, given an attribute a and a number k, we can generate the corresponding constraint enumerating all possible cases. We first write $\mathcal{A}_{|a} = \{(a, v) \mid v \in \mathcal{V}_a\}$ for the set of all attribute values for a. We then write $C_{a,k} = \{s \subseteq \mathcal{A}_{|a} \mid |s| = k + 1\}$ for the set of subsets of $\mathcal{A}_{|a}$ with a cardinality equal to $k + 1$. Finally, the *cardinality constraint* expressing that an attribute can have at most k values can be expressed as:

$$\text{card}_{a,k} = \bigwedge_{s \in C_{a,k}} \neg \bigwedge_{(a,v) \in s} (a, v)$$

Any query containing more than k values for attribute a would have at least one set $s \in C_{a,k}$ for which the conjunction of the attribute values would be true, rendering the whole conjunction $\text{card}_{a,k}$ false.

Example 2. Consider the scenario in Section 3, such that, for the sake of exposition, we only consider six possible nationalities: FR, AT, GB, DE, BE and NL. The constraint that individuals cannot hold more than three nationalities can be expressed by the constraint $card_{nat,3}$, which consists of 30 conjunctions of conjunctions:

$$card_{nat,3} = \quad \neg((nat, FR) \wedge (nat, AT) \wedge (nat, GB) \wedge (nat, DE))$$
$$\wedge \neg((nat, FR) \wedge (nat, AT) \wedge (nat, GB) \wedge (nat, BE))$$
$$\wedge \ldots$$
$$\wedge \neg((nat, GB) \wedge (nat, DE) \wedge (nat, BE) \wedge (nat, NL))$$

As demonstrated by the example above, the cardinality constraint for an attribute a can only be constructed in this form when the attribute domain $\mathcal{V}_a$ is finite. In this paper, our encoding of ABAC policies requires anyway finite domains for attributes, and we leave the investigation of infinite attribute domains for future work. Hereafter, given a set of constraints C, we write $Q_{\mathcal{A}|C}$ for the set $\{q \in Q_{\mathcal{A}} \mid \forall c \in C \; [\![c]\!]_C(q) = 1\}$.

5 EFFICIENT EXTENDED EVALUATION COMPUTATION

In the previous section, we introduced the notion of query constraint. The use of query constraints has the advantage to remove queries that are not possible. We next propose an algorithm for computing the extended evaluation function $[\![\cdot]\!]_E$. Along the lines of previous work (*e.g.*, [1, 8, 9]), our algorithm relies on the use of *binary decision diagram* (BDD) for the representation of ABAC policies, query constraints and the query space. We evaluate this approach in the following section.

We first briefly review the essential concepts behind BDDs and how we use them to represent the aforementioned artifacts. For a more in-depth treatment of the underlying algorithmics for constructing and manipulating BDDs, we refer to [2].

Let *Vars* be a finite set of Boolean variables. A propositional formula over *Vars* can be efficiently represented by a BDD. Formally, a BDD is a graph-based data structure defined as follows:

Definition 1. A binary decision diagram (BDD) is a rooted directed acyclic graph with vertex set V containing the terminal vertices 0 and 1, and non-terminal vertices that are labelled (using a function L) with variables from *Vars*. Non-terminal vertices have exactly one outgoing high edge (denoted *hi*) and one outgoing low edge (denoted *lo*). Terminal vertices have no outgoing edges.

A BDD is said to be *reduced* if it contains no vertex v with $lo(v) = hi(v)$, nor does it contain two distinct vertices v and v' whose subgraphs (*i.e.*, the BDDs rooted in v and v') are isomorphic. In this work, we are only concerned with reduced BDDs.

We assume a fixed ordering $<$ on the Boolean variables *Vars*. A propositional formula can be represented uniquely (up-to-isomorphism) by a (reduced) BDD by labeling each non-terminal vertex v with a Boolean variable $L(v)$, ensuring that each successor vertex v' of v is either a terminal vertex or a vertex labeled with a Boolean variable $L(v') < L(v)$. The formula $F(v)$, represented by a BDD with root v, is obtained as follows:

$$F(v) = \begin{cases} false & \text{if } v = 0 \\ true & \text{if } v = 1 \\ (L(v) \implies F(hi(v))) \wedge (\neg L(v) \implies F(lo(v))) & \text{otherwise} \end{cases}$$

Checking whether a concrete truth-assignment to the Boolean variables is such that the propositional formula represented by the BDD holds reduces to checking whether in the BDD, the path associated with the variable assignment leads to terminal vertex 1. That is, the runtime complexity for evaluating whether such a truth-assignment makes a formula true is linear in the depth of the BDD, which, in turn, is limited by the size of *Vars*. BDDs can be used effectively for representing and computing the extended evaluation; we explain how this is done in the remainder of this section.

Henceforward, let $(Q_{\mathcal{A}|C}, \rightarrow)$ be a fixed constrained query space ranging over a set of attribute names $\mathcal{A}$ and attribute domains $\mathcal{V}_{\mathcal{A}}$. We represent each attribute name-value pair $(a, v) \in \mathcal{A} \times \mathcal{V}_{\mathcal{A}}$ by a Boolean variable a_v. The set of all Boolean variables is denoted $Vars_{\mathcal{A}}$. A truth-assignment to all Boolean variables represents a single query. A set of queries can be represented as a propositional formula over these variables. For instance, the propositional formula $\neg(nat_{AT} \wedge nat_{NL})$ encodes the set of all queries except those queries that contain both attribute name-value pairs (nat, AT) and (nat, NL). A query q induces an *interpretation* $I(q)$ which is defined as $I(q)(a_v) = true$ iff $(a, v) \in q$. Given an interpretation $I(q)$ and a propositional formula ϕ, we write $I(q) \models \phi$ iff the formula evaluates to *true* under interpretation $I(q)$.

The main idea behind our approach is as follows. Given a fixed policy p, we construct a triple $(e_1, e_0, e_\perp)$ of propositional formulae representing sets of queries Q_1, Q_0 and $Q_\perp$ such that $d \in [\![p]\!]_E(q)$ exactly when $q \in Q_d$. We represent these propositional formulae using (reduced) BDDs. For computing the triple of propositional formulae $(e_1, e_0, e_\perp)$, we use the following formulae:

(1) a triple of propositional formulae $(b_1, b_0, b_\perp)$ representing $[\![p]\!]_B$,

(2) a propositional formula S encoding the constrained query space $Q_{\mathcal{A}|C}$,

(3) a propositional formula R encoding relation $\rightarrow^*$ on $Q_{\mathcal{A}|C}$.

The triple of propositional formulae $(b_1, b_0, b_\perp)$ representing $[\![p]\!]_B$ is computed recursively using transformations τ and π employing the inductive definition of the policy language. More specifically, each b_d is a propositional formula representing a set of queries $Q_d \subseteq Q_{\mathcal{A}}$ satisfying $d = [\![p]\!]_B(q)$ whenever $q \in Q_d$. Hereafter, we write $\tau_d(t)$ and $\pi_i(p)$ for the formulae representing decision d in the transformation $\tau(t)$ and $\pi(p)$, respectively. The transformation rules for τ (for targets) and π (for policies) given in Table 2 explain the construction of the propositional formula for decision 1 for all targets, (policy) constants and all (policy and target) operators of Table 1. The rules for constructing the propositional formulae for decisions 0 and $\perp$, given by $\tau_0(t)$, $\pi_0(p)$, $\tau_\perp(t)$ and $\pi_\perp(p)$, are similar (see Appendix). The correctness of the propositional formulae $\tau_d(t)$ and $\pi_d(p)$ is stated by the following lemma.

LEMMA 1. *For all* $q \in Q_{\mathcal{A}}$:
(a) $I(q) \models \tau_d(t)$ *iff* $d = [\![t]\!]_T(q)$,
(b) $I(q) \models \pi_d(p)$ *iff* $d = [\![p]\!]_B(q)$.

Example 3. Let us reconsider policy p introduced in Section 3. By applying transformations τ_1 and π_1 in Table 2 to p, we obtain (after minor simplification) the following propositional formula:

$$\pi_1(p) = nat_{BE} \wedge \neg nat_{NL}$$

$\tau_1((a, v))$	=	a_v
$\tau_1(\neg t_1)$	=	$\tau_0(t_1)$
$\tau_1(\sim t_1)$	=	$\tau_1(t_1)$
$\tau_1(E_1(t_1))$	=	$\tau_\perp(t_1)$
$\tau_1(t_1 \mathbin{\tilde{\sqcap}} t_2)$	=	$\tau_1(t_1) \wedge \tau_1(t_2)$
$\tau_1(t_1 \sqcap t_2)$	=	$\tau_1(t_1) \wedge \tau_1(t_2)$
$\tau_1(t_1 \mathbin{\triangle} t_2)$	=	$(\tau_1(t_1) \wedge \neg\tau_0(t_2)) \vee (\tau_1(t_2) \wedge \neg\tau_0(t_1))$
$\tau_1(t_1 \mathbin{\tilde{\sqcup}} t_2)$	=	$\tau_1(t_1) \vee \tau_1(t_2)$
$\tau_1(t_1 \sqcup t_2)$	=	$(\tau_1(t_1) \wedge \neg\tau_\perp(t_2)) \vee (\tau_1(t_2) \wedge \neg\tau_\perp(t_1))$
$\tau_1(t_1 \mathbin{\triangledown} t_2)$	=	$\tau_1(t_1) \vee \tau_1(t_2)$
$\pi_1(1)$	=	$true$
$\pi_1(0)$	=	$false$
$\pi_1((t, p_1))$	=	$\tau_1(t) \wedge \pi_1(p_1)$
$\pi_1(\neg p_1)$	=	$\pi_0(p_1)$
$\pi_1(\sim p_1)$	=	$\pi_1(p_1)$
$\pi_1(E_1(p_1))$	=	$\pi_\perp(p_1)$
$\pi_1(p_1 \mathbin{\tilde{\sqcap}} p_2)$	=	$\pi_1(p_1) \wedge \pi_1(p_2)$
$\pi_1(p_1 \sqcap p_2)$	=	$\pi_1(p_1) \wedge \pi_1(p_2)$
$\pi_1(p_1 \mathbin{\triangle} p_2)$	=	$(\pi_1(p_1) \wedge \neg\pi_0(p_2)) \vee (\pi_1(p_2) \wedge \neg\pi_0(p_1))$
$\pi_1(p_1 \mathbin{\tilde{\sqcup}} p_2)$	=	$\pi_1(p_1) \vee \pi_1(p_2)$
$\pi_1(p_1 \sqcup p_2)$	=	$(\pi_1(p_1) \wedge \neg\pi_\perp(p_2)) \vee (\pi_1(p_2) \wedge \neg\pi_\perp(p_1))$
$\pi_1(p_1 \mathbin{\triangledown} p_2)$	=	$\pi_1(p_1) \vee \pi_1(p_2)$

Table 2: Transformation rules for τ (for targets) and π (for policies) for the case 1; the rules for the cases 0 and $\perp$ are similar and can be deduced from the semantics of $[\![\_]\!]_T$ and $[\![\_]\!]_B$.

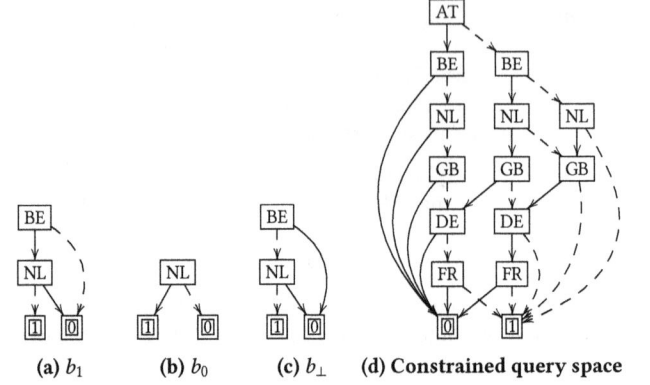

Figure 2: BDDs $(b_1, b_0, b_\perp)$ and constrained query space for the policy in Section 3

Fig. 2a shows the corresponding BDD. The BDDs corresponding to $\pi_0(p)$ (Fig. 2b) and $\pi_\perp(p)$ (Fig. 2c) can be obtained in a similar way. In the figures, solid arrows indicate that the path of the BDD in case a given attribute value is present in the query (*i.e.* the *hi*-edge), whereas dashed arrows indicate that the attribute value is not present (*i.e.* the *lo*-edge); terminal nodes are represented using a double line rectangle. These BDDs show that any query including attribute name-value pair (**nat**, NL) evaluates to 0 and any query including attribute name-value pair (**nat**, BE) (and not (**nat**, NL)) evaluates to 1; if both (**nat**, BE) and (**nat**, NL) are not present, the query evaluates to $\perp$.

The propositional formula S representing the constrained query space $Q_{\mathcal{A}|C}$ can be readily constructed by reusing transformation τ, since the constraint language $C_{\mathcal{A}}$ is essentially a subset of the target language $\mathcal{T}_{\mathcal{A}}$. The constrained query space can therefore be represented by the following propositional formula for S:

$$\bigwedge \{\tau_1(c) \mid c \in C\}$$

Example 4. Fig. 2d shows a BDD encoding a constrained query space. It is obtained by applying transformation τ to the cardinality constraint in Example 2 (*i.e.*, $card_{\mathbf{nat},3}$) in conjunction with a query constraint imposing that individuals having an Austrian nationality cannot have dual nationality. It is easy to observe in the BDD that queries including attribute name-value pair (**nat**, AT) and any other nationalities are invalid (left part of Fig. 2d); queries that contain four nationalities are invalid as well and thus all map to terminal vertex 0.

For representing the relation $\rightarrow^*$, we introduce a set of copies of all Boolean variables; that is, for each variable a_v, we introduce a unique copy a'_v representing the value of a_v in a reachable query. We denote the set of variables consisting of these copies by $Vars'_{\mathcal{A}}$. Since $\rightarrow^*$ is in essence the subset relation, the proposition R encoding this relation is constructed by conjunctively composing the propositional formulae $a_v \implies a'_v$. The correctness of this encoding is given by the following lemma.

LEMMA 2. *Let $q, q' \in Q_{\mathcal{A}}$. Let $I(q)$ denote the interpretation for Vars and $I'(q')$ the interpretation for Vars', defined as $I'(q')(a'_v) = true$ iff $(a, v) \in q'$. We then have $I(q) \cup I'(q') \models \bigwedge\{a_v \implies a'_v \mid a_v \in Vars\}$ iff $(q, q') \in \rightarrow^*$.*

Note that we also need to ensure that only queries from the set represented by S are considered. We achieve this by strengthening the transition relation using the propositional formula S. This leads to the following propositional formula for the transition relation R:

$$S \wedge S[Vars_{\mathcal{A}} := Vars'_{\mathcal{A}}] \wedge \bigwedge\{a_v \implies a'_v \mid a_v \in Vars_{\mathcal{A}}\}$$

The substitution notation we use in this formula is short-hand for replacing each unprimed variable by its primed counterpart in the propositional formula.

Using the triple $(b_1, b_0, b_\perp)$, the constrained query space encoded by S and the transition relation encoded by R, we can compute a triple of propositional formulae $(e_1, e_0, e_\perp)$ representing $[\![p]\!]_E$ using a backwards reachability analysis. Since our transition relation R is transitively closed, it essentially suffices to use R to compute all immediate predecessors of b_1, b_0 and $b_\perp$. The computation of predecessors can be performed effectively on the level of BDDs using a standard encoding of the existential quantification over all primed variables. For e_1, this boils down to computing the (reduced) BDD for the following formula:

$$(S \wedge b_1) \vee \exists Vars'_{\mathcal{A}}.(R \wedge (b_1[Vars_{\mathcal{A}} := Vars'_{\mathcal{A}}]))$$

The computation of e_0 and $e_\perp$ proceeds analogously. We summarize the steps we take to compute the extended evaluation in Algorithm 1. The correctness of the algorithm is stated in the following theorem.

THEOREM 3. *Procedure COMPUTEEXTENDEDEVALUATION computes, for a given policy p and a constrained query space $(Q_{\mathcal{A}|C}, \rightarrow)$, a triple $(e_1, e_0, e_\perp)$ of BDDs representing sets $(Q_1, Q_0, Q_\perp)$ satisfying, for each $q \in Q_{\mathcal{A}}$, $q \in Q_d$ iff $q \in Q_{\mathcal{A}|C} \wedge d \in [\![p]\!]_E(q)$.*

As we explained above, testing whether a truth-assignment to all variables makes a propositional formula true can be done in worst-case time $O(|Vars|)$. As a consequence, the BDDs $(e_1, e_0, e_\perp)$ that are computed by Algorithm 1 can be used to simply and efficiently evaluate a policy p for a concrete query q using the extended evaluation $[\![\cdot]\!]_E$: for each $d \in \{1, 0, \perp\}$, one evaluates at run-time

Algorithm 1 Pseudo code for computing the extended evaluation for a policy p and constrained query space $(Q_{\mathcal{A}|C}, \rightarrow)$.

1: **procedure** COMPUTEEXTENDEDEVALUATION
2: $\quad (b_1, b_0, b_\perp) := (\pi_1(p), \pi_0(p), \pi_\perp(p))$
3: $\quad S := \bigwedge\{\tau_1(c) \mid c \in C\}$
4: $\quad R := S \wedge S[Vars_{\mathcal{A}} := Vars'_{\mathcal{A}}] \wedge \bigwedge\{a_v \implies a'_v \mid a_v \in Vars_{\mathcal{A}}\}$
5: $\quad$ **for** $d \in \{1, 0, \perp\}$ **do**
6: $\qquad e_d := (S \wedge b_d) \vee \exists Vars'_{\mathcal{A}}.(R \wedge (b_d[Vars_{\mathcal{A}} := Vars'_{\mathcal{A}}]))$
7: $\quad$ **end for**
8: $\quad$ **return** $(e_1, e_0, e_\perp)$
9: **end procedure**

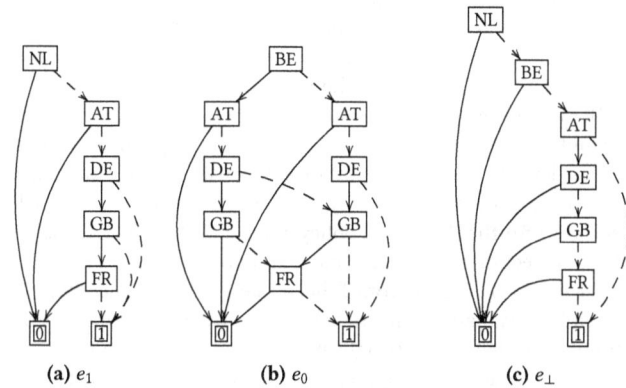

(a) e_1 (b) e_0 (c) $e_\perp$

Figure 3: BDDs $(e_1, e_0, e_\perp)$ for the policy in Section 3

whether $d \in [\![p]\!]_E(q)$ by inspecting BDD e_d, in worst-case time $O(|Vars|)$.

Example 5. Fig. 3 illustrates the BDDs $(e_1, e_0, e_\perp)$ encoding the extended evaluation of the policy in Example 4 augmented with the constrained query space in Fig. 2d. The BDD in Fig. 3a shows that a query will never be evaluated to 1 if it contains attribute name-value pairs (**nat**, NL) and (**nat**, AT). In fact, any query containing (**nat**, NL) is always evaluated to 0 as shown in Fig. 2b and a query containing (**nat**, AT) cannot be extended as imposed by query constraints. The other paths in the BDD indicate that a query not including those attribute name-value pairs can potentially be evaluated to 1 as the query can be extended with attribute name-value pair (**nat**, BE) unless the query already includes three nationalities (the maximum number of nationalities allowed in our scenario). Similar observations holds for the other BDDs in Fig. 3.

6 CASE STUDIES

In this section, we demonstrate our approach to compute BDDs encoding the extended evaluation of ABAC policies using two real-world policies, namely the CONTINUE policy and the SAFAX policy. The approach has been implemented in Python using the dd library[7] (v. 0.5.2). In our experiments, we also compared the standard evaluation function $[\![\cdot]\!]_P$ and the extended evaluation function $[\![\cdot]\!]_E$. To this end, we have also implemented the construction of BDDs encoding function $[\![\cdot]\!]_P$ using the dd library by extending the transformation rules τ and π presented in Section 5. The experiments

---

[7] https://github.com/johnyf/dd

	Policy Size			#Var	#Value Constraints	#Cardinality Constraints
	#PS	#P	#R			
CONTINUE	111	266	298	47	10	2
SAFAX (10)	5	18	35	54	36	5
SAFAX (20)	5	18	35	84	36	5
SAFAX (50)	5	18	35	174	36	5

Table 3: Overview of the datasets used for the experiments

were performed using a machine with 2.30GHz Intel Xeon processor and 16 GB of RAM.

6.1 Datasets

This section provides an overview of the two real-world policies used for our demonstration. Both policies are specified in XACML v2 [13]. XACML has several commonalities with PTaCL; in particular, it has been shown in previous work [12] that XACML policies can be encoded in PTaCL. For the sake of space, we refer to [12] for the details of the encoding. A summary of the policies and datasets constructed from them is given in Table 3. In the table, we report the size of the policies (in terms of number of policysets (**#PS**), policies (**#P**) and rules (**#R**)), the number of variables used to encode the policy (**#Var**) and the number of cardinality and value constraints (*i.e.*, query constraints excluding that two different attribute values can be present at the same time).

CONTINUE: CONTINUE is a conference manager system that supports the submission, review, discussion and notification phases of conferences. The CONTINUE policy[8] consists of 111 policysets that, in turn, consist of 266 policies comprising 298 rules. The target of policysets, policies and rules are defined over 14 attributes ranging from the role of users (role) within the conference management system, the type of resource accessed (resource_class) and the action for which access is requested (action_type) to attributes used to characterize the existence of conflicts of interest (isConflicted) and the status of the review process (isReviewContentInPlace, isPending, etc.). Some of these attributes are Boolean, whereas others, such as role and resource_class, take values from a more complex domain. In total, the union of the attribute domains for the CONTINUE policy consists of 47 attribute values.

Together with the policy we specified 10 value constraints. In particular, 9 constraints were used to enforce that Boolean attributes can be either *true* or *false*. The other value constraint was used to impose that subreviewers cannot be PC members as required by CONTINUE [8]. Moreover, we defined two cardinality constraints to restrict the values that attributes resource_class and action_type can take as suggested in [8].

SAFAX: SAFAX [10] is an XACML-based framework that offers authorization as a service. SAFAX provides a web interface through which users can create, manage and configure their authorization services. The SAFAX policy is used to regulate the action users can perform on the web interface. The SAFAX policy consists of 5 policysets, 18 policies and 35 rules. The target of these policy elements are built over 8 attributes ranging from the group(s) a user belongs to (group), the type of object to be accessed (type) and

---

[8] http://www.margrave-tool.org/v1+v2/margrave/versions/01-01/examples/continue/

the action to be performed on the object (action) to the number of objects a user has already created (count-project, count-demo, count-ppdp) and the relation of the user with the object (isowner, match_project). The last two attributes are Boolean, whereas the others have a more complex domain. In particular, three attributes range over integer numbers. To test the scalability of our approach, we varied the size of the domain of these attributes. In particular, we generated three datasets – SAFAX (10), SAFAX (20) and SAFAX (50) – where the number in parentheses represents the size of the domain of numerical attributes.

We also defined a number of query constraints that reflect the functioning of the system. Besides introducing constraints for Boolean attributes and cardinality constraints for numerical attributes, we restricted the number of object types and actions that can occur in a request. This is motivated by the fact that, in SAFAX, an object can have only one type and access requests are triggered to determine whether a user is allowed to perform a certain action. Moreover, certain actions can be performed only on certain types of objects. We modeled these domain requirements using value constraints. We also defined constraints to restrict the groups a user can belong to simultaneously. Users should register to SAFAX to use the web application. Nonetheless, SAFAX also provides a guest account (with limited functionalities) that allows the use of the application without registration. Guest users are assigned to a special group that is incompatible with other groups. We capture this requirement using value constraints. In total, we complemented the policy with 36 value constraints and 5 cardinality constraints.

6.2 Results

This section presents the results of our experiments. First, we analyze the BDDs obtained using the extended evaluation $[\![\cdot]\!]_E$ and its feasibility in real scenarios. Then, we compare $[\![\cdot]\!]_E$ with the standard evaluation $[\![\cdot]\!]_P$. Finally, we present lessons learned from our experiments and discuss the limitations of the approach.

Analysis of extended evaluation function $[\![\cdot]\!]_E$. For each dataset, Table 4 shows the size of the BDDs obtained using the simplified evaluation function $[\![\cdot]\!]_B$ presented in Section 2.2, and the size of the BDDs obtained using the extended evaluation function $[\![\cdot]\!]_E$ with and without constraints. In particular, for each BDD, the table reports the number of vertices and the depth of the BDD. The depth of BDDs is particularly important as it affects policy evaluation. Table 5 reports the size of the BDDs encoding the constrained query space for the datasets, which represent the set of valid queries (*i.e.*, the queries that satisfy the constraints) along with the number of valid queries. This latter information provides an indication of the size of the constrained query space. Moreover, the table reports the percentage of queries that evaluate to 1, 0 and ⊥ for $[\![\cdot]\!]_B$ and $[\![\cdot]\!]_E$. One can observe that, for $[\![\cdot]\!]_E$, the sum of percentages is greater than 100%. Recall from Section 2 that $[\![\cdot]\!]_E$ is defined over $\mathcal{D}_8 = \wp(\{1, 0, \perp\})$.

The reported statistics were obtained after applying the garbage collection and reordering functions provided by the dd library. The garbage collector function deletes unreferenced nodes. Reordering is used to change the variable order to reduce the size of the BDD representation. In particular, it uses Rudell's sifting algorithm [15], a widely used heuristics for dynamic reordering, to search for a better (fixed) order of variables compared the one currently used. Moreover, the reordering function is nondeterministic in the sense that it can return different orders of variables for the same input set of BDDs. This explains the differences in the number of nodes between the BDDs encoding the simplified evaluation of the SAFAX policy (top-left block of Table 4).[9]

In Table 4 (top-right block), we can observe that the BDDs encoding the extended evaluation without constraints for decision 1 consist of only one vertex. This vertex is the terminal vertex *true*, indicating that all queries can be potentially evaluated to 1. This is due to how the CONTINUE and SAFAX policies are defined. For instance, in the CONTINUE policy positive authorizations have a higher priority than negative authorizations, *i.e.* all XACML policy elements are combined using the first-applicable combining algorithm and *Permit* rules always occur at the top, thus yielding *Permit* whenever they are applicable. Similarly, the SAFAX policy employs a number of *Deny* rules but they are only used as default rules. Thus, if all attribute values are provided in the query, both policies evaluate 1. This demonstrates the importance of constraints. By looking at Table 5, we can observe that only 59% of queries could actually yield decision 1 for the CONTINUE policy and 97% for the SAFAX policy. Thus, neglecting constraints can result in misleading decisions.

We can also observe from Table 4 that the BDDs encoding the simplified evaluation and the extended evaluation without constraints (top-left and top-right blocks, resp.) for ⊥ are the same. This is expected as the applicability of both the CONTINUE and SAFAX policies is monotonic; if they apply to a query, they also apply to all queries that can be constructed from it. Thus, it is not possible that a query evaluates to ⊥ according to $[\![\cdot]\!]_E$ but not according to $[\![\cdot]\!]_B$. We can also observe that, for the SAFAX policy, these BDDs are relative small (7 nodes and depth equal to 6) and, from Table 5, that they cover about 16% of the query space. This is due to the use of default *Deny* rules mentioned above. As a matter of fact, these rules map most of the queries for which a positive authorization is not specified to 0.

As discussed in Section 5, the depth of a BDD is upper bounded by the number of variables. We can observe in Table 4 (bottom-left and bottom-right blocks) that, for the SAFAX policy with constraints, the depth of BDDs is exactly equal to the number of variables. This is due to the fact that the constraints defined for this policy involve all attribute values. This is also visible by observing in Table 3 that the depth of the BDDs representing the constrained query space is equal to the number of variables, indicating that all variables are used to determine the validity of queries.

Feasibility of extended evaluation function $[\![\cdot]\!]_E$. To assess the feasibility of the approach, we considered the time needed to generate the BDDs encoding the extended evaluation of the CONTINUE and SAFAX policies along with the corresponding query constraints and the memory required to store the generated BDDs. Table 6 reports the time required to generate the BDDs encoding the extended evaluation on the constrained query space. From the table, we can observe that the construction of BDDs for the CONTINUE policies required about 1.5s, whereas less than one

---

[9]Recall that these BDDs only encode the evaluation of the given policy and, thus, only constrain the values occurring in the policy, which are the same in all three datasets.

| | | Simplified $[\![\cdot]\!]_B$ | | | | | | Extended $[\![\cdot]\!]_E$ | | | | | |
| | | BDD$_1$ | | BDD$_0$ | | BDD$_\perp$ | | BDD$_1$ | | BDD$_0$ | | BDD$_\perp$ | |
		#Vertex	Depth	#Vertex	Depth	#Vertex	Depth	#Vertex	Depth	#Vertex	Depth	#Vertex	Depth
no constraints	Continue	1085	31	496	29	579	29	1	0	147	24	579	29
	SAFAX (10)	347	24	370	24	7	6	1	0	430	24	7	6
	SAFAX (20)	369	24	407	24	7	6	1	0	450	24	7	6
	SAFAX (50)	343	24	366	24	7	6	1	0	427	24	7	6
constraints	Continue	1156	46	510	46	846	46	594	44	672	46	830	46
	SAFAX (10)	513	54	455	54	108	54	255	54	497	54	108	54
	SAFAX (20)	949	84	920	84	188	84	375	84	762	84	188	84
	SAFAX (50)	1587	174	1551	174	428	174	735	174	1540	174	428	174

Table 4: Overview of the BDDs encoding the simplified $[\![\cdot]\!]_B$ and extended $[\![\cdot]\!]_E$ evaluation with/without constraints

| | #Vertex | Depth | #Queries | Simplified $[\![\cdot]\!]_B$ | | | Extended $[\![\cdot]\!]_E$ | | |
				BDD$_1$	BDD$_0$	BDD$_\perp$	BDD$_1$	BDD$_0$	BDD$_\perp$
Continue	63	44	134,631,720	20.09%	32.28%	47.52%	59.10%	41.48%	47.52%
SAFAX (10)	128	54	7,331,148	55.43%	28.39%	16.18%	97.10%	41.87%	16.18%
SAFAX (20)	188	84	51,009,588	55.36%	28.49%	16.18%	97.06%	43.03%	16.18%
SAFAX (50)	368	174	730,641,708	55.27%	28.55%	16.18%	97.04%	42.14%	16.18%

Table 5: BDD encoding constrained query space and percentage of queries that evaluate $1, 0, \perp$ for $[\![\cdot]\!]_B$ and $[\![\cdot]\!]_E$

	Continue	SAFAX (10)	SAFAX (20)	SAFAX (50)
Time (sec)	1.506	0.673	0.985	2.957
Avg. BDD size (KB)	20.33	7.33	12.33	34.33

Table 6: Time needed to construct the BDDs encoding the extended evaluation on the constrained query space and average BDD size

second was required for the SAFAX (10) and SAFAX (20) datasets; SAFAX (50) required slightly less than 3 seconds.

To estimate the memory required to store the generated BDDs, we exploited the functionalities of the dd library. In particular, the dd library makes it possible to dump a BDD to a pickle file. The average size of the dump files is reported in the last row of Table 6. These results suggest that the precomputed BDDs can be stored and evaluated in resource-constrained devices, like IoT devices, to determine whether a user is allowed to access a device's resources.

Extended evaluation function $[\![\cdot]\!]_E$ vs. standard evaluation function $[\![\cdot]\!]_P$. We also evaluated and compared the outcome yielded by evaluation functions $[\![\cdot]\!]_E$ and $[\![\cdot]\!]_P$ (see Section 2). Tables 7 and 8 report the results of this comparison for Continue and SAFAX (10) datasets, respectively. In particular, for each decision, we report the number of queries returned by each evaluation function and how these queries are evaluated by the other evaluation function. From Table 7, we can observe that the Continue policy is vulnerable to attribute hiding attacks that are not captured when evaluating the policy using $[\![\cdot]\!]_P$. In particular, there exist a number of queries for which $[\![\cdot]\!]_P$ grants access while some extensions of those queries should be denied. On the other hand, $[\![\cdot]\!]_E$ is able to identify the risks of attribute hiding attacks by indicating that some extensions of these queries should be denied. Moreover, from the tables, we can observe that, for both policies, the standard evaluation returns decisions than actually cannot be reached. For instance, the

evaluation of the Continue policy (Table 7) shows that 972 queries evaluate to $\{1, 0\}$ according to $[\![\cdot]\!]_P$ due to missing information, whereas decision 0 can never be reached for any non-deterministic extension of those queries (which follows from the $\{1, 0\}$ entry in the $\{0\}$ row of the $[\![\cdot]\!]_E$ evaluation). A similar situation can be observed for 106920 queries evaluating to $\{1, \perp\}$ according to $[\![\cdot]\!]_E$.

On the other hand, the differences between $[\![\cdot]\!]_P$ and $[\![\cdot]\!]_E$ are less prominent for the SAFAX policy (Table 8). For instance, the SAFAX policy is not vulnerable to attribute hiding attacks, although we can observe from the table that some queries for which access is denied could be eventually permitted when more information is provided. This result can be explained by recalling that the SAFAX policy employs a number of default *Deny* rules that apply when positive authorizations do not apply. In general, the closeness between for $[\![\cdot]\!]_P$ and $[\![\cdot]\!]_E$ for the SAFAX policy is due to the extensive use of constraints (see Table 3). Specifically, these constraints make several queries that would have resulted in an inconclusive decision (*i.e.*, decisions different from $\{1\}$ or $\{0\}$) invalid. From Section 2, it is easy to observe that $[\![\cdot]\!]_P$ and $[\![\cdot]\!]_E$ have the same behavior over singleton decision.

Discussion. The experiment results show the feasibility and applicability of our approach in real scenarios as well as that the extended evaluation function $[\![\cdot]\!]_E$ provides a more accurate evaluation of ABAC policies compared to standard evaluation function $[\![\cdot]\!]_P$.

Nonetheless, the experiments reveal that query constraints have a significant impact on the extended evaluation function $[\![\cdot]\!]_E$. On the one hand, query constraints improve the accuracy of policy evaluation by removing queries that cannot occur in practice, also reducing the query space. On the other hand, they affect the size of the BDDs representing policy evaluation because invalid queries have to be explicitly encoded in the BDDs.

Another factor that largely influences BDD size is the size of attributes' domains (in combination with query constraints). This

157

			Standard $[\![\cdot]\!]_P$						
			{1}	{0}	{⊥}	{1,⊥}	{0,⊥}	{1,0}	{1,0,⊥}
		#Queries	26892810	33023700	41504886	11091006	2519424	10732338	8867556
Extended $[\![\cdot]\!]_E$	{1}	26578854	26577882	0	0	0	0	972	0
	{0}	24249456	0	24249456	0	0	0	0	0
	{⊥}	29865672	0	0	29865672	0	0	0	0
	{1,⊥}	22336560	0	0	11304846	10924794	0	0	106920
	{0,⊥}	944784	0	0	0	0	944784	0	0
	{1,0}	19820538	314928	8774244	0	0	0	10731366	0
	{1,0,⊥}	10835856	0	0	334368	166212	1574640	0	8760636

Table 7: Comparison between extended evaluation and standard evaluation for the CONTINUE policy.

			Standard $[\![\cdot]\!]_P$						
			{1}	{0}	{⊥}	{1,⊥}	{0,⊥}	{1,0}	{1,0,⊥}
		#Queries	4063785	1015916	0	0	390104	1065526	795817
Extended $[\![\cdot]\!]_E$	{1}	4063785	4063785	0	0	0	0	0	0
	{0}	147499	0	147499	0	0	0	0	0
	{⊥}	0	0	0	0	0	0	0	0
	{1,⊥}	197934	0	0	0	0	0	0	197934
	{0,⊥}	64977	0	0	0	0	64977	0	0
	{1,0}	1933943	0	868417	0	0	0	1065526	0
	{1,0,⊥}	923010	0	0	0	0	325127	0	597883

Table 8: Comparison between extended evaluation and standard evaluation for SAFAX (10).

is particularly evident for the SAFAX policy, which contains numerical attributes. In particular, we observe that, in this policy, the number of vertices forming the BDDs increases with the size of attributes' domains and the depth of BDDs is equal to the overall number of attribute values, thus representing the worst case scenario. Nevertheless, the experiments show that our approach remains tractable and it is able to handle such types of policies.

Although in the worst case the number of vertices in a BDD is exponential in the number of variables, in practice the number of vertices is often polynomial [8]. In this respect, the BDD representation used has an impact on the BDD size. The dd library uses a fixed order of variables that is common for all BDDs. This BDD representation can affect the size of the generated BDDs. To reduce the size of BDDs, we used the optimizations offered by the library, namely garbage collection and reordering. Although the use of these optimization provides some benefits in terms of BDD size, we believe that the size of BDDs can be further reduced using different representations (or variants of BDDs), which for instance use a variable order of variables, or by optimizing the order of variables for each BDD independently.

7 RELATED WORK

Attribute-based access control has gained increasing popularity in the last years due to its flexibility and expressiveness. Several mechanisms for the evaluation and enforcement of ABAC policies have been proposed in both academia and industry, especially for XACML [13, 14]. Examples of these mechanisms are SUN-XACML[10], HERAS-AF [7], XEngine [11], enterprise-java-xacml[11] and WSO2 Balana[12]. These mechanisms evaluate policies according to the standard evaluation function. As discussed in Section 2, this function can yield decisions that do not correspond to an

intuitive interpretation of what these decisions means due to missing information.

Tschantz and Krishnamurthi introduced in [16] the problem of missing information, and Crampton and Morisset developed in [4] the notion of attribute-hiding attacks for PTaCL and proposed different restrictions on the definition of a target to prevent such attacks. A different approach to address the problem of missing information is presented in [5], where all queries that can be constructed from the initial query are evaluated to account that attributes could have been hidden, using the PRISM model-checker. Model-checking has been used in the past for access control, for instance Zhang et al. [18] propose a tool checking whether a particular goal can be reached within an access control policy, but not in the context of missing information for ABAC. However, the query space could potentially consist of a huge number of states and its exploration at evaluation time is not practical in real settings. In this work, we improve on [5] by studying how to efficiently compute the extended evaluation of policies while considering more expressive domain constraints.

Recently, Turkmen et al. [17] have proposed a policy analysis framework for XACML policies based on SMT. The framework supports the verification of a large range of properties including the robustness of XACML policies against two types of attribute hiding attacks, namely partial attribute hiding and general attribute hiding. Partial attribute hiding analyzes the case where a user hides a single attribute name-value pair, whereas general attribute hiding extends partial attribute hiding by assuming that a user completely suppresses information about one attribute. However, this work only allows verifying whether a policy is vulnerable to attribute hiding attacks.

In this work, we have proposed the use of binary decision diagram (BDD)-based data structures for the representation of ABAC policies. We are not the first that use such data structures in the context of ABAC. For instance, Hu et al. [9] use BDDs to determine the applicability of policies, whereas other researchers [1, 8] propose an

[10]http://sunxacml.sourceforge.net
[11]http://code.google.com/p/enterprise-java-xacml
[12]http://xacmlinfo.org/category/balana

encoding of ABAC policies using Multi-Terminal BDDs (MTBDDs). Although the use of BDD-based data structures presented in our work shares several similarities with these works, there also several differences. Similarly to our work, these proposals construct BDDs (or MTBDDs) from the policy specification. However, they encode policy evaluation according to the standard evaluation function, which, as discussed in Section 2, is not able to handle missing information properly. Moreover, these approaches typically neglect domain constraints. As shown in Section 6, this can result in misleading decisions. To the best of our knowledge, the only approach that address this issue is Margrave [8], a formal framework for the analysis of XACML policies. In Margrave, domain constraints are incorporated by introducing a terminal node representing queries that do not satisfy the constraints. In our work, we encoded constraints in a separated BDD, which is combined with the BDDs encoding the simplified evaluation of a policy when computing the extended evaluation of the policy.

8 CONCLUSION

The ABAC paradigm is gaining more and more attention due to its flexibility and expressiveness. However, it has been shown that the current way standard ABAC mechanisms (*e.g.*, XACML) handle missing information is flawed, making ABAC policies vulnerable to attribute hiding attacks. Previous work [5] has addressed this issue by providing a novel approach to the evaluation of ABAC policies. However, a naïve implementation of this approach would require exploring the state space for all possible queries, which is exponential in the number of attribute values, and therefore not feasible in practice. In this work, we have presented an efficient method for the computation of the extended evaluation of ABAC policies. The method uses the BDD representation of the policies to compute the extended evaluation directly on the BDD structure. Moreover, we have investigated the use of query constraints to obtain more accurate decisions. We have demonstrated our approach using two real-world policies. The results show that the extended evaluation can be computed in a few seconds and the corresponding BDDs do not require considerable memory for storage. Moreover, the results show that the extended evaluation is able to identify the risk of attribute hiding attacks and provides more accurate decisions with respect to the standard evaluation.

As future work, we plan to extend our approach to support a probabilistic evaluation of ABAC policies. Intuitively, we would like to determine the probability that a certain decision can be reached through the exploration of the (constrained) query space. Moreover, we want to explore the use of other variants of BDD for the representation of the extended evaluation of ABAC policies. In particular, Multi-valued Decision Diagrams (MDDs) and Multi-Terminal BDDs (MTBDDs), as well as their combination, could be suitable alternatives for our purposes. On the one end, MTBDDs allow specifying a single decision diagram encoding all decisions, instead of three separated BDDs, one for each (singleton) decision. On the other hand, MDDs supports the encoding of multi-valued predicates. This would make it possible to bound the depth of decision diagrams to the number of attributes rather to the number of attribute values, thus reducing the time required for policy evaluation.

Acknowledgments. This work is partially funded by the ITEA projects M2MGrids (13011) and APPSTACLE (15017).

REFERENCES

[1] B. Bahrak, A. Deshpande, M. Whitaker, and J. Park. 2010. BRESAP: A Policy Reasoner for Processing Spectrum Access Policies Represented by Binary Decision Diagrams. In *Proc. of Symp. on New Frontiers in Dynamic Spectrum*. IEEE, 1–12.
[2] R. E. Bryant. 1992. Symbolic Boolean Manipulation with Ordered Binary-Decision Diagrams. *ACM Comput. Surv.* 24, 3 (1992), 293–318.
[3] J. Crampton and M. Huth. 2010. An Authorization Framework Resilient to Policy Evaluation Failures. In *Computer Security*. Springer, 472–487.
[4] J. Crampton and C. Morisset. 2012. PTaCL: A Language for Attribute-Based Access Control in Open Systems. In *Principles of Security and Trust (LNCS 7215)*. Springer, 390–409.
[5] J. Crampton, C. Morisset, and N. Zannone. 2015. On Missing Attributes in Access Control: Non-deterministic and Probabilistic Attribute Retrieval. In *Proc. of Symposium on Access Control Models and Technologies*. ACM, 99–109.
[6] J. Crampton and C. Williams. 2016. On Completeness in Languages for Attribute-Based Access Control. In *Proc. of Symposium on Access Control Models and Technologies*. ACM, 149–160.
[7] S. Dolski, F. Huonder, and S. Oberholzer. 2007. *HERAS-AF: XACML 2.0 Implementation*. Tech. Rep. University of Applied Sciences Rapperswil.
[8] K. Fisler, S. Krishnamurthi, L. Meyerovich, and M. Tschantz. 2005. Verification and Change-impact Analysis of Access-control Policies. In *Proc. of Int. Conference on Software Engineering*. ACM, 196–205.
[9] H. Hu, G. Ahn, and K. Kulkarni. 2013. Discovery and Resolution of Anomalies in Web Access Control Policies. *TDSC* 10, 6 (2013), 341–354.
[10] S. P. Kaluvuri, A. I. Egner, J. den Hartog, and N. Zannone. 2015. SAFAX - An Extensible Authorization Service for Cloud Environments. *Front. ICT* (2015).
[11] A. Liu, F. Chen, J. Hwang, and T. Xie. 2011. Designing Fast and Scalable XACML Policy Evaluation Engines. *IEEE Trans. Computers* 60, 12 (2011), 1802–1817.
[12] C. Morisset and N. Zannone. 2014. Reduction of access control decisions. In *Proc. of Symposium on Access Control Models and Technologies*. ACM, 53–62.
[13] OASIS. 2005. *eXtensible Access Control Markup Language (XACML) Version 2.0*. OASIS Standard.
[14] OASIS. 2013. *eXtensible Access Control Markup Language (XACML) Version 3.0*. OASIS Standard.
[15] R. Rudell. 1993. Dynamic variable ordering for ordered binary decision diagrams. In *Proc. of International Conference on Computer Aided Design*. IEEE, 42–47.
[16] M. Tschantz and S. Krishnamurthi. 2006. Towards reasonability properties for access-control policy languages. In *Proc. of Symposium on Access Control Models and Technologies*. ACM, 160–169.
[17] F. Turkmen, J. den Hartog, S. Ranise, and N. Zannone. 2017. Formal analysis of XACML policies using SMT. *Computers & Security* 66 (2017), 185–203.
[18] N. Zhang, M. Ryan, and D. Guelev. 2005. Evaluating Access Control Policies Through Model Checking. In *Information Security*. Springer, 446–460.

A TRANSFORMATION RULES FOR DECISIONS 0 AND ⊥

Tables 9 and 10 present the transformation rules for τ (for targets) and π (for policies) for decisions 0 and $\bot$, respectively. We note that using a simple structural induction, one can show that both $\tau_\bot(t) = \neg(\tau_1(t) \vee \tau_0(t))$ and $\pi_\bot(p) = \neg(\pi_1(p) \vee \pi_0(p))$. Thus, in our proofs, we can focus on the cases $d = 1$ and $d = 0$.

B PROOF OF THEOREM 3

Note that the semantics of a propositional formula is given in the context of an interpretation $\eta : Vars \rightarrow \mathbb{B}$, assigning meaning to variables. Let $\eta : Vars \rightarrow \mathbb{B}$ be such an interpretation. We write $\eta \models \phi$ for propositional formula ϕ ranging over *Vars* iff ϕ holds under interpretation η. A query induces an interpretation $I : Q_{\mathcal{A}} \rightarrow (Vars \rightarrow \mathbb{B})$, given by $I(q)(a_v) = true$ iff $(a, v) \in q$.

The correctness of our algorithm essentially hinges on two lemmata, which we present next. The first one states that transformation τ faithfully characterizes sets of queries, whereas the second one states that transformation τ correctly encodes the simplified evaluation of the policy language.

$\tau_0((a,v))$	$=$	$\neg a_v \wedge \bigvee \{a_{v'} \mid v' \in \mathcal{V}_{\mathcal{A}}\}$
$\tau_0(\neg t_1)$	$=$	$\tau_1(t_1)$
$\tau_0(\sim t_1)$	$=$	$\tau_0(t_1) \vee \tau_\perp(t_1)$
$\tau_0(E_1(t_1))$	$=$	$\tau_0(t_1)$
$\tau_0(t_1 \sqcap t_2)$	$=$	$\tau_0(t_1) \vee \tau_0(t_2)$
$\tau_0(t_1 \tilde{\sqcap} t_2)$	$=$	$(\tau_0(t_1) \wedge \neg\tau_\perp(t_2)) \vee (\tau_0(t_2) \wedge \neg\tau_\perp(t_1))$
$\tau_0(t_1 \triangle t_2)$	$=$	$\tau_0(t_1) \vee \tau_0(t_2)$
$\tau_0(t_1 \sqcup t_2)$	$=$	$\tau_0(t_1) \wedge \tau_0(t_2)$
$\tau_0(t_1 \tilde{\sqcup} t_2)$	$=$	$\tau_0(t_1) \wedge \tau_0(t_2)$
$\tau_0(t_1 \triangledown t_2)$	$=$	$(\tau_0(t_1) \wedge \neg\tau_1(t_2)) \vee (\tau_0(t_2) \wedge \neg\tau_1(t_1))$
$\pi_0(1)$	$=$	*false*
$\pi_0(0)$	$=$	*true*
$\pi_0((t,p_1))$	$=$	$\tau_1(t) \wedge \pi_0(p_1)$
$\pi_0(\neg p_1)$	$=$	$\pi_1(p_1)$
$\pi_0(\sim p_1)$	$=$	$\pi_0(p_1) \vee \pi_\perp(p_1)$
$\pi_0(E_1(p_1))$	$=$	$\pi_0(p_1)$
$\pi_0(p_1 \sqcap p_2)$	$=$	$\pi_0(p_1) \vee \pi_0(p_2)$
$\pi_0(p_1 \tilde{\sqcap} p_2)$	$=$	$(\pi_0(p_1) \wedge \neg\pi_\perp(p_2)) \vee (\pi_0(p_2) \wedge \neg\pi_\perp(p_1))$
$\pi_0(p_1 \triangle p_2)$	$=$	$\pi_0(p_1) \vee \pi_0(p_2)$
$\pi_0(p_1 \tilde{\sqcup} p_2)$	$=$	$\pi_0(p_1) \wedge \pi_0(p_2)$
$\pi_0(p_1 \sqcup p_2)$	$=$	$\pi_0(p_1) \wedge \pi_0(p_2)$
$\pi_0(p_1 \triangledown p_2)$	$=$	$(\pi_0(p_1) \wedge \neg\pi_1(p_2)) \vee (\pi_0(p_2) \wedge \neg\pi_1(p_1))$

Table 9: Transformation rules for τ_0 (for targets) and π_0 (for policies) for decision 0

$\tau_\perp((a,v))$	$=$	$\bigwedge \{\neg a_{v'} \mid v' \in \mathcal{V}_{\mathcal{A}}\}$
$\tau_\perp(\neg t_1)$	$=$	$\tau_\perp(t_1)$
$\tau_\perp(\sim t_1)$	$=$	*false*
$\tau_\perp(E_1(t_1))$	$=$	$\tau_1(t_1)$
$\tau_\perp(t_1 \sqcap t_2)$	$=$	$(\tau_\perp(t_1) \wedge \neg\tau_0(t_2)) \vee (\tau_\perp(t_2) \wedge \neg\tau_0(t_1))$
$\tau_\perp(t_1 \tilde{\sqcap} t_2)$	$=$	$\tau_\perp(t_1) \vee \tau_\perp(t_2)$
$\tau_\perp(t_1 \triangle t_2)$	$=$	$\tau_\perp(t_1) \wedge \tau_\perp(t_2)$
$\tau_\perp(t_1 \sqcup t_2)$	$=$	$(\tau_\perp(t_1) \wedge \neg\tau_1(t_2)) \vee (\tau_\perp(t_2) \wedge \neg\tau_1(t_1))$
$\tau_\perp(t_1 \tilde{\sqcup} t_2)$	$=$	$\tau_\perp(t_1) \vee \tau_\perp(t_2)$
$\tau_\perp(t_1 \triangledown t_2)$	$=$	$\tau_\perp(t_1) \wedge \tau_\perp(t_2)$
$\pi_\perp(1)$	$=$	*false*
$\pi_\perp(0)$	$=$	*false*
$\pi_\perp((t,p_1))$	$=$	$\tau_0(t) \vee \tau_\perp(t) \vee (\tau_1(t) \wedge \pi_\perp(p_1))$
$\pi_\perp(\neg p_1)$	$=$	$\pi_\perp(p_1)$
$\pi_\perp(\sim p_1)$	$=$	*false*
$\pi_\perp(E_1(p_1))$	$=$	$\pi_1(p_1)$
$\pi_\perp(p_1 \sqcap p_2)$	$=$	$(\pi_\perp(p_1) \wedge \neg\pi_0(p_2)) \vee (\pi_\perp(p_2) \wedge \neg\pi_0(p_1))$
$\pi_\perp(p_1 \tilde{\sqcap} p_2)$	$=$	$\pi_\perp(p_1) \vee \pi_\perp(p_2)$
$\pi_\perp(p_1 \triangle p_2)$	$=$	$\pi_\perp(p_1) \wedge \pi_\perp(p_2)$
$\pi_\perp(p_1 \tilde{\sqcup} p_2)$	$=$	$(\pi_\perp(p_1) \wedge \neg\pi_1(p_2)) \vee (\pi_\perp(p_2) \wedge \neg\pi_1(p_1))$
$\pi_\perp(p_1 \sqcup p_2)$	$=$	$\pi_\perp(p_1) \vee \pi_\perp(p_2)$
$\pi_\perp(p_1 \triangledown p_2)$	$=$	$\pi_\perp(p_1) \wedge \pi_\perp(p_2)$

Table 10: Transformation rules for $\tau_\perp$ (for targets) and $\pi_\perp$ (for policies) for decision $\perp$

LEMMA 1(A). *For all $q \in Q_{\mathcal{A}}$, $I(q) \models \tau_d(t)$ iff $d = [\![t]\!]_T(q)$.*

PROOF. By structural induction on t. Let $q \in Q_{\mathcal{A}}$ be arbitrary.

- *Base case*: $t \equiv (a,v)$. We prove correctness for each $d \in \{1,0\}$ separately (Recall that case $d = \perp$ follows from $d = 1$ and $d = 0$).
  - Case $d = 1$. Suppose $I(q) \models \tau_1((a,v))$. By definition, $\tau_1((a,v)) = a_v$. From this, it follows that $I(q) \models a_v$ which, by definition means that $I(q)(a_v) = true$ and, thus, $(a,v) \in q$. By definition of $[\![\cdot]\!]_T$ we also have $[\![(a,v)]\!]_T(q) = 1$.
  - Case $d = 0$ follows identical reasoning using Table 9.
- *Induction hypothesis*: suppose that, for all d', $I(q) \models \tau_{d'}(t_i)$ iff $d' = [\![t_i]\!]_T(q)$ with $i \in \{1,2\}$. We need to consider all unary and binary operators and prove each equivalence for all $d \in \{1,0\}$. We provide details for negation $\neg$ and strong conjunction $\tilde{\sqcap}$; the proofs for all remaining operators are analogous and therefore omitted.
  - Suppose $t \equiv \neg t_1$. We compute:

$I(q) \models \tau_1(\neg t_1)$	$I(q) \models \tau_0(\neg t_1)$
iff {by def.} $I(q) \models \tau_0(t_1)$	iff {by def.} $I(q) \models \tau_1(t_1)$
iff {by induction} $0 = [\![t_1]\!]_T(q)$	iff {by induction} $1 = [\![t_1]\!]_T(q)$
iff {by def. of $\neg$} $[\![\neg t_1]\!]_T = 1$	iff {by def. of $\neg$} $[\![\neg t_1]\!]_T = 0$

- Suppose $t \equiv t_1 \tilde{\sqcap} t_2$. We compute for $d = 1$:

$$I(q) \models \tau_1(t_1 \tilde{\sqcap} t_2) \text{ iff \{by def.\} } I(q) \models \tau_1(t_1) \wedge \tau_1(t_2)$$
$$\text{iff \{by def.\} } I(q) \models \tau_1(t_1) \text{ and } I(q) \models \tau_1(t_2)$$
$$\text{iff \{by induction (2x)\} } 1 = [\![t_1]\!]_T(q) \text{ and } 1 = [\![t_2]\!]_T(q)$$
$$\text{iff \{by def.\} } 1 = [\![t_1 \tilde{\sqcap} t_2]\!]_T(q)$$

Case $d = 0$ follows the same reasoning, employing the encodings of Table 9. □

LEMMA 1(B). *For all $q \in Q_{\mathcal{A}}$, $I(q) \models \pi_d(p)$ iff $d = [\![p]\!]_B(q)$.*

PROOF. The proof of this lemma proceeds by induction on the structure of the policy. Since the proof bears many similarities to that of the previous lemma, we only highlight the interesting case, which is the case $p \equiv (t, p_1)$. Assume, as our induction hypothesis, that for all d', $I(q) \models \pi_{d'}(p_1)$ iff $d' = [\![p_1]\!]_B(q)$.

We separately prove the statement for $d \in \{1, 0\}$. We reason as follows:

$I(q) \models \pi_1((t,p_1))$	$I(q) \models \pi_0((t,p_1))$
iff {by def.}	iff {by def.}
$I(q) \models \tau_1(t) \wedge \pi_1(p_1)$	$I(q) \models \tau_1(t) \wedge \pi_0(p_1)$
iff {by def.}	iff {by def.}
$I(q) \models \tau_1(t)$ and $I(q) \models \pi_1(p_1)$	$I(q) \models \tau_1(t)$ and $I(q) \models \pi_0(p_1)$
iff {by induction}	iff {by induction}
$I(q) \models \tau_1(t)$ and $1 = [\![p_1]\!]_B(q)$	$I(q) \models \tau_1(t)$ and $0 = [\![p_1]\!]_B(q)$
iff {by Lemma 1(a)}	iff {by Lemma 1(a)}
$[\![t]\!]_T(q) = 1$ and $1 = [\![p_1]\!]_B(q)$	$[\![t]\!]_T(q) = 1$ and $0 = [\![p_1]\!]_B(q)$
iff {by def.}	iff {by def.}
$1 = [\![(t,p_1)]\!]_B(q)$	$0 = [\![(t,p_1)]\!]_B(q)$ □

Finally, we observe that the proposition $\bar{R}$, defined as $\bigwedge \{a_v \Longrightarrow a'_v \mid a_v \in Vars_{\mathcal{A}}\}$, indeed encodes the subset relation on $Q_{\mathcal{A}}$. We introduce an interpretation $I' : Q_{\mathcal{A}} \rightarrow (Vars' \rightarrow \mathbb{B})$, which is given by $I'(q)(a'_v) = true$ iff $(a,v) \in q$. We write $\eta \cup \eta' \models \bar{R}$ iff $\bar{R}$ holds under interpretation $\eta : Vars \rightarrow \mathbb{B}$ for variables from $Vars$ and $\eta' : Vars' \rightarrow \mathbb{B}$ for variables from $Vars'$.

LEMMA 2. *For all $q, q' \in Q_{\mathcal{A}}$, $I(q) \cup I'(q') \models \bar{R}$ iff $(q, q') \in \rightarrow^*$.*

PROOF. First, observe that $\rightarrow^*$ is in fact equivalent to $\subseteq$ on $Q_{\mathcal{A}}$.
- Implication from left to right. Suppose $I(q) \cup I'(q') \models \bar{R}$. Then, $I(q) \cup I'(q') \models \bigwedge \{a_v \Longrightarrow a'_v \mid a_v \in Vars_{\mathcal{A}}\}$, and, therefore, for all $a_v \in Vars_{\mathcal{A}}$, we find that $I(q) \cup I'(q') \models a_v \Longrightarrow a'_v$. But then if $I(q)(a_v)$ holds, then so does $I'(q')(a'_v)$. By definition, this means $(a,v) \in q$ implies $(a,v) \in q'$ for all $(a,v) \in Q_{\mathcal{A}}$. But then $q \subseteq q'$, or, equivalently $(q, q') \rightarrow^*$.
- Implication from right to left. Suppose $(q, q') \in \rightarrow^*$, or, equivalently, $q \subseteq q'$. Pick some arbitrary $(a,v) \in Q_{\mathcal{A}}$, and assume $(a,v) \in q$. By definition, we then have $I(q)(a_v)$ holds. Since $q \subseteq q'$, also $(a,v) \in q'$; but then also $I'(q)(a_v)$ holds. So we have $I(q)(a_v)$ implies $I'(q)(a'_v)$. But then $I(q) \cup I'(q') \models a_v \Longrightarrow a'_v$. Since we picked $(a,v) \in Q_{\mathcal{A}}$ arbitrary, we find that $I(q) \cup I'(q') \models \bigwedge \{a_v \Longrightarrow a'_v \mid a_v \in Vars_{\mathcal{A}}\}$. □

The correctness of procedure COMPUTEEXTENDEDEVALUATION (Theorem 3) directly follows from the next proposition, where $R = \bar{R} \wedge S \wedge S[Vars_{\mathcal{A}} := Vars'_{\mathcal{A}}]$ and $S = \bigwedge \{\tau_1(c) \mid c \in C\}$:

PROPOSITION 4. *For all $d \in \{1, 0, \perp\}$, $q \in Q_{\mathcal{A}|C} \wedge d \in [\![p]\!]_E(q)$ iff $I(q) \models (\pi_d(p) \wedge S) \vee \exists Vars'_{\mathcal{A}}.(R \wedge (\pi_d(p))[Vars_{\mathcal{A}} := Vars'_{\mathcal{A}}])$.*

PROOF. Follows from Lemmata 1(a), 1(b) and 2. □

Mining Positive and Negative Attribute-Based Access Control Policy Rules

Padmavathi Iyer
University at Albany – SUNY
Albany, New York
riyer2@albany.edu

Amirreza Masoumzadeh
University at Albany – SUNY
Albany, New York
amasoumzadeh@albany.edu

ABSTRACT

Mining access control policies can reduce the burden of adopting more modern access control models by automating the process of generating policies based on existing authorization information in a system. Previous work in this area has focused on mining positive authorizations only. That includes the literature on mining role-based access control policies (which are naturally about positive authorization) and even more recent work on mining attribute-based access control (ABAC) policies. However, various theoretical access control models (including ABAC), specification standards (such as XACML), and implementations (such as operating systems and databases) support negative authorization as well as positive authorization.

In this paper, we propose a novel approach to mine ABAC policies that may contain both positive and negative authorization rules. We evaluate our approach using two different policies in terms of correctness, quality of rules (conciseness), and time. We show that while achieving the new goal of supporting negative authorizations, our proposed algorithm outperforms existing approach to ABAC mining in terms of time.

CCS CONCEPTS

• **Security and privacy** → **Access control**; **Authorization**;

KEYWORDS

attribute-based access control; policy mining; negative authorization; authorization conflicts

ACM Reference format:
Padmavathi Iyer and Amirreza Masoumzadeh. 2018. Mining Positive and Negative Attribute-Based Access Control Policy Rules. In *Proceedings of The 23rd ACM Symposium on Access Control Models & Technologies (SACMAT), Indianapolis, IN, USA, June 13–15, 2018 (SACMAT '18),* 12 pages.
https://doi.org/10.1145/3205977.3205988

1 INTRODUCTION

Access control is one of the indispensable services of any information system responsible for protecting the underlying data from unauthorized access and inappropriate modifications [8]. *Attribute-based access control (ABAC)*, as one of the more recent models for specifying access control policies, has been shown to overcome major limitations in previous models [10]. Unlike discretionary access control (DAC) or mandatory access control (MAC) models, ABAC is not dependent on user identities or rigid rules to determine authorizations as in DAC and MAC. Also, by allowing composition of flexible rules, it avoids problems such as role explosion [10] in role-based access control (RBAC). As the name suggests, ABAC models employ the attributes of users and resources to determine if an access request should be granted or denied, that is, attribute expressions are used to specify the sets of users and resources to which a policy is applicable [12, 22, 28]. For example, a policy such as *"A manager can read any document in his/her department"* may be directly translated to an ABAC policy: *"if userType=manager, resourceType=document, userDepartment=resourceDepartment, action=read then* PERMIT*"*. Thus, compared to traditional access control models, ABAC is very flexible in specifying access control policies, which makes ABAC a powerful access control model for promoting security.

We explore the problem of *mining ABAC policies* in this paper. Suppose an organization has already implemented some form of access control and wants to migrate to ABAC paradigm. Specifying ABAC policies manually from the existing access control information can be a time-consuming and error-prone job. To reduce the burden and expense of this task, the process of extracting policies from the given access control information can be partially or completely automated. This approach of automating the policy generation process is called *policy mining*. Mining RBAC policies, aka *role mining*, has been heavily studied in recent years [18]. Recently, Xu and Stoller have proposed an approach for mining ABAC policies [27, 26].

One of the limitations of policy mining approaches in the literature, addressing which is a central contribution of this paper, is lack of support for mining negative authorization rules. An ABAC policy can comprise of a set of positive and negative authorization rules, which grant or deny applicable access requests, respectively. Simultaneous use of positive and negative authorization rules are useful in situations when exceptions to more general rules need to be expressed, or when authorization rules with clonflicting outcomes originated from different viewpoints may have overlap. Beside ABAC, various other access control models in the literature allow expressing both positive and negative authorizations [13, 3, 9]. XACML policy language [6], a widely used standard for specifying and enforcing access control policies, also supports them. Negative authorizations have been also supported in products such as operating systems [21], web servers [1], and database systems [2].

Therefore, it is essential for an access control mining approach to be able to mine policies that may contain both positive and negative authorization rules. We note that although policy mining has been largely studied in the context of RBAC, due to lack of support for negative authorization in RBAC, naturally no previous work in that area addresses this problem [18]. The work by Xu and Stoller [27, 26], in the context of ABAC, also supports only mining policies with positive rules.

In this paper, we propose an algorithm for mining ABAC policies that can extract positive as well as negative authorization rules from a given access control information. Rather than designing an algorithm from scratch, we adopt an existing rule mining algorithm from the data mining literature, called *PRISM* [4], and extend that to capture positive and negative authorization rules simultaneously. Therefore, compared to previous work [27, 26], our algorithm provides a more systematic and less heuristic approach to mining access control rules that not only extracts negative authorizations but also performs better in terms of time. Our key contributions in this paper are as follows.

- We propose an algorithm for mining ABAC policies that, to the best of our knowledge, is a first of its kind approach to extract negative authorization rules in addition to positive authorization rules in the access control mining literature.
- We present a detailed approach to generate an authorization log that is needed as input to the mining algorithm, in case it is not readily available for a system.
- We implement a prototype and conduct experiments on the performance of our algorithm in terms of correctness and conciseness of the mined rules and the time taken to generate them. We demonstrate that, when the original (ground truth) policy includes negative authorization rules, our algorithm generates concise set of rules, which is not possible using previous work [27, 26]. Moreover, our algorithm outperforms previous work in terms of time in both cases of positive-only and positive-and-negative authorization policies.

The rest of the paper is organized as follows. Section 2 discusses our reference policy model that we use for specifying ABAC policies. In Section 3, we discuss about the design goals and challenges, and formally define the ABAC policy mining problem. Section 4 will describe the proposed ABAC policy mining algorithm in depth along with its time complexity. We discuss about an approach to generate complete authorization log in Section 5. In Section 6, we run experiments to test our proposed algorithm and analyze the results. Section 7 discusses related work in the field of policy mining and how our approach is novel compared to previous contributions. Finally, in Section 8, we provide additional discussions and conclusions.

2 ABAC POLICY MODEL

In this section, we present a specification and authorization semantics for ABAC policies that will be the basis for defining the policy mining problem and its proposed solution in this paper.

2.1 Policy Specification

An ABAC policy usually contains a disjunctive set of rules comprising attribute expressions on users and resources, actions, and applicable decisions. In the rest of this section, we generally use uppercase letters for denoting a set and lowercase letters for notating an element in a set.

Let U be the set of users in the system and R be the set of resources. A user is characterized by a set of attributes. Let $UATTR$ be the set of user attributes. To get the value of an attribute for a user, we use the notation $u.uattr$, where $uattr \in UATTR$ is the name of the user attribute. Like a user, a resource is characterized by a set of attributes, which will be denoted as $RATTR$. Given a resource attribute $rattr \in RATTR$, the value of that attribute for a resource is denoted by $r.rattr$. Let the *domain* of an attribute be the set of all possible values that the attribute can take. The domain of an attribute $attr \in UATTR \cup RATTR$ is denoted by $dom(attr)$. For simplicity, we consider only categorical attributes in this work. We assume that every user and resource in the system has a *unique identifier* attribute, defined by uid and rid, respectively. Authorizations in an ABAC system are determined for *actions* requested by users over resources. Let ACT be the set of all possible actions in the system.

The main components of an ABAC rule are attribute expressions that together (in a conjunctive format) determine the sets of users and resources to which a rule applies. An attribute expression can be either an *attribute-value* pair or an *attribute-attribute* pair. An attribute-value pair specifies the value corresponding to a user or resource attribute for the given rule to be applicable. An attribute-value pair for a user attribute $uattr$ and a value val is expressed as $u.uattr = val$ and that for a resource attribute $rattr$ and a value val is denoted as $r.rattr = val$. The followings are examples of attribute-value pairs:

- $u.department = CS$
- $r.type = transcript$

In the above examples, the first attribute-value pair indicates the set of users whose department is CS, while the second attribute pair indicates the set of resources whose type is transcript.

An attribute-attribute pair specifies a pair of user and resource attributes that need to match for the rule to be applicable. Formally, an attribute-attribute pair can be expressed as $u.uattr = r.rattr$, where $uattr \in UATTR$ and $rattr \in RATTR$. An example of attribute-attribute expression is as follows:

- $u.department = r.department$

In the above example, the attribute expression is satisfied by that set of users and resources where user department is the same as resource department.

Similar to attribute expressions, in particular attribute-value pairs, an ABAC rule includes an action expression that is denoted by $action = act$, where $act \in ACT$. Such an expression determines the access requests to which a rule will be applicable based on the requested action. Finally, each ABAC rule includes a rule effect, which is interpreted as granting applicable requests (PERMIT) or denying them (DENY). Given the abovementioned components, an *ABAC rule* is formally defined as a pair $\langle \phi, d \rangle$ where ϕ is a conjunctive set of attribute expressions and action expression and $d \in \{\text{PERMIT}, \text{DENY}\}$

is the rule effect. We use the following grammar for rule specification in this paper:

$$rule ::= \langle \phi, d \rangle$$
$$\phi ::= exp \, [; \, exp \,]$$
$$exp ::= u.uattr = value \mid$$
$$r.rattr = value \mid$$
$$u.uattr = r.rattr \mid$$
$$action = value$$
$$d ::= \texttt{PERMIT} \mid \texttt{DENY}$$

The followings are some examples of ABAC rules:

- $\langle u.position = faculty; u.chair = true; r.type = transcript;$ $u.department = r.department; action = read\_transcript,$ $\texttt{PERMIT}\rangle$
- $\langle u.position = manager; u.department = accounts;$ $r.type = budget; action = approve, \texttt{DENY}\rangle$

The first example above is an example of a positive rule, according to which a user who is a faculty and chair of a department can perform read_transcript operation on all the transcripts in his/her department. On the other hand, the second example is an illustration of a negative rule, according to which if a manager from the accounts department tries to approve the budget of a project (project is a resource in this case), then he/she will be denied access.

As mentioned earlier, an ABAC policy is a disjunctive set of rules. We denote the complete set of rules in an ABAC policy by ρ. Along with the authorization rules, an ABAC policy also includes a *default decision* and a *conflict resolution strategy*. A *default decision* applies when none of the rules in the policy are applicable to an access request. A *conflict resolution strategy* applies when there is an overlap between positive and negative authorization rules. In other words, if both PERMIT and DENY rules are applicable to an access request, then the conflict resolution strategy of the policy decides the final decision for that access request [15, 16, 11].

In the context of this paper, in order to avoid overcomplicating our discussion about policy mining, we assume DENY as the default decision and *deny-overrides* as the conflict resolution strategy.

2.2 Authorization Process

An authorization request is a tuple $\langle u \in U, r \in R, a \in ACT \rangle$ indicating the requesting user, requested resource and action, respectively. Given an ABAC policy as described in Section 2.1, an ABAC authorization system evaluates each policy rule's expressions based on the request and determines if the rule is applicable to the request or not. There are three possible scenarios based on such a matching process:

- the access request matches with one or more rules in the policy, all of which contain the same access decision; or
- the access request matches with more than one rule in the policy but the access decisions of those rules are conflicting, i.e., include both PERMIT and DENY decisions; or
- the access request does not match with any rule in the policy.

The first scenario is quite straightforward. In this case, the authorization decision returned by the rule(s) in the policy. In the second scenario, the final authorization decision is resolved according to

the conflict resolution strategy of the policy. For example, if the conflict resolution strategy of the policy is *deny-overrides*, then only one applicable DENY rule in the policy is sufficient to make the final authorization decision to be DENY. Finally, in the third scenario above, the default decision of the policy determines the authorization result. For example, if the default decision of the policy is DENY, then the system denies an access request if the request is not applicable with any of the rules in the policy.

3 PROBLEM STATEMENT

In this section, we present our design considerations and challenges for mining ABAC policies that include both positive and negative rules, and formulate the ABAC policy mining problem.

As input to the policy mining process, we consider a low-level log of authorization decisions in a system, which indicates authorization decision (PERMIT or DENY) for any given access by a user to a resource. Since our goal is to mine rules based on user and resource attributes, such a log needs to be accompanied (and augmented) by attributes of users and resources involved in the log entries. Such an access log may be accumulated by and retrieved from a working authorization system (e.g., as in collected in audit logs or for the sole purpose of mining). Also, in some cases, we may have an already existing access control policy specified using other models such as role-based access control (RBAC [7]) or simple access control lists (ACL [20]). In such cases, based on the existing policy, we may generate the desired log using an authorization engine or a log conversion process in case of simple models such as ACL.

A central design consideration and contribution of this work is coexistence of positive and negative rules in a mined policy. Ability to specify both positive and negative rules is desirable in cases such as handling simple exceptions (e.g., all but one department should be able to access a file) or implementing strict requirements for a group of users/resources (e.g., all employees on administrative leave should not be able to access any resource). This requirement brings on new challenges for mining ABAC policies compared to when mining positive rules only. In order to discuss better about the challenges, we illustrate two sample abstract policies as Venn diagrams in Figure 1. Here, the universe represents all possible access requests and corresponding decisions in the system. Each policy rule has been represented as a circle determining set of access instances to which it is applicable. As such, various overlapping situations can exist among policy rules. An overlap area indicates access instances with multiple applicable policies. As explained in Section 2.2, overlap can lead to a conflict situation if rules result in different decisions. For example, Figure 1(a) represents partial overlaps between two positive rules as well as overlap of the negative rules with the positive rules. Here, negative rules are proper subset of positive rules which may be used to specify exceptions to some permissions. For example, it can be the case that every student except students in the CS department can view the courselist:

- $\langle u.position = student; actions = view\_course\_list, \texttt{PERMIT}\rangle$
- $\langle u.position = student; u.department = CS;$ $actions = view\_course\_list, \texttt{DENY}\rangle$

Figure 1(b) shows another example where a negative rule overlaps with multiple positive rules.

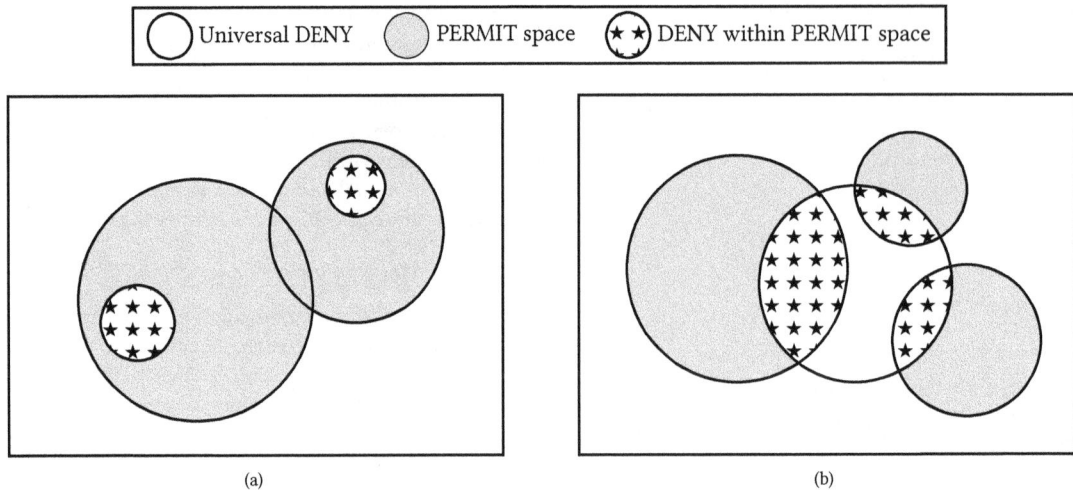

Figure 1: Policy spaces demonstrating PERMIT rules, conflicting DENY rules, and DENY space as default decision (a) Conflicting DENY rules are proper subset of PERMIT rules; and, (b) DENY rules conflict with more than one PERMIT rule.

Looking at the above examples from the viewpoint of a policy mining algorithm, which only sees a flat access log data, it is challenging to discover the rules when both positive and negative rules exist. The solution needs to discern DENY cases that are result of applying negative rules versus those that are result of applying the default rule. Note that we consider DENY as the default decision in this paper as explained in Section 2.1, . In Figure 1 the non-shaded area outside of the rules represents cases to which the default policy applies while the crossed areas represent cases when a negative rule results in DENY. Figure 1(b) highlights another desired characteristic for our solution. Rather than trying to generate three different specific negative rules, each corresponding to the crossed DENY pieces that are cut out of the positive rules, we need to be able to detect that they belong to one more general negative rule.

Finally, a policy mining solution should strive for deriving a policy that is as concise as possible as they are more manageable and easier to interpret. In terms of an ABAC policy, we would like to create less number of rules as well as creating rules with less number of expressions (more general rules). Previous work on mining ABAC policies [26] have adopted the notion of *Weighted Structural Complexity (WSC)*, previously defined in the context of RBAC policy mining [19], as a metric for this purpose. We adopt the same notion here. Informally, WSC of an ABAC policy is the sum of weights of all of its rules, where each rule's weight is calculated as the weighted sum of the number of expressions in that rule. Mathematically, WSC of an ABAC policy composed of the ruleset ρ is given as:

$$WSC(\rho) = \sum_{rule \in \rho} WSC(rule)$$

$$WSC(rule) = w_1|\alpha| + w_2|\beta| + w_3|\gamma|$$

where α, β and γ are, respectively, sets of attribute-value pairs, attribute-attribute pairs, and action expressions in rule's ϕ. Moreover, w_is are user-specified weights that adjust their contribution to rule's conciseness.

Based on the abovementioned considerations, we define the *ABAC policy mining problem* as follows. The ABAC policy mining problem accepts a complete authorization log (augmented with attributes) as input and extracts an ABAC policy (Section 2.1) that is concise and consistent with the authorization log. Based on the notations discussed in Section 2.1, the authorization log is a set of records, each indicating attribute values of a requesting user (*UATTR*), attribute values of requested resource (*RATTR*), an action (*ACT*), and corresponding access decision (PERMIT or DENY). In this work, we assume a complete log as input, meaning that every potential combination of attribute values are provided in the log (or otherwise assumed and set to be equal to the default DENY decision). As the correctness criterion, the mined policy must be consistent with the input authorization, i.e., the authorization of a log entry according to the mined policy and the semantics described in Section 2.2 must result in the same access decision as in the log entry. As the quality criterion, a solution to the mining problem must aim for policies that are as concise as possible. We quantify performance towards achieving this goal using the abovementioned WSC metric.

4 MINING ABAC POLICIES

In this section, we propose an approach for mining ABAC policies that include both positive and negative rules based on the policy model discussed in Section 2. Our proposed algorithm follows a systematic flow to mine optimal rules, as shown in Figure 2, avoiding heuristic and sub-optimal procedures as much as possible. The flow starts with mining positive rules, but also discovers conflicting negative rules simultaneously as a subprocess. In the following, we present our algorithm and analyze its time complexity.

4.1 Positive/Negative Rule Mining Algorithm

In order to mine attribute-based rules from authorization logs, we adopt concepts from a rule mining algorithm, called *PRISM* [4].

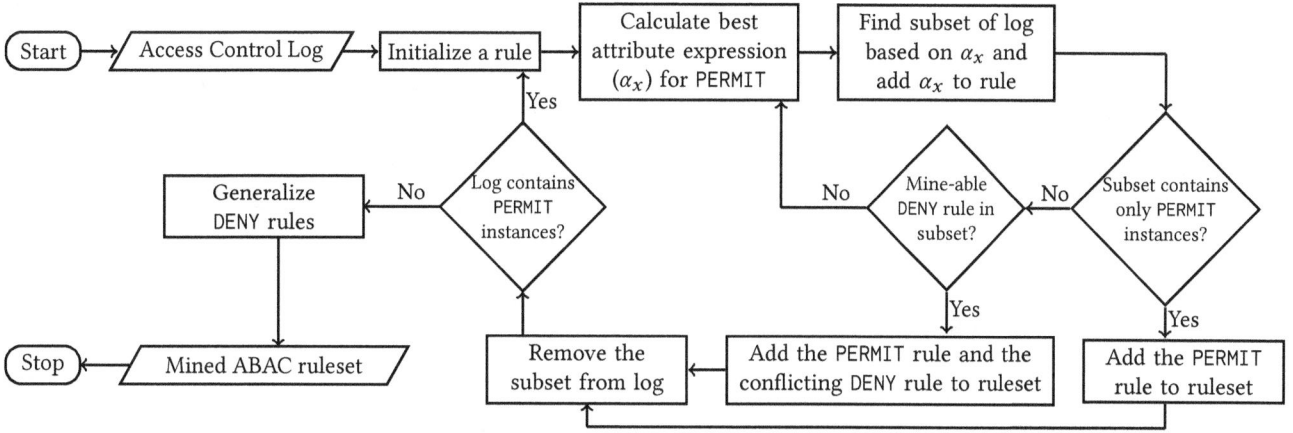

Figure 2: Flow chart of the proposed ABAC policy mining algorithm

The backbone of PRISM algorithm is induction strategy for finding the attribute-value pair, α_x, which yields highest conditional probability for a particular classification, δ_n, that is, for which $P(\delta_n \mid \alpha_x)$ is maximum. In context of this paper, conditional probability $P(\delta_n \mid \alpha_x)$ is the probability of occurrence of PERMIT or DENY decision, δ_n, for a given attribute expression, α_x.

At a high level our ABAC policy mining algorithm works in an iterative manner as shown in Algorithm 1. The input to the algorithm is an authorization log (augmented with user/resource attributes) as described in Section 3. The *getLastCol* function returns all the access decisions, in order, from the input dataset. The outer while loop runs until the log does not contain any PERMIT instances, to ensure that all positive rules have been mined. The inner while loop runs until a subset of the log contains all PERMIT instances or a conflicting DENY rule is encountered. Basically, the inner while loop is used to mine either a positive rule or a pair of positive and conflicting DENY rules. Within the inner loop, lines 7-17 returns the attribute expression, either attribute-value or attribute-attribute pair, that yields the highest conditional probability for PERMIT. If equal probabilities are encountered, then the one with larger coverage is returned. An attribute expression has larger coverage over another if the number of instances in the dataset that contains the former is greater than that for latter. The selected attribute expression is then added to the positive rule. *getInstances* function returns a subset of the log containing those instances that satisfy the selected attribute expression. Within this subset, existence of a conflicting DENY rule is checked using *findDenyRule* function (Algorithm 4). If it does, the conflicting DENY rule is added to ruleset and the inner loop breaks. Otherwise, inner loop repeats over the subset created in the previous iteration, until the subset comprises of only PERMIT instances. Lines 24-25 add PERMIT rule, which is created by taking the conjunction of all selected attribute expressions in the inner loop, to the ruleset, and remove all instances from the log that are covered by this rule. *generalizeDenyRules* function (Algorithm 5) generalizes all the negative rules in the ruleset by removing redundant attribute expressions from those rules. The output of the ABAC policy mining algorithm is a set of positive and conflicting negative rules.

Algorithm 1: mineRules

Input : *log* (complete authorization log)
Output: List of rules

1   $decision\_col \leftarrow getLastCol(log)$
2   **while** PERMIT $\in decision\_col$ **do**
3     $X \leftarrow log$
4     $Y \leftarrow decision\_col$
5     $\phi \leftarrow \emptyset$
6   **while** DENY $\in Y$ **do**
7       $(attr, val, prob) \leftarrow$ findAttrValPair (X, PERMIT)
8       $coverage1 = length(getInstances(X, attr, val))$
9       $(attr1, attr2, prob2) \leftarrow$ findAttrAttrPair (X, PERMIT)
10      $coverage2 = length(getInstances(X, attr1, attr2))$
11   **if** $prob = prob2$ and $coverage1 > coverage2$ **then**
12        $(expr\_LHS, expr\_RHS) \leftarrow (attr, val)$
13   **else if** $prob2 < prob$ **then**
14        $(expr\_LHS, expr\_RHS) \leftarrow (attr, val)$
15   **else**
16        $(expr\_LHS, expr\_RHS) \leftarrow (attr1, attr2)$
17      $\phi.add(expr\_LHS = expr\_RHS)$
18      $X \leftarrow getInstances(X, expr\_LHS, expr\_RHS)$
19      $Y \leftarrow getLastCol(X)$
20      $deny\_rule \leftarrow findDenyRule(X, \phi, Y)$
21   **if** $deny\_rule! = null$ **then**
22        $ruleset.add(deny\_rule)$
23   **break**
24     $ruleset.add(\langle \phi, \text{PERMIT} \rangle)$
25     $log.removeInstances(\phi)$
26     $decision\_col \leftarrow getLastCol(log)$
27   $ruleset \leftarrow generalizeDenyRules(ruleset, log)$

Algorithms 2 and 3 manifest two functions for returning attribute expressions, attribute-value pair and attribute-attribute pair, with highest conditional probability for PERMIT. The inputs to both these functions are the same. The loop in the *findAttrValPair* function

---

Algorithm 2: findAttrValPair

Input : X (log of access requests and decisions), *class* (PERMIT or DENY)

Output: Attribute-Value pair

1 $(maxProb, attr, val) \leftarrow (0, null, null)$
2 **for** $i \leftarrow 1$ **to** $(numAttributes(X)\text{-}1)$ **do**
3   **foreach** $j \in getUniqueValues(X.getColumn(i))$ **do**
4       $prob \leftarrow P(class \mid i_j)$
5   **if** $maxProb < prob$ **then**
6          $(maxProb, attr, val) \leftarrow (prob, i, j)$
7   **else if** $maxProb = prob$ **then**
8   **if** $attr = null$ **and** $val = null$ **then**
9             $(attr, val) \leftarrow (i, j)$
10   **else if** $length(getInstances(X, attr, val)) <$
            $length(getInstances(X, i, j))$ **then**
11             $(maxProb, attr, val) \leftarrow (prob, i, j)$
12 **return** $(attr, val, maxProb)$

Algorithm 3: findAttrAttrPair

Input : X (log of access requests and decisions), *class* (PERMIT or DENY)

Output: Attribute-Attribute pair

1 $uAttr \leftarrow getUserAttributes(X)$
2 $rAttr \leftarrow getResourceAttributes(X)$
3 $(maxProb, attr1, attr2) \leftarrow (0, null, null)$
4 **for** $i \leftarrow 1$ **to** $(numAttributes(uAttr)\text{-}1)$ **do**
5   **for** $j \leftarrow 1$ **to** $(numAttributes(rAttr)\text{-}1)$ **do**
6       $prob \leftarrow P(class \mid [i, j])$
7       $actual\_i \leftarrow getActualIndex(i, X)$
8       $actual\_j \leftarrow getActualIndex(j, X)$
9   **if** $maxProb < prob$ **then**
10          $(maxProb, attr1, attr2) \leftarrow$
            $(prob, actual\_i, actual\_j)$
11   **else if** $maxProb = prob$ **then**
12   **if** $attr1 = null$ **and** $attr2 = null$ **then**
13             $(attr1, attr2) \leftarrow (actual\_i, actual\_j)$
14   **else if** $length(getInstances(X, attr1, attr2)) <$
            $length(getInstances(X, actual\_i, actual\_j))$ **then**
15             $(maxProb, attr1, attr2) \leftarrow$
            $(prob, actual\_i, actual\_j)$
16 **return** $(attr1, attr2, maxProb)$

Algorithm 4: findDenyRule

Input : X (log of access requests and decisions), ϕ (a permit rule), Y (list of decisions for access requests in X)

Output: A deny rule

1 $flag \leftarrow false$
2 $decision\_col \leftarrow getLastCol(X)$
3 **while** $\textbf{not}(getUniqueValues(decision\_col) = \{DENY\})$ **do**
4    $(attr, val, prob) \leftarrow getAttrExp(X, DENY)$
5    $coverage = length(getInstances(X, attr, val))$
6    $(expr\_LHS, expr\_RHS) \leftarrow (attr, val)$
7   **if** $getUniqueValues(X.getColumn(attr)) \equiv dom(attr)$
   then
8       $\phi.add(expr\_LHS = expr\_RHS)$
9       $flag \leftarrow true$
10    $X \leftarrow getInstances(X, rule\_LHS, rule\_RHS)$
11    $decision\_col \leftarrow getLastCol(X)$
12 **if** $flag = false$ **then**
13   **return** $(null)$
14 **else if** $coverage = length(getInstances(Y, DENY))$ **then**
15   **return** $(\langle \phi, DENY \rangle)$
16 **else**
17   **return** $(null)$

Algorithm 5: generalizeDenyRules

Input : *ruleset* (initial ruleset from mining algorithm), *log* (complete authorization log)

Output: Final ruleset with generalized deny rules

1 $covered\_instances \leftarrow \emptyset$
2 **foreach** $rule \in ruleset$ **do**
3   **if** $rule.d = DENY$ **then**
4       $coverage \leftarrow getRuleCoverage(rule)$
5   **if** $coverage \subseteq covered\_instances$ **then**
6          $ruleset.remove(rule)$
7   **else**
8   **foreach** $attrExp \in rule$ **do**
9             $gen\_cov \leftarrow$
            $getRuleCoverage(rule.remove(attrExp))$
10   **if** $\textbf{not}(PERMIT \in gen\_cov)$ **then**
11                $rule \leftarrow rule.remove(attrExp)$
12          $ruleset.add(rule)$
13          $coverage \leftarrow getRuleCoverage(rule)$
14          $covered\_instances \leftarrow$
            $covered\_instances \cup coverage$
15 **return** *ruleset*

---

enumerates all possible attribute-value pairs in the input dataset and calculates conditional probability in case of each attribute-value pair. The *getUniqueValues* function in line 3 returns the set of distinct values from the input set. The conditional probability in line 4 indicates the probability of occurrence of the given class (in this case, the class is PERMIT), given an attribute-value pair. If two attribute-value pairs have the same probability, then the one with higher coverage is selected (lines 7-11). The *findAttrAttrPair* function is similar to the *findAttrValPair* function, except that, instead of attribute-value pairs, the loop in *findAttrAttrPair* function enumerates all possible pairs of *uattr* and *rattr*, where *uattr* $\in$ UATTR,

$rattr \in RATTR$, and *uattr* and *rattr* have the same domain, that is, $dom(uattr) = dom(rattr)$. The conditional probability in line 6 (Algorithm 3) indicates the probability of occurrence of PERMIT, given an attribute-attribute pair.

The *findDenyRule* function in Algorithm 4 mines a conflicting negative rule within a positive rule. The loop runs until all the instances in the input dataset contain only DENY. Within this loop, the attribute expression yielding the highest conditional probability for DENY is selected. Lines 7-9 ensure that the selected attribute expression is added to the input rule only if the set of distinct values contained in attribute *attr* equals the domain of *attr*. The *flag* variable indicates whether any attribute expression was added to the input rule. A subset of the input dataset is created comprising of all instances containing the selected attribute expression. The loop is then repeated on this subset, until it contains only instances of DENY. At this point, a negative rule is created by taking the conjunction of all selected attribute expressions in the loop. The mined negative rule is indeed a conflicting negative rule if it covers all DENY instances in the input dataset (lines 12-17).

After generating the initial ruleset from the access control log, the policy mining algorithm generalizes the DENY rules in the ruleset as specified in Algorithm 5. For every DENY rule in the ruleset, we initially check if it is a subset of a generalized DENY rule, and if it is, then it is removed from the ruleset. Otherwise, the DENY rule is generalized by removing its components (attribute expressions) one at a time. Each time a component is removed, we check if the new DENY rule covers any PERMIT instances. If it does not, then the redundant component is removed from the original DENY rule. Finally, the generalized DENY rule is added to the ruleset. The *getRuleCoverage* function returns the set of instances covered by a rule in the access log.

4.2 Time Complexity

The time complexity of ABAC policy mining algorithm (Algorithm 1) can be calculated as follows. Let n be the number of records or instances and d be the number of attributes in the access log. The outer loop runs as many times as the number of PERMIT instances in the log. So, the running time of the outer loop is $O(n)$.

The inner loop runs as many times as the total number of attributes involved, including all the attribute expressions, within a particular PERMIT rule. In the worst case, a PERMIT rule can be formed by all attributes for attribute-value pairs and all combinations of attributes for attribute-attribute pairs. Since a rule cannot contain duplicate attribute expressions, total number of attributes included in attribute-value pairs is d and that for attribute-attribute pairs is of the order d^2. So, the running time of inner while loop is $O(d^2)$.

Calculating the optimal attribute-value pair (line 7 in Algorithm 1; Algorithm 2) takes $O(nd)$ in the worst case when all the attributes in the log contains n distinct values. Further, calculating the optimal attribute-attribute pair (line 9 in Algorithm 1; Algorithm 3) takes $O(d^2)$ time. So, total time taken for calculating the optimal attribute expression is $O(nd)$.

Computing a conflicting DENY rule (line 20 in Algorithm 1; Algorithm 4) takes total $O(nd^3)$ time. This is because the while loop in Algorithm 4 takes $O(d^2)$ time in the worst case when a DENY rule contains all attributes for attribute-value pairs and all combinations of attributes for attribute-attribute pairs. Moreover, calculating the optimal attribute expression (line 4 in Algorithm 4) takes $O(nd)$ time.

Generalizing the DENY rules (line 27 in Algorithm 1; Algorithm 5) consumes a total of $O(nd)$ time. This is because the loop in Algorithm 5 runs for each attribute, within every DENY rule in the initial

ruleset. Since rules represent instances of the access log, the number of DENY rules in the initial ruleset is of the order n.

The total running time of our ABAC policy mining algorithm is, therefore, $O(n^2 d^5)$. The time complexity of our policy mining approach is much less than $O(n^3)$, which is the worst case running time of [26] (details in Section 7). Suppose, every attribute in the log contains exactly two values in its domain, then total number of instances in a complete log, n, is 2^d. Besides, in a realistic application, domain of attributes have more than two values. So, for large values of d, $d^5 << m^d (= n)$, where $m \in \{2, 3, 4, ...\}$ depending on the application.

5 GENERATING ACCESS LOGS

In this part, we discuss the algorithm used for generating the log, in detail. The proposed algorithm can be used as a framework for generating synthetic logs, which can be utilized for various analysis purposes. For example, we use synthetic logs, generated from ABAC policies, for evaluation of our policy mining approach, so that we can have the ground truth while comparing the mined ABAC policy with original ABAC policy.

Log generation is an important phase in our proposed approach, because the log outputted from this phase serves as the input for the ABAC policy mining algorithm. Our goal is to understand the behavior of an underlying access control model. So we consider all possible combinations of all possible users, resources and actions, in short all possible scenarios of access requests, while generating the log, to be able to interpret all possible operations of the underlying access control model.

The log generation algorithm works as follows. Using the set of user attributes and domain for each user attribute, all possible users in the system are created by enumerating all possible combinations of values for user attributes. Similarly, all possible resources in the system are created using the set of resource attributes and domain for each resource attribute. A unique identifier is allocated to each user and resource. Then, using the complete set of users, resources and actions in the system, all possible *(user, resource, action)* combinations are determined, to enumerate all possible access requests that can be created from the system. While generating the complete set of access requests, each request is evaluated against the given XACML policy to determine the access decision for that request, following which the access request and corresponding access decision are written to a file.

Each record in the log indicates if a certain user can perform certain action on a certain resource. In other words, each row in the log contains the tuple (A_u, A_r, *Action*, *Decision*), where A_u and A_r are, respectively, the set of requesting user and requested resource attributes, *Action* is the requested action, and *Decision* $\in$ {PERMIT, DENY } is the access decision corresponding to that access request.

5.1 Determining domains for each attribute

A challenge that we encountered while generating the log was to determine the domain for each user and resource attribute, because based on this domain information, all possible combinations of values for user and resource attributes can be created. In the context of this paper, we assume four types of columns or attributes: columns appearing only in the set of user attributes or resource attributes (but not in both) referred to as *usr-only* attribute and *res-only* attribute respectively, columns that appear in the intersection of user and resource attribute sets referred as *usr-res* attributes, a user column dependent on the resource identifier column called as *usr-foreign-key* column, and a resource column dependent on the user identifier column referred to as *res-foreign-key* attribute.

The basic algorithm for defining the domain for all attributes is as follows:

Step 1: Determine the domain for all usr-only and res-only attributes.
Step 2: For every column $c \in$ usr-res, repeat:
- First determine the domain of c.
- Then the domain of each *uattr* and *rattr*, where *uattr* $\cap$ *rattr* $= c$, is the same as the domain of c, that is, $dom(uattr) = dom(rattr) = dom(c)$.
Step 3: If the set of user attributes contains a column $c \in$ usr-foreign-key, then the domain of c, $dom(c)$, is the set or subset of resource identifiers, as required by c.
Step 4: If the set of resource attributes contains a column $c \in$ res-foreign-key, then the domain of c, $dom(c)$, is the set or subset of user identifiers, as required by c.

6 EVALUATION

We have implemented the proposed algorithms in Section 4 and report our experimental evaluation in this section. As our evaluation approach, rather than starting from an access log, we conduct our experiments by generating an access log from an ABAC policy, and then mine policies based on the generated log. Such an approach ensures that we have access to *ground truth* policies (i.e., original policies) with which we can compare the results of our mining algorithm. We follow a systematic approach to generate a comprehensive as well as minimal log as proposed in Section 5.

We compare the performance of our algorithm with the previously proposed algorithm by Xu and Stoller [26], which we refer to as XSAM in the rest of this section. We should note that XSAM is only capable of mining positive attribute-based access control policies. Therefore, we conduct our experiments on both policies that contain only positive rules, and policies that include positive as well as conflicting negative rules.

6.1 Datasets

We perform our experiments on two policy datasets that we have have adapted from [26] to include negative authorizations. The university policy, University, authorizes accesses to applications, gradebooks, rosters and transcripts, requested by students, faculties, applicants and staff in registrar/admissions office. The project management policy, Project, controls accesses by accountant, auditor, planner and manager to tasks, schedules and budgets associated with projects.

In order to provide a fair assessment and comparison of our algorithm versus XSAM, we use two different versions of University and Project policies. Policies UniversityP and ProjectP contain only postive authorization rules, while policies UniversityPN and ProjectPN have both positive and negative authorization rules. We have included the policies in Appendix A.

6.2 Implementation

Our log generation implementation works based on list of all possible user attributes and resource attributes along with the domain for each attribute, list of all possible actions, and an ABAC policy written in XACML 3.0 [6] (Section 5). Each policy in XACML comprises of a set of rules, where each rule consists of a sequence of attribute expressions to determine which access requests the rule applies to and a rule effect to determine the access decision in case the rule is satisfied by an access request. Consistent with our policy model, we use *deny-overrides* rule-combining algorithm for XACML policies. The log generation algorithm is implemented in Java (JDK 1.8). We use WSO2 Balana [25], an open-source XACML implementation, to determine access decisions corresponding to each access request for a given XACML policy. The policy mining algorithm is written in Python (Python 3.5). We performed each experiment 10 times and report the average time measurement in our experiments. The experiments were performed on a 64-bit Windows 10 machine having 12 GB RAM and Intel Core i7-6700HQ processor.

Table 1 summarizes the access logs generated for university and project management policies. We note that the same number of access requests were generated regardless of positive-only vs. positive/negative policy versions. $|attr_u|$ is the number of user attributes, including the unique identifier attribute. Similarly, $|attr_r|$ is the number of resource attributes, including the identifier attribute. $|U|$, $|R|$ and $|O|$ are, respectively, the total number of user, resources and actions in the system. $|log|$ is the total number of records in the generated log, which is computed as $|U|$ x $|R|$ x $|O|$.

6.3 Experiments with Positive Authorizations

We first compare the performance of our policy mining algorithm with XSAM [26] on policies consisting of only positive authorizations. This can provide an insight on how performances comapre on solving a mining problem that both approaches should be able to solve by design. We use the complete log as input to our algorithm, and provide only the PERMIT instances as input to XSAM since it works based on access control lists (ACLs).

The first four rows in Table 2 show the results of our algorithm and XSAM on UniversityP and ProjectP policies. The table compares approaches on the basis of quality, with respect to preciseness and conciseness, of mined rules and total time taken for execution. $|\rho_{orig+}|$ and $|\rho_{orig-}|$ are the number of positive and negative rules in the original ABAC policies, whereas $|\rho_{mined+}|$ and $|\rho_{mined-}|$ are the number of positive and negative rules in the mined ABAC policies. Further, WSC_{orig} and WSC_{mined} are, respectively, the WSC measure for original and mined policies. When calculating WSC for the experiments, we consider all user-specified weights w_i to be equal to one. Finally, *Run time* is the total time, in seconds, taken for mining ABAC policies from the given access control information.

As demonstrated in Table 2, both approaches, XSAM [26] and our proposed work, perform exactly the same in terms of mining concise rules that are syntactically and semantically similar to the original policy. However, our approach outperforms XSAM in terms of running time.

Table 1: Details of the access logs created from original ABAC policies

Policy	$|attr_u|$	$|U|$	$|attr_r|$	$|R|$	$|O|$	$|log|$
University	6	128	5	2048	9	2359296
Project	8	4608	6	72	7	2322432

Table 2: Comparison of our proposed algorithm with XSAM [26] for university and project management policies

Mining Alg.	Policy	$|\rho_{orig+}|$	$|\rho_{orig-}|$	$|\rho_{mined+}|$	$|\rho_{mined-}|$	WSC_{orig}	WSC_{mined}	Time (s)
XSAM	UniversityP	5	-	5	-	19	19	1540
Proposed work	UniversityP	5	-	5	-	19	19	936
XSAM	ProjectP	11	-	11	-	49	48	1328
Proposed work	ProjectP	11	-	11	-	49	48	896
XSAM	ProjectPN	11	4	20	-	67	4324	1370
Proposed work	ProjectPN	11	4	11	4	67	64	1032
XSAM*	UniversityPN	11	3	-*	-*	56	-*	7200+*
Proposed work	UniversityPN	11	3	11	3	56	53	1123

*XSAM [26] did not terminate nor produced any output for the UniversityPN policy even after running for more than two hours.

6.4 Experiments with Positive and Negative Authorizations

Our second set of experiments is on policies consisting of both positive and negative authorization rules. The last four rows in Table 2 show the performance of the two approaches on ProjectPN and UniversityPN policies. Our observations show that our approach precisely mines concise positive and negative rules for both policies, whereas XSAM [26] computes verbose rules that are more identity-based rather than attribute-based. For example, in case of ProjectPN, while our proposed algorithm mines total of 15 rules with WSC of 64, XSAM produces 20 rules with significantly large WSC (4332). Furthermore, in our experiments, XSAM was not able to terminate and produce an output for UniversityPN even after running for more than two hours. The result clearly demonstrate the need for mining negative authorization rules along with positive rules.

6.5 Discussion of Results

6.5.1 Overall Analysis. As shown in Table 2, our policy mining algorithm precisely mines all the positive and negative rules from the generated log. Although the input access control log contains records belonging to both types of DENY spaces, the DENY space as a result of negative authorization rules and the default DENY space, our policy mining algorithm successfully mines all and only the required DENY authorization rules.

Our manual observation of the mined rules showed that they never reference any identity-based attributes like unique user identifier attribute and unique resource identifier attribute. Further, the experiment results verified that the mined ABAC policy is equivalent to the original ABAC policy. Moreover, the WSC of mined policy is constantly less than or equal to the WSC of original policy, i.e., $(WSC)_{mined} \leq (WSC)_{original}$. This manifests that our algorithm mines policies that are at least as concise as the original policies, while maintaining the semantic meaning of the original policies.

6.5.2 Comparison with XSAM. Our policy mining algorithm and the XSAM approach perform similar when only positive authorization rules need to be mined. However, there is a significance difference when both positive as well as negative authorization rules are considered. More particularly, when experimenting on policies containing negative authorization, XSAM either does not terminate in reasonable time (after two hours for UniversityPN) or produces verbose positive rules containing identifier attributes (which should be avoided for ABAC policies). In addition, our policy mining approach always runs faster than that of XSAM.

Although it may be argued that XSAM considers negative instances implicitly (i.e., any access not permitted is denied), it fails badly when considering both positive and negative rules as demonstrated in our experiments. This is because the policies ProjectPN and UniversityPN are particularly hard to express using only positive rules, which emphasizes the need for explicitly mining negative authorization rules along with positive authorization rules.

7 RELATED WORK

One of the areas in policy mining that received great research interest was role mining. The problem of role mining is to determine an optimal set of roles R from the user-permission assignments (UPA) for obtaining RBAC configuration that is equivalent to the given user-permission assignments, that is, decomposing the given UPA into User-role Assignments (UA) and role-Permission Assignments (PA) [18]. Vaidya at al. defined the Basic-RMP problem for finding a minimal set of roles from the given UPA [23]. Edge-RMP, a variant of Basic-RMP, aims to minimize, along with number of roles, |UA|+|PA| [14, 24]. |S| denotes the cardinality of a set S. Furthermore, Colantonio et al. presented a cost-based metric for mining optimal set of roles [5]. Another metric , proposed by Molloy et al., called *Weighted Structural Complexity* (WSC) [19], is the weighted sum of the number of elements in R, UA, PA and other components of an RBAC system. The aim of WSC optimization problem is to find an RBAC configuration, consistent with the given UPA, such that

WSC of the mined RBAC policy is minimized. Consistent with [26], we adopt the notion of WSC for measuring the complexity of mined ABAC policies.

The limitation of RBAC policy mining is that, for obtaining RBAC configuration from the given User Permission Assignments, role mining problems consider only the positive authorizations, in terms of what permissions are assigned to users, based on their roles. Our ABAC mining approach on the other hand, considers both positive and negative authorizations while obtaining ABAC policy.

Xu and Stoller were the first to introduce the concept of ABAC policy mining [26]. The motivation behind the idea of ABAC mining is to ease the burden of migration to ABAC framework from an existing access control paradigm, by partially automating the process of migration. At a high level, their policy mining algorithm works as follows. Initially, they generate an Access Control List (ACL), which they refer as the User Permission Relation, from an ABAC policy and attribute data. Then their policy mining algorithm, while iterating over the tuples in the given User Permission Relation, select a user permission tuple that is used as the seed for creating a candidate rule. This candidate rule is then generalized by replacing conjuncts in attribute expressions with constraints. The goal of their generalization process is to increase the coverage of the rule in terms of the additional tuples that can be covered by the rule in the User Permission Relation. The set of candidate rules, which altogether cover the entire ACL, is then optimized by removing redundant rules and merging pairs of rules. A rule is redundant if it covers instances in the User Permission Relation already covered by some other rule. Two different rules, having the same constraints, are merged by taking the union of conjuncts, in those rules, for every attribute. However, their algorithm does not deal with negative authorizations. Moreover the ABAC policy mining algorithm presented in [26] is very heuristic and complicated to interpret. Importantly, their running time is cubic in the size of the ACL, whereas the time complexity of our ABAC mining approach is much less than cubic time as explained in detail in Section 4.2.

Recently, Medvet et al. [17] proposed an evolutionary, separate and conquer approach for mining ABAC policies, using the same policy language and case studies as in [26]. In their work, a new rule is generated and the set of access requests decreases to a smaller size during each iteration. Similar to Xu and Stoller [26] and unlike our proposed approach, their work is not capable of mining negative authorization rules. Moreover, there is not much difference in terms of performance compared to [26]. Therefore, we only compare our performance against [26].

Our policy mining algorithm is closely related to the PRISM rule mining algorithm [4] by Cendrowsk. PRISM is an established data mining algorithm for inducing rules corresponding to a given dataset. It serves as a solution for the traditional data mining classification problem. Given a training dataset, containing different classifications, PRISM outputs a set of modular rules, where each rule contains combination of attribute-value pairs for arriving at a particular classification. To yield a set of disjunctive rules, PRISM uses an induction strategy for finding the attribute-value that delivers the most information about a particular classification. In other words, when determining a rule for a particular classification δ_n, PRISM finds the attribute-value pair α_x that gives the highest conditional probability for the classification δ_n, that is, PRISM selects the α_x for which the probability of occurrence of the classification δ_n, given the attribute-value pair α_x, is maximum. However, the limitation of PRISM in the context of this paper is that, for a particular rule, PRISM tends to find only attribute-value pairs, but not attribute-attribute pairs. As a result, when PRISM is run on the access control log, which serves as a suitable training dataset comprising of two classifications PERMIT and DENY, PRISM creates rules containing the identifier attributes like the unique user identifier attribute and unique resource identifier attribute. As a result, the output is verbose since it contains large number of rules. Our policy mining algorithm, although based on PRISM, overcomes this drawback by also considering attribute-attribute pairs, along with attribute-value pairs, while constructing a rule for PERMIT or DENY.

8 DISCUSSIONS AND CONCLUSIONS

In this paper, we proposed an algorithm for mining ABAC policies capable of discovering both positive and negative authorization rules simultaneously. While previous approaches in access control policy mining literature had focused on positive-only authorization rules (including more recent work on ABAC mining [26]), our work significantly contributes to the area by discovering negative authorization rules as well. We evaluated our policy mining algorithm on logs generated from two synthetic but realistic policies. Our observations from experiments show that the mined rules never reference identity-based attributes like user identifier and resource identifier attributes. Also, the results demonstrate that the mined rules are equivalent to the original ABAC policy, and that the mined policies are concise compared to them. Furthermore, we demonstrated that our approach outperforms previous ABAC mining algorithm [26] through the experiments and theoretical analysis.

Our mining algorithm attempts to mine positive and negative rules simultaneously. An alternative strategy would be to mine all possible positive rules first and then combine rules in a way to resolve in more general set of positive and negative rules. However, such an alternative strategy will lead to many granular positive rules which then need to be considered for generalization. Combining granular rules is a complex problem itself to solve optimally. We note that the previous ABAC mining approach [26] followed such an strategy (for positive rules only). But it relied on heuristics for generalization (by considering only pairs of rules). A main objective of design of our mining approach was to avoid such heuristic, suboptimal strategies.

The proposed mining algorithm is feasible to be employed in practice based on our experimental results and theoretical analysis. Running time of the algorithm was in the order of a few minutes for the synthetic policies. Theoretically, the time complexity of our policy mining algorithm depends on size of complete log, which is exponential to number of attributes. While we acknowledge this limitation, we note that it is applicable to any log mining algorithm that aims to avoid false positives/negatives. Moreover, we note that policy mining is inherently an offline and less time-sensitive task.

As future work, we plan to extend our approach to incorporate other ABAC features such as support for numerical data and other relational operators such as subset in attribute expressions. We will also explore algorithmic improvements, and more extensive quantitative analysis based on policies of different sizes.

ACKNOWLEDGEMENTS

We would like to thank the anonymous reviewers for their valuable comments and helpful suggestions that guided us in improving the final manuscript.

REFERENCES

[1] Apache Tutorials - Apache HTTP Server. URL: https://httpd.apache.org/docs/2.0/misc/tutorials.html.

[2] E. Bertino, P. Samarati, and S. Jajodia. An extended authorization model for relational databases. *IEEE Transactions on Knowledge and Data Engineering*, 9(1):85–101, Jan. 1997. ISSN: 1041-4347.

[3] E. Bertino, S. Jajodia, and P. Samarati. A Flexible Authorization Mechanism for Relational Data Management Systems. *ACM Trans. Inf. Syst.*, 17(2):101–140, Apr. 1999. ISSN: 1046-8188.

[4] J. Cendrowska. PRISM: An algorithm for inducing modular rules. *International Journal of Man-Machine Studies*, 27(4):349–370, Oct. 1, 1987. ISSN: 0020-7373.

[5] A. Colantonio, R. Di Pietro, and A. Ocello. A Cost-driven Approach to Role Engineering. In *Proceedings of the 2008 ACM Symposium on Applied Computing*, SAC '08, pages 2129–2136, New York, NY, USA. ACM, 2008.

[6] eXtensible Access Control Markup Language (XACML) Version 3.0. URL: http://docs.oasis-open.org/xacml/3.0/xacml-3.0-core-spec-os-en.html.

[7] D. F. Ferraiolo, R. Sandhu, S. Gavrila, D. R. Kuhn, and R. Chandramouli. Proposed NIST standard for role-based access control. *ACM Transactions on Information and System Security*, 4(3):224–274, 2001.

[8] E. Ferrari. Access Control in Data Management Systems. *Synthesis Lectures on Data Management*, 2(1):1–117, Jan. 1, 2010. ISSN: 2153-5418.

[9] N. Gal-Oz, E. Gudes, and E. Fernández. A Model of Methods Access Authorization in Object-oriented Databases. In *Proc VLDB*, pages 52–61, Jan. 1, 1993.

[10] V. C. Hu, D. Ferraiolo, R. Kuhn, A. R. Friedman, A. J. Lang, M. M. Cogdell, A. Schnitzer, K. Sandlin, R. Miller, and K. Scarfone. Guide to attribute based access control (abac) definition and considerations (draft). *NIST special publication*, 800(162), 2013.

[11] F. Huonder. Conflict Detection and Resolution of XACML Policies. *Master's thesis, University of Applied Sciences Rapperswil*, 2010.

[12] X. Jin, R. Krishnan, and R. Sandhu. A Unified Attribute-Based Access Control Model Covering DAC, MAC and RBAC. In *IFIP Annual Conference on Data and Applications Security and Privacy*, LNCS, pages 41–55. Springer, Berlin, Heidelberg, July 11, 2012.

[13] M. A. Al-Kahtani and R. Sandhu. Rule-based RBAC with negative authorization. In *20th Annual Computer Security Applications Conference*, pages 405–415, Dec. 2004.

[14] H. Lu, J. Vaidya, and V. Atluri. Optimal Boolean Matrix Decomposition: Application to Role Engineering. In *2008 IEEE 24th International Conference on Data Engineering*, pages 297–306, Apr. 2008.

[15] A. Lunardelli, I. Matteucci, P. Mori, and M. Petrocchi. A prototype for solving conflicts in XACML-based e-Health policies. In *Proceedings of the 26th IEEE International Symposium on Computer-Based Medical Systems*, pages 449–452, June 2013.

[16] M. St-Martin and A. P. Felty. A Verified Algorithm for Detecting Conflicts in XACML Access Control Rules. In *Proceedings of the 5th ACM SIGPLAN Conference on Certified Programs and Proofs*, CPP 2016, pages 166–175, New York, NY, USA. ACM, 2016.

[17] E. Medvet, A. Bartoli, B. Carminati, and E. Ferrari. Evolutionary inference of attribute-based access control policies. In *International Conference on Evolutionary Multi-Criterion Optimization*, pages 351–365. Springer, 2015.

[18] B. Mitra, S. Sural, J. Vaidya, and V. Atluri. A Survey of Role Mining. *ACM Comput. Surv.*, 48(4):50:1–50:37, Feb. 2016. ISSN: 0360-0300.

[19] I. Molloy, N. Li, Y. A. Qi, J. Lobo, and L. Dickens. Mining Roles with Noisy Data. In *Proceedings of the 15th ACM Symposium on Access Control Models and Technologies*, SACMAT '10, pages 45–54, New York, NY, USA. ACM, 2010.

[20] R. S. Sandhu and P. Samarati. Access Control: Principles and Practice. *IEEE Communications Magazine*, 32(9):40–48, 1994.

[21] M. Satyanarayanan. Integrating Security in a Large Distributed System. *ACM Trans. Comput. Syst.*, 7(3):247–280, Aug. 1989. ISSN: 0734-2071.

[22] D. Servos and S. L. Osborn. HGABAC: Towards a Formal Model of Hierarchical Attribute-Based Access Control. In *International Symposium on Foundations and Practice of Security*, LNCS, pages 187–204. Springer, Cham, Nov. 3, 2014.

[23] J. Vaidya, V. Atluri, and Q. Guo. The Role Mining Problem: A Formal Perspective. *ACM Trans. Inf. Syst. Secur.*, 13(3):27:1–27:31, July 2010. ISSN: 1094-9224.

[24] J. Vaidya, V. Atluri, Q. Guo, and H. Lu. Edge-RMP: Minimizing administrative assignments for role-based access control. *Journal of Computer Security*, 17(2):211–235, Jan. 1, 2009. ISSN: 0926-227X.

[25] WSO2 Balana. URL: https://github.com/wso2/balana.

[26] Z. Xu and S. D. Stoller. Mining Attribute-Based Access Control Policies. *IEEE Transactions on Dependable and Secure Computing*, 12(5):533–545, Sept. 2015. ISSN: 1545-5971.

[27] Z. Xu and S. D. Stoller. Mining Attribute-Based Access Control Policies from Logs. In *IFIP Annual Conference on Data and Applications Security and Privacy*, LNCS, pages 276–291. Springer, Berlin, Heidelberg, July 14, 2014.

[28] X. Zhang, Y. Li, and D. Nalla. An Attribute-based Access Matrix Model. In *Proceedings of the 2005 ACM Symposium on Applied Computing*, SAC '05, pages 359–363, New York, NY, USA. ACM, 2005.

A POLICY DATASETS

In the following tables, we list the rules in the policies that we used in the experiments. Table 3 lists the rules in the ProjectP policy. In addition to those rules, the ProjectPN policy includes the DENY rules listed in Table 4. Tables 5 and 6 show the rules in the UniversityP and UniversityPN policies, respectively.

- $\langle u.adminRole = manager; r.type = budget; u.department = r.department; action = read, \text{PERMIT}\rangle$
- $\langle u.adminRole = manager; r.type = budget; u.department = r.department; action = approve, \text{PERMIT}\rangle$
- $\langle r.type = schedule; u.projectLed = r.project; action = read, \text{PERMIT}\rangle$
- $\langle r.type = budget; u.projectLed = r.project; action = read, \text{PERMIT}\rangle$
- $\langle r.type = schedule; u.projectLed = r.project; action = write, \text{PERMIT}\rangle$
- $\langle r.type = budget; u.projectLed = r.project; action = write, \text{PERMIT}\rangle$
- $\langle r.type = schedule; u.project = r.project; action = read, \text{PERMIT}\rangle$
- $\langle r.type = task; u.task = r.rid; action = setStatus, \text{PERMIT}\rangle$
- $\langle r.type = task; r.proprietary = false; u.project = r.project; u.expertise = r.expertise; action = read, \text{PERMIT}\rangle$
- $\langle r.type = task; r.proprietary = false; u.project = r.project; u.expertise = r.expertise; action = request, \text{PERMIT}\rangle$
- $\langle u.isEmployee = true; r.type = task; u.project = r.project; u.expertise = r.expertise; action = read, \text{PERMIT}\rangle$
- $\langle u.isEmployee = true; r.type = task; u.project = r.project; u.expertise = r.expertise; action = request, \text{PERMIT}\rangle$
- $\langle u.adminRole = auditor; r.type = budget; u.project = r.project; action = read, \text{PERMIT}\rangle$
- $\langle u.adminRole = accountant; r.type = budget; u.project = r.project; action = read, \text{PERMIT}\rangle$
- $\langle u.adminRole = accountant; r.type = budget; u.project = r.project; action = write, \text{PERMIT}\rangle$
- $\langle u.adminRole = accountant; r.type = task; u.project = r.project; action = setCost, \text{PERMIT}\rangle$
- $\langle u.adminRole = planner; r.type = schedule; u.project = r.project; action = write, \text{PERMIT}\rangle$
- $\langle u.adminRole = planner; r.type = task; u.project = r.project; action = setSchedule, \text{PERMIT}\rangle$

Table 3: ProjectP policy rules

- $\langle u.adminRole = manager; u.department = dept2; r.type = budget; action = read, \text{DENY}\rangle$
- $\langle u.adminRole = manager; r.type = budget; r.project = proj21; action = approve, \text{DENY}\rangle$
- $\langle u.adminRole = planner; u.department = dept3; u.expertise = testing; r.type = schedule; action = read, \text{DENY}\rangle$
- $\langle r.type = task; r.department = dept2, \text{DENY}\rangle$

Table 4: DENY rules in ProjectPN policy. PERMIT rules are the same as in ProjectP (Table 3)

- $\langle r.type = gradebook; u.courseTaken = r.course; action = readScore, \text{PERMIT}\rangle$
- $\langle r.type = gradebook; u.courseTaught = r.course; action = readScore, \text{PERMIT}\rangle$
- $\langle u.position = faculty; r.type = gradebook; u.courseTaught = r.course; action = assignGrade, \text{PERMIT}\rangle$
- $\langle u.position = student; r.type = transcript; u.uid = r.student; action = readTranscript, \text{PERMIT}\rangle$
- $\langle u.position = faculty; u.isChair = true; r.type = transcript; u.department = r.department; action = readTranscript, \text{PERMIT}\rangle$

Table 5: UniversityP policy rules

- $\langle r.type = gradebook; u.courseTaken = r.course; action = readMyScores, \text{PERMIT}\rangle$
- $\langle r.type = gradebook; u.courseTaught = r.course; action = addScore, \text{PERMIT}\rangle$
- $\langle r.type = gradebook; u.courseTaught = r.course; action = readScore, \text{PERMIT}\rangle$
- $\langle u.position = faculty; r.type = gradebook; u.courseTaught = r.course; action = changeScore, \text{PERMIT}\rangle$
- $\langle u.position = faculty; r.type = gradebook; u.courseTaught = r.course; action = assignGrade, \text{PERMIT}\rangle$
- $\langle u.isChair = true; r.type = gradebook; u.department = r.department; action = readScore, \text{PERMIT}\rangle$
- $\langle r.type = gradebook; u.courseTaken = r.course; action = addScore, \text{DENY}\rangle$
- $\langle r.type = gradebook; u.courseTaken = r.course; action = readScore, \text{DENY}\rangle$
- $\langle r.type = gradebook; u.courseTaken = r.course; action = changeScore, \text{DENY}\rangle$
- $\langle r.type = gradebook; u.courseTaken = r.course; action = assignGrade, \text{DENY}\rangle$
- $\langle u.department = registrar; r.type = roster; action = read, \text{PERMIT}\rangle$
- $\langle u.department = registrar; r.type = roster; action = write, \text{PERMIT}\rangle$
- $\langle u.position = faculty; r.type = roster; u.courseTaught = r.course; action = read, \text{PERMIT}\rangle$
- $\langle r.type = transcript; u.uid = r.student; action = read, \text{PERMIT}\rangle$
- $\langle u.position = student; u.department = dept1; r.type = transcript; action = read, \text{DENY}\rangle$
- $\langle u.isChair = true; r.type = transcript; u.department = r.department; action = read, \text{PERMIT}\rangle$
- $\langle u.department = registrar; r.type = transcript; action = read, \text{PERMIT}\rangle$
- $\langle r.type = application; u.uid = r.student; action = checkStatus, \text{PERMIT}\rangle$
- $\langle u.department = admissions; r.type = application; action = read, \text{PERMIT}\rangle$
- $\langle u.department = admissions; r.type = application; action = setStatus, \text{PERMIT}\rangle$
- $\langle u.department = admissions; r.type = application; r.department = dept2; action = read, \text{DENY}\rangle$
- $\langle u.department = admissions; r.type = application; r.department = dept2; action = setStatus, \text{DENY}\rangle$

Table 6: UniversityPN policy rules

Towards a Privacy-Aware Quantified Self
Data Management Framework

Bhavani Thuraisingham
The University of Texas at Dallas
800 W Campbell Rd, Richardson
Texas
bxt043000@utdallas.edu

Murat Kantarcioglu
The University of Texas at Dallas
800 W Campbell Rd, Richardson
Texas
muratk@utdallas.edu

Elisa Bertino
Purdue University
610 Purdue Mall, West Lafayette
Indiana
bertino@purdue.edu

Jonathan Z. Bakdash
U.S. Army Research Laboratory
Field Element at University
of Texas at Dallas
800 W Campbell Rd,
Richardson, Texas
jonathan.z.bakdash.civ@mail.mil

Maribel Fernandez
King's College, University of London
Strand, London WC2R 2LS
London
maribel.fernandez@klc.ac.uk

ABSTRACT

Massive amounts of data are being collected, stored, and analyzed for various business and marketing purposes. While such data analysis is critical for many applications, it could also violate the privacy of individuals. This paper describes the issues involved in designing a privacy aware data management framework for collecting, storing, and analyzing the data. We also discuss behavioral aspects of data sharing as well as aspects of a formal framework based on rewriting rules that encompasses the privacy aware data management framework.

CCS CONCEPTS

• **Security and privacy** → **Database and storage security** → Data anonymization and sanitization

KEYWORDS

Data privacy, quantified self, privacy preserving, data analytics.

ACM Reference Format:
B.Thuraisingham, M. Kantarcioglu, E. Bertino, J. Z. Bakdash and M. Fernandez. 2018. Towards a Privacy-Aware Quantified SelfData Management Framework. In Proceedings of ACM *SACMAT '18, June 13–15, 2018, Indianapolis, IN, USA*, ACM, NY, NY, USA, 12 pages. https://doi.org/10.1145/3205977.3205997

1 INTRODUCTION

1.1 The Problem

Mobile devices such as smartphones have become a prevalent computing platform, with just over 968 million smartphones sold in 2013 around the world [27], a 36% increase in the fourth quarter of 2013. In particular, Android devices accounted for 78.4% of the market share, an increase of 12% year-on-year. Moreover, smartphone app downloads from app stores have seen a steady rise, reaching 102 billion in 2013 with total revenue of $26 billion [28], and including a multitude of apps for monitoring personal data such as health, food intake, exercise, and sleep patterns, among others. With the recent emergence of the *Quantified Self (QS)* movement, personal data collected by wearable devices and smartphone apps are being analyzed to give guidance to users in improving their health or personal life habits. These data are also being shared with other service providers (e.g., retailers) using cloud-based services, bringing potential benefits to users (e.g., information about health products). But such data collection and sharing are often being carried out without the user's knowledge, bringing grave danger that personal data may be used for improper purposes. For example, data collected by a device monitoring blood glucose levels might be used by an insurance company to deny coverage to a user or even a user's blood relatives. Such privacy violations could easily get out of control if data collectors could aggregate financial and health-related data with tweets, Facebook activity, and purchase patterns. This could result in lawsuits against data collectors and psychological and physical distress in individuals. To address these growing challenges, we urgently need tools and techniques for privacy protection in QS applications.

1.2 Motivational Scenario:

To understand the impact of environmental (e.g., air pollution) and lifestyle (e.g., sleep quality) factors on childhood asthma attacks, the U.S. National Institutes of Health (NIH) recently started a "Pediatric Research using Integrated Sensor Monitoring Systems (PRISMS)" program. The goal of this program is "to address significant data science and tool development challenges associated with integrated monitoring systems datasets to enable important advances in our understanding of environmental determinants of pediatric asthma" [54]. As a part of this study, it is expected that monitoring devices will be attached to children to collect data about their lifestyles (e.g., physical activity, blood oxygen levels, etc.) and these lifestyle datasets will be combined with environmental (e.g., air pollution near the child's home) and medical (e.g., number of hospitalizations due to asthma attacks) datasets to better understand and predict asthma attacks. This NIH program requires researchers to have "demonstrated expertise to enable data security and maintain confidentiality of personally identifiable information" since parents need strong assurances about their children's privacy before participating in such a study. Similarly, QS data gathered about employees (e.g., sleep quality, activity data, etc.) could be used to predict employee stress levels and to improve employee well-being provided that adequate measures for protecting privacy are adopted. According to a recent survey by PwC (Price Waterhouse Coopers) only "more than half of employees would consider wearing a smartwatch from their employer if their data was used to improve things such as working hours, stress levels and where they can work from." The good news is that according to the survey, "people are also more open to the idea if the data is anonymized and shared at an aggregate level, rather than being personalized." These examples show the potential of collecting and sharing QS data to improve healthcare outcomes and employee productivity, provided, however, that individual privacy is protected. Therefore, we need a framework to enforce appropriate privacy-aware policies guided by users' privacy needs to determine which data are to be collected, stored and shared by whom, when, where, why and how, as well as tools and techniques to efficiently enforce the policies while getting as much utility as possible from the QS data.

1.3 Contributions of this Paper

Our work is motivated by examples and scenarios such as the ones discussed in Section 1.2 in order solve the problem stated in Section 1.1. Specifically, our objective is to develop novel mobile and cloud-based data storage architectures combined with innovative cryptographic protocols, access control techniques, privacy enhancing techniques, information leakage analysis, and usability analysis to securely store, process and share privacy sensitive QS data without violating individual privacy. In particular, our goal is to develop a privacy-aware QS data management framework that controls the entire life cycle of QS data and consists of the components (i) privacy aware data collection, (ii) privacy aware data storage and access, and (iii) privacy aware data analytics/mining and sharing. The organization of this paper is as follows: Section 2 describes the research challenges; Section 3 describes the high-level design of the framework; Section 4 discusses novel directions such as the behavioral aspects of information sharing as well as aspects of developing a formal framework; Section 5 concludes the paper.

2 PRIVACY-AWARE QUANTIFIED SELF DATA MANAGEMENT FRAMEWORK

2.1 Architecture Overview

We need to develop a privacy-aware QS data management framework that controls the entire lifecycle of the QS data (Figure 1). We envision that different data sources and devices will be providing sensitive information to our Data Collection Layer (Section 2.3) running on the mobile device based on the privacy-aware data collection policies. These policies will specify when, where, and what can be collected and stored by the device. For example, a device that automatically captures all of the images (e.g., Narrative Clip [53]) may not be used in certain locations such as the immigration status check area at an international airport. Such data collection restrictions will be automatically managed by the privacy-aware data collection manager running on the device.

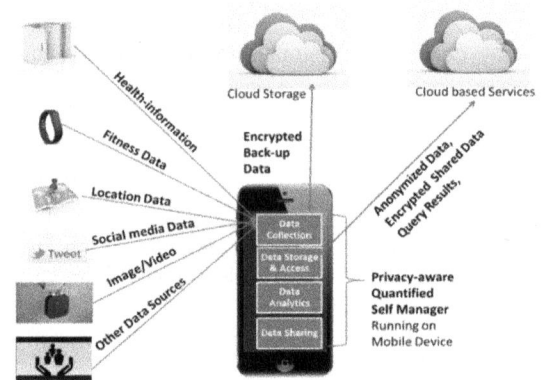

Figure 1: Architecture Overview

In our platform, we assume that only the mobile device is trusted, for example, that it adopts state-of-the art techniques for smartphone security such as containerization [6, 56], and is allowed to access all the incoming data in plaintext form; the mobile device plays the role of "gatekeeper" in controlling what information is released. However, cloud-based services and apps running on the device are not trusted. Later on, the collected data will be indexed and certain statistics (e.g., average sleep per day for the last 12 months) and basic data analytics functions (e.g., correlation coefficients between two data streams) will be computed locally on the incoming QS data. As more data are collected, the storage on the device will not be sufficient to store all of the data. We envision an encrypted cloud storage component where older data and/or less frequently accessed data are pushed to cloud. For example, pictures captured from a prior event may be stored in encrypted form in the cloud. Appropriate local indexes will be maintained to efficiently retrieve the encrypted data stored in the cloud as needed. In addition, based on the access control policies, local apps running on the device will be given access to some of the collected data. When needed, these apps will be allowed to access some of the encrypted data stored in the cloud via a simple query interface. We emphasize that our architecture does not require change to any existing application or device. For example, if a user is happy to use the Fitbit app, the user can continue using it as it is. On the other hand, using the application programming interface (API) provided by Fitbit, our agent running on the mobile device can collect the necessary activity data and can combine them it with location data collected from the mobile device to enforce some policies or enable other applications. As a part of this project, we will develop a proof of concept architecture integrating different types of data using the APIs provided by device manufacturers.

The Data Storage and Access Layer will also deal with managing the lifecycle of the data. In some cases, the data may not be needed in fine-grained form any longer. For example, storing 20-year-old daily weight data may not be necessary; instead storing and mining monthly average weight data could be sufficient for supporting various medical applications. In other cases, the data may have to be deleted to preserve privacy (e.g., delete and/or generate fake location data to hide the fact that the user participated in a protest). Such data deletion policies will be automatically managed by the storage layer and the potential privacy impact of such deletions would be analyzed using quantitative information flow analysis (e.g., only deleting sensitive information may create some inference side channels). Since people change or lose their mobile devices frequently, we envision that the information stored on **the mobile device will be continuously backed up** using another cloud service provider. Thus, in the event that the mobile device is lost, a new mobile device could be set up using the encrypted back-up copy. Of course, cloud service providers need to make sure that the stored encrypted data are reliably accessible.

Another key component of the architecture is a set of secure and privacy-aware mechanisms to mine and share the collected data (i.e., the Data Analytics/Mining and Sharing Layer). We envision that such data sharing and mining will be carried out using the services running in the cloud. Based on different scenarios some of the data could be sent without any modification (e.g., heart rate data for medical diagnosis), some will be sent after sanitization (e.g., randomized response-based techniques [24] to hide user's true response) and some will be sent in an encrypted format that will enable the distributed computation of exact data mining results as needed. To provide such capabilities, we need to develop novel approaches that combine cloud-based distributed data mining, and secure multi-party computation techniques with mobile device-based data sanitization, randomized response, efficient stream pre-processing, and local data caching. Our main assumption in the framework is that the mobile device is trusted. Other than that, our architecture could be easily modified if the research carried out shows us different needs. One major contribution of this project would be to understand the best ways to integrate different components running on the device and the cloud while preserving privacy.

2.2 Related Work

Our work touches on many different topics ranging from personal data stores to access control policy issues. In this section, we discuss some prior research in the context of quantified self-data lifecycle (i.e., capturing, storage and sharing of QS data).

Access Control Policies, Privacy and Usability. Previous work on access control policies has not addressed the problem of the continuous collection of personal data. The only previous

work focusing on personal data collected by mobile devices is the FENCE system (short for "Continuous Access Control Enforcement in Dynamic Data Stream Environments") [53] by the project PI and collaborators. However, FENCE does not associate context information with policies, and, thus, it is unable to automatically select the policy to be associated with specific data. Previous work on security for mobile operating systems focuses on restricting applications from accessing sensitive data and resources, but lacks efficient techniques for enforcing those restrictions according to fine-grained contexts that differentiate between closely located subareas [12]. Moreover, much of this work focuses on developing policy systems that do not restrict privileges per application and are only effective system-wide [43]. Also, existing policy systems do not cover all of the possible ways in which applications access user data and device resources. Finally, existing location-based policy systems only provide a single mechanism, such as special hardware or location devices, for detecting the location [12, 40, 42]. In most cases, such systems assume the context as given without providing or evaluating the context detection methods of mobile devices [12, 32].

Setting of policy rules relating to privacy and access is a topic that has been investigated in several domains of computer science and human-computer interaction, including system access control, privacy policies of organizations [4], and policy management for online social networks [10]. Research in these domains has examined users' comprehension of policies and how to present the privacy information in a manner that is easy for users to comprehend. In general, users do not comprehend policies of any type very well [67, 70], and they will seldom engage in the time and effort needed to try to comprehend them. Whether a user will purchase a product from an internet vendor is influenced by the perceived security of their personal data provided by the vendor [26]. Similarly, it can be expected that allowing one's personal data to be shared more widely will depend on trust that this sharing will be done as intended and that unauthorized access to the data will be prevented. Sociological and theoretical literature has emphasized the significance of perceptions about context to the appropriateness of data flows such as those envisioned in our design [55].

Effort has been devoted by researchers to develop alternative mechanisms for privacy and security that reduce the cognitive demands on the users, while at the same time enabling them to make informed decisions. For the authoring of policies, evidence for the effectiveness of a template-based approach has been provided [37, 38]. Such an approach reduces the cognitive demands on the policy author by providing templates (developed by policy experts and domain experts) that decompose the overall task into subtasks composed of relevant policy elements. Reduction of cognitive demands was also the idea behind the tool Privacy Bird developed to provide a signal (red, yellow, or green bird) to indicate whether a website's policy is consistent with the user's specified preferences prior to the user entering information into the site [15]. Laboratory and crowd-sourcing studies have shown that users tend to make less risky app-selection decisions when a summary risk score is provided, particularly when that information is conveyed as the amount of safety associated with the app [11, 29].

Personal Data Stores. There have been recent efforts to manage personal data collected by smartphones. One of the most notable efforts is the OpenPDS project that provides an open-source implementation of Personal Data stores for mobile platforms [51]. Similarly, companies such as Mydex [52] provide cloud-based personal data stores. Recently, Apple released an app called Health [5] to enable the storage of health and fitness data on mobile devices. To our knowledge, such systems do not integrate mobile devices with cloud storage in a secure manner to enable a wide range of data access and/or querying functionalities, and work under the assumption that the cloud-based service provider is trusted. One way to securely process QS data stored in the cloud is to encrypt the data prior to moving it to the cloud and to perform secure analysis over encrypted QS data. Although the research community has made significant progress in developing cryptographic approaches that allow some computation over encrypted data such as searchable encryption techniques (e.g., [16, 31, 66]), order preserving encryption (e.g., [8]), fully homomorphic encryption (e.g., [30]), and practical Oblivious RAM techniques (e.g., [64, 65])—no generic and cost-efficient solution for the QS data storage setting has yet emerged. In this project, we will leverage existing cryptographic advances as much as possible in the context of QS data back-up in the cloud. Especially, we will focus on how best to use the mobile device storage and potential processing of the data on the device to enable efficient privacy-preserving QS data processing.

Mining Quantified Self Data. We need to leverage existing research and significantly improve and enhance the state-of-the-art in several important directions. Recent studies have reported on mining QS data to provide useful results. For example, "collaborative recommendation" is an evidence-based recommendation technique in which information such as ratings from many training users is leveraged to make recommendations for a specific test user [1, 34, 60]. However, such previous work has not addressed the problem of (i) assessing the quality of recommender systems obtained when data used for training such systems is anonymized and (ii) whether and how such systems could be personalized for specific users using non-anonymized data in the context of mobile QS data collection. In addition, there are many projects that try to mine user data collected by mobile phones. For example, the Reality mining project [22] tries to infer individuals' habits from data collected by the mobile device. MoodSense [46] leverages the collected mobile data to infer the mood of the user. BeWell [44] tries to infer metrics such as user's sociality by mining various mobile phone sensors. Eigenbehaviors [23] uses principal component analysis techniques to predict daily activity. Recently, the Lifestreams project [35] tries to provide a platform where other data mining tasks can be built by leveraging the analytics building blocks provided by the system. To our knowledge, none of the existing work and platforms tries to integrate privacy-aware technologies with a wide range of QS data mining tasks.

Differential Privacy and Privacy-Preserving Data Mining. Recently, many differentially private data mining tools have been developed, ranging from generic differential private statistical estimation framework (e.g., [21]) to machine learning algorithms such as differentially-private support vector machines (e.g., [9]). Although these developments are quite interesting, they are not directly applicable to our case since they assume that the data are already collected in a database controlled by the curator. On the other hand, recent randomized response-based differential private data collection techniques [24] are relevant but it is not clear how such randomized response ideas could be leveraged for mining QS

data. As a part of this project, we will extend noise addition techniques combined with distributed cryptographic protocols (e.g., [20]) to produce differentially-private data mining results and leverage cloud infrastructure to scale to millions of individuals by delegating some work to cloud-based services. Our work on privacy-preserving distributed data mining has explored how to leverage cryptographic techniques to mine data from different parties (e.g., [39]). Many of the existing privacy-preserving distributed data mining protocols implicitly assume that the number of parties participating is small. Scaling these protocols to potentially millions of mobile devices remains an important challenge. We need to tackle these challenges by combining peer-to-peer cryptographic protocols with secure outsourcing of some computation to the cloud using secret sharing-based techniques.

3. HIGH LEVEL DESIGN OF THE FRAMEWORK

3.1 Privacy-Aware Data Collection

Users typically carry and use their smartphones and other personal devices in public and private places and in a variety of different contexts, some of which are privacy sensitive. For example, a user is likely to consider being in a hospital or doctor's office as personally-sensitive information. Therefore, we must allow users to specify policies restricting which data can be collected in which contexts. These policies allow an individual to specify his/her own personal privacy policies with respect to the collection of his/her own personal data. Policies must be tightly coupled with the data because the policies may change over time and, for accountability reasons, it is important to keep track of the policies under which data were collected. Also, in many contexts, a user is not alone; therefore, use of certain devices may have to be prevented or controlled as these devices may record information about other users, thus violating their privacy. Moreover, corporations and other organizations may forbid their employees and visitors to bring, or use, camera-enabled devices to the workplace, including smartphones, even though employees might need to have their devices with them at all times (e.g., an employee who uses his/her device to store information relevant to his/her health). Furthermore, default privacy policies are needed for aggregated and individual data that reveals the location and even layout of sensitive facilities, such as fitness data within military bases outside of the U.S. We thus need fine-grained context-based access control policies by which certain devices or resources within devices can be blocked from acquiring data. We refer to these policies *as context-based device resource usage policies*. An essential requirement for supporting the enforcement of both types of policies is the support for context information acquisition. In addition, such collection decisions needs to be analyzed to address potential privacy implications (e.g., not collecting images may disclose that the user is in a sensitive location). To address the above challenges, we need to design a privacy aware data collection system. Our high level design consists of the following four components:

1) *A policy language for specifying context-based data collection policies and context-based device resource usage policies.* A key element in such a language is the constructs for specifying contexts. As discussed by Nissembaum [55], the appropriateness of information handling is best judged by

the situational context of a disclosure. Even though her work did not address the specific case of personal data, advanced by our notion of QS data, we believe that her idea nicely maps onto it. Our notion of a context-based policy language, and a corresponding enforcement engine, is our approach to introducing such an idea into our system. We need to support three different types of contexts: location, time, and situation. Situation refers to application-specific context, such as a task that the user is currently engaged in. For all the context types, we will allow users to associate symbolic names with specific contexts. For example, consider a hospital located in a certain street in a given city. The hospital can be denoted in many ways, for example by using geographical coordinates or by using a postal address. However, it will be easier for the user to associate his/her shorthand name to the hospital. Our policy language will support different constructs for the specification of contexts and also the specification of complex contexts by which one can combine different types of contexts, and will incorporate social constraints where the absence and/or presence of other users nearby impact the data collection process [44]; an example would be a policy specifying that images can be acquired in a given location only if no one else is present.

2) *A policy authoring tool for the specification of policies according to our policy language.* The tool will provide an easy-to-use interface for the specification of policies as well as a mechanism to import policies (e.g. the corporate policies that have to be enforced on user devices). We need to leverage existing work on policy-by-example [10]; however, this approach has been developed for social networks and mainly deals with grouping friends in order to assign them permissions. We need to borrow the notion of "policy-by-example" and tailor it to our context. The authoring tool will also support graphical location-based interfaces for the specification of location information.

3) *A flexible location and presence detection mechanism.* We need to develop a suite of mechanisms for detecting the location of the user, so that the most convenient mechanism can be used depending on the type of location (such as closed/open location), and networks and sensing devices available. Our location detection system will leverage Wi-Fi-based positioning techniques to retrieve the location of the device. In addition to these techniques, our system will also collect location data retrieved from GPS and cellular networks for situations where there is no Wi-Fi coverage in the areas of interest. As part of the system, we will develop a user-specific database of Wi-Fi access points, recording the areas that the user has visited and thus allowing the user to associate names with these areas and refer to them in policies. Concerning presence detection, we will develop mechanisms based on the use of near field communication (NFC) techniques [44], physical access control, motion sensors, surveillance devices and other approaches [32].

4) *A policy enforcement engine.* The engine, located in the devices, will be in charge of enforcing the policies. A major challenge is the enforcement of policies requiring that certain resources on a device not be used in a particular context. Our initial approach will address this problem on Android and

leverage our previous work in the IdentiDroid anonymity system [50, 62] on dynamically revoking Android permissions. In our system, a main challenge is that permissions must be dynamically revoked or re-instated based on the context, whereas in IdentiDroid the switch is executed when the user requires to enter or exit the anonymous mode.

A detailed analysis needs to be carried out to identify privacy issues that are specific to our target environment consisting of continuous/pervasive personal data collection by each individual about himself/herself. In addition, we need to explore ways of designing the following:

1) *Policy languages for privacy-aware data collections:* We need to develop a policy language as an extension of the well-known XACML standard [72].

2) *Policy authoring tool:* We need to adapt or develop a user-friendly tool supporting the specification of policies expressed in our language. One possibility is using conversational agent with a high-level representation of information [58]. The tool needs to support the analysis and evolution of policies, based on user feedback and policy overrides. The tool also needs to support policy integration supporting the merging of different policies (for example, a corporate policy on what data can be captured while working in the office and the personal policy defined by the user) and include simple mechanisms and defaults for policy conflict resolution.

3) *Location and presence detection mechanism:* We need to design location detection mechanisms for devices such as the smart phones.

4) *Policy enforcement engine:* We need to design the engine to apply the policies. An important challenge in the design of the engine is to ensure that the policies are not bypassed by (possibly) malicious users, in the case of corporate policies by users who do not want to comply with the policies, or by malicious software whose goal is to gather private data about users. To address such challenge we need to integrate and extend Trusted Platform Management? TPM technology, containerization techniques, and application profiling techniques originally developed for protecting data from insider threats [36].

3.2 Privacy-Aware Data Storage and Access

After collecting QS data from different sensors (e.g., health monitors), devices (e.g., Narrative clip), and mobile sources (e.g., tweets and text messages sent by the mobile device user), we need to store these data for mining and analysis to extract interesting patterns. In some cases (e.g., correlating location data with air quality data to understand long term asthma trends), there may be long-term value in storing all of the data captured based on the policies. Storage of such collected data creates interesting research challenges. First, the smartphones that are currently becoming the hub for all the captured data may not be able to store all the data on the device. To address the storage limitations of smartphones, one can leverage cloud storage. Many mobile devices support automatic cloud back-up and storage mechanisms. For example, iPhone comes with a default iCloud-based data backup support. Unfortunately, as recent events show [19], privacy-sensitive data stored in the cloud in plaintext format could be vulnerable to attacks. Encrypting such data before moving them to the cloud prevents some of these attacks, but straightforward data encryption results in many query execution and data retrieval challenges. There are recent advances in querying encrypted data that could be leveraged to enable secure cloud data storage while allowing selective retrieval of the data, but important challenges remain, that need to be addressed to satisfy the requirements of various QS applications. Existing techniques such as range queries (e.g., [63]), key-word search (e.g., [16, 31, 66]), and attribute-based encryption (e.g., [71]) and fully homomorphic encryption (e.g., [30], do not directly support queries such as "find the pictures taken in New York City that have Jim in the picture". Adapting and improving existing encrypted data querying techniques while leveraging the capabilities of the smartphones remains an important research direction. As we discuss below, we plan to address these challenges by extracting important features from the QS data and then modify existing searchable encryption techniques to work with these extracted features.

Another important requirement is to support mobile apps that provide valuable services to users. Consider an app that accesses movement data to automatically extract sleep patterns and correlate it with weight information to understand the impact of someone's weight on sleep patterns. To support such an app, we may want to provide motion sensor data only in the evening, hiding the activity pattern during the day. Providing fine-grained access to collected QS data would be the first step in allowing useful QS applications while protecting privacy. Given the large number of potential apps that may combine different types of QS data to provide value-added services, enabling users to define access control policies for each app becomes a challenge. Understanding users' needs for easy-to-use mechanisms is critical; otherwise users will end up not making use of fine-grained access control policies.

Finally, keeping all the collected data forever creates significant privacy challenges. For instance, remembering all location data forever might allow a malicious app or malicious party to infer important information about user movement patterns going back many years. To enhance privacy, we envision certain scenarios where users may want to delete some information based on pre-defined conditions. For example, a user may want to delete some information captured (e.g., photos taken) during a visit to a particular location (e.g., Las Vegas) after a certain period (e.g., 10 years). Of course, facilitating such secure deletion of data would require us to track where the data are stored. To support automatic QS data deletion policies, efficient techniques are needed to track and delete sensitive data.

To address the above challenges we need to design a Privacy-Aware Data Storage and Access System. Our high level design is illustrated in Figure 2, where all the data coming from different sources will first be processed and stored on the mobile device. The local storage will keep different types of indexes locally (i.e., on the smartphone) to help in querying the stored data. In addition, the framework will manage the data access policies for different mobile apps. We need to make the framework compatible with existing efforts such as OpenPDS [51] so that multiple different apps can be used on top of the framework by

using basic mechanisms to access the stored data. Later on, as the mobile device storage space fills up, some of the stored QS data will be pushed to the cloud using different heuristics. For example, heart rate data from the previous month may be pushed to the cloud in an encrypted format. Before such an action, appropriate local indexes will be updated to enable easy retrieval later. Furthermore, locally-built models will be kept to enable certain tasks. For example, a time series model that is built to find anomalies in the heart rate could be updated locally even if the underlying data is shifted to the cloud using stream processing

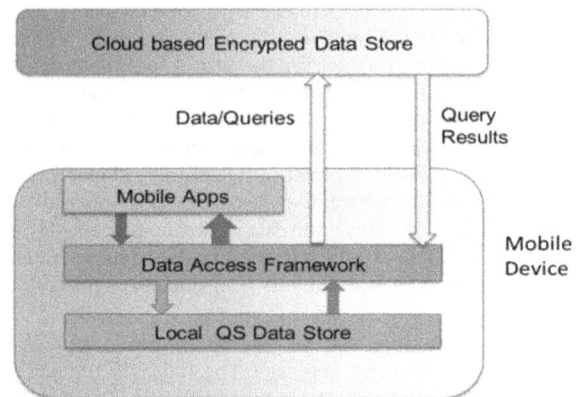

Figure 2 Storage Architecture

techniques. In addition, the framework will keep track of which apps accessed which data (i.e., keep basic provenance information) to facilitate data deletion in the future. Clearly, enabling such a framework will require us to address many research challenges. Below, we summarize the activities that need to be explored.

1) *Secure long-term storage of QS data:* We envision that a typical user may generate terabytes of data during his/her life. Based on current smartphone capabilities, clearly it is not possible to store all the data locally. At the same time, as discussed earlier, we must push data in encrypted format to the cloud to protect individual privacy. We need to explore how existing searchable encryption techniques could be applied seamlessly to query local and (encrypted) cloud data. Because most of the QS data will be indexed, queried, and accessed based on time and location, we will start by building encrypted indexes on these two dimensions for different types of QS data. To be able to leverage existing keyword search techniques, we need to discretize each dimension (e.g., discretize time based on day, month and year) and convert a given search into a keyword search and/or simple one dimensional range-query search. This simple approach will provide us with basic capabilities for data querying based on location and time. Such encrypted querying may form the basis for building data mining models from QS data. Furthermore, we need to explore ways of pre-computing certain interesting functions on the data before the QS data are pushed to the cloud. For example, a face detection algorithm can be used to automatically detect faces in a given image. Later on, such information related to a detected face

may be inserted into an appropriate index for fast image retrieval. We need to explore pre-computation of various interesting features from the data (e.g., faces in a given image, moving averages of sensor information) to build indexes to enable fast retrieval of encrypted data from the cloud using existing range and keyword search techniques.

2) *Secure and privacy-aware query interfaces for QS Apps:* To enable a wide range of applications, we need to provide interfaces for apps to access the stored data. Some of the data that are used by an app may need to be retrieved from the cloud as well as from the local mobile storage. During this data access, we want to make sure that apps only access data at a granularity that does not violate individual privacy. Providing a full-fledged query language support, such as SQL, in a secure and privacy preserving manner to QS apps may be too costly. We need to explore simple interfaces (e.g., a limited subset of SQL) to enable apps to provide value-added services while simplifying the access control and privacy policy enforcement requirements. We also need to explore aggregation (i.e. disclose results aggregated to hide sensitive data) and noise addition techniques (i.e., local differentially private techniques).

3) *Usability/Human Factors:* Because end-users must interact through the interfaces to define policies, set the data management options, and use the data for their own purposes, interfaces must be designed consistent with human capabilities. Of critical importance, users need to understand recommendations and suggestions given by the applications/recommenders. We need to exploit our knowledge and experience dealing with comprehension of organizations' privacy policies and specification of users' privacy preferences [59], as well as comprehension of the permissions requested by Android app's [29], to design and evaluate interfaces that are easy and intuitive to use for the different types of users who will be involved in the different phases of the QS data lifecycle.

4) *QS Data Deletion/Sanitization Support:* As we discussed earlier, we may want to delete or sanitize some of the data for privacy and efficiency reasons. Assessing the efficiency implications of data deletion or sanitization is straightforward, but it is more challenging to assess the implications for privacy. A striking example was given by the *William Weld re-identification* [69], which was not prevented by sanitizing records down to just (Date of birth, Sex, Zip Code). One fruitful approach is to study the effectiveness of particular sanitizations against particular adversaries [33]. But we believe that stronger privacy guarantees could be achieved through quantitative information flow analysis. The idea is to view a deletion/sanitization mechanism as an information-theoretic channel that takes the original data to a sanitized output. The amount of leakage of this channel quantifies the effectiveness of the sanitization against arbitrary adversaries. As discussed in Section 2.2, a challenge is that there are *many* leakage measures that might be most appropriate, depending on the operational scenario. For this reason, it is attractive to focus on *min-capacity*, which by the Miracle Theorem of [2] is an upper bound on leakage in all scenarios. Min-capacity is also relatively easy to compute; in the case of a deterministic channel, for instance, it just requires calculating the number of feasible channel outputs.

For the (Date of birth, Sex, Zip Code) channel, for example, the number of feasible outputs can be crudely estimated to be about 240 million. (There are around 40,000 Zip Codes, each with an average population of around 8000, or about 4000 of each sex. Since there are 36,500 possible dates of birth, we can presume that the 4000 people of each sex in a given Zip Code have mostly distinct dates of birth, giving 40,000×2×3000 = 240 million feasible outputs.) Hence if the secret is a uniformly-distributed American, the channel increases its vulnerability to being guessed correctly by a factor of 240 million, giving a posterior vulnerability of 240/320 = 0.75, showing that this sanitization is completely inadequate. We need to, then, to develop sanitization mechanisms with small min-capacity, allowing precise statements about the privacy protection that they provide. One challenge is the possibility of *correlations* among secrets. Some leakage bounds in the presence of arbitrary correlations are shown in [3], but we need to explore this further.

3.2 Privacy-Aware Data Analytics and Sharing

We believe that to create more value from the QS data, we need to support more functionality on top of the storage and querying framework. Personal data collected by each individual can be used in different ways to the benefit of the individual, others, and to society in general. For example, running a large-scale medical research project on understanding the impact of regular exercise on high blood pressure could easily be carried out by collecting and aggregating sport activity data with blood pressure data from millions of individuals. However, even though individuals may have incentives to share data, privacy concerns may impede such sharing. Thus, it is critical that privacy-aware sharing be supported. Consequently, we need techniques allowing one to specify and evolve access control policies to support selective sharing of personal data with other individuals.

In certain scenarios, directly allowing apps to access even a subset of the data may disclose sensitive information, so, instead we may want to share results that are mined locally. For example, incoming QS data can be mined locally to find interesting association rules (e.g., a fitness app that is used to enter food intake information may be combined with blood pressure data measurements to find associations). This way we can limit the app's access to a few data mining or query results (e.g., local association rule results). Furthermore, the user's data can be mined locally by an app developed by a third party, but the results may be shared only when a user explicitly approves sharing the result.

Also, data coming from different individuals may need to be integrated to create aggregated/sample-level/population-level models. One way to facilitate such data sharing would be to send data using techniques such as Onion routing (e.g., using Tor [18]) to avoid data being linked to the individual who is donating the data. However, previous research on identifiability [69] clearly indicates that even if data contains no identifiers and are sent using Onion routing, it can still be used to identify individuals. Another option could be to add noise to the data so that the shared data become less accurate (e.g., randomized response type application [24]) and therefore, less likely to cause negative outcomes for individuals. We believe the right combination of techniques for QS data that can support a large number of applications needs to be explored. Especially, important is that suitable privacy-aware techniques are in place and tools and guidelines be available for individuals to be able to trade off privacy risks with personal benefits.

Finally, as indicated by this paper's previous sections, for the data sharing scheme to accomplish its goal of enforcing personalized privacy policies for individual users, the interface will need to be designed to fulfill users' needs and to be "user friendly." For users to allow data sharing, they must trust their data will be protected in the manner that they intend and will not be vulnerable to leakage and attacks. Also, users must be able to comprehend the policy management options so they understand their choices and the possible consequences of their selections. Because these options involve the data that can be collected and the contexts in which they can be collected, as well as who will be allowed access to their data, policy specification by the user will necessarily be a complex process. Consequently, the interactions with the interface necessary for a user to define his/her policies and set the data management options need to be as straightforward as possible and allow for personalization. Not all users may desire to have detailed control over their personal information, so the interface needs to support decisions at different levels of granularity and smart default settings that would be acceptable to the majority of users. Smart default settings are critical because the majority of users do not change privacy/security settings (e.g., > 90% of Google accounts do not have two factor authentication enabled [68]).

Our high-level design for data sharing consists of multiple components. The first component comprises a personal access control system supporting the specification and enforcement of access control policies for personal data as well as the evolution and merging of different policies ranging from event-based sharing to data donations by the individual for research. The access control system will also include an authoring tool. The second component is a data mining system able to work on sanitized data. An important issue is to assess the quality of data mining models derived from sets of anonymized data. More importantly, it is crucial to determine whether and how a data mining model built from a large population can then be refined by using non-anonymized personal data of each user or if the predictions obtained by such a public data mining system can be combined with recommendations obtained by a local data mining system (i.e., a local data mining system based on the data of the specific users). The goal would be to create global data mining models based on the sanitized data of multiple users and then personalize these models for each a specific user.

We need to build a framework where the QS streams coming from different sources will be analyzed locally. Using the computational power of the mobile device, important statistics as well as the data mining models for the individual will be computed. In addition, as needed, the encrypted querying mechanisms discussed earlier will be used to retrieve data archived in the cloud to improve the local models and statistics. Later on, these models and statistics will be shared based on the policies and events registered by the user. We also need to develop cloud-based secure distributed data mining techniques to allow individuals to securely donate and/or sell data to the various data mining needs. Based on the data sharing policies, the data that will be submitted to data mining models will be automatically extracted. In certain scenarios, the data also will be aggregated using the information coming from the peers (i.e.,

information coming from nearby friends). In some cases, the information will be sanitized by adding noise before sharing with the cloud-based services (e.g., by leveraging randomized response based differential-privacy techniques [24]). This locally computed information will be shared using secret sharing-based techniques [13] with multiple servers located on the public cloud using service such as Tor [18] so that linking back the data to a particular individual will be harder. Once the data are sent to multiple servers using secret sharing mechanisms, secret sharing-based secure protocols will be executed among the servers to build the population-level data mining models. To scale to a large number of users, we plan to combine effective sampling and randomized response techniques in conjunction with secret sharing-based, secure multi-party ideas. For example, we may want to combine user data from a certain subpopulation (e.g., people above age 65 with hypertension) to build a linear regression model.

If user i is participating in the system with their data vectors x_i where $1 \le i \le n$, we can write the data mining process as secure multi-party evaluation of linear regression function f as $f\left(I_{C(x_1)} \cdot x_1, I_{C(x_2)} \cdot x_2, \ldots, I_{C(x_n)} \cdot x_n\right)$ where $I_{C(x_i)}$ is the indicator function that describe the selection condition for the user data. First of all, since this is a data mining model, to be statistically significant, we may not need to get all the samples. Given the selection condition C, we may estimate the number of users t that can satisfy the condition C, if $t \gg s$ where s is the number of samples required for statistical significance, than we can subsample from the user population that matches the condition with probability $\frac{s}{t}$ to reduce the amount of data that is secretly shared for SMC phase. Of course, while doing sampling, we may disclose which users match condition C. To prevent this we may want to sample from the users for whom condition C is not satisfied as well. The sampling rates could be adjusted to balance individual privacy protection versus efficiency. Once user data are selected after this sampling step, noise addition techniques or secret sharing techniques with multiple servers could be used to send the data to a cloud-based secret sharing-based SMC framework. In some cases, these built models will be sent back to the users to locally customize to improve their utility for the user.

Finally, in order to investigate data sharing from a human factors point of view, we need to take a multi-method approach in which a variety of methods, including interviews, surveys, laboratory experiments, and crowd-sourcing experiments, are used to obtain qualitative and quantitative data in naturalistic and controlled settings [59]. This information will be used to determine smart defaults. We need to leverage our access to various user populations at Purdue University and through its Center for Education and Research in Information Assurance and Security (CERIAS) partners to develop and test our interface design concepts on groups that are most relevant to the particular issue in QS data storage. For research requiring large samples of experienced computer users, we will conduct studies on Amazon Mechanical Turk (MTurk) for which we obtain performance measures as well as survey and demographic information, as we have done in our app-selection research [11, 29]. As a first stage of our approach, we will identify human factors issues related to personal data sharing by determining the risks and benefits associated with QS data storage, including consideration of legal rules under which those risks can be created (e.g. search warrants) or avoided (e.g. bans on certain data-handling practices in statutes such as the Health Insurance Portability and Accountability Act [HIPAA]). As a next stage, we will establish whether typical users are aware of these risks and benefits, and perceive them to be substantial. A third stage will be to evaluate usability issues involved in specifying personal privacy policies. A central focus of this stage will be to focus on ways to present the policy information in a comprehensible manner during the specification process. We need to evaluate not only the usability of alternative interfaces but also whether the users have an accurate understanding of what their policy specifications allow and do not allow. The following six items outline the activities that need to be explored.

1) *A risk-aware access control system for personal data:* The system will include a policy language for the specification of policies, based on extensions/customizations of the XACML standard, a policy authoring tool able to merge and evolve access control policies, and a policy enforcement engine. In addition, we will also explore quantitative methods to analyze and quantify risks in sharing QS data and automatically adjust policies in the light of existing risks. In our past work [7], we explored risk-based data sharing issues in the context of sharing large datasets. We need to integrate the risk acceptance behaviors captured during human subject experiments into quantitative models to better account for human behavior in real life. We need to explore how event-based sharing policies can be built on top of XACML extensions.

2) *A local data analytics framework to build models and local statistics based on streaming data and encrypted data stored in the cloud:* We need to explore how existing stream mining techniques [47, 48] could be used to maintain local statistics and data sketches for different data mining tasks. However, current stream learning algorithms [49] may not be readily used in the context of privacy-aware or encrypted data. A small change in the training set may affect the quality and performance of the learned model. For this, we will explore ways of maintaining basic statistics such as correlations among multiple streams. As needed some of the older models and statistics will be backed-up encrypted in the cloud. In some cases, such learned models and statistics will be combined to answer important questions based on approximation. Such approximations generally utilize a sliding window or sampling approach. For example, to answer a question as to how an individual's sleep quality is affected by his/her weight, previous models about sleep patterns and weight data (stored in the cloud) will be selectively utilized to compute such correlations.

3) *A global recommender system able to work on sanitized data:* We need to develop a recommender system able to work on data value ranges, rather than precise values. Furthermore, noise addition techniques such as randomized response will be explored to add noise to the data before sharing it. We need to test the relative effectiveness of the recommender systems built using sanitized data following the same testing approach we used to test the quality of classifiers learned on anonymized data.

4) *Cloud-based privacy-aware distributed data mining protocols to build population-level data mining models:* In addition to noise addition/sanitization techniques discussed earlier, we need to build distributed data mining techniques that do not disclose any information about the individuals other than the final data mining model. Initially, we will explore whether each user can push his/her data to few non-colluding, semi-honest servers sitting in the cloud. For example, to facilitate a scientific study that tries to find the impact of regular exercise, the location of the user, and air pollution on asthma attacks, a local data mining model can automatically create statistics about weekly exercise numbers combined with the user's demographic information and asthma attacks (assuming the user keeps an electronic journal) and location information. These statistics will be divided into secret shares [14, 17] and will be sent to different servers. Later on, existing data about local pollution information will be securely linked to user's location data by using secret sharing-based distributed data mining techniques. Building such an application will have unique challenges on how best to summarize local data so that the secret sharing-based protocols in the cloud could be best leveraged and scaled to a large number of users. In addition, we may need to explore how additional external sources of data can be used locally to improve the efficiency of the global distributed data mining protocols. For example, each mobile device may download the local pollution data from the internet and do the linkage locally (again using a system like TOR to prevent linkage to an individual). This will reduce the amount of cryptographic protocol execution needed in the public cloud.

5) *A customization system able to refine the global recommender system for specific users:* We need to investigate an approach based on the multiple mixture model [45], by which we will combine the recommendations obtained by a local recommender, built on the non-sanitized data of a single user, with the recommendations obtained by the global recommender system, in order to obtain customized recommendations for the specific user. It is important to note the local recommender system will be obtained based on a very small set of data, very precise because it is not sanitized. Whereas the global recommender system will be based on a very large set of data, which is less precise because of the potential data sanitization. Extensive experimental analysis will be carried out to assess the accuracy of such a two-step approach.

6) *A human-factors analysis to determine the risks and benefits associated with QS data sharing perceived by both expert and typical users:* One-on-one interviews and online survey methods will be used for such an analysis. Policy experts will be invited for one-on-one, semi-structured interviews and asked about their thoughts concerning the possible risks and benefits associated with QS data storage. Different categories of risks and benefits, and their perceived importance, will be identified from the interview data. Typical users will be recruited through MTurk to answer a questionnaire that will allow us to determine whether they distinguish the same categories as the policy experts and perceive their relative importance similarly. In both studies, users will be asked about the degree to which they have trust in the QS data storage, and the categories of risks and benefits will be analyzed as a function of different levels of trust. If the typical users' perceived risks and benefits differ from those

identified by the expert users, ways of educating users about these risks and benefits will be devised and tested by comparing users' responses before and after the education. We need to also compare findings concerning user preferences to legal doctrine defining adequate consent to data collection or processing and identify ways to ensure that user decisions constitute legally effective limitations. To enable personalization of privacy policies for QS data sharing, the different options for setting the privacy policies should be identified. We need to query the policy experts and typical users with regard to the choices that they would like a privacy specification interface to accommodate. From this information we will evaluate the identified design features in controlled experiments conducted in the lab with a population of college-student computer users or on MTurk with a broader range of computer users. Many users will not want to engage in detailed specifications because of the high information-processing demands, so we will develop smart defaults, settings that are acceptable to the majority users, and also evaluate ways of presenting pre-set options that allow relatively simple setting of policies, but at a more aggregate level than specifying each factor separately. We need to incorporate the results of the experiments in the design of one or more possible interfaces, for which we will perform usability evaluations.

4. NOVEL DIRECTIONS

Section 3 described our high-level design of the privacy-aware data management framework for data collection, data storage, data sharing and data analysis. Our design consisted of concrete solutions such as specific languages and models (e.g., XACML) for data collection as well as privacy-aware data storage and analysis. In order to develop a useful framework, we need to take into consideration some additional aspects such as (i) the security of user devices and (ii) formalizing the framework so that we can prove properties such as consistency and completeness. We discuss these additional aspects in this section.

4.1 Security of User Devices

In order privacy to be maintained, user devices must remain secure over time. Privacy risks throughout the data lifecycle (collect, store, and analyze) can be mitigated by informing users about device vulnerabilities that are found over time. More importantly, the framework can help users update their smart phones and especially Internet of Things (IoT) devices. Almost half of all users never update IoT devices [61]. In addition, users can be notified if they are using (vulnerable) devices that are no longer receiving updates.

While security and privacy have to be a major consideration in designing data management systems for the IoT devices, usability is also important. For example, what happens if the user has forgotten his or her password and is unable to access the smart home or smart hospital records. Therefore, it is important to consider multifactor authentication for the user and also we need appropriate standards to be developed. For example, standards such as SAML and XACML have to be considered for authentication and authorization. Therefore, the user interface framework has to be integrated with the data management framework so that we can ensure security, privacy and usability of the IoT devices.

4.2 Towards a Formal Framework

In order to be able to accommodate any solutions, we need to develop a formal framework. In a recent paper we discussed some aspects of a formal framework based on rewriting rules [25]. In particular, we described a general framework, whereby users cannot only specify how their data are managed, but also restrict data collection from their connected devices as well as the storage and analysis of this data. More precisely, we discussed the use of data collection policies to govern the transmission of data from various devices (e.g., IoT devices), coupled with policies to ensure that once the data have been transmitted, it is stored and shared in a secure and privacy-preserving way. In other words, we discussed a framework for secure data collection, storage and management, with logical foundations that enable verification of policy properties. Our main focus however was on the aspect of specifying and reasoning about the policies for data collection.

While the work discussed in [25] is the first step towards designing such a formal framework for specifying and reasoning about security and privacy policies, we need to explore the use of such a framework for the privacy-aware data management framework we have discussed in Section 3. This is a research direction we are pursuing while we continue to carry out a more detailed design of the data management framework.

5. SUMMARY AND DIRECTIONS

This paper discussed the problem of securing, collecting, storing, and analyzing the data with a motivational example. Then we discussed the challenges involved in designing a privacy-aware data management framework for data collection, management and analysis. We also discussed the behavioral aspects of information sharing as well as some aspects of a formal framework for privacy-aware policy management. Finally, we discussed briefly the need for formalizing the framework so that one can specify and reason about the security and privacy policies regardless of the implementation solutions.

This paper mainly raises the awareness of the need for incorporating security and privacy policies at all levels of data management. The next step is to carry out a detailed design and implementation of the framework. We also have to design the formal framework so we can specify and reason about the policies regardless of the solutions implemented.

6. ACKNOWLEDGEMENTS

The views and conclusions contained in this document are those of the authors and should not be interpreted as representing the official policies, either expressed or implied, of the U.S. Army Research Laboratory or the U.S. government.

7. REFERENCES

[1] G. Adomavicius and A. Tuzhilin. Toward the next generation of recommender systems: A survey of the state-of-the-art and possible extensions. IEEE Transactions on Knowledge and Data Engineering, 17(6):734–749, 2005.

[2] Mário S. Alvim, Kostas Chatzikokolakis, Catuscia Palamidessi, and Geoffrey Smith. Measuring Information Leakage using Generalized Gain Functions. In Proc. CSF 2012: 25th IEEE Computer Security Foundations Symposium, pp. 265–279, Cambridge, MA, June 2012.

[3] Mário S. Alvim, Konstantinos Chatzikokolakis, Annabelle McIver, Carroll Morgan, Catuscia Palamidessi, and Geoffrey Smith. Additive and multiplicative notions of leakage, and their capacities. In Proc. CSF 2014: 27th IEEE Computer Security Foundations Symposium, pp. 308–322, Vienna, Austria, July 2014.

[4] Annie I. Anton, Elisa Bertino, Ninghui Li, and Ting Yu. A Roadmap for Comprehensive Online Privacy Policy Management. Communications of the ACM. 50(7):109–116, July 2007.

[5] Apple Health Web Site. https://www.apple.com/ios/whats-new/health/. Access 2014 November.

[6] N. Asokan, Lucas Vincenzo Davi, Alexandra Dmitrienko, Stephan Heuser, Kari Kostiainen, Elena Reshetova, Ahmad-Reza Sadeghi: Mobile Platform Security. Synthesis Lectures on Information Security, Privacy, and Trust, Morgan & Claypool Publishers, 2013

[7] Alain Bensoussan, Murat Kantarcioglu and SingRu Hoe. A Trust-Score-Based Access Control in Assured Information Sharing Systems: An Application of Financial Credit Risk Score Model. Risk and Decision Analysis, IOS Press, 2014.

[8] A. Boldyreva et al. Order-preserving Symmetric Encryption. In EUROCRYPT, 2009.

[9] Kamalika Chaudhuri, Claire Monteleoni, and Anand D. Sarwate. Differentially Private Empirical Risk Minimization. J. Mach. Learn. Res. 12 (July 2011), 1069–1109. 2011.

[10] Gorrell P. Cheek, Mohamed Shehab: Policy-by-example for online social networks. Proceedings of 17th ACM Symposium on Access Control Models and Technologies, SACMAT '12, Newark, NJ, USA. June 20–22, 2012, pp. 23–32.

[11] Jing Chen, Christopher S. Gates, Robert W. Proctor, and., Ninghui Li. Framing of summary risk/safety information and app selection. In Proceedings of the 2014 Annual Meeting of the Human Factors and Ergonomics Society. Santa Monica, CA: HFES, 2014.

[12] Mauro Conti, V. T. N. Nguyen, and Bruno Crispo: Crepe: context-related policy enforcement for android. Proceedings of the 13th international conference on Information security. ISC '10. Berlin, Heidelberg: Springer-Verlag, 2011, pp. 331–345.

[13] Ronald Cramer, Ivan Damgård, and Ueli Maurer. General secure multi-party computation from any linear secret-sharing scheme. In Proceedings of the 19th international conference on Theory and application of cryptographic techniques (EUROCRYPT'00), Bart Preneel (Ed.). Springer-Verlag, Berlin, Heidelberg, 316–334. 2000.

[14] Ronald Cramer, Serge Fehr, Yuval Ishai, and Eyal Kushilevitz. Efficient multi-party computation over rings. In Advances in Cryptology—EUROCRYPT 2003, pp. 596–613. Springer Berlin Heidelberg, 2003.

[15] Lorrie Faith Cranor, Praveen Guduru, Manjula Arjula. User interfaces for privacy agents. ACM Transactions on Computer-Human Interaction, 13, 135–178, 2006.

[16] R. Curtmola, J. Garay, S. Kamara, and R. Ostrovsky. Searchable Symmetric Encryption: Improved Definitions and Efficient Constructions. Journal of Computer Security, 19(5):895–934, 2011.

[17] Yvo Desmedt, Yair Frankel: Perfect Homomorphic Zero-Knowledge Threshold Schemes over any Finite Abelian Group. SIAM J. Discrete Math. 7(4): 667–679 (1994)

[18] R Dingledine, N Mathewson, P Syverson. Tor: The second-generation onion router. 13th USENIX Security Symposium. 2004.

[19] Alan Duke. Five Things to Know about the Celebrity Nude Photo Hacking Scandal. CNN. October 2014.

[20] Cynthia Dwork, Krishnaram Kenthapadi, Frank McSherry, Ilya Mironov, and Moni Naor. Our data, ourselves: privacy via distributed noise generation. In Proceedings of the 24th annual international conference on The Theory and Applications of Cryptographic Techniques (EUROCRYPT'06), Serge Vaudenay (Ed.). Springer-Verlag, Berlin, Heidelberg, 486–503. 2006. DOI=10.1007/11761679_29 http://dx.doi.org/10.1007/11761679_29

[21] Cynthia Dwork and Jing Lei. Differential privacy and robust statistics. In Proceedings of the forty-first annual ACM symposium on Theory of computing (STOC '09). ACM, New York, NY, USA, 371–380. 2009.

[22] N. Eagle and A. Pentland. Reality mining: sensing complex social systems. Personal and Ubiquitous Computing, 10(4):255–268, 2006.

[23] N. Eagle and A.S. Pentland. Eigenbehaviors: Identifying structure in routine. Behavioral Ecology and Sociobiology, 63(7): 2009.

[24] Úlfar Erlingsson, Vasyl Pihur, Aleksandra Korolova. RAPPOR: Randomized Aggregatable Privacy-Preserving Ordinal Response. In CCS 2014.

[25] M. Fernandez, M. Kantarcioglu, B. Thuraisingham, A Framework for Secure Data Collection and Management for Internet of Things, Proceedings ACSAC Conference Workshop (ICSS), Los Angeles, CA, December 2016.

[26] Carlos Flavián & Miguel Guinalíu. Consumer trust, perceived security and privacy policy. Industrial Management & Data Systems, Vol. 106, Issue 5, pp. 601–620, 2006.

[27] Gartner. 2014 Gartner Says Annual Smartphone Sales Surpassed Sales of Feature Phones for the First Time in 2013. February. http://www.gartner.com/newsroom/id/2665715.

[28] Gartner. 2013. Gartner Says Mobile App Stores Will See Annual Downloads Reach 102 Billion in 2013. September. http://www.gartner.com/newsroom/id/2592315.

[29] Christopher S. Gates, Ninghui Li, Hao Peng, Bhaskar Pratim Sarma, Yuan Qi, Rahul Potharaju, Cristina Nita-Rotaru, Ian Molloy: Generating Summary Risk Scores for Mobile Applications. IEEE Trans. Dependable Sec. Comput. 11(3): 238–251 (2014).

[30] Craig Gentry. A Fully Homomorphic Encryption Scheme. PhD thesis, Stanford University, 2009. crypto.stanford.edu/craig

[31] E.J. Goh. Secure Indexes. In Cryptology ePrint Archive, Report 2003/216, 2003.

[32] Aditi Gupta, Markus Miettinen, N. Asokan, and Marcin Nagy: Intuitive security policy configuration in mobile devices using context profiling. IEEE International Conference on Social Computing, SOCIALCOM-PASSAT '12. Washington, DC, USA: IEEE, pp. 471–480.

[33] Raymond Heatherly, Murat Kantarcioglu, Bhavani M. Thuraisingham. Preventing Private Information Inference Attacks on Social Networks. IEEE Trans. Knowl. Data Eng., v.25, 2013, p. 1849.

[34] J.L. Herlocker, J.A. Konstan, L.G. Terveen, and J.T. Riedl. Evaluating collaborative filtering recommender systems. ACM Transactions on Information Systems (TOIS), 22(1):5–53, 2004.

[35] Cheng-Kang Hsieh, Hongsuda Tangmunarunkit, Faisal Alquaddoomi, John Jenkins, Jinha Kang, Cameron Ketcham, Brent Longstaff, Joshua Selsky, Betta Dawson, Dallas Swendeman, Deborah Estrin, and Nithya Ramanathan. Lifestreams: a modular sense-making toolset for identifying important patterns from everyday life. In Proceedings of the 11th ACM Conference on Embedded Networked Sensor Systems (SenSys '13). ACM, New York, NY, USA.

[36] Syed Rafiul Hussain, Asmaa Sallam, Elisa Bertino: DetAnomDetecting Anomalous Database Transactions by Insiders. CODASPY 2015: 25–35

[37] Mark Johnson, John Karat, Claire-Marie Karat, and J. Grueneberg. Optimizing a policy authoring framework for security and privacy policies. Symposium on Usable Privacy and Security (SOUPS) 2010, Redmond, WA.

[38] Mark Johnson, John Karat, Claire-Marie Karat, and J. Grueneberg. An empirical study of policy template authoring. In ACITA '10, 2010.

[39] Murat Kantarcioglu and Chris Clifton. Privacy-preserving Distributed Mining of Association Rules on Horizontally Partitioned Data. IEEE TKDE, 16(9):1026–1037, September 2004.

[40] Michael S. Kirkpatrick and Elisa Bertino: Enforcing spatial constraints for mobile RBAC systems. Proceedings of the 15th ACM symposium on Access control models and technologies, ser. SACMAT '10. New York, NY, USA: ACM, 2010, pp. 99–108.

[41] Michael S. Kirkpatrick, Maria Luisa Damiani, Elisa Bertino: Prox-RBAC: a proximity-based spatially aware RBAC. Proceedings of 19th ACM SIGSPATIAL International Symposium on Advances in Geographic Information Systems, ACM-GIS 2011, November 1–4, 2011, Chicago, IL, USA, pp. 339–348.

[42] Sandeep Kumar, Mohamed Abdul Qadeer, and Archana Gupta: Location based services using android. Proceedings of the 3rd IEEE international conference on Internet multimedia services architecture and applications, ser. IMSAA '09, 2009, pp. 335–339.

[43] Amit Kushwaha1, Vineet Kushwaha: Location Based Services using Android Mobile Operating System. International Journal of Advances in Engineering & Technology, Mar 2011, pp. 11–20.

[44] N.D. Lane, M. Mohammod, M. Lin, X. Yang, H. Lu, S. Ali, A. Doryab, E. Berke, T. Choudhury, and A.T. Campbell. Bewell: A smartphone application to monitor, model and promote wellbeing. In Pervasive Health '11.

[45] Jason D. Lee, Ran Gilad-Bachrach, Rich Caruana: Using multiple samples to learn mixture models. NIPS 2013: 324–332.

[46] R. LiKamWa, Y. Liu, N.D. Lane, and L. Zhong. Can your smartphone infer your mood. In Phone Sense '11.

[47] M. Masud, J. Gao, L. Khan, J. Han, and B. Thuraisingham. "A practical approach to classify evolving data streams: Training with limited amount of labeled data." IEEE ICDM, 2008.

[48] M. Masud, Q. Chen, L. Khan, C. Aggarwal, J. Gao, H. Han, A. Srivastava, and N. C. Oza. Classification and adaptive novel class detection of feature-evolving data streams. IEEE Transactions on Knowledge and Data Engineering, Volume 25, 2013.

[49] M. Masud, Q. Chen, L. Khan, C. Aggarwal, J. Gao, J. Han, and B. Thuraisingham. Addressing concept-evolution in concept-drifting data streams, IEEE ICDM, 2010.

[50] Daniele Midi, Oyindamola Oluwatimi, Bilal Shebaro, Elisa Bertino: Demo Overview: Privacy-Enhancing Features of IdentiDroid. ACM Conference on Computer and Communications Security 2014, pp.1481–1483.

[51] Yves-Alexandre de Montjoye, Erez Shmueli, Samuel S. Wang, Alex Sandy Pentland. openPDS: Protecting the Privacy of Metadata through SafeAnswers. PLoS ONE 9(7): e98790.

[52] Mydex website. URL http://mydex.org/. Accessed 2014 October.

[53] Narrative Clip, 2014, http://getnarrative.com/

[54] Rimma V. Nehme, Hyo-Sang Lim, Elisa Bertino: FENCE: continuous access control enforcement in dynamic data stream environments. Proceedings of Third ACM Conference on Data and Application Security and Privacy, CODASPY '13, San Antonio, TX, USA, February 18–20, 2013, pp. 243–254.

[55] NIH. Pediatric Research Using Integrated Sensor Monitoring Systems (PROSMS): Informatics Platform Technologies for Asthma (U54).

[56] Helen Nissembaum. Privacy in Context: Technology, Policy, and the Integrity of Social Life (Stanford Law Books) – November 24, 2009.

[57] Oyindamola Oluwatimi, Daniele Midi, Elisa Bertino: Mobile Device Containerization: Survey and Open Research Directions. Submitted for publication, July 2015.

[58] Christos Parizas, Diego Pizzocaro, Alun Preece, Petros Zerfos: Managing ISR sharing policies at the network edge using Controlled English. In Ground/Air Multisensor Interoperability, Integration, and Networking for Persistent ISR, SPIE, Vol. 8742, 2013.

[59] Proctor, R. W., & Vu, K.-P. L. A multimethod approach to examining usability of Web privacy policies and user agents for specifying privacy preferences. Behavior Research Methods, 39, 205-21, 2007.

[60] P. Resnick and H.R. Varian. Recommender systems. Communications of the ACM, 40(3):56–58, 1997.

[61] T. Rouffineau. Research: Consumers are terrible at updating their connected devices, Ubuntu Insights Blog: https://insights.ubuntu.com/2016/12/15/research-consumers-are-terrible-at-updating-their-connected-devices/

[62] Bilal Shebaro, Oyindamola Oluwatimi, Daniele Midi, Elisa Bertino: IdentiDroid: Android Can Finally Wear its Anonymous Suit. Transactions on Data Privacy 7(1): 27–50 (2014)

[63] Elaine Shi, John Bethencourt, T-H. Hubert Chan, Dawn Song, and Adrian Perrig. Multidimensional Range Query over Encrypted Data. In SP '07: Proceedings of the 2007 IEEE Symposium on Security and Privacy, pages 350–364, Washington, DC, USA, 2007. IEEE Computer Society.

[64] E. Stefanov, E. Shi, and D. Song. Towards practical oblivious ram. In NDSS '12, 2012.

[65] E. Stefanov and E. Shi. Oblivistore: High performance oblivious cloud storage. In S&P '13, 2013.

[66] E. Stefanov, C. Papamanthou, and E. Shi. Practical dynamic searchable encryption with small leakage. In NDSS '14, 2014.

[67] K. Strater and H. R. Lipford. Strategies and struggles with privacy in an online social networking community. In Proceedings of the 22nd British HCI Group Annual Conference on People and Computers: Culture, Creativity, Interaction - Volume 1, BCS-HCI '08, pages 111–119, Swinton, UK, UK, 2008. British Computer Society.

[68] A. Sulleyman, GMAIL Two-step verification: Less than 10% of Google users have its most important security feature enabled, The Independent, 2018: http://www.independent.co.uk/life-style/gadgets-and-tech/news/gmail-two-step-verification-2fa-google-account-users-security-feature-cyber-crime-a8172391.html

[69] Latanya Sweeney. K-anonymity: A model for Protecting Privacy. International Journal of Uncertainty, Fuzziness and Knowledge-Based Systems 10: 557–570. 2002.

[70] K.-P.L. Vu, V. Chambers, F.P. Garcia, B. Creekmur, J. Sulaitis, D. Nelson, R. Pierce, R.W. Proctor, How users read and comprehend privacy policies, in: M.J. Smith, G. Salvendy (Eds.), Human Interface. Part II. HCII 2007, Lecture Notes in Computer Science 4558, Springer-Verlag, Berlin, 2007, pp. 802–811.

[71] Guojun Wang, Qin Liu, and Jie Wu. Hierarchical Attribute-based Encryption for Fine Grained Access Control in Cloud Storage Services. In Proceedings of the 17th ACM Conference on Computer and Communications Security, CCS '10, pages 735–737, New York, NY, USA, 2010. ACM.

[72] OASIS https://www.oasis-open.org/committees/tc_home.php?wg_abbrev=xacml, accessed on 11/11/2014.

Access Control in the Era of Big Data: State of the Art and Research Directions

Pietro Colombo
DiSTA, University of Insubria
Varese, Italy
pietro.colombo@uninsubria.it

Elena Ferrari
DiSTA, University of Insubria
Varese, Italy
elena.ferrari@uninsubria.it

ABSTRACT

Data security and privacy issues are magnified by the volume, the variety, and the velocity of Big Data and by the lack, up to now, of a standard data model and related data manipulation language. In this paper, we focus on one of the key data security services, that is, access control, by highlighting the differences with traditional data management systems and describing a set of requirements that any access control solution for Big Data platforms may fulfill. We then describe the state of the art and discuss open research issues.

CCS CONCEPTS

• **Security and privacy** → **Access control**;

KEYWORDS

Big Data; Access control; Privacy; NoSQL Data Management Systems

ACM Reference format:
Pietro Colombo and Elena Ferrari. 2018. Access Control in the Era of Big Data: State of the Art and Research Directions. In *Proceedings of The 23rd ACM Symposium on Access Control Models & Technologies (SACMAT), Indianapolis, IN, USA, June 13–15, 2018 (SACMAT '18)*, 8 pages.
https://doi.org/10.1145/3205977.3205998

1 INTRODUCTION

The last years have seen changes related to the organization of business models and work styles, caused by the rapid evolution of data analysis and data management systems. Business strategies are more and more driven by the integrated analysis of huge volumes of heterogeneous data, coming from different sources (e.g., social media, IoT devices). Data have become a key factor for making business decisions: we have entered the Big Data era [32].

The term Big Data refers to a phenomenon characterized by "5 V": starting from datasets collecting huge Volumes of data with a high Variety of formats, Big Data analytic platforms allow one to make predictions with high Velocity, thus, in a timely manner, low Veracity, therefore with low uncertainties, and with a high Value, namely, with an expected significant gain [27]. The phenomenon has been pushed by numerous technological advancements. The

most significant include: the birth of NoSQL datastores [7], that is, modern data management systems which, by means of innovative data models, provide highly efficient storage and analysis services for structured, unstructured, and semi structured data, such as transactions, electronic documents and emails; and distributed computational paradigms, like MapReduce [18], which have opened the way to the systematic analysis of semi-structured and unstructured data.

Overall, the support provided by Big Data platforms for the storage and analysis of huge and heterogeneous datasets cannot find a counterpart within traditional data management systems. In addition, the advantages of these new systems are not only related to the outstanding flexibility and efficacy of the analysis services, as Big Data platforms outperform traditional systems even with respect to performance and scalability. However, the optimization of these aspects goes to the detriment of data protection. As a matter of fact, for what data privacy and security are concerned, in contrast with traditional systems, for which a variety of data protection framework exist (e.g., see [1, 6, 10–12, 21]), the majority of Big Data platforms integrate quite basic access control enforcement mechanisms [13]. The unconstrained access to high volume of data from multiple data sources, the sensitive and private contents of some data resources, and the advanced analysis and prediction capabilities of Big Data analytic platforms, represent a serious threat. For instance, the analysis capabilities can be exploited to derive correlations between sensitive and personal data. As an example, think about the retail sector, where the analysis of the purchases associated with customer fidelity cards done for marketing purposes, may allow the identification of individuals who suffer from food intolerances. As a consequence, although the potential benefits of Big Data analytics are indisputable, the lack of standard data protection tools open these services to potential attackers.

The definition of proper data protection tools tailored for Big Data platforms is as a very ambitious research challenge. State of the art enforcement techniques proposed for traditional systems cannot be used as they are, or straightforwardly adapted to the Big Data context for manifold reasons, such as the required support for semi structured and unstructured data (Variety), the quantity of data to be protected (Volume), and the very strict performance requirements (Velocity). Therefore, the challenge is protecting privacy and confidentiality while not hindering data analytics and information sharing. Additional aspects contribute to raise the complexity of this goal, such as the variety of data models and data analysis and manipulation languages which are used by Big Data platforms. Indeed, different from RDBMSs, Big Data platforms are characterized by various data models [7], the most notable being the key-value, wide column, and document oriented ones.

SACMAT '18, June 13–15, 2018, Indianapolis, IN, USA
© 2018 Association for Computing Machinery.
ACM ISBN 978-1-4503-5666-4/18/06...$15.00
https://doi.org/10.1145/3205977.3205998

In this paper, we first identify a set of requirements that any access control solution for Big Data platforms should address (cfr. Section 2). Then, we classify and analyze the related literature (Sections 3, 4, and 5), and discuss key research challenges (Section 6). Finally, we conclude the paper in Section 7.

2 REQUIREMENTS

In this section, we provide an overview of the key requirements behind the definition of an access control mechanism for Big Data platforms.

- **Fine-grained access control**. In terms of features the access control mechanism should support, fine grained access control (FGAC) has been widely recognized as one of the fundamental component for an effective protection of personal and sensitive data (e.g., see [1, 39]). Since data processed by Big Data analytics platforms often refer user personal characteristics, it is important that access control rules can be bound to data at the finest granularity levels. However, the related enforcement mechanisms need to be invented from scratch, as those proposed for traditional systems rely on data referring to known schema, while in the context of Big Data, data are heterogeneous and schemaless.
- **Context management**. Another key aspect that should be considered is the support for context based access constraints, as these allow highly customized access control forms. For instance, they can be used to constrain access to specific time periods or geographical locations. In case contexts are used to derive access control decisions, access authorizations are granted when conditions referring to properties of the environment within which an access request has been issued are satisfied.
- **Efficiency of access control**. The characteristics of the Big Data scenario, such as the distributed nature of the considered platforms, the complexity of the queries, and the focus on performance, require enforcement strategies that do not compromise the usability of the hosting analytic frameworks. Indeed, based on the considered queries, the number of checks to be executed during access control enforcement can match or be even greater than the number of data records, and, in the Big Data scenario, data sets can include up to hundreds of millions of such records. This requires efficient policy compliance mechanisms. FGAC has been enforced in traditional relational DBMSs according to two main approaches. The first is the view-based one, where users are only allowed to access a view of the target dataset that satisfies the specified access control restrictions, whereas the second one is based on query rewriting. Under such an approach instead of pre-computing the authorized views, the query is modified at run-time by injecting restrictions imposed by the specified access control rules. It is therefore important to determine to what extent these approaches are suitable for the Big Data scenario and how they can be possibly customized or extended.

As it should be clear from the previous discussion, one of the main difficulties in developing an access control solution for Big Data platforms is the lack of a standard model and related manipulation languages to which access control rules and the related enforcement monitor can be bound.

3 STATE OF THE ART

In the literature various proposals exist which address the issue of access control for Big Data platforms. They can be classified in two main categories:

- **Platform specific approaches**. Access control solutions under this category are designed for one system only (e.g., MongoDB, Hadoop), and possibly leverage on native access control features of the protected platform. The main advantage of this approach is that the devised access control solution can be optimized for the target system, however, its usability and interoperability is greatly limited.
- **Platform independent approaches**. The approaches falling under this category propose access control solutions which do not target a specific platform only. Existing proposals in this category mainly leverage on recent research efforts that aim at defining a unifying query language for NoSQL datastores (e.g., JSONiq [22] and SQL++ [35]). An approach designed for a unifying query language has the advantage of being more general than platform specific solutions, being applicable to the protection of data sources managed by heterogeneous platforms.

In what follows, we analyze the related literature in view of this classification, then we discuss related research challenges. A summary of the surveyed access control frameworks and of the supported requirements (cfr. Section 2) is shown in Table 1.

4 PLATFORM SPECIFIC APPROACHES

The great majority of access control frameworks targeting Big Data platforms propose enforcement approaches designed on the basis of platform specific features and which can only be used with the platform for which they have been defined.

In the remainder of this section, we analyze platform specific approaches defined for MapReduce-based analytics platforms,[1] and NoSQL datastores, which together cover the majority of existing BigData systems.

4.1 MapReduce systems

MapReduce is a distributed computational paradigm that allows analyzing very large data sets [18]. Within MapReduce systems, data resources are partitioned into multiple chunks of data and distributed in a cluster of commodity hardware nodes. Data are analyzed in parallel by means of MapReduce tasks, characterized by users defined Map and Reduce functions. These tasks operate by first extracting and then manipulating flows of key-value pairs, each modeling a portion of the target data resource. The considered computation paradigm allows processing unstructured and semi-structured data resources.

In [41], a framework denoted GuardMR has been proposed, to enforce fine grained Role-based Access Control (RBAC) [20] within

---

[1]MapReduce-based analytics platforms are hereafter denoted MapReduce systems for the sake of brevity.

Table 1: Summary of the surveyed access control frameworks

AC framework	Target platform	AC model	Max granularity	Context support	Efficiency
GuardMR[41]	Hadoop	RBAC	K,V pair	No	Medium/High
Vigiles[42]	Hadoop	DAC	K,V pair	No	Medium/High
HeAC[23]	Hadoop	RBAC	K,V pair	No	Not available
K-VAC[29]	Cassandra/ HBase	DAC	Cell	Yes	High
[40]	Cassandra	RBAC	Cell	No	Not available
Mem[15]	MongoDB	RBAC	Document	No	High
ConfinedMem[14]	MongoDB	DAC	Field	Yes	Medium/Low
[16]	All those supporting SQL++	ABAC	Cell/Field	Yes	Medium
[31]	Not clear	ABAC	Cell/Field	Yes	Not available

Hadoop[2], a very popular Big Data analytics platform built on top of MapReduce. GuardMR enforces data protection by filtering, and possibly altering, the key-value pairs derived from a target data resource by a MapReduce task, which are then provided as input to the Map function. Filters are used for generating views of the analyzed resources, from which all contents resulting unauthorized for the subject who requires the execution of the MapReduce task are removed or obfuscated. More precisely, filters specify: i) pre-conditions to the processing of any key-value pair p extracted from a target resource under analysis, as well as ii) the rationale for deriving from p, a new pair p', which models the authorized content of p. The use of filters had previously been considered in Vigiles [42], a fine grained access control framework for Hadoop. In [42] authorization filters are handled by means of per-user assignment lists, and filters are coded in Java by security administrators. In contrast, in GuardMR, filters are assigned to subjects on the basis of the covered roles, and a formal specification approach to the definition of filters is proposed, which allows specifying selection and modification criteria at a very high level of abstraction using the Object Constraint Language (OCL)[3] [9, 43]. GuardMR relies on automatic tools[4] to generate Java bytecode from OCL-based filter specifications, as well as to integrate the generated bytecode into the bytecode of the MapReduce task to be executed. GuardMR has been used with MapReduce tasks targeting both textual and binary resources [41], showing the flexibility of the approach. GuardMR and Vigiles do not require Hadoop source code customization, however, they rely on platform specific features, such as the Hadoop APIs and the Hadoop control flow for regulating the execution of a MapReduce task. A reasonably low enforcement overhead has been observed with both Vigiles and GuardMR. Neither Vigiles nor GuardMR provide support for context aware access control policies.

A recent work targeting access control enforcement within MapReduce systems is described in [23]. More precisely, [23] introduces the foundations of an access control model, called HeAC, which formalizes the authorization model of Apache Ranger[5] and Apache Sentry[6], as well as the native access control features of Hadoop.[7] Authorization assignments are specified for operations and objects,

possibly on the basis of object tags, namely attributes specifying properties, like sensitivity, content or expiration date. Moreover, [23] introduces the foundation of Object Tagged RBAC, an RBAC model which, while preserving RBAC role based permission assignments, introduces support for object attributes. A prototypical implementation of the model has been defined by introducing role support into Apache Ranger. The proposed enforcement approach is again platform specific as it has been designed on top of Hadoop specific features. No support is given to context related properties, and no performance evaluation is presented.

4.2 NoSQL datastores

NoSQL datastores represent highly flexible, scalable, and efficient data management systems for Big Data, based on different data models. Cattell [7] classifies NoSQL systems on the basis of the adopted data model into three classes, namely key value, wide column, and document-oriented datastores, each suited to specific application scenarios. Key-value datastores (e.g., Redis[8]) can be seen as big hash tables with persistent storage services. Data are modeled by means of key-value pairs, where values of primitive or complex type are directly addressed by means of a key. Wide column stores (e.g., Cassandra[9]) model data as records with variable structures, which are then grouped into tables with flexible schema. Document-oriented datastores (e.g., MongoDB [10]) model data as hierarchical records, denoted documents, whose fields either specify a primitive value, or are in turn records composed of multiple fields. Documents are partitioned into collections, which in turn are grouped in a database.

Fine grained access control within NoSQL datastore management systems is still in the very early stage, and only few access control frameworks have been proposed so far for wide column and document oriented datastores.

K-VAC [29] is among the earliest fine grained access control frameworks targeting wide-column NoSQL datastores which have been proposed in the literature. K-VAC supports the enforcement of content-based, and context-based access control policies possibly specified at different levels of the data model hierarchy (e.g., for a column or for a row). Two prototypical versions of K-VAC have been released. One has been specifically designed as an internal module of Cassandra, a popular wide-column datastore whose

---

[2]http://hadoop.apache.org/
[3]https://www.omg.org/spec/OCL
[4]Dresden OCL Toolkit, http://st.inf.tu-dresden.de/oclportal
[5]https://ranger.apache.org/
[6]https://sentry.apache.org/
[7]Apache Ranger and Apache Sentry represent state of the art technologies for the enforcement of fine grained access control in Hadoop ecosystems.

[8]https://redis.io/
[9]http://cassandra.apache.org/
[10]https://www.mongodb.com

source code has been modified to host K-VAC's enforcement monitor. In contrast, the latter version has been released as an external library, with the aim to enforce access control on multiple datastores. However, the use of the proposed library still requires *ad-hoc* implementation of binding criteria, which so far have been only defined for Cassandra and HBase[11]. Overall the integration of K-VAC requires deep customizations of the hosting platform. Empirical performance evaluations show the efficiency of both the proposed prototypes, with a lower overhead measured with the customized version of Cassandra.

Another work targeting Cassandra has been proposed in [40], where an approach to the cryptographic enforcement of RBAC policies has been defined. Predicate encryption [28] and second level encryption [33] are used for the definition of an efficient scheme for RBAC enforcement which operates within Cassandra distributed architecture. The proposed approach is an example of platform specific solution designed on top of platform specific features, such as the distributed architecture of Cassandra. Also in this case no support is given for context-aware policies, and, unfortunately, the enforcement overhead is not discussed.

For what document-oriented datastores is concerned, efficient solutions to the integration of fine-grained purpose-based access control into MongoDB have been proposed in [14] and [15]. In [15] the RBAC model natively integrated in MongoDB has been enhanced with the support for the specification and enforcement of purpose-based policies [6] regulating the access up to document level. The proposed approach refines the granularity level at which the native MongoDB RBAC model operates. An enforcement monitor, called Mem (MongoDB enforcement monitor), has been designed, which monitors and possibly manipulates the flow of messages exchanged by MongoDB clients and the MongoDB server, thus acting like a proxy. Once Mem intercepts a message m issued by a MongoDB client on behalf of a subject s, it forwards m to the server, or it temporary blocks m, and issues additional messages finalized at profiling s. If m models a query q, Mem rewrites m as m' in such a way that m' encodes a query q' that only accesses those documents accessed by q which result authorized by the applicable access control policies. Mem's proxy based architecture allows the straightforward integration of the enforcement monitor into existing MongoDB deployments with basic configuration tasks. Experimental evaluations show the efficiency of the proposed approach, however also in this case no support is given for context-aware policies.

In [14], the framework presented in [15] has been significantly extended, introducing support for access control policies regulating the access up to field level, and providing support to specification and enforcement of content and context based policies. The proposed enforcement monitor, denoted ConfinedMem, applies the same logic as Mem, but it operates according to a two-steps process, which consists of: 1) the derivation of the authorized views of all documents to be accessed by a submitted query q included in a message m requiring the access to data resources, 2) the rewriting of m as m' in such a way that m' specifies a query q' which can only access the authorized views of the documents to be accessed by q. Different implementation techniques have been considered

for queries specifying different operations (e.g., selection and aggregations) with the aim to minimize the overhead. Experimental evaluations show that overall, the enforcement overhead which has been observed with access control policies specified at field level is significantly higher than the one measured for document level policies.

5 PLATFORM INDEPENDENT APPROACHES

The great majority of the research contributions in the field of access control for Big Data analytics platforms propose a platform specific solution. This is probably due to the high heterogeneity of the considered application scenarios. Indeed, the lack of a reference standard for query languages and data models has caused the birth of a variety of proprietary solutions. As a matter of fact, numerous NoSQL datastores exist, most of which operate with a platform specific query language (e.g., the query language of MongoDB can only be used with that platform), and adopt a different data model. Even different datastores that nominally refer to the same data model can use different data organization and terminology. For instance, both MongoDB and CouchDB[12] use the document oriented data model, however the concept of collection is not supported by CouchDB, whereas collections are basic data organization features of MongoDB. The great heterogeneity of the scenario has significantly raised the complexity of devising enforcement solutions that can work with multiple platforms. Overall, the definition of a general access control enforcement approach represents a very ambitious task.

In the recent years, academia and industry started collaborating to the definition of unifying query languages for NoSQL datastores. To the best of our knowledge, JSONiq [22] and SQL++ [35] represent the most relevant results that have been so far achieved towards the fulfillment of this goal. JSONiq is an Xquery[8] based language that has been defined with the aim to analyze data handled by NoSQL datastores adopting a JSON-based data model. Unfortunately, at present JSONiq is only supported by Zorba,[13] and Sparksoniq,[14] which allow processing data serialized in JSON format, and by a platform denoted 28msec, [15] which supports the execution of JSONiq queries on MongoDB databases.

SQL++ [35] is a recent proposal of unifying query language that allows analysing semi-structured data handled by NoSQL datastores as well as structured data of traditional DBMSs. SQL++ has been recently adopted by Couchbase[16] and AsterixDB,[17][3] whereas Apache Drill [18] is in the process of aligning with SQL++. The diffusion of this language is thus growing, and the adopted SQL based syntax and the backward compatibility with relational DBMSs promise to further increase the popularity and diffusion of this language.

In [16] an SQL++ based Attribute-based Access Control (ABAC) [25, 26] framework for NoSQL datastores has been proposed. The choice to base the framework on SQL++ allows protecting any

---

[11]HBase is a popular wide-column store, https://hbase.apache.org/

[12]http://couchdb.apache.org/
[13]http://www.zorba.io
[14]http://sparksoniq.org/
[15]https://www.28msec.com/
[16]https://www.couchbase.com/
[17]https://asterixdb.apache.org/
[18]https://drill.apache.org/

NoSQL datastore which provides support to this language. Therefore, the proposal distinguishes from all other work introduced in Section 4 for higher generality and applicability, which may even grow with a future potential wider diffusion of SQL++. The framework operates at a very fine grained level, in that it allows regulating the access up to single data fields.[19] Enforcement is based on query rewriting and operates with heterogeneous data with no assumption on data schema, thus overcoming state of the art query rewriting techniques proposed for RDBMSs [30, 39]. Query rewriting techniques finalized at enforcing cell-level access control within traditional DBMSs operate by projecting or nullifying the value of each cell to be accessed by a query q on the basis of the compliance of the access performed by q with the applicable access control policies [30]. More precisely, a query q submitted for execution is rewritten in such a way to: i) include a subquery s for each table t accessed by q, which, cell by cell, generates an authorized view of t, and ii) perform the same analysis tasks as q on the result set of s. The subquery s specifies projection criteria conditioned by the compliance of the accesses operated by q with the cell level access control policies that have been specified for t's cells. A similar approach can only be used if the scheme of any accessed table is *a priori* known, as the projection criteria of the subqueries need to refer to table columns. The schemaless and highly heterogeneous nature of the data within Big Data platforms does not allow to use similar techniques. In [15] this issue has been handled by means of SQL++ operators that allow achieving the projection without knowing in advance the accessed fields. The approach operates by visiting, field by field, the data unit[20] du of an analyzed resource, and adding a visited field f to the authorized view du' of du only if the access to f complies with the ABAC policies specified for f. The proposed approach allows deriving in-memory authorized views of the data resources to be analyzed, and executing the analysis tasks of the original queries on such derived views. The ABAC framework proposed in [15] supports the specification and enforcement of context-aware access control policies. Empirical performance assessments show an enforcement overhead that varies with the characteristics of the specified policies and the number of fields of the analyzed documents. The overhead is high when field level policies cover high percentage of data units fields.

Another language-based ABAC approach has been proposed in [31], with the goal to be usable with traditional data management systems, Mapreduce systems, as well as NoSQL datastores. The work proposes a query rewriting approach that targets user transactions specified with an SQL-like language. Unfortunately, a detailed description of the adopted query language and data model is missing, which makes unclear how the approach could be used with different platforms, and how the heterogeneity of schemaless data can be handled by means of an SQL-like language.

6 RESEARCH ISSUES

In what follows we discuss some open research issues in the field of Big Data access control.

6.1 Unifying access control model and mechanism

State of the art review done in Sections 4 and 5 has highlighted that, although research in the area of access control for Big Data platforms is progressing, no solution has been proposed so far for a unifying access control framework which can combine generality and efficiency of access control. The heterogeneous schemaless nature of the managed data significantly complicates the definition of this framework, and so far this has lead mainly to ad-hoc platform specific solutions (see Section 4). In contrast, language centric approaches still suffer of limited applicability (see Section 5).[21]

One key element that may be instrumental to fill this void is the definition of a unifying data model capable of representing data resources of the different data models currently adopted by Big Data platforms. The ability to represent data resources is a fundamental requirements for binding access control policies to the protected data, as well as for the specification of policies regulating the access on the basis of the protected objects' attributes. Indeed, in the literature on access control, multiple models allow enforcing content-based access constraints (e.g., [14, 29]), as well as access control rules that refer to various security meta-data related to the protected data resources (e.g., [12]).

The key-value, wide column, and document-oriented models adopt different data modeling criteria, however, in all these models data are hierarchically organized as tree structures, where nodes at different height of the tree represent resources at different granularity levels of the related data model (e.g., database, table, row and cell). Data models differ among them for the height of the tree with which data resources can be represented. This may range from 2, within key-value datastores[22] to a height of variable length n (n > 2) for document-oriented datastores.[23] A data resource of a data model corresponds to a node n of the tree representing all the resources handled by a platform, and it can be accessed traversing the path from the root of the tree to n. Therefore, we believe that a unifying representation of data resources of multiple models should take into account the identification of proper modeling strategies for the nodes of the above mentioned resource tree. In particular, nodes should be specified in such a way to keep track of: i) any structural property related to the modeled resource, ii) hierarchical relations with other nodes (e.g., a parent of relationship), iii) possible meta-data, and iv) access control policies specified for the modeled resource. The considered policies may refer to different access control models, specifying context aware access control rules as well as content-based constraints.

Going one step further, the specified unifying model could also be used for enforcement purposes. We believe that enforcement mechanisms should be achieved by means of bidirectional mappings between resources represented with a platform specific native data model and the unifying data model. Overall, the analysis of related work has revealed that fine grained access control with schemaless

---

[19]The supported granularity is thus equivalent to cell level within relational DBMSs.

[20]SQL++ can be used with datastores adopting different data models, thus, the term data unit is used to denote a table row, or a document.

[21]Although the popularity of the SQL++[35] initiative is growing, the support provided to this language is still limited to a small number of platforms.

[22]All key-value pairs (leaf nodes), belong to a key-space (root node).

[23]A database (root node), groups a variable number of collections (level 2 nodes), which in turn include a variable number of documents (level 3 nodes), each composed of a variable number of fields, which in turn are possibly hierarchically organized into a tree structure (level 4 to n).

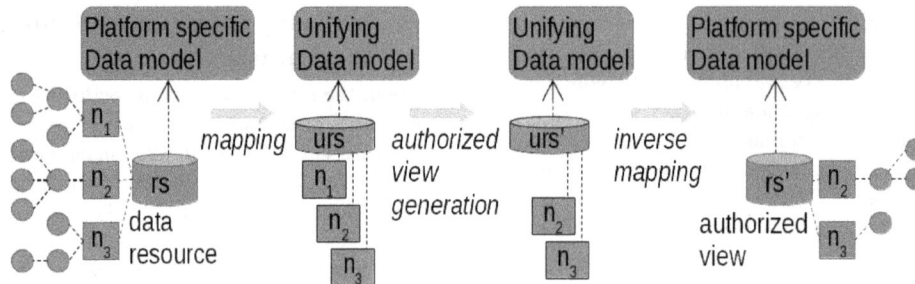

Figure 1: The pipeline of operations at the basis of the enforcement mechanism

data is usually enforced executing the submitted analysis tasks on authorized views of the accessed resources (e.g., see [16]). Therefore, a platform independent strategy to handle fine grained access control enforcement may consist of a pipeline of operations supported by any platform, which, by means of the unifying data model, handle the generation of authorized views. The generated view can then be analyzed by the originally submitted query without additional platform specific rewriting activities. The above mentioned pipeline is illustrated in Figure 1. For each accessed resource rs, represented as a tree characterized by different nodes n_i, the process: i) derives a unifying model-based representation urs of rs, ii) derives the authorized view urs' of urs, where the unauthorized contents have been removed, and, finally, iii) maps back the authorized view urs' to the native data model, so that the generated view rs' can be analyzed by the originally submitted analysis task. In order to support such approach within multiple platforms, the above mentioned mapping and view generation mechanisms should be defined in such a way that any platform, independently from the supported query language and data model, could handle the execution of this process. To the best of our knowledge, the majority of today Big Data platforms provide support for MapReduce computational paradigm, independently from the adopted data model and query language. Therefore, a promising approach could be that of specifying mapping and view generation mechanisms by means of MapReduce operations.

The enforcement overhead of the above discussed technique is expected to depend on the platform hosting the data to be protected, as different behaviors are expected to be observed. For instance, Apache Spark,[24] integrates a highly efficient computation engines, which promises to be significantly faster than Hadoop[2] (up to 100 times faster.[25]) The overhead is expected to be reasonably contained in all those platforms supporting in-memory MapReduce computations, as well as data streams.

6.2 Policy analysis tools

The availability of a unifying data model on which access control policies can be specified would also allow to support policy analysis and reasoning at an abstract layer independent from any specific platform. As a matter of fact, the variety of data models, access control models, and related configuration options, such as policy

propagation and conflict resolution criteria, adopted by Big Data platforms, can make really hard for security administrators to understand the effect of a set of access control policies on the data resources which are managed by their systems, as well as assessing the quality of the specified policies. Most of the research efforts in this field have been devoted to correctness verification, detection of inconsistencies and redundancies, and policy sets completeness analysis (e.g., see [2, 4, 38]). A more recent work [5] has proposed the use of provenance techniques to check the quality of the specified access control policies for a scenario where collaborations are carried out by autonomous cognitive devices. However, to the best of our knowledge, so far no proposal has yet targeted Big Data platforms. The model centric approach previously discussed may be exploited as a basis for the definition of such policy analysis framework. For instance, it may be used to generate views of the protected resources that show the authorized and unauthorized contents when different policies and configuration options are used, as well as to quantify policy coverage for a requesting subject with respect to an execution context.

The definition of a policy reasoning tool is also instrumental to fulfill the new EU General Data Protection Regulation, (GDPR)[26] which is intended to strengthen data protection for all individuals within the European Union. GDPR applies regardless of where a company is located, provided that the company manages data of EU residents. GDPR introduces a set of very important principles for Big Data management, such as privacy by-design and by-default. The new regulation also emphasizes accountability for data controllers to demonstrate compliance to GDPR, whereas article 35 requires controllers to carry out Data Protection Impact Assessments in cases of potentially high-risk processing activities. All such principles require tools to clearly assess the effect of access control policies on the managed data.

Finally, a policy analysis framework is also required for community centered collaborative systems, such as online social networks and collaborative editing platforms, which may be seen as federated applications that handle Big Data. Recent surveys pointed out that these systems typically provide rudimentary forms of access control [37] A key requirement for access control models tailored for collaborative systems is to allow users to understand collaborative decisions, as well as to inspect users access preferences, and to evaluate their effects [37]. Paci et al. [37] claim that, although a few work exist which explain the effect of access decisions[24], and the

---

[24]https://spark.apache.org/
[25]https://www.datamation.com/data-center/hadoop-vs.-spark-the-new-age-of-big-data.html

[26]https://www.eugdpr.org/

reasons for which certain decisions have been taken [19], the above mentioned requirements are still largely understudied. Therefore, the definition of a reasoning framework capable of operating within such federated environments with multiparty access control models appears as a research challenge of paramount importance.

6.3 Access control for Big Data streaming analytics

In recent years, the number of Big Data platforms that provide support to data stream management is growing. Apache Spark[27] is probably the most popular open source framework which supports the analysis of continuous streams of data. Apache Storm[28] is another open source distributed real-time computation system which can also be used for real-time analytics and continuous computation. In addition, several commercial solutions exist, such as, for instance, Amazon Kinesis[29], which is a service for real-time processing of streaming data on the cloud, and IBM Streaming analytics,[30] a platform supporting risk analysis and decision making in real-time. Due to the growing emphasis to real-time analysis of data flows, a future research goal is the support of enforcement mechanisms targeting continuous flows of data. Some results have been presented in the past years in the field of Data Stream Management Systems. For instance, in [34], a framework called FENCE has been proposed, which supports continuous access control enforcement. Data and query security restrictions are modeled as meta-data, denoted security punctuations, which are embedded into the data streams. Different enforcement mechanisms have been proposed, which operate by analyzing security punctuations, such as special physical operators which are integrated within query execution plans with the aim to filter the tuples which can be analyzed, and rewriting mechanisms targeting continuous queries. The definition of similar approaches for the Big Data scenario is an open issue. A possible system centric strategy may consist in designing the mechanism on top of one of the existing streaming framework. However, similar to the platform specific approaches presented in Section 4, such a solution would suffer from a limited applicability. Moreover, existing solutions (e.g., FENCE [34]) operate at tuple level, whereas cell/field level granularity may be necessary in the Big Data scenario (see Sections 4 and 5), requiring a data filtering approach that operates at a finer granularity level. The development of an enforcement mechanisms based on language centric approaches seems still impracticable, as no standard continuous query language exists. In contrast, since some of these platforms can implement MapReduce tasks (e.g., Apache Spark, Apache Storm), a model centric approach may be a possible strategy, however, thorough investigations are required to support this intuition.

6.4 Access control for IoT ecosystems

Internet of Things (IoT) ecosystems are representative cases of Big Data applications. IoT applications are rapidly getting popularity in a variety of domains for the indisputable improvements of people life style. For instance, a growing number of users cannot do without wearable devices that continuously track their sport activities and health conditions. Due to the personal and sensitive nature of the handled information, security and privacy of these systems have become a major concern. As a consequence, in the recent years, several research efforts have been devoted to security and privacy of IoT applications, and a variety of access control models have been proposed (see, for instance, [36] for a compendium). These initial efforts have mainly produced models adopting centralized enforcement mechanisms (e.g., see [17]). However, multiple IoT ecosystems may be connected to each other exchanging data. As a matter of fact, federated systems where multiple IoT applications cooperate cannot be handled with centralized enforcement mechanisms. Multiparty access control solutions for IoT ecosystems are thus needed, which are suited to operate at Big Data scale. The definition of such access control frameworks still represent a big open research challenge.

7 CONCLUSIONS

Security services for Big Data represent a key feature instrumental to foster trust on how data are managed and analyzed by Big Data platforms. This paper has focused on one of the key security service, that is, access control, by discussing the requirements that an access control solution for Big Data platforms should address. Moreover, the paper has provided a review of the state of the art in view of the devised requirements, and it has also discussed future research challenges in the area.

REFERENCES

[1] R. Agrawal, J. Kiernan, R. Srikant, and Y. Xu. 2002. Hippocratic databases. In *28th International Conference on Very Large Data Bases (VLDB)*.
[2] Gail-Joon Ahn, Hongxin Hu, Joohyung Lee, and Yunsong Meng. 2010. Representing and reasoning about web access control policies. In *Computer Software and Applications Conference (COMPSAC), 2010 IEEE 34th Annual*. IEEE, 137–146.
[3] Sattam Alsubaiee, Yasser Altowim, Hotham Altwaijry, Alexander Behm, Vinayak Borkar, Yingyi Bu, Michael Carey, Inci Cetindil, Madhusudan Cheelangi, Khurram Faraaz, et al. 2014. AsterixDB: A scalable, open source BDMS. *Proceedings of the VLDB Endowment* 7, 14 (2014), 1905–1916.
[4] Lujo Bauer, Scott Garriss, and Michael K Reiter. 2011. Detecting and resolving policy misconfigurations in access-control systems. *ACM Transactions on Information and System Security (TISSEC)* 14, 1 (2011), 2.
[5] E. Bertino, A. A. Jabal, S. B. Calo, C. Makaya, M. Touma, D. C. Verma, and C. Williams. 2017. Provenance-Based Analytics Services for Access Control Policies. In *2017 IEEE World Congress on Services, SERVICES 2017, Honolulu, HI, USA, June 25-30, 2017*. 94–101.
[6] J.W. Byun and N. Li. 2008. Purpose based access control for privacy protection in relational database systems. *The VLDB Journal* 17, 4 (2008).
[7] Rick Cattell. 2011. Scalable SQL and NoSQL Data Stores. *SIGMOD Rec.* 39, 4 (May 2011), 12–27. https://doi.org/10.1145/1978915.1978919
[8] Don Chamberlin, Daniela Florescu, Jonathan Robie, Jerome Simeon, and Mugur Stefanescu. 2003. XQuery: A query language for XML. In *SIGMOD Conference*, Vol. 682.
[9] Tony Clark and Jos Warmer. 2002. *Object Modeling With the OCL: The Rationale Behind the Object Constraint Language*. Vol. 2263. Springer.
[10] P. Colombo and E. Ferrari. 2014. Enforcement of Purpose Based Access Control within Relational Database Management Systems. *IEEE Transactions on Knowledge and Data Engineering (TKDE)* 26, 11 (2014). https://doi.org/10.1109/TKDE.2014.2312112
[11] P. Colombo and E. Ferrari. 2014. Enforcing Obligations within Relational Database Management Systems. *IEEE Transactions on Dependable and Secure Computing (TDSC)* 11, 4 (2014). https://doi.org/10.1109/TDSC.2013.48
[12] P. Colombo and E. Ferrari. 2015. Efficient Enforcement of Action aware Purpose Based Access Control within Relational Database Management Systems. *Knowledge and Data Engineering, IEEE Transactions on* (2015). in press.
[13] Pietro Colombo and Elena Ferrari. 2015. Privacy Aware Access Control for Big Data: A Research Roadmap. *Big Data Research* 2, 4 (2015), 145 – 154. https://doi.org/10.1016/j.bdr.2015.08.001

---

[27] https://spark.apache.org/
[28] http://storm.apache.org/
[29] https://aws.amazon.com/kinesis/
[30] https://www.ibm.com/cloud/streaming-analytics

[14] Pietro Colombo and Elena Ferrari. 2016. Towards Virtual Private NoSQL datastores. In *32nd IEEE International Conference on Data Engineering, ICDE 2016, Helsinki, Finland, May 16-20, 2016.* 193–204.

[15] Pietro Colombo and Elena Ferrari. 2017. Enhancing MongoDB with Purpose-Based Access Control. *IEEE Trans. Dependable Sec. Comput.* 14, 6 (2017), 591–604. https://doi.org/10.1109/TDSC.2015.2497680

[16] Pietro Colombo and Elena Ferrari. 2017. Towards a Unifying Attribute Based Access Control Approach for NoSQL Datastores. In *33rd IEEE International Conference on Data Engineering, ICDE 2017, San Diego, CA, USA, April 19-22, 2017.* 709–720.

[17] Pietro Colombo and Elena Ferrari. 2018. Access Control Enforcement within MQTT-based Internet of Things Ecosystems. In *Proceedings of the ACM Symposium on Access Control Models and Technologies (SACMAT).* ACM.

[18] Jeffrey Dean and Sanjay Ghemawat. 2004. MapReduce: Simplified Data Processing on Large Clusters. In *Proceedings of the 6th Conference on Symposium on Opearting Systems Design & Implementation - Volume 6 (OSDI'04).* USENIX Association, Berkeley, CA, USA, 10–10. http://dl.acm.org/citation.cfm?id=1251254.1251264

[19] Jerry den Hartog and Nicola Zannone. 2016. A Policy Framework for Data Fusion and Derived Data Control. In *Proceedings of the 2016 ACM International Workshop on Attribute Based Access Control (ABAC '16).* ACM, New York, NY, USA, 47–57. https://doi.org/10.1145/2875491.2875492

[20] D.F. Ferraiolo, R. Sandhu, S. Gavrila, D.R. Kuhn, and R. Chandramouli. 2001. Proposed NIST standard for role-based access control. *ACM Transactions on Information and System Security (TISSEC)* 4, 3 (2001).

[21] Elena Ferrari. 2010. *Access Control in Data Management Systems.* Morgan & Claypool Publishers.

[22] D. Florescu and G. Fourny. 2013. JSONiq: The History of a Query Language. *IEEE Internet Computing* 17, 5 (Sept 2013), 86–90. https://doi.org/10.1109/MIC.2013.97

[23] Maanak Gupta, Farhan Patwa, and Ravi Sandhu. 2017. Object-Tagged RBAC Model for the Hadoop Ecosystem. In *Data and Applications Security and Privacy XXXI,* Giovanni Livraga and Sencun Zhu (Eds.). Springer International Publishing, Cham, 63–81.

[24] H. Hu, G. J. Ahn, and J. Jorgensen. 2013. Multiparty Access Control for Online Social Networks: Model and Mechanisms. *IEEE Transactions on Knowledge and Data Engineering* 25, 7 (July 2013), 1614–1627. https://doi.org/10.1109/TKDE.2012.97

[25] Vincent C Hu, David Ferraiolo, Rick Kuhn, Arthur R Friedman, Alan J Lang, Margaret M Cogdell, Adam Schnitzer, Kenneth Sandlin, Robert Miller, Karen Scarfone, et al. 2013. Guide to attribute based access control (ABAC) definition and considerations (draft). *NIST special publication* 800, 162 (2013).

[26] V. C. Hu, D. R. Kuhn, and D. F. Ferraiolo. 2015. Attribute-Based Access Control. *Computer* 48, 2 (Feb 2015), 85–88. https://doi.org/10.1109/MC.2015.33

[27] Xiaolong Jin, Benjamin W. Wah, Xueqi Cheng, and Yuanzhuo Wang. 2015. Significance and Challenges of Big Data Research. *Big Data Research* (2015). https://doi.org/10.1016/j.bdr.2015.01.006

[28] Jonathan Katz, Amit Sahai, and Brent Waters. 2013. Predicate encryption supporting disjunctions, polynomial equations, and inner products. *Journal of cryptology* 26, 2 (2013), 191–224.

[29] Devdatta Kulkarni. 2013. A fine-grained access control model for key-value systems. In *Proceedings of the third ACM conference on Data and application security and privacy.* ACM, 161–164.

[30] Kristen LeFevre, Rakesh Agrawal, Vuk Ercegovac, Raghu Ramakrishnan, Yirong Xu, and David DeWitt. 2004. Limiting disclosure in hippocratic databases. In *Proceedings of the Thirtieth international conference on Very large data bases-Volume 30.* VLDB Endowment, 108–119.

[31] Jim J. Longstaff and Joanne Noble. 2016. Attribute Based Access Control for Big Data Applications by Query Modification. In *Second IEEE International Conference on Big Data Computing Service and Applications, BigDataService 2016, Oxford, United Kingdom, March 29 - April 1, 2016.* 58–65.

[32] Viktor Mayer-Schönberger and Kenneth Cukier. 2013. *Big data: A revolution that will transform how we live, work, and think.* Houghton Mifflin Harcourt.

[33] Mohamed Nabeel and Elisa Bertino. 2014. Privacy preserving delegated access control in public clouds. *IEEE Transactions on Knowledge and Data Engineering* 26, 9 (2014), 2268–2280.

[34] R. V. Nehme, H. S. Lim, and E. Bertino. 2010. FENCE: Continuous access control enforcement in dynamic data stream environments. In *2010 IEEE 26th International Conference on Data Engineering (ICDE 2010).* 940–943. https://doi.org/10.1109/ICDE.2010.5447899

[35] Kian Win Ong, Yannis Papakonstantinou, and Romain Vernoux. 2014. The SQL++ unifying semi-structured query language, and an expressiveness benchmark of SQL-on-Hadoop, NoSQL and NewSQL databases. *CoRR, abs/1405.3631* (2014).

[36] Aafaf Ouaddah, Hajar Mousannif, Anas Abou Elkalam, and Abdellah Ait Ouahman. 2017. Access control in the Internet of Things: Big challenges and new opportunities. *Computer Networks* 112 (2017), 237 – 262. https://doi.org/10.1016/j.comnet.2016.11.007

[37] Federica Paci, Anna Squicciarini, and Nicola Zannone. 2018. Survey on Access Control for Community-Centered Collaborative Systems. *ACM Comput. Surv.* 51, 1, Article 6 (Jan. 2018), 38 pages. https://doi.org/10.1145/3146025

[38] Edelmira Pasarella and Jorge Lobo. 2017. A Datalog Framework for Modeling Relationship-based Access Control Policies. In *Proceedings of the 22nd ACM on Symposium on Access Control Models and Technologies.* ACM, 91–102.

[39] S. Rizvi, A. Mendelzon, S. Sudarshan, and P. Roy. 2004. Extending query rewriting techniques for fine-grained access control. In *ACM SIGMOD 2004.* 551–562.

[40] Yossif Shalabi and Ehud Gudes. 2017. Cryptographically Enforced Role-Based Access Control for NoSQL Distributed Databases. In *Data and Applications Security and Privacy XXXI,* Giovanni Livraga and Sencun Zhu (Eds.). Springer International Publishing, Cham, 3–19.

[41] H. Ulusoy, P. Colombo, E. Ferrari, M. Kantarcioglu, and E. Pattuk. 2015. GuardMR: Fine-grained Security Policy Enforcement for MapReduce Systems. In *ACM ASIACCS 2015.*

[42] Huseyin Ulusoy, Murat Kantarcioglu, Kevin Hamlen, and Erman Pattuk. 2014. Vigiles: Fine-grained Access Control for MapReduce Systems. In *IEEE BigData.*

[43] Jos B Warmer and Anneke G Kleppe. 1998. The object constraint language: Precise modeling with uml (addison-wesley object technology series). (1998).

Authorization Framework for Secure Cloud Assisted Connected Cars and Vehicular Internet of Things

Maanak Gupta and Ravi Sandhu
Institute for Cyber Security (ICS),
Center for Security and Privacy Enhanced Cloud Computing (C-SPECC),
Department of Computer Science, University of Texas at San Antonio
Email: gmaanakg@yahoo.com, ravi.sandhu@utsa.edu

ABSTRACT

Internet of Things has become a predominant phenomenon in every sphere of smart life. Connected Cars and Vehicular Internet of Things, which involves communication and data exchange between vehicles, traffic infrastructure or other entities are pivotal to realize the vision of smart city and intelligent transportation. Vehicular Cloud offers a promising architecture wherein storage and processing capabilities of smart objects are utilized to provide on-the-fly fog platform. Researchers have demonstrated vulnerabilities in this emerging vehicular IoT ecosystem, where data has been stolen from critical sensors and smart vehicles controlled remotely. Security and privacy is important in Internet of Vehicles (IoV) where access to electronic control units, applications and data in connected cars should only be authorized to legitimate users, sensors or vehicles. In this paper, we propose an authorization framework to secure this dynamic system where interactions among entities is not pre-defined. We provide an extended access control oriented (E-ACO) architecture relevant to IoV and discuss the need of vehicular clouds in this time and location sensitive environment. We outline approaches to different access control models which can be enforced at various layers of E-ACO architecture and in the authorization framework. Finally, we discuss use cases to illustrate access control requirements in our vision of cloud assisted connected cars and vehicular IoT, and discuss possible research directions.

CCS CONCEPTS

• **Security and privacy** → **Security requirements**; **Access control**; **Authorization**;

KEYWORDS

Access Control; Internet of Things; Vehicular Internet of Things; Connected Cars; Vehicular Cloud; Internet of Vehicles; Big Data; Attributes Based; Trust; Fog Computing; Cloud Computing

ACM Reference Format:
Maanak Gupta and Ravi Sandhu. 2018. Authorization Framework for Secure Cloud Assisted Connected Cars and Vehicular Internet of Things. In *Proceedings of 23rd ACM Symposium on Access Control Models and Technologies (SACMAT'18)*. ACM, New York, NY, USA, 12 pages. https://doi.org/10.1145/3205977.3205994

1 INTRODUCTION

Internet of Things (IoT) is the new era of technology which envisions to make human lives smarter. The concept has attracted wide applications and services in variety of domains including health-care, homes, industry, transportation, power grids etc. The magnitude of this technology is illustrated by the number of devices which are estimated to be more than 20 billion by year 2020 [32]. The prime asset delivered by such massive interconnection and networking of smart devices is Big Data, which is analyzed to gather insights and deliver valuable information.

IoT requires the use of multiple technologies including identification (naming and addressing), sensing (sensor devices, RFID tags etc.), communication technologies (Bluetooth, WiFi etc.), computation technologies involving hardware or software platforms like Cloud, multiple IoT services [35] and the applications which provide functionalities to the end user [9, 13, 36]. Several IoT architectures have been demonstrated to incorporate physical objects, object abstraction (virtual objects), middleware or service, application and business layers with variations in architecture stack and nomenclature [9, 13]. Cloud computing is also an important domain in today's world which offers boundless applications and resources (storage and compute) to multiple users. Therefore, the merger of IoT and cloud is arguably indispensable to harness the full potential of IoT smart objects which have limited storage, processing and communication capabilities. The literature has recognized this desirable integration using terms such as cloud-assisted, cloud-enabled, and cloud-centric IoT [8, 16, 18, 20, 21, 25, 50].

Smart cities and intelligent transportation has been a vision of future society. IoT plays an important role to make transportation smarter by introducing connected cars and vehicular communication. Vehicular IoT involves interaction and V2X data/messages exchange between several entities including vehicle to vehicle (V2V), vehicle to road infrastructure (V2I), vehicle to human (V2H), intra-vehicle, and vehicle to cloud (V2C). Vehicular Ad-hoc Networks (VANETs) provide necessary connectivity which is extended with use of smarter devices and cloud or fog infrastructures. Several sensors in and around connected car 'talk' to each other for smarter decisions and convenient transportation experience to user. Our vision of vehicular IoT harness computation and storage capabilities of cloud and the concept of virtual objects (e.g. AWS shadows [14]).

Security and privacy have been a serious concern and challenge for the adoption of IoT. The gravity of these issues is magnified when we think about implications in vehicular IoT and the emerging concept of autonomous cars. This ecosystem has connected cars as its most important, and also most vulnerable, entity. With over 100 millions lines of code, more than 100 electronic control units (ECUs) and broad attack surface opened by features such as onboard diagnostics, driver assistance systems and airbags, it becomes a challenge to protect this smart entity. Further, the communication among smart objects (vehicle to vehicle, vehicle to infrastructure etc.), mobility, and dynamic network topology makes it even harder to secure the system. Some of the potential risks in vehicular IoT involves untrustworthy or fake messages from smart objects, data privacy, critical ECU hacking and control, spoofing connected vehicle sensor, and injecting malicious software. The US Department of Transportation (USDOT) and National Highway Traffic Safety Administration (NHTSA) have focused on vehicular security and have released important cyber-security guidelines in this regard [52, 53]. USDOT's strategic plan also outlines the direction and goals of Intelligent Transportation System (ITS) Program [15].

Access control is an important mechanism to prevent unauthorized access to resources in any system. This paper focuses on access control and authorization requirements in Vehicular Internet of Things and Connected Cars, which we also refer to collectively as the Internet of Vehicles (IoV). We envisage cloud and virtual objects as an important component of cloud-assisted vehicular IoT. We propose an extended access control oriented architecture (E-ACO) for IoV, which is an extension to the recently proposed ACO architecture for IoT [10]. The prime difference between these architectures is the introduction of clustered objects, which are objects with multiple sensors, and possible interaction between sensors in same clustered object or between different object's sensors. Clustered objects are particularly relevant in case of connected cars, traffic lights or other smart devices which have multiple sensors and ECUs mounted on them. Our authorization framework illustrates different interaction and data exchange scenarios in vehicular IoT and proposes access control models at various E-ACO layers including physical, virtual objects, cloud layer and applications. We further discuss different cloud or fog based architectures in IoV, and the concept of vehicular cloud and its relevance. Comprehensive use cases and research directions are also elaborated to illustrate the need for an authorization framework in vehicular IoT ecosystem.

The paper is organized as follows. Section 2 discusses important technologies and concepts relevant to vehicular IoT including connected cars, vehicular clouds, virtual objects, IoV security and privacy concerns, and ACO architecture. Section 3 elaborates IoV characteristics, various cloud or fog architectures, and our proposed extended access control oriented (E-ACO) architecture. Authorization framework with different IoV entities interactions and some access control approaches, is discussed in Section 4. Real world use cases reflecting access control requirements in single and multiple cloud systems are discussed in Section 5, followed by some proposed research agenda in Section 6 and conclusion in Section 7.

2 RELEVANT BACKGROUND

Vehicular IoT is a novel domain where networking and communication among cars, traffic infrastructure, pedestrians, homes or ultimately anything is proposed. This emerging concept involves several new and established technologies which needs to be discussed to understand IoV systems and our authorization framework. This section reviews IoV building blocks which we believe are fundamentally required and are the basis of our work.

2.1 Connected Cars

The prime goal of IoV is inter-connectivity among smart entities in which vehicles are most important. As stated [4] by Wikipedia , "A Connected car (or Connected Vehicle (CV)) is a car equipped with internet access and usually also with the wireless area network. This allows the car to share internet access with other devices both inside as well as outside the vehicle". Gartner predicts a quarter billion connected cars by year 2020 [31] which will form a significant portion of the overall connected devices. The communication among vehicles and infrastructure, driving assistance and autonomous driving, automatic braking and emergency calling, weather and accident warnings, parking areas, E-toll, and predictive maintenance, are among the most desired and available features in today's connected cars. These cars have more than 100 ECUs and 100 millions lines of code in support of such functionality. CVs have controller area network (CAN) bus, FlexRay, Ethernet and other protocols which are used for ECU communication within the car. Messages are broadcasted to all ECUs attached to bus. Multiple buses are connected via a gateway, usually a TCU (Telematics Control Unit), which also provides interface to external environment. These vehicles generate, exchange and process huge amounts of data and are often referred to as 'smartphones on wheels' [63]. Some of the most hackable and exposed attack surfaces in a connected car include airbag ECU, Bluetooth, TPMS, and remote key [22]. As vehicles with a broad attack surface get connected to the internet, they get exposed to remote malicious activities. Cyber attacks can be orchestrated from in-vehicle network, from a user inside the car using a smartphone, from external entities in proximity, or even through cloud.

2.2 Vehicular Clouds

Vehicular Ad-hoc Networks (VANETs) have been proposed in the literature to support vehicle to vehicle and vehicle to infrastructure communication to enable advanced services to the drivers. The network nodes in VANETs (cars, infrastructure etc.) have storage, computation and communication modules to provide such services. However, most of these on-board resources are usually under-utilized with the set of applications offered, and can be utilized for additional services to stakeholders [27, 56]. The concept of vehicular cloud (VC) has been proposed which blends the two separate ideas of VANETs and Cloud computing. Cloud computing provides the idea of boundless storage, compute or network resources in the form of IaaS, PaaS and SaaS, which are extended to the inter-networked cars and infrastructure provided by VANETs. Vehicular Cloud [27, 33, 34, 56] utilizes coordinated on-board resources of cars and infrastructure to offer the capabilities of 'cloud on the fly' to users that need them.

The vision of IoV requires cooperation among entities for smooth and efficient traffic flow with information and entertainment (infotainment) to driver. All such applications have local relevance which need time and location sensitive computation of information avoiding the latency and bandwidth problems when the information is loaded and processed in central cloud. Therefore, the surrounding vehicles can form autonomous clouds to solve driver's locally relevant queries about traffic ahead or parking nearby. Several architectures have been proposed for the formation of vehicular clouds like stationary VC, VC linked with a fixed infrastructure or dynamic VC, where each has different formation scenarios [45, 71].

The key features to distinguish conventional cloud and VC are mobility, agility and autonomy of vehicles, which are computation and storage nodes in vehicular cloud. In VCs, one vehicle is selected as the broker by surrounding vehicles which mediates resource sharing among vehicles in and around specific geographic boundary (for example in 2 miles radius). The broker asks permission for cloud formation from relevant authorities and also sends request to neighbouring vehicles to share resources. Once approved by authorities (DMV or transportation agency), these vehicles pool their resources to form a virtual environment which is shared by all VC users. Further, large scale federation of VCs can be established in case of emergency situations like earthquake, providing temporary infrastructure when conventional cloud is unreachable.

We believe vehicular IoT will involve single or multiple cloud/fog instances supporting different service models – SaaS, PaaS and IaaS. These instances can cover wide geographic area using central cloud, fog instances within 1-2 miles radius or even fog instances at each connected car level based on different use cases. These architectures can be public, private (for example by a car manufacturer) or hybrid and involve single internet clouds, vehicular clouds, fog instances or any combination of them as discussed further in Section 3.

2.3 Virtual Objects

The cyber-physical ecosystem of vehicular IoT has heterogenous objects with different operating conditions, communication technology, and functionalities. Further, the issues related to object connectivity, scalability, object and service discovery, security and privacy, quality management, and identification are challenges in any IoT system [55]. To counter these issues the concept of virtual objects is introduced in several IoT architectures [60, 70]. Amazon AWS IoT [17] also incorporates virtual objects as device shadows where in case a physical device is not connected, its cyber counterpart (i.e. shadow) will have the last received state or desired future state information. Therefore, whenever the physical device gets connected to its virtual entity, it gets updated to the state of its cyber object and also mitigates the problem of sporadic object connectivity. Microsoft Azure [7] has device twins which are JSON documents maintained in Azure IoT hub for each device connected and stores device state information. Different association scenarios exist between physical and virtual objects: single virtual object for one physical object irrespective of the number of services and functionalities provided by physical object; whereas for object with multiple services, it is possible to have many virtual objects for each service of same physical object. Similarly, other configurations such as many physical to one virtual or many physical to many virtual mappings are also possible depending on different use-case requirements. The creation and location of virtual objects is primarily proposed in the cloud and their communication uses RESTful technologies [55]. Since high latency and low bandwidth issues will exist in virtual objects creation, for real time applications

like vehicular IoT, we envision to keep the virtual objects near to the physical objects, i.e at the fog level or in vehicular cloud (VC).

2.4 Security and Privacy Concerns

Most security vulnerabilities like trojan horse, buffer overflow exploits, malware, ransomware, and privilege escalation can be exploited on connected vehicles and other IoV entities. Connected vehicle with more than 100 ECUs, with broad attack surface interacting both in-vehicle systems and a wide range of external networks including WiFi, cellular networks, and internet to data exchange between service garages, toll roads, gas stations, and several automotive and aftermarket applications [22], present a big challenge for security. Recently Tesla Model X was hacked [66] with many other incidents of attacks noticed in past. Security is vital in IoV and CVs where attacks (like disabling brakes) can even lead to loss of life. Several studies and reports [2, 5, 58, 59, 69] have been published to illustrate potential risks and attacks which can be orchestrated on smart entities in IoV. Some examples of cyber attacks in connected cars and IoV as discussed in [24, 26, 30, 44, 62] include: user impersonation to exchange fake basic safety messages (BSM) or false information about an accident, stealing personal data or credit card information, controlling critical sensors of connected vehicle, gaining knowledge of vehicle and driver movement, spoofing CV's sensors, coordinated attacks on infrastructure, unauthorized over-the air firmware updates, and infecting a CV with ransomware. CAN bus used for internal ECU communication must also be secured to prevent unauthorized gain of data and manipulation of software on ECU and sensor systems. An unauthorized party that gains access to the bus can block legitimate messages and transmit illegitimate ones. On board equipments (OBEs) integrate with the CAN bus to provide information such as vehicle speed and brake system status to participating entities. This bring us back full circle to needing to protect the internal components of a vehicle in order to maintain confidence that V2V, V2I and V2X messages are legitimate. Securing IoV and connected vehicles will require protecting control systems (on-board diagnostic (OBD) port, CAN bus etc.), protecting infotainment systems, securing smartphone applications, securing infrastructure, securing over-the air updates, and securing hardware from manual tampering. Security mechanisms become hard to implement considering intrinsic IoV characteristics like dynamic topology, mobile limitation, and large scale network.

US Department of Transportation initiated the ITS (Intelligent Transportation Systems) program to enable communication among vehicles and other smart infrastructures while ensuring security and privacy of the stake-holders. The BSMs exchanged among entities must not include personally identifiable information and must be broadcasted in limited geographic area [67]. Dedicated short range communications (DSRC) is used to exchange information across entities which is used by several safety and other applications to generate alerts for drivers. Therefore, the confidentiality and integrity of such messages is imperative so that drivers can trust their source and information in them. Security Credential Management System (SCMS) [68] has been proposed to ensure trust and message security using public key infrastructure (PKI) approach where certificate generated by certificate authority (CA) is attached with the BSM to ensure trust between talking entities. European

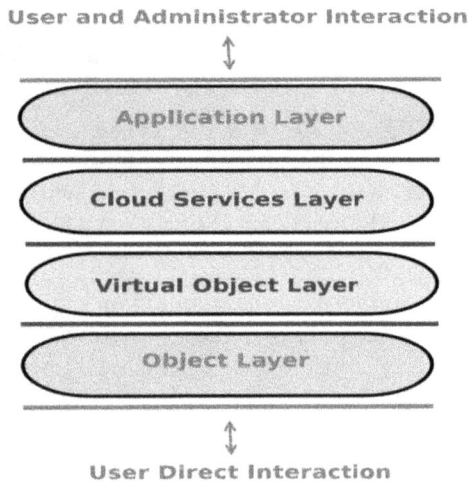

Figure 1: ACO Architecture [10]

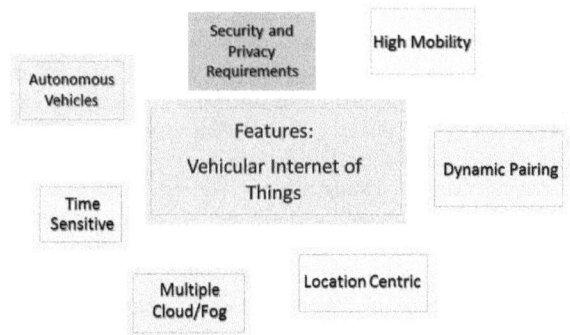

Figure 2: IoV Distinguishing Characteristics

Union Agency for Network and Information Security (ENISA) has also released a study in year 2017 [28] which enlists critical assets in smart cars, threats, potential risks, and proposed good practices mainly segmented into three categories, policy and standards, organizational measures, and security functions, to ensure security of smart cars against cyber threats. European Commission has set up Cooperative Intelligent Transport Systems (C-ITS) Deployment Platform to foster cooperative, connected and automated vehicles, and has released security frameworks [65] and certificate policy [64] documents. National Institute for Standards and Technology (NIST) also proposed a framework [54] for cyber-physical systems (CPS) which address conceptualization, realization and assurance of CPS including security and interoperability.

2.5 ACO Architecture

In general, all proposed IoT architectures [9, 13, 20, 36, 55] have three layers: object, middleware (with multiple sub-layers) and application layer. Recently, Alsehri and Sandhu proposed an IoT architecture, referred as access control oriented architecture (ACO) [10], taking into consideration the access control requirements in IoT and incorporation of models at various layers. As shown in Figure 1, ACO architecture has four layers – object, virtual object, cloud services and application – with user and administrators interacting at object and application layers. Since, our proposed extended ACO architecture for vehicular IoT (discussed in Section 3) adds to/refines generic IoT based ACO architecture, we will outline ACO architecture layers below.

- **Object Layer:** The bottom layer of ACO architecture comprises physical smart devices like sensors, RFIDs, beacons, and ECUs, which are responsible for data sensing and accumulation, and for sending data to upper layers. These devices can communicate with other devices using different communication technologies including Bluetooth, WiFi, Zigbee, LAN and LTE. Physical devices communicate with their cyber counterparts (virtual objects) using protocols like HTTP, MQTT, DDS or CoAP [9]. Users can also directly access physical objects at this layer.

- **Virtual Object Layer:** As discussed, virtual objects represent the digital counterpart of physical objects which maintain the status of physical objects even when they are not connected. ACO architecture recommends virtual object layer as a part of middleware to support communication between heterogenous objects and overcome IoT challenges of scalability or locality.

- **Cloud Services Layer:** With the number of IoT devices proliferating, the storage and computation of data will be done in cloud, where different applications can harness it to make valued decisions. Single or multiple cloud scenarios can exist to support federation or trusted collaboration between them. Some important IoT cloud platforms include Amazon AWS [14], Microsoft Azure IoT Hub [7], and Google Cloud IoT Core [6].

- **Application Layer:** The applications offered by IoT systems to end users are situated in this layer, which leverage the services and functionalities of the lower cloud services layer. Users and administrators can remotely send commands and instructions to smart devices at bottom layer using these applications, but such interaction has to pass via other two ACO middleware layers (cloud services and virtual object). Administrators can also define access control policies for various IoT resources using this layer.

3 CLOUD ASSISTED VEHICULAR INTERNET OF THINGS

The vision of smart city and intelligent transportation encompasses connected cars and vehicular IoT as an important component. The eventual goal of IoV is the integration of vehicles, infrastructure, smart things, homes or ultimately any thing to promote efficient transportation, accidental safety, fuel efficiency etc. and for pleasant travel experience to the driver. The technology involves communication between vehicles (V2V), vehicle to human (V2H), vehicle to cloud (V2C), vehicle to infrastructure (V2I) etc. to exchange vehicle telematics [12, 29] and gather information about surroundings to offer services to the users. Safety applications in IoV require basic safety messages (BSM) to be exchanged among smart entities, which contain information about vehicle position, heading, speed, etc, related to vehicle state and predicted path [1]. Such interaction can happen using dedicated short-range communications (DSRC) technology (similar to WiFi, secure and reliable) which allows rapid communications (up to 10 times per second) between elements of IoV network required for end user applications.

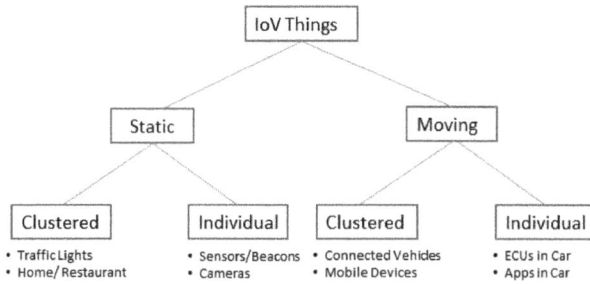

Figure 3: Smart Object Types in IoV

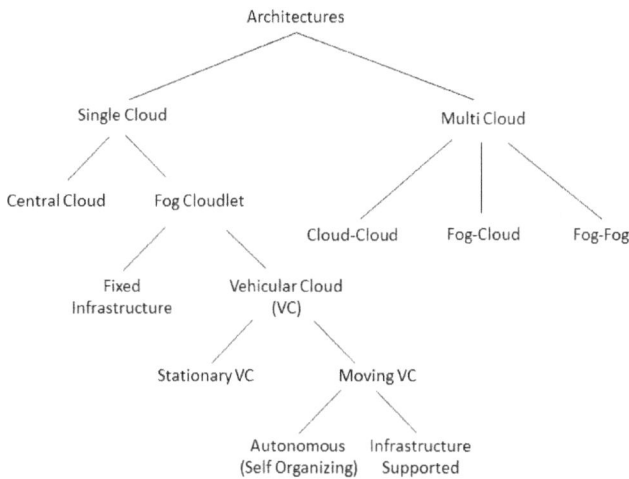

Figure 4: Different Cloud and Fog Architectures in IoV

3.1 Characteristics and Cloud Architectures

Vehicular IoT inherits intrinsic IoT characteristics of data sharing, communication and accumulation in cloud. However, dynamic topology structures, dynamic communication, mobility, network scale, and non-uniform nodes distribution (shown in Figure 2) are some features that distinguish it from other IoT domains, resulting in new security and privacy challenges. Further, several applications in IoV domain are very time and location sensitive; for example, BSM information about traffic congestion from a neighbouring vehicle or a traffic light, or about ice on bridge or an accident report to a nearby hospital etc. makes IoV ecosystem very dynamic. Internet of Vehicles involve different kinds of objects (as shown in Figure 3) based on their mobility, functionalities or processing capabilities. Some smart objects are static in nature; for example, beacons outside a restaurant, or sensor on a smart traffic light whereas moving objects include connected cars, pedestrian with mobile phones, etc. Further, some of these are individual objects with single sensor performing only one function whereas some are clustered objects having multiple sensors associated with them. A connected car has several ECUs and sensors on it, and hence is referred as a clustered object whereas a single ECU in a car generally performs one function and is an individual object. Such characterization is necessary as it drives our access control framework and models. Several applications of connected cars and vehicular IoT are envisioned

for smart city intelligent transportation initiative, including the following.

- **Safety and Assistance:** With machine to machine (M2M) communication among vehicles and infrastructure, these applications provide real-time information about other vehicles and traffic to control speed, in-lane position control or road work warning from signboards. Further, in inclement weather, in non-ideal driving conditions, or blind spots, even pedestrian with mobile phones can exchange safety messages with incoming vehicle such as while crossing roads.
- **Diagnostic and Maintenance:** Remote diagnostic and predictive maintenance of vehicles through manufacturer or authorized mechanic will save time and money. Vehicle sensor data can be send to cloud for processing to predict vehicle mechanical issues. Over the air (OTA) updates can also be issued by manufacturer for fixing car firmware which will obviate the need to go to mechanic. Fleet management applications provide real-time telematics, driver fatigue detection and package tracking.
- **Information and Entertainment:** Driving based insurance models have been introduced which will assess the driver behaviour to determine insurance premiums. Real-time parking information can be shared between parking garages and vehicles. Restaurant and gas stations can send offers to nearby vehicle's dashboard. Car-pooling, connected driving [47], web-browsing, music etc. are some additional IoV applications.

We believe cloud platforms like Amazon AWS, Microsoft Azure etc. will play an important role to fully harness the potential and applications of IoV. Further, the use of edge or fog computing [19] is imperative to resolve the issues of high latency, low bandwidth and communication delays pertinent to using central cloud, which are very critical in time and location sensitive IoV applications [3]. Figure 4 shows various single and multi cloud scenarios viable in IoV. Single cloud architectures may involve only one central cloud which manages user applications, virtual objects and data generated from smart entities in a wide geographic area, such as a city. This architecture is not feasible because of latency and other issues mentioned above. Fog or edge computing is essential, and we believe IoV can either use vehicular cloud (i.e the resources offered by smart vehicles and infrastructure on road) or a fixed infrastructure setup along the road where compute and storage clusters are dedicated for small areas. It is also possible to use fog structure for each connected vehicle, and sensors in the vehicle have virtual objects in the fog which can be used to enable intra-vehicle communication. Vehicular cloud (VC) can be stationary where the vehicles are standing in a mall parking lot and offering their resources for an incentive (like a free parking) or moving VC where vehicles while moving may form cloud using broker [33, 34, 45, 56, 71] and can leave or join the cloud if in specified geographic range. Further, these moving VCs can be supported by fixed infrastructure (example, a traffic light on the roadside acting as a broker) or moving vehicles in autonomous manner can form a VC. In multi-cloud IoV architectures, we envision to have either multiple clouds, cloud-fog or multiple fogs setup. However, we believe single central cloud and multiple fog architectures are a good fit to cover most connected car and IoV applications, as discussed later in our extended ACO architecture.

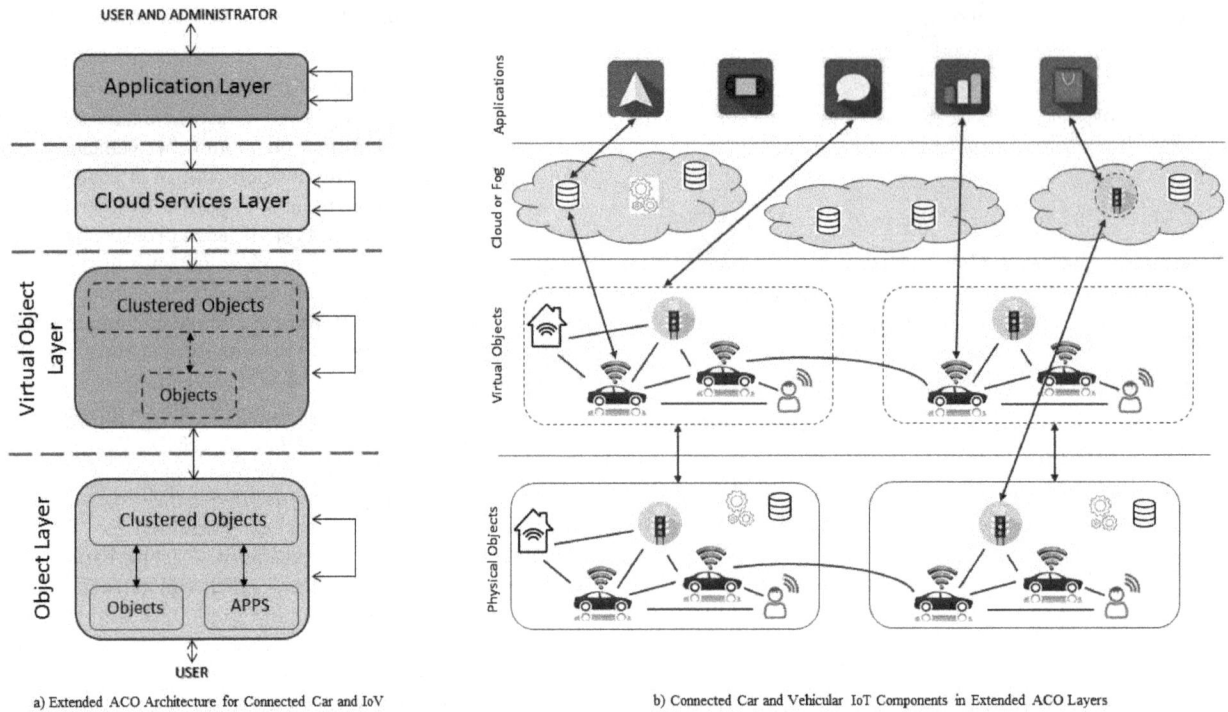

a) Extended ACO Architecture for Connected Car and IoV

b) Connected Car and Vehicular IoT Components in Extended ACO Layers

Figure 5: Extended ACO Architecture for Connected Cars and Vehicular IoT

3.2 Extended ACO Architecture

Connected Cars and Vehicular IoT ecosystem has several heterogenous devices (individual or clustered) and in-built car applications which cooperate to provide services to the end users. Some devices are independent (camera on street, beacons on restaurant) whereas some belong to a larger clustered object (ECU or sensor in a connected car). Hence, we propose to incorporate this distinction into previously defined access control oriented architecture (ACO) [10] to address IoV ecosystem access control requirements. An important reason to incorporate clustered objects is to reflect cross-vehicle and intra-vehicle communication. The fact that two connected cars can exchange basic safety messages (BSM) with each other reflects clustered object communication. Such concept is not defined in ACO architecture which is proposed for generic IoT systems. Besides objects, these clustered objects may have applications running in them; for example, a car may have a navigation application installed in it, or a safety warning application, which may interact with sensors on a smart sign-board to warn the driver via car dashboard or seat vibration or buzzer. It should be noted that these sensors or applications may access sensors in car they belong to or possibly sensors on other cars also.

Figure 5 shows our proposed extended ACO (E-ACO) architecture along with the corresponding vehicular IoT components at different E-ACO layers in Figure 5 (b). E-ACO architecture has four layers similar to ACO: Object layer, Virtual Object layer, Cloud services and Application layer, where the communication can happen within a layer (shown as self loop in Figure 5 (a)) and the adjacent layers above and below. We will now discuss layers in more detail:

Object Layer: The object layer introduces clustered objects which have multiple individual sensors or smart objects. The clustered objects may also have several built-in applications (like tire-pressure monitoring) installed within them. These applications can communicate with ECUs and sensors in same car (or neighbouring car) to get data and update information to the drivers. Some of these applications accumulate data and send it to the cloud infrastructure for further analysis; for example diagnostic applications installed by the manufacturer which will collect data from critical engine sensors and send to the cloud for processing and offering customers with OTA maintenance services. The in-vehicle communication for applications, ECUs and sensors is supported by different networking technologies including Controller Area Network (CAN), Local Interconnect Network (LIN), Ethernet, Media Oriented Systems Transport (MOST) etc. Communication can occur between objects (and clustered objects) in the object layer and also with the layers above (virtual object) and below it (user). Communication across objects (within the object layer) among different vehicles or clustered objects is feasible via technologies like dedicated short-range communications (DSRC), Bluetooth, WiFi, and LTE. An example interaction in object layer is BMW connect application in phone which reads address from phone and send to the car navigation system, or V2V BSM exchange using DSRC.

It should be noted that instead of introducing clustered objects as a separate layer in E-ACO, we have added them to the same object layer of ACO architecture, which reflects the binding between objects, applications and the clustered object to which they belong. We believe the relationship between objects and clustered objects is important, for example, a lane departure sensor in car will have some attributes (like vehicle id) it inherits from the car and such binding is shown by putting them in same layer. These clustered objects and cars also have applications associated with them which offer services to drivers inside. For example, a rear vision system is an application in cars to get rear-view, which gets data from rear-camera (an object) to provide dashboard view to the driver. Other applications include tire-pressure monitoring system which talks to sensor installed in tire, cabin monitoring system, info-tainment systems etc. are in-built in connected cars and can communicate with sensors or other applications in system. These applications in object layer of E-ACO is add-on to the object layer in ACO architecture and reflects its importance in IoV ecosystem which is very dependent on in-built applications supported by smart cars.

Virtual Object Layer: Communication of sensors, vehicles and other smart entities may also involve virtual objects or cyber entities to eliminate connectivity, heterogeneity and locality issues. The most important smart entity in IoV, a smart car, is usually in motion and passing through areas with low or no internet connectivity all times. In such scenario, it is imperative to create a cyber entity of smart car (and its sensors) in the cloud so that the last state and desired state information of car (and sensors) can be sent to the virtual entity when car is not connected. Once the physical object gets back internet connectivity, the virtual entity will push information/state to its physical counter part. For example, if a problem is diagnosed in powertrain control ECU of a car and a command needs to be sent by mechanic to ECU to control air-fuel ratio. In case a car has internet connectivity, message can be sent directly to ECU, but if no connectivity message should be sent to virtual entity of the ECU which will push message to physical ECU when car gets connectivity and syncs virtual and physical entity. We envision the virtual object layer in E-ACO architecture will have one or many cyber entity (virtual object or device shadow) for both clustered and individual objects. Physical objects can communicate with their cyber counterpart using HTTP, MQTT, AMQP or CoAP protocols. When sensors s_1 and s_2 across different vehicles or clustered objects communicate with each other, the sequence of communication via virtual object layer should follow starting s_1 to vs_1 (virtual entity of s_1), vs_1 to vs_2 and vs_2 to physical sensor s_2. Similar communication can be envisioned for in-built car applications which can indirectly exchange information from physical sensors through their cyber counterparts created in cloud, vehicular cloud or fog architecture. It is possible to create a fog cloudlet for each vehicle where cyber entities will reside and support the indirect communication within physical sensors and ECUs inside car. Our E-ACO architecture does not support cyber-entity for in-car applications supported by IoV and will not create virtual objects for such applications [1].

Cloud Services and Application Layer: Since most user IoV applications are cloud supported (i.e. use cloud infrastructure and services), we explain them together to provide a better understanding of these two mutually dependent E-ACO layers. Cloud layer provides storage and processing whereas application layer provides application interface to users to control and interact with object layer components as discussed in ACO architecture [10]. Over the

air (OTA) updates for firmware and other software components in the cars are through the cloud service layer where only authorized users are allowed to issue OTA. User and applications can access the data pushed into the cloud by smart infrastructures for offering value added services to customers. Our proposed architecture assumes to have both central cloud and fog (instantiated by vehicular cloud) component in IoV ecosystem but are collectively represented as cloud services. An important use for cloud layer in IoV and connected cars involves defining security policies for authorized vehicular communication, which we understand is missing in literature. Further, we assume that virtual entities of various objects can be created in both central cloud and fog depending on the use-cases and the scope of applications which are accessing the objects. For example, an accidental safety application will have limited geographic scope and hence will access virtual objects created in fog (to overcome latency issues); whereas, a health-monitoring application may access body sensors via virtual objects created in central cloud. Cloud services and applications can access information and data from virtual objects using MQTT or other relevant protocols. It should be noted that most IoV architectures and use-cases we studied [24, 34, 47] don't have virtual object layer and include only object, cloud services and application layer. Communication between cars, sensors and applications in object layer do not involve virtual objects and is done using lower layer protocols like DSRC, WAVE, Bluetooth or WiFi. Sensors can directly send data to cloud storage for processing without involving virtual objects, which is then used by applications. However, connectivity issues in moving cars and communication heterogeneity among entities supports the need for virtual layer, as discussed earlier in this section.

Figure 5 (b) shows an instance of IoV with physical objects (car, traffic light) along with cyber counterparts in virtual objects layer, and other E-ACO layers. It can be seen that physical objects communicate with virtual objects, and applications are accessing data through cloud which is pushed by virtual entity of an object. Storage and processing icons at object layer symbolizes road-side infrastructures which can help to store data from vehicles and filter before pushing data to cloud. Virtual objects are created at both fog and central cloud to satisfy different application needs.

4 AUTHORIZATION FRAMEWORK FOR INTERNET OF VEHICLES

The dynamic and distributed nature of vehicular IoT brings in challenges to secure the ecosystem. Broad attack surface and numerous external interfaces along with the intrinsic characteristics of IoV makes it hard to ensure security and privacy of the components and data inside. Access controls are important to restrict unauthorized access to data, sensors, applications, infrastructure and other resources in connected cars and IoV. Applications like MobEyes [51] and CarSpeak [49] allow vehicles (or sensors) to access not only its own sensors but also neighbouring vehicle sensors to get data and information. The exchange of BSM messages among vehicles and smart entities, and their use must be trusted and checked. Further, in-vehicle communication along buses between ECUs and applications should be secured. Such exchange must be authorized to ensure confidentiality and integrity of vehicle's and user's personal data, and to prevent remote (or physical) control of connected smart

---

[1]Note that Amazon AWS IoT does allow applications to have a thing shadow [14] but comprehensive IoV use-cases to support the functionality are still missing in literature.

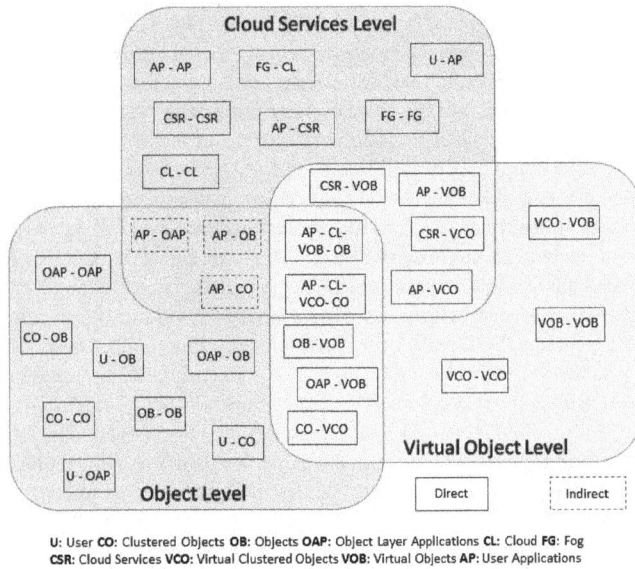

Figure 6: Different Interactions in IoV Ecosystem

entities. In this section, we define an access control framework that reflects authorization needs at various layers of extended ACO architecture discussed earlier. We also discuss some access control models and authorization approaches relevant for IoV ecosystem.

4.1 Authorization Framework

Several interaction scenarios exist in Internet of Vehicles which makes it hard to comprehend different access control decision and enforcement points, together with other security requirements. Based on the extended ACO architecture, we have put together various vehicular IoT communications into three categories: Object Level, Virtual Object Level and Cloud Services Level as shown in Figure 6. Since most user applications are cloud based which use services and resources in cloud, we have bundled the interaction of IoV entities with cloud and applications together. As discussed in the E-ACO architecture, each layer components interact with themselves (components in same layer) and the components in layers immediately above and below it. Two types of interactions exist in E-ACO, direct and indirect, marked with solid and dashed boxes shown in figure. Communication between adjacent and same layer is direct communication whereas indirect includes interaction beyond adjacent layers i.e. two or more layers above or down in E-ACO. For example, interaction between clustered object and objects inside the clustered object is direct, as they belong to the same object layer whereas interaction between an application in application layer and object will be indirect as applications will interact with object via its virtual entity created in cloud. It is possible to have interactions overlapping in two categories, e.g., cloud service (CSR) and virtual object (VOB) interaction is part of both cloud services and virtual object category. Following are the authorization framework categories and some IoV communication scenarios:

- **Object Level:** This category covers object layer interaction within itself and with adjacent layers (virtual objects and users)

in E-ACO architecture. Some interaction types (shown in Figure 6) include between clustered objects (CO-CO), between clustered object and object (CO-OB) for example smartphone and car USB port, between user and sensors (U-OB), between sensor and any application running inside car (OB-OAP), and between ECUs (OB-OB). Access control models to authorize each of these interactions and resulting data exchange are required. BSM exchanges between connected cars using DSRC is an example communication that needs entity authorization to ensure integrity of message, which must be addressed by appropriate access control methods.

- **Virtual Object Level:** This includes communication of virtual entities with real objects, with cloud services or with user applications. Some examples include, between virtual objects (VCO-VCO, VOB-VOB), between application and virtual objects (AP-VOB), cloud services and virtual objects (CSR-VOC, CSR-VOB) etc. Most of these communications are through publish-subscribe protocols like MQTT, DDS or through HTTP, CoAP. Recently, Alsehri and Sandhu [11] presented access control models for VOB-VOB interaction in topic based communication using CapBAC (Capability based access control), ACLs and ABAC.

- **Cloud Services Level:** Cloud provides necessary storage, processing and services to unleash true IoT potential. Further, most applications are also cloud based with their software and hardware components supported in cloud. Therefore, this category includes both application and cloud interactions with IoV entities and virtual objects. The layer also considers multi-cloud or fog-cloud interactions which are important in distributed IoV. Some interactions in this category (shown in Figure 6) include: between user application and cloud services (AP-CSR), multi-cloud or fog interaction (CL-CL, FG-CL), indirect interaction between application and objects (AP-OB), cloud services (CSR-CSR) etc.

In-vehicle network allows interaction among sensors and applications inside the car, which also needs protection. Such communication can fit into above categories depending if entities involved are physical, virtual or applications. CAN bus and other intra-vehicle communication can be protected by assigning ACLs and capabilities to ECUs to prevent spoofing and other attacks. TCUs or Gateways have been used to separate critical ECUs from non-important subnetworks and also act as a common external interface to connected car. Access control models should be developed for various interactions in each category to control communication and data exchange. Note that our authorization framework does not include physical tampering and OBD port connectivity which is excluded from discussion. In next subsection, we will discuss some access control approaches relevant to fit in the IoV authorization framework.

4.2 Access Control Approaches

Researchers have investigated authorization requirements in IoT systems and proposed several access control models and implementations [23, 42, 43, 48, 57, 61, 72]. Recently, an access control model for virtual objects was proposed [11] using ACLs, CapABAC and ABAC. AWS access control model for IoT is discussed [17] which uses policies to control physical, virtual, cloud services and other communications in a publish subscribe exchange protocol.

We believe that IoV environment requires access control policy decision and enforcement at two levels: external communication

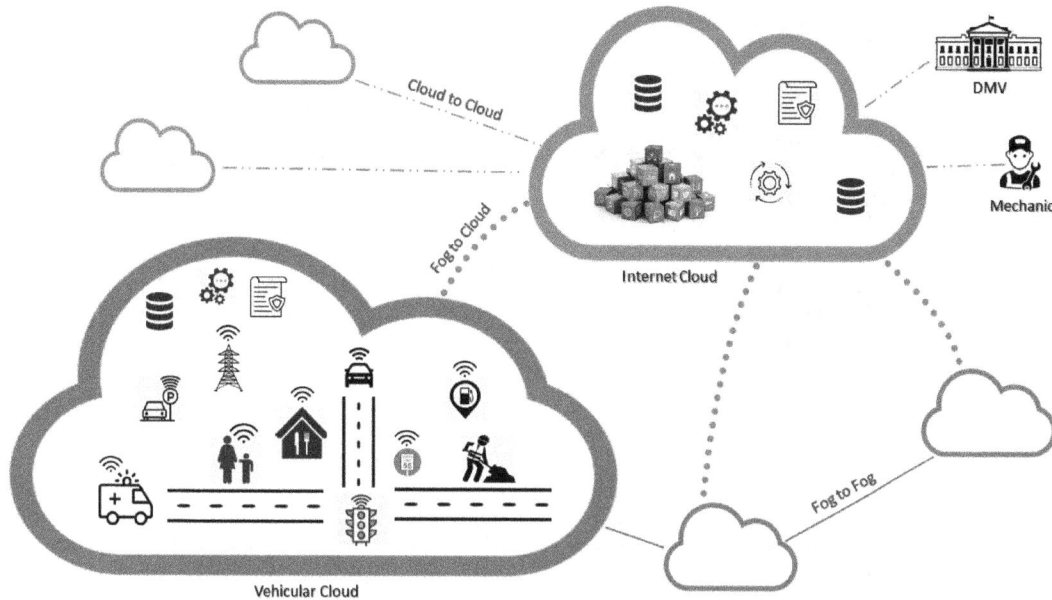

Figure 7: Connected Cars and Internet of Vehicles Ecosystem

and in-vehicle internal communication. Access control for external interface will secure authorized access to vehicle's data, sensors, ECUs and applications from external entities (like vehicle, traffic light, smartphones or user applications etc.) whereas internal mechanisms will secure ECUs and in-car applications communication and data exchange in a connected car supported by CAN bus, Bluetooth, WiFi etc. Securing external interface may not be enough to stop hackers, as they could impersonate a trusted device and bypass external access control. Also, in case if some ECUs with external interface are compromised, second level access control will protect critical systems in connected car. Vehicles discover new vehicles and infrastructure and start exchanging BSMs with them. Vehicular IoT mainly has two data exchange scenarios: static and dynamic, where static considers interaction due to long lasting relation for example, vehicle and owner or car manufacturer. Dynamic communication is temporary and occurs when entities are at certain place, or in geographic range with no prior relation between them. Also, static relation may share more private information which might not be the case in dynamic relation. These relations can help understand and develop access controls in IoV. Another approach may require multi-layered access control where the type of action required on an object determines the authority who can take access decision. For example, controlling an autonomous vehicle may require permissions from both owner and transportation authority, whereas reading data from vehicle may only need owner's consent.

We believe that clustered objects are important in access control decisions and can help to make preliminary decision. In case of vehicles, it is not only the vehicles which share BSMs, but also the sensors or applications in them which communicate. Therefore, first level check will ensure if two vehicles (as clustered objects) are allowed to talk, without considering their in-built sensors. If authorized at first level, next level access control will include sensors,

applications and ECUs of the vehicles to make the final decision. Concept of trust can be introduced where only trusted entities can communicate. Trust can be established based on interaction, or relationships among two entities. For example, entities who have exchanged data earlier are more trusted; home and vehicle belonging to same owner are more trusted and can communicate. PKI based trust establishment in Security Credential and Management System (SCMS) [68] supported by USDOT is an important system to ensure BSM confidentiality and integrity in V2V communication. Further, attribute based [46] solutions can be added where IoV entities can inherit set of attributes from their geographic location, or from manufacturer. In such cases, attribute based policies can be used to determine sensors communication after trust is checked between their vehicles. Attributes which can be used in access decisions include geographic position, current speed, acceleration, deceleration, road surface temperature or other vehicle telemetry. Two level policy may be required: one at cloud level (to control V2V, V2I like communication) and another at fog or vehicular cloud level (to control intra-vehicle ECU's, applications or sensors interaction). Both single and multi-cloud scenarios can exist in which vehicles in same or across clouds can interact, which will also require access controls. Administrative models [11, 41] are also needed to support administration of IoV operational access control models.

5 USE CASES

In this section, we will discuss some use-cases in relevance to our authorization framework, incorporating the extended ACO architecture (shown in Figure 5), various IoV communication exchange scenarios (shown in Figure 6), using cloud and fog architectures, and entities of vehicular IoT ecosystem as shown in Figure 7. We have classified our use-cases into single cloud and multi cloud systems to reflect local or global scope of entity communications and user IoV applications, however, all applications in single cloud can be extended to multi-cloud and vice versa. Our prime objective is to describe how interactions and data exchange takes place in distributed and dynamic vehicular IoT ecosystem and various access control decision, enforcement points requirements.

Most applications in vehicular IoT are time and location sensitive, which require real time processing of information gathered from smart vehicles, sensors, ECUs and other smart objects present in a limited geographic area. To resolve issues related to latency and bandwidth pertinent to using central cloud, we believe vehicular cloud (VC) will play an important role, where the storage and computation present in smart vehicles or road side infrastructures (smart traffic lights, sign boards etc.) can be used to support IoV applications. Hence, our single cloud applications are supported by fog or cloudlet instance in the form of a VC where physical objects will have their cyber counterpart (virtual objects). It is also possible to have a fog instance for each connected car and any communication within the car is supported through it. Other scenarios may need to have multiple virtual objects for a single physical object where some objects are in VC and some in central internet cloud, required for more persistent state or for non-time sensitive applications or where the interacting IoV entities are not present in the range of same vehicular cloud. Such use-cases are discussed in multi cloud or fog-cloud architecture scenarios.

5.1 Single Cloud System

Single cloud applications include entities in limited geographic area communicating and exchanging information. A pedestrian crossing a road sends an alert message to an approaching car, or remote parking capability in BMW 7 series assists driver to park car using touch screen key are some examples of short-range communication. It is also possible to have a nearby restaurant or a gas station sending offers to connected vehicles on their dashboard, or in case of cruise mode cars, speed sign board automatically reduces the speed of car when a message is exchanged between them. Each IoV entity (clustered object, sensors, ECU's) in physical layer will have a cyber entity (one-to-one) created in virtual object layer, which is part of vehicular cloud or cloudlet or fog. MQTT and other IoT topic or content based publish subscribe model where publishers (sensors, applications) can publish to certain topics which are subscribed by other sensors or applications, and message broker passes relevant messages to desired subscribers whenever a publisher publishes on these topics. Besides cross entity interactions, in-vehicle communication also occurs, where sensors, ECUs and applications in a connected car exchange messages or interact with a smart device of a passenger sitting inside the car. In-vehicle communication is supported by fog architecture for each car where virtual entities can be created for each ECU, sensor or device. Further, in case of CAN bus communication critical ECUs are separated using gateway which also provides external interface to connected car. This ensures authentication and authorization to over-the-air (OTA) updates and enforces access control policies for in-vehicle communication.

Access control points are needed at physical, virtual object and cloud services layer, where the interaction and data exchange between legitimate and authorized entities is only allowed. At object layer V2V, V2I and other V2X communications using DSRC, WiFi etc. between clustered objects need access controls to ensure BSM confidentiality and prevent malicious activity. Direct access of user using a remote key to unlock a car or through a smart-phone application also needs authorization. It is also possible to store credit card information on vehicle storage or with a cyber entity of the vehicle, which can ease payment process on a toll road, or in a parking garage. In such cases, only authorized applications can access credit card information, which if leaked to nefarious actors can have huge financial implications. Within object layer, access controls are also needed to ensure authorized communication among sensors or applications and clustered devices, for example in case smart-phone accessing info-tainment systems or plug-in device into car needs security. Access controls are needed when physical objects communicate to their virtual entities in the cloud. For example, an airbag ECU or sensor in the car should only be able to contact its corresponding virtual entity to update its state or push messages via topics. Our concept of IoV ecosystem incorporates virtual objects (for every physical object) which will be important for message and information exchange among heterogenous objects. Virtual entity will be also created for smart devices inside the car that can issue commands to connected vehicle. Therefore, access control is required at virtual object layer also which will control interaction between cyber entities. In-built applications in cars also access on-board sensors for example, tire-pressure monitoring, lane-departure warning system etc., which must be authorized to legitimate applications only. Communication between ECUs also needs authorization using gateway or TCUs. Attribute based access controls can provide fine grained policies and use contextual information to secure data exchange and communication for both physical and virtual object layer. Hence, to secure critical ECUs first level access control restricts external interface and then in-vehicle access control provides second level check.

Connected cars generate lot of data and are referred as 'datacenters on wheels'. Applications use this data to provide real time information regarding traffic, road safety, weather, or road maintenance. Applications can also diagnose issues of vehicles and offer predictive and precautionary advices to the drivers on road. Such actions through mechanics or users via cloud must be authorized. Further, access controls are required for applications and virtual objects communication, in case any application wants to send a command to a sensor in car. Data generated can be sent to cloud servers for storage and processing. As most of these applications are relevant to geography they can harness the vehicular cloud and use its storage and processing capabilities. Data security is important in the cloud. Proper access controls are required to allow only relevant entities to access and process the data in multi-tenant data lake. Applications and cloud services must be authorized to ensure privacy of user data. The most common platform to analyze big data is Hadoop where several access control models have been proposed including [37–40]. This data can be used by applications inside vehicles or user applications at E-ACO application layer.

5.2 Multiple Cloud System

Some IoV applications and use-cases require multiple cloud instances to offer services in vast geographic area or non-time sensitive conditions. For example, assume a vehicle manufacturer has a private cloud where it gathers all data generated from its vehicles, performs analysis for potential problems and offers over the air (OTA) solutions like firmware or software updates. This data can sometimes also reflect problems in the vehicle which needs immediate attention and hence to be sent to a mechanic nearby. Now, the mechanic has its own private cloud and cannot access the vehicle's data which is stored in original equipment manufacturer (OEMs) cloud. In such a scenario, trust has to be established among two clouds so that vehicle's data can be shared between mechanic's cloud and manufacturer's cloud, with the approval of vehicle owner. If a mechanic needs to send messages to sensors in vehicle, cross cloud communication must take place between vehicular cloud (where virtual object of sensor in the car is created) and application in mechanic cloud, which also needs access controls and trust.

Applications like CarSpeak [49] gather data from different sensors not only in the same car but across different cars which may or may not be in the same vehicular cloud. In such cases, the application will access the virtual entity across different vehicular clouds also, which may require trust across different cloud infrastructures. It is also possible to have two vehicular clouds or a vehicular cloud and central cloud exchanging information. For example, suppose a vehicle is approaching the driver's home, and it needs to send a message to the thermostat to turn on the air conditioner. It is possible that the home is in a different cloud, and hence will have its cyber entity in other cloud. In such a scenario cross cloud communication will take place where the application from vehicle will communicate with the virtual object corresponding to the thermostat in the home in other cloud. Since, in this case the home and vehicle belongs to the same owner, we can create a level of trust between them across clouds and use it to make faster access decision without using policy based controls. In another example, suppose department of motor vehicle (DMV) or local police issues a notice about a stolen car or some nefarious elements in city, a vehicle dashboard will start displaying alert messages. These applications will be running in DMV cloud or cloud owned by police department, which will send messages to the cars running in the city, which also requires multi cloud access scenarios. In such cases, DMV can also have dedicated infrastructure installed around the city or highway which will receive messages over cloud and will then pass to nearby vehicles or relevant sensors (through cyber objects or WiFi communication) within a geographic area.

Hence, access controls across single and multiple cloud architectures are needed to ensure secure interaction among physical, virtual objects and applications in Internet of Vehicles ecosystem.

6 PROPOSED SECURITY FOCUSED RESEARCH AGENDA

The main objective of authorization framework and extended ACO architecture for IoV is to understand security requirements and present some security focused research directions. In this section, we will highlight some research problems as discussed below:

- **External Interaction:** The exposure of smart entities to external actors and internet opens doors for remote attacks and data theft. Connected Cars and personal devices have private data which need user-centric privacy policies where user can accept or reject the disclosure. Further, the need to control data in critical

ECUs and issuing command to actuate an action must be secured by authorized entity. Trusted entities should be allowed to share more as compared to someone randomly on the road sending messages. An important question here is: How to establish trust between objects? V2X BSM messages must be encrypted and entities must be properly authenticated before performing operation. The dynamic and short-lived interaction in IoV makes it hard to prevent or detect attacks from compromised entities.

- **In-Vehicle Interaction:** The broadcast CAN communication bus and other protocols inside car are used to support ECUs and application communication using gateway. This gateway provides firewall functionality and isolates critical sensors from other applications installed in the vehicle and also provides a secure external interface. Authentication is required to prevent spoofing of ECU along with isolation of critical sensors. Data inside ECUs should be protected and over-the-air firmware updates must be secured. US GAO [30] have stated how short range communication to vehicle's Bluetooth unit can allow attackers to gain access to vehicle, also needs security. Physical tampering and direct OBD port access to ECU must be restricted.

- **Cross-Cloud Interaction and Sharing:** The cloud assisted vision of vehicular IoT supports multiple cloud or fog infrastructures. To ensure secure cross cloud or fog interactions, trust must be established between two providers which can determine the level of sharing and data exchange. IoT specific cross cloud access controls and relevant security models are still at infancy stage and need more focused attention.

- **Data in Cloud:** User and vehicle data gathered in cloud must be secured from malicious users and be shared, processed based on user and cloud provider defined privacy policies. Further cloud applications and virtual entities must be securely communicating. Also the issues related to moving vehicular cloud (VC) and its security needs require further research. The problems like virtual machine transfer when a participating vehicle leaves VC or VC formation are still not discussed broadly in literature.

7 SUMMARY

This paper provides an authorization framework for cloud assisted connected cars and vehicular IoT. It provides security requirements and discusses several access control decision and enforcements points necessary in the dynamic ecosystem of IoV. The paper first outlines some background study for relevant concepts including connected cars, virtual objects, vehicular cloud and ACO architecture. We proposed an extended ACO (E-ACO) architecture which introduces the novel concept of clustered objects (cars, infrastructure, home), which have several individual smart objects, sensors and applications. We envision IoV to have both fog and cloud instances where fog can be static or dynamically built using vehicle infrastructure or fixed roadside units. Different communication and data exchange scenarios have been discussed followed by access control approaches in E-ACO layers. Real-world use-cases with single and multi-cloud scenarios and access control requirements reflect the need and use of authorization framework for vehicular IoT. We envision to develop access control models for different communication and data exchange needs in cloud assisted connected cars and IoV based on the proposed research agenda.

ACKNOWLEDGMENTS

This work is partially supported by NSF CREST Grant HRD-1736209, NSF grants CNS-1111925, CNS-1423481, CNS-1538418 and DoD ARL Grant W911NF-15-1-0518.

REFERENCES

[1] 2014. *Connected Vehicles and Your Privacy.* https://www.its.dot.gov/factsheets/pdf/Privacy$_f$actsheet.pdf
[2] 2015. *Building Autonomous and Connected Vehicle Systems with the Vortex IoT Data Sharing Platform. Prismtech* (2015).
[3] 2016. *Convergence Of Secure Vehicular Ad-Hoc Network And Cloud In Internet Of Things.* http://mahbubulalam.com/convergence-of-secure-vehicular-ad-hoc-network-and-cloud-in-iot/ [Online; Accessed: 2018-02-01].
[4] 2017. Connected Car. (2017). https://en.wikipedia.org/wiki/Connected$_c$ar
[5] 2017. Securing The Connected Vehicle. *Thales E-Security* (2017).
[6] 2018. *Cloud IoT Core.* https://cloud.google.com/iot-core/
[7] 2018. *Device Twins.* https://docs.microsoft.com/en-us/azure/iot-hub/iot-hub-devguide-device-twins [Online; Accessed: 2018-02-03].
[8] M. Aazam and et al. 2014. Cloud of Things: Integrating Internet of Things and cloud computing and the issues involved. In *Proc. of IBCAST.* 414–419.
[9] A. Al-Fuqaha and et al. 2015. Internet of things: A survey on enabling technologies, protocols, and applications. *IEEE Comm. Surveys & Tutorials* (2015), 2347–2376.
[10] Asma Alshehri and Ravi Sandhu. 2016. Access control models for cloud-enabled internet of things: A proposed architecture and research agenda. In *Proc. of CIC.* IEEE, 530–538.
[11] Asma Alshehri and Ravi Sandhu. 2017. Access Control Models for Virtual Object Communication in Cloud-Enabled IoT. In *Proc. of IRI.* IEEE, 16–25.
[12] Mikio Aoyama. 2012. Computing for the Next-Generation Automobile. *IEEE Computer* 45, 6 (2012), 32–37.
[13] Luigi Atzori, Antonio Iera, and Giacomo Morabito. 2010. The internet of things: A survey. *Computer networks* 54, 15 (2010), 2787–2805.
[14] Amazon AWS. 2017. *Thing Shadows for AWS IoT.* http://docs.aws.amazon.com/iot/latest/developerguide/iot-thing-shadows.html [Accessed: 2018-01-25].
[15] Jim Barbaresso and et al. 2014. USDOT's Intelligent Transportation Systems ITS Strategic Plan 2015- 2019. (2014).
[16] S. Bhatt, F. Patwa, and R. Sandhu. 2017. An Access Control Framework for Cloud-Enabled Wearable Internet of Things. In *Proc. of CIC.* IEEE, 328–338.
[17] Smriti Bhatt, Farhan Patwa, and Ravi Sandhu. 2017. Access Control Model for AWS Internet of Things. In *Proc. of NSS.* Springer, 721–736.
[18] A. R. Biswas and R. Giaffreda. 2014. IoT and cloud convergence: Opportunities and challenges. In *Proc. of WF-IoT.* IEEE, 375–376.
[19] F. Bonomi, R. Milito, J. Zhu, and S. Addepalli. 2012. Fog computing and its role in the internet of things. In *Proc. of MCC Workshop.* ACM, 13–16.
[20] A. Botta, W. de Donato, V. Persico, and A. Pescapé. 2014. On the Integration of Cloud Computing and Internet of Things. In *Proc. of FiCLOUD.* IEEE, 23–30.
[21] Alessio Botta and et al. 2016. Integration of Cloud computing and Internet of Things: A survey. *Future Generation Computer Systems* (2016), 684 - 700.
[22] David Brown et al. 2015. Automotive Security Best Practice. *Intel Security* (2015).
[23] V. G. Cerf. 2015. Access Control and the Internet of Things. *IEEE Internet Computing* 19, 5 (Sept 2015), 96–c3.
[24] J. Contreras, S. Zeadally, and J. A. Guerrero-Ibanez. 2017. Internet of Vehicles: Architecture, Protocols, and Security. *IEEE Internet of Things J.* (2017), 1–9.
[25] M. DÄnaz and et al. 2016. State-of-the-art, challenges, and open issues in the integration of Internet of things and cloud computing. *J. of Network and Computer Applications* (2016), 99 - 117.
[26] A. Elmaghraby and M. Losavio. 2014. Cyber security challenges in Smart Cities: Safety, security and privacy. *J. of advanced research* 5, 4 (2014), 491–497.
[27] Mohamed Eltoweissy and et al. 2010. Towards Autonomous Vehicular Clouds. In *Ad Hoc Networks.* Springer, 1–16.
[28] ENISA. 2017. *Cyber Security and Resilience of smart cars: Good practices and recommendations.* https://www.enisa.europa.eu/publications/cyber-security-and-resilience-of-smart-cars [Online; Accessed: 2018-01-27].
[29] Y. Fangchun and et al. 2014. An overview of internet of vehicles. *China Communications* 11, 10 (2014), 1–15.
[30] US GAO. 2016, March. Vehicle Cybersecurity . *GAO-16-350* (2016, March). https://www.gao.gov/assets/680/676064.pdf
[31] Gartner. 2015. *Gartner Says By 2020, a Quarter Billion Connected Vehicles Will Enable New In-Vehicle Services and Automated Driving Capabilities.*
[32] Gartner. 2017. *Gartner Says 8.4 Billion Connected "Things" Will Be in Use in 2017, Up 31 Percent From 2016.*
[33] M. Gerla. 2012. Vehicular cloud computing. In *Proc. of Med-Hoc-Net.* IEEE.
[34] M. Gerla, E. Lee, G. Pau, and U. Lee. 2014. Internet of vehicles: From intelligent grid to autonomous cars and vehicular clouds. In *Proc. of WF-IoT.* IEEE, 241–246.
[35] Matthew Gigli and Simon Koo. 2011. Internet of things: services and applications categorization. *Advances in Internet of Things* 1, 02 (2011), 27.

[36] J. Gubbi and et al. 2013. Internet of Things (IoT): A vision, architectural elements, and future directions. *Future generation computer systems* 29, 7 (2013), 1645–1660.
[37] M. Gupta and et al. 2017. Multi-Layer Authorization Framework for a Representative Hadoop Ecosystem Deployment. In *Proc. of SACMAT.* ACM, 183–190.
[38] M. Gupta and et al. 2018. An Attribute-Based Access Control Model for Secure Big Data Processing in Hadoop Ecosystem. In *Proc. of ABAC'18.* ACM, 13–24.
[39] Maanak Gupta, Farhan Patwa, and Ravi Sandhu. 2017. Object-Tagged RBAC Model for the Hadoop Ecosystem. In *Proc. of DBSec.* Springer, 63–81.
[40] Maanak Gupta, Farhan Patwa, and Ravi Sandhu. 2017. POSTER: Access Control Model for the Hadoop Ecosystem. In *Proc. of SACMAT.* ACM, 125–127.
[41] Maanak Gupta and Ravi Sandhu. 2016. The GURA$_G$ Administrative Model for User and Group Attribute Assignment. In *Proc. of NSS.* Springer, 318–332.
[42] Sergio Gusmeroli, Salvatore Piccione, and Domenico Rotondi. 2013. A capability-based security approach to manage access control in the internet of things. *Mathematical and Computer Modelling* 58, 5 (2013), 1189–1205.
[43] J. Hernandez-Ramos and et al. 2013. Distributed capability-based access control for the internet of things. *J. of Internet Services and Info. Sec.* 3, 3/4 (2013), 1–16.
[44] Jean-Pierre Hubaux, Srdjan Capkun, and Jun Luo. 2004. The security and privacy of smart vehicles. *IEEE Security & Privacy* 2, 3 (2004), 49–55.
[45] Rasheed Hussain and et al. 2012. Rethinking vehicular communications: Merging VANET with cloud computing. In *Proc. of CloudCom.* IEEE, 606–609.
[46] Xin Jin, Ram Krishnan, and Ravi Sandhu. 2012. A unified attribute-based access control model covering DAC, MAC and RBAC. In *Proc. of DBSec.* Springer, 41–55.
[47] O. Kaiwartya and et al. 2016. Internet of vehicles: Motivation, layered architecture, network model, challenges, and future aspects. *IEEE Access* 4 (2016), 5356–5373.
[48] Sun Kaiwen and Yin Lihua. 2014. Attribute-role-based hybrid access control in the internet of things. In *Proc. of APWeb.* Springer, 333–343.
[49] Swarun Kumar and et al. 2012. CarSpeak: A Content-centric Network for Autonomous Driving. *SIGCOMM Comput. Commun. Rev.* 42, 4 (Aug. 2012), 259–270.
[50] R. Lea and M. Blackstock. 2014. City Hub: A Cloud-Based IoT Platform for Smart Cities. In *Proc. of CloudCom.* IEEE, 799–804.
[51] U. Lee and et al. 2006. Mobeyes: smart mobs for urban monitoring with a vehicular sensor network. *IEEE Wireless Communications* (2006), 52–57.
[52] NHTSA. 2016. NHTSA and Vehicle CyberSecurity. *NHTSA Report* (2016).
[53] NHTSA. 2016, October. Cybersecurity Best Practices for Modern Vehicles. *NHTSA Report No. DOT HS 812 333* (2016, October).
[54] NIST. 2016. *Framework for Cyber-Physical Systems.* https://www.nist.gov/itl/applied-cybersecurity/nist-initiatives-iot [Online; Accessed: 2018-01-13].
[55] M. Nitti and et al. 2016. The virtual object as a major element of the internet of things: a survey. *IEEE Comm. Surveys & Tutorials* (2016), 1228–1240.
[56] Stephan Olariu and et al. 2011. Taking VANET to the clouds. *International Journal of Pervasive Computing and Communications* 7, 1 (2011), 7–21.
[57] Aafaf Ouaddah and et al. 2017. Access control in The Internet of Things: Big challenges and new opportunities. *Computer Networks* 112 (2017), 237–262.
[58] Christopher Poulen. 2014. Driving security: Cyber assurance for next-generation vehicles. *IBM Global Business Services* (2014).
[59] Brian Russell and et al. 2017. Observations and Recommendations on Connected Vehicle Security. *Cloud Security Alliance* (2017).
[60] Chayan Sarkar and et al. 2015. DIAT: A scalable distributed architecture for IoT. *IEEE Internet of Things journal* 2, 3 (2015), 230–239.
[61] Ludwig Seitz, Göran Selander, and Christian Gehrmann. 2013. Authorization framework for the internet-of-things. In *Proc. of WoWMoM.* IEEE, 1–6.
[62] Yunchuan Sun and et al. 2015. Security and Privacy in the Internet of Vehicles. In *Proc. of IIKI.* IEEE, 116–121.
[63] Toyota. 2011. *Toyota-to-launch-smartphone-on-wheels.* https://www.2wglobal.com/news-and-insights/articles/features/Toyota-to-launch-smartphone-on-wheels/ [Online; Accessed: 2018-02-03].
[64] European Union. 2017. *Certificate Policy for Deployment and Operation of European Cooperative Intelligent Transport Systems (C-ITS).* https://ec.europa.eu/transport/sites/transport/files/c-its$_c$ertificate$_p$olicy$_r$elease$_1$.pdf
[65] European Union. 2017. *Security Policy & Governance Framework for Deployment and Operation of European Cooperative Intelligent Transport Systems (C-ITS).* https://ec.europa.eu/transport/sites/transport/files/c-its$_s$ecurity$_p$olicy$_r$elease$_1$.pdf
[66] USAToday. 2017. *Chinese group hacks a Tesla for the second year in a row.*
[67] USDOT. 2016. *Connected Vehicles and Your Privacy.* https://www.its.dot.gov/factsheets/pdf/Privacy$_f$actsheet.pdf
[68] USDOT. 2016. *Securty Credential Management System.* https://www.its.dot.gov/resources/scms.htm [Online; Accessed: 2018-01-13].
[69] Timo van Roermund. 2015. Secure Connected Cars for a Smarter World. *NXP Semiconductors* (2015).
[70] Evan Welbourne and et al. 2009. Building the internet of things using RFID: the RFID ecosystem experience. *IEEE Internet computing* 13, 3 (2009).
[71] Md Whaiduzzaman and et al. 2014. A survey on vehicular cloud computing. *Journal of Network and Computer Applications* 40 (2014), 325–344.
[72] Ning Ye and et al. 2014. An efficient authentication and access control scheme for perception layer of internet of things. *Applied Mathematics and Information Sciences* 8, 4 (2014), 1617–1624.

Poster: Reactive Access Control Systems

Maryam Davari
Purdue University
West Lafayette, Indiana
davari@purdue.edu

Elisa Bertino
Purdue University
West Lafayette, Indiana
bertino@purdue.edu

ABSTRACT

In context-aware applications, user's access privileges rely on both user's identity and context. Access control rules are usually statically defined while contexts and the system state can change dynamically. Changes in contexts can result in service disruptions. To address this issue, this poster proposes a reactive access control system that associates contingency plans with access control rules. Risk scores are also associated with actions part of the contingency plans. Such risks are estimated by using fuzzy inference. Our approach is cast into the XACML reference architecture.

KEYWORDS

Context-aware applications, reactive access control system, contingency plan, risk, Fuzzy inference, XACML

ACM Reference Format:
Maryam Davari and Elisa Bertino. 2018. Poster: Reactive Access Control Systems. In *SACMAT '18: The 23rd ACM Symposium on Access Control Models & Technologies (SACMAT), June 13–15, 2018, Indianapolis, IN, USA*. ACM, New York, NY, USA, 3 pages. https://doi.org/10.1145/3205977.3208947

1 INTRODUCTION

Recent access control models and standards, such as XACML, are context based. A context-based access control system uses context (i.e., a condition or requirement on the current state and attributes of subjects, protected objects, and their environments) to evaluate access requests. Well known context-based access control models include T-RBAC [6] and GEO-RBAC [13] that consider, respectively, time and location as the contextual information relevant for access control. In a context-based access control system, rules determine which access prohibitions or permissions can be applied with respect to specific circumstances. For example, in a health care domain, physicians have different permissions in particular contexts (e.g., "urgency", "industrial medicine") [11].

In a pervasive environment, users are mobile and access resources (e.g., services, sensors) that utilize mobile devices; in addition, such environments continuously evolve. A critical issue is that the context of the subject (e.g., location, time, network state, network security configuration) can dynamically change. Thus accesses that were permitted based on certain contextual conditions may not any longer be permitted. If such a change were not

anticipated, the accesses may have to be blocked and this may result in severe application disruptions. To address such problem, mechanisms are required to minimize service disruption.

To address such need, we propose the notion of a reactive access control that extends the context-based access control mechanism in order to handle unexpected context changes. We define an event as an activity that occurs in time (e.g., leaving a room) and can change the behavior of the system. Anticipating all events is not easy. Therefore, we use the contingency plan concept to handle the events. A contingency plan finds an alternative decision to deal with unexpected events and it is separated from a normal operation. However, a contingency plan can have a potential to add risks to the system. Hence, an appropriate action should be selected such that to keep the risks under control.

We cast our model into XACML [1] by adding to it a specialized component referred to as reactive-XACML (R-XACML, for short) - see Figure 1.

2 OVERVIEW OF THE PROPOSED APPROACH

Assume a scenario in which an access request has been already permitted; then the context changes and the request cannot be completed as the rules under which the access had been permitted are not applicable in the new context. Suppose also that the PDP cannot find any rule that allows the access to continue. In such a case, instead of sending an immediate service interruption notification to the application, the PDP sends notifications to the PIP and the Contingency Plan Manager (CPM). The PIP computes contingency plan parameters (described in the following subsection) and pushes them to the CPM. We use the push-based model (used in the reactive programming) [2] to automatically propagate new attribute values to the CPM when an event occurs.

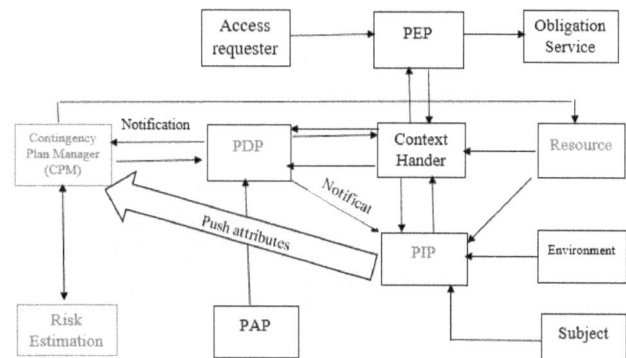

Figure 1: Architecture of R-XACML

The current access continues temporarily until receiving a response from the CPM. The CPM either allows the current access to be completed or proposes an alternative action. Then, the action is submitted to the risk estimation component to estimate the risks associated with the action. If the estimated risk is low, the action will be submitted to the PDP. Otherwise, the interaction between the CPM and risk estimation is repeated until identifying an appropriate action with a low risk. The CPM and risk estimation components are described in the following subsection in more details.

2.1 Contingency Plan Manager (CPM)

Policies are specified under assumptions about environments and events. The applications can do certain actions when specific context conditions hold. The question is "what if" the determined actions cannot complete in time. The importance of developing alternative actions (invoked by contingency plans) in access control application is undeniable as shown by the following example.

In an American health care center, medical records can be read only during office hours and from inside of the USA but what if an access is requested from another country and outside of office hours. Assume that a patient has some medical records managed by this health care center and that he travels to Spain for a couple of days. Suppose that he is badly hurt in a car crash and taken to a hospital. An emergency doctor needs to view the medical records of the patient to check if he has allergies to specific substances. The access request is submitted from outside of the USA and office hours. According to the mentioned health care policy, the doctor is not allowed to access the patient's medical record. A contingency plan is required (e.g., giving the reading access to the emergency doctor after validating the identity of the emergency doctor and notifying the patient's physician).

Due to the importance of alternative actions especially for access control applications, we develop the CPM component for XACML. The CPM contains three main components supporting event specification, event detection, and contingency plans for events (P1-P3) described as follows:

P1. Event specification: Events can be classified as the primitive events (a single event) and composite events (the disjunction, sequence, or conjunction of a set of primitive events) based on the number of events happing synchronously [16].

P2. Event detection: The predefined events are recognized from the contexts and stored in a chronological order.

P3. Contingency plans for events: After identifying involved events in the request, the CPM follows five steps to make a final decision.
Step 1. Parameter set: The CPM defines a set of parameters including the type of event (primitive, composite), type of each involved primitive event (temporal, non-temporal), type of action, type of resource, time of event occurrence, action start time, and action completion time. The parameter values are automatically collected by the PIP from the current request by using the push-based model. Then, the parameter values are sent to step 2 for the evaluation.
Step 2. Event evaluation: The CPM checks if the event is temporary

by waiting (using the system clock) and monitoring the event. If the event value becomes acceptable (by the rules of the application), it resumes continuing the current action (i.e., the action before interruption). Also, for rules with composite events, decisions are made base on the number of events with acceptable values and the value of the most effective event. If it can satisfy the rule, the access resumes. Otherwise, it goes to step 3.
Step 3. Event occurrence time comparison: The time of event occurrence is compared with the action start time and estimated action completion time. If the time of event occurrence is almost closed to the estimated completion time, the access continues. While if the event occurs right after the start of the action, step 4 is followed.
Step 4. Resource sensitivity identification: Some resources are more sensitive than others (e.g., sensitive medical information). If a resource is not sensitive, the access is granted. However, for sensitive information, the type of action is required to make a final decision. Step 5 is followed for this purpose.
Step 5. Action Type recognition: In access control systems, most of the actions are database operations including "read", "insert", "delete", "update", etc. They take a finite amount of time for execution. If the access does not change the data, the event is ignored and the system resumes the action. However, for actions changing the data (including insert, delete, and update), the CPM gives only the access to the copy of the resource. In this case, when a new request is received from the user, the user's confirmation of changes is required. In the case of discarding the changes by the user, the actual data is not updated.

2.2 Risk Estimation

Contingency plans can be associated with risks. Assume a government building containing sensitive information is on fire while firemen are waiting for the security clearance (that is not received in time). In this case, a contingency plan is essential that can let the firemen access the building after signing a non-disclosure agreement. However, the risk resulting from the given access can be high. Contingency plans should be chosen wisely to minimize risks.

The risk estimation predicts the probability of risks incurred by employing contingency plans. One appropriate solution for the risk assessment implementation is fuzzy inference. This technique has been employed in many areas, including medicine, engineering, management application [17]. To implement this technique, first, we collect previous experience containing a set of rule and risk factor information (e.g., an experience shared by system administrators and security researchers). Second, the vague concepts (e.g., low, high) in the collected experience are explained by membership functions in fuzzy inference. Third, fuzzy rules can be any arbitrary function. Actual risk estimation functions can be used in the case of existence.

3 RELATED WORK

3.1 Context-Aware Access Control

Several context-based access control models have been proposed. DRBAC [10] adjusts roles and permission assignments dynamically according to the context information. CA-RBAC [19] includes temporal and spatial constraints by using context-based constraints. GTRBAC [6] uses temporal constraints to enable and disable roles.

Or-BAC [14] introduces abstractions for actions and objects named activities and views, respectively. In Or-BAC, contextual information can be specified to manage given contexts. Despite the importance of alternative actions especially for all time-constraint applications, none of the mentioned approaches consider the use of contingency plans.

An emergency access control model that can manage information sharing was proposed by Carminati et al. [5]. It uses Complex Event Processing (CEP) systems (e.g., Oracle CEP) to automatically detect emergency situations from the contextual information. Break-glass [9], [3] is another approach to handle emergency situations. The Break-glass access control model allows subjects to override decisions without considering the reason for request denial. Rumpole [15] enhances the traditional Break-glass model by checking if the user is allowed to override denial decisions according to accepted obligations. These paradigms only focus on emergency situations. However, the reactive access control system can handle unexpected context changes in different situation.

3.2 XACML

Approaches have been proposed for testing, analyzing, and modeling XACML policies [18], [12]. Such approaches introduce environmental and contextual roles (i.e., roles which are activated/deactivated as a result of an event occurrence in the system). Several formal models, such as the ones based on description logics [4] and model-oriented specification languages [8], and verification techniques [7] have been proposed for XACML. To the best of our knowledge, however, no approach has been proposed for dealing with context changes in XACML.

4 CONCLUSION

In context-aware applications, access requests are permitted based on the contexts of requests. If the context of an access request cannot satisfy the access requirements in the time-constraints, the access will be blocked. To address this issue, we propose the notation of reactive access control mechanism by extending the traditional context-aware applications. We present the reactive XACML in which the contingency plans handle the context changes in the system. In the R-XACML, the user's access is continuously adapted for the contingency environments. The risks associated with the contingency plans are also calculated by using fuzzy inference to keep risks as low as possible.

ACKNOWLEDGMENTS

The work reported in this paper has been partially supported by the U.S. Army Research Laboratory and the U.K. Ministry of Defense under Agreement Number W911NF-16-3-0001. The views and conclusions contained in this document are those of the authors and should not be interpreted as representing the official policies, either expressed or implied, of the U.S. Army Research Laboratory, the U.S. Government, the U.K. Ministry of Defense or the U.K. Government. The U.S. and U.K. Governments are authorized to reproduce and distribute reprints for Government purposes notwithstanding any copyright notation hereon.

REFERENCES

[1] Anne Anderson, Anthony Nadalin, B Parducci, D Engovatov, H Lockhart, M Kudo, P Humenn, S Godik, S Anderson, S Crocker, et al. 2003. extensible access control markup language (xacml) version 1.0. *OASIS* (2003).

[2] Engineer Bainomugisha, Andoni Lombide Carreton, Tom van Cutsem, Stijn Mostinckx, and Wolfgang de Meuter. 2013. A survey on reactive programming. *ACM Computing Surveys (CSUR)* 45, 4 (2013), 52.

[3] Achim D Brucker and Helmut Petritsch. 2009. Extending access control models with break-glass. In *Proceedings of the 14th ACM symposium on Access control models and technologies*. ACM, 197–206.

[4] Jeremy W Bryans and John S Fitzgerald. 2007. Formal engineering of XACML access control policies in VDM++. In *International Conference on Formal Engineering Methods*. Springer, 37–56.

[5] Barbara Carminati, Elena Ferrari, and Michele Guglielmi. 2011. Secure information sharing on support of emergency management. In *Privacy, Security, Risk and Trust (PASSAT) and 2011 IEEE Third Inernational Conference on Social Computing (SocialCom), 2011 IEEE Third International Conference on*. IEEE, 988–995.

[6] Yehia ElRakaiby, Frederic Cuppens, and Nora Cuppens-Boulahia. 2008. Interactivity for reactive access control. *Sar Ssi 2008* (2008), 257.

[7] Kathi Fisler, Shriram Krishnamurthi, Leo A Meyerovich, and Michael Carl Tschantz. 2005. Verification and change-impact analysis of access-control policies. In *Proceedings of the 27th international conference on Software engineering*. ACM, 196–205.

[8] Daniel Jackson, Ilya Shlyakhter, and Manu Sridharan. 2001. A micromodularity mechanism. In *ACM SIGSOFT Software Engineering Notes*, Vol. 26. ACM, 62–73.

[9] NEMA Joint. 2004. COCIR/JIRA Security And Privacy Committee (SPC). *Break-glass: An approach to granting emergency access to healthcare systems* (2004).

[10] James BD Joshi, Elisa Bertino, Usman Latif, and Arif Ghafoor. 2005. A generalized temporal role-based access control model. *IEEE Transactions on Knowledge and Data Engineering* 17, 1 (2005), 4–23.

[11] Anas Abou El Kalam, R EI Baida, Philippe Balbiani, Salem Benferhat, Frédéric Cuppens, Yves Deswarte, Alexandre Miege, Claire Saurel, and Gilles Trouessin. 2003. Organization based access control. In *Policies for Distributed Systems and Networks, 2003. Proceedings. POLICY 2003. IEEE 4th International Workshop on*. IEEE, 120–131.

[12] Vladimir Kolovski, James Hendler, and Bijan Parsia. 2007. Analyzing web access control policies. In *Proceedings of the 16th international conference on World Wide Web*. ACM, 677–686.

[13] Devdatta Kulkarni and Anand Tripathi. 2008. Context-aware role-based access control in pervasive computing systems. In *Proceedings of the 13th ACM symposium on Access control models and technologies*. ACM, 113–122.

[14] Kim Tuyen Le Thi, Tran Khanh Dang, Pierre Kuonen, and Houda Chabbi Drissi. 2012. STRoBAC–spatial temporal role based access control. In *International Conference on Computational Collective Intelligence*. Springer, 201–211.

[15] Srdjan Marinovic, Robert Craven, Jiefei Ma, and Naranker Dulay. 2011. Rumpole: a flexible break-glass access control model. In *Proceedings of the 16th ACM symposium on Access control models and technologies*. ACM, 73–82.

[16] Deepak Mishra. 1991. *SNOOP: an event specification language for active database systems*. Master's thesis. University of Florida.

[17] Qun Ni, Elisa Bertino, and Jorge Lobo. 2010. Risk-based access control systems built on fuzzy inferences. In *Proceedings of the 5th ACM Symposium on Information, Computer and Communications Security*. ACM, 250–260.

[18] Que Nguyet Tran Thi and Tran Khanh Dang. 2012. X-STROWL: A generalized extension of XACML for context-aware spatio-temporal RBAC model with OWL. In *Digital Information Management (ICDIM), 2012 Seventh International Conference on*. IEEE, 253–258.

[19] Guangsen Zhang and Manish Parashar. 2004. Context-aware dynamic access control for pervasive applications. In *Proceedings of the Communication Networks and Distributed Systems Modeling and Simulation Conference*. 21–30.

Poster: Toward A Code Pattern Based Vulnerability Measurement Model

John Heaps, Rocky Slavin, Xiaoyin Wang
The University of Texas at San Antonio
{john.heaps,rocky.slavin,xiaoyin.wang}@utsa.edu

ABSTRACT

Many access control patterns, both positive and negative, have been identified in the past. However, there is little research describing how to leverage those patterns for the detection of access control bugs in code. Many software bug detection models and frameworks for access control exist, however most of these approaches and tools are process-based and suffer from many limitations. We propose a framework to detect access control bugs based on code pattern detection. Our framework will mine and generate bug patterns, detect those patterns in code, and calculate a vulnerability measure of software. Based on our knowledge we are the first pattern-based model for the detection and measurement of bugs in software. As a proof of concept, we perform a case study of the relational database access control pattern "Improper Authorization".

ACM Reference Format:
John Heaps, Rocky Slavin, Xiaoyin Wang. 2018. Poster: Toward A Code Pattern Based Vulnerability Measurement Model. In *SACMAT '18: The 23rd ACM Symposium on Access Control Models & Technologies (SACMAT), June 13–15, 2018, Indianapolis, IN, USA*. ACM, New York, NY, USA, 3 pages. https://doi.org/10.1145/3205977.3208948

1 INTRODUCTION

The security and vulnerabilities of software systems are essential in making decisions for real-world problems. Many process-based approaches and models have been developed to mitigate and quantify software vulnerabilities. However, these approaches, while useful, have many limitations. First, the existing models require data from software processes to estimate model parameters, but fine-grained monitoring of software processes is not always possible. Second, these models cannot always handle new or upgraded software components. Third, these models often cannot differentiate between different types of defects. To address these issues, the proposed project will develop a pattern-based vulnerability measurement model, which checks software artifacts for the existence of negative patterns to estimate the risk of software failures and data security, their impact, and determine overall software vulnerability.

The model will quantitatively estimate the vulnerability of software based on negative pattern instances in software artifacts, as well as the importance and the activation probability of the patterns. Recent studies show that software reuse and code clones are prevalent throughout software systems. In addition, software projects are continually becoming more based on existing software frameworks, which have a limited number of usage patterns. Therefore, it is reasonable to assume that most of the design fragments and code portions of a new software product follow existing patterns. Furthermore, the vulnerability of a software application can be predicted by combining effects of all instances of negative bug patterns. The project will yield a **learning engine** to mine online bug repositories and project hosting websites; a **pattern checker** to detect the existence and invocation of patterns; and a **vulnerability model** for the estimation of the vulnerability of a software project based on the detected patterns and their invocation probabilities.

The project will achieve the following major objectives: 1) Estimate the vulnerability of a software project based on code patterns; 2) Support separate estimation of different aspects of software vulnerability, enabling fine-grained prediction of the effect of software failures; 3) Confirm the existence of negative patterns (i.e., identify the location of access control bugs) using test-coverage-based approach; 4) Evaluate the feasability of the model's ability to perform software vulnerability estimation on real-world software projects.

2 FRAMEWORK

In this section we will discuss our framework for the identification of bug patterns, detection of bugs in code, and proposed measurement model, as shown in Figure 1.

2.1 Learning Engine

The learning engine acts as a repository of known patterns. These patterns will be used to identify bugs in code during pattern detection. To create this initial repository, we first surveyed popular online bug repositories, such as Github, Bugzilla, Common Weakness Enumeration (CWE)[1], Jira, etc. We decided to initially support CWE and Github, as they often have code examples and code fixes linked with their bug reports. Further, they both offer very large, robust data sets of access control patterns and bugs.

CWE is a database that catalogs and categorizes known bugs. Our method crawls bug reports from CWE and categorizes them according to the common keywords in their descriptions and CWE classification categories. We are thus able to extract bug descriptions, code examples, and code solutions.

The goal of bug collection for Github is to identify the most common bugs on Github. We obtain thousands of issues from Github projects by making requests to Github's REST API v3. For each of these issues we are able to extract bug descriptions, solutions, and sometimes sections of code from before and after an issue was resolved. In our initial implementation we searched the top 1,000 Java-based repositories, and used the most recent 100 closed issues with the label "bug" from each.

[1]CWE website URL: https://cwe.mitre.org/

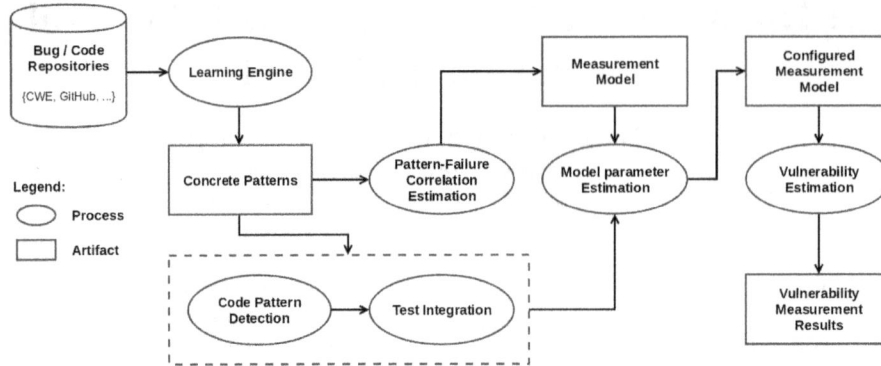

Figure 1: Bug Pattern Framework

After we collected the data from CWE and Github, we applied the clone detection tool CCFinder [2] to detect clones from the set of code commits and identify common buggy code and their fixes. Then, for the most popular common code bugs we manually extracted concrete code patterns from them, which were stored to be used in pattern detection and code analysis.

2.2 Pattern Detection

There is limited literature available on bug pattern detection. Work by Joseph Near and Daniel Jackson [5] describes the tool "SPACE" which is able to detect violations of access control vulnerability patterns. However, this tool requires that a user completely define and map software components and design to the role-based access control model. Not all software systems specifically use role-based access control, though. It can be difficult, or not possible, for systems that use other access control designs to define that system in the role-based model. Further, this approach is based on seven access control patterns, not code-level bug patterns on access control. Other work by Guangtai Liang et al. [3] introduces the tool "PatBugs" which detects temporal bugs in cross-platform mobile applications, focusing on API usage. The scope of this tool is too narrow for our purposes, it's focus being solely on temporal bug patterns in mobile applications.

To conduct the pattern detection in our framework, we utilized SpotBugs[2], a fork of the static analysis tool FindBugs [1]. The tool analyzes Java bytecode and detects the existence of bug patterns.

To study the effectiveness of SpotBugs on detecting bug code patterns, we downloaded the top 1,000 Java GitHub repositories that are under 50MB for a total of 826 repositories. From these repositories, we were able to compile 763 repositories using a program for automatic compilation of various types of Java projects. For each compiled repository, we ran SpotBugs to generate a list of bug types, which detected 217 bug pattern instances.

After identifying bug patterns, they further needed to be linked to abstract quality aspects to calculate a vulnerability, or risk, measure. Specifically, we consider four major aspects of vulnerability including: (1) **Control Integrity** which measures how likely the software may incorrectly interact with its users; (2) **Data Integrity** which measures how likely the software may provide incorrect output; (3) **Data Confidentiality** which measures how likely the

software may release data to entities not authorized to receive it; and (4) **Data Availability** which measures how likely the software may not be able to provide data that should be in storage. Through linking bug code patterns with high-level quality aspects, we are able to estimate the vulnerability, or risk, on different aspects based on detected patterns related to them.

Finally, the detection of a bug pattern is not enough to determine that a bug actually exists, only that a bug possibly exists. We integrate testing techniques to test if the section of code identified by the pattern actually produces an error, showing it truly is a bug.

2.3 Measurement Model

The model used to calculate a vulnerability score must consider as many different types of bugs (related to access control) as possible, and must cover the abstract quality aspects mentioned previously. We began by considering existing measurement models (e.g., Common Vulnerability Scoring System (CVSS) [4], Common Weakness Scoring System (CWSS) [3], etc.), however these models only calculate a scoring for a single bug and not for an entire system. Further, the amount of possible automation in these models is also very limited and requires manual parameter assignments. Therefore, we created our own measurement model.

The basic idea of our measurement model is to estimate the vulnerability of a software based on the detected instances of code patterns in its code base. For a bug pattern instance, we determine the impact it will have on the software in relation to the identified abstract quality aspects. Further, we determine how likely the instance will be triggered at runtime, which was found from the testing performed previously. The more instances of bug patterns detected and the more likely those instances will be triggered, the higher (or worse) the vulnerability score should be.

At the most abstract level, for multiple detected instances of bug patterns, we use the following formula to generate a vulnerability value, normalized to the range [0, 1]. Here *Detected* is the set of bug instances detected in the code using patterns and *Risk(b)* denotes the risk value of a given bug *b*.

$$Vulnerability = 1 - \frac{R}{R + \sum_{Detected} Risk(b)} \qquad (1)$$

R is a constant, which is the average risk sum per software project, which can be estimated using a large number of training software projects. With this formula if there are no bugs in a software project,

---

[2]SpotBugs URL: https://spotbugs.github.io/

[3]CWSS URL: https://cwe.mitre.org/cwss/cwss_v1.0.1.html

the vulnerability score will be 0. If the risk sum of all bugs in a project is R, the vulnerability score will be 0.5. So vulnerability scores above 0.5 indicate above average vulnerability, and lower than 0.5 indicate below average vulnerability. When the risk sum goes very high, the vulnerability value will be close to 1.

The current, top-level formula for the risk of a bug is:

$$Risk = Impact * Susceptibility \qquad (2)$$

Impact represents how the behavior and data of the software are affected by the bugs present in it. *Susceptibility* defines how easy or often those bugs are executed.

We divide *Impact* into four different sub-aspects: Control Integrity, Data Integrity, Data Confidentiality, and Data Availability, which cover our abstract aspects. They are modeled by the equation:

$$Impact = A * Integrity_{Control} + B * Integrity_{Data}$$
$$+ C * Confidentiality_{Data} + D * Availability_{Data} \qquad (3)$$

A, B, C, and D, model the relative importance (or weight) of $Integrity_{Control}$, $Integrity_{Data}$, $Confidentiality_{Data}$, and $Availability_{Data}$, respectfully. The weights of different aspects may be changed according to the actual usage scenarios. It should be noted that, although the formula currently models only negative patterns, positive patterns and mitigations can also be considered in the same way by changing the *Impact* value in a negative way.

Susceptibility indicates how likely the bug may be triggered during runtime. That is, when a software is executed, a bug that is triggered very often is more of a risk than a bug that is triggered rarely. *Susceptibility* can be estimated using the results from the integrated testing mentioned in Section 2.2. The more tests that trigger the bug, the higher the *Susceptibility* should be.

3 IMPROPER AUTHORIZATION EXAMPLE

In this section we briefly discuss how an access control pattern would move through the framework. We will use the "Improper Authorization" bug example, shown in Figure 2, to help explain the flow of our framework.

```
public ResultSet runEmployeeQuery(Connection conn, String name){
    PreparedStatement stmt = conn.prepareStatement("SELECT * " +
        "FROM employees WHERE name = ?");
    stmt.setString(1, name);
    ResultSet rs = stmt.executeQuery()
    return rs;
}
...

//Both "dbConn" and "employeeName" have been defined elsewhere
ResultSet employeeRecord = runEmployeeQuery(dbConn, employeeName);
```

Figure 2: Improper Authorization Bug Code Example

We begin by mining the bug from CWE. Improper Authorization is ID 285 in CWE[4] and occurs when software does not perform, or incorrectly performs, an authorization check when an actor attempts to access a resource or perform an action. After being stored in our learning engine repository, a concrete pattern is developed. For most bugs, multiple code patterns are needed to cover and identify as many variations of the bug as possible. These concrete code patterns are then fed into SpotBugs.

SpotBugs will then execute over a system and when it encounters a piece of code that matches one of the Improper Authorization patterns, it will mark its location in the code. Based on the location

---

[4]https://cwe.mitre.org/data/definitions/285.html

we are able to do testing, specifically targeting that piece of code to find if any input would lead to errors, especially errors that correlate with our abstract aspects from Section 2.2. The output of the testing is then used as input to the model.

The model receives all identified and tested bugs. The *Impact* is determined by the possible errors each bug can produce. For example, the Improper Authorization can effect Data Confidentiality and Data Availability. Based on testing, *Susceptibility* of each bug is determined. The overall *Risk* for each bug is then calculated, and finally the Vulnerability score for the system is produced.

4 CONCLUSION AND FUTURE WORK

We have developed an initial vulnerability model and corresponding tool set to support automatic measurements of software vulnerability of access control violations. While initial studies are promising, the project can be further enhanced and extended.

Our current learning engine is based on bug reports collected from Github and CWE. We plan to enlarge our dataset to mine bugs from a more broad variety of bug datasets. Further, we are currently producing bug patterns manually, which is a tedious and slow process. We will investigate possible machine learning applications to help automatically generate bug patterns.

We are currently using Spotbugs to detect code patterns. One limitation of this tool is that it is Java specific, and requires built software projects to work with. To overcome this limitation, we plan to consider PMD, which takes source code as input and works with many different programming languages (which will also allow us to extend our learning engine to include other programming languages). One issue with PMD is that it may not support some bug code patterns that are currently supported in Spotbugs. Therefore, we plan to adapt such code patterns to PMD.

Our current integration with test coverage is rather preliminary. Currently, we need manual generation and execution of test cases for each software feature. In the next phase, we will automate test execution and the insertion of test coverage build plug-ins.

Finally, we plan to detect positive code patterns to estimate the mitigation of risks in the software project. Specifically, we will first reverse engineer code to class diagrams, and then extract design patterns from those class diagrams.

ACKNOWLEDGEMENTS

We would like to thank Dr. Jianwei Niu, Rodney Rodriguez, MSI STEM Research & Development Consortium (Award #D01_W911SR-14-2-0001-0012), and National Science Foundation (Award #1736209) for their contributions to this project.

REFERENCES

[1] Nathaniel Ayewah, David Hovemeyer, J David Morgenthaler, John Penix, and William Pugh. 2008. Using static analysis to find bugs. *IEEE software* 25, 5 (2008).
[2] Toshihiro Kamiya, Shinji Kusumoto, and Katsuro Inoue. 2002. CCFinder: a multilinguistic token-based code clone detection system for large scale source code. *IEEE Transactions on Software Engineering* 28, 7 (2002), 654–670.
[3] Guangtai Liang, Jian Wang, Shaochun Li, and Rong Chang. 2014. PatBugs: A Pattern-Based Bug Detector for Cross-platform Mobile Applications. In *Mobile Services (MS), 2014 IEEE International Conference on*. IEEE, 84–91.
[4] Peter Mell, Karen Scarfone, and Sasha Romanosky. 2006. Common vulnerability scoring system. *IEEE Security & Privacy* 4, 6 (2006).
[5] Joseph P Near and Daniel Jackson. 2016. Finding security bugs in web applications using a catalog of access control patterns. In *Software Engineering (ICSE), 2016 IEEE/ACM 38th International Conference on*. IEEE, 947–958.

Poster: Using Gini Impurity to Mine Attribute-based Access Control Policies with Environment Attributes

Saptarshi Das
IIT Kharagpur, India
saptarshidas13@iitkgp.ac.in

Shamik Sural
IIT Kharagpur, India
shamik@cse.iitkgp.ernet.in

Jaideep Vaidya
Rutgers University, USA
jsvaidya@business.rutgers.edu

Vijayalakshmi Atluri
Rutgers University, USA
atluri@rutgers.edu

ABSTRACT

In Attribute-based Access Control (ABAC) systems, utilizing environment attributes along with the subject and object attributes introduces a dynamic nature to the access decisions. The inclusion of environment attributes helps in achieving a more fine-grained access control. In this paper, we present an ABAC policy mining algorithm that considers the environment attributes and their associated values while forming the rules. Furthermore, we use gini impurity to form the rules. This helps to minimize the number of rules in the generated policy. The experimental evaluation shows that our approach is quite effective in practice.

KEYWORDS

ABAC; Policy mining; Environment attributes; Gini impurity

ACM Reference Format:
Saptarshi Das, Shamik Sural, Jaideep Vaidya, and Vijayalakshmi Atluri. 2018. Poster: Using Gini Impurity to Mine Attribute-based Access Control Policies with Environment Attributes. In *SACMAT '18: The 23rd ACM Symposium on Access Control Models & Technologies (SACMAT), June 13–15, 2018, Indianapolis, IN, USA*. ACM, New York, NY, USA, 4 pages. https://doi.org/10.1145/3205977.3208949

1 INTRODUCTION

In recent years, ABAC has emerged as the *de-facto* standard for providing controlled access to organizational resources in scenarios involving inter-organizational sharing of resources. Additionally, ABAC is capable of providing the benefits of all the existing access control models. Although traditional access control models like Role-based Access Control (RBAC) are adequate in providing controlled access to organizational resources in situations involving a known set of users, they have been shown to be incompetent in providing efficient fine-grained access control in dynamic environments. This often

necessitates organizations using traditional access control models to migrate to ABAC.

One of the crucial steps for migrating to ABAC is to construct a set of ABAC authorization rules, collectively called an ABAC policy. Each rule consists of a conjunction of subject, object and environment attributes along with their corresponding values and an operation permitted by the rule. Since manually developing ABAC policies is difficult and costly [4], computational approaches have been deployed to partially automate the process of developing an ABAC policy from a given Access Control Matrix (ACM). Although there exist many ABAC policy mining algorithms, none of these consider the environment attributes and their associated values. Inclusion of environment attributes not only gives a dynamic nature to the access decisions, it also helps in achieving more fine-grained access control.

In this context, we propose a policy mining algorithm that takes an ACM as input and aims to generate an ABAC policy having minimum number of rules. From a broad perspective, as there can be only two possible outcomes of an access request, i.e., a *yes* or a *no*, it is possible to classify the accesses given in the ACM on the basis of the attribute data of the subject, object, and environment attributes. We recursively find the attribute data which affects the access decisions most using gini impurity [1] and construct the rules.

While there is some work on mining ABAC policies [3] [5], and also on constrained versions of the ABAC policy mining problem [2], to the best of our knowledge, this is the first attempt towards formulating and solving ABAC policy mining problem which involves environment attributes.

2 ABAC POLICY SPECIFICATION

An ABAC system comprises a set of subject attributes (SA), object attributes (OA), environment attributes (EA) and a set of possible operations (OP). Each attribute $a \in SA \cup OA \cup EA$ has a set (AV_a) of possible values. For a set (S) of users, the attribute data for all $s \in S$ is represented using a matrix (SV) of size $|S| \times |SA|$, where each row corresponds to a subject $s \in S$ and each column corresponds to an attribute $a \in SA$. Each $SV[i][j]$ contains the value of the jth attribute of the ith subject. For instance, Table 1 shows a subject attribute data matrix from which we can see that Alice is a professor and Bob is a student of the department of CSE. The matrices OV and EV are defined

Subject	Designation	Department
Alice	*Professor*	*CSE*
Bob	*Student*	*CSE*

Table 1: Subjects and their attributes with associated values

similarly for object attribute data and environment attribute data, respectively. For the sake of brevity, in this work we consider only one operation named as *access*. However, multiple operations can easily be incorporated in the present work. An ABAC authorization rule is represented as a 4-tuple $\langle SC, OC, EC, OP \rangle$, where SC, OC, EC and OP, respectively represent a set of subject attribute data, object attribute data, environment attribute data and the name of an operation. For instance, a rule of the form $\langle \{Designation = Student\}, \{Type = Assignment\}, \{Location = Lab\}, view \rangle$ conveys that any *Student* can *view* documents of type *Assignment* when inside the *Lab*.

3 ABAC POLICY MINING (APM) PROBLEM

The policy mining problem takes an ACM as input. In this scenario, the ACM is a 3-dimensional matrix of size $|S| \times |O| \times |E|$ where, each dimension contains the subjects, objects and the environments, respectively. An element $ACM[i][j][k]$, also represented as (s_i, o_j, e_k) and referred as an access, is 1, if the ith subject can *access* the jth object in the kth environment or 0, otherwise.

3.1 Problem Definition

Definition 3.1. ABAC Policy Mining (APM) Problem: Given a set of subjects S, a set of objects O, a set of environments E, a subject attribute matrix SV, an object attribute matrix OV, an environment attribute matrix EV, and an ACM A, construct an ABAC policy P such that the following conditions are met: *(i)* each entry in the ACM A is covered by at least one rule in P *(ii)* no extraneous *access* is permitted *(iii)* number of rules in P is minimum.

3.2 Solving APM involving Environment Attributes

In [5], the decision version of APM (D-APM) is proved to be a NP-Complete problem. Thus, it is unlikely that a deterministic polynomial time algorithm exists for solving D-APM. We solve D-APM using a greedy heuristic which involves computing the gini impurity of each attribute data. First, from the given subject, object, and environment attribute data matrices, we construct the attribute data for each possible access. For a given access (s, o, e), the attribute data associated with s, o and e are concatenated along with the corresponding access decision from the access control matrix. This procedure is given in Algorithm 1.

After obtaining the access-data, we construct the ABAC policy. The algorithm for our proposed approach for policy mining is given in Algorithm 2. First, we compute the gini impurity for each of the attribute data to select the attribute data that best divides the accesses into *yes* and *no* decisions (Lines 2-6). For instance, Table 2 consists of attribute data

---

Algorithm 1: Prepare access attribute data

Input: S, O, E, SV, OV, EV, A
Output: *access-data*

1    $Policy \leftarrow \phi$
2   **for** $i \leftarrow 1$ *to* $|S|$ **do**
3   **for** $j \leftarrow 1$ *to* $|O|$ **do**
4   **for** $k \leftarrow 1$ *to* $|E|$ **do**
5             $T \leftarrow concatenate(SV[i], OV[j], EV[k], A[i][j][k])$
             access-data.*append*(T)
6   **end**
7   **end**
8   **end**
9   **return** *access-data*

Department	Designation	Decision
CSE	*Professor*	*no*
CSE	*Professor*	*no*
CSE	*Professor*	*no*
CSE	*Professor*	*no*
ECE	*Professor*	*no*
ECE	*Professor*	*yes*
ECE	*Student*	*yes*
CSE	*Student*	*yes*
ECE	*Professor*	*yes*
CSE	*Professor*	*yes*

Table 2: Sample access data with decisions

and their corresponding access decisions. There are 2 Departments (*Dept.*) namely, *ECE* and *CSE* and two Designations (*Desg.*) namely, Professor (*Prof.*) and Student (*Stu.*). First, considering the attribute *Dept.*, proportions of *ECE* and *CSE* are $\frac{4}{10}$ and $\frac{6}{10}$, respectively. We compute the gini coefficient for $<Dept. = ECE>$. From Table 2, we can see that out of all the instances of *ECE*, $\frac{3}{4}th$ and $\frac{1}{4}th$ instances correspond to *yes* and *no* decsions, respectively. Gini coefficient (GC) for an attribute a having value v is calculated as:

$$GC(a = v) = 1 - P_{yes}{}^2 - P_{no}{}^2 \quad (1)$$

Where, P_{yes} is the probability of getting a *yes* decison when value of attribute a is v. P_{no} is similarly defined. Therefore, gini coefficient for $<Dept. = ECE>$ is:

$$GC(Dept. = ECE) = 1 - ((\frac{3}{4})^2 + (\frac{1}{4})^2) = 0.375$$

Similarly, the gini coefficient for $<Dept. \, ! = ECE>$ which in this example, is same as $<Dept. = CSE>$ is computed as:

$$GC(Dept. \, ! = ECE) = 1 - ((\frac{2}{6})^2 + (\frac{4}{6})^2) = 0.444$$

Now, we compute the Gini impurity (GI) for an attribute a having value v as follows:

$$GI(a = v) = (P_{a=v} * GC(a = v)) + (P_{a!=v} * GC(a =!v)) \quad (2)$$

Therefore, GI for $<Dept. = ECE>$ is computed as:

$$GI(Dept. = ECE) = (\frac{4}{10} * 0.375) + (\frac{6}{10} * 0.444) = 0.417$$

Algorithm 2: APM

Input: access-data, access-decisions, attributes
Output: *Policy*

1 *Policy* ← φ
2 *GI_list* ← φ
3 **for** *i* ← *1 to |attribute-data|* **do**
   // attribute-data is obtained from access-data
4   *temp = GI(attribute-data)*
5   *GI_list.append(temp)*
6 **end**
7 *GI_list* ← *sort(GI_list)*
8 **for** *i* ← *1 to |GI_list|* **do**
9   **while** *attribute-data corresponding to GI_list$_i$ splits*
       access-data comprising both permit and deny accesses **do**
10   *add attribute-data corresponding to GI_list$_i$ to a*
           temporary-rule
11   **end**
12   *add temporary-rule to Policy*
13 **end**
14 **return** *Policy*

Likewise, $GI(Desg. = Prof.)$ is computed to be 0.375. Since, $GI(Desg. = Prof.) < GI(Dept. = ECE.)$, we select the former as the part of a rule (Line 10). Moreover, we can see that, $GC(Desg. != Prof.)$ is computed to be 0, this implies that $<Desg. != Prof.>$, i.e., $<Desg. = Stu.>$ contains instances which correspond to a single decision (yes). Thus, $<Desg. = Stu.>$ is a rule. The rest of the accesses are recursively divided following the different gini impurities unless groups of accesses leading to a single decision are obtained (Lines 9-11). Likewise, the rest of the rules are obtained.

4 EXPERIMENTAL RESULTS

We implemented our proposed algorithm described in Section 3 in Python 3.6. The implemented algorithm was executed on an Intel i5 processor clocked at 2.70 GHz having 4 GB RAM. We represent the results using a number of subjects ($|S|$), objects ($|O|$), number of subject attributes ($|SA|$), object attributes ($|OA|$), number of rules formed using the algorithm given in [5] ($R_{[5]}$), and our proposed approach (R). First, we evaluated our proposed approach on the data sets given in [5]. As the data sets given in [5] do not consider environment attributes, we execute the algorithm of our proposed approach excluding the environment attributes. From the obtained results, given in Table 3, we can see that the number of rules formed using our proposed approach is less than the number of rules formed in [5]. For smaller data sets like the *video library* data set, the number of rules formed by our proposed approached is the same. As the data sets grow in size and involve more subject and object attributes along with an increase in the number of subjects and objects, the number of rules formed using our proposed approach is less.

As there are no available data set which contains environment attributes, to evaluate the performance of our proposed approach we synthetically generate various data sets. Table 4 shows the variation in the number of rules in the generated policy and weight of the generated policy with different number of subjects and objects. In our experiments, we have fixed

Data set	$|S|$	$|SA|$	$|O|$	$|OA|$	$R_{[5]}$	R
video library	12	2	13	2	6	6
university	20	6	34	5	10	9
healthcare	21	6	16	7	11	9
project	16	7	40	6	19	14

Table 3: Comparison of number of generated rules with [5]

S/O	100	200	300	400	500	1000
20	6	9	12	13	16	19
50	10	14	21	24	28	31
100	12	15	23	26	31	35
200	14	20	28	30	34	41

Table 4: Variation in #rules with #subjects and #objects

the number of subject, object and environment attributes to be 5, 5 and 3, respectively. The number of environments was set to 5. Each cell of Table 4 contains the number of rules in the generated policy for a specific number of subjects and objects. It is observed that the number of rules generated increases with the number of subjects and objects. The proposed approach was also observed to mine an ABAC policy in a considerably less amount of time. For instance, for 200 subjects and 1000 objects, it took only 23.63 seconds to generate a policy comprising 41 rules. Therefore, we have included the environment attributes in policy mining to achieve a more fine-grained access control. Moreover, our proposed approach generates policies having less number of rules as compared to the existing work. A policy having less number of rules is not only compact, but also helps in faster access decisions in case of an actual access request when deployed in an organization.

5 CONCLUSION

This paper presents a policy mining algorithm that uses gini impurity to determine the rules for ABAC systems involving environment attributes. Minimizing the number of rules in the generated ABAC policy helps in taking faster access decisions. In the future, we plan to explore other heuristics to further reduce the number of roles as well as attributes used in the generated policy.

ACKNOWLEDGMENTS

This work was supported by the National Institutes of Health under award R01GM118574 and by the National Science Foundation under award CNS-1624503.

REFERENCES

[1] L. Breiman. Technical Note: Some Properties of Splitting Criteria. *Machine Learning* (1997), 41–47.
[2] M. Gautam, S. Jha, S. Sural, J. Vaidya, and V. Atluri. Poster: Constrained Policy Mining in Attribute Based Access Control. *Sym. on Acc. Con. Mod. and Tech.* (2017), 21–23.
[3] T. Talukdar, G. Batra, J. Vaidya, V. Atluri and S. Sural. Efficient bottom-up Mining of Attribute Based Access Control Policies. *IEEE CIC* (2017), 339–348.
[4] D. Servos and S. L. Osborn. Current Research and Open Problems in Attribute-Based Access Control. *ACM Comp. Sur.* (2017), 1–45.
[5] Z. Xu and S. D. Stoller. Mining attribute-based access control policies. *IEEE Trans. Dep. and Sec. Com.* 12, 5 (2015), 533–545.

Poster: Towards Greater Expressiveness, Flexibility, and Uniformity in Access Control

Jiaming Jiang
Computer Science Department,
North Carolina State University
Raleigh, North Carolina
jjiang13@ncsu.edu

Rada Chirkova
Computer Science Department,
North Carolina State University
Raleigh, North Carolina
rychirko@ncsu.edu

Jon Doyle
Computer Science Department,
North Carolina State University
Raleigh, North Carolina
Jon_Doyle@ncsu.edu

Arnon Rosenthal
The MITRE Corporation
Bedford, Massachusetts
arnie@mitre.org

ABSTRACT

Attribute-based access control (ABAC) is a general access control model that subsumes numerous earlier access control models. Its increasing popularity stems from the intuitive generic structure of granting permissions based on application and domain attributes of users, subjects, objects, and other entities in the system. Multiple formal and informal languages have been developed to express policies in terms of such attributes.

The utility of ABAC policy languages is potentially undermined without a properly formalized underlying model. The high-level structure in a majority of ABAC models consists of sets of tokens and sets of sets, expressions that demand that the reader unpack multiple levels of sets and tokens to determine what things mean. The resulting reduced readability potentially endangers correct expression, reduces maintainability, and impedes validation. These problems could be magnified in models that employ nonuniform representations of actions and their governing policies.

We propose to avoid these magnified problems by recasting the high-level structure of ABAC models in a logical formalism that treats all actions (by users and others) uniformly and that keeps existing policy languages in place by interpreting their attributes in terms of the restructured model. In comparison to existing ABAC models, use of a logical language for model formalization, including hierarchies of types of entities and attributes, promises improved *expressiveness* in specifying the relationships between and requirements on application and domain attributes. A logical modeling language also potentially improves *flexibility* in representing relationships as attributes to support some widely used policy languages. Consistency and intelligibility are improved by using *uniform* means for representing different types of controlled actions—such as regular access control actions, administrative actions, and user logins—and their governing policies.

SACMAT'18, June 13–15, 2018, Indianapolis, IN, USA
© 2018 Copyright held by the owner/author(s).
ACM ISBN 978-1-4503-5666-4/18/06...$15.00
https://doi.org/10.1145/3205977.3208950

Logical languages also provide a well-defined denotational semantics supported by numerous formal inference and verification tools.

CCS CONCEPTS

• **Security and privacy** → **Formal security models**; **Access control**; *Authorization*; • **Theory of computation** → **Formalisms**;

KEYWORDS

Attribute-based access control; security; policy formalism; logical models

ACM Reference Format:
Jiaming Jiang, Rada Chirkova, Jon Doyle, and Arnon Rosenthal. 2018. Poster: Towards Greater Expressiveness, Flexibility, and Uniformity in Access Control. In *SACMAT'18: 23rd ACM Symposium on Access Control Models & Technologies, June 13–15, 2018, Indianapolis, IN, USA.* ACM, New York, NY, USA, 3 pages. https://doi.org/10.1145/3205977.3208950

1 INTRODUCTION

Access control (AC) concerns the problems of designing, expressing, and mechanizing policies that decide whether a party, such as a human *user* or one of a user's *subject* computational processes, has been granted *permissions* sufficient to perform some *action*, such as reading or writing, on a specific *object*, such as a file in a computer system. *Attribute-based access control* (ABAC) models, summarized in [8] and surveyed in [16], provide generality and subsume many other AC models by allowing definitions of domain-dependent properties called *attributes*. Translations have shown how one can simulate in ABAC the discretionary access control (DAC), mandatory access control (MAC), and role-based access control (RBAC) models [10, 11] .

Research on formalizing ABAC currently takes two major directions. One develops policy languages for use with ABAC models [2, 3, 13, 14]. The other develops means for representing the high-level structure and components of ABAC models and for determining how different components relate to each other [7, 9–11, 18, 19].

Many formal languages for specifying policies often have a uniform syntax and well-defined semantics [2, 3, 13, 14]. In contrast, the high-level structure for ABAC models in the current literature lack the expressiveness and uniformity often found in formal policy languages. The languages used to specify the ABAC model underlying some policies do not provide a clear *expression* of how the main components interact with each other, leading to less readable models and greater chances of errors. For example, hierarchies of users or subjects and of attributes cannot be conveniently and efficiently represented in an authorization policy. Thus if an attribute is only defined on some subset of the users, administrators have the burden of making sure the other users do not have a value for that attribute. The languages used to specify ABAC models are also not *uniform* in the sense of representing different types of actions and their corresponding governing policies in a consistent format. For instance, [10] specifies three types of actions and their governing policies are in different representations. One type of actions is for administrators creating and deleting a user, governed by fixed policies that are implicitly encoded in the model. Another type of action is for non-administrative users creating and modifying a subject and an object, governed by restricted forms of "constraints". The third type consists of other domain-dependent actions, such as read and write. Such non-uniform representation limits the usability of the model.

Our aim is to bridge the gap between policy and model languages by developing an ABAC model formalism that (a) uses representations with well-defined semantics to set out the high-level structure of the model, and that (b) supports expressive embedded policy languages with a uniform treatment of actions and their governing policies. Such a formalization would complement well the current policy language specifications and have the benefits of clearer high-level models.

The formalism would also be *flexible* in that it could be adjusted to incorporate additional desirable features, such as whether time is a factor in making policy decisions regarding a requested action. In the many applications in which DAC, MAC, and RBAC are sufficient, the time of when an action is requested does not play a role. While in more complicated scenarios, such as large corporations and hospitals, whether an action can be authorized often depends on the time of the request. For example, a senior care facility might authorize its manager to delete the medical records of a resident only after at least seven years have passed since the resident left the facility. Offering such flexibility by allowing the designers of an ABAC system to tailor the functionalities of the underlying ABAC model to their requirements is a desirable feature of an ABAC formalism. The formalism in [18] shows how to incorporate conflict resolution and default policies. We seek a more generic framework that incorporates a variety of widely used features, including the time component, common mathematical domains, conflict resolution mechanisms, and default and exception policies.

2 PROBLEMS AND RESPONSES

We now discuss some common problems to be addressed in current high-level ABAC models, especially vis-a-vis models that use a symbol-set representation, such as [10, 11, 15].

Semantics. The $ABAC_\alpha$ model [10, 11] uses representations based on sets of tokens or symbols that denote users, subjects, objects, attributes, roles, and actions. $ABAC_\alpha$ regards attributes as functions whose domains and ranges are also sets of symbols. Thus $ABAC_\alpha$ regards a user attribute symbol a as a function on the set of users, one that maps each user u to the value $a(u)$ of the attribute exhibited by the user. Each $ABAC_\alpha$ authorization policy consists of a condition expressed in first-order predicates on sets, such as "is an element of" ($\in$) and "is a subset of" ($\subseteq$). For example, one $ABAC_\alpha$ expression of DAC [11, Table 6, p. 51] expresses the condition for authorizing a subject s to read an object o as $SubCreator(s) \in reader(o)$, meaning that the user who created s must be in the set of users authorized to read o.

Unfortunately, interpreting an attribute symbol as standing for a mapping from symbols to other symbols or sets of symbols adds indirection that divorces attributes from their intuitive meaning.

Suppose, for example, that the value of user *Alice*'s organizational position attribute *orgPos* is the set {*Employee, Manager*}. What does it mean for *Manager* $\in$ *orgPos(Alice)* to be true? Only that the symbol *Manager* is in the set {*Employee, Manager*}, which, although true, is a statement about a representation, not about the world. The intended meaning, however, is that Alice is a manager, which is just the condition under which the simple predication *Manager(Alice)* is true in the standard semantics of logic. If one wants to say that managers can access all files owned by their subordinates, a direct statement would use predicate symbols to state properties of things. Stating this in terms of sets of symbols is an indirect expression that still leaves symbols such as *Manager* without their intended interpretations.

Response: Mere use of logic does not necessarily address the semantical issue. Indeed, the symbol-set view of ABAC is visible in several ABAC efforts that employ logical expressions [5, 17, 18]. For example, [18] presents a logic-programming formalization of ABAC that uses predicates over sets, elements, and subsets, as in $ABAC_\alpha$, and that uses a different vocabulary to specify authorization conditions. The consistency and completeness proofs given for the formalization only concern its handling of sets of symbols, not direct conclusions about what is true of entities in the AC system. In the more recent works, in order to place AC entities within taxonomic hierarchies [5] recasts RBAC using OWL [4] and [17] recasts $ABAC_\alpha$ using OWL and N3 [1]. These translations mainly use the description logic formalism to describe sets of attribute symbols, thus providing a description logic twist to the standard syntax approach of [18].

Extensibility. One hallmark of a convenient representation is that one can use it to describe the key things of interest in a simple and direct way, and that when time comes to modify the description, one can describe simple changes simply. Unfortunately, symbol-set representations fall short of this ideal with respect to simple extensibility, exceptions, and generalizations. For instance, to extend a symbol-set model such as $ABAC_\alpha$ with new attributes, one must change the elements of one or more sets. If sets are defined by explicitly listing their elements, say by using $U = \{Alice, Bob, Carol\}$ to define the set of users and $UA = \{a_1, a_2, \dots\}$ to define the set of user attributes, adding a new user requires replacing the former list with a new one, say $U = \{Alice, Bob, Carol, David\}$, and making corresponding changes in other lists, such as the value of each of the attributes in *UA*. Modifying numerous lists offers numerous chances to make an error of omission, which one can expect to become more frequent as protected systems and organizations become larger and larger.

Response: One step toward minimizing the potential for error is to employ a more modular representation in which one just *adds* the new information about additions, say by stating that *David* is a user, along with the values of *David*'s attributes. Such modularity of statement lies at the heart of standard logical languages, and carries over to description logics as well. One can make specification of non-additive changes, such as changing *David*'s address, modular as well, as is common in transactional database systems.

Prohibitions. In many ABAC systems, authorization decisions are made with a bias toward denial, meaning that a request is authorized only if the antecedent of some authorization rule evaluates to true. This approach can run into problems when the system lacks means to determine that a true condition is true, especially in cases in which the default is that everyone has access apart from some exceptions. For example, all medical personnel in a hospital might have blanket permission to see any patient's medical records, except for the records of other medical personnel at the same hospital. Moreover, [12] has shown that having prohibitions along with authorization policies would reduce the total number of rules, and hence, the time for evaluating access requests.

Response: Direct specification of the actual policies would benefit from using explicit prohibitions in tandem with explicit authorizations. Thus, a policy language that handles both prohibitions and authorization would be suitable for AC models.

3 PROPOSED DIRECTION OF WORK

Description logics have been used in representing ontologies in various application domains, such as in diagnostic and configuration systems. We propose to follow the lead of [5, 17] in using description logics to formalize AC models, but aim for a direct representation of the high-level structure of AC models. Other work [6, 9] uses description logics to formalize AC models, but uses terminological axioms of description logics to represent policies rather than to construct a high-level ontology of the components of a model. Even though terminological axioms are "syntactic sugar" of certain first-order formulas, treating policies as terminological axioms can be confusing and does not fully utilize the power of description logics in constructing a readable and maintainable ontology. For instance, the axioms $Manager \sqsubseteq User$ and $Intern \sqsubseteq User$ for specifying managers and interns as two types of users are obviously not policies. However, they are treated similarly as policies in a description logic knowledge base.

Furthermore, description logics cannot handle the cases where an attribute value is missing. This makes policy languages such as that of [3], which is specifically designed to handle missing attribute values, more appropriate. We expect to obtain a formal ABAC model with improved expressiveness, flexibility, and uniformity by combining such a formal policy language with a high-level ontology and underlying logical representation.

REFERENCES

[1] Tim Berners-Lee and Dan Connolly. 2011. *Notation3 (N3): A readable RDF syntax.* Technical Report. World Wide Web Consortium (W3C). http://www.w3.org/TeamSubmission/n3/

[2] G. Bruns and M. Huth. 2011. Access control via Belnap logic: Intuitive, expressive, and analyzable policy composition. *ACM Transactions on Information and System Security (TISSEC)* 14, 1 (2011), 9.

[3] Jason Crampton and Charles Morisset. 2012. PTaCL: A Language for Attribute-Based Access Control in Open Systems. In *Proceedings of the First International Conference on Principles of Security and Trust POST 2012 (Lecture Notes in Computer Science)*, Pierpaolo Degano and Joshua D. Guttman (Eds.). Springer-Verlag, Berlin Heidelberg, 390–409. DOI: http://dx.doi.org/10.1007/978-3-642-28641-4_21

[4] Mike Dean, Guus Schreiber, Sean Bechhofer, Frank van Harmelen, Jim Hendler, Ian Horrocks, Deborah L. McGuinness, Peter F. Patel-Schneider, and Lynn Andrea Stein. 2004. *OWL Web Ontology Language Reference.* World Wide Web Consortium (W3C), Cambridge, MA, USA. http://www.w3.org/TR/owl-ref/

[5] T. Finin, A. Joshi, L. Kagal, J. Niu, R. Sandhu, W. Winsborough, and B. Thuraisingham. 2008. ROWLBAC: Representing Role Based Access Control in OWL. In *Proceedings of the 13th ACM Symposium on Access Control Models and Technologies (SACMAT '08)*. ACM, New York, NY, USA, 73–82. DOI: http://dx.doi.org/10.1145/1377836.1377849

[6] Fausto Giunchiglia, Rui Zhang, and Bruno Crispo. 2008. RelBAC: Relation based access control. In *Fourth International Conference on Semantics, Knowledge and Grid, SKG '08, Beijing, China, December 3-5, 2008.* IEEE Computer Society, Los Alamitos, CA, 3–11. DOI: http://dx.doi.org/10.1109/SKG.2008.76

[7] Vipul Goyal, Omkant Pandey, Amit Sahai, and Brent Waters. 2006. Attribute-based encryption for fine-grained access control of encrypted data. In *Proceedings of the 13th ACM Conference on Computer and Communications Security (CCS 2006).* ACM, New York, NY, 89–98. DOI: http://dx.doi.org/10.1145/1180405.1180418

[8] Chung Tong Hu, David F. Ferraiolo, David R. Kuhn, Adam Schnitzer, Kenneth Sandlin, Robert Miller, and Karen Scarfone. 2014. *Guide to Attribute Based Access Control (ABAC) Definition and Considerations.* Special Publication (NIST SP) 800-162. National Institutes of Standards and Technology (NIST), Gaithersburg, Maryland. DOI: http://dx.doi.org/10.6028/NIST.SP.800-162

[9] Peng Jin and Yang Fang-chun. 2006. Description Logic Modeling of Temporal Attribute-Based Access Control. In *2006 First International Conference on Communications and Electronics*, Ngyuen Quoc Trung, Kazuo Tanaka, and Hyukjae Lee (Eds.). IEEE, Los Alamitos, CA, 414–418. DOI: http://dx.doi.org/10.1109/CCE.2006.350888

[10] Xin Jin. 2014. *Attribute-Based Access Control Models and Implementation In Cloud Infrastructure as a Service.* Ph.D. Dissertation. The University of Texas at San Antonio, San Antonio, TX.

[11] Xin Jin, Ram Krishnan, and Ravi Sandhu. 2012. A Unified Attribute-Based Access Control Model Covering DAC, MAC and RBAC. In *Data and Applications Security and Privacy XXVI (DBSec 2012)*, N. Cuppens-Boulahia et al. (Ed.). Lecture Notes in Computer Science, Vol. 7371. Springer Verlag, Heidelberg, 41–55.

[12] John C. John, Shamik Sural, and Arobinda Gupta. 2017. Attribute-based access control management for multicloud collaboration. *Concurrency and Computation: Practice and Experience* 29, 19, Article e4199 (2017), 14 pages. DOI: http://dx.doi.org/10.1002/cpe.4199

[13] Carroline Dewi Puspa Kencana Ramli, Hanne Riis Nielson, and Flemming Nielson. 2011. The Logic of XACML. In *Formal Aspects of Component Software - 8th International Symposium, FACS 2011, Oslo, Norway, September 14-16, 2011, Revised Selected Papers.* Springer, Springer, Berlin Heidelberg, 205–222. DOI: http://dx.doi.org/10.1007/978-3-642-35743-5_13

[14] Prathima Rao, Dan Lin, Elisa Bertino, Ninghui Li, and Jorge Lobo. 2009. An algebra for fine-grained integration of XACML policies. In *Proceedings of the 14th ACM symposium on Access Control Models and Technologies (SACMAT 2009).* ACM, New York, NY, 63–72. DOI: http://dx.doi.org/10.1145/1542207.1542218

[15] Daniel Servos and Sylvia L. Osborn. 2014. HGABAC: Towards a Formal Model of Hierarchical Attribute-Based Access Control. In *Seventh International Symposium on Foundations and Practice of Security (Lecture Notes in Computer Science)*, Frédéric Cuppens, Joaquín García-Alfaro, A. Nur Zincir-Heywood, and Philip W. L. Fong (Eds.). Springer, Cham, Switzerland, 187–204. DOI: http://dx.doi.org/10.1007/978-3-319-17040-4_12

[16] Daniel Servos and Sylvia L. Osborn. 2017. Current Research and Open Problems in Attribute-Based Access Control. *Comput. Surveys* 49, 4 (January 2017), 65:1–45. DOI: http://dx.doi.org/10.1145/3007204

[17] Nitin Kumar Sharma and Anupam Joshi. 2016. Representing Attribute Based Access Control Policies in OWL. In *Tenth IEEE International Conference on Semantic Computing, ICSC 2016, Laguna Hills, CA, USA, February 4-6, 2016.* IEEE Computer Society, Los Alamitos, CA, 333–336. DOI: http://dx.doi.org/10.1109/ICSC.2016.16

[18] Lingyu Wang, Duminda Wijesekera, and Sushil Jajodia. 2004. A Logic-based Framework for Attribute based Access Control. In *Formal Methods in Software Engineering (FMSE'04).* ACM, ACM, New York, NY, 45–55. 100045.

[19] Xinwen Zhang, Yingjiu Li, and Divya Nalla. 2005. An attribute-based access matrix model. In *Proceedings of the 2005 ACM Symposium on Applied Computing (SAC)*, Hisham Haddad, Lorie M. Liebrock, Andrea Omicini, and Roger L. Wainwright (Eds.). ACM, New York, NY, 359–363. DOI: http://dx.doi.org/10.1145/1066677.1066760

How Inadequate Specification, Buggy Implementation, and Deficient Platform-Support Hinder Security

Omar Chowdhury
Department of Computer Science
The University of Iowa
Iowa City, Iowa
omar-chowdhury@uiowa.edu

ABSTRACT

Developing a secure system (or, protocol) in general boils down to having a correct and robust specification which developers faithfully implement with the available platform support. Vulnerabilities can thus crop up due to inadequate specification, buggy implementations, or the lack of appropriate security constructs in the platform. In this talk, I will present examples of insecurity due to inadequate specification, wrong implementations, and deficient platform support. I will particularly focus on how automated reasoning and formal verification techniques can greatly contribute towards detecting vulnerabilities.

In the first example, I will show how 4G LTE telecommunication protocol specification lacks security considerations which can be exploited by adversaries to have catastrophic impacts [2]. Next, I will present how incorrect X.509 certificate validation implementations in open-source SSL/TLS libraries leave users prone to impersonation attacks [1]. Finally, I will conclude my talk with a discussion of how lack of hardware support makes enforcing Digital Rights Management (DRM) policies infeasible for mobile devices.

CCS CONCEPTS

• **Security and privacy** → **Logic and verification**; **Security protocols**; **Mobile and wireless security**; *Mobile platform security*;

KEYWORDS

Implementation bugs; Inconsistent Specification; X.509 Public-key Infrastructure; 4G LTE; Digital Rights Management; Inadequate platform constructs

ACM Reference Format:
Omar Chowdhury. 2018. How Inadequate Specification, Buggy Implementation, and Deficient Platform-Support Hinder Security. In *SACMAT'18: 23rd ACM Symposium on Access Control Models & Technologies, June 13–15, 2018, Indianapolis, IN, USA.* ACM, New York, NY, USA, 1 page. https://doi.org/10.1145/3205977.3206002

BIOGRAPHY

Dr. Omar Haider Chowdhury is an Assistant Professor of Computer Science at the University of Iowa. Dr. Chowdhury's research focuses on leveraging formal machinery and techniques to solve practically-relevant security and privacy problems of emerging systems and protocols. At Iowa, Dr. Chowdhury currently co-directs the Computational Logic Center (CLC) and is also an active member of the Informatics Initiative (UI3).

Before joining the University of Iowa, he held post-doctoral researcher positions at Carnegie Mellon University and Purdue University. He received his Ph.D. in Computer Science from the University of Texas at San Antonio. Dr. Chowdhury's research is currently supported by the National Science Foundation (NSF) and Defense Advanced Research Projects Agency (DARPA).

ACKNOWLEDGEMENT

The results reported in this keynote is partially supported by the National Science Foundation (NSF) grant CNS-1657124. Any opinions, findings, or recommendations conveyed during the keynote are those of the author, and do not necessarily reflect those of NSF.

REFERENCES

[1] S. Y. Chau, O. Chowdhury, E. Hoque, H. Ge, A. Kate, C. Nita-Rotaru, and N. Li. 2017. SymCerts: Practical Symbolic Execution for Exposing Noncompliance in X.509 Certificate Validation Implementations. In *2017 IEEE Symposium on Security and Privacy (SP).* 503–520.
[2] Syed Rafiul Hussain, Omar Chowdhury, Shagufta Mehnaz, and Elisa Bertino. 2018. LTEInspector: A Systematic Approach for Adversarial Testing of 4G LTE. In *2018 Network and Distributed System Security Symposium (NDSS).* https://doi.org/10.14722/ndss.2018.23319

Access Control Enforcement within MQTT-based Internet of Things Ecosystems

Pietro Colombo
DiSTA, University of Insubria
Varese, Italy
pietro.colombo@uninsubria.it

Elena Ferrari
DiSTA, University of Insubria
Varese, Italy
elena.ferrari@uninsubria.it

ABSTRACT

Confidentiality and privacy of data managed by IoT ecosystems is becoming a primary concern. This paper targets the design of a general access control enforcement mechanism for MQTT-based IoT ecosystems. The proposed approach is presented with ABAC, but other access control models can be similarly supported. The solution is based on an enforcement monitor that has been designed to operate as a proxy between MQTT clients and an MQTT server. The monitor enforces access control constraints by intercepting and possibly manipulating the flow of exchanged MQTT control packets. Early experimental evaluations have overall shown low enforcement overhead.

CCS CONCEPTS

• Security and privacy → Access control;

KEYWORDS

Access control; Internet of Things; MQTT;

ACM Reference format:
Pietro Colombo and Elena Ferrari. 2018. Access Control Enforcement within MQTT-based Internet of Things Ecosystems. In *Proceedings of The 23rd ACM Symposium on Access Control Models & Technologies (SACMAT), Indianapolis, IN, USA, June 13–15, 2018 (SACMAT '18),* 12 pages.
https://doi.org/10.1145/3205977.3205986

1 INTRODUCTION

Internet of Things (IoT) applications are becoming a fundamental part of our daily life. People cannot do without wearable devices that continuously track their status, sport activities, and health conditions. Smart home technologies started to be extensively used, and a wider diffusion has been prospected for the next years [17]. Overall a great variety of IoT applications exists, and these are getting a growing popularity and diffusion for the indisputable improvements of our life style.

Although the benefits of IoT services are manifold, IoT represents a potential serious threat for user personal and confidential data,

which are continuously exposed to unauthorized accesses. Recognized the seriousness of this risk, in the recent years, research has extensively investigated aspects related to security and privacy of IoT ecosystems. In particular, for what access control is concerned, a variety of access control models tailored for IoT applications have been proposed (see, for instance, [20] for a compendium). Several proposals are based on Capability Based Access Control - CapBAC - (e.g., [7, 9, 16]), according to which users directly show their authorization capabilities to service providers, and access privileges are granted on the basis of the provided information. Centralized [7] and distributed [9] implementations of CapBAC have been proposed, but the approach has been criticized since it does not take context awareness into account [19]. Other proposals (e.g., [8, 13, 22]) are based on Role Based Access Control (RBAC) [6]. An extension of RBAC is proposed in [22], which introduces contextual constraints to fit IoT dinamicity. However, as pointed out in [21], the same shortcomings affecting RBAC, such as role explosion, can also be found in [22]. Other proposals are based on Attribute-based Access Control (ABAC) [10, 11]. An ABAC model has been proposed in [13], which extends RBAC with attributes finalized to handle the dynamic assignment of roles to users. However, no support for other attributes is provided. In [8], a CoAP[1] based implementation of an ABAC model has been presented, which works with a predefined set of attributes. However, no formalization of the supported policies and of the implemented enforcement mechanism is provided.

A very recent line of research investigates access control for cloud-enabled IoT (see e.g., [1–4]). In [1], an access control oriented (ACO) architecture is proposed, which serves as a framework to build access control models [2] for cloud-based IoT services. Different solutions have been defined on top of ACO, such as models designed for specific IoT platforms [3], and applications [4]. The proposed approach is general and suited to support different access control models, but it only targets cloud-enabled IoT ecosystems.

A few recent proposals (e.g., [15, 18]) are based on Usage Control (UCON) [23]. A fault tolerant framework supporting the enforcement of UCON policies within IoT is proposed in [18], and its use is illustrated for the protection of a Smart Home environment. However, technological and architectural assumptions limit the generality of the proposal.

The analysis of related work has shown that a general approach to the smooth integration of access control into IoT ecosystems is still missing. In this paper, we do a step to fill this void, by proposing a general enforcement mechanism that allows enforcing policies of different access control models within MQTT-based IoT ecosystems.

---

[1]http://coap.technology/

We have designed our mechanism on top of MQTT, since MQTT-based environments represent a significant subset of IoT ecosystems. MQTT[2] is a standard application layer protocol that enables the communication of IoT devices by means of the publish/subscribe architecture, with a message broker that handles message passing among a set of connected devices.

The main peculiarity of the proposed approach is that it can be smoothly integrated into any MQTT-based IoT deployment, as it does not require modifications to MQTT message brokers or clients. Among the various access control paradigms, ABAC [10, 11] has been chosen for presenting the proposed mechanisms for its outstanding flexibility,[3] as well as for the dynamic and context aware nature of the supported policies, which seems a perfect fit for the pervasivity of IoT applications. However, in the current paper, we do not aim to propose a novel ABAC model for IoT, as the focus of the work is on the enforcement mechanism, and ABAC has only been used as reference model for presentation purposes. The proposed enforcement mechanism may also be used with other access control models, such as RBAC, CapBAC, and UCON.

Our solution supports two different classes of access control policies. The first class includes policies specified by security administrators. These represent general rules regulating the right to receive/publish messages on specific topics. However, some users may want to specify additional constraints, on the basis of their scenario dependent needs, through user-defined preferences that restrict the privileges granted by access control policies. For instance, let us consider an IoT environment related to a gym with smart gym apparatuses that track data related to gym frequenters. A policy may grant gym coaches read access to data generated by gym frequenters with any exercise machine. A user preference specified by a frequenter of the gym, may instead forbid a specific coach to access the tracked data. Similarly, in a smart home domain, access control policies may regulate the publishing of data generated by thermometers, humidity and movements sensors at given weekly schedules, as well as the read access to comprehensive reports of the generated data through smart home apps given to trusted users. User preferences specified by a family member may be used to restrict the privileges granted by access control policies, for instance allowing a trusted neighbor to access sensors data only during a vacation period.

The analysis of all previously considered related work has revealed that none of them supports both access control policies and user preferences. In addition, the proposed approach differs from previously considered ABAC frameworks for a wider variety of supported attributes, which makes it more flexible and thus suitable to a wider range of application scenarios.

We have defined an enforcement monitor suited to be deployed on low capacity devices, which typically compose IoT ecosystems. The monitor allows regulating MQTT-based message passing within deployments with a not a priori known number of heterogeneous clients. The proposed enforcement mechanism, rather than focusing on ad hoc customization of client/server functionalities, is based on the analysis and manipulation of the exchanged MQTT control packets. A prototypical version of the monitor has been released, and preliminary evaluations of the monitor have shown satisfactory efficiency levels, with a reduced time overhead.

To the best of our knowledge, we are aware of two other MQTT-based solutions, i.e. [15] and [14], where UCON policy enforcement is directly handled by the message broker. However, the generality of both these solutions is limited by ad-hoc designed message brokers.

The remainder of this paper is organized as follows. Section 2 shortly presents background information related to MQTT, whereas Section 3 presents the adopted access control model. Section 4 provides an overview of the proposed solution, whereas Section 5 discusses the management of access control policies and user preferences. Section 6 introduces the enforcement mechanism. Section 7 presents experimental evaluations. Finally, Section 8 concludes the paper.

2 BACKGROUND

This section presents some basic concepts related to MQTT, which are instrumental to the definition of the proposed access control enforcement mechanism.

MQTT is a communication protocol designed to enable the interaction of multiple peers within a publish/subscribe architecture. A *client* is a peer that represents a program or a device that exchange application messages[4] over given *topics* with other clients through a *server*, also referred to as *message broker*. It is not required that clients know each other, as clients interaction is always mediated by a server.

Clients communicate by requesting the server to receive or publish messages on given topics. Clients wishing to publish a message jointly specify the *payload* and the *topic* of the message to be published, whereas clients wishing to receive messages subscribe to a set of topics, specified through *topic filter* expressions.

Topics are hierarchically organized into tree structures, and topic filter expressions allow referring to all the elements at given hierarchical levels of the tree. This allows the delivery of messages referring to multiple topics on the basis of the same routing criteria.

A *topic* is a string structured as a sequence of alphanumeric tokens, referred to as *topic levels*, and separated by a topic level separator.[5]

Example 2.1. Let us assume a topic hierarchy related to a smart home application, where the first topic level encodes the considered building, the second level specifies the floor, the third the room, and the forth a physical quantity (e.g., humidity, temperature). A message that encodes the temperature of the bathroom at the ground floor of the house may have a topic name specified as: *house/groundfloor/bathroom/temperature*.

A *topic filter* is a string structured as a sequence of topic levels, each specifying an alphanumeric token or the wildcard characters '+' or '#', which denote placeholders for one or more alphanumeric tokens. The wildcard + can be substituted by a single token, whereas the wildcard # by a sequence of tokens of arbitrary length.[6]

---

[2]MQTT Ver. 3.1.1: http://docs.oasis-open.org/mqtt/mqtt/v3.1.1/mqtt-v3.1.1.html
[3]It has been proved that ABAC can be used to express policies of the most popular access control models [12].

[4]Hereafter, for the sake of brevity, we refer to an application message simply as message.
[5]The forward slash character '/' is the default topic level separator.
[6]# can only be used as terminal topic level.

Example 2.2. Let us consider the scenario introduced in Example 2.1. The topic filter expression *house/+/+/humidity* denotes the topics names of the messages that encode the humidity of any room in each floor of the house, whereas the expression *house/firstfloor/#* those encoding any physical quantity that has been measured in any room of the first floor.

The server delivers published messages to the right subscribers using the specified topic names as routing information. More precisely, on request of publishing a message *m* on a topic name *tn*, the server matches *tn* against the topics implied by the topic filter expressions of all requested subscriptions, and forwards *m* to any subscribed client *c* whose topic filter expression denotes a set of topic names that includes *tn*.

Example 2.3. Let us consider a scenario where a client c_1 has subscribed the topic names denoted by the topic filter expression *house/+/+/humidity*, whereas a client c_2 has subscribed the topics denoted by the filter expression *house/firstfloor/#* (see Example 2.2). Let us now suppose that a client c_3, which corresponds to a humidity sensor, requests the server to publish the sensed humidity value 0.62 to the topic name *house/basement/basementroom/humidity*. The server matches the topic name of the message against the topic filter expressions of its subscriptions, and dispatches the message to c_1.

Client communication can only be achieved if clients are connected with the server. Clients connect and communicate with the server by means of control packets exchanged over a network connection. The control packets defined by MQTT are shown in Table 1.

Table 1: MQTT control packets

CONNECT	Client requests a connection to a Server
CONNACK	Acknowledge connection request
PUBLISH	Publish message
PUBACK	Publish acknowledgement
PUBREC	Publish received
PUBREL	Publish release
PUBCOMP	Publish complete
SUBSCRIBE	Subscribe to topics
SUBACK	Subscribe acknowledgement
UNSUBSCRIBE	Unsubscribe from topics
UNSUBACK	Unsubscribe acknowledgement
PINGREQ	PING request
PINGRESP	PING response
DISCONNECT	Disconnect notification

The server opens a connection with a client *c* on response to a connection request (control packet *CONNECT*) that has been issued by *c*. Once *c* has received the acknowledge of the established connection (control packet *CONNACK*), it can request: i) to *publish* a message on a *topic*, conveying the message in a control packet *PUBLISH*), ii) to *subscribe* to messages satisfying a *topic filter* expression (control packet *SUBSCRIBE*), iii) to *unsubscribe*, namely to remove a previously issued subscription request (control packet *UNSUBSCRIBE*), or iv) to *disconnect* from the server (control packet *DISCONNECT*).

MQTT allows clients to require that given message delivering guarantees are satisfied. Three Quality of Service (QoS) levels can be chosen by clients on the basis of network reliability and the considered application scenario, requesting that the message is delivered at most once (0), at least once (1), or exactly once (2). The lowest QoS level is used in scenarios where missing or lost messages are tolerated by the clients. In contrast, the higher QoS levels enables client communication even over unreliable networks, as message retransmission and delivery guarantees are handled at protocol level by means of dedicated control packets. The interested reader can refer to the MQTT specification[2] for a thorough presentation of sequences of control packets that are exchanged by a client and the server to ensure QoS level 1 and 2.

3 THE ACCESS CONTROL MODEL

We use the Attribute Based Access Control (ABAC) paradigm [10, 11] due to its generality, flexibility, and increasing adoption, and we customize it to be used in MQTT-based IoT ecosystems. In our context, ABAC is used to regulate the reception of messages by subscribed clients, as well as the publishing of new messages, on the basis of access control policies and user preferences.

Let us start to consider how basic concepts of ABAC, namely subjects, objects, environments, and related attributes, can be mapped to elements of the considered scenario.

A *subject* represents a client who connects to a server with the aim to publish or receive messages, possibly on behalf of a user.[7] It is worth noting that a client, at most, can be handled by a single user (at a time), whereas multiple clients can be handled by the same user.

A subject *s* is thus characterized by an attribute *cid*, which represents the identifier of the client who requests to connect to the server, and, optionally, by an attribute *uid*, which specifies the identifier of the user who handles *cid*.

Protection *objects* correspond to application messages. They are characterized by attributes that model message properties, which can be used for access control purposes. More precisely, an object *o* is characterized by an attribute *tp*, which specifies the topic of the message modeled by *o*, and an attribute *pl*, which specifies the message payload.

Environment attributes characterize the context within which a message is delivered, and can be used to influence an access decision. For the sake of simplicity, in this paper, we only focus on temporal properties. Therefore, we assume that an environment *e* specifies an attribute *t*, which models a message delivery instant (as perceived by the server) as a timestamp.[8] However, a variety of other context properties, such as, for instance, location and purposes may also be supported.

Access control policies are specified by security administrators to grant subjects the read or write access to messages referring to a set of topics. A read authorization corresponds to the right to receive

---

[7]MQTT allows specifying a user name within CONNECT control packets (see Table 1), with the aim to support authentication mechanisms. However, user names are not mandatorily specified.
[8]The timestamp specifies the number of milliseconds that have passed since an epoch (e.g. the Unix Epoch is Jan 1, 1970 00:00:00 UTC).

messages on a subscribed topic, whereas a write authorization corresponds to the authorization to publish a new message. Users can further constrain the reception of the messages published on their behalf, through user preferences.

The joint enforcement of users preferences and access control policies allow highly customized forms of data protection, which access control policies alone can hardly achieve. Indeed, multiple users may publish data on the same topic, but each user can have a different perception of the sensitivity of the published data, and may desire to protect the access to his/her data accordingly. For instance, let us consider a fitness app deployed on the tapis roulant of a gym, which allows users to share data of a running session. Users may wish to constrain, through user preferences, the set of data which can be shared within a running session, such as the current and average speed, race length, duration, step rates, and heart bit frequency. In contrast, access control policies are used to constrain the type of data that can be published and received by a gym frequenter, independently from a specific running session. For instance, an access control policy may authorize the app of a gym coach to access any information that is published by gym frequenters, and the app of a frequenter to see the running speed, running length, and duration of other frequenters registered for the same gym course. A user, at any time, can specify preferences restricting the read access to his/her published data by other users.

Access control policies and user preferences are specified by specifying predicates over subject, object and context attributes.

Definition 3.1 (Parametric predicate). A parametric predicate is a boolean expression built by composition of subject, object and environment attributes, mathematical operators ($>, <, =, +, -, *, /, \%$), logical operators ($\wedge, \vee, \neg$), set operators ($\in, \subset, \subseteq, \cap, \cup, \setminus$), logical quantifiers ($\forall, \exists$), and predefined functions allowing the processing of attributes values.

Definition 3.2 (Access control policy). An access control policy p is a tuple $\langle sid, tf, exp, pr \rangle$, where sid refers to the identifier of the client or user constrained by p[9], tf specifies a topic filter expression, exp is a parametric predicate,[10] whereas pr specifies the *read* /*write* privileges granted to sid if exp is satisfied.

Example 3.3. Let us assume that *Bob* is the owner of a smart home, and let us consider the specification of an access control policy p which authorizes all thermometers to publish the sensed temperature at the minutes 0, 5, 10 ... 55 of any hour. The topic filter expression of p may be specified as *home/+/+/temperature*, whereas the parametric predicate as *getMinutes(t)%5==0*, where *getMinutes(t)* is a function which returns the minute denoted by t. p can therefore be specified as follows: $\langle Bob, home/+/+/temperature, getMinutes(t)\%5==0, w \rangle$.

User preferences are defined to constrain the access to messages published by a user, on the basis of parametric predicates.

Definition 3.4 (User preference). A user preference up is a tuple $\langle uid, tf, sub\_exp \rangle$, where uid specifies the identifier of a user who wishes to protect the access to messages published by any of the

clients it handles, whereas tf specifies a topic filter expression which denotes the messages, among those that have been published on behalf of uid, to which the preference applies, whereas sub_exp is a parametric predicate specifying a precondition to the receiving of a protected message to be satisfied by the subscribed clients.

Example 3.5. Let us consider the specification of a user preference up, which regulates the access to some of the messages that have been published by *Bob* clients. More precisely, let us consider the specification of a user preference which grants *Alice*, a trusted family member, the access to temperature, humidity and states of the windows of any room at the first floor of the house during Bob's vacation $[vp_1..vp_2]$. The topic filter expression may be specified as *home/groundfloor/+/+*, whereas the preference predicate as *uid='Alice'*$\wedge vp_1 <=t<=vp_2$. Therefore, up is specified as $\langle Bob, home/groundfloor/+/+, uid='Alice'\wedge vp_1<=t<=vp_2 \rangle$.

User preferences restrict the read access privileges which are granted by access control policies. Therefore, a subscriber subject s can read, at time t, a message m published by a user u on a topic tp iff: i) there exists an access control policy p that grants s read access to tp at time t, and ii) there exists at least one user preference up among those specified by u with a topic filter expression that is matched by tp, which grants s read access to tp.

4 OVERVIEW

The proposed mechanism, which has been designed to be used within any IoT ecosystems that use MQTT as communication protocol, leverages on an enforcement monitor which operates as a proxy between an MQTT message broker (the server) and multiple clients. It relies on a key-value datastore for the management of access control policies and user preferences. An high level view of the system architecture is shown in Figure 1.

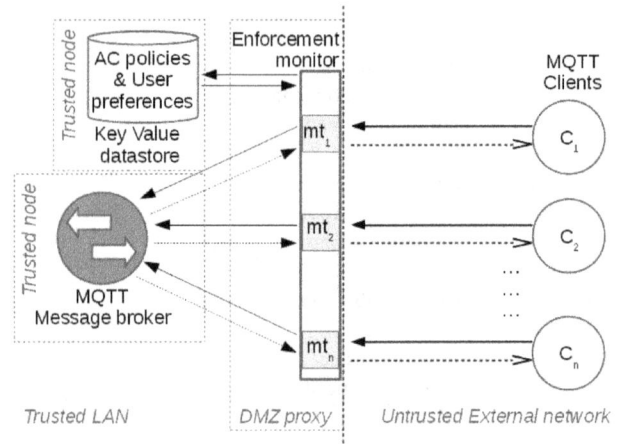

Figure 1: An high level view of the system architecture

The mechanism relies on a common architecture for proxy-based monitors (e.g., see [5]) which has been sketched in Figure 1, where: 1) MQTT brokers are deployed in a trusted LAN, 2) MQTT clients are deployed on untrusted external networks, and 3) the enforcement monitor is deployed on a DMZ proxy which operates as

---

[9]In current work we explicitly refer to subject identifiers to keep the description as simpler as possible. However, the approach can be easily extended by providing support to intensional binding expressions defined by composition of subject attributes.

[10]If no restriction is required, the predicate should be specified as a tautology.

unique interface of the trusted LAN with the external networks. We assume that firewalls placed at the interfaces of the DMZ proxy prohibit clients to open a communication channel with the message broker, which is not mediated by the DMZ proxy.

The proposed enforcement approach does not require the specification of ad-hoc designed clients or server, it only requires that clients are configured to connect to the proxy rather than directly to the server. The mechanism is independent from specific client and server versions as the proxy can operate within heterogeneous environments, where different versions of clients and server cooperate.

In order to ensure that read and write accesses to application messages comply with the specified access control policies and user preferences, the enforcement monitor analyzes and possibly alters the flow of MQTT control packets exchanged by the clients and the server. More precisely, upon receipt of a connection request cp_{CN} by a client c_i, the enforcement monitor activates a monitoring task mt_i, dedicated to the management of the flow of all control packets transiting through the considered connection. mt_i extracts the credentials of the subject from the *CONNECT* control packet received by c_i, and forwards the packet to the server. The server authenticates the requesting client and replies with a *CONNACK* control packet cp_{CA}, which is received by the proxy. mt_i forwards the control packet to the client c_i, without modifying the received packet cp_{CA}. The forwarded *CONNACK* packet cp_{CA} encodes a status code specifying whether the client request has been accepted or refused by the server, and, in the latter case, the cause. If cp_{CA} encodes the acceptance of the connection request, the client starts a communication session with the server through the proxy, otherwise no additional packet can be forwarded. The connection will be kept open by the server as long as c_i sends a *DISCONNECT* packet or the network connection is accidentally interrupted. Once connected, the client c_i can send any other control packet.

In case c_i sends a *SUBSCRIBE* control packet cp_{SB} specifying tf as topic filter, mt_i directly forwards cp_{SB} to s. The server keeps track of the topic filter tf specified by the subscription request, and sends back a *SUBACK* packet which notifies the receiving of the request. The acknowledge is received by the enforcement monitor and forwarded to the requesting client c_i.

In case of successful subscription, a client c_j, connected to s through the enforcement monitor, can send a publishing request cp_{PB} for a message on a topic tp. The monitoring thread mt_j, activated for c_j's connection, derives the access control policies that should be applied to regulate the processing of the request issued by c_j. The selected policies are those specified to constrain the publishing of messages by c_j (or by the user on behalf of whom c_j has sent the publishing request cp_{PB}), which specify a topic filter expression tf that is matched by tp. If no access control policy authorizes the publishing request, cp_{PB}'s transit is blocked, otherwise, if the request complies with at least one of the applicable policies, the publishing of cp_{PB} is authorized.

However, the publishing authorization does not imply that any subscriber of a topic filter that is matched by tp can receive the message, as the read access to cp_{PB} by a rightful subscriber rs is constrained by the access control policies that regulate the receiving of messages by rs, as well as by user preferences specified by the user on behalf of whom cp_{PB} has been issued. In order to reach a rightful subscriber, the packet still has to pass through the enforcement monitor, which, on the basis of the applicable policies and preferences, either authorizes or blocks the transit. Therefore, the monitoring task mt_j is defined in such a way to embed the user preferences of cp_{PB} sender in the payload of cp_{PB}, and to forward the resulting packet to the server. The server receives cp_{PB}, and, on the basis of the specified topic tp, transmits cp_{PB} through the connections with the rightful subscribers. If the topic tp of cp_{PB} matches the topic filter expression of cp_{SB}, the message forwarded by the server towards c_i is received by the enforcement monitor and analyzed by the monitoring task mt_i, which derives: 1) the access control policies regulating the read access to messages on topic tp by c_i, and ii) the preferences specified within cp_{PB}. The read access to cp_{PB} by c_i is authorized iff the access complies with at least one applicable access control policy, and the user preferences specified within cp_{PB} are satisfied. In case of granted authorization, mt_i removes the user preferences from cp_{PB} payload and forwards the resulting packet to c_i.

Except for *PUBLISH* control packets, all packets issued by a client or the server through an open connection which are received by the enforcement monitor are directly forwarded to the respective counterpart with no additional processing activities.

5 POLICY MANAGEMENT

The low computational capabilities of the devices typically used within IoT ecosystems require an efficient data management system with very low footprint on system resources for the management of access control policies and user preferences. The analysis of the literature in the light of these requirements, lead us to select a key-value datastore. The main service to be supported by the datastore is the derivation of the access control policies and user preferences that regulate the access to a message. Key-value datastores do not natively integrate operators supporting efficient data selection (based on data values), and the execution of exhaustive scanning of the key-space appears as an inefficient solution. We address this issue by adopting data modeling criteria which favor efficient selections. However, few key-value datastores (e.g., Redis[11] and Oracle NoSQL[12]) allow structuring the value component of the collected pairs. Value components of complex type, such as components structured as sets and data records, may be used to partition the key-space. A value in a set may correspond to the key of a record. Therefore, through the adoption of complex types, key-spaces can be organized into chunks of data, each mapped by a key, thus favoring a more efficient content-based analysis.

Let us now consider in more details the adopted modeling choices. The proposed modeling strategy aims at optimizing the execution of queries, which respectively derive:

a) the access control policies that can be applied to regulate the publishing of a message / read access to a message with a given topic by a subject.

b) the user preferences that can be applied to regulate the read access to a message with a given topic.

---

[11]https://redis.io/

[12]http://www.oracle.com/technetwork/database/database-technologies/nosqldb/documentation/index.html

To better explain the proposed design choices, let us consider how this could be handled within a traditional data management system. Let p and up be tables with a schema corresponding to the tuples in Def. 3.2 and Def. 3.4, respectively, and let us consider a pair of SQL queries, denoted qa and qb, which respectively implement the previously introduced queries a and b. Let $isMatched(tf,tp)$ be a function that checks whether a topic filter tf is matched by a topic tp. Query qa can be expressed as:

```
select p.exp from p
where p.sid=ID and isMatchedBy(p.tf,TP) and p.pr= AT
```

where ID is a parameter which refers to the identifier of the subject who wishes to publish a message / read a message on topic TP, whereas AT specifies the type of access (w/r).

Similarly, qb can be expressed as:

```
select up.sub_exp from up
where up.sid=ID and isMatchedBy(up.tf,TP)
```

where ID refers to the identifier of the user wishing to regulate the read access to a message on a topic TP by means of a user preference.

On the basis of the specified queries, let us now consider which components of p and tp should be defined as keys, and which as values of the pairs that model p and up. Within qa and qb, the projected attributes are never referred to within the *where* clauses. Therefore, the components $p.exp$ and $up.sub\_exp$ cannot be used to refer other components, and therefore, they should be specified within the value components of the respective pairs. In contrast, all attributes in the *where* clauses refer to properties of tuples included in the result set, and are compared with external parameters to perform the selection. However, for the cases of $p.sid$, $p.pr$, and $up.sid$ the value of the attribute is used as selector (it refers to a set of access control policies / user preferences), whereas for $p.tp$ and $up.tp$, an indirection is introduced, as the policies are selected on the basis of the value returned by function *isMatched*. Therefore, components $p.sid$, $p.pr$ and $up.sid$ should be part of the key components, whereas $p.tp$ and $up.tp$ should be treated as values.

It is worth noting that multiple access control policies / user preferences can be specified for the same subject /by the same user. As a consequence, we handle this *one to many* relationship modeling p by means of two pairs $\langle k_1^p, v_1^p \rangle$ and $\langle k_2^p, v_2^p \rangle$. k_1^p represents the searching key of p, and it is defined by concatenating the values of $p.sid$ and $p.pr$. Component v_2^p specifies the topic filter and the parametric predicate of p, and is thus modeled as a data record characterized by the fields tp and exp. Finally, k_2^p and v_1^p relate the topic filter and the parametric predicate within v_2^p to the searching key k_1^p, by modeling v_1^p as a set of identifiers that also includes k_2^p, the key of v_2^p.

A similar structure is defined for user preferences. up is thus modeled by the pairs $\langle k_1^{up}, v_1^{up} \rangle$ and $\langle k_2^{up}, v_2^{up} \rangle$, where k_1^{up} corresponds to $up.sid$, v_2^{up} is a data record characterized by the fields tp and sub_exp, v_1^{up} is a set of references that also includes the value of k_2^{up}, which represents the storing key of v_2^{up}.

Due to the ability to handle structured values, such as sets and hash-sets (records), the low system requirements and very good

performance, the enforcement mechanism has been developed on top of Redis[11], a very popular key-value datastore.[13]

6 THE ENFORCEMENT MECHANISM

Let us now focus on the proposed enforcement mechanism, which is presented referring to the system architecture that is shown in Figure 2. The enforcement monitor has been designed in such a way to include a connection handler that continuously listens for upcoming network connection requests by MQTT clients which desire to interact with the server.

Once the enforcement monitor receives the request to open a network connection from a client c_i, it enables a communication channel cc_{c_i} with c_i, and a channel $cc_s^{c_i}$ with the server s. Simultaneously, a monitoring task mt_i is instantiated to regulate the control packets flowing through cc_{c_i} and $cc_s^{c_i}$, and four message queues, denoted in_{c_i}, out_{c_i}, $in_s^{c_i}$ and $out_s^{c_i}$ [14] are associated with cc_{c_i}, and $cc_s^{c_i}$, to temporary collect the input packets for the enforcement monitor, and the output packets for s and c_i, respectively. A set of packet handlers operate encoding the control packets that have been issued by s and c_i, and adding them to the respective input queues, whereas, a second set dequeues the packets directed to s and c_i from the output queues, and transmit them through the related channels.

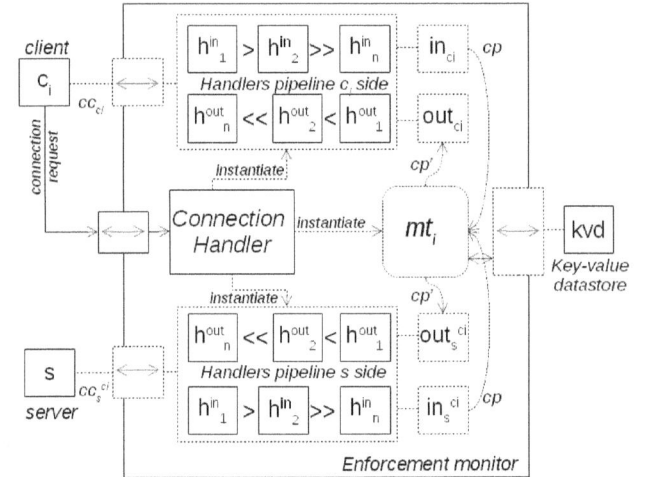

Figure 2: Enforcement monitor architecture

The monitoring task mt_i forwards to the server all control packets cp received by the enforcement monitor that have been issued by a client, except for those packets encoding connection and publishing requests, which are first analyzed and manipulated, and then sent to the server, back to the client, or blocked. Similarly, it sends all packets received from the server to the rightful clients, with the exception of PUBLISH packets, which once analyzed, are either modified and forwarded to the clients, or blocked.

mt_i executes different sub-tasks on the basis of the type t of cp, or directly forwards the packet to the respective receiver, if no

---

[13]Recent surveys show Redis as the most diffused key-value datastore, see https://db-engines.com/en/ranking

[14]in and out denote the verse of the packet flow with respect to the monitor, whereas the subscript c_i /s^{c_i} denote the sender/receiver of the flow.

additional analysis is required. All sub-tasks return a control packet cp', which, on the basis of cp type, content and provenance, and of the applicable access control policies and user preferences may: i) specify the same content as cp; ii) specify a new content while preserving t as control packet type, iii) specify a new content and type, or iv) specify a null content. If not null, the returned packet is added to one of the output message queues (the choice depends on cp sender and cp' content), from which it will be withdrawn and forwarded to the rightful receiver. In contrast, if cp' is null, the flow is blocked.

In the remainder of this section, we discuss the monitoring activities for control packets of different types.

6.1 Connection requests

When a client c_i wishes to publish or receive messages, it issues a control packet cp_{CR} of type CONNECT through cc_{c_i}, which models a connection request to a server. cp_{CR} specifies the identifier of c_i, and, optionally, the identifier of the user who has forwarded the request by means of c_i.

The monitor relies on the authentication mechanism of the message broker for authenticating the requesting user. The monitor simply identifies the requesting user by extracting credential data from the CONNECT packet cp_{CR}. More precisely, the monitoring sub-task $handleConnect(cp_{CR})$ executed by mt_i, extracts the client and user identifiers from cp_{CR} and adds them to ch, an hash table field of the monitoring task mt_i, which keeps track of all properties related to the monitored connection. Properties are thus modeled as key-value pairs, and the derived user and client identifiers are referred to by the keys uid and cid. The execution of $handleConnect(cp_{CR})$ returns to mt_i a control packet cp_{CR}' that exactly matches the control packet cp_{CR} received as input. Finally, mt_i adds cp_{CR} to the output message queue of channel $cc_s^{c_i}$, forwarding the request to the server on behalf of the subject.

6.2 Publishing requests by clients

A client c_i requests to publish a message on a topic by issuing a PUBLISH control packet through an open connection. Let us denote with cp_{PB} a PUBLISH control packet that has been issued by c_i through cc_{c_i}, which includes the message payload pl, the message topic tp, and the requested quality of service level qos. The enforcement monitor must check whether the subject is entitled to publish messages on tp or the request must be blocked. Therefore, it calls function $handlePublishFromClient$, whose pseudocode is shown in Listing 1. The function first calculates the key dk to be used with the key-value datastore, referred to as kvd, for selecting the applicable access control policies (see Section 5). dk maps a set $pSet$ of identifiers, each representing the storing key of an access control policy that grants to the subject write privileges for messages on a set of topics. An access control policy acp belonging to the set referred to by dk is applicable to the publishing request if the topic filter expression tf of acp is matched by tp, the topic of the message to be published, referred to within cp_{PB}. $handlePublishFromClient$ relies on function $isMatched(tp, tf)$ to check whether the topic tp specified within cp_{PB} matches the filter expression of the candidate policy acp.

Listing 1: Function handlePublishFromClient

```
1  function handlePublishFromClient(cpPB){
2    boolean authorized=false;
3    var dk=getPolicyKey(ch,cpPB);
4    if(kvd.exists(dk){
5      var pSet=dkv.smembers(dk);
6      for(pid ∈ pSet){
7        var acp=dkv.get(pid);
8        if(isMatched(acp.tf,topicOf(cpPB){
9          authorized=authorized ∨ evalPP(acp.exp,cpPB,ch);
10         if(authorized) break;
11       }
12     }
13   }
14   if(!authorized){
15     switch(qos(cpPB)) {
16       case 2: return genPUBREC(cpPB);
17       case 1: return genPUBACK(cpPB);
18       case 0:
19       default: return null;
20     }
21   }
22   else{
23     var upk=getUserPreferenceKey(ch);
24     var cpp="true"
25     if(kvd.exists(upk){
26       var upidSet=dkv.smembers(upk);
27       cpp="false"
28       for(upid ∈ upidSet){
29         var up=dkv.get(upid);
30         if(isMatched(up.tf,topicOf(cpPB){
31           cpp=cpp+" ∨ ("+up.exp+")";
32         }
33       }
34     }
35     return embedCPP(cpp, cpPB);
36   }
37 }
```

If this is verified, acp is evaluated. The enforcement monitor is defined in such a way to grant the publishing privilege to the subject, if the request encoded by cp_{PB} complies with at least one of the applicable access control policies. Therefore, if the parametric predicate exp referred to by acp is satisfied, the forwarding of cp_{PB} to the server can be authorized. $handlePublishFromClient$ relies on function $evalPP$ for the evaluation of the parametric predicate exp of acp. The evaluation is performed wrt the set of subject, object and environment attributes characterizing the context within which cp_{PB} has been received. Then, the enforcement monitor integrates into the payload of cp_{PB}, the parametric predicates of the user preferences possibly specified by the user on behalf of whom cp_{PB} has been sent, which may be used to regulate the read access to cp_{PB} by any rightful subscriber. To this aim, $handlePublishFromClient$ has to select the set of user preferences which should be used to protect the access to cp_{PB}, and derive a composite parametric predicate cpp to be integrated into cp_{PB}. The predicate is defined by disjunction of the predicates of the applicable preferences. If no applicable user preference exists, no further restrictions are specified to constrain the access to cp_{PB}, and, therefore, cpp is set to $true$.

Function $getUserPreferenceKey$ is invoked by $handlePublishFromClient$ to calculate the key upk to select, from kvd, the applicable user preferences. For any identifier $upid$ in $upidSet$, the user preference up referred to by $upid$ can be applied to cp_{PB} iff the topic filter expression tf of up is matched by the topic tp specified within cp_{PB}. cpp is initialized to $"false"$, and if the topic filter expression tf of up

is matched by the topic tp,[15] the parametric predicate within up is added as disjunct to cpp. Finally, function $embedCPP$ is invoked to integrate cpp into the cp_{PB} payload. $embedCPP$ derives the number of bytes required to represent cpp, referred to as $cppsize$, and then reinitialize the payload of cp_{PB} placing $cppsize$ and cpp before the original payload of the packet. The updated PUBLISH control packet cp'_{PB} is finally returned to mt_i, which, once identified the type of the returned control packet, adds it to $out_s^{c_i}$, the queue of packets for s, from which it will be withdrawn and forwarded to the server.

In contrast, if the access performed by cp_{PB} does not comply with any of the applicable access control policies, the control packet cannot be forwarded to the server. In this case, on the basis of the quality of service level qos specified within cp_{PB}, three different scenarios can occurr. If qos is set to 0, $handlePublishFromClient$ returns a $null$ object, and, as a consequence, mt_i blocks the control packet. In contrast, if cp_{PB} specifies 1 / 2 as quality of service level, c_i must be informed that cp_{PB} has been received, by means of a PUBACK / PUBREC packet, respectively. These acknowledgement packets are directly generated by the enforcement monitor, which simulates the behavior of a server upon receipt of a PUBLISH control packet with quality of service level 1 / 2. The generated packet is finally returned to mt_i, to be forwarded to c_i.

6.3 Publishing requests by the server

Once the server receives a publish request cp_{PB} from the enforcement monitor (as a consequence of a publish request originally sent by a client), it forwards a copy of cp_{PB} via all the communication channels through which it has received a subscription request with a topic filter that is matched by the topic of cp_{PB}. Any copy of cp_{PB} that is forwarded by s is received by the enforcement monitor and analyzed by a distinct monitoring task that has been activated for a specific client-server connection. Let us hereafter focus on a single monitoring task, denoted mt_j, activated for the connection related to the subscriber client c_j. cp_{PB} is recognized by mt_j as a publishing request that has been issued by the server. Therefore, mt_j calls function $handlePublishFromServer$, whose pseudocode is shown in Listing 2.

The initial tasks of $handlePublishFromServer$ are the same as those performed by function $handlePublishFromClient$ (cfr. Listings 2 and 1). Therefore, $handlePublishFromServer$ extracts from kvd, all access control policies which grant read access privileges to c_j, selects the policies whose topic filters are matched by the topic within cp_{PB}, and finally evaluates the related parametric predicates. If at least one of these predicates is satisfied, $handlePublishFromServer$ analyzes the user preferences specified within cp_{PB}. $handlePublishFromServer$ relies on function $deriveCPP$ to extract from cp_{PB} payload the composite parametric predicate specifying the user preferences. The first 4 bytes of cp_{PB} payload encode $cppsize$, namely the number of bytes that have been used to encode the composite parametric predicate cpp.

Therefore, the parametric predicate expression cpp is derived from the bytes in the range $5..cppsize$, and it is finally analyzed by function $evalPP$, which evaluates cpp with respect to the set of attributes characterizing the connection at current time. If cpp is

---

Listing 2: Function handlePublishFromServer

```
1  function handlePublishFromServer(cpPB){
2    var authorized=false;
3    var dk=getPolicyKey(ch,cpPB,r);
4    if(kvd.exists(dk){
5      var pSet=dkv.smembers(dk);
6      for(pid ∈ pSet){
7        var acp=dkv.get(pid);
8        if(isMatched(acp.tf,topicOf(cpPB){
9          authorized=authorized ∨ evalPP(acp.exp,cpPB,ch);
10         if(authorized) break;
11       }
12     }
13   }
14   if(authorized){
15     var cpp=deriveCPP(cpPB);
16     if(evalPP(cpp,cpPB,ch)) return pruneCPP(cpPB);
17   }
18   return null;
19 }
```

satisfied, $handlePublishFromServer$ invokes function $pruneCPP$ to delete the initial $cppsize+4$ bytes of cp_{PB} payload, restoring the payload of the control packet originally sent by cp_{PB} publisher. The resulting packet is returned to mt_j, which adds the packet to the queue out_{c_j}, from which it will be withdrawn and forwarded to c_j.

In contrast, if the keyspace of kvd does not include dk, or if an access control policy authorizing the read access to cp_{PB} by c_j does not exist, or if cpp is not satisfied, $handlePublishFromServer$ returns $null$, and, consequently, mt_j blocks the transit of cp_{PB} towards c_j.

7 PERFORMANCE ANALYSIS

In this section we assess the performance of the proposed enforcement mechanism in a variety of scenarios. The monitor has been implemented by a Java-based prototype relying on:

- Netty[16], a popular Java-based asynchronous event-driven network application framework, for the management of network connections as well as the handling of MQTT control packets encoding and decoding;
- Redis [17], for the management of access control policies and user preferences;
- Jedis[18], a lightweight Java-based Redis client, to manage the interaction of the enforcement monitor with Redis.

In particular, we analyze the *message transmission time*, namely the time spent by a published message to reach a rightful subscriber. The overhead is calculated by comparing the transmission time in a deployment where a set of access control policies have been specified, and an enforcement monitor is active, with deployments with the same clients configuration, but where clients are directly connected to the server.

With the proposed experiments we aim to assess the performance of the enforcement monitor prototype in stressful conditions, considering a variety of system configurations. In particular, each configuration is characterized by: i) a server, hosted by a node; ii) the enforcement monitor, hosted by a node which is not necessarily

---

[15]The check is performed by function $isMatched(tp, tf)$.

[16]https://netty.io/
[17]https://redis.io
[18]https://github.com/xetorthio/jedis

the same that host the server, and a set of subscriber and publisher clients, all deployed on a third node. For the experiments, we used *Mosquitto* 1.4.10[19] as MQTT message broker, whereas the related publisher / subscriber processes mosquitto_pub / mosquitto_sub have been used as MQTT clients. Finally, a Raspberry Pi 3 Model B[20] (64bit Quad Core and 1 GB RAM) and two desktop PCs both equipped with an i7 64bit Quad Core CPU and 16GB of RAM have been used as hosting nodes. The five different deployments that have been considered for the experiments are summarized in Table 2.

Table 2: System deployments

	Server	Proxy	Clients
d_1	Raspberry Pi	Not active	PC_2
d_2	Raspberry Pi	Raspberry Pi	PC_2
d_3	PC_1	Raspberry Pi	PC_2
d_4	PC_1	Not active	PC_2
d_5	PC_1	PC_1	PC_2

The overhead has been analyzed comparing the transmission times measured for the same configuration of clients, access control policies and user preferences in each of the considered deployment.

With the aim to assess the scalability of the proposed approach, the analysis is repeated by varying the number of clients which are contemporary connected to the server, either through the proxy, or directly, if the enforcement monitor is not included in the considered scenario. A different set of experiments has been executed for scenarios composed of 50, 100, 250, 500, 750 and 1000 subscribers, each including 1000 publishers. The above mentioned scenarios, hereafter referred to as $s_1..s_6$, are summarized in Table 3.

Table 3: Configuration scenarios

	s_1	s_2	s_3	s_4	s_5	s_6
subscribers	50	100	250	500	750	1000
publishers	1000	1000	1000	1000	1000	1000

7.1 Experiments configuration

Let us now consider key aspects related to clients set up and policy/preference specification for a given scenario s_i.

Let *USet* and *CSet* denote the set of user and client identifiers considered for scenario s_i. The topic tree *tt* to be considered in a given scenario has been randomly generated in such a way that each node can have 0 to 5 children, the maximum height of the three is 5, and each node is labeled with a unique identifier. We believe that these dimensions are sufficient for assessing complex routing scenarios. The proposed values are in line with the use cases presented in MQTT's literature (e.g., see https://www.hivemq.com/blog/mqtt-essentials-part-5-mqtt-topics-best-practices). The topic tree has been generated as we are not aware of complete topic trees with comparable dimensions.

Any subscriber client *sc* within s_i is configured in such a way to issue a subscription request specifying: i) *cid* / *uid* as client / user identifier (where *cid* ∈ *CSet* and *uid* ∈ *USet*), ii) a topic filter *tf* randomly generated starting from *tt*, and iii) a random *qos* level from the admissible values 0..2.

Similarly, any publisher client *pc* within s_i issues a publishing request specifying: i) *cid* / *uid* as client / user identifier (where *cid* ∈ *CSet* and *uid* ∈ *USet*), ii) a topic *tp* randomly selected from *tt*, iii) a payload *pl*, specifying a message identifier, and the timestamp related to the publishing request, and iv) a *qos* level randomly selected from the range of admissible values.

The access control policies and user preferences specified for s_i have been synthetically defined, as we are not aware of benchmarks for policies and user preferences tailored for the considered application scenario. The generation process has been carried out as follows. The topic filter expressions of both access control policies and user preferences (components *tf* of *p* / *up* in Def. 3.2/ Def. 3.4, respectively) have been randomly generated starting from the topic tree *tt*. The parametric predicates of access control policies (component *exp* in Def. 3.2) have been defined by randomly specifying the daily time slots during which the access is allowed (e.g., *8≤t.getHours()≤17*), whereas the predicates of user preferences (component *sub_exp* in Def. 3.4) specify time slots and/or the identifiers of the users who can perform the access (*s.uid='u5'*). The privileges granted by access control policies (component *pr* of *p* in Def. 3.2) have been randomly selected, whereas, by definition, user preferences only grant read access privileges. The subjects constrained by access control policies (component *sid* of *p* in Def. 3.2) have been randomly selected from *CSet* and *USet*, whereas those specifying the user preferences, have been selected from *USet*.

7.2 Logging facilities

The subscriber clients involved in a scenario are configured to keep track of the transmission time of the received messages. More precisely, the subscribers are invoked in such a way that each line of the client standard output is redirected to an analyzer process.[21] The analyzer task extracts the timestamp within the payload of the received message, and subtracts it from the timestamp associated with the received message (i.e., the time at which the analyzer task has been invoked). Since in each considered scenario the subscriber and publisher clients are hosted by the same node (see Table 3), all clients share the same clock, and thus, the resulting value represents the milliseconds elapsed from the publishing request to the receiving of the message. The analyzer task also extracts the identifier of the received message from the payload, and keeps track of the measured transmission time within a key value datastore (an additional instance of Redis hosted by the same node that hosts all clients). Along with the transmission time, the analyzer keeps track of the identifiers of : i) the received message, ii) the receiver subject, iii) the considered scenario, and iv) the deployment within which the measure has been done.

The proposed logging facility favors the analysis of the enforcement overhead. More precisely, the transmission time of a message *msg* measured for a subject *sid* in a scenario s_i related to a deployment d_j where the enforcement monitor is active, can be compared

---

[19]Eclipse Mosquitto, is an open source lightweight MQTT broker - https://mosquitto.org/

[20]https://www.raspberrypi.org/

---

[21]*xarg* and *awk* have been used for this purpose.

with the transmission time related to *msg* received by *sid*, within s_i in a deployment d_j where all clients are directly connected to the server. The observed offset provides a fine grained measure of the enforcement overhead related to the receiving of a single message. These values can be aggregated to derive the average overhead that has been observed per subject, and per scenario.

7.3 Experiments

A first set of experiments have been run to analyze the overhead in deployments where devices with reduced computational capacity host the enforcement monitor or the server. The considered deployments aim at showing the behavior of the proposed mechanism with devices with computational capacity aligned with the one typically characterizing the devices used within IoT ecosystems.

The diagram in Figure 3 shows the average transmission time per scenario (see Table 3), which has been measured within deployments d_1, d_2 and d_3 (see Table 2).

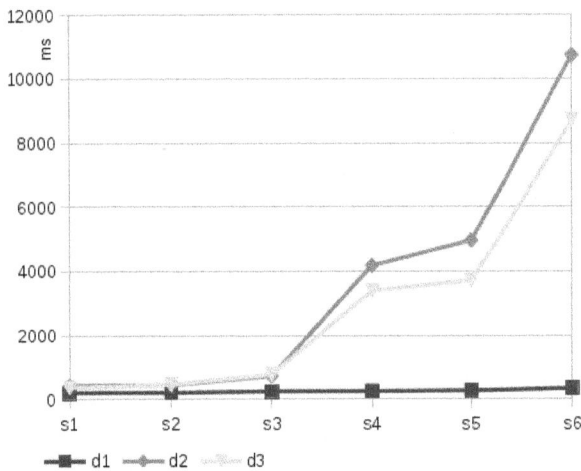

Figure 3: The average message transmission time (in ms) per scenario s_i within the deployments d_1, d_2 and d_3. The scenarios s_1, s_2, s_3 s_4, s_5 and s_6 respectively consider 50, 100, 250, 500, 750 and 1000 subscribers, receiving messages generated by 1000 publishers.

The measures have been derived starting from a set of messages generated by the involved publisher clients (one message per client), which are received, in each scenario, by a different number of clients.

The measures observed with d_1, where no enforcement monitor is configured, clearly show the lowest values, with a small growth of the transmission time associated with the growth of the involved clients. The red line shows the transmission time related to deployment d_2, where the enforcement monitor and the server are hosted by the same node, a Raspberry Pi. The observable enforcement overhead is reasonably low (~150ms) for scenarios s_1, s_2 and s_3, but it significantly grows for s_4, s_5 and s_6, where the number of contemporary connected clients goes over 1500 units. This sudden and unexpected growth seems ascribable to the inefficient

garbage collection mechanism implemented by Netty[22], the library implementing the networking facilities of the enforcement monitor prototype. The more messages are sent, the more garbage is created, and if the rate with which new messages are generated is higher than the rate with which the garbage collector is called, the enforcement monitor consumes all its random access memory. Once no more RAM memory is available, time expensive swap operations are necessary, with related significant overhead, which is visible in Figure 3. It is worth noting that this technological issue, which affects the prototype is not directly related to the enforcement mechanism, and can be addressed using alternative networking technologies (e.g., CoralReactor) for future monitor versions, which promise to handle message transmission without producing any garbage (e.g., see http://www.coralblocks.com/index.php/coralreactor-vs-netty-performance-comparison/).

A similar trend is also visible with deployment d_3, where the proxy and the server are hosted by different nodes. The time overhead observed for s_1, s_2 and s_3 matches the one of d_2 for the same scenarios. A significant growth of the average transmission time is again observable for s_4, s_5 and s_6, however the growth is lower than the one observed with d_2. As a matter of fact, within d_3 the enforcement monitor does not need to share memory with the message broker process, as this is hosted by a separate node, and thus the activation of the swapping mechanism is delayed. Overall, the performed empirical analysis shows better results for deployments where the server and the monitor are hosted by separate nodes.

A second set of experiments have been executed to assess the time overhead in scenarios with full fledged general purpose hardware. As a matter of fact, in some application contexts, a message broker may be hosted by a commodity server, which might also host the enforcement monitor.

Figure 4 shows the average transmission time that has been measured for scenarios $s_1..s_6$ (see Table 3) within deployments d_4 and d_5 (see Table 2).

The blue line shows the average transmission time (per scenario), related to deployment d_4, which does not include any enforcement monitor. The derived values show a small growth of the transmission time consequent to an higher number of active clients. The observed trend is almost linear.

The red line shows the measures related to d_5, a deployment where the enforcement monitor and the server are hosted by the same node. The observed transmission time grows jointly with the number of connected clients. The related overhead is generally very low (<100ms) for all scenarios, except s_6, where it significantly grows up until it reaches ~300ms, but which still appears as a reasonable cost. In this case, due to the higher quantity of RAM that can be used by the enforcement monitor, the inefficient garbage collection management operated by Netty has a lower impact on system performance. Indeed, the observed measures shows that in this scenario, the monitor can handle up to 1750 contemporary connections with a small impact on the overhead.

It is worth noting that smart home and smart fitness scenarios similar to those considered in previous sections of the paper, are expected to include no more than a few hundreds of clients

---

[22]http://www.coralblocks.com/index.php/coralreactor-vs-netty-performance-comparison/

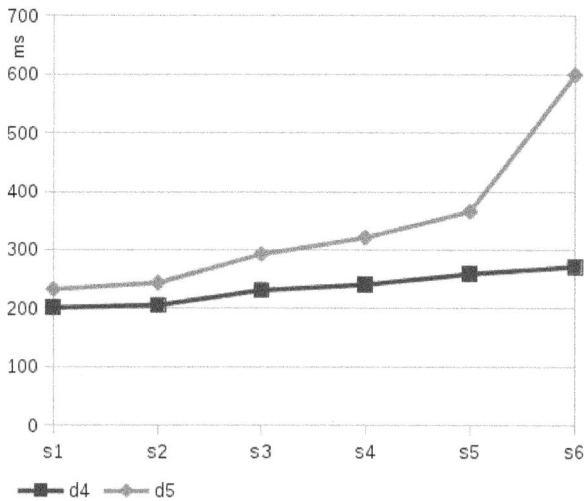

Figure 4: The average message transmission time (in ms) per scenario s_i within the deployments d_4, and d_5. The scenarios s_1, s_2, s_3 s_4, s_5 and s_6 respectively consider 50, 100, 250, 500, 750 and 1000 subscribers, receiving messages generated by 1000 publishers.

monitor that allows enforcing CapBAC policies, and, in the future we will target additional access control models, such as UCON and RBAC. Further, we are investigating extensions of the proposed enforcement mechanism that aim at supporting content based access control policies. We believe that their efficient enforcement within MQTT-based environments represents a very ambitious research challenge.

For future versions of the enforcement monitor we are also considering the adoption of networking technologies with a lower impact on system resources, which would allow handling a higher number of contemporary connected clients with lower time overhead. We are also working on extensions of the proposed framework to handle ecosystems where multiple message brokers are bridged together, and message topics are possibly remapped before they are forwarded to the respective clients. Finally, we are starting to apply the proposed framework to a realistic case study related to a smart home application.

contemporary producing and consuming messages. Overall, both the rate with which the messages are generated and the number of contemporary connected clients are expected to be lower than those which have been considered in this stress use case.

Considering all these aspects, and the overhead which has been measured with both the experiments sets, we derive that the enforcement monitor prototype shows a satisfactory efficiency level when it handles up to 1250 connections, with an average overhead lower than 150ms observed in deployments where the monitor is hosted by a Raspberry (see $d2$ and $d3$ in Figure 3), and even lower than 80ms in deployments where the monitor is hosted by a PC (see $d5$ in Figure 4).

8 CONCLUSIONS

This paper presented an effective solution to enforce access control within MQTT-based IoT ecosystems. An ABAC model is used to regulate message passing by means of access control policies and user preferences. The corresponding enforcement monitor has been designed to operate as a proxy between MQTT clients and an MQTT server. The monitor enforces access control policies and user preferences by intercepting and possibly manipulating the flow of exchanged MQTT control packets. Early experimental evaluations have overall shown low enforcement overhead.

Our work is still progressing in manifold directions.

We are working on tools supporting user preferences and access control policies specification, which provide predefined templates of access control rules specified in natural language to the end users, and wizards supporting composition of access control rules. The goal of this specification toolkit is to hide syntactical aspects of policy specification, favoring a security and privacy aware use of IoT applications. We are also designing an extended version of the

REFERENCES

[1] A. Alshehri and R. Sandhu. 2016. Access Control Models for Cloud-Enabled Internet of Things: A Proposed Architecture and Research Agenda. In *2016 IEEE 2nd International Conference on Collaboration and Internet Computing (CIC)*. 530–538. https://doi.org/10.1109/CIC.2016.081

[2] A. Alshehri and R. Sandhu. 2017. Access Control Models for Virtual Object Communication in Cloud-Enabled IoT. In *2017 IEEE International Conference on Information Reuse and Integration (IRI)*. 16–25. https://doi.org/10.1109/IRI.2017.60

[3] Smriti Bhatt, Farhan Patwa, and Ravi Sandhu. 2017. Access Control Model for AWS Internet of Things. In *Network and System Security*, Zheng Yan, Refik Molva, Wojciech Mazurczyk, and Raimo Kantola (Eds.). Springer International Publishing, Cham, 721–736.

[4] S. Bhatt, F. Patwa, and R. Sandhu. 2018. An Access Control Framework for Cloud-Enabled Wearable Internet of Things. In *2017 IEEE 3rd International Conference on Collaboration and Internet Computing (CIC)*, Vol. 00. 328–338. https://doi.org/10.1109/CIC.2017.00050

[5] P. Colombo and E. Ferrari. 2017. Enhancing MongoDB with Purpose-Based Access Control. *IEEE Transactions on Dependable and Secure Computing* 14, 6 (Nov 2017), 591–604. https://doi.org/10.1109/TDSC.2015.2497680

[6] David F. Ferraiolo, Ravi Sandhu, Serban Gavrila, D. Richard Kuhn, and Ramaswamy Chandramouli. 2001. Proposed NIST Standard for Role-based Access Control. *ACM Trans. Inf. Syst. Secur.* 4, 3 (Aug. 2001), 224–274. https://doi.org/10.1145/501978.501980

[7] Sergio Gusmeroli, Salvatore Piccione, and Domenico Rotondi. 2013. A capability-based security approach to manage access control in the Internet of Things. *Mathematical and Computer Modelling* 58, 5 (2013), 1189 – 1205. https://doi.org/10.1016/j.mcm.2013.02.006 The Measurement of Undesirable Outputs: Models Development and Empirical Analyses and Advances in mobile, ubiquitous and cognitive computing.

[8] M. Hemdi and R. Deters. 2016. Using REST based protocol to enable ABAC within IoT systems. In *2016 IEEE 7th Annual Information Technology, Electronics and Mobile Communication Conference (IEMCON)*. 1–7. https://doi.org/10.1109/IEMCON.2016.7746297

[9] José L Hernández-Ramos, Antonio J Jara, Leandro Marin, and Antonio F Skarmeta. 2013. Distributed capability-based access control for the internet of things. *Journal of Internet Services and Information Security (JISIS)* 3, 3/4 (2013), 1–16.

[10] Vincent C Hu, David Ferraiolo, Rick Kuhn, Arthur R Friedman, Alan J Lang, Margaret M Cogdell, Adam Schnitzer, Kenneth Sandlin, Robert Miller, Karen Scarfone, et al. 2013. Guide to attribute based access control (ABAC) definition and considerations (draft). *NIST special publication* 800, 162 (2013).

[11] V. C. Hu, D. R. Kuhn, and D. F. Ferraiolo. 2015. Attribute-Based Access Control. *Computer* 48, 2 (Feb 2015), 85–88. https://doi.org/10.1109/MC.2015.33

[12] Xin Jin, Ram Krishnan, and Ravi Sandhu. 2012. A Unified Attribute-Based Access Control Model Covering DAC, MAC and RBAC. In *Data and Applications Security and Privacy XXVI*, Nora Cuppens-Boulahia, Frédéric Cuppens, and Joaquin Garcia-Alfaro (Eds.). Springer Berlin Heidelberg, Berlin, Heidelberg, 41–55.

[13] Sun Kaiwen and Yin Lihua. 2014. Attribute-Role-Based Hybrid Access Control in the Internet of Things. In *Web Technologies and Applications*, Weihong Han, Zi Huang, Changjun Hu, Hongli Zhang, and Li Guo (Eds.). Springer International Publishing, Cham, 333–343.

[14] Antonio La Marra, Fabio Martinelli, Paolo Mori, Athanasios Rizos, and Andrea Saracino. 2017. Improving MQTT by Inclusion of Usage Control. In *Security, Privacy, and Anonymity in Computation, Communication, and Storage*, Guojun

Wang, Mohammed Atiquzzaman, Zheng Yan, and Kim-Kwang Raymond Choo (Eds.). Springer International Publishing, Cham, 545–560.

[15] Antonio La Marra, Fabio Martinelli, Paolo Mori, Athanasios Rizos, and Andrea Saracino. 2018. Introducing Usage Control in MQTT. In *Computer Security*, Sokratis K. Katsikas, Frédéric Cuppens, Nora Cuppens, Costas Lambrinoudakis, Christos Kalloniatis, John Mylopoulos, Annie Antón, and Stefanos Gritzalis (Eds.). Springer International Publishing, Cham, 35–43.

[16] Parikshit N Mahalle, Bayu Anggorojati, Neeli R Prasad, Ramjee Prasad, et al. 2013. Identity authentication and capability based access control (iacac) for the internet of things. *Journal of Cyber Security and Mobility* 1, 4 (2013), 309–348.

[17] Y. D. Marinakis, S. T. Walsh, and R. Harms. 2017. Internet of Things Technology Diffusion Forecasts. In *2017 Portland International Conference on Management of Engineering and Technology (PICMET)*. 1–5. https://doi.org/10.23919/PICMET.2017.8125435

[18] A. L. Marra, F. Martinelli, P. Mori, and A. Saracino. 2017. Implementing Usage Control in Internet of Things: A Smart Home Use Case. In *2017 IEEE Trustcom/BigDataSE/ICESS*. 1056–1063. https://doi.org/10.1109/Trustcom/BigDataSE/ICESS.2017.352

[19] A. Ouaddah, I. Bouij-Pasquier, A. Abou Elkalam, and A. Ait Ouahman. 2015. Security analysis and proposal of new access control model in the Internet of Thing. In *2015 International Conference on Electrical and Information Technologies (ICEIT)*. 30–35. https://doi.org/10.1109/EITech.2015.7162936

[20] Aafaf Ouaddah, Hajar Mousannif, Anas Abou Elkalam, and Abdellah Ait Ouahman. 2017. Access control in the Internet of Things: Big challenges and new opportunities. *Computer Networks* 112 (2017), 237 – 262. https://doi.org/10.1016/j.comnet.2016.11.007

[21] Qasim Mahmood Rajpoot, Christian Damsgaard Jensen, and Ram Krishnan. 2015. Integrating Attributes into Role-Based Access Control. In *Data and Applications Security and Privacy XXIX*, Pierangela Samarati (Ed.). Springer International Publishing, Cham, 242–249.

[22] Guoping Zhang and Jiazheng Tian. 2010. An extended role based access control model for the Internet of Things. In *2010 International Conference on Information, Networking and Automation (ICINA)*, Vol. 1. V1–319–V1–323. https://doi.org/10.1109/ICINA.2010.5636381

[23] Xinwen Zhang, Francesco Parisi-Presicce, Ravi Sandhu, and Jaehong Park. 2005. Formal Model and Policy Specification of Usage Control. *ACM Trans. Inf. Syst. Secur.* 8, 4 (Nov. 2005), 351–387. https://doi.org/10.1145/1108906.1108908

A Lazy Approach to Access Control as a Service (ACaaS) for IoT
An AWS Case Study

Tahir Ahmad
Security & Trust Unit, FBK-ICT, Trento, Italy
DIBRIS, University of Genova, Italy
ahmad@fbk.eu

Umberto Morelli
Security & Trust Unit, FBK-ICT, Trento, Italy
umorelli@fbk.eu

Silvio Ranise
Security & Trust Unit, FBK-ICT, Trento, Italy
ranise@fbk.eu

Nicola Zannone
Eindhoven University of Technology, The Netherlands
n.zannone@tue.nl

ABSTRACT

The Internet of Things (IoT) is receiving considerable attention from both industry and academia because of the new business models that it enables and the new security and privacy challenges that it generates. Major Cloud Service Providers (CSPs) have proposed platforms to support IoT by combining cloud and edge computing. However, the security mechanisms available in the cloud have been extended to IoT with some shortcomings with respect to the management and enforcement of access control policies. Access Control as a Service (ACaaS) is emerging as a solution to overcome these difficulties. The paper proposes a lazy approach to ACaaS that allows the specification and management of policies independently of the CSP while leveraging its enforcement mechanisms. We demonstrate the approach by investigating (also experimentally) alternative deployments in the IoT platform offered by Amazon Web Services on a realistic smart lock solution.

CCS CONCEPTS

• **Security and privacy** → **Access control**; **Authorization**;

KEYWORDS

Internet of Things; Policy specification and management; Attribute-Based Access Control; IoT platforms; Edge Computing

ACM Reference Format:
Tahir Ahmad, Umberto Morelli, Silvio Ranise, and Nicola Zannone. 2018. A Lazy Approach to Access Control as a Service (ACaaS) for IoT: An AWS Case Study. In *SACMAT '18: The 23rd ACM Symposium on Access Control Models & Technologies (SACMAT), June 13–15, 2018, Indianapolis, IN, USA*. ACM, New York, NY, USA, 12 pages. https://doi.org/10.1145/3205977.3205989

1 INTRODUCTION

The Internet of Things (IoT) holds the promise to bring huge benefits for users, industry, and society by combining the capabilities of collecting large amount of data over long periods of time

with substantial processing capabilities and low-latency communication. However, the convergence of these technologies raises significant security and privacy concerns. To mitigate these risks, access control plays a key role for providing controlled information sharing—a necessary condition to build privacy into IoT solutions—and integrity guarantees—a crucial pre-requisite for the correct functioning of an entire IoT system.

Traditional approaches to access control (see, e.g., [16]) are not adequate for IoT due to several sources of complexity, including the heterogeneity and large number of connected devices (e.g, different types of sensors distributed in many locations), resource constraints (on processing, storage and communication), interaction patterns (from stable and long-lived to casual and short-lived), and augmented context awareness (such as time, location, and mode of operation of a system) [13]. As a result, the management and enforcement of access control policies become daunting tasks that hinder the deployment of secure and privacy-aware IoT solutions with negative consequences on their adoption by users because of a lack of trust.

In an attempt to combine large scale data processing and low-latency communication for IoT solutions, Cloud Service Providers (CSPs)—such as Amazon, Google, and Microsoft—started extending their cloud computing platform with support for edge computing. At the same time, CSPs offer refinements of their access control mechanisms with the aim of satisfying the requirements posed by IoT solutions on the management and enforcement of security policies. Unfortunately, such offerings are not satisfactory as they suffer serious drawbacks such as: *(D1)* limited support for policy administration, *(D2)* proprietary policy languages (which increase the risk of vendor lock-in), and *(D3)* limited expressiveness in specifying complex authorization conditions that depend on a multitude of resources and contextual attributes.

To alleviate drawbacks *(D1)*, *(D2)* and *(D3)*, we propose a *lazy* approach to Access Control as a Service (ACaaS) tailored to IoT solutions and built on top of existing IoT platforms. ACaaS allows one to outsource the administration and enforcement of access control policies to a trusted third party. The advantages of ACaaS are several and include a comprehensive and uniform support for policy administration—addressing *(D1)* together with an expressive and high-level (independent of a particular CSP) policy specification language—addressing both *(D2)* and *(D3)*.

The main difference between ours and most existing ACaaS solutions [1, 6, 7, 10] is that we outsource the management but not the enforcement of policies and prefer to reuse the enforcement mechanisms provided by each CSP. Following and extending the approach introduced in [12], we do this by translating a high-level policy language based on Attribute Based Access Control (ABAC) [9] to the policy language adopted by a given CSP. This allows us, on the one hand, to reuse well-engineered, robust, and tested enforcement mechanisms and, one the other hand, reduce the overhead due to the invocation of an external evaluation point for every authorization request. An additional advantage is in speeding up authorization request evaluation by exploiting the support for edge computing that is available in most IoT platforms from CSPs.

Two remarks are in order. First, we have chosen ABAC as the underlying access control model for the high-level language used in our ACaaS solution as recommended by previous works (see, e.g., [3]) that argue for its adequacy to express context-dependent authorization requirements of IoT systems. Second, we have chosen the Amazon Web Service (AWS) IoT platform to conduct our experiments since it is one of the more advanced solution available on the market and allows us to perform a thorough validation of the flexibility and adequacy of our approach.

IoT solutions can be developed in many and heterogeneous application domains. Each domain induces a different emphasis on the security requirements to be met (see, e.g., [13] for an in-depth discussion). For instance, in healthcare and smart home applications, confidentiality, integrity, and privacy are crucial as the data collected by smart devices are personal and sensitive. Instead, for smart community services, availability becomes of paramount importance whereas confidentiality and privacy are less relevant as the data collected by the devices are usually less sensitive. Since access control has been traditionally used to guarantee confidentiality and integrity, we have selected a smart lock system in the smart home domain as the reference application to elicit the requirements of the access control solutions for IoT. We also discuss scalability and availability issues when the smart lock system is lifted to the enterprise level in the context of hotel chains or geographically distributed company buildings.

The remainder of the paper is organized as follows. Sec. 2 introduces the smart lock system and the requirements for access control. Sec. 3 briefly discusses the AWS IoT platform and its shortcomings. Sec. 4 presents our lazy approach to ACaaS, illustrates four possible deployments, and shows how it supports the smart lock system. Sec. 5 evaluates the approach both qualitatively and experimentally with respect to the requirements identified in Sec. 2. Sec. 6 discusses related work, and Sec. 7 draws some conclusions and summarizes future work.

2 USE CASE & REQUIREMENTS

We describe a smart lock system as a realistic use case scenario, identify the requirements that access control solutions for IoT should meet, and guide future developments of similar solutions.

2.1 Smart lock system

Smart locks are cyber-physical devices that aim to replace traditional locks with smart cylinder remotely controlled through a mobile application or a web portal. They can be deployed by individuals (in homes) or enterprise customers (typically hotels) to

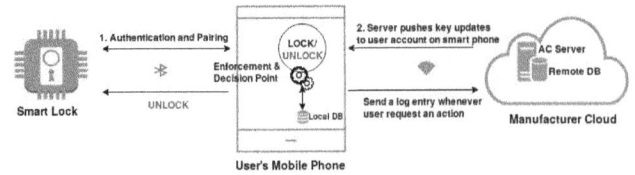

Figure 1: Architectural design of the smart lock system

reduce management costs and improve service quality; they can also be used as a smart work enabler (in smart offices) or to provide innovative services. Amazon Key in-home delivery service[1] is one such innovative service that is based on cloud-based Amazon camera and a smart door lock. Using this service, the owner can authorize a delivery company to temporary gain access to his home and monitor the activity using a cloud-based camera. The service can be expanded to include other in-home services such as house cleaning, pet sitters, etc. Similarly, Sofia locks[2] provide smart lock solutions for residential, commercial, industrial and public buildings.

Our use case is inspired to real world smart lock solutions that we had the opportunity to analyze and it features their most important characteristics. The architectural design of most commercial smart lock systems is based on a centralized IoT architecture in which the application logic is governed by a central entity (deployed in a private cloud) that provides a limited set of well-known entry points (e.g., APIs). Figure 1 presents an abstract view of the architecture. The main components are an electronically augmented deadbolt, which includes a smart cylinder lock and a controller, and a user mobile phone acting as an Internet gateway. The smart lock lacks direct Internet connectivity and, thus, relies on the user's mobile phone to communicate with the manufacturer cloud when the phone enters the Bluetooth range of the lock.

The smart lock employs an access management system, deployed in the manufacturer's private cloud, where smart lock owners can configure user permissions through an API. The access management system is based on Group Based Access Control (GBAC) [5] in which the access of users to resources is regulated using the notion of group, i.e. a logical collection of one or more entities that have common properties. The owner can add/remove a person to one of the groups predefined by the smart lock manufacturer (e.g., "Owner", "Resident", "Recurring Guest", "Temporary Guest"). Listing 1 shows a simple access rule of the smart lock system. This access rule indicates that users belonging to `persongroup` "Temporary Guest" can open doors in `doorgroup` "V3I6G5LSQGWL". Field `accessprofile` indicates the time scheme in which the rule is applicable (e.g., during office hours). A default `accessprofile` "*always*" is assigned if this field is not defined. Fields `valid_from` and `valid_to` denote the validity of the permission. The list of authorized users is also maintained in the local database of the smart lock (see below for the process used to update the smart lock database).

The smart lock system also provides an access logging mechanism. Whenever a user interacts with the lock, it sends a log entry recording the action, the user who performed it and the timestamp to the logging mechanism hosted in the manufacturer cloud. Sample access logs are shown in Listing 2, where `token_uuid` identifies the

[1]https://www.amazon.com/key
[2]https://www.sofialocks.com/it/smartlocks/

Listing 1: Access Control Policy

```
1  <xml version="1.0" encoding="UTF-8">
2  <accessrule>
3    <description>description of customer</description>
4    <doorgroup >V3I6G5LSQGWL</doorgroup>
5    <accessprofile>18HLFPN293</accessprofile>
6    <persongroup>Temporary Guest</persongroup>
7    <valid_from>2018-01-06 00:00:00+00:00</valid_from>
8    <valid_to>2018-12-06 23:59:00+00:00</valid_to>
9  </accessrule>
```

Listing 2: Access Logs

```
1  <xml version="1.0" encoding="UTF-8">
2  <accesslog>
3    <token_uuid>2WSROEJSJ72R</token_uuid>
4    <code>1</code>
5    <timestamp>2018-01-03 12:27:03</timestamp>
6    <lockid>30EBG7RQG12R</lockid>
7  </accesslog>
8  <accesslog>
9    <token_uuid>2WSROEJSJ72RP</token_uuid>
10   <code>2</code>
11   <timestamp>2018-01-03 12:28:17</timestamp>
12   <lockid>30EBG7RQG12R</lockid>
13 </accesslog>
```

user and code refers to the action performed. In the listing, code 1 corresponds to UNLOCK and code 2 to LOCK. Field timestamp records the date-time when the action was performed, and field lockid indicates the specific lock on which the action was performed.

Below we describe the key processes supported by the smart lock system.

- **User Registration & Permission Configuration:** The smart lock manufacturer provides users with a mobile application and a unique authorization code along with the smart lock. After installing the application, the owner pairs the application with the smart lock using the provided unique authorization code. Then, the owner can generate short term and long term digital keys for various types of users (family members, visiting friends, etc.) by accessing the access management system in manufacturer's private cloud. The access to the private cloud is controlled with the usage of One Time Password (OTP) generated by the application on the owner's mobile device.

- **Locking and Unlocking Process:** The smart lock is controlled through a smart lock application provided by the manufacturer and installed on the user mobile device. A user can LOCK or UNLOCK the lock through the smart lock's mobile application. As shown in Figure 1, when a user enters the Bluetooth range of the smart lock, his mobile phone is authenticated and paired with the smart lock through the Bluetooth protocol. Once connected, the smart lock receives the key status of the specific user from the remote access management system via the user's mobile device and uses the received key status to determine whether access should be granted. The key status is also stored in the local database of the smart lock. In case the remote access management system cannot be reached, the smart lock system ensures availability and maintain access by making decision based on the entries in its local database.

- **Key Revocation Process:** The owner is allowed to detach his or any other (authorized) device from the smart lock by accessing the access management system. Specifically, the owner can revoke access from a user by revoking the key assigned to that user

and updating the key status inside the key repository in the access management system on the manufacturer cloud. The changes are then propagated to the local database of the smart lock system when the user connect to the lock through his mobile device.

2.2 Analysis of the Use Case Scenario

We now analyze the smart lock system and discuss its limitations. First, we focus on the security issues affecting the adopted access control mechanism and, then, we consider other aspects that can influence the design of an access control solution for IoT.

The access management system provided within the smart lock system only allows smart lock's owners to specify simple policies in the GBAC model. Specifically, owners can assign users to predefined groups and define their permissions with respect to group(s) they belong to. Although this model provides users with a simple and intuitive approach for policy specification, it is rather limited in the policies that can be specified and it is not suitable when fine grained control is needed or access should be granted decision under certain contextual conditions. For example, it is not possible to specify that access should be granted to a temporary guest only if a member of the "Resident" group is at home.

Moreover, the smart lock system has intrinsic vulnerabilities and weaknesses in its design that can be exploited by users to compromise the system:

V1: The smart lock lacks direct connectivity to the Internet and relies on the user's smart phone to interact with the manifacturer's cloud. Therefore, the smart lock implicitly trusts the user to behave faithfully.

V2: The smart lock receives key status updates from the remote access management system only when a user interacts with the smart lock. Moreover, the received updates only concerns the interacting user. Therefore, the smart lock remains unaware of changes in the policies while it cannot connect to the manufacturer's cloud (via the user's smart phone).

V3: The access control logic is implemented in the access management system hosted in the manufacturer's cloud whereas access control policies are enforced locally by the smart lock. If the smart lock is unable to retrieve key status updates, it uses the policies stored in the local database, which however can be outdated (V2).

V4: The smart lock owner can grant, update or revoke a digital key through the remote access management system. However, these actions are subject to a final approval through the mobile application on the owner's mobile phone.

We hereby present two threat models that are typical for smart lock systems like the one described in our scenario.

(1) *Control of a user's mobile device*: The adversary is assumed to be a legitimate user of the system or to be in control of the mobile device of a legitimate user. Therefore, the adversary can block the connectivity between the smart lock and the manufacturer's cloud, for instance, by turning ON airplane mode when interacting with the smart lock.

(2) *Control of the owner's mobile device*: The adversary is assumed to be in control of the owner's mobile device. Besides the capabilities described in the previous threat model, the adversary is

also in control of the application to configure the smart lock system installed on the owner's mobile device.

Next, we discuss some attacks, also identified by [8], based on the aforementioned threat models and the vulnerabilities of the access control mechanism adopted within the smart lock system. **Revocation Evasion:** An adversary can exploit the above mentioned vulnerabilities to retain access to the smart lock when his permissions have been revoked by blocking the connectivity between the smart lock and the access management system. Consider, for instance, a housekeeper that has recently been relieved from duty. Accordingly, the owner revokes her permissions for entering his house by performing the key revocation procedure described above. However, by exploiting vulnerabilities V1, V2 and V3 of the smart lock system, the housekeeper can still maintain (unauthorized) access. In particular, she can turn ON the airplane mode on his mobile phone when interacting with the smart lock, thus preventing the smart lock from receiving key status updates. Due to vulnerabilities V1 and V2, the smart lock remains unaware of the revoked permissions. Since the smart lock makes decisions based on the policies in the local database when it is unable to contact the access management system (V3), the housekeeper is still able to enter the apartment.

Logging Evasion: An adversary, who can block the connectivity between the smart lock and the manufacturer's cloud, can also hide his interaction with the smart lock by blocking log messages from reaching the access management system by simply turning ON the airplane mode when interacting with smart lock.

Update Evasion: In case the smart lock's owner looses his mobile device or his mobile device is stolen, he has to remove the device from the smart lock system. To this end, he can access the access management system and revoke the digital key assigned to that device. However, if the adversary posses the owner's mobile device, he can ignore the request for approving the revocation (V4) and, thus, he can access the lock system using the owner's mobile device. In these situations, a user often has no other option than returning the smart lock back to the manufacturer, as happened in the case of Lockstate after sending users a wrong firmware update [11].

Besides the security considerations above, other orthogonal aspects should be considered when designing an access control solution for IoT.

Management: Smart lock solutions not only can be deployed on small scale in homes and small offices, as described in our scenario, but also on larger scale, for instance, in industrial setups and hotels. This requires an access control mechanism to be able to manage the access for a potentially large number of smart locks. The analyzed smart lock system allows assigning a smart lock to a single user account. This means, for instance, that a hotel manager has to manage a large number of accounts, one for each smart locks. This solution is clearly impractical when deployed on large scale. Moreover, policy specification is known to be difficult and error-prone [18]. For instance, when a policy is updated, it is difficult to determine whether the revised policy works as intended. Even small errors can lead to unauthorized accesses. Ensuring the correctness of access control policies is thus a crucial task to guarantee the security of the smart lock system. Finally, the smart lock system provides very little support in the configuration of security mechanisms. For

instance, it does not allow the smart lock's owner to configure the access logging system. This can affect user privacy as he cannot prevent his or any other user's interaction with the smart lock to be recorded (recall that access logs are stored in the manufacturer's cloud and, thus, he has not control over them).

Latency: Users standing in front of a door typically expect a response from the smart lock in the order of milliseconds. In our system, the smart lock has to retrieve the key status from the access management system hosted on the manufacturer's cloud to determine whether a user is allowed to open the door. However, the response time from a cloud might vary from milliseconds to seconds or even minutes depending on the geographic location of the cloud. This can affect the functioning of the system as well as user satisfaction in the smart lock solution. Therefore, it is important to consider the response time required by the specific IoT application [4] and to guarantee that the access control solution does not introduce an intolerable delay for users.

Platform-Independence: The analyzed smart lock system is bounded to the manufacturer's private cloud. This, together with the employment of ad-hoc mechanisms, makes the portability of smart lock configurations and policies to another cloud service provider difficult, if possible at all. This is known as *vendor lock-in* and is one of the main issues to the widespread adoption of cloud-based services and applications [6].

2.3 Requirements for Access Control

Based on the discussion above, we have identified a number of requirements to guide the development of access control solutions for smart locks and similar IoT applications (cf. Table 1).

(AC1) **Expressibility:** An access control system for IoT should be applicable in all security contexts by allowing the specification of policies that fit the desired level of granularity. In fact, many IoT applications require enforcing access restrictions that depend on several attributes of users, resources, and the environment. It is thus desirable from an access control policy to be expressive enough to capture the access restrictions to be enforced. In the case of our smart lock system, for instance, the smart lock owner should be able to specify that access should be denied to temporary guests if no member of "Resident" group is at home.

(AC2) **Administration:** The way in which an access control system is configured and managed is very critical to ensure security and privacy within IoT systems. The definition of access control policies is far from being a trivial process due to the interpretation of complex and ambiguous security polices that have to be translated into well-defined, unambiguous and enforceable rules. This requires the access control system to provide users with an administration point for easy translation of security requirements into enforceable access control policies and for the verification of their correctness. The administration point should also provide users with capabilities for the configuration of security mechanisms.

(AC3) **Portability:** Besides affecting the administration of access control policies, the inherent difficulties in defining access control restrictions have also an impact on the migration of the smart lock system across different cloud service providers (CSP), resulting in vendor lock-in. Consider, for instance, a chain of hotels with branches in different parts of the world, where branches in different

Table 1: Requirements of Access Control Systems for IoT

ID	Requirement	Description
AC1	Expressibility	The access control system must allow users to specify fine-grained access control policies.
AC2	Administration	The access control system must provide an administration point to easily configure policies for connected devices and available resources.
AC3	Portability	The access control system needs to be platform independent.
AC4	Extensibility	The access control system must support the enforcement of arbitrary security constraints.
AC5	Latency	The access control system must be designed according to the latency requirements of the IoT application.
AC6	Reliability	The access control system must provide a reliable access decision in every system state.
AC7	Scalability	The access control system must be able to handle a growing number of devices and amount of data generated and processed by those devices.

countries rely on a different CSP, e.g. for legal and/or economic reasons. Each CSP can adopt a different access control mechanism along with a different policy language, which makes the management of smart locks across different branches difficult as policies have to be specified with respect to each CSP. This raises the need of portability for access control policies so that a user can specify policies that can be reused across different CSPs.

(AC4) **Extensibility:** To maximize its viability, an access control system should provide extensibility points to customize policy evaluation with respect to the needs of the application domain. The most noteworthy extensibility point is the possibility to augment the access control system with event driven functions for the evaluation of custom constraints in access control policies [10].

(AC5) **Latency:** Service provision in a cloud-centric IoT architecture might lead to congestion and arbitrary delays due to the large number of requesting services and devices that generate and consume data [15]. Several IoT applications have stringent latency requirements, which impose constraints also on data transfer and decision making processes. To address these concerns, new trends are emerging to move part of the computational logic closer to the physical devices. In particular, new computing paradigms like edge computing and fog computing propose to move cloud capabilities towards network edge to minimize the need to interact with the cloud [19]. However, there is a gray scale between the two extremes – pure cloud and pure edge – that allows a spectrum of possible architectures to distribute the access control logic and responsibilities. The choice of the type of architecture should be driven by the requirements of the IoT application at hand.

(AC6) **Reliability:** The use of cloud has also an impact on the security of the system and, in particular, on the reliability of access decisions. As shown in our scenario, the lack of connectivity between the smart lock and the access management system hosted in the manufacturer's cloud can be exploited by an adversary to maintain the access to the smart lock when his permissions have been revoked (revocation evasion). We advocate that an access control mechanism should be reliable in every system state.

(AC7) **Scalability:** The exponential growth of IoT deployments is highly expected in terms of new devices and amount of data generated and processed by these devices. In our scenario, each smart lock is managed by a single account. However, in case of deployment on large scale (e.g., hotels or industrial setups), the management of smart locks might become a serious concern. Therefore, we envision that an access control mechanism for IoT should be able to scale in size, structure and number of users and resources.

3 AWS IoT

First, we give a brief overview of the Amazon Web Services platform for IoT (AWS IoT). Then, we discuss the problems we encountered in realizing the smart lock system of Sec. 2 on top of AWS IoT.

3.1 AWS IoT & Greengrass

AWS IoT is an extension of the Amazon Web Services platform for IoT. This platform provides support to collect and analyze data from Internet-connected devices and to connect those data to AWS cloud applications, allowing to tie data into applications. The dashed (rounded) rectangle labeled with "DM1: Pure Cloud Architecture" in Fig. 2 shows a high-level view of the AWS IoT architecture with the following components:

- **Device Gateway:** enables IoT devices to securely and efficiently communicate with AWS IoT.
- **Message Broker:** provides IoT devices with a secure mechanism to publish and receive messages to and from each other using the MQTT protocol.
- **Lambda Function:** is a stateless piece of code whose execution can be triggered by a wide range of sources, both internal and external to AWS like web and mobile applications.
- **AWS Management Console:** is a web application providing an built-in user interface for the management of AWS services.
- **Authentication:** AWS IoT provides mutual authentication and encryption to every connected IoT device. It supports two authentication methods: X.509 certificates and Custom Authorizers (authentication based on custom tokens).
- **Access Control:** AWS IoT employs an access control mechanism based on a limited variant of ABAC. An AWS policy is a JSON file that is attached to the certificate of an entity and comprises three main parts: *Effect* (allow or deny), *Action* (e.g., IoT:publish) and *Resources* (e.g., an AWS resource name). A policy can also include a *Condition* that refines the scope of a permission and may contain up to three attributes of the entity. Listing 3 shows a sample AWS access control policy for the smart lock scenario. This policy allows operations "Connect" and "Subscribe" on any resource ("*") whereas it allows operations "Publish" and "Receive" only on the device with *ID* "Thing_ID_1" provided that it belongs to Alice (*Owner*) and is associated to "Room_1" (*Room*). For more details on AWS IoT access control policies, see [3].

To overcome potential latency issues (that are typical of pure cloud platforms for IoT), AWS IoT provides an additional service, called AWS Greengrass, that integrates edge computing. IoT devices connected to the same Greengrass instance (typically on the same network) can be configured as a Greengrass group. In case an IoT device loses connection with the back-end cloud, it can continue to communicate with other IoT devices in the same Greengrass

Listing 3: AWS IoT policy for the smart lock use case

```
{"Version": "2012-10-17",
 "Statement": [
 {"Effect": "Allow",
  "Action": ["iot:Connect","iot:Subscribe"],
  "Resource": "*" },
 {"Effect": "Allow",
  "Action": ["iot:Publish","iot:Receive"],
  "Resource":"arn:aws:iot:us-west-2:X:topic/Test",
  "Condition": {
   "StringEquals": {
    "iot:Connection.Thing.Attributes[Owner]":"Alice",
    "iot:Connection.Thing.Attributes[ID]":"Thing_ID_1",
    "iot:Connection.Thing.Attributes[Room]":"Room_1"}}}
      ]}
```

group over the local network. Greengrass maintains a subscription table defining the messages that can be exchanged within a Greengrass group, where each entry in the subscription table specifies a source (message sender), a target (message recipient) and a topic over which messages can be sent/received. Messages can be exchanged only if an entry exists in the subscription table matching the source, target, and topic; this provides a rudimentary access control mechanism.

3.2 Limitations of AWS IoT & Greengrass

We discuss the limitations encountered in using AWS IoT and Greengrass to realize the smart lock system in Sec. 2 with respect to the requirements in Tab. 1:

- AWS IoT does not allow the specification of fine-grained access control policies (AC1). AWS IoT imposes a restriction on the number of attributes that can be used for policy specification. Only three attributes of the entity can be used in a policy, resulting in coarse grained access control policies, whereas the dynamic nature of IoT might demand to express more complex authorization conditions involving a larger number of attributes and/or refer to properties of the requested resource and environment as in the policy of Sec. 2.2.

- AWS IoT provides limited support for policy administration (AC2). Every service has a different administrative interface inside the AWS Management Console, making policy administration across services cumbersome. Moreover, the policy specification interface provides very little assistance in policy verification. In particular, it does not provide any mechanism to validate and debug the specified policy before enforcement; it only warns the user in case of a syntactic problem.

- AWS IoT uses a proprietary access management system that employs an ad-hoc language for policy specification (cf. Listing 3), thus hindering the migration to other IoT platforms and resulting in vendor lock-in (AC3).

- The use of AWS Greengrass can potentially help meet latency (AC5) and reliability (AC6) requirements by bringing the access logic closer to physical devices. However, Greengrass relies on a rudimentary access control mechanisms based on subscriptions, which does not allow for fine-grained control (AC1). Moreover, it limits the number of IoT devices that can be configured within a deployable instance to 200 and restricts to 50 the number of those who can receive messages from AWS IoT.

- AWS IoT and Greengrass access control mechanisms can be extended by using Lambda functions; unfortunately, the burden of

doing this is entirely left on the shoulder of programmers with little or no assistance (AC4).

- To the best of our knowledge, AWS IoT has only been tested with small scale deployments whereas large scale deployments (AC7) with different set of requirements as the ones given in Section 2.3, are still unclear [17].

4 A LAZY APPROACH TO ACaaS

We now explain how to overcome the limitations of the AWS IoT platform discussed in Sec. 3.2 using our lazy approach to ACaaS.

First of all, we observe that the first four requirements in Tab. 1 are readily satisfied by adopting ACaaS. In fact, by using standard policy specification languages (such as XACML) usually based on the Attribute Based Access Control (ABAC) model [9], existing ACaaS solutions support the expressiveness necessary to specify fine grained access control policies (AC1), abstraction from the details of the access control models available in different CSP platforms (AC2), portability across different CSPs (AC3), and extensibility to enforce complex authorization constraints (AC4). An in-depth discussion of how the proposed approach satisfies all the requirements in Tab. 1 is presented in Sec. 5 with particular attention to (AC5), (AC6), and (AC7). Here, we introduce the main idea underlying our approach.

While most ACaaS frameworks (e.g., [1, 10]) outsource activities pertaining to policy specification, management, and evaluation, we follow [12] and choose to outsource only policy specification and management while reusing the policy evaluation mechanism provided by the various CSPs. We do this by translating from the high-level policy specification language used in the ACaaS tool to the proprietary specification language of the various CSPs. Technically, we use a policy specification language with a formal semantics rooted in the ABAC framework [9] that is independent of a particular CSP platform. This allows us to reuse automated tools for the security analysis of policies to understand whether the defined policies meet designer expectations and perform automated policy analysis (see, e.g., [2, 18]). More importantly for this work, the formal semantics of the language of the ACaaS tool allows us to design a translation to the language available in a given CSP that can be readily enforced by the mechanisms provided by the CSP platform. Additionally, it is possible to argue the correctness of the translation, i.e. an authorization query is allowed by the formal semantics of the ACaaS tool if it is so by the access control system available in the CSP platform. This paves the way to the exploitation of the efficient integration of policy evaluation and enforcement mechanism available in CSP platforms (such as the combination of cloud and edge computing that are crucial, for instance, to reduce latency in IoT systems) and streamlines separation of concerns and identification of responsabilities.

We have implemented these ideas by extending the ACaaS tool SecurePG[3] [12] for cloud computing platforms to target IoT systems on top of the AWS IoT platform (Sec. 3.1). The extension of SecurePG (Sec. 4.2) results in the capabilities of specifying and enforcing more fine-grained policies with respect to AWS IoT and of enforcing policies in four different IoT architectures (Sec. 4.1)—integrating cloud and edge computing together with event-driven

---

[3]https://sites.google.com/view/securepg/

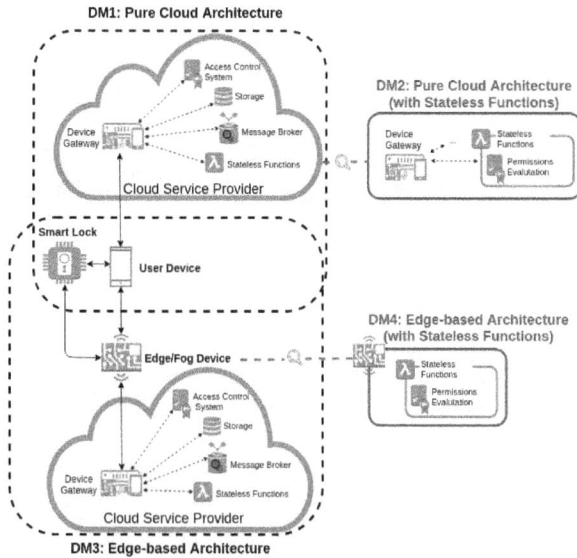

Figure 2: Four Possible Deployment Scenarios

stateless functions (Lambda function in AWS)—without additional burdens to policy designers or administrators. We show how to use the extended version of SECUREPG (Sec. 4.3) to realize the smart lock system of Sec. 2.

4.1   IoT Architectures

By building upon our experience with AWS IoT and Greengrass, we identified four different architectures that exploits the capabilities of cloud and edge computing. Figure 2 provides an overview of these architectures. Red boxes highlight the delegation of policy evaluation from the native access control mechanism to stateless functions.

DM1: Pure Cloud Architecture. The access control mechanism along with IoT entities' configurations and permissions is deployed and managed in the cloud. When a user requests access to a resource, his device connects with the device gateway, which forwards the request to the native authorization mechanism for evaluation and notifies, if authorized, the device hosting the resource (e.g., a smart lock exploiting the user device Internet access).

DM2: Pure Cloud Architecture with stateless functions. As in DM1, device configurations and permissions are stored and managed in the cloud. However, this architecture extends the access control mechanism provided by CSPs through the use of cloud-hosted stateless functions (Lambda functions in AWS). Intuitively, stateless functions implement the authorization mechanism responsible for intercepting access requests and, after retrieving the needed attribute values from a database, evaluate them against the appropriate policies (eventually also fetched from the database).

DM3: Edge-based Architecture. Access control and devices management are performed in edge devices. When a user requests access to a resource, his device and the one hosting the resource interact with the edge node that evaluates the request using the native authorization mechanism (e.g., the rudimentary one based on subscriptions of AWS Greengrass).

Table 2: IoT Entities and Actions supported by SECUREPG

Entities		Actions	Description
IoT Subject	Client	Connect	Support the IoT physical devices connection.
	Thing, Thing type, Things group	Subscribe, Publish, Receive	Support the IoT virtual devices subscription to Topics and, afterwards, the possibility to publish and receive messages on the Topics.
IoT Resource	Topic	Publish, Receive	Support the possibility to publish and receive messages on a Topic.
	Topic Filter	Subscribe	Support the subscription to a set of Topics.

DM4: Edge-based Architecture with stateless functions. As in DM3, device management and policy evaluation are performed locally in edge devices. However, this architecture extends the access control mechanism provided by the CSP through the use of stateless functions along the lines of DM2.

4.2   Extending SECUREPG for IoT

To support the configuration of the access control mechanism in the four architectures defined in Sec. 4.1, we have extended SE-CUREPG [12], a policy authoring framework for cloud environments that provides users with a single point of administration to (i) define authorization requirements using a CSP-independent policy specification language, (ii) automatically analyze and validate policies, (iii) translate access control requirements into platform-dependent entities and policies, and (iv) export local components and policies in pre-existing cloud environments. Next, we discuss how SECUREPG has been extended to support the configuration of an arbitrary number of IoT entities with an unbounded number of attributes and their deployment in AWS IoT and Greengrass.

First, we have provided SECUREPG with the capability to configure IoT entities and their primary interactions (e.g., devices connection, subscriptions to topics, publishing and receiving of messages). Table 2 presents the concepts that have been integrated in SECUREPG, namely a representation of the physical devices, called *clients*, and their virtual counterpart (in the cloud), named *things*. Things can be organized in groups and possess a specific set of attributes. As in AWS, the types of subjects and resources specified by policy administrators in their policies are bound to specific actions.

To support the evaluation of policies with an arbitrary number of attributes (DM2 and DM4), we have implemented four Lambda functions, two for AWS IoT (referred to as LF1 and LF2) and two for Greengrass (referred to as LF3 and LF4). LF1 and LF3 evaluate access requests against an AWS thing's policy (i.e., its certificate's policy) and grant access if there is at least one attribute in the request that matches those in the policy and no attributes have different values. LF2 and LF4 extend LF1 and LF3 respectively by allowing the retrieval of the attributes needed for the evaluation of the request from a database. Lambda functions have been implemented in Java 8 (code available as Maven projects in the repository folder[4]) and are integrated in SECUREPG. When configuring AWS IoT and Greengrass, SECUREPG deploys these Lambda functions according to the selected architecture as described below; thereby completely relieving policy administrators from the burden of developing the code of Lambda functions.

Figure 3 shows the configuration and deployment procedure followed by SECUREPG (red dashed rectangles denotes the functionalities developed in this work). First, users configure IoT entities

---

[4]Deployment models results, data and configuration: https://goo.gl/xybfGf

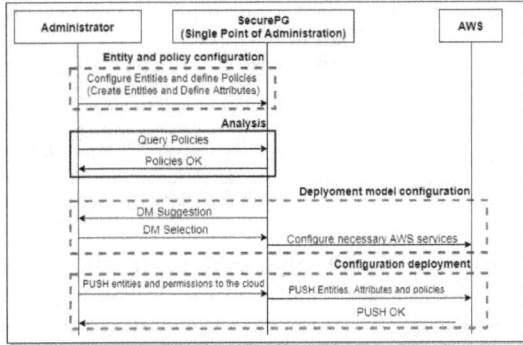

Figure 3: SECUREPG configuration and deployment procedure for IoT

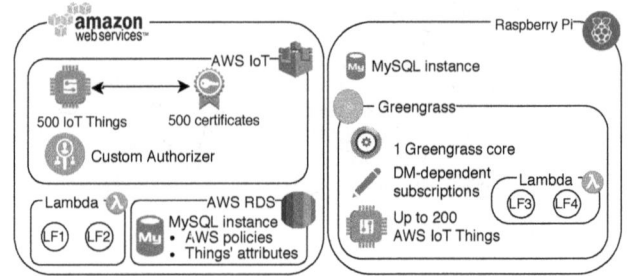

Figure 4: Prototype configuration components

and associated policies in a high level language. These policies can be analyzed and validated using a module available in SECUREPG that analyzes the defined policies using an SMT solver and reports possible policy misconfigurations before their deployment (see [12] for details).

In addition, SECUREPG assists users in the deployment of entities' configurations and permissions by suggesting a possible deployment based on the IoT platform and granularity of permissions. If the policy contains three or less attributes (in *Condition*), all entities are configured using AWS IoT native mechanisms (DM1). If policies contain more than three attributes, SECUREPG creates and configures the AWS Lambda infrastructure to support policy evaluation using stateless functions (DM2); this requires to configure an AWS *Custom Authorizer* to coordinate policy evaluation (see Sec. 4.3). The use of attributes not supported by AWS, e.g. those associated to resources, also triggers the creation and configuration of the environment necessary to fetch policies and attributes for their evaluation.

When indicated by the user, SECUREPG configures the Greengrass environment (DM3 or DM4) by triggering the deployment of the configuration on a pre-existing Greengrass-enabled device. In case policies include at least one attribute, SECUREPG creates and coordinates the AWS Lambda infrastructure to support policy evaluation as in DM2 (but to be deployed on the specified Greengrass-enabled device) along with, if necessary, a local database.

When an appropriate architecture is selected, SECUREPG deploys IoT entities' configurations and policies in the IoT platform. In particular, it synchronizes the necessary data (e.g., certificates) by interacting with the cloud, invokes the creation of AWS self-generated certificates and updates their local relations with the corresponding things.

4.3 The Smart lock system and SECUREPG

To assess the architectures described in Section 4.1, we developed the smart lock scenario in Sec. 2 in AWS IoT and Greengrass. Figure 2 shows the interaction among connected IoT devices (smart lock and user's mobile device), AWS cloud, edge/fog device and IoT services. Entities' configurations and policies were generated and deployed using SECUREPG. Here, we discuss how we did this and detail the configuration and components in Figure 4.

We simulated the interactions between smart locks and user devices by sending and receiving MQTT messages with the following software clients: JMeter[5], and a device instance of the AWS JavaScript SDK[6] via NodeJS[7] . All clients use MQTT protocol with TLS security to communicate with the AWS IoT and Greengrass services.

To implement the smart lock system using pure cloud architectures (DM1 and DM2), we configured the AWS IoT service. AWS IoT allows users to create virtual objects (things) for each physical device (using the AWS management console), create X.509 certificates (through the "one click certificate" functionality) in order to support devices interaction, and assign policies to these certificates. These certificates are attached to specific virtual objects (things) and downloaded into the corresponding IoT device. SECUREPG assists policy administrators in the execution of these steps by providing a single point of administration and deploying the desired configuration on the AWS IoT platform as described in Sec. 4.2.

Additionally, for DM2 we extended the access control mechanism of AWS IoT by configuring a *Custom Authorizer* (hereafter CA). This is a special lambda function used to authorize already authenticated IoT devices by invoking LF1 or LF2. To use this function, access requests from IoT devices should contain a JSON-token and the CA signature. While the latter is verified by the AWS device gateway to authenticate the device, the token is verified by the CA with a public key (uploaded during CA's configuration).

To enable the use of LF2 in DM2, we also deployed a MySQL instance configured with *AWS Relational Database Service (RDS)*. This service provides cost-efficient and resizable capacity while automating time-consuming administration tasks such as hardware provisioning, database setup, patching and backups. The MySQL instance comprises two tables: one for JSON policies (specified using the AWS syntax) and one to store the attributes of AWS things. AWS RDS was configured with default settings.

To support edge-based solutions (DM3 and DM4), we deployed a AWS Greengrass core on a board Raspberry Pi 3 Model B and configured a Greengrass group by taking into account AWS limitations: up to 200 subscriptions and a reference to a single Greengrass core, the dedicated lambda functions (LF3 and LF4) and up to 200 AWS IoT Things' name.

---

[5] http://jmeter.apache.org/ - MQTT Plugin: https://github.com/emqtt/mqtt-jmeter
[6] AWS JS IoT SDK: https://github.com/aws/aws-iot-device-sdk-js
[7] https://nodejs.org

When connecting to the IoT endpoint (i.e., the Greengrass core IP address on the Raspberry Pi), clients have to provide the certificate of the Greengrass group. This has been configured with a reference to the Greengrass core, the sender and receiver IoT things, and subscription rules. The Greengrass core authenticates the connecting clients through the certificates and authorize them according to the subscription rules. These rules, however, differ between DM3 and DM4. In DM3, subscription rules have the form <sender_name, MQTT_topic_name, "IoT Cloud"> and <"IoT Cloud", MQTT_topic_name,receiver_name> representing the permission to send and receive a message respectively. On the other hand, DM4 uses subscription rules of the form <sender_name, MQTT_topic_name, Lambda_function_name> and <Lambda_function_name, MQTT_topic_name, receiver_name>. When connecting to the IoT endpoint the Greengrass core not only authenticates the client through its certificates as in DM3 but, in the case of a sender client, it also triggers the lambda function referenced in the subscription rule (the other subscription rule allows the same function to send the message to the receiver client).

Lambda functions deployed on Greengrass (LF3 and LF4) are configured as *long-lived*. Using this feature thing's attributes are cached for 30 seconds, improving the performance of policy evaluation. To support DM4 with LF4, we deployed a MySQL instance on the Raspberry Pi.

5 EVALUATION

To understand to what extent the deployment models presented in Section 4.1 meet the requirements identified in Section 2.3, we assessed the smart lock system in Section 4.3. Given the heterogeneous nature of the requirements, we evaluated them using different approaches: latency (AC5) and scalability (AC7) were evaluated by means of experiments (Sec. 5.1) while the others through a qualitative analysis (Sec. 5.2). Here we report our findings.

5.1 Experimental analysis

To evaluate the *latency* and *scalability* of the deployment models, we performed two sets of experiments using our prototype. To evaluate the latency, we configured two IoT clients using AWS IoT JavaScript SDK: one creates a timestamp when sending an MQTT message on a specific topic; the other client listens on the same topic and generates a timestamp when receiving the message. The difference between the timestamps allowed us to determine the communication and processing time for the evaluation of a IoT client's request in AWS. Clients were deployed on a 8GB ram, 8-core i7 Windows 10 machine.

The number of attributes allowed in the message (if any) and in the clients' policies (if any) varies depending on the deployment model (NodeJS Clients and configuration files available in the repository folder[4]).In DM1, the sender client is configured with a certificate that holds (in the cloud) a policy including up to three attributes. The receiver client is configured similarly with a policy that holds different attributes' values. The guarantees on clients' identity offered by assigning a certificate to each client allowed us to use clients whose policy does not contain a condition tag (i.e., no attributes are used in the policy). When connecting to the IoT endpoint (i.e., the AWS device gateway), clients provide the

AWS certificate authority digital certificate, a *ClientID* (that must be equal to an AWS IoT thing's name) and its related certificate and private key. When receiving a request, the AWS IoT authorization mechanism fetches the attributes retrieved via the *ClientID* (i.e., three among the 50 specified beforehand when creating the AWS IoT thing) and evaluates their value against those retrieved via the certificate (i.e., up to three in the condition tag of the associated policy).

In DM2, the sender client is configured with a certificate that holds no condition tag; the receiver client is configured as in DM1. When connecting to the IoT endpoint, similarly to DM1, the sender client provides a *ClientID* and, instead of the certificates and key, the set of AWS CA headers to enable policy evaluation through lambda functions LF1 and LF2 as described in Section 4.3. Headers can include tokens containing up to 80 attributes due to the maximum header length supported by AWS. The lack of the certificates and keys in the requests, here and in DM4, led us to consider valid only requests sent with at least one attribute.

Since Greengrass uses a rudimentary access control mechanism based on subscriptions (cf. Sec. 3.2), we were unable to consider any policy attributes in DM3. On the other hand, lambda functions LF3 and LF4 allow the retrieval of a potentially unlimited number of attributes from MQTT messages. Thus, we tested DM4 with up to 80 attributes to compare it with DM2.

To evaluate the scalability of the deployment models, we configured a fleet of 500 policy-enabled IoT things in AWS IoT, named *test_lock_1* to *test_lock_ 500*, all belonging to a single type named *Lock*. Each thing is configured with 50 attributes, of which up to three referenced in the specific AWS IoT policies, an AWS self-generated certificate and the private key provided during its generation. Certificates hold four versions of the same policy (a sample policy for test_lock_1 is available in the repository folder[4]), enabled one at a time based on the necessary number of attributes in the condition. We assessed the deployment models by measuring the time necessary to send and receive up to 500 messages (pseudo-parallelism as supported by JMeter) from as many individual sender clients. By analysing the difference between the first timestamp (of a sender) and the last timestamp generated by the single receiver, we were able to establish the communication and processing time of all clients' messages.

In our experiments we could not test more than 500 connecting devices (499 senders and one receiver) due to the limitations of AWS IoT[8]. Moreover, the throttling on the number of parallel requests (imposed by AWS) allowed us to only evaluate policies using the attributes provided in the request (in the header or in the payload of MQTT messages). Moreover, constraints on Greengrass prevented us to evaluate more than 150 parallel requests for DM3 and 130 for DM4.

Results. We now provide a summary of the results of our experiments. Detailed results are available in the repository folder [4]. Figure 5 presents a boxplot showing the distribution of the processing time for deployment models DM1, DM2 (with LF1 for 1 to 50 attributes and with LF2 for 80 attributes) and DM4 (LF4). Lacking

---

[8]https://docs.aws.amazon.com/general/latest/gr/aws_service_limits.html

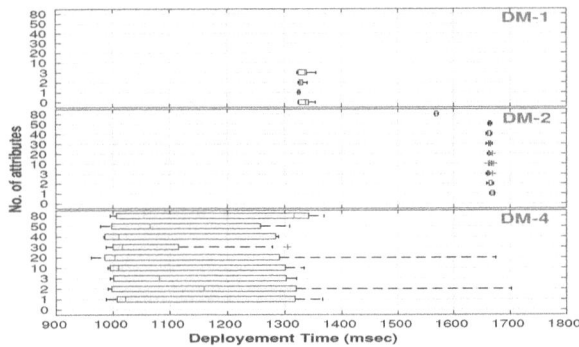

Figure 5: Distribution of time intervals (ms) to send and receive a message on a topic for the deployment models

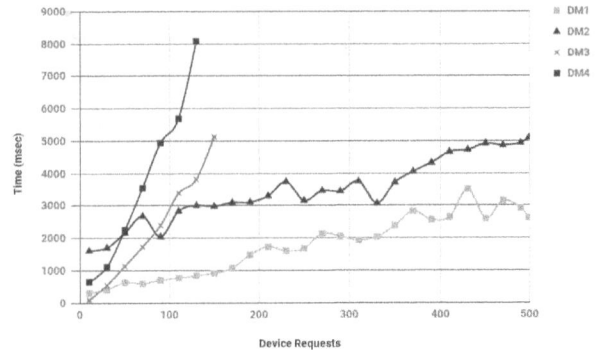

Figure 6: Time intervals (ms) necessary to send and receive multiple parallel requests

the possibility to evaluate clients' attributes in the implementation of DM3, we decided to omit this deployment model from the diagram.

From the figure, we can observe that the number of attributes specified in the policies (as in DM1), in the header (as in DM2) or in the payload (as in DM4) of the MQTT message does not significantly affect the processing time: when passing from three attributes, as supported in DM1, to the 50 attributes supported by DM2 (with LF1), the computation time varies from 1325 ms to 1668 ms. Even when DM2 executes LF2 (and connects to the AWS RDS MySQL instance to support 80 attributes), processing time ranges from 1571 ms to 1578 ms.

Our experiments show that edge-based solutions outperform pure cloud solutions for the evaluation of single requests when employing simple mechanisms (like the subscription-based mechanism provided by Greengrass and implemented in DM3) but also when interacting with a local database (as in DM4 with LF4).

It is worth mentioning that, when DM2 triggers LF1, the first client's request may take up to 4.6 times (1.9 times when DM2 executes LF2, i.e. when interacting with AWS RDS). These performance discrepancies are probably due to the caching mechanism employed by AWS to handle the container that runs lambda functions, which speeds up subsequent requests.

Figure 6 shows the results of the experiments on scalability regarding DM1, DM2 (with LF1), DM3 and DM4 (with LF4). We can observe that pure cloud architectures (DM1 and DM2) scale linearly with the number of requests, supporting up to 499 parallel requests within 2617 ms in DM1 and 5090ms in DM2. We speculate that those results are due to the scalable infrastructure offered by AWS. In contrast, we observe an exponential grow of the processing time for edge-based solutions. Our experiments also showed, as described in the full results[15], a high message loss (up to 51% when configuring 150 sender devices) for edge-based solutions.

5.2 Qualitative analysis

The prototype implementation described in Section 4.3 and our experience when assessing the four deployment models with AWS, provide important insights on how those solutions truly address the requirements identified in Section 2.3. Below we provide an in-depth discussion, which is summarized in Table 3.

DM1: Pure Cloud Architecture. This solution strongly depends on the cloud services offered by the CSP and its access control capabilities. Based on our experience with AWS, we believe that most cloud-based IoT platforms fail to fully support AC1. For instance, when handling a fleet of smart locks and user devices, system administrators would require more than three subject's attributes and, most importantly, resource's attributes to configure their policies. Similarly, the use of a proprietary, ad-hoc access control mechanisms could prevent the satisfaction of AC4 and limit the portability of access control policies (AC3). Our experiments show that AWS IoT only partially satisfies AC5 and AC7. In fact, AWS IoT processes single requests within 1.4 seconds and up to 499 parallel requests always within 4 seconds, while users of the smart lock system would expect a response time in the order of milliseconds. Moreover, we experience message loss starting from 330 parallel requests. DM1 is also not resilient in case of connection problems between users' devices and the cloud, thus not satisfying AC6.

DM2: Pure Cloud Architecture with stateless functions. Some IoT platforms like AWS IoT allow system administrators to customize and extend the provided access control mechanism, hence supporting AC1 and ACR4. This can be achieved using CSP's specific functionalities, e.g. a custom authorizer to execute LF1, or using platform independent components, e.g. a MySQL instance to fetch policies and things' attributes when executing LF2. While LF1 allows DM2 to support AC4, LF2 enables in addition the fulfillment of AC3. However, the increased empowerment corresponds to greater responsibilities for administrators. Functionalities like the recently launched AWS Custom Authorizer, which currently lacks a clear documentation, need to be fully understood to avoid design flaws that would lead to the unauthorized disclosure of sensitive resources. Our experiments show that the performances of DM2 are comparable to the ones of DM1. Moreover, we experience a message loss similar to the one we encountered in DM1 when increasing the number of (parallel) requests; thus, we mark AC6 not satisfied also for DM2.

DM3: Edge-based Architecture. As DM1, this solution is strongly bounded to the given IoT platform. However, the lack of expressibility (AC1) and extensibility (AC4) is even more evident for DM3. Edge nodes have typically reduced capabilities compared to a cloud and, thus, a simple authorization mechanism is often employed. For

Table 3: Comparison of Architectures. Green check (✓) means satisfied; orange star (✳) means partially satisfied, red cross (✗) means not satisfied.

Architectures	AC1	AC2	AC3	AC4	AC5	AC6	AC7
DM1 (AWS IoT)	✳	✗	✗	✗	✳	✗	✳
DM2	✓	✗	✳	✓	✳	✗	✳
DM3 (Greengrass)	✗	✗	✗	✗	✓	✗	✗
DM4	✓	✗	✳	✓	✓	✗	✗

instance, Greengrass uses a simple subscription-based authorization mechanism in which access rights are granted only considering the device's identifier. This approach can introduce even additional issues. For instance, we observed that, when a thing is removed from the AWS IoT service, a client was still allowed to send and receive messages using its certificates. Although single requests were processed within 500ms, due to Greengrass limitations, we experienced an exponential growth in processing time and were not able to support more than 150 parallel requests. This suggests that solutions based on DM3 can potentially satisfy AC5 but not AC7. The high message loss rate observed in our experiments suggests that additional measures have to be taken into account to address reliability (AC6).

DM4: Edge Cloud Architecture with stateless functions. By enabling ABAC through the use of stateless functions (e.g., AWS lambda functions), this solution is able to leverage the best of the pure cloud and edge-based solutions: supporting AC1 and AC4 as in DM2 and AC5 as in DM3. Our experience with AWS highlighted two important limitations that should be addressed: the evaluation of AWS IoT things' policies and the limit on the number of things that can subscribe to a given topic. In our experiments, the throttling introduced by AWS prevented us to exploit the former under heavy loads and the latter was addressed by configuring LF4 as the client sender. Although in our analysis single requests were processed within 1.5 seconds, IoT platform and edge devices' limitations might reduce DM4's potentials. For instance, within Greengrass, we experienced an exponential growth in the processing time when a single edge device was deployed. Further experiments should be performed to evaluate latency and scalability when more Greengrass cores are deployed.

Final considerations. The lack of scalability (AC7) and reliability (AC6) experienced in our experiments with DM3 and DM4, can be attributed to the way Greengrass processes MQTT messages on the Raspberry Pi, sequentially and at most 30 per second, and the language in which lambda functions have been implemented (Java). Further investigations is needed to determine if other CSPs offer edge solutions similar to Greengrass and the impact of the programming language on the results. Despite this, we believe that by employing multiple endpoints and strongly optimizing stateless functions, it is possible to efficiently handle a large number of parallel requests and to improve reliability.

It is worth noting that AWS IoT and Greengrass provide users with very little, almost no support for policy administration (AC2). To this end, we have extended SecurePG to support the semi-automated deployment of AWS Lambda functions (LF1 to LF4), the RDS configuration and all the IoT-specific components needed to manage a fleet of devices according to the specific authorization mechanism. Thus, SecurePG allows system administrators to configure and deploy their access control policies for all deployment models from a single administration point, thus satisfying AC2. Moreover, using SecurePG, administrators are not forced to specify their policies in a proprietary language. The tool offers a platform-independent language for policy specification along with components that automatically translate policy specifications into platform-specific policy specification, thus enhancing portability of policies across different CSPs (AC3).

6 RELATED WORK

Security and privacy are the primary concerns that hinder the widespread adaption of IoT. Roman et al. [14] provides an explicit analysis of the features and security challenges such as interoperability and management of access control w.r.t. various architectural approaches in the IoT. The coexistence of centralized and distributed architectural approaches is stressed for providing the foundation of full-fledged IoT. Ouaddah et al. [13] performed detailed analysis of existing access control solutions for IoT based upon domain specific IoT requirements. Alonso et al. [1] identifies special requirements (application-scoped, client-independent, flexible, delegated and configurable) that need consideration to foster new approaches for access control mechanism in IoT. Ho et al. [8] examine the security mechanisms employed in home smart lock solutions. Their study reveals flaws in the architectural design and interaction models of existing locks, which can be exploited by an adversary to learn private information about the user and gain unauthorized home access. In our work, we analyzed a vendor specific smart lock as a sample use case of IoT to devise requirements for access control to guide future development of smart locks and similar real-time IoT applications.

Access control mechanisms adopted by CSPs are typically generic and, thus, are often unable to completely capture the specific security requirements of the application domain. Moreover, they are based upon proprietary protocols leading to vendor lock-in situations, which makes the concurrent usage of different CSPs or switching between CSPs difficult for users. To address these issues, recent years have seen the emergence of several solutions adhering the principles underlying the Access Control as a Service (ACaaS) paradigm. Fitiou et al. [6] present access control as a third party service that gives data owner the flexibility to move between CSPs or concurrent usage of multiple CSP. Kaluvuri et al. [10] proposes SAFAX, a XACML-based authorization service provided by trusted third party and designed to address challenges in multi-cloud environment. It provides users with a single point of administration to specify access control policies in a standard format and augment policy evaluation with information from user selectable trust services. Alonso et al. [1] propose IoT Application-Scoped Access Control as a Service (IAACaaS) based on OAuth 2.0 protocol, an IETF standard for authorizing access to resources over HTTP that requires the resource owner to be online during the user authorizing procedure. Similarly, Fremantle et al. [7] makes use of OAuth 2.0 protocol to enable access control to information using MQTT protocol.

Outsourcing access control to trusted third party has several advantages like relieving application developers and CSPs of the burden of designing and maintaining the access control mechanism.

Moreover, it facilitates users in the configuration of their access control policies, since they can be managed from a single, central point. However, this approach is subject to the willingness of a CSP to allow the use of third party services to handle the protection of the data and resources. To the best of our knowledge, none of the existing public CSPs supports such extension. This motivated us to propose a lazy approach to ACaaS by only outsourcing activities pertaining to the specification and configuration of access control policies. This allows the definition of fine grained access control policies, employing an arbitrary number of attributes, along with dedicated function for their evaluation, which can be enforced by the native access control mechanism of the IoT platform.

7 CONCLUSION

We analyzed a realistic smart lock solution and identified the main requirements that access control systems for IoT should satisfy. Driven from this analysis and the current state-of-the-art IoT platforms, we presented an ACaaS solution that outsources the specification and administration of access control policies to a trusted third party, while leveraging the access control mechanism available in the IoT platform for policy evaluation and enforcement. We investigated the practical feasibility of the proposed approach and discussed how the identified requirements are satisfied.

Our lazy approach to ACaaS provides an initial blueprint for developing access control mechanisms for edge-cloud enabled IoT, which can be incrementally enhanced to incorporate new access control capabilities. We observed the main challenge in doing this, namely the simultaneous satisfaction of all requirements in Tab. 1 (cf. Tab. 3). The main reason for this seems to be the combination of heterogeneous technologies—such as cloud, edge and mobile computing together with communication protocols for resource constrained devices (e.g., BLE and MQTT)—that enlarge the attack surface of the access control system, hindering the possibility of confining its core functionalities to a trusted base as it is the case with more traditional systems (such as databases, operating systems, or web services). For instance, policy evaluation becomes unreliable when updates to the latest version of the policies are prevented by features of mobile computing devices such as switching to air mode in order to guarantee availability; there is an obvious trade-off between reliability (AC6) and latency (AC5). As a consequence of this state-of-affairs, it is no more possible to separate the concerns of validating and enforcing policies as typically done in the access control literature (see, e.g., [16]) that assumes that enforcement is correctly implemented by analyzing policies with respect to the abstract semantics of the specification language. Such as assumption seems be too coarse because of the subtle interactions among the technologies used in major IoT platforms. For this reason, we believe that new approaches to design and implement access control mechanisms for IoT systems must be developed and we regard this work as a first step towards this research goal. To further investigate these issues, in future work, we plan to investigate other IoT use cases and extend our ACaaS tool to support more IoT platforms.

Acknowledgments. This work is partially funded by the ITEA2 project M2MGrids (13011), the ITEA3 project APPSTACLE (15017) and the RSA-B project SeCludE.

REFERENCES

[1] Álvaro Alonso, Federico Fernández, Lourdes Marco, and Joaquín Salvachúa. 2017. IAACaaS: IoT Application-Scoped Access Control as a Service. *Future Internet* 9, 4 (2017), 64.

[2] A. Armando, S. Ranise, R. Traverso, and K. S. Wrona. 2016. SMT-based Enforcement and Analysis of NATO Content-based Protection and Release Policies. In *Proc. of the ABAC@CODASPY 2016*. 35–46.

[3] Smriti Bhatt, Farhan Patwa, and Ravi Sandhu. 2017. Access Control Model for AWS Internet of Things. In *Int. Conf. on Network and System Security*. Springer, 721–736.

[4] Charles C Byers. 2017. Architectural imperatives for fog computing: Use cases, requirements, and architectural techniques for FOG-enabled IoT networks. *IEEE Communications Magazine* 55, 8 (2017), 14–20.

[5] David F Ferraiolo, Ravi Sandhu, Serban Gavrila, D Richard Kuhn, and Ramaswamy Chandramouli. 2001. Proposed NIST standard for role-based access control. *ACM Transactions on Information and System Security* 4, 3 (2001), 224–274.

[6] Nikos Fotiou, Apostolis Machas, George C Polyzos, and George Xylomenos. 2015. Access control as a service for the Cloud. *J. of Internet Services and Applications* 6, 1 (2015), 11.

[7] Paul Fremantle, Benjamin Aziz, Jacek Kopecký, and Philip Scott. 2014. Federated identity and access management for the Internet of Things. In *International Workshop on Secure Internet of Things*. IEEE, 10–17.

[8] Grant Ho, Derek Leung, Pratyush Mishra, Ashkan Hosseini, Dawn Song, and David Wagner. 2016. Smart locks: Lessons for securing commodity Internet of Things devices. In *Proc. of Asia Conf. on Computer and Communications Security*. ACM, 461–472.

[9] V. C Hu, D. Ferraiolo, R. Kuhn, A. R. Friedman, A. J Lang, M. M Cogdell, A. Schnitzer, K. Sandlin, R. Miller, and K. Scarfone. 2013. Guide to ABAC Definition and Considerations. Number 800-162 in NIST.

[10] Samuel Paul Kaluvuri, Alexandru Ionut Egner, Jerry den Hartog, and Nicola Zannone. 2015. SAFAX–an extensible authorization service for cloud environments. *Frontiers in ICT* 2 (2015), 9.

[11] Nolan Mondrow. 2017. LockState 6i/6000i Update. (Aug. 2017). Retrieved Feb 13, 2018 from https://marketing.lockstate.com/acton/rif/18500/s-016e-1708/-/l-00fd:3d3/l-00fd/showPreparedMessage?cm_mmc=Act-On%20Software-_-email-_-UPDATE%20LockState%206i%2F6000i%20Issue-_-Click%20here&sid=TV2:3iibu2UNq

[12] Umberto Morelli and Silvio Ranise. 2017. Assisted Authoring, Analysis and Enforcement of Access Control Policies in the Cloud. In *IFIP International Conference on ICT Systems Security and Privacy Protection*. Springer, 296–309.

[13] Aafaf Ouaddah, Hajar Mousannif, Anas Abou Elkalam, and Abdellah Ait Ouahman. 2017. Access control in The Internet of Things: Big challenges and new opportunities. *Computer Networks* 112 (2017), 237–262.

[14] Rodrigo Roman, Jianying Zhou, and Javier Lopez. 2013. On the features and challenges of security and privacy in distributed Internet of Things. *Computer Networks* 57, 10 (2013), 2266–2279.

[15] Stavros Salonikias, Ioannis Mavridis, and Dimitris Gritzalis. 2015. Access control issues in utilizing fog computing for transport infrastructure. In *International Conference on Critical Information Infrastructures Security*. Springer, 15–26.

[16] Pierangela Samarati and Sabrina Capitani de Vimercati. 2000. Access control: Policies, models, and mechanisms. In *International School on Foundations of Security Analysis and Design*. Springer, 137–196.

[17] William Tärneberg, Vishal Chandrasekaran, and Marty Humphrey. 2016. Experiences creating a framework for smart traffic control using AWS IoT. In *Proc. of Int. Conf. on Utility and Cloud Computing*. ACM, 63–69.

[18] Fatih Turkmen, Jerry den Hartog, Silvio Ranise, and Nicola Zannone. 2017. Formal analysis of XACML policies using SMT. *Computers & Security* 66 (2017), 185–203.

[19] Xiaomin Xu, Sheng Huang, Lance Feagan, Yaoliang Chen, Yunjie Qiu, and Yu Wang. 2017. EAaaS: Edge Analytics as a Service. In *IEEE International Conference on Web Services*. IEEE, 349–356.

HCAP: A History-Based Capability System for IoT Devices

Lakshya Tandon
Philip W. L. Fong
Reihaneh Safavi-Naini
University of Calgary, Alberta, Canada
{lakshya.tandon,pwlfong,rei}@ucalgary.ca

ABSTRACT

Permissions are highly sensitive in Internet-of-Things (IoT) applications, as IoT devices collect our personal data and control the safety of our environment. Rather than simply granting permissions, further constraints shall be imposed on permission usage so as to realize the Principle of Least Privilege. Since IoT devices are physically embedded, they are often accessed in a particular sequence based on their relative physical positions. Monitoring if such sequencing constraints are honoured when IoT devices are accessed provides a means to fence off malicious accesses. This paper proposes a history-based capability system, HCAP, for enforcing permission sequencing constraints in a distributed authorization environment. We formally establish the security guarantees of HCAP, and empirically evaluate its performance.

CCS CONCEPTS

• Security and privacy → Logic and verification; Access control;

KEYWORDS

Internet of Things, distributed authorization, History-Based Access Control, capability system, formal verification, safety, liveness, performance evaluation

ACM Reference Format:
Lakshya Tandon, Philip W. L. Fong, and Reihaneh Safavi-Naini. 2018. HCAP: A History-Based Capability System for IoT Devices. In *SACMAT '18: The 23rd ACM Symposium on Access Control Models & Technologies (SACMAT), June 13–15, 2018, Indianapolis, IN, USA.* ACM, New York, NY, USA, 12 pages. https://doi.org/10.1145/3205977.3205978

1 INTRODUCTION

Internet-of-Things (IoT) devices collect our personal data (e.g., wearables, sensors) and control the safety of our environment (e.g., thermostat, smart locks). Granting permissions to access IoT devices often comes with significant privacy, security and even safety implications. Yet, authority delegation is a common use case in IoT applications. For example, envision the wide deployment of smart locks on an organization campus. Permissions to unlock various

entrances must now be properly granted to members of that organization. In this work, we are concerned with the potential misuse of permissions by users of IoT devices.

Rather than simply granting permissions, further usage constraints shall be imposed on permissions in order to rule out potentially malicious usage patterns. Simple examples of this would include contextual constraints such as not allowing entry after midnight. Such constraints are a way of realizing the Principle of Least Privilege [33]. But we can do even better than contextual constraints. Since IoT devices are physically embedded, they are often accessed in a particular sequence based on their relative physical positions. Monitoring if such sequencing constraints are honoured provides a means to fence off malicious accesses to devices.

Example 1.1 (Physical Embeddedness). Alice often stays after office hour, when all the doors of her organization are locked. Special permissions are granted to her to unlock certain doors. When Alice leaves for the day, she passes through entrances A, B and C (corresponding respectively to the lab door, the computer science building entrance, and the campus gate) in that physical order. Not only does Alice require the permissions to unlock the smart locks at A, B and C, ordering constraints shall also be imposed so that, during off hours, C (campus gate) is not unlocked before the authorization system registering her unlocking A (lab door) and B (building entrance). Directly unlocking C (campus gate) without going through A (lab door) and B (building entrance) could very well mean her smartphone has been picked up by an unauthorized party trying to enter the campus from the outside.

Permission sequencing constraints are also important when device accesses must conform to a workflow specification. Kortuem *et al.* use the term **process awareness** to refer to the ability of smart objects to guide their users in following operational procedures [21]. Procedure guiding is envisioned to be a key feature of, say, smart construction objects [29].

Example 1.2 (Process Awareness). Suppose an industrial process follows an explicitly articulated workflow, in which two conceptual steps, S_1 and S_2, are sequentially ordered. Permissions to operate equipments are assigned to each step [9, 41]: e.g., permissions p_1 and p_2 can be exercised in step S_1, and permissions p_2 and p_3 can be exercised in step S_2. The permission assignment and the ordering of workflow steps jointly induce sequencing constraints on permission usage: Once p_3 is exercised, it is obvious that S_2 is being executed, and thus p_1 shall no longer be allowed (i.e., no p_1 after p_3). Violation of this sequencing constraint is a sign of equipment misuse.

Constraining the order in which permissions are exercised is in fact the spirit of History-Based Access Control (HBAC) [12, 13, 22, 25, 35, 39, 40], in which the authorization decision of an access request is a function of the access history. HBAC policies can be imposed to restrict permission usage once an access pattern has been detected (no p_1 after p_3). This feature can be leveraged for enforcing the following forms of permission usage control.

Example 1.3 (Permission Usage Control). Suppose a campus visitor is only allowed to access a facility (e.g., a smart coffee dispenser) no more than four times during her visit. In other words, we want the authorization system to deny the usage of a permission after it has been exercised for a number of times. In short, permissions are seen as consumable resources. A second form of permission usage constraint is the **cardinality constraint**, which demands that no more than k of the permissions in a set P can be exercised [34]. In the special case of $|P| = 2$ and $k = 1$, the constraint enforces permission-level **mutual exclusion**. Similarly, the Chinese Wall policy [8] can be seen as a third form of permission usage constraints: Once a resource has been accessed, access to resources in conflict with the former will be denied.

Enforcing HBAC policies requires support from the authorization system. The growing scale of smart devices and casual users makes it necessary for device administrators to be able to manage access control policies centrally, while enabling devices to enforce such policies in a decentralized manner (i.e., without the mediation of a centralized reference monitor). Typically, an unforgeable capability (aka security token) is issued by a centralized authorization server to a client, who in turn presents the capability to the resource custodian as a proof of authorization. Examples of such distributed capability systems include the Identity-based Capability System (ICAP) [16], CapaFS [32], O'Auth [18], OpenID [31], and Macaroons [5]. The dual requirements of centralized policy administration and decentralized policy enforcement are the main driver behind the recent push by access management solution providers [15, 30] to adopt the User-Managed Access standard [27] as the choice platform for access management in IoT applications. More generally, distributed capability systems have emerged as a popular choice for decentralized access control in the IoT literature [17, 19, 26]. Unfortunately, none of the distributed capability systems surveyed above offers adequate support for HBAC. The crux of the problem is that policy enforcement in HBAC is a stateful process. A traditional capability, however, captures a static set of authorized permissions. Such capabilities will have to be revoked and reissued by the centralized authorization server whenever the state of HBAC enforcement changes, causing the authorization server to be contacted frequently, thereby nullifying the benefit of decentralized access control promised by distributed capability systems.

This paper proposes a History-Based Capability System, HCAP, for regulating the order in which permissions are exercised in a distributed authorization environment. HCAP is an extension of ICAP [16]. HCAP capabilities carry sequencing constraints in the form of security automata (SA) [35]. Exercising a permission produces an SA state transition, invalidates the existing capability, and generates a new capability reflecting the new SA state. Since the proposed scheme minimizes communication with the central authorization server, and does not require the IoT devices to know about the access control policies, HCAP makes a good building block for UMA-style combination of centralized policy administration and decentralized policy enforcement. We claim four contributions:

(1) We describe the design of HCAP, a distributed capability system that can enforce history-based access control policies (see §3).
(2) We formally establish the security guarantees of HCAP in the form of a safety property and a liveness property (see §4).
(3) In the formulation of core HCAP, it is assumed that the permissions associated with an SA are all related to a single device. We propose an extension to HCAP that relaxes this restriction, thereby allowing an SA to regulate the permission usage of multiple devices (see §5).
(4) We empirically evaluate the performance of HCAP (see §6).

2 RELATED WORK

There are two kinds of distributed authorization system [37]. The first kind are the **credentials-based authorization systems** (F. Schneider's terminology), in which the client presents a set of certificates to an authorization system as a proof of policy compliance [1–3, 24]. The certificates in the compliance proof are typically issued by different authorities, and each certificate corresponds to an assertion in a logical language used for specifying conditions of authorization. The authorization system is presumed to know the access control policy, which is specified in the aforementioned logical language. The second kind are the **distributed capability systems**, in which the authorization system, upon successful check of policy compliance, issues to the client an unforgeable capability (aka security token) [5, 16, 18, 31, 32]. The client then presents the capability to resource custodians to gain access without further mediation of the authorization system. The resource custodians are thus freed from needing to know and manage the access control policies. This work contributes to the literature of the second kind. To the best of our knowledge, HCAP is the first distributed capability system to support History-Based Access Control (HBAC). We advocate the employment of this feature for sequencing permission usage in IoT environments.

HCAP is an extension of ICAP [16] in order to enforce HBAC policies. While an ICAP capability carries the list of granted permissions, an HCAP capability carries a partial specification of an SA, which we call an SA fragment. In the degenerate case when the SA has only one state, an HCAP capability is structurally equivalent to an ICAP capability. Another point of comparison concerns the exceptions. Exceptions are created in ICAP when the authorization server informs the resource server of capability revocations. In HCAP, an exception is created when the resource server exercises a permission that leads to SA state transition, thereby invalidating an existing capability. In addition, HCAP exceptions are much more complex: each exception chronicles the history of SA state transition, rather than a single event of revocation.

ICAP has also been extended by Mahalle *et al.* for IoT applications [26]. Their extension does not support HBAC.

The State-Modifying Policy (SMP) language is an authorization logic that supports the specification of changes to the protection state as a result of authorization [4]. SMP is designed particularly for HBAC policies. Its enforcement model, however, assumes a centralized resource guard (aka PEP), and is therefore incapable of supporting decentralized access control in the manner of HCAP.

In history-based access control, the history of access is tracked by a reference monitor, and this access history forms the basis of making authorization decisions [12, 13, 22, 25, 35, 39, 40]. Schneider proved that only safety properties are enforceable using a reference monitor that tracks execution history, and proposed the Security Automata as an automata-theoretic representation of reference monitors [35]. In this work, permission sequencing constraints are encoded as a Security Automaton and embedded in a capability. State transition occurs when the capability is presented to a resource custodian, who may not immediately relay this change back to the central authorization server. The representation of the current automaton state is therefore distributed across multiple participants. The technical challenge addressed by HCAP are (a) to ensure the coherence of this distributed representation, (b) to provably prevent replay attacks, and (c) to achieve the above while minimizing communications with the authorization server.

3 A HISTORY-BASED CAPABILITY SYSTEM

3.1 Overview

Protocol Participants. We envision a distributed authorization system akin to UMA [27], consisting of resource servers, clients and an authorization server.

Resource servers. Each resource server encapsulates a number of resources within a single device, and acts as their custodian. For example, a smart weather station tracks a number of weather readings, each considered a separate resource. Operations can be performed on the resources. In the smart weather station, an operation for a given weather reading (e.g., temperature) can be "retrieve" or "post reading to Facebook." A *permission* is an operation-resource pair. An access request is a request for the resource server to *exercise* a permission: i.e., perform the operation on the resource.

Clients. Clients are users who, mediated by software systems (e.g., smartphone apps), direct access requests to resource servers.

Authorization server. The authorization server is responsible for access management. Administrators of resource servers and their resources may specify access control policies to indicate which permission is granted to which client. We assume that an Application Programming Interface (API) is in place for an administrator to specify resources and operations to be protected. What is unique in HCAP is that the access control policy not only grants a set of permissions to a client, but also prescribes constraints on the order in which the permissions are to be exercised. As we shall see below, such constraints will take the form of a *security automaton* [35].

The authorization server issues capabilities [10] to clients, who in turn present the capabilities to resource servers.

Trust Assumptions. The following are assumed. (1) The authorization server and resource servers are trusted parties. (2) Clients are not trusted: they actively attempt to forge, share with others, or replay capabilities (and other tickets). They are also unreliable: they may lose capabilities (and other tickets) that have been issued to them. (3) A public key infrastructure (PKI) is in place, so that the authorization server and the resource servers can authenticate one another, as well as the identity claims of clients. It is assumed that the authorization server can verify membership of the resource servers and clients that belong to the organization. (4) Each resource server has established a shared secret with the authorization server.

(5) Devices are equipped with a secure untamperable hardware that holds their secret values. (6) We assume a central clock that is used to synchronize all individual clocks in the system, and assume entities communicate over secure channel.

Design Objectives. HCAP is designed with the following objectives in mind.

O1 Resource servers shall not maintain knowledge of client identities and sequencing constraints. The authorization server alone is responsible for access management. In other words, when access control policies evolve, the resource servers do not need to be reconfigured.

O2 Communication with the authorization server shall be minimized, because that server is a communication bottleneck. A protocol in which every access request is mediated by the authorization server is considered a non-solution.

O3 The computational demand for resource servers shall be minimized, as these servers are hosted on IoT devices that may have limited computational capabilities.

Solution Approach. The sequencing constraints for permissions are essentially safety properties [23], encoded as security automata (an automata-theoretic representation of reference monitors) [35]. When a client initiates a protocol session, a security automaton is started to monitor the order in which permissions are exercised in that session. The authorization server tracks the current state of that automaton. Since the resource server does not know the security automaton (**O1**), and the authorization server shall not be involved in policy mediation (**O2**), part of or all of the security automaton is carried in the capability. When the client presents the capability to a resource server for gaining access, the resource server simulates the automaton's state transition. State transition is not communicated immediately to the authorization server (**O2**). Instead, the resource server records the state transition, and issues a new capability to the client (while revoking the previous one). To conserve the computational resources of the resource server, the HCAP protocol has the resource server flushes its record of state transitions back to the authorization server from time to time, a process known as garbage collection (**O3**). For the same reason, the capability may not carry the full specification of the security automaton, thereby making capability processing lightweight (**O3**).

As the knowledge of the authorization server in the automaton state may lag behind the state transitions carried out remotely by resource servers, the current state of the security automaton is a datum distributed between the authorization server and the resource servers. The design of HCAP ensures the coherence of this distributed representation of the automaton state, and that outdated capabilities are not replayed by the client to gain access illegally.

Core HCAP. To facilitate presentation, this and the next section will present *core HCAP*, in which there is only one resource server. The extension of core HCAP to handle multiple resource servers is deferred to §5.

Preliminaries. We write $dom(f)$ and $ran(f)$ respectively for the domain and range of function f. A *partial function* $f : A \nrightarrow B$ is a function f with domain $A' \subseteq A$ and codomain B. A finite partial function (i.e., finite domain) is also called a *map*.

3.2 Building Blocks

Security Automata. A **security automaton** is an automata-theoretic encoding of a safety property [35]. Here, we adopt the finitary variant of deterministic security automaton as defined by Fong [13]. A **Deterministic Finite Security Automaton (DFSA)**, or simply **Security Automaton (SA)** in this work, is a tuple (Σ, Q, q_0, δ), where Σ is a finite set of permissions, Q is a finite set of automaton states, $q_0 \in Q$ is an initial state, and $\delta : Q \times \Sigma \nrightarrow Q$ is a partial transition function (i.e., $\delta(q, p)$ may be undefined for some pair of state $q \in Q$ and permission $p \in \Sigma$). An SA is essentially like a deterministic finite automaton in which every state is a final state. An SA accepts a sequence of permissions so long as the transition function defines a transition for every step. Policy violation is detected when there is no transition for a permission in the current state. For instance, the two SA below enforce the policies described in Example 1.1 (left) and Example 1.2 (right).

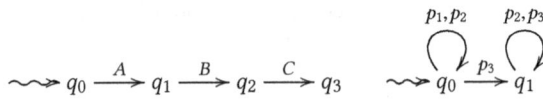

When the SA M is in a state q, the permissions that bring M back to q are **stationary** permissions, and the permissions that cause a transition to a different state are **transitioning** permissions. We define $\text{stat}_M(q) = \{p \in \Sigma \mid \delta(q, p) = q\}$ to be the set of stationary permissions in state q. Similarly, we define $\text{trans}_M(q) = \{p \in \Sigma \mid \exists q' \in Q . q' \neq q \wedge \delta(q, p) = q'\}$ to be the set of transitioning permissions in state q.

Tickets. The authorization server and resource server issue **tickets** to the client, who in turn uses them to justify requests. To ensure ticket authenticity and non-transferability, each ticket carries an authentication tag obtained from (a) the shared secret k between the authorization server and the resource server (trust assumption 4 in §3.1), and (b) the client identity *uid*. In this work, we follow the lightweight tagging mechanism of ICAP [16]. Suppose α is an assertion, the ticket $\langle\!\langle \alpha \rangle\!\rangle_{k,uid}$ derived from secret key k for client *uid* is $\alpha \mid h(\alpha \mid uid \mid k)$, where h is a hash function and "$x \mid y$" means the concatenation of x and y. Upon receiving a ticket $\langle\!\langle \alpha \rangle\!\rangle_{?,?}$ from a client *uid*, the resource server can check the ticket's authenticity by checking that the hash value in $\langle\!\langle \alpha \rangle\!\rangle_{?,?}$ is equal to $h(\alpha \mid uid \mid k)$. The use of *uid* to compute the hash value also ensures that the ticket is non-transferrable.

There are two kinds of ticket, capabilities and update requests, which we introduce in turn.

Capabilities. Capabilities are tickets issued by either the authorization server or the resource server to assert that certain permissions can be exercised by the client. A client may present an access request along with the capability to gain access. A capability issued to client *uid* for session *sessid* has the form $\langle\!\langle sessid : \text{cap}(t_{ser}, F) \rangle\!\rangle_{k,uid}$. Every capability asserts that the SA is in a certain state q, and thus some corresponding permissions can be exercised for *sessid*. The timestamp t_{ser}, also called the **serial number** of the capability, identifies q indirectly by identifying the time when the SA entered into state q. The component F is an **SA fragment**, which identifies the permissions (stationary and transitioning) allowed in state q, as well as the transitions emanating from q. In some sense,

an SA fragment is a partial specification of the SA, with current state q (formal definition to be given below). The specification is partial, because the authorization server is not obligated to encode the entire SA in one capability. This may be because full encoding causes the capability to be bloated, or because the authorization server desires to be synchronized with the resource server more often, or because the underlying communication protocol limits the capability size.

SA Fragments. An SA fragment is a representation of two things: (a) a (possibly incomplete) transition diagram, and (b) the current state of the transition diagram. States in the transition diagram are identified by symbolic names. We assume there is a countably infinite set $\mathcal{N}$ of symbolic names as well as a distinct marker $\circ$ (pronounced 'unknown') such that $\circ \notin \mathcal{N}$. An SA fragment F is a pair $(defs, n_\star)$. The component $defs$ is a finite partial function in which $dom(defs) \subset \mathcal{N}$ identifies the states of a transition diagram. For each name $n \in dom(defs)$, $defs(n)$ specifies the transitions emanating from the state with name n. More specifically, $defs(n)$ is a pair $(SP, trans)$, so that $SP \subseteq \Sigma$ is the set of stationary permissions of n, and $trans : \Sigma \nrightarrow \mathcal{N} \cup \{\circ\}$ maps each transitioning permission of n to either a next state or the marker $\circ$. When $trans(p) = \circ$, the transition diagram permits the transition but does not identify the next state of the transition (thus F is a fragment rather than a complete SA). We further require that $SP \cap dom(trans) = \emptyset$, and $ran(trans) \setminus \{\circ\} \subseteq dom(defs)$. Lastly, the second component $n_\star$ of F identifies the current state of the transition diagram, such that $n_\star \in dom(defs)$. It is easy to see that one can use an SA fragment to partially specify an SA (i.e., a subset of states plus a subset of transitions). An SA fragment can be encoded as a JSON (JavaScript Object Notation) object in a straightforward manner [11].

Transitions can be computed efficiently when SA fragments are encoded in JSON. Given an SA fragment $F = (defs, n_\star)$ for which $defs(n_\star) = (SP, trans)$, $\Delta(F, p)$ is defined to be (a) F if $p \in SP$, (b) the fragment $(defs, trans(p))$ if $trans(p) \in \mathcal{N}$, and (c) $\circ$ if $trans(p) = \circ$. Otherwise $\Delta(F, p)$ is undefined.

Our security guarantees depend on the condition that the SA fragments embedded in capabilities are "conservative" partial specification of the corresponding SA: i.e., the SA fragment does not allow transitions that are not supported by the corresponding SA, a notion that we formalize in the following. Let $F = (defs, n_\star)$ be an SA fragment, $M = (\Sigma, Q, q_0, \delta)$ be an SA, and $q \in Q$ be an SA state. Then F is **safe for** M **in state** q if and only if there exists a function $\pi : dom(defs) \to Q$ such that (a) $\pi(n_\star) = q$, and (b) for every $n \in dom(defs)$, where $defs(n) = (SP, trans)$, the three conditions below hold: (i) $SP \subseteq \text{stat}_M(\pi(n))$; (ii) $dom(trans) \subseteq \text{trans}_M(\pi(n))$; (iii) for every $p \in dom(trans)$, either $trans(p) = \circ$ or $\pi(trans(p)) = \delta(\pi(n), p)$.

LEMMA 3.1. *Suppose $M = (\Sigma, Q, q_0, \delta)$ is an SA, $q \in Q$, and SA fragment $F = (defs, n_\star)$ is safe for M in q. Let $defs(n_\star) = (SP, trans)$. Then the following properties hold: (1) $\Delta(F, p)$ is defined only if $\delta(q, p)$ is defined. (2) If $p \in SP$, then p is stationary for q. If $p \in dom(trans)$, then p is transitioning for q. (3) If $\Delta(F, p)$ is an SA fragment (rather than $\circ$), then $\Delta(F, p)$ is safe for M in $\delta(q, p)$.*

Update Requests. A second kind of ticket is an **update request**, which has the form $\langle\!\langle sessid : \text{upd}(e) \rangle\!\rangle_{k,uid}$. An update request is issued by the resource server, asserting that since last synchronized with the authorization server, e is the list of transitioning permissions that have been exercised by the resource server for the session $sessid$. The construct e is called an **exception**, for it describes how the knowledge of the authorization server has been out of sync.

Exceptions. An **exception** e records the history of the resource server having exercised certain permissions in the past. It is defined inductively as follows:

$$e ::= \text{nil}(t) \mid \text{ex}(p, t, e)$$

where $p \in \Sigma$ and $t \in \mathbb{N}$. Essentially, e is a list of permission-timestamp pairs. Each pair contains a permission p and the time t at which p was exercised. The permissions are listed in descending order of time (more recent ones are listed first). We write $times(e)$ for the set of all timestamps appearing in e, as well as $first(e)$ and $last(e)$ respectively for the minimum (least recent) and maximum (most recent) timestamps in $times(e)$.

We write $\delta^*(q, e)$ to signify the SA state obtained by starting at state q and exercising the permissions of e in chronological order. That is, $\delta^*(q, \text{nil}(t)) = q$, and $\delta^*(q, \text{ex}(p, t, e)) = \delta(\delta^*(q, e), p)$. δ^* is undefined if one of the recursive calls is undefined.

A similar notation, $\Delta^*(F, e)$, can also be defined for SA fragments: $\Delta^*(F, \text{nil}(t)) = F$, and $\Delta^*(F, \text{ex}(p, t, e)) = \Delta(\Delta^*(F, e), p)$. As expected, $\Delta^*(F, e)$ is not defined if the nested calls are not defined, or if they return $\circ$.

Sometimes we want to apply only some of the transitions in an exception list to an SA fragment. Suppose $e = \text{ex}(p_m, t_m, \text{ex}(p_{m-1}, t_{m-1}, \ldots \text{ex}(p_1, t_1, \text{nil}(t_0)) \ldots))$ for some $m \geq 0$. We then write $\Delta^*_{\leq t_i}(F, e)$ to denote $\Delta(\ldots \Delta(\Delta(F, p_1), p_2) \ldots, p_i)$, and $\Delta^*_{> t_i}(F, e)$ to denote $\Delta(\ldots \Delta(\Delta(F, p_{i+1}), p_{i+2}) \ldots, p_m)$. It is not hard to see that $\Delta^*(F, e) = \Delta^*_{> t_i}(\Delta^*_{\leq t_i}(F, e), e)$.

3.3 Protocol Description

Server Internal States. The authorization server and the resource server maintain a shared secret k. In addition, the authorization server maintains three maps for session administration: (a) $monitor[sessid]$ is the SA for session $sessid$, (b) $state[sessid]$ is the state of $monitor[sessid]$ last known by the authorization server, and (c) $serial[sessid]$ is the timestamp when $monitor[sessid]$ is registered by the authorization server to have entered into state $state[sessid]$. The timestamp $serial[sessid]$ will be used as the serial number of the next capability issued by the authorization server for session $sessid$. Lastly, the authorization server precomputes an SA fragment $fragment[M, q]$ for every SA M stored in $monitor[\cdot]$ and every state q of M. It is assumed that $fragment[M, q]$ is safe for M in q.

The resource server maintains two pieces of information: (a) a timestamp t_{rs}, which marks the minimum serial number of capabilities that the server considers valid, and (b) a map $ex[\cdot]$, which records, for each known session ID $sessid$, the exception that chronicles the transitioning permissions the resource server has exercised since the SA of $sessid$ has entered the state $state[sessid]$.

Session Initialization. A client uid who intends to access a resource server shall first authenticate itself to the authorization server, and then request the initiation of a new protocol session for that resource server. The authorization server will consult an

---

Algorithm 1: Authorization procedure of the resource server.

Input: A client access request (uid, p, cap), where uid is the client's authenticated identity, p is the permission to be exercised, and cap is a capability $\langle\!\langle sessid : \text{cap}(t_{ser}, F) \rangle\!\rangle_{?,?}$ for session $sessid$, such that $F = (defs, n_\star)$ and $defs(n_\star) = (SP, trans)$.

Output: A set of tickets, or a failure response.

Data: The resource server maintains the following persistent data: (a) a secret k it shares with the authorization server, (b) a timestamp t_{rs}, and (c) a map $ex[\cdot]$ that assigns an exception to each known session ID.

1 **if** cap is not signed by k for uid, or $t_{ser} < t_{rs}$ **then**
2   **return** *failure*
3 **if** $ex[sessid]$ is undefined, or $t_{ser} > last(ex[sessid])$ **then**
4    $ex[sessid] \leftarrow \text{nil}(t_{ser})$
5 **else if** $t_{ser} < last(ex[sessid])$ **then**
6   **return** *failure*
7 **if** $p \in SP$ **then**
8   Exercise permission p;
9   **return** $\emptyset$
10 **else if** $p \in dom(trans)$ **then**
11   Exercise permission p;
12    $t \leftarrow current\_time()$;
13    $ex[sessid] \leftarrow \text{ex}(p, t, ex[sessid])$;
14    $F' \leftarrow \Delta(F, p)$;
15   **if** $F' = \circ$ **then**
16   **return** $\{\langle\!\langle sessid : \text{upd}(ex[sessid]) \rangle\!\rangle_{k, uid}\}$
17   **else**
18   **return** $\{\langle\!\langle sessid : \text{cap}(t, F') \rangle\!\rangle_{k, uid}\}$
19 **else return** *failure* ;

---

access control policy, and decide if access shall be granted.[1] If the authorization decision is positive, a new session ID $sessid$ is created. The access control policy will grant a set Σ of permissions to the session, and also prescribe an SA $M = (\Sigma, Q, q_0, \delta)$ to regulate the order in which permissions are to be exercised within that session. The session $sessid$ is initialized as follows:

$$monitor[sessid] \leftarrow M;$$
$$state[sessid] \leftarrow q_0;$$
$$serial[sessid] \leftarrow current\_time();$$

The capability $\langle\!\langle sessid : \text{cap}(t_{ser}, F) \rangle\!\rangle_{k, uid}$ is then issued to client uid, where k is the shared secret between the authorization and the resource server, $t_{ser} = serial[sessid]$, and $F = fragment[M, q_0]$.

Authorization. The client uid requests the resource server to exercise a permission p by presenting a triple $(uid, p, \langle\!\langle sessid : \text{cap}(t_{ser}, F) \rangle\!\rangle_{?,?})$, where the capability is the justification for access. The identity of uid is first authenticated, and then the request is authorized according to Algorithm 1. The resource server first checks

---

[1] The authorization decision can take into account identities, roles (RBAC) [34], attributes (ABAC) [20] and relationships (ReBAC) [14].

the authenticity of the capability (line 1). It also rejects capabilities with serial numbers earlier than t_{rs}. As we shall see below, t_{rs} is the time of the last garbage collection, whereby the authorization server and the resource server synchronize their knowledge of the SA's current states. Such a synchronization invalidates all capabilities with serial numbers earlier than t_{rs}.

The serial number of the capability is then compared to $last(ex[sessid])$ in lines 3–6. The goal is to see how current the capability is in comparison to the knowledge of the resource server. Line 3 corresponds to the case when the capability is issued by the authorization server, and the latter's knowledge of the SA state is more current than that of the resource server. Consequently, $ex[sessid]$ is reset. Line 5 corresponds to the case when the capability captures an SA state that is older than what the resource server knows. The capability is therefore rejected. The fall-through case of lines 3–6 is when t_{ser} equals $last(ex[sessid])$, meaning that the capability is as current as the knowledge of the resource server, and nothing needs to be done in this case.

Lines 7–9 handle requests that involve the exercising of stationary permissions. No new ticket is issued.

Lines 10–18 specify the case when the request involves a transitioning permission. The permission is exercised, and the transition is recorded in $ex[sessid]$ (line 13). The provided SA fragment is then used for computing the next SA fragment (line 14). A new capability is issued for the new SA fragment (line 18). Line 16 will be discussed below under the heading *Update Requests*.

If the permission requested is neither stationary nor transitioning, then the request is denied (line 19).

Update Requests. An update request is issued when the SA fragment embedded in the capability does not provide enough information for the resource server to construct the next capability (line 16). The client is expected to take the update request to the authorization server, so that the latter can update its record of the current SA state. The authorization server will only accept an update request $\langle\!\langle sessid : upd(e)\rangle\!\rangle_{k,uid}$ if $first(e) = serial[sessid]$. The result is that $serial[sessid]$ is updated to the current time, and $state[sessid]$ is updated to $\delta^*(state[sessid], e)$, where δ is the transition function of $monitor[sessid]$. Lastly, the authorization server will issue to the client a fresh capability, in which the SA fragment is $fragment[monitor[sessid], state[sessid]]$.

Garbage Collection. The resource server accumulates exception information in $ex[\cdot]$ due to the creation of new sessions and exercising transitioning permissions. Tracking exception information strains the resource server, which is hosted on constrained hardware. That is why "garbage collection" needs to be performed from time to time. This involves the resource server (a) sending the contents of $ex[\cdot]$ (e.g., encoded as a JSON object) to the authorization server, (b) resetting $ex[\cdot]$ to an empty map, and (c) setting t_{rs} to the current time (i.e., time of garbage collection). Step (c) invalidates the tickets issued prior to garbage collection, forcing clients to obtain fresh capabilities from the authorization server.

Upon receiving $ex[\cdot]$, the authorization server updates the SA state on record for each $sessid$ defined in $ex[\cdot]$. More specifically, $state[sessid]$ is updated to $\delta^*(state[sessid], ex[sessid])$, and $serial[sessid]$ to the time of garbage collection.

Ticket Recovery. Clients are unreliable, and may accidentally misplace tickets. As tickets contain crucial information for the proper execution of the protocol, two mechanisms of ticket recovery are in place.

First, a client may contact the authorization server, and have the capability with serial number $serial[sessid]$ reissued. The SA fragment of that capability is $fragment[monitor[sessid], state[sessid]]$. This is the standard means for obtaining a working capability after garbage collection.

The method above may not be sufficient for recovering the latest tickets. In particular, if transitioning requests have already been made since $serial[sessid]$, then the resource server has issued more recent tickets. So a second ticket recovery mechanism is in place, in which the client may present to the resource server a previously issued capability $\langle\!\langle sessid : cap(t_{ser}, F)\rangle\!\rangle_{k,uid}$, such that $t_{ser} \in times(ex[sessid])$, and then the resource server will use $ex[sessid]$ together with F to reconstruct the latest ticket for $sessid$ (either an update request or a capability). Details of this mechanism are provided in the next section in transition rule T-Rcv. The latest ticket for a session can always be recovered by applying the first and second recovery mechanism in sequence.

3.4 Discussions

Authorization server. The authorization server has freedom to construct any SA fragment as $fragment[M, q]$ so long as the fragment is safe for M in q. The following are some possibilities:

- If the SA M contains a single state, then the HCAP protocol degenerates to ICAP, as all permissions are stationary.
- Consider the case when every capability issued by the authorization contains an SA fragment $F = (defs, n_\star)$ such that $defs(n_\star) = (SP, trans)$, $dom(defs) = \{n_\star\}$, and $ran(trans) = \{\circ\}$. That is, all transition targets are unknown. Such a capability describes only the stationary and transitioning permissions (via SP and $dom(trans)$ respectively) of the current SA state. This results in highly lightweight capabilities, and the processing overhead for the resource server is minimized. An update request will be returned every time a transitioning permission is exercised, thereby forcing the client to communicate with the authorization server whenever a transition occurs.
- Capabilities may be constructed to capture several levels of transition. For example, if it is known that the most frequent transitions will oscillate among a small number of states, then that region of the transition diagram can be embedded in the capability. Update requests will be returned infrequently.
- If M is small, then the entire specification can be captured in the capability. No update requests will ever be returned.

Resource server. There are two approaches to decide when garbage collection should be triggered:

(1) Garbage collection can be invoked on regular intervals (e.g., every 8 hours). This ensures that sessions that are no longer active will not occupy resources indefinitely.

(2) Garbage collection can also be invoked when $ex[\cdot]$ reaches a certain size threshold, or when one of the exception lists exceeds a certain length threshold. With this approach, $ex[\cdot]$ is guaranteed to never grow beyond a predetermined capacity.

A combination of both approaches is recommended for a realistic implementation: perform garbage collection in regular intervals as well as when the capacity/length threshold is reached.

4 SECURITY GUARANTEES

Replay attacks are the main security concern for HCAP: Is it possible for the client to gain illegal access by presenting a previously issued capability to a resource server after the SA has already transitioned to a state q in which that capability is no longer representative of q. In this section, we formulate a formal model for an HCAP protocol session, and demonstrate that replay attacks are impossible (Safety). We also demonstrate that the protocol is resilient to unreliable clients who misplace tickets (Liveness).

We model the HCAP protocol as a state transition system. Each protocol state captures the state of the entire distributed authorization system, including the internal states of the authorization server, the resource server and the client. A protocol state transition occurs when the protocol participants interact with one another. The main goal of verification is to establish a correspondence between the distributed authorization system and a reference monitor that runs in a centralized system (Theorem 4.2).

Our state transition model abstracts away the following aspects of HCAP: (1) Ticket forging is not modelled as we assume that it is adequately prevented by authentication tags. (2) As protocol sessions are independent from one another, the model specifies the behaviour of one protocol session only. (3) We omit the minor detail of $ex[sessid]$ becoming undefined after garbage collection.

Protocol States. Throughout this section, we assume that $M = (\Sigma, Q, q_0, \delta)$ is the SA for the protocol session being modelled. We further assume that the authorization server has pre-computed, for each state $q \in Q$, an SA fragment $F_{M,q}$ that is safe for M in q.

Definition 4.1 (Protocol States). A **protocol state** γ is a 4-tuple (t_{clo}, A, R, C), where the four components are defined as follows.

- The component $t_{clo} \in \mathbb{N}$ is the **global clock value**.
- The **authorization server state** A is a pair (q_{as}, t_{as}), where $q_{as} \in Q$ is the state of M last known by the authorization server, and $t_{as} \in \mathbb{N}$ is the time when the above knowledge is registered by the authorization server.
- The **resource server state** R is a pair (t_{rs}, e_{rs}), where $t_{rs} \in \mathbb{N}$ is the minimum serial number for capabilities that the resource server considers valid, and exception e_{rs} records the transitioning permissions that have been exercised by the resource server since M enters into state q_{as}.
- The **client state** C is the set of **tickets** that have been issued to the client throughout the protocol session. A ticket tic is of one of two forms: (a) an update request $upd(e)$, where e is of the form $ex(p, t, e')$, or (b) a capability $cap(t_{ser}, F)$.

Let $\Gamma(M)$ be the set of all protocol states γ of the above form.

Initial State. The protocol is intended to begin at the initial state $\gamma_0 = (2, A_0, R_0, \emptyset)$ where $A_0 = (q_0, 1)$, $R_0 = (1, nil(0))$.

State Transition. A **transition identifier** λ identifies a protocol event that causes a change to the protocol state:

$$\lambda ::= issue() \mid request(p, tic) \mid flush() \mid update(tic) \mid$$
$$recover(tic) \mid drop(Ts)$$

where p is a permission, tic is a ticket, and Ts is a set of tickets. Let $\Lambda(M)$ be the set of all transition identifiers induced by M.

We specify below a transition relation $\cdot \overset{\cdot}{\longrightarrow} \cdot \subseteq \Gamma(M) \times \Lambda(M) \times \Gamma(M)$. The relation is specified in terms of transition rules, which identify the conditions under which $(t_{clo}, A, R, C) \overset{\lambda}{\longrightarrow} (t'_{clo}, A', R', C')$, where $A = (q_{as}, t_{as})$, $R = (t_{rs}, e_{rs})$, $A' = (q'_{as}, t'_{as})$, and $R' = (t'_{rs}, e'_{rs})$. By default, $t'_{clo} = t_{clo} + 1$, $A' = A$, $R' = R$ and $C' = C$, unless the rules explicitly say otherwise.

T-Iss *The authorization server issues a capability to the client.*
  Precondition: $\lambda = issue()$
  Effect: $C' = C \cup \{ cap(t_{as}, F_M, q_{as}) \}$.

T-ReqS *The client requests to exercise a stationary permission.*
  Precondition: $\lambda = request(p, tic)$, $tic \in C$, $tic = cap(t_{ser}, F)$, $t_{ser} \geq t_{rs}$, $t_{ser} \geq last(e_{rs})$, $F = (defs, n_\star)$, $defs(n_\star) = (SP, \_)$, $p \in SP$.
  Effect: $e'_{rs} = nil(t_{ser})$ if $t_{ser} > last(e_{rs})$.

T-ReqT *The client requests to exercise a transitioning permission.*
  Precondition: $\lambda = request(p, tic)$, $tic \in C$, $tic = cap(t_{ser}, F)$, $t_{ser} \geq t_{rs}$, $t_{ser} \geq last(e_{rs})$, $F = (defs, n_\star)$, $defs(n_\star) = (\_, trans)$, $p \in dom(trans)$.
  Effect: First, $e'_{rs} = ex(p, t_{clo}, e_0)$, where $e_0 = nil(t_{ser})$ if $t_{ser} > last(e_{rs})$, or $e_0 = e_{rs}$ if $t_{ser} = last(e_{rs})$. Second, $C' = C \cup \{ tic_0 \}$, where $tic_0 = upd(e'_{rs})$ if $\Delta(F, p) = \circ$, or $tic_0 = cap(t_{clo}, \Delta(F, p))$ otherwise.

T-Fsh *Garbage collection.*
  Precondition: $\lambda = flush()$.
  Effect: First, $t'_{as} = t_{clo}$, $t'_{rs} = t_{clo}$, and $e'_{rs} = nil(last(e_{rs}))$. Second, $q'_{as} = \delta^*(q_{as}, e_{rs})$ if $t_{as} = first(e_{rs})$.

T-Upd *The client updates the internal state of the authorization server.*
  Precondition: $\lambda = update(tic)$, $tic \in C$, $tic = upd(e)$, and $first(e) = t_{as}$.
  Effect: $t'_{as} = t_{clo}$, $q'_{as} = \delta^*(q_{as}, e)$.

T-Rcv *The client asks the resource server to recover a lost ticket.*
  Precondition: $\lambda = recover(tic)$, $tic \in C$, $tic = cap(t_{ser}, F)$, and $t_{ser} \in times(e_{rs})$.
  Effect: Let $F' = \Delta^*_{>t_{ser}}(F, e_{rs})$. There are three cases. (1) If F' is undefined, then $C' = C$. (2) If $F' = \circ$, then $C' = C \cup \{upd(e_{rs})\}$. (3) Otherwise, $C' = C \cup \{ cap(last(e_{rs}), F') \}$.

T-Drp *The client accidentally drops some of its tickets.*
  Precondition: $\lambda = drop(Ts)$, $Ts \subseteq C$.
  Effect: $C' = C \setminus Ts$.

Appendix A of [38] enumerates the state invariants that are satisfied by the initial state and perserved by the state transition relation.

Security Properties. Consider protocol state $\gamma = (t_{clo}, A, R, C)$, where $A = (q_{as}, t_{as})$ and $R = (t_{rs}, e_{rs})$, such that γ satisfies the state invariants in [38, Appendix A]. The **effective SA state** of protocol state γ, denoted $eff(\gamma)$, is q_{as} if $t_{as} > last(e_{rs})$, or $\delta^*(q_{as}, e_{rs})$ otherwise. The internal states of the authorization and resource server is a distributed representation of the effective SA state. The main theorem below asserts that the distributed authorization system mimics the behaviour of the centralized reference monitor that M represents.

THEOREM 4.2 (SAFETY). *Suppose γ satisfies the state invariants in [38, Appendix A], and $\gamma \xrightarrow{\lambda} \gamma'$. Then the following statements hold: (1) If $\lambda = \text{request}(p, tic)$ then $\delta(\text{eff}(\gamma), p) = \text{eff}(\gamma')$. (2) If λ is not of the form request$(\_,\_)$ then $\text{eff}(\gamma) = \text{eff}(\gamma')$.*

A proof of the theorem above can be found in [38, Appendix B].

The next theorem asserts that the client can eventually obtain a working capability (before garbage collection occurs), even if tickets are misplaced.

THEOREM 4.3 (LIVENESS). *Suppose γ satisfies the state invariants in [38, Appendix A]. Then there exists a (possibly empty) sequence of transitions $\gamma = \gamma_0 \xrightarrow{\lambda_1} \gamma_1 \xrightarrow{\lambda_2} \ldots \xrightarrow{\lambda_n} \gamma_n = \gamma'$, such that each λ_i is neither flush() nor drop$(\_)$, $\gamma' = (\_,\_,(\_,e'_{rs}),C')$, and C' contains a capability cap$(t_{ser},\_)$ for which $t_{ser} \geq t_{rs}$ and $t_{ser} \geq last(e'_{rs})$.*

A proof of liveness is given in [38, Appendix B].

5 MULTIPLE RESOURCE SERVERS

We have been assuming that, when the client requests the authorization server to grant access to a pool of resources, the entire pool is guarded by a single resource server. This section presents an extension to HCAP for accommodating resource pools guarded by multiple resource servers.

Every resource server has a unique identifier *rsid*. We write k_{rsid} to denote the shared secret established between the resource server *rsid* and the authorization server. In §3.1, a permission is defined to be an operation-resource pair. We assume that the resource identifier within a permission p also identifies the resource server $RS(p)$ that holds the named resource, and that it takes only $O(1)$ time to reconstruct $RS(p)$ from p. (This is true if the resource is identified by a URI, as in the implementation reported in §6.)

New Concepts. Our design of the multiple resource servers extension aims to preserve the security guarantees of §4. To this end, the design is based on three concepts.

(1) Baton holding. A global invariant is that, at most one resource server tracks the exception list *ex*[*sessid*] for a session *sessid*. That resource server is said to be "holding the ***baton*** (i.e., *ex*[*sessid*]) for session *sessid*." This allows the security proofs in §4 to (mostly) transfer to this new setting, with one exception. Suppose a resource server *rsid* does not hold the baton for *sessid*. Then a malicious client may replay to *rsid* an outdated capability for *sessid*. The resource server would not be able to differentiate between the following two cases: Is it the case that (i) no resource server holds the baton (i.e., the baton is garbage collected), or (ii) another resource server holds the baton (a replay attack)? Therefore, in the extended HCAP scheme, the authorization server tracks an additional boolean flag for each session to differentiate between (i) and (ii).

(2) Remote capability validation. A capability *cap* for session *sessid* is signed by a specific shared secret, say k_{rsid_1}, so that only $rsid_1$ knows how to check the hash value of *cap*. Capability validation also involves consulting *ex*[·], and thus $rsid_1$ needs to hold the baton for *sessid* as well. When *cap* is presented along an access request to a resource server $rsid_2$ different from $rsid_1$, $rsid_2$ will now have to request $rsid_1$ to perform capability validation on its behalf (aka ***remote capability validation***).

To facilitate remote capability validation, a capability now has the form $\langle\!\langle vid, sessid : \text{cap}(t_{ser}, F)\rangle\!\rangle_{k, uid}$. The new element *vid* explicitly identifies the resource server who knows the secret key k. In other words, $k = k_{vid}$, and thus *vid* can validate the capability.

To preserve the efficiency of stationary transitions, we further assume the SA satisfies the property below:

$$\forall q, q' \in Q . \forall p, p' \in \Sigma . \delta(q, p) = \delta(q', p') \rightarrow RS(p) = RS(p') \quad (1)$$

Intuitively, transitions going into a state are triggered by permissions that can be exercised on the same resource server. Consequently, exercising a stationary permission never causes remote capability validation (and baton passing, see below). This ensures stationary transitions are always efficient. Property (1) also makes it natural to associate a resource server $RS(q)$ to every state q: transitions into q can always be conducted on resource server $RS(q)$.

(3) Baton passing. When $rsid_2$ requests $rsid_1$ to perform remote capability validation, $rsid_1$ will pass *ex*[*sessid*] to $rsid_2$ after validation succeeds. This step is known as ***baton passing***. The intention is that stationary transitions performed on $rsid_2$ after that point will be efficient (i.e., not involving remote capability validation).

Server States and Session Initialization. In addition to *monitor*[·], *state*[·], *serial*[·] and *fragment*[·, ·], the authorization server maintains a boolean flag *baton*[*sessid*] for each session *sessid*. The invariant is that *baton*[*sessid*] is true if and only if at least one of the resource servers has the baton for *sessid* (i.e., *ex*[*sessid*] is defined on that resource server). When a new session *sessid* starts, the authorization server sets *baton*[*sessid*] to false, since *ex*[*sessid*] is not yet defined on any resource server.

Authorization. When a request $(uid, p, \langle\!\langle vid, sessid : \text{cap}(t_{ser}, F)\rangle\!\rangle_{k, uid})$ is presented to a resource server *rsid*, authorization is performed via Algorithm 2, which is composed of three sections.

(1) The first section, consisting of line 1 only, has no counterpart in Algorithm 1. That line checks whether the resource server *rsid* can actually exercise the permission p. This check is necessary because p can only be exercised by $RS(p)$.

(2) The second section, made up of lines 2–10, has the same role as lines 1–6 in Algorithm 1. The section validates the integrity of the capability, and initializes *ex*[*sessid*] if necessary.

If *rsid* is specified as the validator, then Algorithm 3 is invoked locally on *rsid* to perform the validation logic. Algorithm 3 is mostly equivalent to lines 1–6 in Algorithm 1, with one exception. When *rsid* does not hold the baton (i.e., *ex*[*sessid*] is not defined), it is because either (i) no resource server holds the baton, or (ii) another resource server holds the baton. Case (ii) corresponds to a replay attack. This is prevented by lines 3–4 of Algorithm 3, which contact the authorization server to confirm case (i).

If the validator *vid* is a resource server other than *rsid*, then *rsid* requests *vid* to run Algorithm 3 remotely (line 6). (During remote capability validation, the identifier *rsid* in Algorithm 3 refers to the validator *vid*.) If validation succeeds, then the baton is passed to *rsid* (lines 8–10).

(3) The third section is composed of lines 12–24. This last section of Algorithm 2 plays the same role as lines 7–19 in Algorithm 1. Two points are worth noting. First, the capabilities and update requests issued by *rsid* are signed by the k_{rsid} instead of k_{vid} (lines 21 &

Algorithm 2: Authorize access request (mult. res. servers)

Input: A client access request (uid, p, cap), where uid is the client's authenticated identity, p is the permission to be exercised, and cap is a capability $\langle\!\langle vid, sessid : \mathrm{cap}(t_{ser}, F)\rangle\!\rangle_{?,?}$ for session $sessid$ and validator vid, such that $F = (defs, n_\star)$ and $defs(n_\star) = (SP, trans)$.

Output: A set of tickets, or a failure response.

Data: The resource server maintains the following persistent data: (a) its identity $rsid$, (b) a secret k_{rsid} it shares with the authorization server, and (c) a map $ex[\cdot]$ that assigns exceptions to session IDs.

1   **if** $RS(p) \neq rsid$ **then return** *failure*;

2   **if** $vid = rsid$ **then**

3   Invoke Algorithm 3 locally on $rsid$ to validate cap ;

4   **if** *Algorithm 3 fails* **then return** *failure*;

5   **else**

6   Request vid to run Algorithm 3 to validate cap ;

7   **if** *Algorithm 3 succeeds* **then**

8   vid sends $rsid$ the contents of $ex[sessid]$;

9   vid deletes its copy of $ex[sessid]$;

10      $rsid$ stores the received contents locally in $ex[sessid]$;

11   **else return** *failure*;

12   **if** $p \in SP$ **then**

13   Exercise permission p;

14   **return** $\emptyset$;

15   **else if** $p \in dom(trans)$ **then**

16   Exercise permission p;

17     $t \leftarrow current\_time()$;

18     $ex[sessid] \leftarrow ex(p, t, ex[sessid])$;

19     $F' \leftarrow \Delta(F, p)$;

20   **if** $F' = \circ$ **then**

21   **return** $\{\langle\!\langle rsid, sessid : \mathrm{upd}(ex[sessid])\rangle\!\rangle_{k_{rsid}, uid}\}$;

22   **else**

23   **return** $\{\langle\!\langle rsid, sessid : \mathrm{cap}(t, F')\rangle\!\rangle_{k_{rsid}, uid}\}$;

24   **else return** *failure*;

Algorithm 3: Validate capability

Input: An authenticated client identifier uid and a capability cap of the form $\langle\!\langle vid, sessid : \mathrm{cap}(t_{ser}, F)\rangle\!\rangle_{?,?}$.

Output: Success or failure.

Data: The resource server maintains the following persistent data: (a) its identity $rsid$, (b) a secret k_{rsid} it shares with the authorization server, and (c) a map $ex[\cdot]$ that assigns exceptions to session IDs.

1   **if** cap is not signed by k_{rsid} for uid **then return** *failure* ;

2   **if** $ex[sessid]$ is undefined **then**

3   Request the authorization server to confirm that (a) $baton[sessid] = false$, and (b) $t_{ser} = serial[sessid]$; on confirmation $baton[sessid]$ is set to $true$;

4   **if** *(a) and (b) are not confirmed* **then return** *failure*;

5     $ex[sessid] \leftarrow \mathrm{nil}(t_{ser})$

6   **else if** $t_{ser} > last(ex[sessid])$ **then** $ex[sessid] \leftarrow \mathrm{nil}(t_{ser})$;

7   **else if** $t_{ser} < last(ex[sessid])$ **then return** *failure*;

8   **return** *success*

---

23). Second, when p is stationary, assumption (1) guarantees that $rsid = vid$, and thus no new capabilities need to be issued (line 14).

Baton Compression. Resource servers have different memory capacities, and thus when a large baton is passed, the receiving resource server may not have enough memory to store the baton. This concern is addressed by an implementation technique known as **baton compression**, which allows us to bound the length of batons by the size of SA fragments.

The key observation is that, when a transition is performed on an SA fragment (Algorithm 2, line 19, $\Delta(F, p)$), the underlying transition diagram (*defs*) remains unchanged. Thus the transitions recorded in an exception list visit states from the same transition diagram. Eventually, a state will be revisited when the length of the transition history exceeds the number of states in the transition diagram. When this happens, the transition sequence contains a

loop. Even if loops are eliminated from the transition history, the authorization server can still reconstruct the current SA state.

With the baton compression mechanism, when a transitioning permission is exercised by a resource server for a session *sessid*, the resource server will check that the length of the resulting exception list $ex[sessid]$ does not exceed the number of states in the SA fragment of the capability associated with the request. If the check fails, then the transition history is examined for the presence of loops. Any discovered loops are eliminated, and thus $ex[sessid]$ is "compressed" into a loop-free transition history with a length bounded by the size of the SA fragment stored in the capability of the request. Consequently, baton passing involves only very small payloads with sizes proportional to that of capabilities.

Hard and Soft Garbage Collection. Recall that a design objective of HCAP is to minimize communication with the authorization server (**O2**). Compared to core HCAP (§3), the extended protocol has one additional communication with the authorization server: line 3 in Algorithm 3. To make this additional communication an infrequent event, we have devised an optimization technique by enriching the garbage collection mechanism as follows.

When garbage collection is triggered on the resource server, two types of garbage collection may be performed for each session *sessid*. Session *sessid* undergoes **hard garbage collection** when $ex[sessid]$ is reset to undefined (i.e., deallocated). This is the same sort of GC performed by core HCAP. Session *sessid* undergoes **soft garbage collection** when $ex[sessid]$ is set to $\mathrm{nil}(t)$, where t is the largest timestamp in the exception list $ex[sessid]$ prior to garbage collection. Soft GC clears the exception list without relinquishing the baton (i.e., a nil entry is kept). The resource server is configured in such a way that a session with lots of activities will only undergo soft GC, and a session that has been inactive for an extended time will undergo a hard GC. The effect is that batons are retained for active sessions. Therefore, the extra communication with the authorization server (line 3 of Algorithm 3) is only performed when a session that has remained inactive for an extended time becomes active again. What constitutes "extended time" is a configurable parameter, meaning that the extra communication with the authorization server can be made as infrequently as possible.

As in core HCAP, the garbage-collected (whether hard or soft) exception lists are sent to the authorization server. Along with each exception list, we now have to also indicate, by way of a boolean flag, whether the baton of the corresponding session has been retained (i.e., soft GC). The authorization server will use these boolean flags to update its $baton[\cdot]$ map.

6 IMPLEMENTATION AND EXPERIMENTS

6.1 Implementation

We implemented the extended HCAP protocol in Java.[2] The implementation is based on CoAP [36], a lightweight, UDP-based variant of HTTP commonly used in IoT environments. An HCAP permission in this context is a pair composed of a CoAP method (e.g., GET) and an URI. We rely on the Californium-core library to provide CoAP functionalities. DTLS, which provides TLS-like features for UDP, is used to enable secure communication and mutual authentication. X.509 certificates are used by DTLS for authentication. DTLS features are provided by the Scandium-core library.

Tickets, as well as the contents of $ex[\cdot]$ that are sent during GC, are encoded as either JSON [11] or CBOR [6] objects. JSON is a human readable, lightweight data interchange format which is a subset of the JavaScript Programming Language. CBOR is a variant of JSON that represents data in a compact binary format. We used the jackson-dataformat-cbor and jackson-dataformat-json libraries respectively for CBOR and JSON encoding/decoding.

Our implementation consists of three reusable components (Fig. 1). The first is a client-side library ("HCAP Client API" in Fig. 1), which allows client code to issue HCAP requests to the authorization server and the resource servers. The payload of an HCAP request contains both a capability and the actual payload which the client might want to deliver. Thus our request payload is a JSON map with two keys, mapping to the capability and the actual payload. The second component is a CoAP server that acts as the authorization server ("HCAP Authorization Code" in Fig. 1). It offers RESTful services [28] for issuing capabilities, processing update requests, and performing garbage collection. The third component allows IoT vendors to add HCAP access control functionalities to a resource server that runs on the Californium framework. More specifically, we developed a *message deliverer* for mediating accesses. Within the Californium framework, a message deliverer is a hook method which intercepts a CoAP request before it reaches the intended resource. We developed a custom message deliverer that checks a capability for its validity before passing the request to the resources ("HCAP Access Mediation Code" in Fig. 1).

CoAP is designed for small data transfers, but sometimes the size of data being transferred might be too large to fit in a single packet (e.g., during garbage collection). In this case we make use of blockwise transfers [7], another functionality provided by CoAP to segment large chunks of data as blocks and send them over. This allows us to perform garbage collection in an efficient manner.

---

[2]The implementation is available at http://github.com/HCAPDevTeam/hcap.

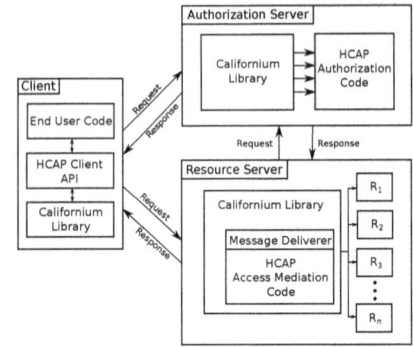

Figure 1: Architecture of our implementation.

6.2 Empirical Evaluation

We conducted four experiments to assess the performance of our HCAP implementation. The focus of our empirical study is in assessing the network overhead incurred by HCAP, since the computation involved in the protocol is relatively lightweight.

All clients were hosted on a single machine. Each of the authorization and resource servers ran on a separate machine. Experiment 1–3 involves a single resource server, while Experiment 4 involves two resource servers. Clients and the resource servers were hosted on 3.6 Ghz Intel Core i7 (4790) machines with 8 GB of RAM, running Fedora 24 4.8 and OpenJDK Runtime Environment (1.8). The authorization server was hosted on a 2.66 Ghz Intel Xeon(R)(X5355) machine with 24 GB of RAM, running Fedora 22 4.8 and OpenJDK Runtime Environment (1.8). All machines were connected via wired LAN on a 1 Gbps line.

The first communication between the client and the servers takes considerable amount of time, this is due to a DTLS session being established between the two communicating parties. To eliminate this confounding factor, we send a dummy request (ping) to the servers before the experiments start. We used "SHA256withECDSA" to generate signatures, and the key size was 256 bits.

Experiment 1: Incomplete SA Fragments. If the SA fragment in a capability does not provide enough information for the resource server to construct its next capability, an update request is returned to the client (Algorithm 2, line 21), causing an extra communication with the authorization server. The purpose of this experiment is to assess the performance impact of incomplete SA fragments.

The experimental protocol session involves an SA $M = (\{p_0, p_1\}, \{q_0, q_1\}, q_0, \delta)$, such that $\delta(q_i, p_0) = q_i$, $\delta(q_i, p_1) = q_{1-i}$. In short, p_0 is stationary, and p_1 is transitioning. Every capability issued by the authorization server carries an SA fragment $F = (defs, n_\star)$ for which $defs(n_\star) = (SP, trans)$ and $ran(trans) = \{\circ\}$. In other words, the resource server returns an update request whenever the request involves p_1. In each experimental configuration, we had a client generating 100 access requests, so that $P\%$ of the requests involved p_1. The client would then bring any update request to the authorization server before the next access request was generated. We repeated this for $P = 0, 10, \ldots, 100$. We measured the average time it took for the client to complete an access request, including

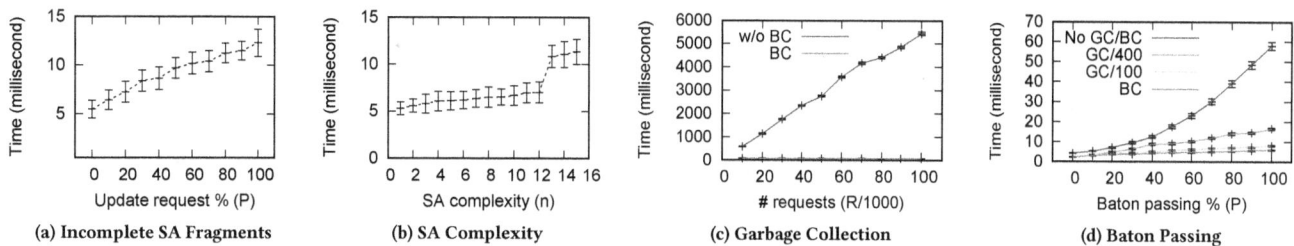

Figure 2: Performance impact of various features of extended HCAP (95% confidence interval).

the overhead of contacting the authorization server in case an update request was returned.

The results are depicted in Fig. 2(a). The average request handling time is between 5.5 to 12.3 milliseconds (10^{-3} sec), an acceptable range considering that the high-end (12.3 millisec) corresponds to the case when every access request results in an update request ($P = 100\%$).

Experiment 2: SA Complexity. The purpose of this experiment is to assess the performance impact of embedding a complex SA in a capability. The experimental protocol sessions involve SA of the following form: $M_n = (\Sigma_n, Q_n, q_0, \delta_n)$, where $\Sigma_n = \{p_0, \ldots, p_{n-1}\}$, $Q_n = \{q_0, \ldots, q_{n-1}\}$, and $\delta_n(q_i, p_j) = q_j$. In short, there is a transition between every ordered pair of states in M_n. The SA fragments embedded in capabilities incorporate the *full* specification of the SA. We varied n from 1 up to 15. For each value of n, a client issued 100 randomly generated access requests to the resource server. We measured the average time for the client to complete one request.

The results are depicted in Fig. 2(b). As n increases, the number of transitions in M_n grows quadratically, so does the size of the SA fragment. When the value of n increased from 12 to 13, we see a sudden jump in the request handling time. This is because, when $n \le 12$, the entire SA fragment can be fitted into a single UDP packet, but multiple packets are needed when $n > 13$. That was when CoAP blockwise transfer kicked in. This highlights the advantage of keeping SA fragments moderate in size.

Experiment 3: Garbage Collection. The purpose of this experiment is to evaluate the performance impact of garbage collection (GC). Reusing the SA M_{12} from Experiment 2, we deployed 100 clients to issue transitioning requests to the resource server. As each transitioning request for session *sessid* was served, a new exception entry was added to $ex[sessid]$. Once all the requests were issued, GC was triggered, and the entire contents of $ex[\cdot]$ were transfered to the authorization server for updating $state[\cdot]$. We measured the time for GC to complete. Let R be the total number of requests made by the clients right before GC was triggered. The experiment was repeated for $R = 10{,}000, 20{,}000, \ldots, 100{,}000$. In addition, for each R, the experiment was repeated 100 times to obtain the average GC overhead. These experiments were conducted in two experimental configurations: (1) **w/o BC**, in which baton compression was turned off, and (2) **BC**, in which baton compression was turned on. This allowed us to observe how GC interacted with baton compression

The results are depicted in Fig. 2(c), with the horizontal axis corresponding to R divided by 1,000. Without baton compression

(**w/o BC**), the size of $ex[\cdot]$ grew in proportion to R (i.e., the number of transitioning requests issued to the resource server), and GC time grew accordingly. If we amortize GC time over individual requests, then the per-request GC overhead ranges between 54 and 58 microseconds (10^{-6} sec), that is, between 0.78% and 0.83% of the average request handling time (Experiment 2, $n = 12$).

When baton compression was turned on (**BC**), the overhead of garbage collection was significantly reduced. This was because the length of an exception list $ex[sessid]$ is bounded by 12 (i.e., the number of states in M_{12}). Thus the total size of $ex[\cdot]$ is never above $12 \times 100 = 1{,}200$. Amortizing the GC overhead over individual requests, the per-request GC overhead ranges between 0.72 and 7.5 microseconds (10^{-6} sec), that is, between 0.01% and 0.10% of the average request handling time.

Experiment 4: Baton Passing. The purpose of this experiment is to evaluate the performance impact of baton passing. Two resource servers were involved. The SA M_2 from Experiment 2 was reused, so that the two resource servers played the role of $RS(q_0)$ and $RS(q_1)$ respectively. Consequently, baton passing was triggered when and only when a transitioning permission was exercised. A single client was configured to issue a total of 1,000 requests to the resource servers, so that $P\%$ of the requests involved baton passing. The experiment was repeated for $P = 0, 10, \ldots, 100$. The average time required to complete one authorization request was recorded for each P. In addition, the experiments were conducted in four different experimental configurations, so that we could observe how the overhead of baton passing was affected by garbage collection and baton compression:

(1) **No GC/BC**. Both garbage collection and baton compression were turned off.

(2) **GC/400**. Garbage collection was triggered after every 400 transitioning requests, but baton compression was turned off.

(3) **GC/100**. This configuration is similar to GC/400 except that garbage collected was triggered after every 100 requests.

(4) **BC**. Baton compression was turned on, but garbage collection was turned off.

The results are depicted in Fig. 2(d). In the case of **No GC/BC**, the baton sizes (i.e., lengths of exception lists) grew indefinitely because neither garbage collection nor baton compression was turned on. Therefore, baton passing incurred significant overhead (approximately 60 milliseconds per authorization request when $P = 100\%$). Turning on garbage collection (**GC/400** and **GC/100**) significantly reduced the overhead of baton passing, because a baton was reduced to empty every time it was garbage collected, and thus batons were never given the chance to grow too long. We also notice that the more frequently garbage collection was triggered (e.g., more frequently in **GC/100** than in **GC/400**), the overhead of baton passing became smaller. The most promising result, however, is that of **BC**, in which baton compression was turned on (even without the help of GC): it took only 6 milliseconds to complete an authorization request even when $P = 100\%$. This is because the batons (i.e., exception lists) are kept to a size of 2 (M_2 has only two states). In this case, baton passing involved only the sending of a single UDP packet.

7 CONCLUSION AND FUTURE WORK

We argued that the physical embeddedness and process awareness of IoT devices impose a natural sequencing of accesses, which can be exploited for realizing Least Privilege. To this end, we proposed HCAP, a distributed capability system for enforcing history-based access control policies in a decentralized manner. We formally established the security guarantees of HCAP and empirically demonstrated that the performance of HCAP is competitive.

The following are some directions for future work: (1) integrating HCAP into UMA or OpenID, (2) adding fault tolerance into HCAP, (3) compilation of workflow specification and/or UMP specification [4] into SA fragments for use in HCAP, and (4) incorporating context awareness (e.g., time, location, sensor inputs) into HCAP.

ACKNOWLEDGMENTS

This work is supported in part by an NSERC Discovery Grant (RGPIN-2014-06611) and a Canada Research Chair (950-229712).

REFERENCES

[1] Martín Abadi, Michael Burrows, Butler Lampson, and Gordon Plotkin. 1993. A Calculus for Access Control in Distributed Systems. *ACM Transactions on Programming Languages and Systems* 15, 4 (Sept. 1993), 706–734.

[2] Andrew W. Appel and Edward W. Felten. 1999. Proof-Carrying Authentication. In *Proceedings of the 6th ACM Conference on Computer and Communications Security (CCS'99)*. Singapore, 52–62.

[3] Moritz Y. Becker, Cédric Fournet, and Andrew D. Gordon. 2010. SecPAL: Design and Semantics of a Decentralized Authorization Language. *Journal of Computer Security* 18 (2010), 597–643.

[4] Moritz Y. Becker and Sebastian Nanz. 2010. A Logic for State-Modifying Authorization Policies. *ACM Transactions on Information and System Security* 13, 3 (July 2010), 20.1–20.27.

[5] Arnar Birgisson, Joe Gibbs Politz, Úlfar Erlingsson, Ankur Taly, Michael Vrable, and Mark Lentczner. 2014. Macaroons: Cookies with Contextual Caveats for Decentralized Authorization in the Cloud. In *Proceedings of the 2014 Network and Distributed System Security Symposium (NDSS)*. San Diego, CA.

[6] Carsten Bormann and Paul Hoffman. 2013. Concise Binary Object Representation (CBOR). (2013).

[7] C. Bormann and Z. Shelby. 2011. Blockwise transfers in CoAP. *draft-ietf-core-block-04 (work in progress)* (2011).

[8] David F. C. Brewer and Michael J. Nash. 1989. The Chinese Wall security policy. In *Proceedings of the 1989 IEEE Symposium on Security and Privacy (S&P'89)*. Oakland, California, 206–214.

[9] Jason Crampton, Gregory Gutin, and Anders Yeo. 2013. On the Parameterized Complexity and Kernelization of the Workflow Satisfiability Problem. *ACM Transactions on Information and System Security* 16, 1 (June 2013).

[10] Jack B. Dennis and Earl C. Van Horn. 1983. Programming Semantics for Multiprogrammed Computations. *Commun. ACM* 26, 1 (Jan. 1983), 29–35.

[11] ECMA International. 2013. ECMA-404: The JSON Data Interchange Format.

[12] D. Evans and A. Twyman. 1999. Flexible policy-directed code safety. In *In Proceedings of the 1999 IEEE Symposium on Security and Privacy (S&P'1999)*. Oakland, California, 32–45.

[13] Philip W. L. Fong. 2004. Access control by tracking shallow execution history. In *Proceedings of the 2004 IEEE Symposium on Security and Privacy (S&P'04)*. Berkeley, CA, 43–55.

[14] Philip W. L. Fong. 2011. Relationship-Based Access Control: Protection Model and Policy Language. In *Proceedings of the First ACM Conference on Data and Application Security and Privacy (CODASPY'11)*. San Antonio, Taxas, USA, 191–202.

[15] ForgeRock 2018. ForgeRock. http://www.forgerock.com

[16] Li Gong. 1989. A Secure Identity-Based Capability System. In *Proceedings of the 1989 IEEE Symposium on Security and Privacy (S&P'89)*. Oakland, California.

[17] Sergio Gusmeroli, Salvatore Piccione, and Domenico Rotondi. 2013. A capability-based security approach to manage access control in the Internet of Things. *Mathematical and Computer Modelling* 58 (2013), 1189–1205.

[18] D. Hardt. 2012. *The O'Auth 2.0 Authorization Framework*. RFC 6749. IETF.

[19] José L. Hernández-Ramos, Antonio J. Jara, Leandro Marin, and Antonio F. Skarmeta Gómez. 2016. DCapBAC: Embedding authorization logic into smart things through ECC optimization. *International Journal of Computer Mathematics* 93, 2 (2016), 345–366.

[20] Vincent C. Hu, David Ferraiolo, Rick Kuhn, Adam Schnitzer, Kenneth Sandlin, Robert Miller, and Karen Scarfone. 2014. *Guide to Attribute Based Access Control (ABAC) Definition and Considerations*. NIST Special Publication 800-162. NIST.

[21] Gerd Kortuem, Fahim Kawsar, Daniel Fitton, and Vasughi Sundramoorthy. 2010. Smart Objects as Building Blocks for the Internet of Things. *IEEE Internet Computing* 14, 1 (2010), 44–51.

[22] K. Krukow, M. Nielsen, and V. Sassone. 2008. A logical framework for history-based access control and reputation systems. *Journal of Computer Security* 16, 1 (2008), 63–101.

[23] Leslie Lamport. 1977. Proving the Correctness of Multiprocess Programs. *IEEE Transactions on Software Engineering* 3, 2 (March 1977), 125–143.

[24] Ninghui Li, Benjamin N. Grosof, and Joan Feigenbaum. 2003. Delegation Logic: A Logic-based Approach to Distributed Authorization. *ACM Transactions on Information and System Security* 6, 1 (Feb. 2003), 128–171.

[25] Jay Ligatti, Lujo Bauer, and David Walker. 2009. Run-Time Enforcement of Nonsafety Policies. *ACM Transactions on Information and System Security* 12, 3 (Jan. 2009).

[26] Parikshit N. Mahalle, Bayu Anggorojati, Neeli R. Prasad, and Ramjee Prasad. 2013. Identity Authentication and Capability Based Access Control (IACAC) for the Internet of Things. *Journal of Cyber Security and Mobility* 1, 4 (2013), 309–348.

[27] Eve Maler, Maciej Machulak, and Domenico Catalano. 2015. *User-Managed Access (UMA) Profile of O'Auth 2.0*. Kantara Initiative.

[28] Mark Masse. 2011. *REST API Design Rulebook: Designing Consistent RESTful Web Service Interfaces.* " O'Reilly Media, Inc.".

[29] Yuhan Niu, Weisheng Lu, Ke Chen, George G. Huang, and Chimay Anumba. 2016. Smart Construction Objects. *Journal of Computing in Civil Engineering* 30, 4 (July 2016).

[30] Nulli 2018. Nulli. http://www.nulli.com

[31] OpenID 2018. OpenID. http://openid.net/

[32] Jude T Regan and Christian D. Jensen. 2001. Capability File Names: Separating Authorization from User Management in an Internet File System. In *Proceedings of the 10th USENIX Security Symposium*. Washington, D.C.

[33] Jerry H. Saltzer and Mike D. Schroeder. 1975. The protection of information in computer systems. *Proc. IEEE* 63, 9 (Sept. 1975), 1278–1308.

[34] Ravi S. Sandhu, Edward J. Coyne, Hal L. Feinstein, and Charles E. Youman. 1996. Role-Based Access Control Models. *IEEE Computer* 29, 2 (Feb. 1996), 38–47.

[35] Fred B. Schneider. 2000. Enforceable Security Policies. *ACM Transactions on Information and System Security* 3, 1 (Feb. 2000), 30–50.

[36] Z. Shelby, K. Hartke, and C. Bormann. 2014. *RFC 7252: The Constrained Application Protocol (CoAP)*. IETF.

[37] Ankur Taly and Asim Shankar. 2016. Distributed Authorization in Vanadium. In *Foundations of Security Analysis and Design VIII, FOSAD 2015/2016 (LNCS)*, Vol. 9808. Springer, 139–162.

[38] L. Tandon, P. W. L. Fong, and R. Safavi-Naini. 2018. HCAP: A History-Based Capability System for IoT Devices. *ArXiv e-prints* (March 2018). arXiv:cs.CR/1804.00086

[39] Úlfar Erlingsson and F. B. Schneider. 2000. IRM enforcement of Java stack inspection. In *Proceedings of the 2000 IEEE Symposium on Security and Privacy (S&P'2000)*. Berkeley, California, 246–255.

[40] D. S. Wallach, A. W. Appel, and E. W. Felten. 2000. SAFKASI: A security mechanism for language-based systems. *ACM Transactions on Software Engineering and Methodology* 9, 4 (Oct. 2000), 341–378.

[41] Qihua Wang and Ninghui Li. 2010. Satisfiability and Resiliency in Workflow Authorization Systems. *ACM Transactions on Information and System Security* 13, 4 (Dec. 2010).

Author Index

NOTES

www.ingramcontent.com/pod-product-compliance
Lightning Source LLC
Chambersburg PA
CBHW061356210326
41598CB00035B/5997